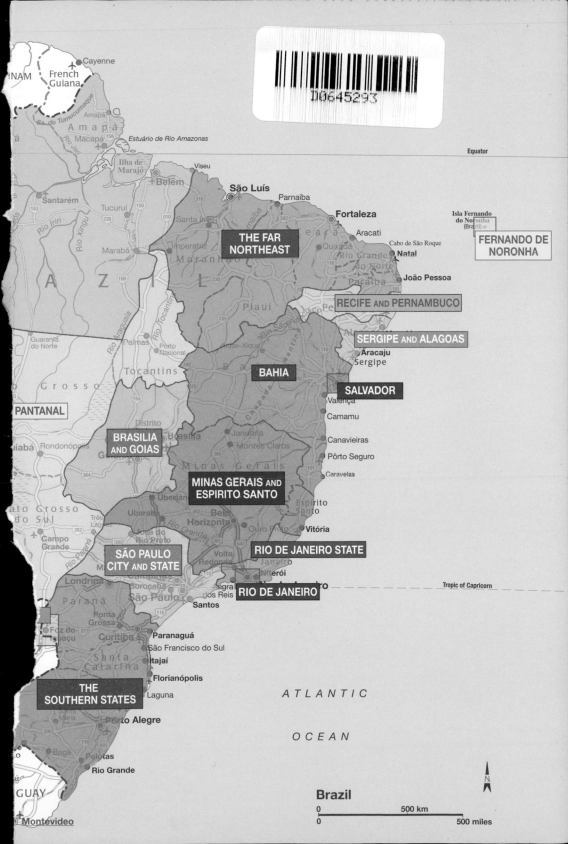

Cayenne

SURINAM
French
Guiana

Sa. do Tumucumaque

Amapá

Macapá 156

Estuário de Río Amazonas

Equator

Santarém

Ilha de
Marajó

Belém

Viseu

São Luís

Parnaíba

Fortaleza

Isla Fernando
do Noronha
(Brazil)

FERNANDO DE NORONHA

Tucurui 150

Santa Inês

Maranhão

Aracati

Cabo de São Roque

THE FAR NORTHEAST

Ceará

Quixadá

Rio Grande
do Norte

Natal

Marabá

Imperatriz

Piauí

Paraíba

João Pessoa

RECIFE AND PERNAMBUCO

Rio Xingu

Rio Iriri

Rio Tocantins

Guaranã
do Norte

Palmas

Porto
Nacional

Xique-Xique

Rio São Francisco

Chapada Diamantina

SERGIPE AND ALAGOAS

Aracaju
Sergipe

BAHIA

SALVADOR

Tocantins

Grosso

PANTANAL

Distrito

BRASILIA AND GOIAS

Brasilia

Goiás

Januária

Montes Claros

Minas Gerais

Valença

Camamu

Canavieiras

Pôrto Seguro

Caravelas

Cuiabá

Rondonópolis

MINAS GERAIS AND ESPIRITO SANTO

Uberlândia

Espirito
Santo

Mato Grosso
do Sul

Três
Lagoas

Uberaba

Belo
Horizonte

Ouro Preto

Vitória

Campo
Grande

Rio Grande

São José do
Rio Preto

RIO DE JANEIRO STATE

SÃO PAULO CITY AND STATE

Volta
Redonda

Janeiro

Niterói

Rio de Janeiro

Londrina

Maringá

Campinas

Sorocaba

Tropic of Capricorn

Paraná

São Paulo

Angra
dos Reis

RIO DE JANEIRO

Ponta
Grossa

Santos

Foz do
Iguaçu

Curitiba

Paranaguá

São Francisco do Sul

Santa
Catarina

Itajaí

Florianópolis

Laguna

THE SOUTHERN STATES

ATLANTIC

Santa
Maria

Porto Alegre

OCEAN

Bagé

Pelotas

Rio Grande

URUGUAY

N

Montevideo

Brazil

0   500 km

0   500 miles

INSIGHT GUIDES
BRAZIL

Contents

Introduction

The Best of Brazil.................... **4**
A Land without Frontiers **15**
The People of Brazil.............. **17**
The Amerindians **24**

History

Decisive Dates...................... **30**
The Making of Brazil............. **35**
Country of the Future........... **49**

Features

From Sandy Beaches to
   Amazon Jungle.................. **61**
Carnival **69**
Festivals............................... **75**
Saints and Idols.................... **81**
A Passion for Soccer **89**
Food and Drink **94**
A Nation in Tune................... **98**
Cinema.............................. **108**
Art and Artists **113**
Modern Architecture **120**

Insights

PHOTO FEATURES

Brazilian Dishes.................... **96**
Brazilian Baroque.............. **204**
Mistura Fina....................... **284**
The Riches of the
   River Amazon................. **338**

MINI FEATURES

The golden age of Pedro II ... **38**

The disappearing rainforest. **64**
Boi-Bumba............................ **79**
Seu Jorge **106**
TV Globo............................ **111**
Rio's favelas **150**
Rio's 2016 Olympics **160**
Wine country..................... **232**
Tours and lodges **254**
Bahian cuisine.................. **266**
São Francisco river........... **289**
The lost city of El Dorado... **324**
An American dream........... **328**

Places

Introduction **129**
The Southeast **133**
Rio de Janeiro **137**
Rio de Janeiro State **165**
São Paulo: City and State.. **183**
Minas Gerais and
   Espirito Santo **207**
Iguaçu Falls....................... **220**
The Southern States **223**
The Center-West............... **239**
Brasília and Goiás **241**
The Pantanal..................... **251**
The Northeast................... **261**
Bahia................................. **263**
Salvador............................ **273**
Sergipe and Alagoas **286**
Recife and Pernambuco.... **293**
Fernando de Noronha **302**
The Far Northeast............. **305**
The Amazon **319**

Travel Tips

TRANSPORTATION
Getting there...................... 342
Getting around.................. 343

ACCOMMODATIONS
Hotels................................ 347
Budget accommodations.. 347
Charming hotels 347
Booking hotels.................. 347
Hotel groups 347
Rio de Janeiro................... 348
Rio State 349
São Paulo City and
    State.............................. 350
Minas Gerais..................... 352
Southern States 353
Brasília.............................. 354
Center West (Pantanal) 355
Bahia................................. 355
Salvador............................ 356
Sergipe and Alagoas 357
Recife and Pernambuco.... 357
The Far Northeast............. 358
Amazon 359

ACTIVITIES
The arts............................. 360
Nightlife 361
Festivals............................ 361
Sports............................... 362
Children's activities........... 363
Shopping........................... 364

A – Z
Admission charges............ 366
Airport taxes...................... 366
Budgeting for the trip 366
Business hours.................. 366
Climate.............................. 366
Crime and safety 367
Customs and duty free...... 367
Disabled travelers 367
Electricity 368
Embassies and
    consulates.................... 368
Entry regulations 368
Etiquette 369
Gay and lesbian travelers . 369
Health 369
Internet 370
Lost property..................... 370
Maps 370
Media 370
Money 371
Postal services 371
Public holidays.................. 371
Public toilets 372
Religious services............. 372
Student travelers............... 372
Telecommunications......... 372
Time zones........................ 373
Tipping.............................. 373
Tourist offices 374
Travel agents and
    tour operators............... 374
Websites 374
Weights and measures 375
What to bring 375

LANGUAGE 376

FURTHER READING 379

Maps
Brazil 130
Central Rio 134
Copacabana, Ipanema
    and Pão de Açúcar......... 151
São Conrado and
    Barra da Tijuca.............. 158
Rio de Janeiro State 166
Petrópolis.......................... 168
São Paulo City................... 186
São Paulo State 198
Minas Gerais and
    Espírito Santo 208
Ouro Preto......................... 211
Southern States 226
Brasília.............................. 244
Wild West and Goiás 252
Northeast States 260
Central Salvador................ 274
Recife 294
Amazonia 322
Belém................................ 326
Manus............................... 330
Inside front cover Brazil
Inside back cover Greater Rio
de Janerio and Northeast States

THE BEST OF BRAZIL: TOP ATTRACTIONS

Amazing beaches, a vast array of wildlife, and historical colonial towns are only a sample of the best that Brazil has to offer. Here are the top sights you simply have to see.

△ **Corcovado, Rio de Janeiro.** Voted one of the New Seven Wonders of the World, you can't go to Rio without taking the train to the top of Corcovado, where the views are phenomenal. See page 154.

◁ **World Cup 2014/Olympics 2016.** Brazil's attention will be focused on the FIFA World Cup in 2014 and in Rio on the Olympic and Paralympic games as it prepares to host in 2016. See page 160.

▷ **The Pantanal.** The Pantanal is home to 650 bird species. Lots of mammals, too, including the capybara, caiman, marsh deer, and armadillos. See page 251.

△ **Iguaçu Falls.** 'Poor Niagara!' Eleanor Roosevelt exclaimed upon first seeing the magnificent falls at Iguaçu. The world's greatest collection of waterfalls is simply breathtaking. See page 220.

△ **Amazon.** Amazonia, the lungs of the world, supports 30 percent of all known plant and animal species, including 2,500 fish species, 50,000 higher plant species, and millions of insects. See page 319.

△ **Pelourinho, Salvador.** According to Unesco, the Pelourinho is the most important grouping of 17th- and 18th-century colonial architecture in the Americas. See page 275.

△ **Historic towns of Minas Gerais.** Gold and diamonds made Ouro Preto rich, and financed the Baroque architecture and sculpture that led Unesco to declare it a World Cultural Monument. But the historic state is much more than just Ouro Preto. Equally memorable is Congonhas do Campo, site of the two greatest works of the 18th-century sculptor Aleijadinho. See page 207.

△ **Sugar Loaf, Rio de Janeiro.** There are those who claim the views of Rio and the bay are even better from the top of Sugar Loaf mountain than from Corcovado. It's a hard one to decide, so go see for yourself. See page 147.

◁ **Paraty.** A masterpiece of colonial architecture and charm that is also home to one of the world's most prestigious literary festivals. See page 177.

▷ **Carnival.** Brazil is justifiably famous for its huge, exuberant pre-Lent Carnival, the biggest and brashest in the world. Like the beaches, it would seem unfair just to highlight one, as Brazil has an embarrassment of riches that start with Rio, Salvador, Recife, and Olinda. See page 69.

THE BEST OF BRAZIL: EDITOR'S CHOICE

Breathtaking views, tropical beaches, a vast array of wildlife, a tempting selection of restaurants, and a calendar of festivals that would be hard to beat anywhere in the world. Brazil has it all, and these essential tips reveal where you can find the best of everything.

Brazil is blessed with many gorgeous beaches.

BEST BEACHES

Búzios. White-sand beaches, crystalline water, palm trees, and coconuts. See page 169.

Lopes Mendes, Ilha Grande, Rio State. A glorious stretch of beach where the fine white sand squeaks beneath your feet. See page 175.

The Rio–Santos Highway. The road passes more than 400km (240 miles) of glorious beaches. See page 173.

Taipús de Fora, Bahia State. On the remote Maraú Peninsula, this is considered by many to be one of the finest beaches in Brazil. See page 173.

Praia do Forte. Thousands of coconut palms stand on 12km (7 miles) of white sandy beach, some 85km (53 miles) from Salvador. See page 267.

Praia Pajuçara, Maceió, Alagoas State. Maceió beaches are famous for the transparent, bright emerald green water. Praia Pajuçara, which becomes an enormous wading pool at low tide, is a prime example. See page 290.

Jericoacoara, Ceará State. Ceará has innumerable beautiful beaches, but perhaps the finest is the remote Jericoacoara, declared a national park in 2002. See page 312.

Praia do Sancho, Fernando de Noronha. Its waters are home to dolphins, sharks, and multicolored fish, but in Praia do Sancho, this island has one of the country's best beaches and dive sites. See page

OUTDOOR ADVENTURE

Fernando de Noronha. Scuba diving and snorkeling are popular activities here. There are ships to visit and you might meet a shark on a night dive. See page 302.

Rio da Prata, Bonito. Very different snorkeling is found in the rivers that surround Bonito. Float with the current in a natural aquarium. See page 257.

Iguaçu Falls. Aboard sturdy, 20-seater inflatable boats you can get right up to the base of the falls. See page 220.

Amazon. Take treks into the forest, canoe trips, or go piranha-fishing or torchlight caiman-spotting. See page 319.

Lençóis Maranhenses. Rolling sheets of white sand, dotted by transparent pools of water. See page 314.

Ilha do Mel, Paranaguá. The island is a nature reserve with natural pools, grottoes, beaches, and no vehicles. Its unspoiled nature makes it a popular spot. See page 227.

Parque Nacional de Brasília. An area of savannah and low forest where birds, wolves, and monkeys find refuge. There are forest trails, and swimming pools. See page 247.

Brazil's beaches are excellent places to swim, surf, dive, or sail.

TOP MUSEUMS

Sculptures at Museu Nacional de Belas Artes or National Fine Arts Museum in Rio de Janeiro.

Museu Nacional de Belas Artes, Rio. Houses one of Latin America's finest art collections, including works by the great 20th-century Cândido Portinari. See page 142.

Museu de Arte do Rio (MAR), Rio. First of the new museums and galleries projected for Rio's redeveloped port area. The underlying theme of this museum is Rio itself. A perfect introduction to the city for any visitor. See page 140.

Museu de Arte Contemporânea, Niterói. Designed by

Gathering on Rio's Copacabana beach for New Year's Eve celebrations.

Oscar Niemeyer, the building may be the best attraction. The views back to Rio are gorgeous. See page 147.

Museu Afro-Brasileiro, Salvador. A fascinating collection of objects that highlight the strong African influence on Bahian culture. See page 274.

Museu do Homem do Nordeste, Recife. The museum is a tribute to the cultural history of this fascinating region. See page 296.

Museu de Arte de São Paulo (MASP). Rembrandt, Renoir, Goya, Picasso and Monet are just a few of the European artists represented here. There's also a sweeping survey of Brazilian art. See page 193.

Museu do Futebol, São Paulo. This state-of-the-art football museum is the one the five-time World Champions deserved. Located in the Pacaembu Stadium. See page 194.

Museu Imperial, Petrópolis. An Imperial gem that shines an illuminating light on Brazil's early rulers. See page 166.

BEST FESTIVALS

Rio Carnival. Rio de Janeiro hosts the world's most famous Carnival, and it deserves its reputation. The parade of the top samba schools is one of the entertainment world's genuine wonders. See page 69.

Salvador, Bahia. Carnival in Salvador is quite a different thing. The centerpiece is a glittering music festival on wheels called trio elétrico. See page 73.

Boi-Bumba. The last weekend of June marks the Parintins Folk Festival in Amazonia, a huge festival centered on the Amerindian Boi-Bumba fable. A rival to Carnival, it is the most complete

Celebrating Carnival in Rio.

mixture of Amerindian, European, and African cultural elements in Brazil. See page 79.

June Festivals. Celebrating the feast days of St Anthony (June 12), St John (June 23–4), and St Peter (June 28–9) they are characterized by brightly illuminated balloons, and bonfires blazing through the night; as well as fireworks and music. See page 75.

Bom Jesus dos Navegantes. Celebrated at New Year in Salvador. A procession of small craft decked with streamers and flags carries a statue of the Lord of Seafarers from the harbor to the Boa Viagem church. See page 78.

Círio de Nazaré. A four-hour procession in Belém on the second Sunday of October, centered on a colorfully decorated carriage bearing the image of Our Lady of Nazareth. See page 77.

SOUNDS OF BRAZIL

Bossa Nova. Brazil's most popular music, led by the likes of Tom Jobim, Sergio Mendes, João Gilberto, and his daughter Bebel. See page 102.

Samba. The driving rhythm and cornerstone of Rio's carnival, but so much more. See page 100.

Axé. A melting pot of Afro, Caribbean, and Brazilian music. Leading exponents include Ivete

Sangalo, Cláudia Leitte, Daniela Mercury, and Olodum. See page 99.

Tropicalia. A musical wave that flowed from Salvador to Rio thanks to the work of Caetano Veloso, Gilberto Gil, Gal Costa, and Maria Bethania, to name a few. See page 103.

Choro. Hear Brazil cry (choro) through the sound of flute, guitar, and cavaquinho. See page 100.

Sugar Loaf Mountain looms over
the Bay of Botafogo.

Local boys dive in, Trancoso.

A LAND WITHOUT FRONTIERS

Since first landing in Brazil in 1500, visitors have always been slightly dazed by the sheer size of the country and its hidden riches; Brazilians are no less captivated.

Colonial architecture in Salvador.

Since its colonization by the Portuguese in the 16th century, Brazil has held a constant fascination for foreigners. First it was gold, then rubber and coffee, and more recently, the exotic sights and sounds of the nation. For Brazilians, too, it is an intriguing land. There is a feeling that, hidden in some far corner of this great nation, there may be an immense treasure just waiting to be discovered. The main problem lies in identifying the corner.

Brazilians and foreigners alike have been gradually occupying the enormous empty spaces of this continent-sized country ever since the 16th century. They have populated them with some 193 million souls, composing one of the world's most heterogeneous populations. They live amid modern splendor in sprawling cities and in squalid deprivation in rural backwaters. They work in high-tech industries and push wooden plows behind laboring beasts. Within the confines of this country live indigenous people in near Stone Age conditions, semi-feudal peasants and landlords, pioneers hacking out jungle settlements, and wealthy entrepreneurs and business people.

Perhaps nowhere on earth is the process of development as tangible as in Brazil. The dynamism of the country is its greatest achievement. Even in periods of stagnation, Brazilians continue to get on with the process of nation-building, and can now look forward to the responsibility of hosting the world at the FIFA World Cup in 2014 and the Olympic and Paralympic Games in 2016.

Brazilians are united by a common language, Portuguese; a common religion, Catholicism (though mixed with indigenous faiths); and a common dream that Brazil will be a great nation. Despite enormous social and economic difficulties, Brazilians are a remarkably spontaneous, enthusiastic, and high-spirited people, who tend to live in the moment. After all, at any moment, you may just find treasure.

Catedral Metropolitana, Brasilia.

THE PEOPLE OF BRAZIL

Brazil is sometimes referred to as a melting pot, but this implies that people from many different backgrounds have blended together. They are, in fact, proudly different, but also proud to be Brazilians.

Brazil is a diverse nation. Its people share only a common language and a vague notion of Brazil's cultural shape. They worship a dozen gods, and their ancestors came from all over the globe. This is a legacy of Brazil's colonial past. Among the countries of the New World, it is unique. Whereas the Spanish-American colonies were ruled by rigid bureaucracies, and the future United States by a negligent Britain, Brazil's colonial society followed a flexible middle course. The Portuguese colonists were not outcasts from their native land like the Puritans of New England. Nor were they like the grasping Spanish courtiers fulfilling a brief colonial service before returning home. They were men – and for decades, *only* men – who retained an allegiance to the old country but quickly identified with their new home.

In his classic work on Brazil's origins *Raízes do Brasil (Roots of Brazil)*, historian Sérgio Buarque de Holanda (father of songwriter Chico Buarque) writes: 'He [the Brazilian male] is free to take on entire repertoires of new ideas, outlooks and forms, assimilating them without difficulty.'

Racial mixing

The Spanish grandees hated the New World, the Puritans were stuck with it, but the Portuguese *liked* Brazil – particularly its native women – and the colonizers' desire married with the beauty of the indigenous females to begin a new race. The first members of that race – the first Brazilians – were *mamelucos*, the progeny of Portuguese white men and native Amerindian women. Later, other races emerged – the *cafusos*, of Amerindian and African blood, and the *mulatos*, of African and European.

Resident in Cachoeira town, Bahia.

INDIGENOUS LANGUAGES

Around 274 languages are used in Brazil, including an estimated 180 Amerindian languages, and 158 of them are endangered because they are spoken by groups of fewer than 1,000. Many are almost extinct, spoken only by a handful of people, mostly elderly. Most speakers of indigenous languages are bilingual (in Portuguese and their own tongue), but there are parts of Amazonas and Pará where most women and children speak only their own language – Mundurukú – although men speak some Portuguese. Kayapó is another language that is flourishing orally, but only a small proportion of the estimated 5,000 speakers are literate in it.

The fusion of race is more complete in Brazil than in many Latin American countries. Pedro Alvares Cabral is honored by all Brazilians as the country's 'discoverer,' yet the Amerindian past is not disdained. Diplomat William Schurz, in his 1961 book *Brazil*, notes that numerous Amerindian family names have been preserved. He lists Ypiranga, Araripe, Peryassu, and many others, some of which belong to distinguished families in Pernambuco and Bahia.

But in contemporary Brazil, Schurz might have pointed out, the Amerindian is only a shadow of the other races. Historians believe

the north and northeast, many nominal Caucasians are in fact *mestiços*.

African culture

The history of African and the associated mixed-race people in Brazil has been complex. Despite now having the largest black population outside of Africa, Brazilians are known for being ambivalent about their black heritage. In the past, racism existed but was simply denied. In recent years, however, there has emerged an awareness of both Brazilian racism and the rich legacy that Africans have introduced to Brazil.

Passengers on the ferry from Itaparica island to Salvador, Bahia.

that as many as 5 million Amerindians lived in the area at the time of the European discovery in 1500. According to Amerindian leader Ailton Krenak, approximately 700 tribes have disappeared since that time, victim of disease, extermination, or gradual absorption through miscegenation. About 180 tribes have survived, as have a similar number of languages or dialects. They comprise about 900,000 people, mostly living on government reservations in Mato Grosso and Goiás, or in villages deep in the Amazon.

Brazil's *mestiço (mestizo)* population, meanwhile, has tended to melt into the white category. Only about 2 to 3 percent of Brazilians, mostly in the Amazon or its borders, consider themselves *mestiços*, but in reality, throughout

Pernambucan sociologist Gilberto Freyre wrote, in his 1936 volume *Casa Grande e Senzala*: 'Every Brazilian, even the light-skinned and fair-haired one, carries about with him in his soul, when not in soul and body alike, the shadow, or even the birthmark, of the aborigine or the negro. The influence of the African, either direct or remote, is everything that is a sincere reflection of our lives. We, almost all of us, bear the mark of that influence.'

Starting in colonial days, entire portions of African culture were incorporated wholesale into Brazilian life. Today, they are reflected in the rhythmic music of samba, the varied and spicy cuisine of Bahia, and the growth of African-origin spiritist religions, even in urban centers. And the mark of that influence, as Freyre said, goes far beyond mere religious and culinary conventions.

Change in racial views

Recent years have seen the rediscovery and redefinition of Brazil's African past, including the revision of racist views of history. Brazilian history books at the turn of the century often contained racist passages. One text noted that 'negroes of the worst quality, generally those from the Congo, were sent to the fields and the mines.' The preamble of an early 20th-century immigration law said, 'It is necessary to pre-

Lobsters and prawns for sale on the beach at Trancoso.

serve and develop the ethnic composition of our population by giving preference to its most desirable European elements.'

Modern social scientists, starting with Freyre, have catalogued the real achievements of Brazil's early black residents. For example, the Africans often possessed highly developed manual skills in carpentry, masonry and mining. Much of the best Baroque carving that graces Bahia's colonial churches was done by Africans.

In Minas Gerais, the illegitimate son of a Portuguese builder and a black slave woman led Brazilian sculpture and architecture into the high Baroque. Antônio Francisco Lisboa, called Aleijadinho ('The Little Cripple', because of a deformation some have attributed to arthritis,

others to leprosy), started late in the 18th century with his elegant São Francisco church in Ouro Preto and the larger, more elaborate São Francisco in São João del Rei. He also created 78 sinuous and lifelike soapstone and cedar carvings at the Basílica do Senhor Bom Jesus de Matosinhos, in Congonhas do Campo.

Aleijadinho's miracle is that he created an informed yet innovative artistic idiom at the edge of Western civilization. During his remarkable 80-year lifetime he never studied art and never saw the ocean. Yet his Congonhas statues are numbered among the greatest collections of Baroque art in the world (see page 214).

In addition to their artistic attributes and manual skills, many Africans, especially the Yorubás of West Africa who dominated in Bahia, brought sophisticated political and religious practices to Brazil. Historians noted that they practiced the Islamic religion and were literate in Arabic. Their culture was rich in music, dance, art, and unwritten but majestic literature. Writes Freyre, 'In Bahia, many ... were, in every respect but political and social status, the equal or superior of their masters.'

Rebellion against slavery

These proud Africans did not simply accept their bondage. Brazil's previous view of its African slavery as 'less rigorous than that practiced by the French, English or North Americans' has been revised by historians, who note that nine violent slave rebellions rocked the province of Bahia between 1807 and 1835.

A German visitor to a Bahian plantation in the 19th century, Prince Adalbert of Prussia, reported that 'the loaded guns and pistols hanging up in the plantation owner's bedroom showed that he had no confidence in his slaves and had more than once been obliged to face them with his loaded gun.'

The story of Brazilian slavery is inevitably harrowing. Historians believe that 12 million Africans were captured and shipped to Brazil between 1549 and the outlawing of the Brazilian slave trade in 1853. Of that number, about 2 million people died on the slave boats before reaching Brazilian shores.

Once in Brazil, white masters treated their slaves as a cheap investment. An African youth enslaved by the owner of a sugar plantation or gold mine could expect to live eight years. It was cheaper to buy new slaves than preserve the health of existing ones. Enslaved Africans in the northeast were often in flight. Historians know of at least 10 large-scale *quilombos,* or slave retreats, formed during colonial days in the interior of the northeast. The largest of these, Palmares, had a population of 30,000 at its peak, and flourished for 67 years before being crushed in 1694. Palmares, like the other great *quilombos* of the 17th and 18th centuries, was run along the lines of an African tribal monarchy, with a king, a royal council, community and private property, a tribal army, and a priestly class.

dos Pretos discriminated against whites.

Brazilian slavery finally came to an end in 1888, when Princess Regent Isabel de Orléans e Bragança signed the Lei Aurea (Golden Law) abolishing the institution. This law immediately freed an estimated 800,000 slaves.

Socioeconomic development

Brazil's history of racism and slavery left its non-white population unprepared for the 21st century. Today, Afro-Brazilians lag behind in socioeconomic terms, creating a vicious circle that has resulted in persistent discrimination.

An Afro-Brazilian family on Coroa Vermelha beach.

In some respects, however, Brazilian slavery was more liberal than its equivalents elsewhere. Owners were prohibited by law from separating slave families, and were required to grant slaves their freedom if they could pay a fair market price. A surprising number of slaves were able to achieve manumission. Freed slaves often went on to form religious brotherhoods, with the support of the Catholic Church, particularly Jesuit missionaries. The brotherhoods raised money to buy the freedom of more slaves, and some of them became quite wealthy.

In Ouro Preto, one such brotherhood built one of the most beautiful colonial churches in Brazil, the Igreja da Nossa Senhora do Rosário dos Pretos. In a backlash against slavery, Rosário

SOCIAL ISSUES

Divorce and abortion are two areas where Brazilian laws have lagged behind. Until 1977, divorce was unlawful, but there was a provision for legal separation – a desquite. This guaranteed that a woman could claim alimony, but the marriage was not legally terminated, so neither party could remarry. The law was streamlined and modernized in 2007. Abortion is more problematic. In 2005 and 2008, a bill to legalize abortion was presented to Congress, but quashed by the Catholic Church and the pro-life movement. A 2010 poll by Vox Populi showed that 82 percent of those polled were still happy with the current abortion legislation.

According to São Paulo human-rights attorney Dalmo Dallari, 'We have, in our Constitution and laws, the explicit prohibition of racial discrimination. But, it is equally clear that such laws are merely an expression of intentions with little practical effect.' Dallari and others point to persistent, widespread discrimination. Blacks being barred at the doors of restaurants and told to 'go to the service entrance' by apartment-building doormen is among many examples.

There is also a more subtle face to Brazilian racial discrimination. São Paulo's ex-State Gov-

Woman from the former gold-mining town of Ouro Preto.

ernment Afro-Brazilian Affairs Coordinator, Percy da Silva, said: 'While it may be true that blacks are no longer slaves, it is also a fact blacks do not have the same opportunities as whites. We are, to a great extent, stigmatized, seen as inferior. We must show a double capacity, both intellectual and personal, to be accepted in many places, especially the workplace.'

Thankfully, this began to change with the appointment, by President Lula in 2002, of the first black cabinet officials, though there still remain very few black diplomats, corporate leaders, or legislators.

The economic condition of Afro-Brazilians was amply documented in a 2006 report published by the Brazilian Census Bureau (IBGE).

The report showed that, while whites formed 49.9 percent of the total population, 88.4 percent of the richest 1 percent of Brazilians were white. Over half of whites in the 18 to 24 age bracket – 51.6 percent – attended college. On the other hand, when it came to the 48 percent

> Although there are no official records, it is estimated that around 2.5 million Brazilians live outside Brazil. There are sizeable communities in the US, the UK, in Canada, Italy, France, Germany, Spain, and, of course, Portugal.

of Brazil's population categorized as Afro-Brazilian or mixed-race, only 19 percent in the same age bracket attended college. Of Brazil's richest 1 percent, only 11.6 percent were black or brown, but of the poorest 10 percent, almost two-thirds were black or brown.

In 2004, the richest 10 percent of Brazilian society still controlled 45 percent of the nation's wealth, while the poorest 50 percent had to divide a mere 14 percent of the nation's riches. Fully one quarter of Brazil's population lived below what officials stunningly dubbed 'the misery line,' defined as personal income of about US$50 per month or less, but these numbers are falling thanks to new social programmes, such as Bolsa Família, which have seen the real earnings of the poorest 10 percent of the Brazilian population increase by nearly 30 percent since 2009.

But social inequalities are an old story in Brazil. In his classic study contrasting US and Brazilian development, *Bandeirantes e Pioneiros*, author Vianna Moog writes, 'Right from the start, there was a fundamental difference of motivation between the colonization of North America and that of Brazil. In the former case, the initial sentiments were spiritual, organic and constructive, while in the latter, they were predatory and selfish, with religious influences only secondary.' The foundations were laid for a lasting pattern of social inequalities.

Women's role

Historically, the treatment afforded to women in Brazil has not been much better than that extended to blacks or the poor. Mrs Elizabeth Cabot Agassiz, wife of the famed Swiss-born naturalist, Louis Agassiz, noted that, during their 1865 visit to Brazil, special permission was needed from Emperor Dom Pedro II for her to attend one of her husband's lectures. 'Ordinarily, no women were allowed,' she wrote later. 'Having one on hand was evidently too great an innovation of national habits.'

But the position of women in Brazilian society has changed greatly. In 2010, two of the three candidates for the presidency of the country were women, and, on October 31, 2010 Dilma Rousseff was duly elected as the first female president of Brazil. She took office on January 1, 2011.

was even more telling, finding that among professionals and managers, women with exactly the same qualifications and experience as men earned only 91 percent of what their male colleagues earned. According to a report published by the United Nations in 2010, income inequality between races in Brazil has narrowed over the past decade, but a black woman still earns only half of what a white man makes. The difference in income between blacks and whites in Brazil narrowed by 31 percent between 1995 and 2005, according to the study.

Brazilian President Dilma Rousseff.

As part of Rousseff's plan to stimulate the presence of women in business and leadership, 26 percent of her cabinet were female in 2013, and the number of female CEOs in the private sector has also risen sharply.

But while welcome progress has been made, women still lag behind in terms of most economic indicators. According to the IGBE, as of 2004, women members of the workforce were still disproportionately represented in the lowest income brackets, with 71 percent of women earning US$200 a month or less, against only 55 percent of men. Overall, women's earnings in 2005 were estimated to be only 70 percent of men's. A 2006 study by the Brazilian Development Bank (BNDES)

A nation of immigrants

Like the United States, Brazil is a nation of immigrants, and not just from Portugal, the original colonizing country. Rodrigues, Fernandes, de Souza and other Latin names dominate the phone book in some Brazilian cities. But, in others, names such as Alaby or Geisel, Tolentino, or Kobayashi appear more than once.

The presence of many ethnic groups in Brazil dates from the 1850s, when the imperial government encouraged European immigration to help rebuild the labor force as the slave trade declined. The first incomers were German and Swiss farmers who settled mainly in the three southern states of Rio Grande do Sul, Santa Catarina and Paraná, where the soil and climate were most similar to those in Europe.

For decades, some communities, such as Novo Hamburgo in Rio Grande do Sul and Blumenau in Santa Catarina, were more German than Brazilian. Protestant religious services were as common as Roman Catholic ones, and German rather than Portuguese was the first language of most residents. Such towns still bear the distinctive mark of their Teutonic heritage, with Alpine-style architecture dominating the landscape and restaurant menus offering more *knackwurst* and *eisbein* than *feijoada*.

By the turn of the century, Brazil was hosting immigrants from around the globe. According to records held by the foreign ministry, a total of 5 million immigrants arrived on Brazilian shores between 1884 and 1973, when restrictive legislation was adopted. Italy sent the greatest number, 1.4 million; Portugal sent 1.2 million people; Spain sent 580,000; Germany 200,000; and Russia 110,000, including many Jews who settled in São Paulo and Rio.

The call for immigrants reached beyond the borders of Europe. Starting in 1908, with the arrival in Santos harbor of the *Kasato Maru*, 250,000 Japanese left their homeland to live in Brazil. The descendants of these people, who were fleeing crop failures and earthquakes in their native islands, still live in metropolitan São Paulo, most visibly in the Japanese Liberdade district (see page 191). By the millennium it was estimated that around 1.5 million people of Japanese descent were living in Brazil – the largest Japanese population outside of Japan.

The Middle East sent 700,000 immigrants, mostly from Syria and Lebanon, during the early 20th century. Sprawling commercial districts in two cities – around Rua do Ouvidor in Rio and Rua 25 de Março in São Paulo – feature shops owned by people of Middle Eastern origin.

Despite the impact of mass communications and the trend toward political centralization, the process of molding diverse populations into one is far from complete. One reason is the strength of regionalism: when this comes to the fore, all shades of the racial and religious spectrum blend together, and regional solidarity becomes the defining factor.

A young Japanese man in São Paulo.

THE ITALIAN INFLUENCE

Starting in the 1870s, nearly a million Italian immigrants, fleeing poverty and hardship in Europe, flooded into São Paulo state. Many worked on coffee plantations, while others entered the growing urban workforce in São Paulo and neighboring cities. Within a generation, the Italians were established in the trades and professions; within two they were a new elite, thanks to families such as the Martinellis and the Matarazzos. One of Brazil's first skyscrapers was the 30-story Martinelli Building, built in 1929. A few decades later, the 46-story Itália Building went up on Ipiranga Avenue – the tallest building in South America when it was completed in 1965.

Another half a million Italians arrived in Brazil during the late 19th century. Used to working on the land, they had little taste for city life, so many of them headed south and settled in a temperate, hilly region of the southern state of Rio Grande do Sul. They brought the secrets of viniculture to a country where wine production was negligible. Today, the industry is flourishing, and Brazil's best wines are produced in the region around Caxias do Sul (see page 232). In 1931, Caxias inaugurated its signature event, the biennial Festival of the Grape, held in February to March in even years (2014, 2016, and so on), which celebrates the Italian heritage and culture.

THE AMERINDIANS

The survival of Brazil's indigenous people, and their
many different languages, hangs in the balance. In
recent years, some of their expropriated land has been
returned to them, but there is still a long way to go.

The first contact Brazilian Amerindians
had with European civilization was in
1500, when the Portuguese explorer,
Pedro Alvarez Cabral, blown off course on a
voyage to India, reached the shores of their
country. For many years, Brazilian historians
estimated that there were about 4 million
Amerindians in Brazil at that time, but more
recently, some anthropologists have begun to
believe there may have been far more, possibly as many as 30 million. This new way
of thinking came about because many old
Amerindian settlements are still being uncovered as new areas of Amazon rainforest are
cut down.

Pieces of the past

Until recently, anthropologists also agreed that
the ancestors of all Amerindians had migrated
from Central Asia across the Bering Strait and
down through the Americas about 10,000 years
ago. However, ancient-pottery finds in the Amazon and the wide variety of indigenous cultures
have led some experts to believe that Amerindians have lived in Brazil much longer, and may
have come across the Pacific.

Tropical forest provides abundant timber, but
it is a poor source of stone, and the Amerindians' shifting lifestyle left behind few of the
lasting monuments considered the mark of
advanced civilizations.

Yet any assumption that Stone Age Amerindian culture was primitive has been chal-
lenged by recent archeological discoveries,
which suggest, on the contrary, that substantial, permanent, and highly organized cities
existed in pre-Columbian Amazonia. Once
again, the accepted view of Amerindian history is under scrutiny.

Over 200 tribes vanished in the early 20th century.

Mixed messages

Early Portuguese explorers were greatly
impressed by the Amerindians' innocence and
generosity. They were regarded as 'noble sav-
ages,' and some were shipped to Europe to be
paraded before royalty. Thus, in the early post-
contact years, the Amerindians were relatively
well treated, but soon the colonizers' greed and
the serious shortage of labor on the sugar plantations led them to overcome any moral scru-
ples. Raiders – known as *bandeirantes* – traveled
up from São Paulo to bring back Amerindians
as slaves. Their brutality was legendary, and
appalled Jesuit missionaries who opposed
enslaving the indigenous people. The Jesuits
tried to protect and convert the Amerindians by

forcing forest-dwelling tribes to live in *aldeias* (settlements). The missions replaced native culture with Christianity and hard labor, but encouraged the people to resist enslavement. There is still debate over whether the Jesuits defended or helped crush the Amerindians. Whatever their motives, both missionaries and *bandeirantes* introduced Western diseases such as measles and influenza, and hundreds of thousands of Amerindians died as a result.

Slavery and violence

In 1755, Portugal freed all Amerindians from slavery, but the effects were sadly negligible. The Jesuits were soon after expelled, and their missions were put under the control of lay directors who could make profits from the indigenous people's forced labor. Under the Jesuits, the seven Guarani missions held 30,000 Amerindians. By 1821, unable to adapt to life in crowded settlements, forced to labor as debt slaves, and at the mercy of alien diseases, only 3,000 had survived. Furthermore, the introduction of alcohol had corrupted Amerindian culture, and whites consequently regarded them as lazy, shiftless, and incapable of integration.

The advance of cattle ranchers across the northeastern plains, and of gold miners in the south, resulted in bloody conflicts. By the time the Portuguese royal family fled to Brazil in 1807 (see page 37), whites outnumbered Amerindians. A new edict was issued, permitting the enslavement of Amerindians in the south. In 1845, the indigenous people were restored to mission life, just in time for their labor to be exploited for extracting rubber from the rainforest.

As the need for labor declined, extreme racial 'solutions' came to the fore. In 1908, Hermann von Ihering, the director of São Paulo Museum, defended the extermination of all remaining Amerindians in Santa Catarina and Paraná who threatened German and Italian immigrants. In the early 1900s, *bugreiros*, paid hunters hired by the colonists, prided themselves on poisoning, shooting, or raping Kaingáng people who attempted to stop the construction of a railroad line.

The Fundação Nacional do Indio

Fewer than a million Amerindians survived, but public opinion was beginning to turn. In 1910, the explorer and humanist soldier, Cândido Mariano da Silva Rondon – who instructed his troops: 'Die if you have to, but never shoot!' – formed the Fundação Nacional do Indio. It was nevertheless too late to stop the widespread destruction of indigenous cultures.

In 1960, anthropologists found that one-third of the 230 tribes known to exist 60 years earlier had vanished. As the agricultural frontier moved west, then north, one group of Amerindians after another became extinct, and the population dropped to 200,000. When, in the 1960s and 1970s, the government built a huge network of roads across the Amazon jungle and encouraged white settlers to move in, it seemed

Indigenous Brazilian wearing a quill.

FAIR-WEATHER FRIENDS

Despite the relatively fair treatment accorded them by the Europeans in the early years of colonization, some indigenous people were suspicious, realizing that attitudes could change to suit circumstances. 'Do not trust the whites. They are the men who control the lightning, who live without a homeland, who wander to satisfy their thirst for gold. They are kind to us when they need us, for the land they tread and the rivers they assault are ours. Once they have achieved their goals, they are false and treacherous.' So wrote Rosa, a Borôro Amerindian, and she was right: the men 'without a homeland' had little respect for the lands they conquered.

that the few remaining Amerindians would soon be exterminated. But since then they have staged a remarkably successful comeback.

The Panara

At the end of the 1960s, the Panara (or Kreen-Akore and Krenakore, as they were known at the time) were rumored to be a fierce and elusive people. They were seen as an obstacle in the drive to open up the interior of Brazil to economic development through the construction of the Cuiabá–Santarém highway across the hitherto isolated Amazon basin. The Panara

> Modern Brazilians are reminded of their country's indigenous roots daily, through place names, foods, and rituals.

in northern Mato Grosso and southern Pará in the Amazon basin. They found much of the land devastated by mining, ranching, and logging. Even so, the Panara are slowly reconstructing their old life, with its myths, rituals, songs, dances, and rhythms of work; and an area comprising more than 490,000 hectares (1.2 million

Yanomami people crossing a river by boat.

were contacted by anthropologists just days before the highway construction teams reached their land.

Once contacted, they were devastated by disease and reduced to begging. In 1975, 79 demoralized survivors were taken by plane to the Xingú Amerindian reserve over 1,000km (620 miles) away, an action that caused outrage at home and abroad. With the help of a group of anthropologists, the Panara waged a campaign to regain their land. The political climate, in Brazil and internationally, changed and their demands began to receive a more sympathetic hearing.

Some 20 years after their expulsion, the tide turned. In October 1995, a small group of Panara people were taken back to their traditional lands

acres) of unoccupied forest was recognized in the Brazilian courts as their reserve in 1996.

The attitude of the establishment has evolved since the creation of the Xingú Park reserve, where several different tribes coexist. Though flawed, the reserve can be considered a success. The Xingú retain their tribal organization because contact with 'civilization' is limited, but many have developed business activities and been elected as government officials.

Amerindian affairs are now under the jurisdiction of FUNAI (Fundação Nacional do Indio), Rondon's agency, which was rehabilitated in 1967 and greatly expanded its activities during the Fernando Henrique Cardoso and Lula governments. FUNAI is responsible for demarcating Amerindian tribal land as protection against ranchers, miners, and loggers.

Staging a recovery

The Panara's return to their ancestral land is symbolic of a revival in the fortunes of Amerindians. The 2000 census showed numbers had increased by 138 percent since 1990; while the 2010 census recorded that there are now an estimated 900,000 Amerindians in the country, 460,000 of whom live on their own lands. Once the demarcation process is complete, their territories will cover about 10 percent of Brazil's total landmass.

Gold-panners frequently invade the reserve allocated to the 27,000-strong Yanomami who live near the border with Venezuela. These illegal prospectors, *garimpeiros*, whom the government is either unable or unwilling to police – have brought violence, pollution, and disease.

Other Amerindian groups have found it difficult to deal with the strains imposed by the modern world. There are about 25,000 Guarani-Kaiowa Amerindians in some 22 villages scattered over largely deforested scrubland in Mato Grosso do Sul in central Brazil. Without adequate provisions or reserves to sustain them, many are forced to work as farm laborers. A large proportion of them are unable to cope with the traumatic change this brings to their lifestyle, and there has been an alarmingly high rate of suicides. Government health agency FUNASA reported that 555 Guarani committed suicide between 2000 and 2011, the majority of them in their teens or early twenties.

The Guarani-Kaiowa Amerindians have started to fight back. They have carried out a series of *retomadas* – retaking the lands from which they had been expelled. *Retomadas* are often violent, as the occupants, predominantly cattle-rearers, struggle to retain their hold on the land. Between 2010 and 2012, 71 murders were registered on the reserve.

In 2007 FUNAI reported that it had confirmed the presence of 67 different uncontacted tribes in Brazil, up from 40 in 2005. Dia dos Indios was introduced by President Getúlio Vargas in 1943. The day is to encourage the Brazilian population to think about the Amerindians and part they have played in the country's history.

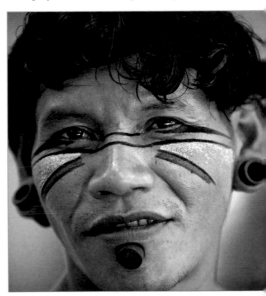

Portrait of a Pataxo Indian man at the Reserva Indigena da Jaqueira.

THE STRUGGLE FOR SURVIVAL

The unhappy history of Amerindian contact with whites means that today, casual visitors are not encouraged to visit the reserves administered by FUNAI (www.funai. gov.br). Even bona fide researchers must be willing to apply in advance and wait for permission.

Amerindians in parts of Brazil are still in crisis, and some have taken desperate measures. In March 2003, the Cauruaia in the southwest of Pará seized hostages in protest at miners on their reserve poisoning rivers and wildlife with mercury in order to extract gold.

Although indigenous groups initially welcomed the election of President Lula da Silva in 2002, the following year saw a disturbing escalation of murders and attacks throughout the country. President Lula's ratification, in April 2005, of the Raposa Serra do Sol territory in the northern state of Roraima, a 16,800 sq km (6,500 sq mile) area that is the traditional home of some 20,000 Macuxi, Wapichana, Ingarikã, Patamona, and Taurepang people, represented a victory for Amerindians in the region, who have struggled for more than 30 years for recognition of their land rights. Progress has been slow, partly because the reserve borders both Venezuela and Guyana, but in 2009, Brazil's Supreme Court ruled that the reservation should be solely for indigenous people, and ordered the government to remove any remaining rice producers and farm workers from the region.

Pataxó Indian ceremonial house.

DECISIVE DATES

Colonial era (1500–1822)

1409
The Treaty of Tordesillas divides the non-European world between Portugal and Spain. Portugal gets present-day Brazil.

1500
Portuguese explorer Pedro Alvares Cabral is the first European to set foot in Brazil, which he names Ilha de Vera Cruz.

1501–2
Amerigo Vespucci sails along the Brazilian coast, naming places after the saints on whose days they were first sighted.

1533
The colony is divided into 15 captaincies (capitanias), each governed by a Portuguese courtier.

1549
A central administration based in Salvador oversees the captaincies. Colonists and

Pedro Alvares Cabral.

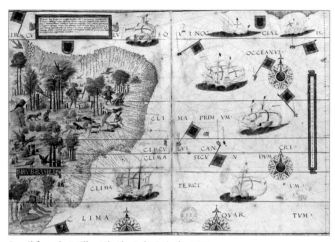

Brazil from the 'Miller Atlas' by Pedro Reinel, c.1519.

Jesuit missionaries argue about the treatment of Amerindians.

1549
Royal decree gives Jesuits control over Christianised Amerindians; colonists are allowed to enslave those captured in war. Colonists import slaves to boost workforce.

1550–1800
Sugar cane, grown on huge plantations worked by African slaves, is the most important crop, supplemented by tobacco, cattle and, later, cotton and coffee.

1555
The French build a garrison on the site of present-day Rio de Janeiro, but are driven out in 1565 by governor general Mem de Sá, who founds a city.

1580–1640
Portugal and Spain are united.

1600s
Expeditions (bandeiras) of settlers delve into the interior in search of gold and slaves. Many Amerindians are wiped out by European diseases, enslavement and massacres.

1624–54
The Dutch West India Company conquers much of the northeast. A Dutch prince, Maurice of Nassau, rules Pernambuco, in the heart of the sugar cane-growing region, 1637–44.

1695
Discovery of gold in Minas Gerais leads to the growth of gold-rush towns in the interior.

1759
After years of disputes with colonists and Portuguese government, Jesuits are expelled.

1763
Rio de Janeiro becomes the capital city.

1789

An independence movement, the Inconfidência Mineira, springs up in Ouro Preto. In 1792 its leader, Joaquim José da Silva Xavier (Tiradentes) is hanged and the movement collapses soon afterwards.

1807

King João VI flees Portugal to escape Napoleon, and establishes his court in Rio. He introduces many reforms; Brazil is allowed to trade freely.

1821

João returns to Portugal and names his son, Pedro, as prince regent and governor of Brazil.

The Empire (1822–89)

1822

Pedro I proclaims independence from Portugal, and establishes Brazilian Empire, which is recognized by the US and, in 1825, by Portugal.

1831

Pedro I abdicates in favour of his five-year-old son (also Pedro). Political leaders run the country, and face revolts and army rebellions.

1840–89

The reign of Pedro II sees the population increase from 4 million to 14 million. Wars with neighboring countries strengthen the military, while the emperor's opposition to slavery makes him enemies among the landowning class.

1853

Importation of slaves ends.

1870–1914

Manaus becomes prosperous from Amazonian rubber trade, but declines when Asia starts producing the crop, using seeds smuggled out of Brazil.

1871

All children born to slaves are declared free.

1888

The last slaves are freed.

Republican Brazil (1889–1963)

1889

Pedro II overthrown by the military and sent into exile.

1890s

Coffee makes São Paulo the country's commercial center and dominant power base.

1894

Prudente de Morais becomes first elected civilian president.

1930–45

After riots, the army installs Getúlio Vargas as president. He assumes total power, brings in social security and minimum wage.

1942

Brazil declares war on Germany – the only Latin American country to take an active part in World War II.

1950

Brazil hosts the fourth World Cup, the first after World War II. It is played in six cities and 13 teams take part.

1950–4

Vargas again made president, this time in a democratic election. In 1954, on the brink of a military coup, he commits suicide.

1953

Founding of national oil company, Petrobras.

1956

President Juscelino Kubitschek unveils a five-year plan aiming to achieve rapid industrialization.

1958

With Pelé in its side, Brazil wins World Cup in Sweden.

1960

The new capital city, Brasília, is inaugurated.

Doctor Getulio Vargas singing the decree appointing his Cabinet in 1930.

Pelé playing in the 1958 World Cup.

1961
President Jânio Quadros resigns, after only seven months in office.

1962
Brazil retains the World Cup in Chile.

Military dictatorship (1964–84)

1964–7
General Castelo Branco rules as president after a successful military coup.

1968
General Arthur da Costa e Silva closes Congress and institutes a program of repression.

1969–74
Under General Emílio Garrastazu Medici, state terrorism is used against insurgents, but the economy soars.

1970
In Mexico, Brazil wins the World Cup for third time to win Jules Rimet Trophy outright.

1972
Emerson Fittipaldi becomes the first Brazilian to win the Formula One drivers' championship. He wins again in 1974, becoming CART champion in 1989 and two-time winner of Indianapolis 500.

1974–9
General Ernesto Geisel begins a gradual relaxation of the military regime.

1979
João Baptista Figueiredo becomes military president. Political rights restored to the opposition.

1981
Nelson Piquet is Formula One World Champion. He wins again in 1983 and 1987.

1982
Latin American debt crisis – Brazil has the largest national debt in the Third World.

1984
1.5 million Brazilians demonstrate in São Paulo for the return of democratic rights, 'Direitos Já.'

1985–present

1985
Tancredo Neves becomes president, but dies six weeks later. José Sarney succeeds him.

1985
Rock in Rio, Brazil's largest rock festival takes place. The crowd is estimated at 1.5 million. Further festivals are held in 1991, 2001, 2011, and 2013.

1986
Sarney's economic package, the Cruzado Plan, attempts unsuccessfully to curb rampant inflation.

1988
A new constitution is introduced. Chico Mendes, defender of the rainforest, is murdered.

1988
Ayrton Senna is Formula One World Champion. He wins again in 1990 and 1991.

Chico Mendes.

1989
Fernando Collor de Mello is elected president.

1992
UN Earth Summit is held in Rio, at the time the largest-ever gathering of heads of state and government.

1992
Collor resigns amid corruption scandals.

1994
National hero Ayrton Senna dies after a crash at the San Marino Grand Prix.

1994
Brazil wins the World Cup in the US.

1994
Fernando Henrique Cardoso is elected president. His Plano Real brings inflation under control and he is re-elected in 1998.

2000
Brazil celebrates its 500th anniversary as a country.

2001
Such is the potential of Brazil, Russia, India and China to be the dominant global economies by 2050, they become known as the 'BRIC' countries.

Preparing a campaign billboard for then presidential-hopeful Luiz Inacio Lula da Silva in 2002.

2002
Brazil wins World Cup for a fifth time in Japan and Korea. Financial markets in Brazil and abroad panic at the prospect of victory of Luiz Inácio Lula da Silva. He becomes the country's first left-wing president for 40 years.

2003
Twenty-one people killed when a space satellite explodes at the Alcântara space center.

2004
Brazil, with Germany, Japan, and India, launches a bid to become a member of the UN Security Council. Brazil's first space rocket launched.

2005
Senior figures in Lula's Workers' Party resign after serious allegations of corruption.

2006
A private executive jet en route to the US collides with a Gol Boeing 737 over Mato Grosso; 154 passengers and crew are killed. In the second round of voting in the presidential elections, Lula is re-elected to a second four-year term.

2007
Government recognizes human-rights abuses carried out under the military dictatorship between 1964 and 1985. Rio de Janeiro hosts the Pan American Games. Awarded the 2014 FIFA World Cup.

2008
Environment minister Marina Silva resigns from the government and joins the Green Party. She is the party's presidential candidate in 2010. Brazil turns down an invitation to join OPEC.

2009
Brazil offers $10 billion to the IMF to improve the availability of credit in developing countries. President Obama says at the G20 in London that President Lula is 'most popular politician on earth,' Rio de Janeiro awarded the 2016 Summer Olympic Games. Massive 'Pré-sal' (pre-salt) oil and gas fields discovered off the coast of Brazil.

2010
Dilma Rousseff is elected as Brazil's first female president, with 56 percent of the vote.

2012
Brazil's main airline, TAM, merges with Chile's LAN to form LATAM, the largest airline in South America. Brazilian architect Oscar Niemeyer, who designed some of the 20th Century's most famous modernist buildings, dies on December 5 at the age of 104.

2013
A fire in a nightclub in Santa Maria, Rio Grande do Sul, kills at least 242 people. Brazilian Roberto Azevedo is appointed director general of the World Trade Organization. Pope Francis, born in neighboring Argentina, makes his first overseas trip to Brazil to take part in World Youth Day in Rio de Janeiro. Brazil hosts and wins the Confederations Cup. There is widespread civil unrest during the tournament as sections of the public protest about the behavior of politicians and a series of diverse issues.

2014
Brazil to host the FIFA World Cup Tournament. Twelve cities will host the games, with 32 countries taking part. Presidential election to be held.

2016
Rio de Janeiro to host the Olympic and Paralympic games.

Funeral cortège of Pedro II, 1891.

THE MAKING OF BRAZIL

The only Portuguese-speaking country in Latin America, Brazil became an empire in the 19th century. Throughout the centuries, however, it played only a minor role in shaping the world – but that is now changing fast.

Brazil has often avoided the kind of violent upheavals that have occurred so frequently elsewhere in Latin America. Brazilians feel that they have a way of resolving their disputes through compromise rather than confrontation. Brazil's history sets it apart from the rest of South America. In addition to its size, which dwarfs that of its neighbors, Brazil stands out because of its language, Portuguese; its colonial period, in which it became the seat of government of the mother country; its mostly bloodless path towards independence; and its largely peaceful relations with its neighbors.

Discovery and colonization

The discovery of Brazil in 1500 by Pedro Alvares Cabral occurred during a series of voyages launched by the great Portuguese navigators in the 15th and 16th centuries. Cabral, sailing to India via the Cape of Good Hope, was blown off course. At first he thought he had discovered an island, and named it Ilha de Vera Cruz. When it became obvious that it was the east coast of a continent, it was renamed Terra de Santa Cruz, but eventually became Brazil after one of the colony's primary products, *pau brasil* or brazil wood, highly valued in Europe for red dye extract.

In 1533, the Portuguese crown made its first determined effort to organize the colonization of Brazil. The coastline – the only area that had been explored – was divided into 15 captaincies, given to Portuguese noblemen who received hereditary rights. They were expected to settle and develop them, using their own resources in order to spare the crown this expense. The two most important captaincies were São Vicente in the southeast (now the state of São Paulo) and Pernambuco in the northeast, where the

Pedro Alvares Cabral.

GOLD SPAWNS NEW TOWNS

In the mountains of the central plateau, the bandeirantes found what they had been looking for – gold. In 1695, a gold rush brought thousands of settlers to what is today the state of Minas Gerais (General Mines), the first mass settlement of Brazil's vast interior. Towns sprang up, and by 1750 the city of Ouro Preto had a population of 80,000. The gold found here made Brazil the 18th century's largest producer of this precious metal. All the wealth, however, went to Portugal – a fact that did nothing to please the colonists who were already feeling more Brazilian than Portuguese, and was to lead to calls for independence.

It was because of the Jesuits' initial success in preventing enslavement of the Amerindians that the colony looked elsewhere for manpower. Soon, slave ships were unloading slaves taken from the west coast of Africa.

introduction of sugar plantations quickly made the area the economic center of the colony.

The captaincies, however, couldn't satisfy the needs of either the colonists or Portugal. Left to the whims and financial means of their own-

A Jesuit missionary.

ers, some were simply abandoned. Furthermore, there was no coordination, so Brazil's coastline fell prey to constant attacks by French pirates. In 1549, King João III finally lost patience with the captaincy system and imposed a centralized colonial government on top of the existing divisions. The northeastern city of Salvador became the first capital of Brazil, a status it maintained for 214 years. Tomé de Sousa was installed as the colony's first governor general.

With this administrative reform, colonization again picked up. From 1549 until the end of the century, a variety of colonists arrived – mostly noblemen, adventurers, and Jesuit missionaries, charged with converting the Amerindians to Christianity. Several leading Jesuits, such as

Father José de Anchieta in São Paulo, declared that Amerindians were to be protected, not enslaved, which put them in direct conflict with the interests of the colonizers. The Jesuits built schools and missions, around which Amerindian villages sprang up, in an effort to protect them from slave traders.

French and Dutch occupations

In 1555, the French occupied what is now Rio de Janeiro, the first step towards a major French colony in South America. But they were unable to attract European colonists to the area, and in 1565, the Portuguese drove them out. Two years later, the city of São Sebastião do Rio de Janeiro was founded by the Portuguese.

This would be the last challenge to Portuguese control until the Dutch West India Company sent a fleet, which, in 1630, conquered the economically important sugar-growing region of Pernambuco. This followed Portugal's alliance with Spain (1580–1640), which brought Brazil under fire from Spain's enemies, Holland included. The Dutch established a functioning colony in Pernambuco and remained there until 1654, when they were driven out by a rebellion led by the colonists themselves.

The adventurers

In the same period, in the south of Brazil, bands of adventurers called *bandeirantes* (flag-carriers) began to march out from their base in São Paulo in search of Amerindian slaves and gold. The great marches (*bandeiras*) took them west, south and north into the hinterlands. Some of these treks lasted for years. Through the *bandeirantes*, the colony launched its first effort to define its frontiers. The adventurers clashed with the Jesuits, but there was nothing the missionaries could do to stop the great *bandeiras*, which reached south to Uruguay and Argentina, west to Peru and Bolivia and northwest to Colombia. In the process, the *bandeirantes* crossed the imaginary line of the Treaty of Tordesillas, which carved up South America into two empires. At the time, this had little significance, since Portugal and Spain were united, but after 1640, when Portugal again became an independent nation, the conquests were incorporated into Brazil against the protests of Spain.

As part of this period of nation-building, Jesuit missionaries moved into the Amazon, and the powerful landholders of the northeast expanded their influence and control into the arid backlands of this region. Uniting this huge colony was the Portuguese language and culture, which underlined the distinction between Brazil and Spanish South America. The Treaty of Madrid with Spain in 1750, and succeeding treaties, recognized the incursions of the *bandeirantes* and formally included these areas in the colony of Brazil.

Brazil in the 18th century had grown into a predominantly rural and coastal society. Wealth was concentrated in the hands of

to the southeast. In 1763, this led to Brazil's capital moving from Salvador to Rio de Janeiro. At the same time, the captaincies were taken over by the crown, four years after the last Jesuits were expelled from Brazil.

Liberal ideas

Brazil was isolated, but not entirely shut off from the outside world. By the second half of the 18th century, the liberal ideas popular in Europe began to enter Brazil's consciousness. In 1789, the country experienced its first independence movement, centered on the gold-rush

'Washing Precious Stones in Brazil', by Carlos Juliao.

a few landholding families. The principal products were sugar, tobacco, and cattle, but coffee and cotton were becoming increasingly important. Despite the Jesuit missions, the *bandeirantes* had managed to reduce drastically the Amerindian population through enslavement, disease, and massacre. Meanwhile, the population of African slaves had increased sharply. Brazil traded only with Portugal and, other than the marches of the *bandeirantes*, had little contact with its neighbors. All this, however, was about to change, with the discovery of gold at the end of the 17th century.

Gold shifted the colony's center of wealth from the sugar-producing areas of the northeast

boomtown of Ouro Preto. The catalyst was a decision by Portugal to increase the tax on gold. But the Inconfidência Mineira, as it was called, ended badly, with the arrest of its leaders. One of these, Joaquim José da Silva Xavier, a dentist better known as Tiradentes, or Tooth-Puller, was hanged and quartered.

Other movements would probably have followed but for developments in Europe. In 1807, Napoleon conquered Portugal, forcing the royal family into exile. King João VI fled to Brazil, making the colony the seat of government for the mother country, the only instance of such a turnaround during the colonial period.

Brazil's changed status led to the crown opening up commerce with other nations,

The golden age of Pedro II

The modern world thinks of President Luiz Inácio Lula da Silva as the man who put Brazil on the political map, but it was a reigning monarch that helped shape the country.

Pedro II reigned for 49 years, from 1840 to 1889, using his extraordinary talents to give Brazil its longest continuous period of political stability.

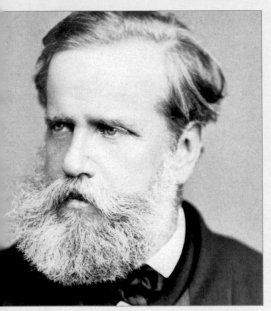

Pedro II.

Despite his royal birth, Pedro was a humble man who felt uncomfortable with the traditional trappings of an emperor, but he was blessed with enormous personal authority and charisma. During the American Civil War, Abraham Lincoln remarked that the only man he would trust to arbitrate between north and south was Pedro.

Born in Rio de Janeiro, Pedro was classically educated. He married Teresa Cristina Maria, daughter of Francis I of Sicily, and fathered four children. Illustrations of Pedro's character and scholarly interests are preserved in the neoclassical summer palace he built in Petrópolis (see page 166).

Pedro was not only learned but also politically astute. He managed to keep regional rivalries in check and, through his own popularity, extend the control of central government. Against this backdrop, Brazil grew wealthy and economically stable, and considerable technological progress was made. Yet Pedro also pursued a series of risky and controversial foreign policies..

Pedro was determined to maintain regional parity in South America, which led him to interfere with developments in Uruguay, Argentina, and Paraguay. As a result, Brazil fought three wars between 1851 and 1870. First, in 1851, to ensure free navigation on the River Plate and its tributaries, Pedro sent troops into Uruguay, gaining a quick victory and a new Brazil-friendly government, with which he then allied in order to overthrow the Argentine dictator Juan Manuel Rosas.

The Paraguayan War

A second incursion against Uruguay in 1864 provoked war with Paraguay. Allied with the losing side in Uruguay, Paraguay's ruler Francisco Solano López struck back against Brazil and Argentina. In 1865, the so-called triple alliance was formed, joining Brazil, Argentina, and Uruguay against Paraguay. After initial successes, the alliance suffered a series of setbacks, and the war dragged on until 1870, becoming the longest in South America in the 19th century.

The consequent elevation to prominence of Brazil's military leaders meant that Pedro needed their support to remain in power – and when he lost it, he quickly fell from grace, in spite of his popularity with the masses. Ironically, the issue that led to his demise was slavery, whose abolition, from today's perspective, was perhaps his greatest achievement. In the latter half of the 19th century, the Brazilian economy was still overwhelmingly agricultural, and slaves continued to play a major role. However, in the 1860s an abolitionist movement gathered pace, which led to the end of slavery in 1888. Slavery was clearly doomed: bringing slaves into the country had been outlawed in 1853, so the existing slave population was in decline, and Brazil was increasingly isolated in maintaining the institution. Nevertheless, its abolition set the nation's landholders against Pedro.

By this time, the military, like the landholders, also felt under-represented, and in November 1889, a military revolt led to a bloodless coup. Pedro II was deposed, and Brazil's most popular leader was forced into exile. He died in Paris in 1891, where he was given a royal funeral. His body, and that of his wife, were returned to Brazil in 1920 and reburied in Petrópolis in 1939.

in particular England, Portugal's ally against Napoleon. When King João at last returned to Portugal in 1821, he named his son, Dom Pedro, regent, making him head of government for Brazil. But the Portuguese parliament refused to recognize Brazil's new situation, and attempted to force a return to colonial dependence. Realizing that Brazilians would never accept this, on September 7, 1822 Pedro declared independence from Portugal, and in the process creating the Brazilian Empire, the first monarchy in the Americas.

With Portugal still recovering from the Napoleonic wars, Brazil faced little opposition from the mother country. Helped by a British soldier of fortune, Lord Alexander Thomas Cochrane, Brazilian forces quickly expelled the remaining Portuguese garrisons. By the end of 1823, the Portuguese had left and the new nation's independence was secured. The following year, the United States became the first foreign nation to recognize Brazil, and in 1825 relations were re-established with Portugal.

Internal divisions

The ease with which independence was won, however, proved to be a false indication of the young nation's immediate future. During its first 18 years, Brazil struggled to overcome bitter internal divisions, which in some cases reached the point of open revolt. The first disappointment was the emperor himself, who insisted on maintaining the privileges and power of an absolute monarch. Pedro I eventually agreed to the creation of a parliament, but fought with it constantly. Already widely disliked, he plunged Brazil into a reckless and unpopular war with Argentina over what was then the southernmost state of Brazil, Cisplatina. Brazil lost the war and Cisplatina, which is now Uruguay.

Pedro I abdicated in 1831 in favor of his five-year-old son, and from 1831 to 1840 Brazil was ruled by a triple regency of political leaders who ran the nation in the name of the young Pedro. The next nine years were the most violent in Brazil's history, with revolts and army rebellions in the northeast, the Amazon, Minas Gerais, and the south. Brazil appeared to be on the verge of civil war as regional factions fighting for autonomy threatened to tear the nation apart. The *farrapos* war, in the south, lasted 10 years and

almost led to the loss of what is today the state of Rio Grande do Sul.

In desperation, it was agreed in 1840 to declare Pedro II of age and hand over rule to a 15-year-old monarch. They were right to do so (see page 38). It is ironic that Brazil's most successful emperor was also its last.

Debts of the military

The end of the monarchy in 1889 marked the arrival of what was to become Brazil's most powerful institution – the military. From 1889 to the present day, the armed forces have been

Slaves making a street in Rio de Janeiro in 1839.

at the center of almost every major political development in Brazil. The first two governments of the republic were headed by military men, both of whom proved better at spending than governing. By the time a civilian president took office (Prudente de Morais, 1894–8), the country was deep in debt. The problem was faced by the country's second civilian president, Manuel Ferraz de Campos Salles (1898–1902), who was the first to negotiate rescheduling the foreign debt, and is credited with saving Brazil from financial collapse.

The astute Campos Salles and his successor, Francisco de Paula Rodrigues Alves (1902–6) managed to put Brazil back on its feet and set an example of success that few presidents have matched since. Brazil went through a period of dramatic social change between 1900 and 1930, when large numbers of immigrants arrived from Europe. Economic and political power shifted to the southeast. While certain states, namely São Paulo and Minas Gerais, increased their power and influence, the federal government had very little of either, becoming a prisoner of regional and economic interests.

Economic woes lead to coup

After World War I, in which Brazil declared war on Germany but did not take an active

The political crisis reached its zenith following the 1930 election of the establishment candidate Júlio Prestes, despite a major effort to mobilize the urban masses in favor of the opposition candidate Getúlio Vargas, governor of the state of Rio Grande do Sul. The opposition dug their heels in and refused to accept the election result. With the support of participants and backers of the lieutenants' movement, a revolt broke out in Minas Gerais, Rio Grande do Sul, and the northeast. Within just two weeks, the army had control of the country, overthrowing Prestes and installing Getúlio Vargas as the new president.

Marching troops in 1939.

role in the conflict, economic woes again beset the country. Spendthrift governments emptied the public coffers, while rumors of widespread corruption led to public unrest. Military movements also resurfaced, with an attempted coup in 1922 and an isolated revolt in São Paulo in 1924, put down with massive destruction by the federal government, whose troops bombarded the city of São Paulo at will.

The dissatisfaction in the barracks was led by a group of junior officers who became known as the *tenentes* (lieutenants). These officers were closely identified with the emerging urban middle class, which was searching for political leadership to oppose the wealthy landholders of São Paulo state and Minas Gerais.

DEMISE OF A DICTATOR

During his final years in office following his 1950 election, Getúlio Vargas tried to safeguard his position by introducing measures, such as the nationalization of oil production; nevertheless, he rapidly lost popularity. A political crisis sparked by an attempt on the life of one of his main political opponents, allegedly planned by an aide, finally brought the Vargas era to an end. When he was given an ultimatum by the military to resign or be forced out of office, Vargas instead chose a third route – on August 24, 1954 he committed suicide in the presidential palace. His death was to have a profound effect on Brazil.

The Vargas era

The rapid ascension of President Vargas signaled the beginning of a new era in Brazilian politics. A man linked to the urban middle and lower classes, Vargas represented a complete break from political control in the hands of the rural elite. The coffee barons of São Paulo and the wealthy landholders of other states and regions, the political power brokers of the old Republic, were suddenly out. The focus of politics in Brazil was shifted to the common man in the fast-growing urban centers.

Ironically, this dramatic upheaval did not lead to increased democracy. Intent on retaining power, Vargas initiated a policy marked by populism and nationalism that kept him at the center of political life for 25 years. During this period, he set the model for Brazilian politics for the rest of the 20th century, which saw the country alternate between populist political leaders and military intervention.

Vargas's basic strategy was to win the support of the urban masses and concentrate power in his own hands. Taking advantage of growing industrialization, Vargas used labor legislation as his key weapon: laws were passed creating a minimum wage and social-security system, paid vacations, maternity leave, and medical assistance. Vargas instituted reforms that legalized labor unions but also made them dependent on the federal government. He quickly became the most popular Brazilian leader since Dom Pedro II. In the new constitution, which was not drafted until 1934, and then only after an anti-Vargas revolt in São Paulo, Vargas further increased the powers of central government.

With the constitution approved, Vargas's 'interim' presidency ended and he was elected president by Congress in 1934. The constitution limited him to one four-year term, with elections scheduled for 1938, but Vargas refused to surrender power. In 1937, using the invented threat of a Communist coup and supported by the military, Vargas closed Congress and threw out the 1934 constitution, replacing it with a new document giving him dictatorial powers. The second part of the Vargas reign, which he glorified under the title The New State, proved far more tumultuous than his first seven years.

Brazil at war

Growing political opposition to Vargas's repressive means threatened to topple him, but the president saved himself by joining the Allies in World War II, declaring war on Germany in 1942. He sent an expeditionary force of 25,000 soldiers to Europe, where they joined the Allied Fifth Army in Italy, making Brazil the only Latin American country to take an active part in the war. Brazilian losses were light (some 450 dead), and the war effort served to distract the public and lessened the pressure on Vargas.

With the war winding down, however, Vargas was under threat from the military that had put him in power, so he approved

President Getúlio Vargas.

measures legalizing opposition political parties and calling for a presidential election at the end of 1945. But while he bargained with the opposition to prevent a coup, Vargas also instigated his backers in the labor movement to join forces with the Communists in a popular movement to keep him in office. Fearful that Vargas might succeed, the military ousted him from power on October 29, 1945, ending a 15-year reign.

In December 1945, Vargas's former war minister, General Eurico Gaspar Dutra, was elected president, serving a five-year term during which a new, liberal constitution was approved. Then, in 1950, Vargas returned to power, this time elected by the people.

New faces

The eventual removal of Vargas from the political scene, after his suicide in 1954, cleared the way for new faces. The first to emerge came again from the twin poles of Brazilian 20th-century politics, São Paulo and Minas Gerais. Juscelino Kubitschek from Minas and Jânio Quadros from São Paulo both used the same path to the presidency, first serving as mayors of their state capitals, and then as governors. Populism, nationalism, and military connections, the three leading themes of modern Brazilian politics, all played a part in their careers.

President Juscelino Kubitschek in Brasília.

Two new factors were the increasing linkage of economic growth with political developments and Brazil's growing economic and political ties with the outside world.

Kubitschek's vision

Kubitschek, an expansive and dynamic leader with a vision of Brazil as a world power, was elected president in 1955. He promised to give the country, 'Fifty years of progress in five.' For the first time, Brazil had a leader whose primary concern was economic growth. Under Kubitschek, there was rapid industrialization: foreign auto manufacturers invited to Brazil provided the initial impetus for what was to become an explosion of growth in the city and

> In 1960 President Quadros shocked Brazil by awarding a medal to Che Guevara. Some believe he did this to curry favor with the Soviet bloc. This might have contributed to his downfall, as he was removed from power after only eight months.

state of São Paulo. Government funds as well as incentives were used to build roads, steel mills, and hydroelectric plants, creating the precedent of direct government involvement in large-scale infrastructure projects. But Kubitschek's biggest project was the building of Brasília.

The idea of a new federal capital in the heart of the country came to obsess Kubitschek. Upon taking office, he ordered the plans drawn up, insisting Brazil would have a new capital before his term ended, designed by Brazil's best architects (see page 241). He wanted to develop the near-deserted central plain by moving thousands of civil servants from Rio. Nothing existed at the chosen site, so he faced enormous opposition from bureaucrats with no desire to leave the comforts and pleasures of Rio de Janeiro for an inland wilderness.

Between 1957 and 1960, construction of the new city continued at full speed, and on April 21, 1960, Kubitschek proudly inaugurated his capital. But while Brasília became a symbol of Kubitschek's dynamism, it also became an unceasing drain on the treasury. Brasília, and other grandiose public-works projects, meant that the Kubitschek administration left office having produced not only rapid growth, but also a soaring public debt, high inflation and vast corruption.

The situation seemed ready-made for Jânio Quadros, a self-styled reformer who used a broom as his campaign symbol, promising to sweep the government clean of all corruption. Instead, he embarked on a short but memorable administration culminating in an institutional crisis that ultimately brought an end to Brazil's experiment with democracy. Quadros was impatient, unpredictable, and autocratic. Insisting that everything be done exactly his way, he attempted to ignore Congress, sparking an open confrontation with the legislative branch, and surprised his followers by moving Brazil closer to the bloc of non-aligned nations. Finally, he resigned from the presidency without warning on August 25, 1961, seven months after taking office, citing the 'terrible forces' that were aligned against him.

The resignation of Quadros created an immediate crisis, once more bringing the military to the center of political developments. Military officials threatened to prevent Quadros's leftist vice-president, João Goulart, from taking office, but Goulart had the support of army units in his home state of Rio Grande do Sul. Fearing a civil war, the military agreed to negotiate a solution to the impasse, permitting Goulart to assume the presidency but also instituting a parliamentary system of government with vastly reduced powers for the president.

Populist program

This compromise solution failed to work in practice, and in 1963 a national plebiscite voted to return to presidential rule. With his powers enhanced, Goulart launched a populist, nationalistic program that moved the country to the left. He announced sweeping land reforms, promised widespread social reforms, and threatened to nationalize foreign firms.

His economic policies, meanwhile, failed to stem inflation. The cost of living soared, contributing to a wave of strikes supported by Goulart's followers in the labor movement. Opposition grew, centered on the middle classes of São Paulo and Minas Gerais whose political leaders appealed to the military to intervene. Finally, on March 31, 1964, claiming that Goulart was preparing a Communist takeover of the government, the military orchestrated a bloodless coup.

While the 1964 coup was the fourth time since 1945 that the military had intervened in the government, this was to be the only instance when the generals remained in power. For the next 21 years, Brazil was governed by a military regime, which clamped down on civilian corruption (while indulging in much of its own). Five army generals occupied the presidency during this period. The first was Humberto de Alencar Castelo Branco, who concentrated on resolving the delicate economic situation. He introduced austerity measures to attack inflation and reduced government spending sharply, thus restoring economic stability, and setting the stage for the strong growth years that were to follow. His administration also adopted

measures to limit political freedom: existing political parties were suspended and replaced by a two-party system, one party (Arena) supporting the government, the other, the liberal Democratic Movement Party (MDB) representing the opposition; mayors and governors were appointed by the military and presidents were chosen in secret by the army.

Military repression

During the presidency of General Arthur da Costa e Silva, Castelo Branco's successor, the military introduced a new constitution making

A street in Rio de Janeiro guarded by tanks a few hours after the escape to Uruguay of President João Goulart, ousted by a military coup.

Congress subordinate to the executive branch. A wave of opposition to the military in 1968 led Costa e Silva to clamp down. The closing of Congress and severe restriction of individual rights marked the beginning of the most repressive years of the military regime. The doctrine of national security gave the government the right to arrest and detain without habeas corpus. The military embarked on a war against 'subversion,' and launched a bid to erase the influence of the left, via imprisonment without trial, torture, and censorship. Editors who opposed the regime were obliged to bring out publications containing blank spaces. When the military banned this, they filled the spaces with recipes and other items before many of them were silenced.

Ruthless military repression peaked during General Emílio Garrastazu Medici's government. He assumed the presidency after Costa e Silva suffered a fatal stroke in 1969. The Medici years were the most dramatic of the military regime, not only because of severe suppression of human rights, but also due to the economic growth that Brazil enjoyed. While in power, Medici and his successor, General Ernesto Geisel (1974–9), saw the economy surge. These

slowed, and then slumped. Following a debt moratorium by Mexico in 1982, the Latin American debt crisis exploded. New foreign loans dried up, and interest charges on previous loans outstripped the resources of the government.

General João Baptista Figueiredo – the last of the military presidents – took office in 1979, promising to return Brazil to democracy, and announced an amnesty for political prisoners and exiles. In addition, press censorship was lifted, new political parties founded, and elections for governors and Congress were held. But

Brazilian forward Jairzinho is carried by fans after Brazil defeated Italy 4-1 in the World Cup final 21 June 1970 in Mexico City.

boom years brought unprecedented prosperity, providing full employment for the urban masses and high salaries for middle-class professionals and white-collar workers. As a result, some Brazilians were inclined to accept military rule and tolerate the lack of personal and political freedom. Winning the 1970 World Cup in Mexico did the popularity of the regime no harm either. Brazil's increasing economic clout led the military to adopt a more independent foreign policy, breaking with traditional adherence to the US-backed positions.

Liberalization

With the advent of the 1980s, the military regime fell on hard times. Economic growth

increasing political freedom did little to offset the gloom of recession from 1981 to 1983.

In January 1985, an electoral college chose Tancredo Neves as Brazil's first civilian president in 22 years. A moderate who had opposed the military regime, he was acceptable to both conservatives and liberals. Brazil's transition to democracy, however, was halted as Neves fell ill the night before he was to be sworn in and died a month later, plunging Brazil into another political crisis. The vice-president, José Sarney, instantly assumed the presidency, but he was a conservative who had little support among the liberals who were now returning to power.

Once in office, Sarney attempted populist measures, such as an ill-fated land reform

> The dramatic economic upturn of the 1970s brought Brazil into the international spotlight and spurred the old dream of becoming a major world power.

program, to secure the support of the liberals who controlled Congress. But the country's economic difficulties worsened. Weighed down with foreign debt and lacking the resources for investments, the government was unable to provide effective leadership for the economy.

The Cruzado Plan, and after

By the start of 1986, with inflation running at an annual rate of 330 percent, Sarney was facing a slump in popularity and pressure from the left for a direct presidential election. His response was the Cruzado Plan, an unorthodox economic package that froze prices while letting wages continue to rise. After years of seeing their spending power eroded by inflation, Brazilians threw themselves into the ensuing consumer boom. The president's popularity rose sharply; claiming co-responsibility for the plan, the politicians of the MDB, who now supported Sarney, swept to victories in the congressional and state elections of November 1986.

However, the long-term success of the Cruzado Plan depended on cuts in government spending, which Sarney, keen to hold on to his newfound popularity, was reluctant to make. Inflation returned with a vengeance, and was to survive a sequence of increasingly ineffectual economic packages introduced throughout the remaining years of the Sarney administration.

The return of high inflation in 1987 coincided with the start of the National Constituent Assembly, charged with drafting a new democratic constitution. Announced in 1988, the Constitution's significant advances included the end of censorship, recognition of Amerindian land rights and increased worker benefits. On the downside, powerful lobbies, and the formation of an informal conservative majority within the Assembly, blocked progress on controversial issues such as land reform. By distributing political favors and government concessions, Sarney won congressional approval to extend his term of office until March 1990. But

his support dwindled as inflation accelerated and discontent grew.

Lula's humble origins

The course of Brazil's ship of state was altered with the arrival of Lula. Luiz Inácio Lula da Silva was born in 1945, in the town of Garanhuns in the drought-stricken northeast, to Aristides, a smallholder, and Eurídice, his wife. Lula was the seventh of the eight children who survived infancy. 'People got up in the morning and had no bread and no money to buy bread,' he relates. 'When it rained, my brothers

Brazilian politician Tancredo Neves (left) is congratulated after his nomination as Prime Minister in 1985.

and sisters made a little dam of sand in the street to catch the water. The alternative was the pond where the animals relieved themselves... There was no education, no knowledge.' Three months before his birth, his father went off to São Paulo with another woman. Lula did not meet his father until years later, when his mother sold everything and took the family on a 13-day truck journey down to São Paulo. Aristides was against the boys going to school, so Lula and Chico cut wood in the mangrove swamps and fetched water for the slum-dwellers. Nevertheless, he learnt to read and write and eventually got a job in a factory, where a press one day took off the index finger of his left hand, marking him for life as a manual worker.

Lula blossomed in industry, rising in trade-union ranks. In São Paulo in 1980, along with other trade unionists, Christians, Social Democrats, and Marxists, he founded the Partido dos Trabalhadores (PT), the Workers' Party. In 1986 he won a seat in the lower house of the Federal Congress with a vote of 650,000, the largest number then achieved.

In the municipal elections of November 1988, control of many state capitals was won by the new Workers' Party. When the long-

A metal smelting facility in 1998.

awaited direct presidential elections were held in November 1989, Luiz Inácio Lula da Silva, the PT candidate, making his first presidential bid, emerged as a strong contender.

The traditional parties suffered overwhelming rejection, while two outsiders ended up in the final round of elections. One of them was Lula. His opponent was Fernando Collor de Mello, the 40-year-old former governor of the politically insignificant northeastern state of Alagoas, running on the ticket of the virtually unheard-of National Reconstruction Party.

Mixing an appeal to youth and modernity with a moralizing discourse that reminded many of Jânio Quadros, and including a hefty dose of preaching against Lula's 'Communism',

> *Such was the potential in 2001 of Brazil, Russia, India, and China to become the dominant global economies by 2050 they became grouped together as the 'BRIC' countries.*

Collor beat the PT candidate by a narrow margin. Taking office in March 1990, with the authority that came from being Brazil's first directly elected president in three decades, he attacked inflation with a brutal fiscal squeeze that included an 18-month 'compulsory loan' of 80 percent of the nation's savings.

Rising inflation

Although these measures forestalled the threat of hyperinflation in the short term, they did not address Brazil's underlying fiscal malaise, and inflation soon crept back and reached a rate of 1,200 percent in 1990. When it came to light that Collor's closest associates had been milking the state of millions of dollars, the middle classes rose against him, taking to the streets in their thousands, demanding his impeachment.

Collor, who resigned before he could be impeached, was replaced by his deputy, Itamar Franco. Although in many ways a lackluster president, Franco won respect for his integrity.

In 1994, Fernando Henrique Cardoso was elected as president by a clear majority. His popularity was based on the success of his Plano Real, the financial plan he introduced as finance minister in Franco's government. This linked Brazil's latest currency, the *real*, to the US dollar in a relationship that retained the flexibility needed to accommodate international financial shocks, while giving the currency an anchor to prevent it being dragged back into a tide of rising inflation. Cardoso pursued the path of privatization started by Collor, and opened up the Brazilian economy, attracting substantial investment from overseas. In October 1998, he was re-elected for a second four-year term, during which he helped to consolidate the recovery and stabilization of the Brazilian economy.

Lula comes to power

In 2002, at his fourth attempt, Lula won the presidency, with over 60 percent of the vote. During the presidency of Cardoso, who was ideologically close to then British prime minister Tony Blair, the accent had been on a continued shrinking of the state, with privatization high on the list. The arrival of Lula meant prejudice against state activity was removed. The state could expand again. Yet Lula, who had suffered the effects of rocketing prices on the poor, was not prepared to let inflation roar away, as many bankers, both local and foreign, had feared. In 2002, the last year of Cardoso's government, prices rose by 12.5 percent, but toward the end of 2006, the end of Lula's first four-year term, they were inching down to half that figure.

The stock market prospered, not least because it tempted foreigners to bring their money into

Rousseff gave continuity to many of Lula's policies, and managed to retain high approval ratings through her term, while distancing herself from a growing number of scandals and mounting corruption linked to the previous Lula government.

As Brazil's first female President, Rousseff has helped increase the profile of women in both Brazil's political and business sectors, and by 2013 over a quarter of her cabinet were women.

Although the Brazilian economy fared better than most, 2013 saw growing unrest in Brazil as sections of the public more vocally ques-

Luiz Inácio Lula da Silva on the campaign trail in 2002.

Brazil to gamble on the share prices. Despite senior officials in his party being implicated in financial scandals, Lula was re-elected in October 2006, again with 60 percent of the vote. While his party and the government experienced the usual ups and downs of political life, Lula's personal popularity continued to soar during his second period in office, when he played a greater and more prominent role on the world stage as Brazil appeared to find its international voice.

Such was the popularity of Lula with the public that he managed to elect his successor, Dilma Rousseff, who had acted as his Chief of Staff. Rousseff, who took office on January 1, 2011, became the first woman to be elected President of Brazil.

tioned government economic and social policies, as well as the Workers Party's behaviour. However, the Presidential elections of October 2014, and Rousseff's chances of re-election, may depend more on the success of the 2014 World Cup, and the Brazilian team, rather than economic indicators.

It is the World Cup, and the Olympic and Paralympic games in 2016, that are going to bring Brazil, its government, its policies, and its economy under the global media spotlight like never before. And, as Brazil sits center stage, it will also give a platform for those who disagree with the government, at Federal, State, and Municipal levels – and its policies – to air their grievances.

Café life in São Paulo.

COUNTRY OF THE FUTURE

Economic cycles of boom and bust plagued the country for decades. This has been replaced by steady growth, and Brazil is now making its presence felt on the international stage.

Brazil is the fifth-largest country in the world, with an area of 8.5 million sq km (3.3 million sq miles). Having expanded over the centuries from a narrow strip of land along the Atlantic Ocean to absorb most of Amazonia and the grassy plains to the south, it won the race with its neighbors to control the largest share of South America's landmass.

The population, 65 percent of which is Catholic, is expected to push up towards 200 million people by 2030 – in 2013 it stood at around 193 million. From being a place of country-dwellers, it is now 83 percent urbanized, even if many of the supposed urban dwellers live in very small towns.

Now, Brazilian governments are beginning to make waves on the world stage, as well as in the rest of Latin America and their own society.

Progress has not been painless. Since colonial times, Brazil has gone through alternating cycles of boom and bust. Industrialization came late. From colonial days until midway through the 20th century, Brazil was primarily a rural society with a monocrop economy. First it was timber, then sugar, shifting in the 18th century to gold. After the rubber boom, coffee emerged as the economy's workhorse. As late as the 1950s, coffee still provided over half of Brazil's export revenue, 65 percent of the workforce was farm-based, and the main function of the banking system was to supply credit to farmers.

Modernization

World War II provided the first stimulus to Brazil's industry when the conflict cut off supplies and manufactured goods, forcing the local development of substitutes. To expand further, however, Brazil's infant industries needed a strong push, and this was provided by the

Bovespa stock exchange, São Paulo

government – more specifically, President Juscelino Kubitschek, who took office in 1955.

Kubitschek made economic growth the primary goal throughout his administration, and this policy has been followed by all succeeding governments. He also established the development model that was copied, with modifications, by his successors: it involved government intervention in managing the economy, and an important role for foreign capital investment.

Kubitschek poured government money into infrastructure projects (highways and power plants) while inviting foreign automakers to establish plants in São Paulo. Government loans also financed the private sector, with the result that during the period 1948–61, the

Brazilian economy grew at an average annual rate of 7 percent.

At this point, two of the great evils of Brazil's 20th-century history – high inflation and political instability – ended the first spurt of economic growth. With the 1964 coup, the new military rulers turned to austerity measures to trim down inflation. By 1968, inflation was under control and the economy was poised for a historic take-off. Starting in 1970, Brazil enjoyed four straight years of double-digit economic growth that ended with a 14 percent expansion in 1973. The rate of growth then slowed, but it never fell below 4.6 percent, and averaged 8.9 percent a year from 1968 to 1980.

The Brazilian Miracle

Between 1960 and 1980, Brazil changed from being a rural nation (with 55 percent of the population living in rural areas) to a majority urban nation (with 67 percent living in the cities), as the boom years attracted waves of peasant migrants fleeing their precarious existence in the nation's rural areas. By 2005, this figure had grown to 85 percent.

São Paulo's skyline.

RENEWABLE ENERGY PROGRAM

Brazil was the first country to embrace a renewable energy source to power motor vehicles. The government-sponsored program to develop the use of sugarcane alcohol as a substitute for imported petroleum was a great technical success and took Brazil to the forefront of ethanol fuel technology. The Pró-Alcool program began in 1975 as a means of reducing dependence on imported oil in the wake of the international petroleum crisis of 1973. A sustainable, renewable, low-pollution fuel was developed, and by 1989 more than 90 percent of it was used by ethanol-only cars.

In 1990 the program collapsed, partly due to the declining price of oil, which made it less economically viable; but 2003 saw a dramatic increase in the production of ethanol, as the government began to revive the scheme. The program received a further boost with the introduction of a new generation of flexible-fuel vehicles that allowed the consumer to choose the fuel depending on current market prices, with the vehicles running on any blend of gasoline or ethanol. Currently around 31 percent of all cars in Brazil are flexible-fuel vehicles, and that number is likely to increase rapidly as older cars are scrapped and new cars take to the roads. Nearly 90 percent of all new cars sold in Brazil are now flexible-fuel vehicles.

Nowhere was this more apparent than in the state of São Paulo. With São Paulo city receiving the bulk of new investments in the private sector, the state's industrial park exploded, emerging as the largest in Latin America and one of the most modern in the world. São Paulo's miracle has continued to the present day. Currently, the gross domestic product of São Paulo state is larger than that of any nation in Latin America except Mexico.

But the miracle years brought more than dramatic social and economic changes. They produced a profound effect on the national psyche. Accustomed to playing down the value and potential of their country, Brazilians in the 1970s saw this sleeping giant begin to stir.

Ecstatic with the success of their economic programs, the generals abandoned their initial goal of providing the framework for growth and embarked on a wildly ambitious scheme to turn Brazil into a world power. Moderation was abandoned and the military drew up massive development projects. The problem, however, was finding a way to finance these dreams. The government, the private sector and the foreign companies did not

Inside Bovespa stock exchange.

MERCOSUL

While North America has the North American Free Trade Area and Europe has the EU, South America has Mercosul – or Mercosur, as it is known in the Spanish-speaking countries. It grew out of a history of ineffectual trade negotiations and treaties stretching back to the 1930s. Progress was impeded by economic and political factors, not least the macho posturing of dictatorial governments in the 1960s and 1970s.

The Treaty of Asunción of 1991 established the mechanism and structure of Mercosul, covering Argentina, Brazil, Paraguay, and Uruguay, with aspirations to promote greater economic integrations than would be offered by a mere free-trade area.

Like the European Union (EU), it swept away customs posts, set standard external tariffs, and outlawed restrictions on trade, ending the post-war years of protectionism and import-substitution policies that had been favored by the military regimes.

The Mercosul bloc has gone from strength to strength in the past decades, with Bolivia, Chile, Colombia, Ecuador and Peru joining as associate members, and Mexico and New Zealand acting as observers. In 2006 Venezuela applied to join as a full member and finally joined the club in July 2012 after Paraguay, who had blocked its entry, was suspended.

The boom years, from 1968 to 1980, became known as the period of the Brazilian Miracle, and they changed the face of Brazil forever. Led by São Paulo, the country's major cities underwent rapid industrialization.

have the resources required. Clearly another partner was needed, and in 1974 that partner appeared. Following the 1973 oil shock, international banks, overflowing with petrodollars, sought investment opportunities in been transferred to Brazil. During these years, money poured into transportation (new highways, bridges, and railroads across the country, and subways for Rio and São Paulo), industry (steel mills, a petrochemical complex, and consumer goods factories), the energy sector (power plants, nuclear reactors, and a program looking into alternative energy and oil exploration), and communications (television, postal services, and telecommunications), in some instances, it also poured into the pockets of generals and technocrats.

Then, in 1979, the second oil shock doubled

Former President Luiz Inácio Lula da Silva looks inside the cockpit of a 100 percent ethanol-powered aircraft made in Brazil.

the developing world. And no other developing nation could match the growth record of Brazil, let alone its potential. Soon, pinstriped bankers were flying down to Rio, Brasília, and São Paulo from New York and London, followed shortly by colleagues from Frankfurt, Tokyo, Paris, Toronto, Geneva, Chicago, and Los Angeles. The rules of the game were disarmingly simple. The generals presented their blueprints for Brazilian superpowerdom and the bankers unloaded the dollars. There was no collateral.

In 1974, Brazil borrowed more money than it had in the preceding 150 years combined. When the decade finally bowed out five years later, a total of US$40 billion had

the price of Brazil's imported petroleum, while interest rates shot up and the prices of commodities on international markets came down. Brazil's trade balance recorded a deficit in 1979 that was nearly three times that of 1978.

At first, however, neither the generals nor the bankers were willing to admit that the party was over. The borrowing continued, only now the incoming dollars went to pay for imported oil and to cover previous loans now falling due.

Lengthy recession

In 1981, the situation worsened, with a recession in the United States that was felt immediately by Brazil. Three years of recession forced Brazil into a lengthy depression. Many small and medium-sized businesses failed, throwing thousands into unemployment. Large industries laid off workers, leaving the poorest increasingly desperate, reliant on woefully inadequate and underfunded welfare provisions.

The decision by Mexico in 1982 to impose a moratorium on international loan interest triggered the so-called Latin American debt crisis. In response, international lending institutions cut off the flow of development loans.

The future looked grim. Twenty years of military government were drawing to a close, leaving the country with rampant inflation and a plethora of inefficient government-owned industries built on the largesse that the generals dispensed to appointees who presided over them. For 20 years the civil service had run amok, creating endless jobs of dubious worth, which nonetheless paid gold-plated salaries and bore a lifetime guarantee. By 1987, a staggering 60 percent of the economy was controlled by the government.

Brazil's manufacturing industries, which were built on import substitution policies pursued by successive governments after World War II, were soft-bellied and inefficient, often run by political appointees who were neither qualified for nor experienced in the jobs they had been given.

Remarkably, Brazil rose to the challenge. Before the debt crisis, exports had been dominated by raw materials and agricultural products, which provided the income to pay for imports of oil and capital goods. But during the 1980s, the overweight industries that had developed in the protected environment of import substitution began to slim down and become more efficient. The need to export opened up new, larger markets, which encouraged the expansion of manufacturing capacity beyond what the domestic market could support. Brazilians often refer to the 1980s as the 'lost decade,' but, in truth, it was a period of positive foundation-building.

However, it was also a decade plagued by inflation, which held back the expansion of Brazil's industries. During these years, Brazil adapted to high inflation by index-linking virtually everything in the economy and, in the process, making market forces a hostage to government policies. All monetary contracts, from salaries and loans to savings and time deposits, were indexed to inflation, receiving adjustments every month.

Financial manipulation

The Brazilian middle class became adept at manipulating their money, timing purchases to their best advantage and using an array of financial mechanisms to maintain their purchasing power. A topic of conversation often heard over breakfast in a business district café was the performance of the 'overnight' – a financial mechanism known to most money dealers the

Chemical plant exterior.

STUNNING STATISTICS

With a GDP of more than US$2.23 trillion in 2013, Brazil is the world's sixth-largest economy. Brazil is one of the world's major steel producers, the seventh-largest car manufacturer, and fourth-largest aircraft manufacturer. Its hydroelectric potential surpasses that of any other nation, and it has the world's largest hydroelectric plant. It is also the largest producer of iron ore, eighth-largest aluminum producer and fifth-largest producer of tin. On top of that, it is the largest exporter of coffee, the largest producer of sugar and orange juice, and second-largest producer of soybeans.

world over but not normally indulged in by the salaried middle class.

During this period the government controlled everything. Prices were indexed, and then they were controlled. Then they were frozen and then controlled again in a constant back and forth that left corporate planners dizzy. Wages, too, were at times frozen, at times linked to a government index that routinely left wage earners with less purchasing power. Exchange rates fluctuated daily, and most transactions, from the purchase of a refrigerator to multimillion-dollar construction contracts, were priced in dollars.

and that would not happen until inflation was brought under control.

Privatization program

Brazil's first directly elected president, Fernando Collor de Mello, although forced from office in 1992 after only three years, set in motion many of the reforms that have brought Brazil into the mainstream of world trade. He instigated a program of privatization, selling off government-owned industries that were viable, and closing down those that were not. He tore down many of the protectionist import tariffs

Mining in the Amazon rainforest.

Similar conditions prevailed at corporate level. A company's principal activity became secondary to its financial planning; its profit primarily dependent on how adept it was at financial manipulation. Planning for the medium term became very uncertain, and long-term objectives were little more than dreams and wishes.

The financial uncertainties of the decade understandably acted as a powerful disincentive to multinational firms who might otherwise have considered investing in Brazil. Curiously, those who were already well established, such as Volkswagen, continued to make healthy profits, but Brazil needed new investment from multinationals to get its industry up to speed,

and restrictions. And he began the taming of the rampant civil service, trimming the excesses of over-employment.

But his attempt to do the same with the economy failed completely. His financial plan went the same way as the four other attempts between 1986 and 1995. Each was announced with a bold, macho fanfare, and a new currency, and each rapidly lost momentum as inflation returned with a vengeance, reaching a remarkable peak of more than 2,100 percent in 1993.

The Plano Real

There followed two years of continued financial mismanagement by provisional president, Itamar Franco, who had been Collor's deputy. Then, in July 1994, the Plano Real was introduced by the then little-known finance minister, Fernando Henrique Cardoso. He managed to link the new national currency, the *real*, to the dollar in a way that left enough flexibility to enable it to withstand regional financial fluctuations without allowing inflation to get going again.

His election as president later the same year was in no small way a result of the effectiveness of the Plano Real. Throughout his first term, Cardoso and Finance Minister Pedro Malan exercised tight fiscal control, bringing inflation down to single figures.

1997 for US$3.3 billion. By the end of 2005, as the world scrambled for iron ore, the worth of the shares had increased 15 times. In 2011 Vale's net profit came to over US$17 billion, although it fell back to $4.5 billion in 2012 due to the global economic crisis.

Brazilian public opinion would not permit even Cardoso to sell off the state company Petróleo Brasileiro (Petrobras), and it repaid the loyalty by making the country self-sufficient in oil in 2006, leading some to speculate that Brazil will join the Organization of Petroleum Exporting Countries (OPEC), although it has

Petrobras' Urucu oil and natural gas plant.

The privatizations carried out during the Cardoso government brought protests from many who said that public property was being sold off at knockdown prices for the sake of pervasive economic orthodoxy, as set out by the international financial institutions. Government receipts from privatization, which in 1995 had come to a mere US$1.6 billion, totalled nearly US$30 billion in 1997 and the following year rose to US$37.5 billion.

Critics of Cardoso said that private individuals and financial institutions were being enriched at the expense of the public good, citing the Companhia Vale do Rio Doce (Vale), the world's biggest single source of iron ore. The government sold 42 percent of the company in

so far declined the invitation to do so.

Brazil's manufacturing industry experienced steady growth during the second half of the 1990s, attracting a rush of foreign investment. The election in October 2002 of left-wing Luiz Inácio Lula da Silva, of the Workers' Party, made the international capital markets jittery, but the new president surprised the markets and his critics by committing to good financial management throughout his two terms in office.

Brazil's industry has survived the opening up of domestic markets to foreign competition, transforming itself into one of the most efficient in the world. Through Mercosul and other trade agreements, Brazil has become both a political and an economic leader in the region, avoiding the political and economic meltdown suffered by other South American countries. As one of the BRIC countries (as Brazil, Russia, India, and China are known), Brazil is expected to have become one of the dominant global economies by 2050, and its economy has certainly weathered the recent global economic crisis better than most.

Rich and poor

However, the education system continues to fail to provide the majority of its young citizens with the skills they need to prosper in the 21st century.

Schoolgirls in Mariana city, in the state of Minas Gerais.

This will leave Brazil's vital and growing industries with a damaging shortage of employees of the quality they need to support their growth. Another major problem is the continuing disparity between rich and poor, which leaves Brazil with huge social and economic problems.

Brazil's predominantly young population (more than 60 percent of the population is under the age of 29) is at once one of its major assets and potentially one of its costliest burdens. Well educated and employed, today's young Brazilians will be the driving force behind the country's future prosperity. Badly educated and possibly condemned to a life of poverty, they will instead become a huge financial and social burden.

The right environment

Industrialization is a messy business, and Brazil is experiencing all the side effects that were seen decades ago in Europe and the United States. Brazilians are well aware that they are getting plenty of criticism from abroad for the damage that has been done to the Amazon forest by mining companies, gold prospectors, ranchers, wood-pulp factories, and pig-iron mills. And the country is slowly beginning to wake up to its responsibility as a protector of a huge tract of the Earth's surface.

Although shocking scenes of flaming trees and polluted rivers frequently appear on television, the Brazilians' view of the problem is somewhat different from that of citizens of wealthier countries. Many people feel that they are being criticized for the same crimes as were committed by the rich nations during earlier decades and centuries. They defend themselves against charges of environmental destruction and human-rights abuses by pointing to the way the United States achieved world supremacy while slaughtering animals, building dirty steel mills, and strip-mining once-beautiful mountains.

Fortunately, both the government and concerned citizens' groups have taken steps to fight pollution, restrain the worst aspects of exploitation in the Amazon, and try to improve the country's image abroad. To continue progressing, Brazil will need aid, since priorities such as housing, health care, and education have first claims on government resources. The environmental issue is helping to teach this young giant that, like it or not, Brazil cannot solve all of its problems on its own. In addition, the world's new set of environmental priorities is giving the country a growing importance.

Future growth

Although in many ways a success, President Cardoso's government had difficulty in driving through critical reforms that were designed to rein in the civil service and exert control over the inefficient social-security system. This left

Brazil's iron ore production is the highest in the world, with enough reserves in the Carajás region alone to satisfy the entire global demand for the next 500 years.

Brazil with a large and intransigent public spending bill, which resulted in a persistent budget deficit.

Meanwhile, Brazil continues to experience unprecedented levels of imports, following the removal of trade barriers. This is partly due to the release of pent-up consumer demand. But the majority of imports are capital equipment, helping Brazil's industry to modernize and increase productivity. This will strengthen manufacturing output and hopefully allow for the rapid growth in export sales to continue once the world's economies improve.

> In the 21st century, Brazil has acquired a new confidence and has become one of the most efficient and economically powerful countries in the world.

The years of rampant inflation filled the coffers of the banks, giving them the resources to develop their expertise and services. The banking system, which came out of the recent global economic crisis relatively unscathed compared with that of other countries, is well developed

A container ship in the Port of Santos.

The election in 2002 of Luiz Inácio Lula da Silva as president signaled a new era for Brazil's presence in international trade. Re-elected to a second term of office in October 2006, Lula was committed to closer ties with the other members of Mercosul, and to greater negotiations with other Latin American countries and the United States on the establishment of new trade agreements.

Minerals will continue to play a key role, having already placed Brazil in the select company of major mining powers. Brazil is a world leader in production of gold and iron ore, as well as so-called 'high-tech' minerals such as titanium, vanadium, zirconium, beryllium, niobium, and quartz, which are now in great demand.

and stands to benefit enormously from the closer trading and financial links being established with other South American countries.

It is also not going to harm Brazil's cause that in 2013 a Brazilian, Roberto Azevedo, was chosen to head up the World Trade Organization. The WTO being the world's most important economic multilateral with 159 member states.

The Brazilian stock market has also prospered immensely in the past 15 years, not least because it has tempted foreign investors and speculators to gamble on the share prices, making the São Paulo-based stock and futures exchange (Bovespa) one of the richest and most important in the world.

Praia Grande beach in Arraial do Cabo, Rio de Janeiro.

FROM SANDY BEACHES TO AMAZON JUNGLE

Brazil, the world's fifth-largest nation, occupies such a large landmass, and is so diverse topographically, socially, and economically, that it is hard to consider it as a single entity.

Although Brazil is the fifth-largest nation on the planet, four times the size of Mexico and more than twice that of India, the Brazil where most people live forms only a small fraction of the country's total landmass of 8,509,711 sq km (3,285,618 sq miles). One in four people crowds into five metropolitan areas in the southern part of the country. Together, the southern and southeastern states contain more than 60 percent of Brazil's population yet account for only 16 percent of the geographical area. More than 115 million people live in an area slightly smaller than Alaska, while another 80 million populate an area the size of the continental US, minus Texas. What Brazil has is space – enormous regions of vast, empty space.

A regional structure

For administrative purposes, Brazil's 26 states and one federal district are divided into five regions; north, northeast, center-west, southeast, and south. The two largest regions are also its least populated. The north, home to the mighty Amazon basin rainforest, occupies 42 percent of Brazil, a country large enough to accommodate all Western Europe, yet its population is smaller than that of New York.

The center-west, just south of the Amazon, is dominated by a vast elevated plateau, and covers 22 percent of Brazil's territory. The

Amazon rainforest canopy.

population here has doubled since the 1970s and now represents 15 percent of the country as a whole. These two great landmasses, which together are larger than most nations, are both the promise and challenge of Brazil's future.

The north's living enigma

The Amazon is one of the planet's last unsolved mysteries. The world's largest river basin, it contains one-fifth of all the fresh water on Earth, and the planet's greatest rainforest, a teeming biological storehouse whose true potential remains largely unknown and untapped.

Despite the encroaching devastation along the forest's frontiers, it is still possible to fly for hours over the Amazon and see no break

The new capital, Brasília, was set in the central plateau to attract settlers and integrate the region with the coast. Brasília has matured into a city of more than 2.6 million people but has so far failed to spawn the hoped-for growth.

in the carpet of greenery except for the sinuous curves of the region's rivers. On boat journeys, the wall of vegetation at the river's edge rolls by for days on end, broken only by the occasional wooden hut.

These huts are clues to a fact that has been largely ignored both by Brazil's development planners and many of the ecologists who campaign to protect the forest as the 'lungs of the world' – the Amazon is no empty wilderness. Aside from the remnants of the Amerindian nations who once ruled the jungle, an estimated 3 million people are scattered

into shanty towns on the margins of the cities. However, as the government starts to take the forest loss seriously (see page 64), there is cause for some optimism. Substantial investment has been poured into the education of settlers, teaching them appropriate forms of agriculture and encouraging them to adopt sustainable extractive techniques.

The wealth of the Amazon is not restricted to its huge land area. Below the surface lie untold riches. In the Serra dos Carajás, 880km (545 miles) southwest of Belém, there is enough iron ore to keep the world supplied for 500 years,

Sacks of unloaded cargo at a dock in Manaus.

over this huge area, eking out a living as their forefathers have for generations. Known as *caboclos*, these true Amazonians are rubber-tappers, brazil-nut gatherers, fishermen, and subsistence farmers.

More recently, cattle ranchers, land speculators, and small farmers were encouraged to move into the area by government incentives, the promise of free land, and the scent of quick profits. Cattle barons and land speculators carved up swathes of virgin forest, employing unscrupulous methods and gangs of gunmen to intimidate anyone who stood in their way. The main victims, along with the trees, plants, and wildlife, were the *caboclos*, many of whom were driven off the land

CHICO MENDES

Chico Mendes (1944–88) was a rubber-tapper and environmental activist, who led the first grassroots organization against logging and forest clearance when he and his followers resisted the loggers' bulldozers in what were known as empates – stand-offs. In 1985 he founded the Xapuri Rural Workers' Union, a national union of rubber-tappers. In 1988 Mendes was murdered, and a local rancher and his father were sentenced to 19 years' imprisonment for the killing. International media pressure resulted in the creation of the Chico Mendes Extractive Reserve, and there are now some 20 such reserves scattered around the region.

while elsewhere gold, tin, rare metals, and oil have been found. Carefully exploited, these commodities could bring development to the region without destroying the forest.

The center-west

In Brazil's other great void, the center-west, the pace of development slowed after a quick burst in the 1970s.

In terms of its geography, the center-west offers none of the natural barriers of the Amazon. An elevated plateau 1,000 meters (3,300ft) above sea level, the Planalto Central

The northeast

Brazil's third-largest region, the northeast, occupying 18 percent of the country, is the nation's poorest. Although sugar plantations made it the original economic and political center in colonial times, the northeast has not developed as fast as the southern and southeastern states. Unlike the north and center-west, the northeast is neither isolated nor underpopulated. Its fatal flaw has been its climate.

The region is divided into four zones: its northernmost state, Maranhão, combines characteristics of the northeast and the Ama-

Looking upstream of the Iguaçu River towards the Devil's Throat, Iguaçu Falls.

is divided into two kinds of area – forest and woodland savannah known as *cerrado*. Made up of stunted trees and grasslands, the *cerrado* appears to be a scrubland with little value. Experience has shown, however, that once cleared, the *cerrado* land is extremely fertile. Farmers from southern Brazil have turned areas of the *cerrado* into sprawling farms and ranches, including the world's largest soybean farm. Roads and bridges have been built, corn and cotton production improved, and an increasing number of qualified people have moved into the area. The grasslands of the southern part of the region have also been adapted to pasture, and some of Brazil's largest cattle herds now graze there.

zon; along the coast from the state of Rio Grande do Norte to Bahia runs a narrow 100 to 200km (60 to 120-mile) strip of fertile land, known as the *zona da mata*; just west of this strip begins a transition zone of semi-fertile land called the *agreste*; the final zone occupies the bulk of the interior of the northeast's states, a dry, arid region known as the *sertão*.

It is the *sertão* that is responsible for Brazil's most devastating poverty. It is an area of periodic drought, of parched earth, of temporary rivers that swell to flood stage in times of rain, and of a thorny scrub called *caatinga*; it is an area of widespread human suffering.

One drought ended in 1984 after five years. Another – a result of El Niño in 1998

The disappearing rainforest

Deforestation in the latter half of the 20th century caused enormous damage, but there are hopes that government initiatives will be in time to save the rainforest.

Being in the rainforest at dusk is an almost spiritual experience, but it is one that the next generation may not have the chance to know, because unless

An area of deforestation scars the Amazon rainforest.

bold steps are taken, evolution's grandest experiment is in danger of coming to a premature end.

When the first Europeans arrived in Brazil in the early 16th century, it was blanketed with a rainforest that stretched along the Atlantic coast from Recife south to Florianópolis. Covering 1 million sq km (386,000 sq miles), it held the most diverse communities of plants and animals on earth. And despite what you might read in the media, Brazil still has the greatest biodiversity of any country on the planet.

The shrinkage of the forest was a direct consequence of Brazil's ever-expanding population, particularly along its Atlantic fringes, now densely populated due to the productive soil. Moreover, fires started by farmers to clear fallen trees and brush often rage out of control, destroying huge tracts of virgin forest.

Once, 600 species of mammal roamed or swung through the glades of the Brazilian forest. One thousand butterfly species fluttered through the canopy. Eight hundred species of trees, more than in the whole of North America, could be found in locations ranging from the Amazon river mouth to the highest mountain.

Amazonia fights back

Amazingly, in view of the widespread destruction, Amazonia still tenaciously holds on to most of its plants and animals – and its secrets. Many of the species here are found nowhere else in the world. The rainforest canopy is one of the last great unexplored regions of the world, and there may be anything from 10 to 30 million species of insect alone that are currently unknown to science.

But a huge loss of biological diversity is happening, and deforestation is the chief cause. No animal or plant can live in a void, and the rate of destruction of their forest habitat has been staggering. Between 1995 and 2000, 2 million hectares (4,942 million acres) were cut down each year. Overall, 51 million hectares (127 million acres) have been deforested, mostly during the 1980s; in the mid-1990s, an area equivalent to over 11 percent of the extent of the original rainforest was lost.

One result of this wholesale destruction is that the Amazon may soon lose some of its most distinguished denizens. The giant otter, for example, which was overhunted in the 1950s and 1960s, now clings to survival in rapidly shrinking habitats. The pet trade has driven several species of blue macaw close to extinction. Other endangered animals include the jaguar and black caiman.

Although reforestation programs are in place, the rate of growth is still far exceeded by the rate of destruction. But there is cause for hope. It was reported in October 2006 that rainforest loss over the previous 12 months was 13,100 sq km (5,057 sq miles). This is a lot, but it is less than 40 percent of the loss suffered in 2004, and the numbers are still falling: in 2011 to just over 6,000 sq km (2,300 sq miles). There are a number of reasons for this, including falling commodity prices, but government conservation initiatives and enforcement laws must also be credited, as well as protected areas such as the vast Tumucumaque Montains National Park. As João Paulo Capobianco, ex-minister of biodiversity and forests, told a press conference: 'We increased enforcement of environmental laws ... and it worked.'

– caused massive destruction, while in 2000, one of the worst droughts in more than 70 years struck the region, propelling millions of the *sertão*'s residents to the urban centers of the southeast, mainly to São Paulo and Rio de Janeiro.

Sparkling beaches

Just a few hours away from the poverty and despair of the *sertão* is the beautiful coastal zone, where white sandy beaches sparkle beneath the tropical sun. It is here that Brazil's renowned beaches begin, and stretch the length

The São Francisco river

Running along the southern edge of the northeast is the São Francisco river, the second of Brazil's main river systems (see page 289). Beginning in the central plateau, the river flows east for more than 3,000km (1,865 miles), reaching into the northeast at its southernmost state, Bahia, and providing a link between the northeast and central Brazil. In addition, the São Francisco river has provided a reliable source of water for the interior through which it passes, creating a narrow belt of productive farmland for a region that has never been able to feed itself.

Porto de Barra, one of the many beaches in Salvador. Although safe for swimming, be aware that many of Salvador's beaches do not have lifeguards.

of this huge country, from Maranhão to the southernmost state of Rio Grande do Sul. Altogether, Brazil's coastline encompasses 7,700km (4,600 miles), making it the longest continuous coastline in the world.

Blessed with adequate rainfall, the northeast coast is the site of the bulk of the region's agricultural production, concentrated in sugar and cocoa, and home to a constantly increasing percentage of the region's population. Lacking investment capital, the economy of the northeast has remained dominated by farming, with a few isolated pockets of industry. Tourism, however, may yet prove to be the northeast's real savior.

The southeast

At the other end of the scale from the northeast is the southeast region. It comprises only 11 percent of the national territory but is home to Brazil's three largest cities, São Paulo, Rio de Janeiro, and Belo Horizonte, and 45 percent of the population. The region is divided between a narrow coastal zone and an elevated plateau, with a coastal mountain region (the Escarpment) beginning in Bahia and running the length of the coast to Rio Grande do Sul.

The dense tropical foliage of the *mata atlântica* has wrapped the coastal mountains in a rich, deep cloak of green. But, ironically, the very development that has brought prosperity to the southeast of the country is threatening the survival of this tropical vegetation. In many parts of São Paulo state, the forest has been destroyed by air pollutants, a by-product of the state's industrial park, the largest in Latin America. The best-preserved example of Brazil's coastal tropical forest is in Paraná.

With the exception of the coastal cities of Rio and Santos (two of Brazil's busiest ports), the southeast's main population centers are on the plateau at an average altitude of 700 meters (2,300ft). This area of rolling hills and temperate climate has a clear distinction between

Cornfield outside Minas Gerais.

winter and summer, and has been the center of Brazil's economic growth since the 1800s.

Minas Gerais, the only state in the region that does not have a seacoast, owes its early development to its mineral wealth. The red earth of Minas Gerais provides graphic testimony to its iron-ore deposits. Part of Brazil's mammoth Precambrian shield area, Minas was the world's leading gold producer in the 18th century. In modern times, it has made Brazil a chief producer of iron ore and gemstones.

The south

The south is the smallest of Brazil's regions, accounting for only 7 percent of the total national territory. Like the southeast, it was blessed with rapid development in the second half of the 20th century, and today is home to 15 percent of the nation's population. Located below the Tropic of Capricorn, the south is the only region of Brazil with a subtropical climate and four distinct seasons, including frosts and even the very occasional light snowfall in winter.

It was in part due to its climate that the three states of the southern region attracted large numbers of immigrants from Italy, Germany, Poland, and Russia in the early 20th century. The rolling farmlands of Paraná and Rio Grande do Sul have made these states, along with São Paulo, the breadbasket of Brazil, growing primarily wheat, corn, soybeans, and rice.

The region is also Brazil's traditional cattle producer, although it has been losing ground to the center-west. In the western half of Rio Grande, pampas grasslands are home to many of Brazil's largest farms and cattle ranches. The eastern half of the state is marked by mountainous terrain with deep, forested valleys where Italian and German immigrants have established Brazil's wine industry (see page 232).

Paraná state has also benefited from vast pine forests, a primary source of lumber for the construction industry, although they are now being depleted. Marking the state's western border is the Paraná river, which, together with the Paraguay farther west, forms Brazil's third great river system. The force of these rivers has been harnessed to produce energy for the industries of the south and southeast, particularly the Paraná, where Brazil (in collaboration with Paraguay) has built the world's largest hydroelectric project, the Itaipú Dam (see page 221).

GRAZING THE PRAIRIES

The prairies of Rio Grande do Sul are the grazing grounds of nearly 14 million head of cattle and 10 million sheep, which has helped turn Brazil into the world leader in beef exports.. The excellence of the beef is widely recognized – rightly so, as anyone who eats at a rodizio will agree. Leather and footwear industries are obvious spin-offs from cattle production. Some of the sheep are of the Karakul breed, from Turkestan, introduced to Brazil in the 1980s. They have a long fleece – some are black, some brown, some gray, and some a pinkish shade. Their broad tails store fat, a source of nourishment, rather like a camel's hump.

CARNIVAL

Carnival in Brazil has a long and fascinating history. While Rio's festivities are the best known, other cities, particularly Salvador and Recife, have equally loud, colorful, and riotous celebrations of their own.

Brazilians are some of the most musical, and most fun-loving, people in the world, and Carnival, 'The Biggest Party on Earth,' is deeply rooted in the nation's ethnic and racial heritage.

Carnival's roots are European, although experts disagree over the origin of the name. According to one school of thought, it comes from the Latin *carrum novalis*, a Roman festival float. A more probable explanation is that it stems from the Latin *carnem levare*, 'putting away meat,' since Carnival and Ash Wednesday mark the last days before Lenten abstinence.

The Romans had more than 100 festivals during their year, of which the most famous was the December Saturnalia, marked by the temporary disappearance of class distinctions. Slaves and masters dined at the same table, drank the same wine, and slept with the same women. Elements of Saturnalia were incorporated into Christmas and Carnival.

Pranksters and Carnival balls

In Brazil, pre-Lenten observances have existed since colonial days, but until the 20th century they were a time for the prankster rather than for good-natured celebration. This aspect of Carnival was called *entrudo* and featured stink bombs and water balloons. *Entrudo* was so bad, decent citizens spent Carnival locked in their homes. One of those who didn't was architect Grandjean de Montigny, who died of pneumonia in 1850 after being doused with water during Carnival. It wasn't until the early 1900s that a stop was finally put to *entrudo*. The indiscriminate tossing of confetti and streamers is all that remains of the bad old days.

The fancy-dress ball was part of European Carnival as early as the 18th century. Paris

People dress up to mark Carnival on the streets of Rio.

CARNIVAL DATES

Carnival is a moveable feast, the date tied to the religious calendar. Activities in Brazil take place from the Friday prior to Ash Wednesday up to Ash Wednesday itself. In some cities, including Rio and Salvador, the celebrations take over the entire week. Most offices and businesses in Brazil will close for the week of Carnival. Forthcoming dates are:
February 28–March 5, 2014
February 13–18, 2015
February 5–10, 2016
February 24–March 1, 2017
February 9–14, 2018
March 1–6, 2019

and Venice had the best masked Carnival balls. This custom hit Rio in 1840 with a chic event at the Hotel Itália on Praça Tiradentes, but it lost money, and it wasn't until 1846 that another one was held, this time in São Cristóvão. The first modern Carnival ball was the High Life, at a Copacabana hotel in 1908. The formal City Ball was inaugurated in 1932 at the Teatro Municipal. By then there were no fewer than 100 fancy-dress balls in Rio at Carnival time.

For Rio's working class, music, dance, and drink were, and still are, the main Carnival

Carnival parade

One of the main contributions of the clubs to modern Carnival in Rio was the parade, complete with elaborate costumes, wheeled floats, and appropriate musical accompaniment. Parade themes stressed Bible stories, mythology, and literature.

The first parade was organized in 1855 by a group grandly named *O Congresso das Sumidades Carnavalescas*, which marched before an elite audience, including the emperor. Overdressed Cossacks and tableaux depicting scenes from French history and *Don Quixote* were featured.

The Sambódromo was built expressly for the Carnival's Samba Parade.

diversions. A Portuguese immigrant, José Nogueira Paredes (nicknamed Zé Pereira), is credited with originating the first Carnival club. One of his ideas was to get everybody in the club to play the same kind of drum, creating a powerful, unified sound. This technique became the basis for the modern samba school *bateria*, or percussion section.

The working- and middle-class clubs, called *blocos*, *ranchos*, or *cordões*, played European-origin ballads known as *choros*. In the 19th century they often had charitable or political aims, and were also active off-season. Many of these predominantly white clubs still exist, including the Clube dos Democráticos, which annually kicks off the downtown street Carnival.

THE ALTERNATIVE CARNIVAL

Followers of African-origin religions bring a more mysterious element to Carnival in the northeast. In Salvador, performers of the afoxé conduct reverent processions during Carnival. They dress in flowing robes and carry banners and canopies. Monotonous music, often sung in African languages, provides an eerie accompaniment. In Recife, Afro-Brazilians maintain a parallel tradition. Maracatu, like afoxé, is a procession that mixes theatrical and musical elements. The central figure is a queen, surrounded by elaborately dressed consorts. Each group is called a nation. The larger the nation, the more consorts surround its queen.

By 1900, the annual downtown parade of such groups, called *Grandes Sociedades*, had become the highlight of Carnival. Black Brazilians first became involved in Carnival in the late 19th century, partly due to the severe drought in the northeast in 1877, which brought many freed slaves, along with their music and dance traditions, to Rio.

Street Carnival draws millions of revelers, many dressed as clowns, television personalities, or animals. The most common sight is men dressed as women: for example, the Bloco das Piranhas is a group of men who always turn up

The samba centerpiece

But the undisputed centerpiece of any Rio de Janeiro Carnival is the main samba school parade, which takes place on Sunday and Monday nights. This is the most African of the Carnival events, due mainly to the popularity of the dance, which is a mix of European folk influences and African techniques. The parade was taken off the streets in 1984 when the Sambódromo, designed by Oscar Niemeyer, was completed in a record nine months. It added new bleachers and boxes in 2012, and now has a capacity for 72,500 people. In 2016,

Elaborately-costumed Carnival participants.

kitted out as prostitutes. Another element that has become an integral part of the Rio Carnival scene is the welcome extended to the international gay community, which has served to enrich the social diversity of the event.

Carnival nights belong to the club balls. Among events attracting both *cariocas* (Rio's residents) and tourists are nightly bashes at the Sírio-Libanês, Flamengo, Fluminense, and Monte-Líbano clubs. The most sought-after ticket is to the ball held at Copacabana Palace Hotel on the Saturday of Carnival. The contest for best costume is held at several balls and features outrageous get-ups, depicting everything from medieval troubadours to Roman Catholic archbishops.

part of the Sambódromo will be used for the Olympic Games.

Modern samba music dates from the 19th century, when the tones of the former slaves met the stylized European sound of Rio. The word 'samba' is believed to derive from the Angolan word *semba*, originating in a ceremony in which men were allowed to select female partners from a circle of dancers.

Today, the samba schools that parade in the Sambódromo are judged by an officially appointed jury. Each presentation must have a central theme – an historical event or personality, or an Amerindian legend. The theme embraces every aspect of the presentation. Costumes must accord with historical time and place. The samba song must recount or develop the theme, and the huge floats must detail it through papier-mâché figures and paintings.

Each school's presentation includes the 'opening wing,' the *Abre-Alas*, a group of colorfully costumed *sambistas* marching next to a large float The float depicts an open book or scroll and is, in effect, the title page of the theme. Behind the *Abre-Alas* is the *Comissão de Frente*, or Board of Directors. Once a line of formally dressed men chosen for their dignified air, today the *Comissão de Frente* is more likely to present a complex dance routine to excite the crowds.

The real event begins with the appearance of the *porta bandeira* (flag bearer) and the *mestre sala* (dance master), in lavish 18th-century dress. The *Porta Bandeira* is a female dancer who holds the school flag during an elaborate dance routine with her consort. The bulk of the samba school follows behind, including a small army of percussion enthusiasts known as the *bateria*. Their role is to maintain a constant rhythm to help other members keep up with the tempo.

Behind the *bateria* are the major samba school *alas*. These groups of *sambistas* illustrate aspects of the school's theme through their

Perfomers ready themselves backstage for their turn in a Carnival parade.

RIO'S CITY OF SAMBA

The first samba school was called Deixa Falar (Let Them Talk), founded by black residents of the Estácio district in 1928. These early groups practiced on school playgrounds, which is how they got the name 'schools,' There are now over 70 registered samba schools in Rio. When the state government decided in the 1980s to build a special stadium for the annual parade, they built it in Estácio to honor the pioneers. Rio's city government and the League of Samba Schools have now built the US$40-million Cidade do Samba (City of Samba) in the port area, and close to the city center. At any time of the year at Cidade do Samba Joãozinho Trinta (http://cidadedosambarj.globo.com), visitors can see how samba school artists put together costumes and parade floats (daily Tue–Sat, with special samba shows on Thu and Fri). The site, which suffered a major fire on the eve of the 2011 carnival, is a cross between a theme park and a Hollywood back lot. The parade of the samba schools has become big business, and major companies including Nestlé and Petrobras swap sponsorship dollars for community good will. The man who practically invented the form of the contemporary samba parade, the late Joãozinho Trinta, after whom the Cidade do Samba is named, attacked the view that Carnival has become too dependent on visual extravaganza, saying, 'Only the rich enjoy poverty. The poor want luxury.'

costumes. If the theme is an Amazon myth, one of its main *alas* might be *sambistas* dressed as Indians; another could have members dressed as Amazonian animals. The compulsory *ala das baianas* group consists of dozens of elderly women dressed in the flowing attire of Bahia. They honor the early history of samba, although in the 1930s they were all men, who, acting as security guards for the schools, used the billowing dresses to conceal knives and razors.

In between the major *alas* are lavishly costumed individuals depicting the main characters of the school's theme. These are *figuras de*

> Today's celebration of Carnival in Rio de Janeiro has three main features: frenzied street events, traditional club balls, and the parade of the major samba schools that takes place on Sunday and Monday nights.

destaque (prominent figures), often played by local celebrities. The preferred personalities for these roles are voluptuous actresses. There will also be groups of dancers known as *passistas* – agile young people who often stop to perform complicated dance routines.

Finally, there are the giant Carnival floats, *carros alegóricos*, created from papier-mâché and Styrofoam, which present the major motifs of a school's theme. The impact of the floats is primarily visual, and some critics argue that they detract from the music, which, they insist, should be the mainstay of the parade.

Carnival in the northeast

Rio is not the only Brazilian city with a tradition of fervent Carnival revelry. Many travelers prefer Carnival in the northeast's coastal cities of Salvador and Recife, and Olinda, where nonstop street action is the highlight.

The centerpiece of Carnival in Salvador (capital of Bahia state) is a glittering music festival on wheels called *trio elétrico*. It began in 1950 when a duo called *Dodô and Osmar* drove a beat-up convertible through the city during Carnival week playing pop and folk tunes. Instead of convertibles, Bahian musicians started using flatbed trucks with flashing lights, streamers, and elaborate sound systems.

Today, there are dozens of *trio elétrico* groups. Their repertoire is dominated by samba; by

a hopped-up northeast dance music called *frevo*; by a more recent style called *deboche*, which blends traditional Carnival sounds with rock'n'roll; and by *axé*, a highly erotic, rhythmic dance music.

The pre-eminent Carnival music of Recife (capital of Pernambuco state) is *frevo*. While Carnival in Bahia moves horizontally, as fans follow musicians through the streets, in Pernambuco the movement is vertical – dancers seem to leap up and down like ballerinas in double time. *Frevo* is a corruption of the Portuguese word for boiling – *fervura* – because it

A group of revelers with a historical theme.

ignites the passions of its listeners. It may have evolved as a musical accompaniment to *capoeira* (see page 105), the northeastern dance and martial art. But modern *frevo* has been simplified musically, and its listeners freed to invent their own dance routines. The best venue for *frevo* is the Recife suburb of Olinda. Olinda residents are Carnival purists who still dance only to acoustic instruments. Three-meter (10ft) wood-and-cloth Carnival figures are another feature of Olinda's celebrations.

Skilled *frevo* dancers, called *passistas*, wear knee britches and carry colorful umbrellas. The attire is a throwback to colonial days and the umbrellas may derive from the ornate canopies used by African kings.

Musician at the annual religious pilgrimage of Menino da Tabua.

FESTIVALS

Brazil is a year-round festival packed with celebrations involving music, dance, and, quite often, fireworks. Many of the festivals are based on Catholic saints' days, but even for the pious these usually involve a lot of fun alongside the religious observances.

Festivals and celebrations in Brazil, as in most Catholic countries, follow the liturgical calendar. After Carnival, the next big event on that calendar is the colorful *Festa do Divino*, held just before Pentecost Sunday (late May or early June). Two of the most strikingly beautiful colonial towns – Alcântara in the northeast state of Maranhão, and Paraty, 250km (150 miles) south of Rio on the coast – feature some classic *Festa do Divino* celebrations.

Townspeople dress in colonial attire, many of them taking the roles of prominent historical figures. The climax is a visit from the 'emperor,' who attends a procession and Mass in the square. In a gesture of royal magnanimity, he frees prisoners from the town jail. Strolling musicians, called *Folias do Divino*, serenade the townsfolk day and night. Banners are emblazoned with a white dove against a red background, symbolizing the coming of the Holy Spirit to the Apostles amid tongues of fire.

Bonfim ribbons.

The June festivals

Soon after Pentecost begins one of Brazil's most interesting celebration cycles, the June festivals (*Festa Junina*). The feasts of saints John, Anthony, and Peter all fall in June – a good excuse for an entire month of festivities.

The feast of St Anthony, patron of lost possessions and women in search of husbands, begins on June 12. Strictly religious observances dominate this saint's day, but the feast days for John and Peter are festive and far more secular. St John's days, June 23 and 24, are characterized by brightly illuminated balloons filling the skies and bonfires blazing through the night – though authorities now discouraged kerosene-powered balloons, on the grounds that they are fire hazards.

St Peter's feast days are June 28 and 29. Fireworks, ample food and drink, and folk music, usually played on an accordion, are the main elements for celebrating this occasion. St Peter is especially honored by widows, who place lighted candles on their doorsteps during the two-day festival.

Most June festivities take place outdoors. Participants dress up like old-fashioned country people, or *caipiras*. Country music, square dancing and mock wedding ceremonies (at which the bride may appear pregnant) feature at the most authentic June festival parties.

In the São Paulo suburb of Osasco, Brazil's largest bonfire (measuring some 20 meters/70ft high) is lit during the last week of June.

Consisting entirely of long-burning eucalyptus logs, the fire takes a week to burn itself out.

October celebrations

October in Brazil is also a month-long cycle of religiously inspired celebrations, including three of Brazil's most characteristic festivals. One of these events, Nossa Senhora de Aparecida, on October 12, is also a national holiday.

In October 1717, 'the miracle of Aparecida' occurred in Guaratingueta, situated about halfway between Rio and São Paulo. The colonial governor of São Paulo was passing through the

> *Brought to Brazil by the Portuguese, June festivals were originally summer solstice fertility rites, attached to convenient Christian saints' days. Ironically, in Brazil they fall in winter.*

The coronation of the original statue in 1931, as the Vatican-anointed patron saint of Brazil, made Aparecida the country's chief religious shrine. This increased the desire to build a bigger church, and by 1978, the main outlines of

Festa do Divino celebrations.

town at lunchtime when he stopped at a fisherman's cottage demanding a meal for his party. The fisherman and two friends hurried to their boats on the Paraíba river but failed to catch any fish. So they prayed. When they cast their nets again, they pulled a small black statue of the Blessed Virgin Mary out of the river. With the image aboard their craft, they landed a catch that nearly burst their nets.

This story quickly spread to the surrounding countryside, and in 1745 a rustic chapel was built to house the statue. Mainly because of the shrine's strategic location on the Rio–São Paulo highway, the cult of Our Lady of Aparecida grew and, in the mid-19th century, a church more grand than the first was built.

the cathedral here were completed. The second church, the world's largest after St Peter's in Rome, stands on a hill overlooking the newer one.

The latter basilica is a massive structure quite out of proportion with its surroundings, but this cathedral, with its enormous nave and network of chapels and galleries, is visited every year by about 7 million pilgrims. About 1 million visit Aparecida in October alone.

In comparison, the pretty Igreja de Nossa Senhora da Penha in Rio is hardly imposing, but it has an unusual history. Located atop a 92-meter (300ft) cone-shaped hill, Penha represents one of Brazil's oldest lay religious organizations. Penitents can be seen climbing its 382 steps on their knees. The order of Penha was founded in the 17th century by a Portuguese landowner named Baltazar Cardoso, who believed he had been saved from death in a hunting accident by divine intervention. The incident took place in Portugal, near a mountain called Penha. Later in the century, the lay order that Cardoso founded as a result of his experience transferred its activities to Brazil, and it found a rocky cone in Rio that was a small-scale copy of Penha in Portugal. The first church was built on the rock in 1635, and two more later went up on the second Sunday of October. A thick rope, 400 meters (1,300ft) long, is used to drag a colorfully decorated carriage bearing the image of Our Lady of Nazareth. Pilgrims who succeed in grabbing hold of the rope believe they are granted favors. When the image reaches the basilica, a 15-day festival, similar to the Penha festivities, begins.

The Círio de Nazaré story tells of a mulatto hunter named José de Sousa, who found an image of the Virgin in the forest. It was later placed in a chapel where it was said to effect miraculous cures. The first procession display-

A Good Friday procession in Aparecida.

same site. The third, built in 1871, now plays host every year to the Penha October festivities. Not only do worshippers participate in religious ceremonies every Sunday in October, they also enjoy a festival at the base of the hill, renowned for its good food, abundant beer, and live music.

Festival in the Amazon

October also marks the chief religious observance in the Brazilian Amazon – the festival of Círio de Nazaré in the city of Belém, at the mouth of the Amazon. Belém annually attracts tens of thousands of penitents and tourists for the remarkable procession, a four-hour cortège along 5km (3 miles) of streets on the

ing the image took place in 1763. The rope was added only in the 19th century.

Christmas

Christmas is the chief religious and family observance. Brazilian children believe that Santa Claus (Papai Noel) distributes gifts to families around the world on Christmas Eve. He enters through an open window, and leaves presents in shoes that have been left for this purpose on the floor or windowsill.

The contemporary celebration of Christmas in Brazil had its origin in the turn-of-the-century influence of German immigrants, who introduced the Christmas tree, gift giving, and Santa Claus. Another aspect of Christmas that hasn't changed is the Christmas Eve supper. Turkey, *rabanada* (a kind of French toast) and ham still feature on many dinner tables.

New Year wishes

New Year's Eve in Brazil rivals Carnival for fun, music, and color. In recent years, Salvador (Bahia) and the São Paulo resort of Guarujá have vied with each other for spectacles, fireworks, and tourist dollars, but the most popular New Year's Eve celebration takes place in Rio de Janeiro. An elaborate firework display splashes brilliant hues across the velvet sky at midnight.

The best place to observe New Year celebrations is on one of Rio's beaches, especially Copacabana. Hundreds of *Filhas de Santo*, white-robed priestesses of the Afro-Brazilian religions, launch wooden vessels on the waters. The tiny boats are filled with flowers and gifts for Iemanjá, the Queen of the Seas. When the tide carries one of the boats to sea it means Iemanjá will grant the gift-giver's wish. Very often, the wish is simple: to spend another New Year's Eve on the beach at Copacabana.

Nearly two million revellers swarm Copacabana beach in Rio to celebrate New Year's Eve

FESTIVALS IN SALVADOR

At New Year, while the rest of Brazil is honoring Iemanjá, Salvador (Brazil's former capital) celebrates the colorful festival of Bom Jesus dos Navegantes. A procession of small craft burdened with streamers and flags carries a statue of the Lord Jesus of Seafarers from the harbor to the Boa Viagem Church. Thousands line the beaches to watch. Legend has it that sailors participating in the event will never die by drowning. (A similar procession takes place on the same day in Angra dos Reis, 150km/90 miles south of Rio.) The tradition dates from the mid-18th century.In mid-January, Salvador prepares for another spectacle unique to this city that so loves pageantry – the Festa do Bonfim. Central to the event, which takes place in a Salvador suburb, is the Washing of the Steps at the Bonfim Church. Scores of Bahian women, dressed in traditional flowing garments, scour the stairs of the church until they are sparkling white. Visitors may take part in a Bahian tradition by buying colorful Bonfim ribbons from hawkers in the square or by the churches. Tie the ribbon around your wrist with several knots, each knot being a wish. When the ribbon finally breaks, your wishes will be granted – but only if the ribbons were a gift, so the trick is to buy and then exchange them. Iemanjá, the festival of the Queen of the Seas, is celebrated in Salvador not at New Year but on February 2.

Boi-Bumba

The Amazon city of Parintins has found a way to make a centuries-old cowboy tale into an annual festival of music, color, and imagination that rivals Rio's Carnival.

The last weekend of June marks the three-day Parintins Folk Festival, organized annually since 1913 and centered on a recounting of the Boi-Bumba fable. Two rival groups – Caprichoso and Garantido – vie with each other for popular acclaim as they fill the town with banners and balloons in their respective colors, blue-and-white for Caprichoso and red-and-white for Garantido. Each group, composed of up to 3,000 marchers and 500 musicians, perform the Boi-Bumba legend. The best show, based on costumes, music, and adherence to Amazon folklore, is the winner.

The story reads like a folk opera. Boi-Bumba recounts the tale of a black ranch hand named Francisco whose pregnant wife, Catirina, pleads for a 'special meal' of succulent bull's tongue. Francisco obliges by slaughtering the ranch owner's favorite bull. But his action turns him into a fugitive. In the trackless jungle, he meets a native shaman and his luck changes. Together they conjure up the Amazon spirits, who bring the bull back to life. Now, it's the ranch owner's turn to slaughter a bull as he welcomes back the prodigal ranch hand.

The Boi-Bumba legend offers broad scope for depicting Amazonian animals and colorful folkloric characters. Costumes, especially the headdress representing the bull, have become more elaborate with each retelling. The story is acted out through intricate dance routines to the beat of the toada, a hypnotic rhythm based on Amazon Indian music.

As with Rio's Carnival, the Parintins Folk Festival has become somewhat commercialized. Laser shows and fireworks have been added. Beer companies have emerged as sponsors, and even Coca-Cola has to have its ads in blue. Some of the better-known toada singers have released albums and turned professional. As many as 35,000 spectators turn up each night for the three days of shows, parades, and regional cuisine, arriving by boat and plane, since Parintins, 420km (260 miles) downriver from Manaus, has no road links to the outside world.

A Brazilian tale

Originally called Bumba-Meu-Boi, the story and dance behind the festivities are thought to have originated in the state of Maranhão in the 18th century. They were based on European models but modified by the region's slaves. In some retellings, Francisco becomes Father Francisco, or Chico, a black slave. The hand of the Jesuits can be seen in the themes of death, resurrection, and redemption. As in the Old Testament, the prodigal is always received 'with great rejoicing.'

Folkloric groups in Maranhão still make Bumba-Meu-Boi presentations in June. The tradition is

A Boi-Bumba legend bull costume.

also kept alive in Manaus and other Amazon-basin cities, and in other Brazilian states, but Parintins has no rival when it comes to fervor and spectacle. In the southern states, it is called Boi-de-Mamão or Boizinho; in some parts of the northeast, it is Boi-de-Reis. The phrase 'Bumba-Meu-Boi' is akin to the American cowboy chant, 'Get along, little doggies.'

The Great Drought of 1877 sent farm workers from Maranhão to the Amazon in search of work as rubber-tappers. The Bumba-Meu-Boi tradition they brought with them was gradually enriched by Amazon music and folklore, making it one of the most comprehensive mixtures of Amerindian, European and African cultural elements in existence in Brazil.

A miracle room with votive offerings and prayers.

SAINTS AND IDOLS

The beliefs of the Brazilian people are derived from a blend of Amerindian, African, and European traditions, which feeds inherent mystical tendencies and embraces faiths – and superstitions – of all kinds.

Se Deus quiser... (God willing...) is one of the expressions you are most likely to come across throughout Brazil, a country where world religions, millenarian cults, and ayahuasca-induced sects co-exist peacefully, setting an example to an intolerant world. Some attribute the force of religion to the people's deeply felt mysticism. Others credit it to the frequent absence of the state, which means that people, especially migrants, turn to religion to fill the gap. Either way, even though 'modernity' and Westernization appear to have made people less religious (or more hesitant to proclaim their faith publicly), religion permeates all levels of Brazilian life.

In the northeastern city of Juazeiro do Norte, women wear black on Friday, and on the 20th of the month. They are in mourning for Padre Cícero, who, according to legend, did not die, but was transported to heaven (see page 308).

Also in the northeast, farmers draw magic circles around sick cows and pray to Santa Barbara (or her Afro-Brazilian equivalent, Iansã) that the animal will not die. They also place six lumps of salt outside their homes on the night of Santa Lucia, December 12. If the dew dissolves the first lump, it will rain in December; if it dissolves the second lump, rain will come in January; and so on. If no dew dissolves the salt, drought will plague the sertão.

Religion and politics

Religion and state are officially separate entities in Brazil, but in practice the various churches have always sought to influence events. Until the end of the 20th century, the vast majority of Brazilians were baptized into the Roman Catholic faith, so a close relationship between the Catholic Church and the state was the norm.

With the growth of new players on the scene,

Misericórdia church, Olinda.

RADICAL RELIGION

In the late 19th century, a preacher called Antônio Conselheiro founded the community of Canudos in Bahia, where land was shared collectively, and there were no police or taxes, landlords or servants. Liberated slaves had equal access to land. This soon became a well-populated town – in four years it was the largest in Bahia, after Salvador. The draining of labor from the surrounding farms and Conselheiro's anti-republican position meant it was only a matter of time before the state and landed interests hit back. Conselheiro's men repelled four heavily armed military incursions, but in 1897 the army slaughtered thousands of his followers.

the Evangelical Churches (particularly the more radical Pentecostal sects), their acquisition of radio stations and television channels to get their message across, and their success in political elections, the crossover between politics and religion has continued.

Brazil is the world's most populous Roman Catholic country, by a large margin, although in the 2010 census only 64.6 percent of the population declared themselves as Catholic, down from 90 percent in 1970. A first South American pope, Pope Francis, may reverse that trend.

When the progressive ideas of liberation the-

Ancient voices

The nation's Amerindian heritage is partly responsible for Brazilians' deep-rooted mystic beliefs. At present the indigenous population of Brazil is composed of around 225 ethnicities, speaking 180 languages or dialects, so there are many different ways of life and perceptions of the afterlife. One common strand is an inextricable link with nature and ancestral lands.

Davi Kopenawa Yanomami, a shaman from the northwestern Amazon, says that since the arrival of the whites, many of the spirits' houses have been burnt and emptied. Today, he claims,

Souvenir dolls wearing traditional dress.

ology flourished in the 1970s and 1980s, many Catholic bishops, priests, and nuns in Brazil decided to fight for the poor and oppose military rule, following, they claimed, the example of Jesus Christ. Instead, they were accused by both the military and the Vatican of being Marxists, and as a result many priests, nuns, and lay-workers were imprisoned and tortured. In 1984, Leonardo Boff, a leading liberation theologian, was summoned to the Vatican to be cross-examined by the then Cardinal Ratzinger, who became Pope Benedict XVI. Boff asked for the date of the audience to be changed because it clashed with the date of the National Assembly of Prostitutes, to whom he was an advisor. After all, he explained, prostitutes are the first in the Kingdom of God.

'The words of the whites have created an obstacle to the voice of the ancients.' Shamans and other indigenous leaders like Davi fight to preserve their cultural heritage as well as their environment. André Baniwa, also from the Amazon, says that missionaries demonized indigenous faiths, and that nowadays it is necessary for schools to pass on traditional knowledge and mythology to children, as oral transmission has lost some of its effectiveness.

Cults of African origin

African beliefs are the second major influence in Brazil's religious culture. Visitors to Brazilian beaches in December, January, and February often find flowers, perfume bottles and cakes of soap still in their wrappers tossed on a shore that is strewn with burned-out candles. Followers of *candomblé* and *umbanda* will have offered these to the West African sea goddess Iemanjá, who is sometimes characterized as the Virgin Mary, sometimes as a sea goddess or a mermaid. If the offerings sink or are carried out to sea, Iemanjá is said to accept them. If they return to shore, however, she has rejected them.

The famous New Year event, when up to 3 million people pack Rio's beaches, began with these ceremonies in the 1970s. By 1992, the city mayor saw it as a chance to attract more tourists. The massive crowds and noise have since caused *candomblé* and *umbanda* groups to move their celebrations to the days leading up to December 31. In Salvador, on the Rio Vermelho beach, there is a huge party to celebrate Iemanjá at the beginning of February.

Although the census of 2010 would have one believe that *candomblé* is numerically unimportant, the National Federation of Afro-Brazilian Tradition and Culture (FENATRAB) has estimated that around 70 million Brazilians are in some way linked to the *terreiros* (sacred land where ceremonies are performed). Until recently, *candomblé* was looked down on as an inferior religion, and those who practiced it would often declare themselves to be followers of other faiths, particularly Catholicism; many people do follow more than one religion.

African slaves brought *candomblé* to Brazil. It was only officially recognized as a religion in Bahia, its stronghold, in 1976. It survived so long, even when outlawed, by adopting the identities of Catholic saints for its deities – the *orixás* – so when a slave appeared to be worshiping St George, he was really paying homage to Xangô, the god of thunder. This element has been incorporated into the religion.

Syncretistic cults such as *umbanda* may also include the god of war, Ogun, godlike figures called *orixás*, and demon-like forces – *exus* – which are part of African rituals. *Umbanda* belongs to a mystic movement called 'spiritism,' which includes African-inspired figures as well as Brazilian mediums and semi-deities such as Pai João, Caboclo and Pomba Gira, plus the mystical theological concepts of Allan Kardec, a European. Some of the most popular images on *umbanda* and spiritist altars are St Cosme and St Damyan, St George slaying the dragon,

Iemanjá in a white flowing dress, or the cigar-smoking figure of Pai João.

During a *candomblé* ritual, when priestesses are ordained, they have their heads ceremonially shaved and the blood of a hen or goat is smeared on their foreheads, along with chicken feathers. The ceremony is accompanied by *atabaque* drums, chants in various African languages, and frenetic dancing that is kept up until the initiates fall into a trance.

Santo Daime, one of the world's fastest-growing cults, was created by Raimundo Irineu Serra, who migrated to the Amazon forest from

Candomblé believers wear strings of beads.

TRACING ANCESTORS

One by-product of Brazil's thriving African religious cults has been the maintenance of an oral history among the Afro-Brazilian community. The leading priestesses of candomblé, such as the late Olga de Alaketu and Mãe Menininha do Gantois, could recite the names of their African ancestors and the ancestors of members of their community, going right back to generations still in their African homeland. They described in detail how their ancestors were captured, bound, and transported on slave ships to Brazil. The priestesses passed this knowledge on to the new spiritual leaders of the community, who memorized the vast genealogy.

the northeast, and Christianized shamanic traditions at the start of the 20th century. During 12-hour rituals accompanied by music, followers ingest a potent drink made from *ayahuasca* (derived from an Amazon vine) in order to

> The Igreja do Rosário dos Pretos in Salvador was built by slaves and freedmen in the 18th century as they were barred from attending 'white' churches. Mass is still occasionally said in the Yoruba language, brought from Nigeria.

A local deity in the ceremonial house of Pataxo Indians.

gain self-understanding and experience God or the Internal Superior Self. *Ayahuasca* was renamed Daime because of the invocations the faithful make while consuming the drink: *Dai-me amor, dai-me luz* (Give me love, give me light). The musician Sting describes his experience at one of these rituals in his autobiography, *Broken Music*.

Voodoo cults, similar to those still practiced in Haiti and elsewhere in the Caribbean, have developed roots in a few parts of Brazil. In Maranhão, in northeastern Brazil, and on the northern national border with the Guianas, the descendants of those slaves who managed to escape to freedom cultivated African sociopolitical structures and cults far removed from the domination of the white man. These practices continued until early in the 20th century.

The cult of Padre Cícero

Padre Cícero gained fame when an elderly woman, Maria Araujo, received the host from his hands at Mass in Juazeiro do Norte church, and then fell to the floor in convulsions. Blood in the form of the Sacred Heart was said to appear on the host. Balladeers wandered the *sertão* singing the praises of the miraculous priest and the 'miracle of the Sacred Heart.' More skeptical observers suggested that Maria Araujo suffered from tuberculosis and had coughed up blood, or suffered from bleeding gums.

Hundreds of woodcarvers have sculpted images of Padre Cícero, and literally millions of plaster of Paris images of him have been sold throughout the country.

Some of Padre Cícero's followers honor him by wearing black on the day of his death (June 20). He was considered a messiah who would turn the dry backlands into a green garden of paradise, where hunger and poverty would cease. A verdant valley was named the *Horto* or Garden of Gethsemane, and the city of Juazeiro do Norte was called the New Jerusalem. Some of his followers even collected his nail clippings, believing they had magical properties.

Through woodcarvings, songs, and poems published in chapbook form, the Padre Cícero legend has been carried forward. A statue of the priest was built in Horto in the 1960s, and his church has become a popular shrine that annually manages to attract thousands of followers.

Since the death of Padre Cícero in 1934, numerous messianic cults have appeared, of which the most famous is found in the northeast, centered around Frei Damião, a Calabrian priest who arrived in Brazil in his youth and who, until his death in 1997, preached with the same fire-and-brimstone images used by other prophetic figures over the past three centuries.

Brasília's millennium sect

Thought by believers to be the center of a magnetic field giving off cosmic energy, the city of Brasília has attracted various modern religious cults. The best known is the Vale do Amanhecer (Valley of the Dawn) movement, based in a valley about 60km (35 miles) from Brasília. Believers have built an enormous temple filled with new deities and religious figures that include Aluxá, Jaruá, White Arrow – an Amerindian deity – and the medium Tia Neiva (Aunt Neiva), the founder of the movement. The valley occupies 9 hectares (22 acres) of land and is currently the largest such center in Brazil (see page 247).

Tia Neiva founded the movement in 1959, and moved to the town of Planaltina 10 years later. Today the valley has more than 20,000 inhabitants, and the movement has also spread to other countries.

On arriving at the Valley of the Dawn, visitors see dozens of women in long robes decorated

Evangelical explosion

It came as something of a surprise when the 2000 census revealed that the Evangelical population had doubled in the space of nine years to some 26 million people, and is now thought to be closer to 35 million. While the numbers of clergy and laymen in the Catholic Church stayed the same, Evangelical churches multiplied. In Brazil people tend to look at Evangelicals (often called *crentes*) with a mixture of suspicion and respect. Scandalous images of some well-known Pentecostal priests enjoying the good life have been widely shown on national television, although

Prayers at Nossa Senhora do Rosário church in Rio de Janeiro.

with silver-sequined stars and quarter-moons. The men wear brown trousers, black shirts, and ribbons that cross their chests, and they carry a leather shield. These are the mediums who lead thousands of the sect.

Tia Neiva believed that there were about 100,000 Brazilians with the powers of a medium, and she herself registered 80,000, according to her follower, Mario Sassi. 'Two-thirds of humanity will disappear at the end of the millennium, but we, here in the Valley of the Dawn, will be saved,' Tia Neiva, who died in 1985, preached. The millennium has passed and they are still there. They believe that the third millennium started many years ago, and we are now in a period of improvement and transition.

not on the networks owned by the Evangelicals. The biggest concentrations of Evangelicals, especially the Pentecostal Churches, are found on the edges of large cities and in agricultural frontier zones. The common thread between these zones is that both have a great number of uprooted migrants in search of a better life in places where the state presence is tenuous. This encourages people to turn to religious networks for support, education, and a sense of belonging.

Islam and Judaism

Islam appears to have arrived in Brazil with slaves brought from West Africa. An attempt at revolution in 1830s Salvador was planned by Muslim freedmen and slaves (*malês*), but the revolt was foiled just before it was about to begin, and the state's response was drastic repression. In the 20th century, Muslim immigrants from the Middle East came to Brazil, and have since built some impressive mosques in many different regions around the country, especially in and around São Paulo.

Judaism arrived in Brazil during the period of Dutch rule, when the Dutch, and their Sephardic Jewish community, controlled Recife and Olinda from 1630 to 1654. During this period Recife was considered one of the world's most cosmopolitan cities. It housed Brazil's

A nun at Nossa Senhora do Pilar church, Ouro Preto.

first synagogue, which is also the first recorded synagogue in the Americas. When the Portuguese and Amerindians fought back and retook the city, many of the Dutch Jewish settlers fled north to set up New Amsterdam, a city that is better known today as New York. It is estimated that there are around 100,000 practicing Jews in Brazil, mainly located in São Paulo and Rio de Janeiro, but the numbers could be much higher.

Patron saint

The patron saint of 'Catholic' Brazil is Nossa Senhora Aparecida, the Virgin of the Conception. Three centuries ago, a broken terracotta image 'appeared' in a fisherman's net in the Paraíba river between Rio and São Paulo. Today, the

> *The mix of Amerindian, African, and European cults results in a rare form of syncretism, where Santa Barbara is Iansã of the Afro-Brazilian cults, and Iemanjá, goddess of the sea, may assume the form of the Virgin Mary.*

Basilica of Aparecida, on the highway between the two cities, houses the terracotta image and receives more than 7 million pilgrims a year A number of legends, stories, superstitions, and presumed miracles have been woven around the image. In 1999, a religious theme park linked to the shrine was constructed at a cost of US$70 million.

Another popular representation of the Virgin Mary is Our Lady of the 'O,' a euphemism for the pregnant Virgin. The upper clergy tried to suppress the cult of this figure in favor of Our Lady of the Conception (without a distended belly). Some Brazilians call this figure 'Our Lady of March 25,' to mark Christ's conception nine months before Christmas. Due to the perils of childbirth, Our Lady of the 'O' is worshiped by pregnant women.

Curative properties of saints

Other saints are believed to have therapeutic or healing properties. Santa Lucia is supposed to cure bad eyesight and blindness. Santa Barbara protects worshipers against lightning. São Brás, the Bishop, protects believers against sore throats and choking on fish bones. Another popular saint, carved in wood or molded in plaster of Paris, is St Jude, who always wears

VOTIVE OFFERINGS

The church in Juazeiro do Norte is filled with wooden *ex votos* (votive offerings) carved in the shape of injured limbs or parts of human bodies. When someone is cured of an illness they carve an image of the wounded body part and, after making a pilgrimage to Juazeiro, hang the carving in the *ex voto* chamber of the church as a token of gratitude. Churches in Caninde and Salvador, as well as the Basilica at Aparecida, are filled with *ex votos*, too, the more recent ones made of wax at the encouragement of the priests, who melt them down and sell them as candles. There are delicately carved femurs, tibias, elbows, eyes, and so on.

high boots. This is the saint who is known in Europe as the patron of lost causes.

Many images that once bore a religious connotation have survived without their former mystical aura. One example is *carrancas*, which were wooden figureheads attached to the prows of paddle-wheel steamers and other vessels sailing the São Francisco river from 1850 to about 1950. Today, on the beach in Nazare, Portugal, fishermen paint eyes on the prows of ships to 'see' the dangers underwater. Similar prow figures served the same purpose in Guinea and other parts of Africa.

Bahia, have malicious features – they are often depicted as wall-eyed or cross-eyed.

As well as angels, the arts-and-crafts fairs of Brazil are full of sculptures of saints. Among the most original are the no-neck images of Santa Ana made by woodcarvers from the northeastern state of Ceará. In *umbanda* shops you can find beautiful and elaborate religious artifacts, as well as potions and concoctions to grant wishes or cure maladies. And you will often find Indians on the street selling artifacts that mimic objects with spiritual meaning.

The state of Minas Gerais is home to hun-

The ornate interior of São Francisco church in Salvador.

The Brazilian *carrancas* were carved in the form of monsters, originally to frighten off the spirits of the waters that were a menace to shipping. The *carranca* gazed downward, and the crew aboard ship saw only the elaborate mane, so as not to be frightened by its terrible features. The São Francisco river is rich with legends of water spirits, such as the *caboclo da agua* (the backwoodsman of the water), who sends ships down to a watery grave.

Religious art

A popular subject for Brazilian artists through the centuries has been the crooked angel. Some of the carved and gilded angels in Salvador's São Francisco church, and in other churches in

dreds of Baroque churches that bear testimony to that institution's wealth and power. In Ouro Preto, Mariana and Diamantina you will see altars covered in gold leaf and sculptures by the great Aleijadinho who, even when crippled by disease, tied chisels to his hands and went on carving eloquent soapstone statues of saints and prophets (see page 211).

Religious dates

If you intend to travel during a national holiday, which is usually a religious date, you should book hotels and flights well in advance. This applies especially to Semana Santa – Holy Week – which precedes Easter and is celebrated 40 days after Ash Wednesday and Carnival.

A PASSION FOR SOCCER

In a game played with passion all over the world, Brazil – the only five-times winner of the World Cup – is pre-eminent. The 'beautiful game' is also a great leveler, arousing equal enthusiasm in people right across the social spectrum.

Brazilians did not invent soccer, they just perfected it. Today Brazil is as well known around the world for its unique style of soccer as it is for its coffee or Carnival. In 2014 the country hosts the FIFA World Cup for the second time. This is a tournament it has already won on five occasions.

The game arrived in the country just before the turn of the 20th century, brought to São Paulo by a young Brazilian-born Englishman named Charles Miller. Upon Miller's return to Brazil as a young adult, he began to teach soccer to his acquaintances at the São Paulo Athletic Club (SPAC), a British community club that was founded in 1888 and still exists today. In 1901, a citywide soccer league was formed, of which SPAC were champions in 1902, 1903, and 1904. But 1904 was the last time a major soccer trophy in Brazil was won by British descendants. Brazilians themselves were quick to learn the game and soon were beating the British at their own sport.

São Paulo is home to one of the world's most outstanding soccer museums. Housed in the Pacaembu Stadium, which, when built in 1940, was the largest and most modern in South America, the Museu do Futebol (www.museudo-futebol.org.br) is located appropriately enough in Praça Charles Miller.

Passion of millions

Every four years, when the World Cup is being played, factory managers and shopkeepers install television sets in the workplace in a mostly futile effort to keep absenteeism to a minimum on the days when the Brazilian squad is playing. In fact, most businesses simply close at game time and let their employees watch the matches – and then join the frenzied celebrations when the

Kicking a ball around in Arraial d'Ajuda, Bahia.

team wins, which is most of the time. One can only guess what will happen when the World Cup is played in Brazil in 2014.

Known as *futebol*, soccer is so hugely popular that some of the world's largest stadia have been erected around the nation with many having been modernized or rebuilt for the 2014 World Cup. Rio de Janeiro's giant oval Maracanã Stadium was able to cram in nearly 200,000 people when first built for the 1950 World Cup (its official record of 183,341 paying spectators was set on August 8, 1969 when Brazil played Paraguay for a World Cup slot). The stadium has been totally rebuilt for the 2014 World Cup with a capacity for 76,000 spectators, and will also be used for the 2016

Olympic and Paralympic games. Morumbi in São Paulo can hold some 70,000 onlookers, as can the city's new World Cup stadium, the Itaquera Arena. There are 17 other Brazilian facilities that can handle between 45,000 and 75,000 fans each.

One of the reasons for soccer's popularity is that it is readily accessible to all; no expensive equipment is required, and makeshift pitches can be set up anywhere. The game has attracted many players from the slums, who see soccer as a ticket out of poverty, and indeed there are a number of rags-to-riches tales of shantytown

Soccer is an all-consuming passion for millions of Brazilian fans around the world, reaching a peak every four years when the World Cup is organized somewhere in the world. In 2014, the hosting of the tournament falls to Brazil.

kids who have excelled at the game, even at international level.

Soccer's greatest players

The richest and most famous of these is Edson Arantes do Nascimento, known to the world by his nickname, Pelé. Legend has it that Pelé, a frail boy from a small city slum in Minas Gerais, had never even owned a pair of shoes when he was contracted, at the age of 15, to play for the Santos Soccer Club. One year later, in 1958, he helped the national team to Brazil's first World Cup win. And four years later, together with another national soccer legend, bandy-legged dribbling genius Garrincha (Manoel Francisco dos Santos), whom many in Brazil claim was even better than Pelé, he was instrumental in propelling Brazil to its second consecutive win of the world's most prestigious soccer trophy. Pelé was injured during the 1966 World Cup finals, staged that year in England, as a result of rough foul play against him, but in 1970 he was back, and at his best, and Brazil won the World Cup title for a record third time and the Jules Rimet Trophy outright. By the time he retired in 1977, Pelé had scored an extraordinary 1,300 goals. To date, only one other player, the Brazilian Romario, has even reached 1,000.

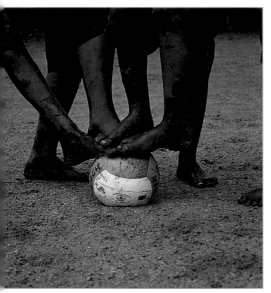

You don't need a lot of expensive gear to play football – some even do it with bare feet.

WORLD CUP VICTORIES

Brazil have won the World Cup five times – one more than Italy and two more than Germany.

Sweden 1958: Brazil had its first taste of raising the winner's cup in 1958 when they defeated the host country, Sweden, in the finals (5-2), and the world got a glimpse of the player who would go on to be considered the greatest footballer of all time: 17-year-old Edson Arantes do Nascimento, or Pelé.

Chile 1962: The Brazilian squad won its second World Cup title, beating Czechoslovakia 3-1 during the final match. Garrincha was the top name in a championship marked by violent play throughout the tournament's first phase.

Mexico 1970: The Brazilian squad, with a host of top players, was irresistible in 1970, beating Italy 4-1 in the final and winning a third world title. However, it was to be 24 years before Brazil would win another World Cup.

Italy 1994: Led by top goal-scorer Romário, Brazil defeated Italy in an emotion-laden final that ended in a 0-0 draw, forcing a penalty shootout, the first time in World Cup history.

Japan/South Korea 2002: Brazil overcame a highly regarded German squad 2-0 in the final, with two goals by leading scorer, Ronaldo. The country went wild, with millions chanting 'Penta Campeão' (five-times champion) in streets across the nation.

Many distinguished commentators consider the 1970 Brazilian squad to be the best ever. The fluid attacking, flexible ball play and clever playmaking, known as *gingado* – the hallmark of Brazilian soccer – enthralled fans around the world. The names of the many great players in that squad – including Pelé, Tostão, Gerson, Jairzinho, and the captain, Carlos Alberto – are still invoked nostalgically today.

Brazil's fourth and final goal in the 1970 final against Italy, scored by Carlos Alberto, but set up by Clodoaldo, Rivelino, Jairzinho and Pelé, is often considered the most beautiful in World

price of admission: at a big match, the fans are as much a part of the action as are the players.

All the major cities have popular football teams and big stadiums, and most Brazilians will know what the week's big games are. Due to the climate, games are normally played late afternoon at the weekend, Sunday being the main match day, while during the week the games will kick off between 7.30 and 9.30pm.

Brazilian Championship

There are two important national soccer tournaments played in Brazil each year. The Bra-

A barefoot game in Cachoeira, Bahia.

Cup history. Jairzinho, who scored seven goals in the 1970 finals, is still the only player to score in every round of the tournament.

The dream of millions of today's Brazilian youths is to follow Pelé's and Garrincha's example and play for one of the large metropolitan clubs. And the ultimate honor is to be picked for the national squad.

Unmissable attraction

One thing that shouldn't be missed while in Brazil is a visit to one of the soccer league matches, such as the classic Flamengo versus Vasco da Gama or Fluminense (the 'Fla-Flu') in Rio's Maracanã Stadium. Even if the game itself is dull, the spectacle of the fans is worth the

sileirão (Brazilian Championship) is disputed by the top 20 Brazilian clubs between March and early December. The four top finishers go on to battle other South American teams for the Copa Libertadores, and since 1960 the winner plays the European champion for the Club World Cup. Brazilian teams to win the world club championship include Santos (1962, 1963); Flamengo (1981); Gremio (1983); São Paulo (1992, 1993, 2005),Internacional (2006) and Corinthians (2012). The top eight finishers in the Brasileirão enter the continent-wide Copa Sudamericana (South American Cup) tournament.

The day of the final game of the Brasileirão is effectively a national holiday: in the home town of the national champion on the evening the title is won, hundreds of thousands of fans emerge into the streets for a night of carousing that rivals Carnival. Rio experienced this atmosphere when Flamengo won the championship for the sixth time in December 2009, its first since 1992, to equal São Paulo's record, and Fluminense won in 2010 and 2012.

The other important event is the Copa do Brasil (Brazil Cup), held during the first half of the year, with the top traditional clubs plus representatives chosen by each state. The winner of the Copa do Brasil also goes forward to play in the Copa Libertadores.

The 2014 FIFA World Cup

Brazil has won an unprecedented five of the 19 FIFA World Cup titles prior to 2014 (see page 92), a clear demonstration of the effectiveness of the unique style that has developed in the country, and the constant emergence of talented players. Brazil is the only nation that has qualified to play in every World Cup tournament since the event was created and first played in Uruguay in 1930.

Kick around on Porto da Barra beach in Salvador.

2014 WORLD CUP HOST CITIES

Due to the sheer size of Brazil, the country was allowed by FIFA to nominate 12 different cities – an unprecedented number – to host games during the 20th World Cup (June 12 through July 13) in 2014. The final game will be played at the most famous stadium of them all, the giant Maracanã Stadium in Rio de Janeiro.

For the World Cup, Brazil built new stadiums in Cuiabá, Manaus, Natal, Recife, Salvador, and São Paulo, while six existing stadiums, including the Maracanã, were completely upgraded for the tournament.

The host cities and their stadiums are:
Belo Horizonte (Mineirão – 70,000 capacity)
Brasília (Estádio Nacional – 71,500)
Cuiabá (Verdão – 42,500)
Curitiba (Arena da Baixada – 41,375)
Fortaleza (Castelão – 66,700)
Manaus (Arena Manaus – 50,000)
Natal (Arena das Dunas – 45,000)
Porto Alegre (Beira Rio – 62,000)
Recife (Cidade da Copa – 46,160)
Rio de Janeiro (Maracanã – 76,000)
Salvador (Fonte Nova – 55,000)
São Paulo (Corinthians – 60,000)

A fan following their team from its first game to the final in Rio de Janeiro is likely to have traveled over 11,800km (7,500 miles) during the tournament.

Brazil won its five titles in Sweden in 1958, Chile in 1962, Mexico in 1970, the United States in 1994 and Japan and Korea in 2002. Brazil came second in 1950, when the tournament was played in Brazil, and in 1998 when the tournament was played in France. Only winning will satisfy the Brazilian fans, and winning with style and flair – the exception to the rule being the 1982 World Cup when a great Brazilian side lost to Italy in the second round. Led by Zico, Sócrates, Falcão, and Éder, the team played the sort of football the country had dreamt of since the 1970 finals,

Thirty-two teams will play in Brazil between June 12 and July 13, 2014. FIFA allowed Brazil to nominate 12 cities to host games, the most ever (see page 92). In 1950, just 13 teams took part and the games were played in six Brazilian cities, all of which host games in 2014.

The 2014 World Cup is the first to be held in South America since Argentina hosted in 1978. Following on from South Africa, it is also the first time that consecutive World Cups have been staged in the Southern Hemisphere. Expectations are high for Brazil to deliver the greatest World Cup ever. Certainly

Celebrating the local teams.

and is considered the best side not to win the World Cup.

Not surprisingly, Brazil and Brazilian players hold a number of World Cup records. Ronaldo is the top overall goal scorer, with 15 goals over three tournaments; Pelé is the only player to win three World Cup winners' medals; Mario Zagallo, along with Germany's Franz Beckenbauer, are the only people to win the World Cup as both player and coach. Brazil has also scored the most goals in the finals and played the most games.

Brazil hosted the fourth World Cup in 1950, the first tournament to be played after World War II, and on October 30, 2007 was selected to host the 20th FIFA World Cup in 2014.

the global anticipation from the fans has been high, and many people will spend the entire month of the tournament in Brazil because if their team doesn't win they still want to be there if Brazil does.

Brazil has also been selected to host the 2016 Summer Olympic Games in Rio de Janeiro. The Olympic gold medal for football is the only major soccer title never to be won by Brazil, with it having lost in three men's finals and two women's finals. Brazil will hope to correct that anomaly on its soccer résumé in Rio in 2016. The Maracanã has been chosen to host the opening and closing ceremonies for the Olympics, as well as the soccer tournament.

FOOD AND DRINK

Fish are fresh from the water, the beef melts in the mouth, and tropical fruits are delicious. To drink: cold beer, *caipirinha*, and an awful lot of coffee.

From giant Amazonian river fish to succulent and beefy steaks, and with an abundance of tropical fruits and vegetables, Brazilian food offers something for all kinds of tastes. The most traditional dishes are variations on Portuguese or African foods, but there is a wonderful variety of dishes, reflecting both on Brazil's size and the influence of its many immigrant groups. A favorite throughout the country is the churrasco, or barbecue, which originated when the southern gauchos roasted meat over open fires while working the herds. Many churrascarias offer a rodizio option: for a set price, you can eat all you wish from a variety of tender meats selected straight from the spit.

In many restaurants a portion is large enough for two people, and it is perfectly acceptable (except in the smartest places) to ask for a dish to share. Comida a kilo restaurants (literally meaning food by weight) are great places where you can get a wide choice of cheap, usually good-quality dishes. Here you can sample unfamiliar foods, and you are not limited by a poor knowledge of Portuguese.

Regional specialties in the northeast and along the coast include seafood dishes such as *peixe a Brasileiro*, a fish stew served with *pirão* (manioc root meal cooked with broth from the stew). In the inland areas, dishes include *carne seca* or *carne de sol* (dried salted beef, often served with squash) and roast kid. Minas Gerais has a hearty pork-and-bean cuisine – the tasty pork sausage is called *linguiça* – and *queijo minas* cheese is good.

In the Amazon, exotic dishes include those prepared with *tucupi* (manioc leaves, which numb the tongue). The rivers produce a great range of fish, including piranha and the giant pirarucu. In some parts of the south, the cuisine reflects a German influence, and Italian

Street-side tables in Rio's buzzing Lapa district.

and Japanese immigrants have brought their culinary skills to São Paulo.

Salgadinhos are Brazilian savory snacks, often served as appetizers or as a quick snack as small pastries stuffed with cheese, chicken, palm heart, and so on. Other tasty snacks include *pão de queijo* (a cheesy bread) and *pastel* (two layers of a thinly rolled, deep-fried dough with a filling sealed inside). Instead of french fries, try *aipim frito* (deep-fried manioc root). A lot of these snacks are served in the traditional *botequims*, (see page 97), which are back in fashion in Rio and across Brazil.

Most desserts are very sweet, and are made from fruit, coconut, egg yolk, or milk. Portuguese-style egg yolk desserts are delicious, especially *quindim* (a rich egg yolk and coconut custard). The custard makes another appearance in *olhos de sogra* (mother-in-law's eyes), in which it is used to stuff prunes. *Docinhos* – little sweets – consumed at all times of the day, are just miniature versions of desserts.

Watermelon, papaya, and pineapple, are among the vast array of fruits on offer. The pink, pellet-like *acerola* is used mainly for juice, and is said to contain the highest concentration of Vitamin C of any fruit in the world. Sticky guava paste, *goiabada*, contrasts with sharp white cheese in a favorite Brazilian dessert, known as Romeu e Julieta.

Brazil's favorite drinks

Brazil and coffee (*café*) are synonymous with each other. Money earned from coffee sales boosted the country's economy in the early 20th century, and it is still one of the most successful exports. Brazilian coffee is roasted dark, ground fine, prepared strong, and drunk with plenty of sugar. Coffee with hot milk (*café com leite*) is the traditional breakfast beverage. Once breakfast is over, it is served black in tiny demitasses. These *cafezinhos* (little coffees), offered to visitors to any home or office, are served piping hot at all *botequims*. There are even *botequims* that serve only *cafezinho*. However you like it, Brazilian coffee makes the perfect ending to a good meal. Decaffeinated coffee is now available in supermarkets, but as Brazilians do not favor the concept, finding it in restaurants is still difficult, but the situation is improving.

Likewise, Brazil was slow to embrace other forms of serving coffee, but has now accepted that there are more than a couple of ways to serve coffee so that coffee stores, even Starbucks, can be found in the main cities. Better restaurants will offer a wider choice of how your coffee can be served.

Rarely seen but widely consumed is *guaraná*. The reddish, seed-filled fruit is borne, in the Amazonian wild, on woody vines that seek the sun in the rainforest by climbing up other trees. The seeds are highly prized and have been used by indigenous people for ages. *Guaraná* was rediscovered in the 20th century; it can be found in capsules, powder or paste form. Its chemical composition is akin to that of ginseng, high in caffeine and other (reputedly aphrodisiac) substances. Visitors and residents are most likely to

encounter the product in canned form, in the refreshing, sparkling soft drink Guaraná, whose sales rival those of the cola producers.

Rio's juice bars are great places in which to familiarize yourself with the local fruits. There's a vast choice – *açaí, acerola, graviola*, as well as fruits that will be more familiar. Or you can opt for a *vitamina*, a thick, creamy shake that will include banana with one or two other types of fruit, and sometimes oat flakes or wheat germ, and is very similar to what is now marketed abroad as a 'smoothie.' If you are watching your calories, you should ask for *sem açúcar* (without sugar).

A man pushes a cart with fresh fruit for sale along the cobbled streets of Olinda.

CACHAÇA

When it comes to alcoholic beverages, the drink of choice in Brazil is *cachaça*, also known as *pinga*, which is produced from fermented sugarcane. It is estimated that Brazilians get through some 1.5 billion litres (390 million gallons) each year, mainly as the basis for the national cocktail, the *caipirinha*, or blended with fresh fruit juices and fruits, when it becomes a *batida*.

There are hundred of brands of *cachaça* on offer in Brazil, all of them strong in terms of alcohol by volume, and the very top *cachaças* can be drunk neat, in very much the same way that a good whiskey or brandy is appreciated.

BRAZILIAN DISHES

Thanks to the diversity of Brazil, visitors will find a wide variety of cooking styles. Even corner bars, the *botequim*, offer a wide variety of gastronomic tastes.

Cooking techniques

The spiciest food in Brazil is found in Bahia, spreading north to Pernambuco, a region of the country where an African influence can be tasted in the dendé palm oil and coconut milk. Dishes can be stew-like or covered in sauce. Famous dishes include bobó de camarão, a dish made with cassava and shrimps *(camarão)*; *vatapá*, a dish featuring shrimps, coconut milk, and palm oil that has been mashed into a creamy paste; and *acarajé*, a popular street food made from black-eyed peas formed formed into a ball and then deep-fried in *dendé*. *Acarajé* are often split in half and then covered with *vatapá*.

One of the great Brazilian dishes, *feijoada*, originated in Bahia, but is now more popular in Rio and São Paulo. It consists of black beans simmered with a variety of dried, salted, and smoked meats. It was developed as food for slaves, whose masters ate all the better cuts of meat, but is now considered Brazil's national dish. It is accompanied by white rice, finely shredded kale *(couve)*, *farofa* (toasted manioc root meal), and sliced oranges. Oranges may seem a strange touch, but they provide a tangy foil for the richness of the dish.

A Portuguese import is bacalhau (dried, salted cod). It is most often served in rissole-like balls – bolinhos de bacalhau – which are meltingly rich.

Alfresco tables at a café in Ipanema, Rio de Janeiro.

Weighing fish at the port in Salvador. Seafood is plentiful on Brazil's coast.

The northeast is particularly known for seafood including shrimps, served simply, as here in Bahia.

Mixing cocktails at a beach bar. Brazil's most famous cocktail is the caipirinha.

THE CORNER BOTEQUIM

Although they have never gone away, *botequims* are back in fashion in Brazil.

They are the legitimate heirs to the old taverns, serving food in healthy portions at accessible prices. They are part of the cultural identity of Rio, and developed from the Spanish *bodega* and Portuguese *botica* to emerge as the Brazilian *boteco* - or *botequim* - in the second half of the 19th century. Today they are found across Brazil, and range from the simple to the sophisticated and fashionable.

A botequim is a place to eat, drink, and be merry. A place where Brazilians – and foreigners – can meet for friendly and lively conversation, good company, and tasty and interesting food in an informal setting. The food can be anything from a full meal to a selection of bite size appetizers and snacks. A *botequim* is great location for visitors to experiment with a range of Brazilian culinary styles and tastes.

Drinks range from ice-cold draft beer to a *caipirinha*. Others might choose Brazil's most popular soft drink, Guaraná, or a coffee, or one of many fruit juices.

Fresh barbequed meats and fish are ever-popular and always easy to find in Brazil.

Cachaça is the national spirit and comes in varying degrees of quality. The very best compare favorably to a top whiskey or brandy.

Just-landed fish.

A NATION IN TUNE

The vast variety of music in Brazil is matched only by its quality. Whatever your musical taste, you should be happy here, where music takes to the streets as well as to the clubs, bars, and concert halls.

On a Saturday night in any sizeable Brazilian town, a vast musical choice presents itself. Will you tap cutlery to a samba *pagode* in a tile-floored bar, or dance hip-to-hip to the simple rhythm of the *forró*? Try the tango-like ballroom virtuosity of the *gafieira*, or converse over the twinkling swirls of *choro* played on mandolins and violas? Alternatively, you could smooch to sensuous bossa novas in the bars of Ipanema once haunted by The Girl. Or wait in line to see ear-bleeding techno-rock bands or hear exhilarating drum-and-bass, hip-hop and electronica DJs perform in small city clubs and bars, or hangar-like *favela* venues from where *baile-funk* spins through cyberspace to Europe's hippest nightspots.

In nightclubs, jazz takes turns with the melancholy of Portuguese *fado*, Brazilian torch singers, and the legends of MPB (Musica Popular Brasileira) such as Roberto Carlos and Elis Regina, and younger favorites, such as Marisa Monte and Céu, perform poetic anthems. Leading lights of the 1970s Tropicalia movement continue to draw young audiences: Gilberto Gil and his collaborator Caetano Veloso still woo with sensual, laid-back singing and eclectic music; Veloso also joins his son Moreno's neo-Tropicalia experimentations; and Tropicalia divas Gal Costa and Maria Bethânia continue to cast their spells. The ageless Jorge Ben Jor, Brazil's James Brown, is seeing his back catalogue of funk-samba cannibalized by a new generation of producers around the world.

Heterogeneous nation

Music changes with geography, and follows migration paths across this vast country, but regional folk music remains very much alive: the gauchos of Rio Grande do Sul sing to accordions like their 19th-century German forebears;

Playing music on the street at night in Olinda.

the *boleros* of Mato Grosso do Sul possess all the drama of the Spanish culture in neighboring Paraguay; and northeastern rhythms – the *baião* and *maracatu* in the interior, and the faster *frevo* on the coast around Recife – dominate wherever *nordestinos* have moved. *Forró*, the mainstay of the *nordestino*, is now universally popular.

Salvador, in Bahia, the original Brazilian capital and a significant slaving port, remains heavily African in cuisine, colloquialisms, religion, and music. Its Carnival is less commercialized than Rio's, and the strong African elements in its music have inspired many national trends.

The extraordinary diversity of Brazil explains why so many musical genres co-exist with equal vigor. Successive waves of immigration have left their imprint: the Portuguese colonists and Jesuit missionaries, the Africans who came as slaves, and the economic and political refugees from 19th- and 20th-century Europe and Asia. Culturally mixed and socially hierarchical, Brazil has one foot in the computer age, the other in the 17th century. It is more than 80 percent urban, yet so recently urbanized that large sectors of the city population retain the cultural habits of the *sertão*. Still predominantly an oral culture, it is nonetheless exposed to the rest of the world through radio, television and the internet, and the latest international hits reach the remotest corners of the country, where folk music is still solidly alive.

Rhythm-makers

Brazilian culture has always been open to a blending and fusion of genres. The 16th-century European missionaries saw Catholic liturgy adapted by the slaves and indigenous people to their ritual songs and choreography; in the northwest of Amazonas state, Tucano Amerindians still sing Gregorian *glorias* and *credos*. Otherwise, the music of indigenous Brazil focuses on rhythm over melody, its principal

Rio Scenarium club in the Lapa area of Rio.

THE TRUTH ABOUT THE GIRL FROM IPANEMA

An intriguing legal action in 2005 sought to prevent an Ipanema woman from calling her boutique The Girl from Ipanema. It was brought by the copyright holders of Brazil's famous song, the sons of the late composers, Antonio Carlos Jobim and Vinicius de Moraes. The woman was Heloisa Pinheiro, the attractive 18-year-old who inspired the song in 1962 as she strolled past the bar where the composers sat.

The song shot to fame in 1963 in a version by Stan Getz and Astrud Gilberto, and was recorded by dozens of singers. The music was originally composed by De Moraes, a prolific poet and lyricist, for a musical comedy, *Dirigível*, and the words of this version, 'Menina que Passa' ('The Girl Who Passes By'), were markedly different from the final version. Jobim and De Moraes did admit to having seen the alluring Heloisa stroll by as they sat at the Veloso bar-café – 'a golden-tanned girl, a mixture of flower and mermaid, full of brightness and grace, but with a touch of sadness,' as De Moraes wrote later. But the legend that they casually composed the song while sitting in the bar belied the hard graft that songwriting often entails.

Today, the bar where the musicians sat is known as A Garota de Ipanema (The Girl from Ipanema), and it is located on the corner of Vinicius de Moraes Street and Rua Prudente de Moraes.

instruments being maracas and rattles, and sometimes simple flutes and panpipes.

For four centuries, the Portuguese colonizers held the dominant influence, defined Brazilian harmonic structures, and established the four-beat bar and syncopation that later blended so well with African rhythms. The Portuguese basis of Brazilian folk dance includes 'drama-tized dances' linked to the Catholic calendar. The liveliest and most profane is *Bumba-Meu-Boi*, a comic representation of the *tourinhos* (Portuguese bullfights), and a colorful, rhyth-mic, essentially African affair, popular in the

came from Angola, Congo, and Sudan, but Brazil's plantation owners, unlike those in the US, broadly tolerated their rhythmic dances and trance rituals. Once freed, and organizing their own religions, they were repressed by the authorities and resorted to disguising their animist gods as Catholic saints – the process known as syncretism that is found throughout the former Spanish and Portuguese colonies.

Origins of samba

For the Afro-Brazilian, music is traditionally both social and religious. The instruments used

Dancing at a Salvador bar.

states of Pernambuco, Maranhão, and Bahia.

Although the Portuguese introduced the *cavaquinho* (similar to the ukulele, but usually steel-stringed), *bandolim* (mandolin), *violão* (Portuguese guitar, resembling a large man-dolin, Indian sitar, or Greek bazouki, with five pairs of strings), bagpipes, piano, viola, and harp, it was the Spanish guitar that became the backbone of Brazil's popular music (although the German accordion is still heard at country parties in many regions).

The Portuguese provided the lyrical-poetic framework and range of themes and emo-tions now central to popular music, but from Africa came *axé* (a Yoruba word meaning joy and strength). The majority of Brazil's slaves

THE CRYING GAME

Choro (meaning crying or sobbing) is a guitar-based song style accompanied by emotional singing to sensual Afro-Brazilian rhythms: the Brazilian 'blues.' It lacks the brash percussive exhilaration of samba. The early 20th-century composer Heitor Villa-Lobos spent his spare time playing *choro* in Rio's bars and cafés, while pro-fessionally weaving together Bach and folk music in his magnificent *Bahianas Brasileiras*. *Choro* thrives in many Brazilian cities, in delightfully old-fashioned bars and clubs, spurred on by the devoted *choro* fan, samba icon, guitarist, and composer Paulinho da Viola.

with varying rhythms in religious ceremonies such as *candomblé*, and at parties, clubs, and concerts, include the *atabaque* drums, *ganza* metal rattles, the *cuíca* drum, whose skin is pulled to make a hoarse rasping sound, and conical *agogo* bells, beaten with a stick or metal rod. With the *violão* or *cavaquinho*, these form the basis of Brazil's national music: the samba.

The word samba derives from the Angolan *semba*, a synonym for *umbigada* – literally, a navel thrust. It was danced originally in a circle, with a soloist in the middle who clapped and danced, then stopped in front of one person, and, with a cheeky *umbigada*, swapped places. Variations of *umbigadas* – *samba de roda*, *jongo*, *tambor-de-crioulo*, *batuque*, and *caxambu* – survive virtually unchanged today in Afro-Brazilian communities all over Brazil.

The Afro-Brazilian rhythms made their first, tentative foray into the salons of white urban society in the late 18th century in the form of the *lundu*, a toned-down couple dance accompanied by viola and sitar. In the second half of the 19th century, slave bands performing on country plantations and in city ballrooms were obliged to copy fashionable European dance rhythms like the polka and the mazurka. But playing for themselves, they injected their own sensuous thrusts and swings, and from those sessions emerged the *maxixe*, an extravagant, rhythmic form of tango. Fred Astaire's version in the 1933 Hollywood film *Flying Down to Rio* coincided with the *maxixe*'s decline in Rio in the face of samba's increasing popularity in Carnival parades. In today's *gafieiras* (dancehalls), couples still mix *maxixes*, *habaneras*, *choros* (samba's precursor, see page 100), and sambas with extravagant virtuosity.

The rise of samba

Samba's official history began in 1916, with *Pelo Telefone*, the first samba on record and an instant hit at Carnival that year. The first samba school, composed of scores of percussionists whose rhythms drive the revelers, was founded in the 1930s, and today every Brazilian town and city has its own. The oldest school, Mangueira, is acknowledged in scores of songs, and the 70-something singer, Elza Soares, whose voice is as huskily sexy as in her 1960s heyday, today mixes sambas and Mangueira tributes with hip-hop fusions.

The best-known samba form is *samba enredo* (story-samba), sung by an amplified voice accompanied by a guitar and *cavaquinho*, to a responding chorus of the thousands of voices in the *desfile* (procession) who 'converse' with the drummers sashaying in their finery. Other subgenres include *samba do morro*, played on percussion instruments only; *samba do breque* (break), which pauses abruptly to allow a wry interjection, then starts again; and the perennial ballad version *samba-canção*, the 'Frank Sinatra of sambas', which is popular in clubs and bars.

With musical frontiers opened and fashions flashing by, samba fusions are virtually limitless. But samba-rock, samba-funk, samba-reggae,

Brazilian singer Bebel Gilberto performs on the opening day of the music festival, Rock in Rio.

and samba-rap must bow to the domination of *samba-pagode*, the sound of Rio's *favelas* since the 1980s. Performed at informal get-togethers, it involves all ages. *Cavaquinhos* and banjos sing out the melodies, and dancers are driven by *pandeiro* (frame drum) and *tamborim* beats. In the late 1980s, David Byrne (ex-Talking Heads) released a significant set of tasters on his Luaka Bop compilation *O Samba*. The compelling collection of classic samba singers it introduced included Zeca Pagodinha, today's *pagode* idol.

Zeca Pagodinha was born in 1959 in Irajá, a traditional samba neighborhood of Rio where he was surrounded by music, samba, and *sambistas*. He started making up the lyrics to his own sambas at a very young age, and became involved in the local *roda-de-samba*, where people sit around singing and composing sambas. As a young child involved in music, he picked up the nickname of 'Pagodinha'. He packs his infectious songs with slang and performs them as casually as a storyteller in a bar. Superstar Seu Jorge (see page 106), who emerged from a generation raised on hip-hop, pays homage to Pagodhina, but his favorite is *samba partido-alto* (high party), with its addictive percussion and sharp beats created with palm-slaps on a *pandeiro*.

Samba, like most great musical genres, is wide open to adaptation, and many samba

Capoeira performance in Salvador.

singers now also include bossa novas in their repertoires. Jazz samba is today an international fusion style, and Tania Maria one of its most popular exponents outside Brazil. The veteran 1960s samba-jazz group Os Ipanemas enjoyed a Buena Vista-style comeback with their album *Samba is Our Gift*, which drops trombone and saxophone into the samba mould.

While Rio holds the world records for numbers of Carnival visitors, samba schools and gyrating feather-clad dancers, Salvador in Bahia offers a more interactive experience in the colonial streets, which echo to the sound of *blocos* (formation drummers). But a rival to Salvador is Olinda, the colonial town attached to Recife (capital of Pernambuco state), whose local *frevo*

rhythm outranks even Rio's sambas in intensity (see page 73).

Bossa nova

Samba is traditionally the voice of black Brazilians and forever associated with Carnival. But bossa nova (new wave) is also synony-

> The construction of bossa nova relied on João Gilberto's wholly original approach to the guitar, which mixed jazz harmonies with a chunky, persistent, offbeat rhythm extracted from the guitar itself.

mous with Brazil, and its birthplace – Rio. Bossa nova exploded on to the world scene in 1964, when the classically trained pianist and composer Antonio Carlos 'Tom' Jobim, the shy young guitarist João Gilberto, and his sultry-voiced wife Astrud, held New York's Carnegie Hall in thrall to *'Garota de Ipanema'* ('The Girl from Ipanema'), *'Desafinado'* ('Out of Tune'), and *'Samba de uma nota só'* ('One Note Samba'). Bossa nova had taken shape several years earlier in Rio, the outcome of a quest by Jobim and other young *carioca* intellectuals for a calmer samba, in response to America's West Coast cool jazz scene led by Stan Getz and Charlie Byrd. Bossa nova would bewitch the world, and inspired scores of schmaltzy covers.

It requires considerable skill to play bossa nova: one musician described it as 'like talking in a long sentence, but one in which you switch language every two words.' The most significant lyricist was the poet and former diplomat, Vinicius de Moraes, whose legacy remains in such exquisite songs as *'Eu Sei Que Vou te Amar'* ('I Know That I Will Love You'). Jobim was a magnificent pianist and a charismatic front man. Working in their apartments and the local bars of Rio's chic Zona Sul neighbourhood, the two men and their collaborators perfected songs that remain in the international repertoire half a century later.

The musicians in favelas overlooking Zona Sul had little interest in this middle-class style, but in today's era of fusion, the classics are now integrated into the mosaic of styles cannibalized by every Brazilian DJ and musician. João Gilberto's daughter Bebel has built a successful reputation in Europe and the US based on such a repertoire.

Tropicalia

In reaction to the cool of bossa nova, the late 1960s saw a very different revolution, born under increasing political turmoil and the impact of Beatles songs and West Coast American rock. 'Tropicalia' was seeded in Salvador, where a group of students, besotted with local folk music and Beatles /songs, included guitarists and songwriters Gilberto Gil and Caetano Veloso, the avant-garde composer Tom Zé, and ex-bossa nova singer Gal Costa. The clan migrated to São Paulo, then the hub of an explosive new arts scene, and Gil's collaborations with the whacky, musically brilliant trio Os Mutantes (The Mutants) led to their anthemic psychedelic song, '*Domingo no Parque*' ('Sunday in the Park'). With Veloso's '*Alegria, Alegria*' ('Joy, Joy'), they launched an era with loud, irreverent songs and Dadaist performances on live TV Globo, shocking the traditionalists but delighting young hippy fans. The song lyrics strikingly juxtaposed concrete poetry with images from pop culture, but pushed the buttons of the establishment, until the military government in 1969 arrested and imprisoned Veloso and Gil, and forced them into exile. They chose to live in London. By the time of their return in 1972, Tropicalia had unified the young generation, and every group was electric – and Tropicalist.

More than 50 years on, the Tropicalia pioneers still carry musical clout: Caetano Veloso, with his sinuous melodies and poetic wit; Gil, until recently the minister of culture, still playful, rhythmic and mesmerizing, and carrying the torch for Bob Marley's songs. The third significant musician of that generation, Chico Buarque, was never a true Tropicalia member but a politically active poet, writer and singer. Today he is still adored and as popular as ever.

Milton Nascimento, leader of Minas Gerais' *Clube de Esquina* generation, a brilliant songwriter and vocalist, has a background in church choral music, but also has Afro-Brazilian influences. The grand lady of Brazilian rock is former Tropicalia star and Os Mutantes singer Rita Lee. Many of these artists still produce significant work more than 50 years after Tropicalia's heyday, and in interesting collaborations with the '*novo tropicalismo*,' electronica generation.

Modern moves

Musical changes still reflect regional differences but, increasingly, in the age of the internet, São Paulo has returned as the hub of a musical revolution, through the proliferation of hip-hop and electronic music. But most challenging to its status is Pernambuco and its capital city, Recife, where Chico Science's Nacao Zumbi, the singer Otto, and DJ Dolores are based.

Occupying a space outside both the electronic dance scene and the post-Tropicalia clan are the Brazilian rockers, who always possessed a certain sweetness: from the teenaged, mini-

Caetano Veloso has been writing and performing since the 1960s.

skirted girls in the mid-1960s; to the innovative 1980s rockers, whose direct, urban and often mocking or humorous songs were a far cry from traditional romanticism; to 1990s rappers, who continue in this vein by tingeing their diatribes with humor. The early Noughties craze for New Rave and the mostly girl group, Cansei de Ser Sexy (CSS), which translates as Tired of Being Sexy, marked a nostalgic return to 1970s post-punk LA girl groups who reject the clichés of girls in rock, and add copious measures of kitsch that Carmen Miranda would surely envy.

Re-Africanization

The late 20th-century shift away from Rio and São Paulo to Salvador and Recife as

> *Brazil has music to suit every taste. The reason for such variety is the country's vast size. Its states are nations, each with its own traditions and customs, its superstars, dances, and musical styles.*

focuses of Brazil's music scene was triggered by the 1970s move for 're-Africanization' in Bahia. Groups of beautifully elegant women dancers, dressed in the white crinolines and headwraps associated with the Afro-Brazilian

Celebrating Rio's Carnival with some freestyle dance moves and an innate sense of rhythm.

candomblé religion, began to make their presence felt during Carnival. Parading through the streets, they danced not to the frenetic *trio elétrico* or samba of Rio but to African rhythms – *afoxés* – beaten out on *agogo* bells. These stately descendants of slaves became the nerve centres of a growing black consciousness movement.

Around the same time, Bob Marley records were arriving in Bahia, and the Baianos immediately identified with reggae. Gilberto Gil adopted Rasta colors, recorded in Jamaica, and inspired a generation. His spine-tingling concert with Jimmy Cliff was a landmark recognition of reggae's connection with black Brazil. Reggae became particularly associated

with the port cities, whose slave descendants lend them a strong African character. In August, the Reggae Festival in the northern port of São Luís sees thousands of reggae fans in Rasta threads flock to see Gil and other Brazilian musicians performing alongside the Jamaican idols.

Inspiring Paul Simon and Michael Jackson

Salvador's post-reggae Carnival generated new dances and new singing stars, led by Margareth Menezes, Daniela Mercury, Ivete Sangalo, the *candomblé*-gospel diva Virginia Rodrigues, and the musician, composer and producer Carlinhos Brown. Their international popularity helped put Salvador on the world music map. The early 1980s saw the formation of the first of the community drumming groups *(blocos afros)*, Olodum, who stirred up Carnival with their massive parades of drummers beating out Afro-Brazilian rhythms. Olodum caught the ear of Paul Simon and provided the rhythmic framework for his *The Rhythm of the Saints* album, as well as performing with him at his concert in Central Park, New York, in August 1991. Olodum also performed with Michael Jackson in his controversial Spike Lee-directed video for *They Don't Care About Us*.

Many of Olodum's 300 or so permanent members were street kids who discovered identity and pride through their involvement. The group offered free classes in Yoruba and Portuguese, literacy, computing, and music at the Olodum centre, and added metalwork and carpentry workshops.

Carlinhos Brown was key to establishing self-supporting, community-based education centers operating through music and culture. 'In Bahia, the drum has become the synonym of employment, education, social ascension, and, of course, polemic,' decreed the leading news magazine *Veja* in June 1998.

Brown described his third solo album, *Bahia do Mundo*, in 2001, as a tribute to the country's black musical traditions, and asserted: 'Drum-and-bass, house, and even funk exist because of samba schools, and trance only exists because of Brazilian Carnival.'

With funds from Unicef, Brown built a school for music, literacy, and maths, and recording studios to nurture musical talent. For a decade, he directed the percussion band

Timbalada, which toured the world, and his 2002 album, *Tribalistas*, recorded with singer-producer and superstar Marisa Monte, and poet and composer Arnaldo Antunes, received five Grammy nominations for a surprisingly low-key, mostly acoustic collection of rock, soul, and samba-influenced songs led by Monte's luminous voice and Antunes' gritty baritone, and a guest appearance by the sultry Salvador vocalist, Margareth Menezes. His well-received 2012 album release was called *Mixturada Brasileira*. Brown also worked on the soundtrack of the animated feature *Rio*.

AfroReggae

In Rio, a similar development to the Olodum phenomenon led to the now internationally renowned community NGO, AfroReggae, which also began life as a drumming troupe. Founded by a young activist, José Jr, it developed through his newssheet *AfroReggae News*, in Rio's most violent *favela*, Vigário Legal. Centro Cultural AfroReggae was established as a landmark offering hope to the youth in a community fighting for survival among gang warfare. Financial, moral, and practical supporters included Caetano Veloso, and the Centro's classes eventually included *capoeira*,

Singer Marisa Monte performs in Rio.

CAPOEIRA

One of the many attractions on the beaches of Brazil is the sight of two young acrobatic men or women caterpillar-looping, doing backflips and high-kicking according to the ancient art of *capoeira*. It is generally accepted that *capoeira*, Brazil's national sport, was brought by slaves from Angola more than 500 years ago. It landed in Salvador and was adopted by all African slaves as a mark of identity. After abolition in 1888, *capoeira* was outlawed, but it remained popular among criminal gangs of freedmen, performing in secret. Legalization followed the opening of the first Academia, in 1937 in Salvador, by Mestre (Master) Bimba, whose style was fast and modern. Five years later, Mestra Pastrinha's Academy promoted the slower, traditional version, Capoeira Angola, which remains popular today. *Capoeira* is a sport and martial art, often incorporated into modern dance and break-dancing. The crucial 'voice' of *capoeira* is a twangy African bow *(berimbau)*, a single steel-stringed instrument, hit with a stick, accompanied by a *pandeiro* (tambourine), metal *agogo* bells, and conga-like *alabaque*. The audience traditionally sits or stands in a circle, cheering and clapping. For observers, it is hypnotic, intense, and often amusing, as the two performers outwit each other with fake moves and false dramas.

Seu Jorge

Seu Jorge is hip, but he is also an old-fashioned singer/songwriter with an ear for a tune and a way with poetic lyrics.

The shockingly realistic film *Cidade de Deus (City of God)*, released in 2003 and nominated for four Oscars, was set in one of Rio's most violent favelas (shantytowns), many of which are just yards from the

Seu Jorge in performance.

most famous beaches in the world. The film launched one of Brazil's most talented and now best-known singers and actors, Seu Jorge, who played Knockout Ned. The role was conceived for the lanky singer/songwriter by the co-director, Fernando Meirelles.

Jorge, who turned 40 in 2010, had grown up in a *favela* like the one in the film, but escaped its poverty and the usual short lifespan through music and community theater after spending several tough teenage years on the streets, busking and involved in risky streetlife. As that film demonstrated, Jorge is a talented actor as well as a singer, and he has become an icon in his native Rio, committed to using his work to transform life in the favelas.

Seu Jorge was already a key player on Rio's exploding new music scene by the time he was cast

for the film. Meirelles knew of his first group, Farofa Carioca, which played electronic versions of the catchy funk-sambas created in the late 1960s hits by Jorge Ben Jor,.

Jorge went solo with his album *Samba esporte fino* (released internationally as *Carolina*), a collaboration with Beastie Boys producer Mario Caldato. The title song was an international club hit and appeared on several compilations released in Europe, which contributed to the interest in the new generation of Brazilian artists, and Seu Jorge in particular.

Songs for a barbecue

Through Meirelles, Jorge was invited by Wes Anderson to appear in his 2004 film *The Life Aquatic with Steve Zissou*, alongside Bill Murray, Anjelica Houston, and Willem Dafoe. Every reviewer mentioned the elusive black guy in the red beanie hat who sang bizarre Portuguese versions of the David Bowie hits *Rebel, Rebel, Rock'n'Roll Suicide, Life on Mars*, and *Starman*. During filming, Jorge recorded his second solo album, *Cru*, in Paris, produced by Gringo de Parada of the Favela Chic club. A collection of guitar-backed songs, it opens with a small samba guitar *(cavaquinho)*, light and jangly against the jumpy samba rhythm that threads through the whole album. Squeaky *cuíca* drums converse with the voice, and earth-shaking beats of a *surdo* (big Carnival bass drum) drive you to dance.

Jorge, who performed at the closing ceremony of the 2012 London Olympics, is part of the new generation of Brazilian performers who are willing to tour outside of Brazil to develop new fans and satisfy their existing overseas fan base. His extensive América-Brasil tour, CD and DVD produced his biggest hits to date, *Burguesinha, Mina do Condominio* and *Trabalhador*. He also found time to perform and record a hit album, *Ana e Jorge*, with another contemporary Brazilian star, Ana Carolina, and released a CD of his show at the 2005 Montreux Jazz Festival.

In 2010 he released Seu Jorge and Almaz, a quirky collection of covers of musicians he admires, from Roy Ayres to Michael Jackson and Kraftwerk, and in late 2011 released the monster hit album, *Músicas para Churrasco Vol.1* (Songs for a Barbecue), that contained a number of hits. A DVD of the live show was released in 2012.

Seu Jorge continues to act and has performed in a number of films since *The Life Aquatic with Steve Zissou*, with a leading role in José Padilha's *Tropa de Elite 2 (Elite Squad 2)*, released at the end of 2010.

literacy and counseling sessions.

The 1992 Funk Festival (whose anti-gangsta publicity featured children holding AK-47s) led to the massively popular *funk-bailes* (balls) to which few outsiders dared go. Young musicians and DJs in this hermetically sealed world produced soundtracks matching their violent lives, and reproduced in the hit movie, *Cidade de Deus (City of God)*. Community projects began to mushroom: at Rio's largest *favela*, Rocinha, a *casa* (community house) offered classes and workshops beyond those geared to Carnival, including sophisticated theater projects, photography and film production in the Audiovisual Center, and music.

Music was the initial draw, and through their performances, AfroReggae became superheroes. José Jr and his team exploited their popularity through music, creating fusions of reggae, hip-hop, funk, and samba. Today, there are AfroReggae centers in several Brazilian *favelas*, and the leaders have conducted workshops in deprived areas of Paris and London.

AfroReggae News now occupies a portfolio including AfroReggae Radio and their internet sites (www.afroreggac.org). The gritty 2005 documentary, *Favela Rising*, followed the story of José Jr and his partner, Anderson Sa (a former trafficker); and the book *Culture is Our Weapon: AfroReggae in the Favelas of Rio* (Patrick Neate and Damian Platt) is a warts-and-all document of the violence, police corruption, tragedies, and triumphs, and the heroism of this radical NGO, which operated with little government support. In 2013 AfroReggae was presented with the Order of Rio Branco, one of Brazil's highest awards, by President Dilma Rousseff.

The electronic century

Recently, the cutting edge of Brazilian music shifted further north through Salvador to Recife, capital of Pernambuco. The 'Pernambuco Sound' is built around a dynamic and diverse music scene that competes with São Paulo's electronica and hip-hop movement for international success, and has been transforming the soundtrack to Brazil.

In the early 1990s, Nação Zumbi (Zumbi Nation, named after a legendary slave leader called Zumbi) were the first to fuse hip-hop, reggae, funk, and rock with local *maracatu* and coco rhythms using electric guitars, samplers with electronic effects, and an overlay of torrential drums. A good sampler is the CD *What's Happening in Pernambuco?*

While Brazil continues to embrace many new musical forms and influences, it has not abandoned its love for the older artists or their musical heritage. Caetano, Gil, Chico, Bethania, Gal, Milton, Toquinho, Martinho da Vila, and many others still sell out on tour, and shift large units of both their new recordings and back catalogs. Roberto Carlos, a contemporary of Elvis Presley, still tops the album charts, and did so in 2009 and 2010 with an album recorded with a selection of Brazilian divas who crossed

The famous A Garota de Ipanema bar, Rio de Janeiro.

the generations, and sang his compositions or duetted with him. Tom Jobim's back catalog is also as popular as ever, and even Sergio Mendes made a comeback after recording with the Black Eyed Peas and producing the soundtrack of the animated hit feature film, *Rio*

Other than those musicians already mentioned, artists to look out for while in Brazil include Adriana Calcanhotto, Ana Carolina, Casuarina, Marcelo D2, Maria Gadú, O Rappa, Vanessa da Mata, Pity, Maria Rita, and Ivete Sangalo. In Brazil you are never very far from the next live show, or a record store, and the internet and stores like iTunes and YouTube make it easier for the world to listen to, watch, discover, appreciate, and purchase Brazilian music.

CINEMA

Brazil's cinema industry is vibrant, and its actors and directors pick up prizes at international festivals with films that are hard-hitting and entertaining. The country has its own film festivals, as well as a landscape that attracts foreign moviemakers.

G iven the diversity and extremes of the Brazilian landscape, it is not surprising that film-makers – both Brazilian and international – have used Brazil as the backdrop, and as a character, in their movies.

The nascent Brazilian film industry had its ups and downs in the early days, reaching its first peak in the 1940s when the Atlântida Studio opened in Rio de Janeiro. For the next 25 years it turned out popular films targeting the masses, many of whom could not read the subtitles on the silent films. Only free delivery into thousands of homes of a similar style of entertainment via television was to burst its bubble (see page 111).

International recognition

The popularity of television did not stifle artistic endeavors on the big screen, however. In 1962, Anselmo Duarte's *O Pagador de Promessas* won the coveted Palme d'Or at Cannes, and it was at the same festival in 1964 that the world started to take notice of Brazil's Cinema Novo. Both Glauber Rocha's *Deus e O Diabo na Terra do Sol* and Nelson Pereira dos Santos's *Vidas Secas* were in competition, while Caca Diegues's *Ganga Zumba, Rei dos Palmares* was the closing film in Critics' Week.

In 1985 it was Hector Babenco's *O Beijo da Mulher Aranha (The Kiss of the Spider Woman)* that made its mark. William Hurt won the best-actor prize in Cannes for his performance and also picked up the best-actor Oscar at the 1986 Academy Awards. The film was also nominated for best picture, director, and screenplay.

If Cannes was good for Brazilian cinema, the Berlin Film Festival was even better, with Brazilian films picking up a string of prizes and critical acclaim over the years. 'Of all the European festivals, Berlin has always been the most

On the set of 'The Elite Squad.'

TICKET SALES

In 2005, Breno Silveira's *2 Filhos de Francisco (Francisco's Two Sons)*, which tells the story of two of Brazil's favorite country-and-western stars, became the biggest Brazilian box-office phenomenon since 1990, with more than 5.3 million tickets sold, surpassing the 4.7 million for Hector Babenco's prison drama *Carandiru* in 2003. In 2010, José Padilha's *Tropa de Elite 2 (Elite Squad: The Enemy Within)* sold over 11 million tickets making it the most popular Brazilian film ever. In 2012, total ticket sales in Brazil were 149 million, with around 16 million of those being for local Brazilian productions: a record.

curious about our film-making,' says Walter Lima Jr, who won a Silver Bear there in 1969 for *Brasil Ano 2000*.

When government production subsidies were pulled in the 1990s, Brazilian film-making virtually came to a halt, but some film-makers never gave up, most significantly Brazil's most successful and prodigious producer, Luiz Carlos Barreto, who had been responsible in 1976 for *Dona Flor e Seus Dois Maridos (Dona Flor and Her Two Husbands)*. Directed by his son, Bruno, it was, until *Tropa de Elite 2*, the most successful Brazilian movie of all time, selling more than 10 million tickets in Brazil.

Academy Award nominations in consecutive years for producer Barreto put the Brazilian film industry back on track and bolstered its confidence in competing critically and commercially. In 1996 and 1997 Brazil received nominations for best foreign-language film, first for Fabio Barreto's *O Quatrilho*, a gentle story of pioneering Italian immigrants in southern Brazil; and then for *O Que é Isso Companheiro?* Bruno's movie (given the English title *Four Days in September*) was based on the true story of the kidnapping of the American ambassador to Brazil by a left-wing group in 1969.

Barreto's most ambitious film was based on the life of Brazilian president, Luiz Inácio Lula da Silva. Directed by Fabio, *Lula: o filho do Brasil (Lula: Son of Brazil)*, the most expensive Brazilian movie ever, was released at the end of 2009.

Glittering prizes

In 1998, Walter Salles Jr's *Central do Brasil* premiered at the Berlin Film Festival. The reception was rapturous. It won the Golden Bear for best film, while its leading lady, Fernanda Montenegro, won the best actress Silver Bear. Over a year later, *Central do Brasil*'s bandwagon rolled into Hollywood, with a nomination for best foreign-language film, Brazil's third nomination in three years. Montenegro was nominated for best actress, a first for a Brazilian performer. The global success of the film, both critically and commercially, turned the spotlight on Brazilian cinema in general, and Salles in particular.

Salles has gone on to direct the highly acclaimed *Diarios de Motocicleta (The Motorcycle Diaries)*, the story of the young Che Guevara's journey through South America; the English-language thriller, *Dark Water;* the Portuguese-language drama, *Linha de Passe;* and in

2012 a big screen adaptation of Jack Kerouac's *On the Road*.

But Salles does not stand alone. In 2003 Fernando Meirelles served up the stunning *Cidade de Deus (City of God)*, a movie about life in Rio's *favelas* that was considered by many to be not only the most innovative and fresh movie of 2003, but also the decade's best. The movie won more than 50 international awards, and was nominated for four Academy Awards. Meirelles has since produced and part-directed a series for TV Globo, *Cidade dos Homens*, and returned to the big screen in 2005 to direct the

Award-winning 'Central do Brasil.'

English-language adaptation of John Le Carré's novel *The Constant Gardener*, a film that won an Academy Award for Rachel Weisz as best supporting actress. In 2008 he directed *Blindness*, a movie based on the novel by Portugal's Nobel Prize-winning author José Saramago, who died in June 2010, and, in 2011 released *360*, which had a screenplay by Peter Morgan.

Another director, José Padilha, first caught the eye of the critics in 2002 with his documentary *Onibus 174 (Bus 174)*. It was his first feature, *Tropa de Elite* (Elite Squad), which premiered at the Rio Film Festival, that made a major impact internationally after winning the Golden Bear in Berlin

From the acclaimed 'City of God.'

in 2008. *Tropa de Elite* is the most pirated Brazilian DVD of all time and in 2010, Padilha released its sequel, *Tropa de Elite*. By selling over 11 million admissions in Brazil alone, it became the highest grossing Brazilian film of all time. Hollywood was never going to ignore those numbers, so Padilha was signed up to direct *Robocop* (2014). Brazil's most commercially successful director internationally is Carlos Saldanha. Saldanha is responsible for Fox's animated *Ice Age* trilogy. As a reward for his success, Fox allowed Saldanha to base his 2011 release, *Rio*, in Brazil. Saldanha's nerdy macaw, Blu, followed in the footsteps of another famous animated bird, Disney's Ze Carioca, a dapper Brazilian parrot created in 1942 for

Saludos Amigos. Such was the success of Rio, that Rio 2 was released in April 2014.

Brazil as backdrop

No consideration of film-making in Brazil would be complete without mentioning the number of foreign films, TV series, pop videos, and advertisements that have used beautiful Rio and the rest of Brazil as part of their backdrop.

One of the first to use Rio is still arguably the most famous – *Flying Down to Rio* of 1933, Thornton Freeland's musical that for the first time paired Fred Astaire and Ginger Rogers. Other notable early films to use Rio include Alfred Hitchcock's 1946 Word War II thriller *Notorious*, which starred Cary Grant, Ingrid Bergman and Claude Rains, and French director Marcel Camus's *Orfeu Negro (Black Orpheus)*.

Premiering at the 1959 Cannes Film Festival, Camus's film, shot largely in the *favelas* of Rio and during Carnival, won the Palme d'Or, and followed that by winning both the Academy Award and Golden Globe for best foreign-language film.

Brazil was also used for the production of the James Bond blockbuster *Moonraker* (1979); Werner Herzog's *Fitzcarraldo* (1982); John Boorman's *The Emerald Forest* (1985); Roland Joffé's *The Mission* (1986); Luis Llosa's *Anaconda* (1997); John Stockwell's *Turistas* (2006); Luis Leterrier's *The Incredible Hulk* (2008) and the comedies *Moon over Parador* (1988), *Woman on Top* (2000), and *Mike Bassett: England Manager* (2001). Rio was also famously the backdrop for Stanley Donen's rom-com *Blame it on Rio* (1984) that starred Michael Caine.

More recently, Brazil was a backdrop for scenes in Michael Mann's *Miami Vice* (2006), while in the same year it was the turn of Bollywood to discover Brazil, with Sanjay Gadhavi's hit action thriller *Dhoom 2*, set in Rio de Janeiro. *CSI: Miami* has also used Rio to good effect, as did Roland Emmerich's *2012*, and the French spy spoof, *OSS117: Rio ne répond plus* (2009), by the director of *The Artist*. Sylvester Stallone used locations throughout the state of Rio for *The Expendables* (2010), as did *Fast and Furious 5: Rio Heist* (2011), and *Twilight: Breaking Dawn* (2011). And the city was the star of Fox's animated *Rio* and *Rio 2* released in 2011 and 2014. Julien Temple also focused on Rio for *Children of the Revolution: This is Rio*, a look at the city's music scene and history (2013).

TV Globo

President Lula declared three days of mourning in August 2003 to mark the death of Roberto Marinho – not a previous president, or even a politician, but a media mogul.

Dubbed the Brazilian Citizen Kane, Roberto Marinho, one of Latin America's richest men, died aged 98, after a career spanning almost eight decades, during which his network reached 99.9 percent of Brazilian homes. Marinho was the head of the nationwide Globo television network, whose soap operas attract a huge following in Brazil and sell in large numbers around the world. The company is the fourth most prolific producer of TV programs in the world, and the biggest network in territorial extent. Its audience comprises around 5 percent of the total worldwide network television audience.

Television had started in a small way in Brazil in 1950, with TV Tupi making the first transmission in South America, but it only truly began to affect the population with the launch of TV Excelsior's daily soaps in 1960. Marinho had taken over *O Globo*, one of Rio de Janeiro's principal newspapers, from his father in the 1920s. Two decades later, he launched Radio Globo, the country's first truly national radio network; and 20 years after that, in April 1965, he did the same with TV Globo.Marinho's timing was near perfect. It was the advent of video, satellite transmission, and other advancements, including the introduction of color television to Brazil in 1972. Sales of television sets were boosted by events such as the moon landing and the World Cup.

The great communicator

Marinho understood that the way to communicate with the Brazilian population – and to deliver the audience sought by advertisers – was through television and radio. Due to poor educational standards, print would always be for the elite. Marinho also made sure that TV Globo's channel was delivered free and had something of interest each night for the entire population.

Anyone who had access to a television set had access to TV Globo, and for years, most sets were never switched to any other channels, which included SBT, Banderiantes, Record, and Cultura.

Pride of place on Globo's small screen goes to its legendary short-run soap operas known as

novelas. The most successful cross all class, regional, and income barriers, and can hold the nation spellbound – from smart lawyers in the rich suburbs of São Paulo to penniless *favelados* in remote Manaus. Between June 1985 and February 1986 *Roque Santeiro*, a parody of the Brazilian government and politicians set in a small town, held an official audience share of 98 percent.

Globo's first true *novela*, *Véu de Noiva*, aired in 1969; the title is the name of a waterfall in Chapada dos Guimarães National Park, but it also means 'bridal veil'. Today Globo produces nearly 4,500 hours of new programing a year for its single

Former Brazilian President Fernando Henrique Cardoso (right) and Globo Television honorific President Roberto Marinho pose for the press.

channel, with three daily *novelas* filling the 6pm to 9.30pm slot, along with the national news, Jornal Nacional. Advertising related to the soap operas, attracting the attention of an audience in excess of 100 million, generates around 60 percent of the network's total billings.

If Marinho had a magic formula, it was for Globo to have its finger firmly on the pulse of the Brazilian public, its tastes and aspirations. Critics may say that it is TV Globo that molds the tastes and opinions of the Brazilian public, yet no other TV network in Brazil (or the international satellite and cable channels) has come close to matching Globo's record of success and audience share.

ART AND ARTISTS

Enriched by artists who began life as the children of poor immigrants, art in Brazil has blossomed since the 1920s, from the abstract work of the mid-20th century to today's vibrant mix of the traditional and the avant-garde.

Contemporary Brazilian art is wonderfully hard to categorize. At first glance, it appears resolutely international and less identifiably Brazilian in character than, for example, Mexican art is identifiable as Mexican. Yet it does have a Brazilian flavor, albeit surprisingly subtle. Brazilian scholar Ivo Mesquita pinpoints a certain lightness of touch as the defining feature: 'The ability to parody others as well as ourselves separates us from the tragic sensibility of our Hispanic neighbors.' And, he could add, a playful delight in the new.

Brazilian artists are among the liveliest participants at the big international shows (the Venice and Sydney Biennales, and the Kassel Documenta). And there is much exchange – *intercâmbio* – between Brazilian artists who do stints abroad, and foreign ones who settle in Brazil.

'The richest, liveliest and most varied range of conceptual and site-specific art has been produced in Brazil,' writes British art historian Edward Lucie-Smith, comparing Brazilian avant-garde with that of the rest of Latin America. 'Site-specific art' – usually large sculptures or installations – might include the cascading plastic curtains of Leda Catunda (b. 1961); the giant hair plaits of Tunga (b. 1952); the eerie silhouettes of Regina Silveira (b. 1937); and the large but restrained sculptures of José Resende (b. 1945), their elegance made physical by arresting surface textures, such as rust on a steel curve.

In painting, there are the thick, vibrant abstract-Expressionist brush strokes of Jorge Guinle (1947–87) and José Roberto Aguillar (b. 1941), and the atmospheric city streets of Gregorio Gruber (b. 1951). In 1996, Ana Maria Pacheco (b. 1943) became the first non-European to be appointed artist in residence at

Sculpture in the National Museum of Fine Arts, Rio de Janeiro.

Britain's National Gallery. Her brief involved developing art that makes reference to works in the national collection.

The birth of Modernism

Given the élan and confidence of Brazilian artists today, it might seem surprising that, up until the early 20th century, the fine arts in Brazil were in the firm grip of an antiquated European academicism, as dictated by Rio's Academia Imperial de Belas Artes, founded in 1826. The rebellion took place in São Paulo, a city that, in the early years of the 20th century, was growing vertiginously, fueled by the wealth of the so-called coffee barons. Unfettered by tradition, these nouveaux riches sank their money into industry, monuments, and mansions, and put São Paulo at the cutting edge of new cultural trends.

The 'Week of Modern Art,' held in São Paulo in 1922, was the watershed. By today's standards, the event was relatively modest – an art exhibition in the lobby of the Municipal Theater and three days of poetry readings and lectures. But art in Brazil was never to be the same again. The exhibition was the gateway into the 'isms' of the age: the angles and refractions of Cubism, Art Deco stylism, Italian Futurism and the metaphors of Symbolism and Surrealism.

Six years later, the poet Oswald de Andrade coined the term *antropofagia* (cannibalism) to describe how Brazilian art had begun to relate to international trends. The word referred to the belief of some Brazilian Amerindian tribes that cooking and eating the bodies of enemies they had killed in battle would endow them with the strength and bravery of the vanquished. Applied to art, this idea was extremely liberating. Brazilian artists dipped into the art world's 'isms' without becoming dominated by them.

Two women played key roles in the modernization of Brazilian art. Anita Malfatti

A Leitura painting by Jose Júnior at Pinacoteca do Estado de São Paulo.

JAPANESE-BRAZILIAN ARTISTS

The post-World War II period saw the emergence of a school of Japanese-Brazilian artists, led by Manabu Mabe (1924–97). At first contracted to work as a field hand, Mabe moved to São Paulo city, where his reputation grew steadily, and his work became gradually more abstract. His stunning colors and forms mingle oriental harmony with bold Brazilian chromatic tones and light. Mabe's works feature bold brush strokes of white exploding in a field of stark reds, blues, and greens.

Far more cerebral and geometrical, using only two or three colors, is the work of Tomie Ohtake, who was born in Kyoto in 1913. Ohtake began painting professionally relatively late, after her family, also indentured farm

workers (like Mabe), moved to São Paulo. Her stage designs for *Madama Butterfly* at Rio's Municipal Theater are a landmark in Latin American scenography.

Mabe's son, Hugo, began his career painting landscapes with an Expressionist vigor, and over the years has gradually reduced them to abstracted form and color. A similar artist is Taro Kaneko, born in a rural region of São Paulo state in 1953, whose mountains and bays of Rio, and São Paulo's Jaragua Peak, are barely perceptible in his intense, thickly massed oils with explosive, unexpected colors. Kaneko's seas are gold or red, his skies green or orange, his mountains yellow or black.

(1889–1964) had studied at the Berlin Academy under Lovis Corinth, and in New York, before returning to Brazil and holding a groundbreaking exhibition in 1917, showing canvases that sung with Cézannesque colors and boldness. The younger generation loved her work, but Malfatti was crushed by a damning newspaper review written by Monteiro Lobato (1882–1948), a well-known novelist, from which she never fully recovered.

In 1923 Tarsila do Amaral (1886–1973) wrote to her parents from Paris, where she was studying under Fernand Léger: 'I want, in art, to be the little country girl from São Bernardo, playing with straw dolls.' She achieved her aim by means of a uniquely sophisticated yet simple style that owed much to the uncorrupted eye of the child. A major retrospective in São Paulo in 1998 put her in the front rank of Brazil's 20th-century painters.

Emiliano di Cavalcanti (1897–1976), a prolific painter and vigorous draftsman, also did a stint in Paris as correspondent for a Brazilian newspaper where he mixed with the great Cubists, Picasso, Léger, and Braque. Returning to Brazil, he spent the next 50 years affectionately portraying the mixed-race *mulata* women in a variety of styles, most notably a decorative form of Cubism.

Europe's Art Deco movement directly influenced two distinctive stylists: Italian-born sculptor Victor Brecheret (1891–1957) and Vicente do Rego Monteiro (1899–1970). Brecheret's impressive *Monument aos Bandeirantes (Monument to the Pioneers)* in São Paulo's Ibirapuera Park dwarfs even the Mussolini school in monumentalism. Monteiro's paintings, often of biblical or indigenous scenes, have the feel of Egyptian bas-reliefs.

José Pancetti (1904–58), perhaps Brazil's best-loved Impressionist, was a tubercular ex-sailor whose moody landscapes and seascapes reflected the state of his mind more than the bright scenery about him.

Candido Portinari

Candido Portinari (1903–62) is Brazil's Diego Rivera. His *War and Peace* fresco adorns the United Nations Building in New York, and his *Discovery and Colonization* painting is hung in the Library of Congress in Washington. Unlike Rivera, however, he never became a fashionable ambassador for his country. Indeed, he painted

so intensively that he contracted cancer from his highly toxic paints and died young.

Born into a family of poor Italian immigrants who worked on the coffee plantations of São Paulo state, Portinari had a deep empathy with uneducated Brazilian laborers. He intentionally exaggerated the size of their hands and feet as if to say, 'These are my only assets. When these are used up, I, too, am tossed aside.' In his youth, Portinari joined the Brazilian Communist Party. In maturity, he painted a searing series on the *retirantes* – peasant farmers driven from their land by drought and debt.

Museu de Arte de São Paulo.

MANET'S INSPIRATION

Legend has it that the sparkling quality of the light reflected in Rio's Guanabara Bay provided the inspiration behind Impressionism. This is based on the occasion when a French frigate carrying the 16-year-old Edouard Manet, the 'father of Impressionism,' docked in Rio harbor for three months in 1849. Manet, whose art was characterized by lively scenes and bright colors, later wrote: 'I learnt a lot in Brazil. I spent endless nights looking at the play of light and shade in the ship's wake. And in the daytime, from the upper deck, I would keep my eyes on the horizon. That's how I learnt how to capture a sky.'

Portinari's influence on other artists was such that his style of social realism became known as 'Portinarism'. His followers include Orlando Teruz (1902–84), Thomaz Santa Rosa (1909–56), Enrico Bianco (1918-2013) and Proença Sigaud (1899–1979). Carlos Scliar painted in the 'Portinarist' fashion for some time, reflecting the conditions of rural workers in Rio Grande do Sul. Gradually, however, he eliminated social elements and concentrated on landscapes with geometrical forms and planes. His best-known work is a pastel-toned teapot, with minimal use of light and shade.

Woodcarver in Mariana, Minas Gerais, which has a tradition of producing such craftsmen.

By contrast, the countryside of Orlando Teruz (1902–84) is a rich, loamy brown, and the rural inhabitants of his paintings are full of a beatific innocence. Fulvio Pennacchi (1905–92), an Italian who settled in Brazil in 1929, also concentrated on country pleasures, such as church fairs and parties. His migrants look like happy families on a pilgrimage, and his villages sometimes reflect the style of those in his native Tuscany. The Hotel Toriba in Campos de Jordão, has a series of five beautifully preserved frescoes painted by Pennacchi.

Another Tuscan émigré, Alfredo Volpi (1896–1988), began his career with paintings of country scenes such as religious *festas*. But by the late 1950s he had reduced his pictures to just one element: the strings of colorful bunting that festoon rural church fairs. Volpi was known as the 'flag painter', and his work was widely reproduced as silk-screen prints. The artist himself always claimed that his overriding interest was color.

The birth of abstract art

At the end of World War II, Brazil was enjoying increased prosperity. The São Paulo Museum of Modern Art (MASP) was built in 1948, Rio's Museum of Modern Art (MAM) opened in 1949, and, in the midst of São Paulo's Ibirapuera Park, the vast, custom-built Bienal Pavilion, designed by Oscar Niemeyer, went up, and hosted the first Bienal in 1951. The 31st will be held in 2014.

The Bienal (www.bienal.org.br) is now held on even-numbered years and lasts for three months, from late September to December. It involves thousands of exhibits and hundreds of events. In the early days, it seemed that the greatest impact was produced by works brought in from abroad, which included Picasso's *Guernica*, Francis Bacon's triptychs and the vast canvases of the US abstract Expressionists. These days, there is a far more equal exchange.

The birth of the Bienal ushered in a phase of abstraction. The rivalry between São Paulo and Rio raged hotly, with artists in the former favoring art that was strictly about color and shape, and the Rio group, who dubbed themselves the 'neo-concretists', permitting some symbolic associations with reality.

Ligia Clarke (1920–88) and Helio Oiticica (1937–80) were among the most influential abstract sculptors of their generation. Clarke created a series of tactile *borrachas* (rubber grubs), and another of feisty, hard-metal *bichos* (animals). Oiticica's work often had the throwaway feel of Carnival props. Bahian-born Rubem Valentim (1922–92) used symbols from Afro-Brazilian *candomblé* ritual to create exuberant, geometrically patterned canvases.

The regions

While São Paulo and Rio monopolize the art trade and are the main centers for international exhibitions and innovative ideas, many artists are rooted in their native regions. Indeed, though they are now becoming fewer in number, Brazil still has a class of uneducated rural

The 2016 Olympic Games in Rio de Janeiro are acting as a catalyst for the opening of a number of exciting galleries in the city. These include the Museu de Arte do Rio (MAR) and Casa Daros.

artisans from which, every now and again, an artistic genius emerges.

Minas Gerais has a tradition of breeding imaginative woodcarvers and potters. Carver Maurino Araujo (b. 1948) has been com-

sharecropper, was so distraught when he lost his land that he simply lay down and stared into the sun until he went blind.)

At the end of the 1980s, a bizarre and tragic accident occurred in Goiás. An illiterate man stole a discarded piece of hospital equipment containing a capsule of radioactive material. Fascinated by the blue glow emitted by the caesium 137, he took it home and passed it around his family, most of whom subsequently died in the protracted agonies of radioactive poisoning. Franco produced a stunning series of paintings based on the

Discovering the Memorial for the Indigenous People, Brasília.

pared to the nation's greatest sculptor, the 18th-century Aleijadinho, whose work can be seen throughout the state. He specializes in myopic, crook-eyed and one-eyed angels, archangels, cherubim and seraphim. From the same region came Geraldo Teles de Oliveira (often known as GTO, 1913–90), whose mandala-like woodcarvings exemplify the best in folk-art sculpture.

In Goiás, near Brasília, Siron Franco (b. 1947) portrays wild animals with magical energy and blazing color. Snakes and the *capivara*, a native rodent with a round snout, are among his favorites. His human and animal faces have bold white, yellow, or fluorescent lines about the eyes. (Siron's father, a

SEBASTIÃO SALGADO

Sebastião Salgado (b. 1944) began his career in the 1970s, but it was his photographs of workers in the Serra Pelada, an open-cast gold mine in the Amazon, that brought him to world prominence in 1986. Whether photographing Bolivian tin miners or Ruhr Valley steelworkers, Salgado has a compassionate eye. Appointed a Unicef Representative in 2001, he concentrates on chronicling the downtrodden and dispossessed. A stunning series of pictures of displaced people, *Migrations*, was published in book form in 2000. While *Genesis*, shows the landscape of places that remain as pristine as they would have been in primeval times.

incident that briefly turned his quiet town into a hotbed of international reporters and scientists.

In the 1960s and 1970s, the new city of Brasília attracted artists from all over Brazil to complete the decoration of Oscar Niemeyer's superb architecture. The meteors of Bruno Giorgi (1905–93) adorn the lake before the Itamarati Palace. A bronze sculpture by Ceschiatti (1918–89) of two seated females combing their hair sits in the pool of the President's Palace, while his mobile of streamlined angels floats permanently beneath the

Naïf painter in Pelourinho.

soaring ceiling of Brasília cathedral, framed by Niemeyer's boomerang-shaped columns.

Recife is solidly represented by João Camara (b. 1944), who first caught the public's attention with his depiction of figures with tortured, non-anatomical limbs in *A Confession*, a protest against the repression of the military government in the early 1970s.

In the neighboring town of Olinda, Gilvan Samico (b. 1928) draws on the *literatura de cordel* (chapbook) tradition of woodcut engraving. He has illustrated the ballads of Charlemagne, and local legends such as those of the charismatic Padre Cícero and the bandit heroes Lampião and Maria Bonita. Samico's engravings are highly prized by museums,

being several grades above the folk art of the northeastern wood engravers.

Aldemir Martins (1922–2006), who was born in Ceará, painted the flora and fauna of his native northeast. His subjects often included exotic fruits such as *jenipapo*, jackfruit, *jabuticaba*, cashew, and the wrinkled *maracujá* (passion fruit).

The best of Bahian art can be found in the sculptures of Mário Cravo Júnior (b. 1923), who experiments in wood and pigmented polyester resin for such creations as *Germination I, II,* and *III*. His son, Mário Cravo Neto (b. 1947), creates wrinkled, untitled forms from materials such as polyester resin and fiberglass.

Rio Grande do Sul is noted for its sculptors, particularly Vasco Prado (1914–98), who was fascinated by pregnant mares. The warriors of bronze and other metals created by Francisco Stockinger, who died in 2009 at the age of 90, have an ominous air, with limbs and faces merely suggested.

Tapestries

The Tangiers-born Madeleine Colaço (1907–2001) invented a form of tapestry stitch registered at the International Biennial of Tapestry in Lausanne as the 'Brazilian Stitch.' She and her daughter, Concessa, use flora and fauna motifs. The French-born Jacques Douchez (1921–2012) and São Paulo's Norberto Nicola (1930–2007), on the other hand, have modernized Brazilian tapestry with their abstract designs and novel use of non-embroidered elements, including native plant fibers.

The sophisticated naïf

For decades, Brazil's art critics have been arguing about whether 'primitive' or *Naïf* (Naïve) art can rank as art at all. Sooner or later, one feels, they will be forced to admit that not only is it art but that the style is currently enjoying a glorious heyday. Indeed, in its range of subject matter, styles and techniques, Brazilian *Naïf* has become supremely sophisticated.

Rodolfo Tamanini (b. 1951), whose paintings are hung in São Paulo's stock exchange, brings *Naïf* technique to contemporary reality. His subjects range from city scenes, such as a block of flats with incidents on every balcony, to luminous coastal vistas of virgin forest, sea, and sky. In direct contrast, Ernani

Pavanelli (b. 1942), a former systems analyst, specializes in nostalgic snatches of daily life from a bygone era, his formally attired couples and family groups painted in Seurat-style pointillism.

Ivonaldo Veloso de Melo (b. 1943) uses strong colors and wry humor – his country people (and animals) all have vividly expressive eyes, whether they be bikini-clad sunbathers, weary cane-cutters, or shy lovers.

Dila (b. 1939), from the interior of Maranhão, paints detailed portraits of backland life, particularly open-air markets, with much haggling

The Museum of Naïve Art

The best collection of *Naïf* art in Brazil – and possibly the world – is found at the Museu Internacional Arte Naïf do Brasil (MIAN) in Rio de Janeiro, close to the Corcovado train station.

The museum is caretaker to what is estimated to be the world's largest collection of Naïve art, with 8,000 works from around Brazil and many other countries. As you walk in, you are immediately hit by the impact of a vast canvas, measuring 4 meters by 7 meters (13ft by 23ft), by Lia Mittarakis (1934–98), entitled

Artist at a Paraty workshop making wooden boat souvenirs.

and mountainous piles of fruit. Isabel de Jesus (b. 1938), a former nun, is internationally recognized for her dreamlike fantasies in delicate gouaches. Her palette of turquoises, purples, yellows, and crimsons blends over delicate line drawings of cats, dogs, fish, horses, children, stars, wolves, and so on.

Several of the *Naïf* artists concentrate more on vegetation than on people. Francisco Severino (b. 1952) paints the landscapes of his native Minas Gerais with botanical accuracy. Ferreira Louis Marius (b. 1953), a fisherman, and Edivaldo Barbosa de Souza (b. 1956), a former commercial artist, create luxuriant seascapes and riverscapes in which people are dwarfed by their environment.

Rio de Janeiro, I Like You, I Like Your Happy People, a quotation from one of the city's favorite old-time waltzes. Another quotation catches the eye, this one by Einstein: 'Imagination is more important than knowledge,' a statement that perfectly sums up the whole concept of Naïve art.

One work in the museum that should not be missed is *Five Centuries of Brazil* by Aparecida Azedos (1929–2006). Viewed from a mezzanine level, it measures 1.40 meters by 24 meters (4ft 7ins by 78ft 8ins). Key events in the development of Brazil are shown with bold simplicity, and explanations of the historical scenes depicted are given on the mezzanine's railings.

MODERN ARCHITECTURE

Brazil's major cities have some stunning examples
of modern architecture, designed by men with
vision. Perhaps their greatest achievement is
Brasília, the capital created in the 1950s at the
instigation of President Kubitschek.

Aselect group of Brazilian architects, all
born in the early years of the 20th century, created a fresh 'tropical' aesthetic
and became the most influential in their pro-
fession. The controversial urban planner Lúcio
Costa, precursor of Modernism in Brazil, the
tropical-landscape magician Roberto Burle
Marx and the architect Oscar Niemeyer have
left dozens of monuments in Brazil's major cities. Niemeyer also counts among his achievements the sweeping French Communist Party
Headquarters in Paris, the National University
Campus in Algeria, the facade of the United
Nations Building in New York, and the Oscar
Niemeyer International Cultural Center in
Asturias, Spain, inaugurated in 2010. Burle
Marx's work can be seen in far flung places
from Venezuela to Japan, and his home in Rio
de Janeiro was bequeathed to the nation on his
death in 1994.

Oscar Niemeyer working on a project, 1969.

The influence of Le Corbusier

Le Corbusier's key themes of simplicity in
design, economy in materials, and open spaces
made their first appearance in Brazil in the
Education Ministry building in Rio de Janeiro,
the Palácio Capanema, built 1937–45 by a team
including Costa, Niemeyer, and Burle Marx,
who landscaped the broad esplanade. The Ministry incorporates a patio made possible by raising the main structure by 9 meters (30ft) on
concrete pillars called pilotis or stilts. Inside, the
floor spaces were left entirely open for flexibility. A sense of space and a magnificent view of
Guanabara Bay were achieved by nearly dou-
bling the normal window size.

Juscelino Kubitschek, then mayor of Belo
Horizonte, brought the same team together
again in the 1940s to create Brazil's most

pleasing park – Pampulha. With its expansive
recreational area built around an artificial lake,
Pampulha combines the landscaper's art with
the discreet placement of public buildings.
These include an art museum, a dance pavilion,
and the Capela de São Francisco, with striking
frescoes by Candido Portinari (see page 115).

Niemeyer erected in Pampulha elegant monuments using curves, ramps, and undulating
roofs. His low-rise, subtropical constructions
include great stretches of ground-floor patios
and breezy esplanades. The overall effect is an
architecture of fresh, light structures that seem
to hover over the green parkland and blue
waters of the lake. Kubitschek was delighted
and critics stood in awe.

The culmination of architectural talents is the capital of Brasília, founded in 1960, but the seeds of modern Brazilian architecture were sown in 1931 when French architect Le Corbusier gave a lecture in Rio on functionalism.

Building Brasília

As Brazil's president in the 1950s, Kubitschek reunited the Pampulha team for an even bolder project, for which he had a personal create a similar effect. City and sky seem to be one. 'I sought forms distinctly characterizing the buildings, giving them lightness, as if they were only tentatively attached to the ground,' said Niemeyer years later.

Burle Marx died in 1994, Costa in 1998, but Niemeyer kept working until.his final weeks – he died in December 2012 at the age of 104. Brazil's premier architect, he created the Memorial of Latin America in São Paulo (1987), Rio's Sambódromo (1983 and 2012), and the stunning Contemporary Art Museum (1991) in Niterói.

Niemeyer designed Brasília's Museo Nacional.

vision – a new capital city for Brazil. An international competition was held to select the best urban plan for Brasília. But, said Burle Marx, 'Everybody knew in advance who was going to win.'

Costa's submission consisted of only a few sketches scratched on notepaper. However, as predicted, this crude effort was enough to win him the contract. Kubitschck recruited Niemeyer to design the main public buildings.

The new capital represented the last stage in Niemeyer's march towards austere design and spare construction. The searing white walls of the main buildings on the Plaza of Three Powers emulate the texture of the clouds in the sky above. Great fields of glass reflect the sky to

In 1988 he was awarded (jointly with US citizen Gordon Bunshaft) the Pritzker Prize, the world's most prestigious award for architecture. The citation read: 'There is a moment in a nation's history when one individual captures the essence of that culture and gives it form. It is sometimes in music, painting, sculpture, or literature. In Brazil, Oscar Niemeyer has captured that essence with his architecture.'

A lifelong Communist, Niemeyer was often in trouble, but remained true to himself. In his memoir, *The Curves of Time*, he wrote: 'I created [my work] with courage and idealism, but also with an awareness that what is important is life, friends, and attempting to make this unjust world a better place in which to live.'

Salvador, capital of Bahia.

Boat cruise around the islands off the coast of Paraty.

São Joaquim market in Salvador.

Ipanema Beach, in the shadow of Sugar Loaf Mountain.

INTRODUCTION

A detailed guide to the entire country, with main
sites cross-referenced by number to the maps.

*Guitarists in the streets of
Paraty, Rio de Janeiro state.*

Brazil is a giant package with a multitude of gifts.
Travelers looking for warm water, white sand, and
tropical beauty will be overwhelmed by the Brazilian
coastline – the longest, and one of the most beautiful, in
the world. The options range from isolated, palm-fringed
inlets to vast stretches backed by sand dunes. Brazilians
argue eternally over which of the beaches is the best, but
reach no consensus.

In the north and northeast, colonial monuments
dot the state capitals, most of which are beside the sea. Salvador and
Recife offer the best combination of beach and history.
In addition, Salvador has a particularly rich culture from
its special mix of African and Portuguese influences. The
succession of beautiful beaches continues south, reaching
its zenith in the all-time leading beach city of the Americas, Rio de Janeiro. But Rio is more than the sum of its
beaches. It is spectacular scenery, samba, Carnival, and a
relaxed, carefree existence. By contrast, in São Paulo, Brazil stops playing and gets down to the serious stuff. The
center of the developing world's largest industrial park,
São Paulo is the most dynamic city in South America, its
hodgepodge of nationalities making it a wonderful Brazilian version of New York.

*Museu da Inconfidência, Ouro
Preto.*

The further south you travel, the more European are the
influences, culminating in the states of Paraná, Santa Catarina, and Rio Grande do Sul, where Italian, German, and Polish settlers
have left their mark. Here, too, the accent is on sand and water, but not all
of Brazil is on the coast. Inland travelers will discover some of the world's
most remarkable natural wonders. Occupying one-third of the nation's
territory is the Amazon rainforest, and below the Amazon region, in an
area drained by its rivers, is the Pantanal, a natural sanctuary for fish,
birds, and mammals. In the south, the wildly beautiful Iguaçu Falls is
considered by many to be the greatest natural attraction of Brazil.

This guide will introduce you to some of Brazil's greatest wonders, and
encourage you to discover more about them for yourself.

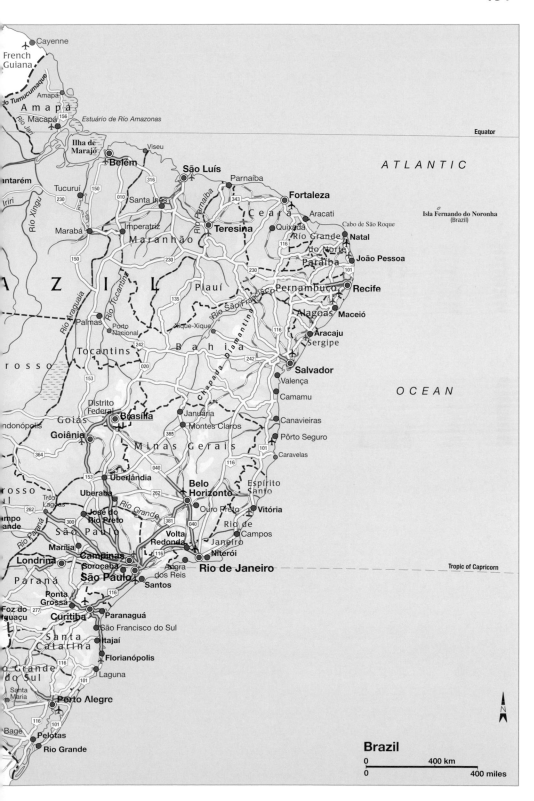

Cayenne

French
Guiana

do Tumucumaque

Amapá

A m a p á

Rio Jari

Macapá 156 Estuário de Río Amazonas

Equator

Ilha de
Marajó

Viseu

Belém

ATLANTIC

São Luís

Parnaíba

antarém

Tucuruí 150

316

010 Santa Inês

Fortaleza

Iriri

Rio Xingu

230

C e a r á

Aracati

Isla Fernando do Noronha
(Brazil)

Marabá

Imperatriz

343

Teresina

Quixadá

Cabo de São Roque

M a r a n h ã o

Rio Parnaíba

Rio Grande
do Norte

Natal

116

150

230

230

Paraíba

João Pessoa

101

A   Z   I   L

P i a u í

Pernambuco

Recife

135

Rio São Fran

Rio Araguaia

Rio Tocantins

Palmas

Porto
Nacional

Xique-Xique

Alagoas

Maceió

116

B a h i a

Aracaju
Sergipe

r o s s o

Tocantins

242

242

020

153

Salvador

Valença

O C E A N

Camamu

Distrito
Federal

Januária

Canavieiras

ndonópolis

Goiás

Brasília

383

Montes Claros

Pôrto Seguro

Goiânia

364

M i n a s   G e r a i s

101

Caravelas

116

040

153

Uberlândia

r o s s o

Uberaba

262

**Belo
Horizonte**

Espírito
Santo

l

Três
Lagoas

Rio Grande

Ouro Preto

Vitória

mpo
ande

262

José do
Rio Preto

300

381

040

Rio de

S ã o   P a u l o

Volta
Redonda

Campos

Marília

Campinas

116

Janeiro

Londrina

Sorocaba

Niterói

Tropic of Capricorn

P a r a n á

São Paulo

Angra
dos Reis

Rio de Janeiro

Ponta
Grossa

Santos

116

Foz do
Iguaçu

277

Curitiba

Paranaguá

São Francisco do Sul

S a n t a
C a t a r i n a

Itajaí

116

Florianópolis

o   G r a n d e
do Sul

Laguna

101

Santa
Maria

Porto Alegre

116

101

Bagé

Pelotas

Rio Grande

N

Brazil

0   400 km

0   400 miles

Fishing Boat in Angra dos Reis.

THE SOUTHEAST

The gateway to Brazil for many, highlights of this region include the hedonism of Rio de Janeiro, the fast-paced nightlife of São Paulo, and the Baroque jewels of Minas Gerais.

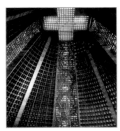

The backdrop to the altar in Rio de Janeiro's Catedral Metropolitana.

Though not large by Brazilian standards, this region contains the nation's most important metropolitan centers and, with its superior infrastructure, services, and leisure facilities, is economically streets ahead of the rest of the country. Partly because of this, and because of the allure of sun and sea, the southeast is also Brazil's premiere tourist destination and international gateway. The industries that have generated wealth and comfortable lifestyles for many in the region, operate mainly inside a triangle of three state capitals – the three most populous cities in Brazil – Rio de Janeiro, São Paulo, and Belo Horizonte, all of which host games during the 2014 World Cup.

Alongside the manufacturing successes of São Paulo in particular, agriculture (from coffee plantations to cattle ranches) is still a major player in the economy. Sugar cane was the region's first money-spinner in the 16th century, followed by gold and diamonds in Minas Gerais, coffee in Rio state (and banking, when Rio de Janeiro was the capital of Brazil), and, most recently, soybeans and biomass. The mines of Minas Gerais now yield mainly iron ore, feeding the region's steel industry, and securing the port of Vitória as the world's biggest exporter of the mineral. The downsides to all this, however, are pollution and social inequality.

For visitors, the southeastern experience is rich with treasures, both natural and man-made. There is the incomparable city of Rio, host to the 2016 Olympic and Paralympic games, with gorgeous beaches, an appealing laid-back lifestyle, and lush, forested mountains looming above. Strung along the coast to either side of the city are hundreds more beautiful beaches and tropical islands. São

Colonial buildings near Praça Minas Gerais.

Paulo state has more stretches of perfect sand, and an infrastructure to match; and in landlocked Minas Gerais there is history and culture to lure those with a yearning to relive the romance of the pioneering days. The colonial towns of this state are showcases for the best of Brazil's Baroque art and architecture, a lasting legacy of the spectacular riches amassed by mineral prospectors.

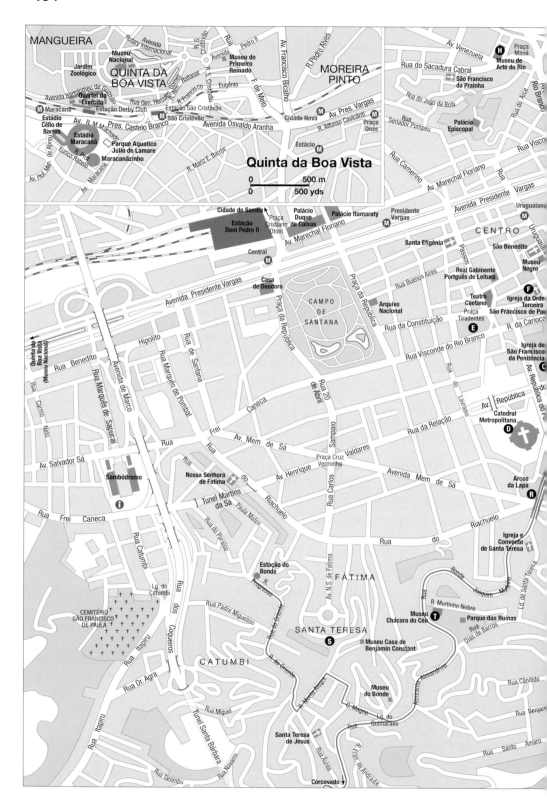

MANGUEIRA

Jardim
Zoológico

QUINTA DA
BOA VISTA

Museu
Nacional

Museu do
Primeiro Reinado

MOREIRA
PINTO

Quartel do
Exército

Estação Derby Club

Estação São Cristóvão

São Cristóvão

Estádio
Célio de
Barros

Estádio
Maracanã

Parque Aquatico
Júlio de Lamare
Maracanãzinho

Pres. Castelo Branco

Avenida Osvaldo Aranha

Cidade Nova

Av. Pres. Vargas

Praça
Onze

Estácio

Av. Venezuela

Praça
Mauá

Museu de
Arte do Rio

Rua do Sacadura Cabral

São Francisco
da Prainha

Rua do Jogo da Bola

Palácio
Episcopal

Av. Marechal Floriano

Quinta da Boa Vista

0   500 m

0   500 yds

Avenida Presidente Vargas

Uruguaiana

Cidade do Samba

Praça
Cristiano
Otoni

Palácio
Duque
de Caxas

Palácio Itamaraty

Estação
Dom Pedro II

Presidente
Vargas

C E N T R O

Av. Marechal Floriano

Central

Santa Efigênia

São Benedito

Museu
Negro

Casa
de Deodoro

CAMPO
DE
SANTANA

Real Gabinete
Português de Leitura

Rua Buenos Aires

Arquivo
Nacional

Teatro
Caetano

Praça
Tiradentes

Igreja da Orde
Terceira
São Francisco de Pau

R. da Carioca

Rua da Constituição

Avenida Presidente Vargas

Hipolito

Quinta da
Boa Vista
(Museu Nacional)

Rua Benedito

Rua Visconde do Rio Branco

Igreja de
São Francisco
da Penitência

Av. República

República

Catedral
Metropolitana

Rua 20 de Abril

Av. Mem de Sá

Praça Cruz
Vermelha

Caneca

Frei

Rua

Sambódromo

Nossa Senhora
de Fatima

Tunel Martins
da Sá

Av. Henrique

Avenida Mem de Sá

Arcos
da Lapa

Av. Salvador Sá

Rua Frei Caneca

Riachuelo

Rua do

Igreja e
Convento
de Santa Teresa

Estação do
Bonde

FÁTIMA

Rua Padre Miguelino

CEMITÉRIO
SÃO FRANCISCO
DE PAULA

Lg. do
Catumbi

SANTA TERESA

Museu
Chácara do Céu

Parque das Ruinas

Museu Casa de
Benjamin Constant

R. Murtinho Nobre

CATUMBI

Rua Dr. Agra

Rua Miguel

Museu
do Bonde

Lg. do
Guimarães

Tunel Santa Bárbara

Santa Teresa
de Jesus

Corcovado

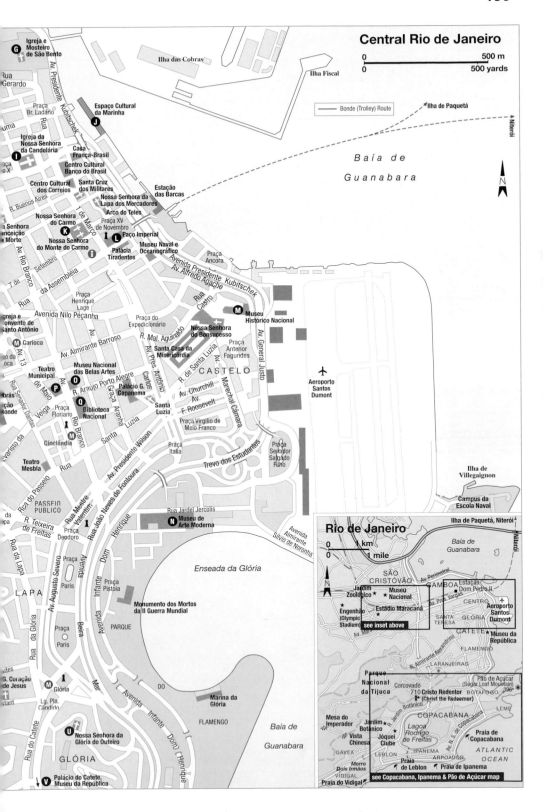

Central Rio de Janeiro

| 0 | 500 m |
| 0 | 500 yards |

—— Bonde (Trolley) Route

G Igreja e Mosteiro de São Bento

Rua Gerardo

Ilha das Cobras

Ilha Fiscal

Ilha de Paquetá

Niterói

B a í a   d e

G u a n a b a r a

N

Praça Br. Ladário

J Espaço Cultural da Marinha

I Igreja da Nossa Senhora da Candelária

Casa França-Brasil

Centro Cultural Banco do Brasil

Santa Cruz dos Militares

Centro Cultural dos Correios

Nossa Senhora da Lapa dos Mercadores

Arco do Teles

Estação das Barcas

a Senhora anceição a Morte

Nossa Senhora do Carmo

K Praça XV de Novembro

L Paço Imperial

Nossa Senhora do Monte do Carmo

Palácio Tiradentes

Museu Naval e Oceanográfico

Praça Ancora

Avenida Presidente Kubitschek

Av. Alfredo Agache

Rua Castro

M Museu Histórico Nacional

Praça Henrique Lage

Praça do Expedicionário

Nossa Senhora do Bonsucesso

Avenida Nilo Peçanha

greja e onvento de Santo Antônio

A Carioca

Av. Almirante Barroso

R. Mal. Aguinaldo

Santa Casa da Misericórdia

Praça Antenor Fagundes

Av. General Justo

C A S T E L O

Aeroporto Santos Dumont

Teatro Municipal

Museu Nacional das Belas Artes

O R. Araújo Porto Alegre

Palácio G. Capanema

Av. Churchill

Av. F. Roosevelt

Santa Luzia

Praça Virgílio de Melo Franco

Praça Senador Salgado Filho

Ilha de Villegaignon

P

Q Biblioteca Nacional

Praça Floriano

Cinelândia

Trevo dos Estudantes

Campus da Escola Naval

Teatro Mesbla

Praça Italia

Rua Jardel Jercolis

N Museu de Arte Moderna

PASSEIO PUBLICO

R. Teixeira de Freitas

Praça Deodoro

Avenida Almirante Silvio de Noronha

Rio de Janeiro

| 0 | 1 km |
| 0 | 1 mile |

Ilha de Paquetá, Niterói

Baía de Guanabara

Niterói

SÃO CRISTÓVÃO

GAMBOA

Estação Dom Pedro II

CENTRO

Aeroporto Santos Dumont

L A P A

Enseada da Glória

Monumento dos Mortos da II Guerra Mundial

PARQUE

Praça Paris

Praça Pistoia

Praça Paris

Marina da Glória

FLAMENGO

Baía de Guanabara

Jardim Zoológico

Museu Nacional

Estádio Maracanã

Engenhão (Olympic Stadium)

see inset above

SANTA TERESA

GLÓRIA

CATETE

Museu da República

FLAMENGO

R. Almirante Alexandrino

LARANJEIRAS

Parque Nacional da Tijuca

Corcovado

710 Cristo Redentor (Christ the Redeemer)

Pão de Açúcar (Sugar Loaf Mountain)

BOTAFOGO

396

Mesa do Imperador

Jardim Botânico

Vista Chinesa

Jóquei Clube

Lagoa Rodrigo de Freitas

COPACABANA

LEME

Praia de Copacabana

ATLANTIC OCEAN

GÁVEA

LEBLON

IPANEMA

ARPOADOR

Morro Dois Irmãos

Praia de Leblon

Praia de Ipanema

VIDIGAL

Praia do Vidigal

see Copacabana, Ipanema & Pão de Açúcar map

G. Coração de Jesus

M Glória

Lg. Pla. Cândido

U Nossa Senhora da Glória do Outeiro

GLÓRIA

V Palácio do Catete, Museu da República

Rua do Catete

Sugar Loaf mountain.

RIO DE JANEIRO

Rio de Janeiro is the country's most iconic and beautiful city, and the host city for the 2016 Olympic and Paralympic games. Everything, from its spectacular natural landmarks to its busy, glitzy beaches must be seen to be believed.

Sprawling in majestic disarray across a strip of land between granite peaks and the South Atlantic Ocean, Rio de Janeiro is a victory of fantasy over fact. Each day, Rio's streets and sidewalks support 12 million people, transported by a million cars, trucks, buses, motorcycles, and scooters, all competing for room in a space designed for less than one-third their number. This spectacular chaos, though, is normal, and does nothing to dampen the enthusiasm of the *cariocas*, Rio's residents. For the *carioca*, all things are relative, except one – the wonder and beauty of their city.

There are just over 6 million residents of Rio proper, but an additional 6 million live in suburbs ringing the city. Many are poor by American or European standards. But there is the beach and there is the samba and there is Carnival. And, not least of all, there is the comforting presence of Rio's extraordinary beauty. The city's residents can also look forward to hosting the World Cup in 2014, including the final, and the Olympic and Paralympic Games in 2016 – events that have brought massive investment in the city's infrastructure.

Nothing quite prepares you for Rio, not the postcards, not the films, not the reports, not even living in Rio really does it. There are other cities that have grown up backed by

mountains and fronted by the sea, but there is none where the play of light, the shifting of shadows, the mix of colors and hues are so vibrant and mobile. Each day is slightly different from the previous one, and all are strikingly beautiful.

Early history

The first tourists arrived in Rio on January 1, 1502, part of a Portuguese exploratory voyage headed by Amerigo Vespucci. He entered what he thought to be the mouth of a river,

Main Attractions
Santa Teresa
Corcovado
Copacabana
Ipanema/Leblon
Corcovado
Lagoa Rodrigo da Freitas

At the beach, Rio-style.

*At Forte de
Copacabana.*

*The view over Rio
from the top of Sugar
Loaf in early evening.*

hence the name Rio de Janeiro (River of January). His river was in reality a 380 sq km (147 sq-mile) bay, still known by its Amerindian name, Guanabara or 'Lagoon of the Sea.'

As the Portuguese slowly settled their colony, they concentrated on regions to the north and south of Rio, leaving in peace the Tamoio Amerindians who at that time inhabited the land surrounding the bay. This peace was eventually broken by raids launched by French and Portuguese pirates who prowled the Brazilian coast in search of riches.

In 1555 a French fleet arrived with the intention of founding France's first colony in the southern half of South America. The efforts to colonize the coastline were largely unsuccessful, and in 1560 the Portuguese attacked, driving out the remnants of the French colony in 1567.

From then on, Rio received increasing attention from Brazil's Portuguese masters. With the expulsion of the French invaders, the city of São Sebastião de Rio de Janeiro was officially founded on 20 January 1567.

Named in honor of St Sebastian (having been established on his feast day), it soon became simply Rio de Janeiro.

By the end of the 16th century, Rio was one of the four largest population centers of the Portuguese colony, and from its port, sugar was exported to Europe. Its importance grew steadily over the next 10 years, challenging that of the capital of the viceroyalty of Brazil, Salvador, in the northeastern state of Bahia.

In the 18th century a gold rush in the neighboring state of Minas Gerais turned Rio into the colony's financial center. Gold became the main export item, and much of it went through Rio to Portugal. In 1763 the colonial capital was transferred from Salvador to Rio as recognition of the latter's newly won status.

Capital city

Until the 1960s, Rio was Brazil's preeminent city. When the Portuguese royal family fled from Napoleon's conquering army in 1808, Rio became capital of the Portuguese Empire. With Brazil's independence in 1822, Rio's title shifted to capital of the Brazilian Empire, changing again in 1889 to capital of the Republic of Brazil. Throughout these years, the city was the economic and political center of Brazil, home to the pomp of the monarchy and the intrigue of the republic.

But the 20th century brought a surge of economic growth in the state of São Paulo. In the 1950s São Paulo surpassed Rio in population and economic importance, a lead that it has never relinquished. Then, in 1960, President Juscelino Kubitschek formally moved the nation's capital to Brasília, a city he had purpose-built for the role in the center of the country, less than five years after taking office in 1956.

Since losing its status as the nation's capital, Rio has suffered on a number of fronts. Its previous rankings as the country's leading industrial and financial center had already been taken

over by the upstart São Paulo, and, although Rio's ruling classes refused to recognize the fact, the city to a large extent had become dependent on tourism, both domestic and international, and on culture. But, even in the unaccustomed role of number two, Rio remains at the heart of the nation's unending political intrigue. Decisions may be made in Brasília and São Paulo, but as the *cariocas* note with some pride, the plots are still hatched in Rio de Janeiro.

Downtown Rio

For visitors there is little sense – other than in the city center – of Rio's historical past, a result of sporadic construction booms and the *cariocas'* insatiable thirst for the new and modern. With space limited by the contours of the city, something must usually come down before something else can go up. The wrecking ball has done away with much of the original Rio, but there are still treasures hidden along the old downtown streets.

In the heart of Rio's downtown area, at the **Largo da Carioca Ⓐ**, is the **Convento de Santo Antônio Ⓑ**. This convent was built over several colonial periods, starting in 1608. The main church was completed in 1780, and next to it stands the **Igreja de São Francisco da Penitência Ⓒ**, built between 1657 and 1772; the interior is rich in gold leaf and woodcarvings.

South of the Largo da Carioca is a modern area dominated by the Roman Catholic **Catedral Metropolitana Ⓓ** on Avenida Chile, which was inaugurated in 1976. This huge, cone-shaped structure can accommodate up to 20,000 people. Four 60-meter (197ft) -high stained-glass windows throw jewel-bright rainbows of light on the interior. The late Pope John Paul II twice visited the cathedral, and Pope Francis visited in July 2013.

Situated north of the cathedral is **Praça Tiradentes Ⓔ**, a public square named after Brazil's most famous revolutionary, Joaquim José da Silva Xavier, better known as Tiradentes (Tooth-Puller). Tiradentes, who came from Minas, was hanged on April 21, 1792, a date that is now celebrated as a national holiday.

Cooling waters in a Praça Floriano fountain.

The modern Metropolitan Cathedral.

Praça Tiradentes is home to two of Rio's principal theaters, Teatro Carlos Gomes and Teatro João Caetano, as well as the **Real Gabinente Português de Leitura** (30 Rua Luis de Camões; www.realgabinete.com.br; Mon–Fri 9am–6pm; free) Opened in 1887, this has the largest and most valuable collection of Portuguese-language literature outside Portugal, with more than 350,000 rare works.

Northeast of Tiradentes, along Rua do Teatro, is Largo de São Francisco, and the **Igreja da Ordem Terceira de São Francisco de Paula ⑤** (1801). The exterior of the church is rococo, and the chapels inside are renowned for paintings by Baroque master Valentim da Fonseca e Silva.

São Bento to Tiradentes Palace

One kilometer (0.5 mile) north, uphill from Rua Dom Gerardo, is the **Mosteiro de São Bento ⑥**, parts of which date from 1633. This monastery overlooks the bay, but more impressive and spectacular than the view from the hill is the splendor of the

Baroque splendour in Mosteiro de São Bento.

monastery's gold-leaf woodcarvings.

The hill on which the monastery stands is one of the few that survive in downtown Rio. The others that existed during the colonial period have fallen victim to one form of *carioca* progress – a penchant for removing hills to fill in the bay. The most tragic example of this trend took place in 1921–2 when the downtown hill of Castelo was carted off, together with most of Rio's remaining 16th- and 17th-century structures. Before the hill disappeared it formed a solid backdrop to Rio's most elegant street, Avenida Central, now better known as Avenida Rio Branco.

Just around the corner from the monastery, at the top of Avenida Rio Branco, is the start of the port area that is being totally redeveloped in time for the 2016 Olympic Games. Results are already being seen; including the new **Museu de Arte do Rio (MAR) ⑧** (www.museudeartedorio.org.br; Tue–Sun 10am–5pm) in Praça Mauá. The museum, which is located in two historic buildings that are linked by their roofs, has an excellent selection of art where the city of Rio de Janeiro itself is the subject matter. The museum is a great option – probably the best – for any visitor who wants to see how the city has developed over the decades, through the eyes of its artists.

The city's most striking church, the **Igreja da Nossa Senhora da Candelária ①**, is situated four blocks south of Praça Mauá, along Avenida Rio Branco at the crossroad with Avenida Presidente Vargas. Built between 1775 and 1811, the domed Candelária stands like a guardian at the head of Avenida Presidente Vargas, one of Rio's wider avenues. The church once stood close to the water, but is now removed from the shoreline, due to the landfills formed by earth from the flattened hills.

The area designated as the **Espaço Cultural da Marinha ①** (Naval Cultural Center; Avenida Alfredo Agache; Tue–Sun noon–5pm) can be found between Candelária and the bay. The center features a number of nautical exhibits that include the imperial barge, built in Salvador in 1808; the torpedo-boat *Bauru*, constructed in the US in 1943, and which took part in World War II; and the submarine *Riachuelo*, built in England in 1973 and decommissioned in 1997. Cruises round the bay (see page 141) visit the Ilha Fiscal, the palace built in 1889 that resembles a 14th-century French castle.

Parallel to the curve of the bay, along Rua Primeiro de Março, you reach **Nossa Senhora do Carmo ⓚ**, completed in 1761. This spectacular church, once the Metropolitan Cathedral, was the site of the coronations of both Brazilian emperors, Pedro I and Pedro II. Next door, separated by a narrow passageway, is the **Ordem Terceira do Monte do Carmo** church (1770).

Both churches sit on the western side of **Praça XV de Novembro**, home of the **Paço Imperial ⓛ**, which dates from 1743; it first served as the capital building for Brazil's governor generals, and later became the Imperial Palace. It was in the Paço Imperial that Princess Isabel signed the Lei Aurea on May 13, 1888 that brought about an end to slavery, and as a result the monarchy itself. Restored in the 1980s, it is now a cultural center incorporating a theater, cinema, library, exhibition spaces, and restaurants. Across Rua da Assembléia is the restored **Tiradentes Palace**, (Mon–Sat 10am–5pm, Sun noon–5pm; free), seat of the State Parliament. The building is an impressive example of the *Belle Epoque* style – don't miss the Grand Salon; there are displays in English.

Arco do Teles

A good way to get to know a bit of old-style Rio is to enter **Arco do Teles**, opposite the Paço Imperial. Here you will find narrow, traffic-free streets, colorful mid-18th-century buildings, quaint restaurants, and storefronts leading to high-ceilinged interiors.

The area from Praça XV up to the Candelária church is known as the Cultural Corridor due the abundance of cultural centers, the majority of which are based in historic buildings. Highlights include the *Centro Cultural Banco do Brasil, Espaço Cultural dos Correios*, and the *Casa França Brasil*.

Fine museums

Less than 500 meters/yds southeast of Praça XV is the **Museu Histórico Nacional ⓜ** (Praça Marechal Ancora; www.museuhistoriconacional.com.br; Tue–Fri 10am–5.30pm, Sat–Sun 2–6pm), whose collection of colonial buildings, one dating to 1603, holds Brazil's national archives of rare documents and colonial artifacts covering the period from Brazil's discovery in 1500 to the Proclamation of the Republic in 1869, along with a collection of photographs by Spaniard Juan Gutiérrez, who documented Rio at the end of the 19th century.

The **Museu de Arte Moderna** (MAM) ⓝ (Parque do Flamengo; www.mamrio.com.br; Tue–Fri noon–6pm, Sat–Sun until 7pm) is close

TIP

When in Rio, take a cruise in the bay aboard the beautifully restored tug, Laurindo Pitta, built in England in 1910. The one-and-a-half hour cruises leave from the Espaço Cultural da Marinha at 1.15pm and 3.15pm Thursday to Sunday.

The Museum of Fine Arts.

Colorful parrots at the zoo.

Museum, is the **Museu Nacional de Belas Artes ⓞ** (Museum of Fine Arts; www.mnba.gov.br; Tue–Fri 10am–6pm, Sat–Sun 2–6pm). It houses one of Latin America's finest art collections, begun by Dom João VI, and includes paintings by the great 20th-century social-realist painter Cândido Portinari (see page 115).

The other fine buildings include the **Teatro Municipal ⓟ** (www.theatro municipal.rj.gov.br), a splendid replica of the Paris Opera House, inaugurated in 1909 and reopened in 2010 after a three-year refurbishment program that has restored it to its former glory; and the **Biblioteca Nacional ⓠ** (National Library; Mon–Fri 9am–8pm, Sat 9am–3pm; free), an eclectic mixture of neoclassicism and Art Nouveau. Holding around 15 million works, it is the largest library in Latin America and the eighth largest in the world. These buildings border the area known as **Cinelândia**, where the city's first movie houses were built in the 1920s and 1930s. The Rio Film Festival, Festival do Rio, is today centered on the beautifully restored

to the downtown airport, Santos Dumont. The museum complements its own national collection with a series of visiting international exhibits. It is also a major venue for concerts and shows, having inaugurated a modern 5,000-capacity concert hall called Viva Rio (www.vivorio.com.br) in 2006, where today many top Brazilian artists choose to perform.

The Modern Art Museum is located just off the southern end of Avenida Rio Branco, which was inaugurated in 1905 as Avenida Central, in response to President Rodrigues Alves's vision of a tropical Paris. Unfortunately, Alves overlooked the fact that downtown Rio de Janeiro, unlike Paris, had no room to grow other than vertically. Through the years, the elegant three- and five-story buildings of Avenida Central were replaced by 30-story skyscrapers. In the process, the avenue also underwent a name change.

Sitting close to the Modern Art Museum, in a strategic location so that it can be viewed along the length of Avenida Rio Branco, is the monument built in memory of all who lost their lives during World War II. Pope John Paul II said mass from its steps in 1980 to a crowd estimated to be over 2 million strong.

Of the 115 splendid buildings that flanked the avenue in 1905, only 10 remain. One of the most impressive, five blocks north of the Modern Art

Odeon Petrobrás, which first opened its doors in 1932.

Most of Rio's principal museums and cultural centers are either downtown or nearby in Flamengo or Botafogo, such as the **Museu do Indio** (Indian Museum; 55 Rua das Palmeiras; www.museudoindio.org.br; Tue–Fri 9am–5.30pm, Sat–Sun 1–5pm). In the Botafogo neighborhood, about 15 to 20 minutes from downtown, depending on traffic, this is an excellent source of information on Brazil's indigenous people. The **Casa Rui Barbosa** (www.casaruibarbosa.gov.br; Tue–Fri 10am–5pm, Sat–Sun 2–6pm), in Rua São Clemente, near the Indian Museum, was home to one of Brazil's famous scholars and politicians. Rui Barbosa (1848–1923) was an abolitionist who (twice) ran unsuccessfully for the presidency. The **Museu Villa-Lobos** (www.museuvillalobos.org.br; Mon–Fri 10am–5.30pm), in the Rua Sorocaba area, honors Heitor Villa-Lobos (1887–1959), considered one of Latin America's greatest composers, whose body of work includes the *Bachianas Brasileiras*.

Close to the **Rio-Sul** mall, the closest of the major malls to the hotels in Copacabana, is **Casa Daros Rio** (www.casadaros.net; Wed–Sat noon–8pm, Sun noon–6pm), one of Rio's most impressive new cultural spaces. The centre is owned and run by the Zurich based Daros Latin America, a well funded institution that specialises in Latin American art. As well as its own collection, which is now put on display at the Casa Daros, it has access to many of the great private collections of Latin American art.

Fifteen minutes west by car from downtown, in the direction of the international airport, is the **Museu Nacional** (Quinta de Boa Vista; www.museunacional.ufrj.br; daily 10am–4pm), the residence of the Brazilian imperial family during the 19th century. The palace is impressive, and houses exhibits on natural history, archeology, and minerals. It is located next door to Rio's zoo, the **Jardim Zoológico** (daily 9am–5pm), the oldest in Brazil, where the exotic and vividly colored birds are the main attraction for most visitors.

TIP

There are tours of Rio's totally refurbished Teatro Municipal, but times are a bit erratic. The best way to appreciate it is to attend a concert, opera, or ballet. The theater has a full diary of events throughout the year, and the forthcoming program can be found on the theater's website (www.theatromunicipal.rj.gov.br) under 'Programação.'

Rio de Janeiro's impressive theatre, the Teatro Municipal.

FACT

The Olympics will not just leave Rio with a sporting legacy, but also a cultural one with the opening of new museums and galleries already including Casa Daros and the Museu de Arte do Rio (MAR).

Maracanã

The Museu Nacional and the zoo are not far from the **Maracanã**, probably the most famous stadium in the world. This is the country's temple of soccer, built for the 1950 World Cup, and is where Pelé scored his 1,000th goal in 1969. Totally rebuilt for the 2014 World Cup and 2016 Olympics (other than the iconic outer ring), major soccer games normally take place here on Saturday and Sunday afternoons and Wednesday evenings. Trips to matches and to the stadium's hall of fame (on non-match days) can be arranged through the concierges of most hotels.

As well as soccer games, the old Maracanã was the venue for major concerts. Artists who have played the stadium include Frank Sinatra, Paul McCartney, Sting, Madonna, Tina Turner, the Rolling Stones, Kiss, and performers in the Rock in Rio festival. The new stadium also hosts major concerts and events.

Big soccer games and concerts also take place at the **Engenhão** (Estádio Olímpico João Havelange). The stadium opened in 2007 for the Pan-American Games and can comfortably accommodate 46,000 spectators. Engenhão is currently closed to allow its capacity to be expanded to more than 60,000 in time for the 2016 Olympic Games, when it will host all the main athletics competitions. The stadium is located in Engenho de Dentro, not far from Maracanã.

Soccer is one Brazilian passion, and samba and Carnival are two others. Between the Maracanã and downtown Rio are found two key elements of both samba and Carnival. In Avenida Marquês de Sapucai is the Passarela do Samba, or **Sambódromo**, where the major samba schools parade on the Sunday and Monday nights of Carnival (see page 71). Designed by Oscar Niemeyer, the facilities double as a school during the rest of the year, and will also be a venue for the 2016 Olympic and Paralympic archery, as well as the start and finish of the marathon.

In 2006, the **Cidade do Samba** (Samba City; http://cidadedosambarj. globo.com; Wed–Mon noon–8pm, special show Thu, Fri 8pm) opened

An old colonial house in Santa Teresa.

HEITOR VILLA-LOBOS

Heitor Villa-Lobos, born in Rio in 1887, showed great musical talent from an early age, and learnt to play the guitar, cello, and clarinet as a boy. After his father died in 1899, Heitor began to play in theater orchestras and with street bands. He began to compose seriously in 1912, and his prolific works drew on many influences, from tango and street music to indigenous Brazilian folk material. European influences were also strong, from Debussy and Satie to his great friend, another French composer, Darius Milhaud. The nationalistic works he composed during the Vargas era engendered some criticism among European musicians, but he later returned to favor. His state funeral was the last major civic event in Rio before the capital was transferred to Brasília.

in Rua Rivadavia Corrêa, close to the docks and downtown Rio, an area that is being totally redeveloped in time for the Olympic and Paralympic games. The purpose-built facilities, which suffered a major fire on the eve of carnival in 2011, give visitors an opportunity to visit the workshops of the major samba schools and see how they prepare for carnival, and to listen to live samba music.

Trolley to Santa Teresa

Departing from downtown in front of the **Petrobrás** building (Brazil's state oil company), and close to the Metropolitan Cathedral, are the open-sided yellow trolley cars of the oldest electric railway in Latin America. The picturesque trolley line climbs up the mountain and along the surprise-filled streets of the Santa Teresa neighborhood. Due to an accident in 2011, the service was suspended, but it is expected to be operating again in time for the 2014 World Cup. The highlight of the trip is crossing the **Carioca Aqueduct**, known as the **Arcos da Lapa ®**, one of downtown Rio's most striking landmarks. Built in the 18th century to carry water from Santa Teresa to the downtown area, the aqueduct became a viaduct in 1896 when the trolley-car service began. Below the aqueduct is the area known as Lapa, one of Rio's hottest nightspots. A place of bars, restaurants and venues for shows of various sizes.

Santa Teresa ⑤ is a tranquil nest of eccentricities perched atop the mountain spine that presses against the city below. According to legend, black slaves used Santa Teresa's mountain trails to escape to freedom during the 18th century, when Rio was Brazil's leading slave port. The neighborhood began to receive more permanent residents when a yellow fever epidemic forced the city's population to move up into the hills to escape from the mosquitoes carrying the disease. By the end of the 19th century, Santa Teresa became a privileged address for

Rio's wealthy, whose Victorian mansions sprouted from its hillsides. Intellectuals and artists were also attracted by its cool breezes and tranquil setting, which were at the same time removed yet close to the hectic downtown area.

One of the neighborhood's most famous 20th-century residents was the 'Great Train Robber' Ronnie Biggs. The best known of a gang that stopped a mail train in England in August 1963 and made off with more than £2.6 million (worth over £46 million/US$75 million in 2013), Biggs escaped from a maximum-security prison in London in July 1965 and made his way to Brazil via Australia. He arrived in Rio in 1970, and made it his home until returning to Britain in May 2001. He was finally released from prison in the UK in 2009. He first moved to 470 Rua Monte Alegre in Santa Teresa in 1979, and was a familiar and popular figure in the area.

Distinctive districts

Today, hanging from its hillsides and flanking its winding, cobblestoned streets, the architectural hodgepodge

Arcos da Lapa.

Cable cars make the journey to the top of Sugar Loaf.

of Santa Teresa's homes is one of Rio's most distinctive features. Gabled mansions with wrought-iron fixtures and stained-glass windows stand beside more staid and proper edifices, all perfectly at home on a mountain that provides a spectacular vista of the Baía de Guanabara. Views are as plentiful as flowers in Santa Teresa. The best are from the second trolley station.

Many houses in Santa Teresa now offer bed-and-breakfast accommodations of varying degrees of sophistication and luxury. Many are part of an organization called Cama e Café (www.camaecafe.com.br) that pioneered the concept in Rio, through which reservations can be made.

There are also now a number of boutique hotels in the area, of which the best known is the Santa Teresa Hotel (see page 348) in Rua Almirante Alexandrino, which in 2010 won a *Wallpaper* magazine design award for the best new hotel suite.

All aboard the trolley to Santa Teresa.

There are several public stairways that lead from Santa Teresa's streets to the neighborhoods of **Glória** and **Flamengo**, hundreds of meters below; and the grounds of the **Museu Chácara do Céu** ❶ (Little House in the Sky Museum; Nobre 93 Rua Murtinho; www.museuscastromaya.com.br; Wed–Mon noon–5pm; free on Wed) that look out over the city, the aqueduct, and the bay. The museum is one of Santa Teresa's main attractions, with a collection of works by Brazilian Modernists, including paintings by Brazil's greatest modern artist, Cândido Portinari see page 115, as well as by a number of European masters.

In the Glória neighborhood to the southeast, perched on a hill overlooking Guanabara Bay, is an architectural gem, the chapel of **Nossa Senhora da Glória do Outeiro** ❶ (http://outeirodagloria.org.br Mon–Fri 8am–5pm, Sat–Sun 8am–noon; free), known simply as the Glória church. This petite 1720s construction, with gleaming white walls and classic lines, is one of the best-preserved examples of Brazilian Baroque, and a Rio landmark. Not surprisingly, the chapel is very popular for weddings.

Nearby in Catete is the **Palácio do Catete** ❶, the residence of Brazilian

presents when Rio was the capital. It now houses the Museu da República (153 Rua do Catete; www.museudar epublica.org.br; Tue–Fri noon–5pm, Sat–Sun 2–6pm; free on Wed), exhibiting paintings and items relating to the presidency and the republic from 1889 to 1960. The bedroom of President Getúlio Vargas has been preserved as it was on the night of his suicide on August 24, 1954. Adjoining the palace is the **Museu do Folclore Edison Carneiro** (Tue–Fri 11am–6pm, Sat–Sun 3–6pm), with displays on everyday life and religion.

The bay

Ever since its 'discovery' in 1502, Rio de Janeiro's **Baía de Guanabara** has delighted visitors. Charles Darwin wrote in 1823: 'Guanabara Bay exceeds in its magnificence everything the European has seen in his native land.' Views of the bay, which had been mistaken for the mouth of a river, are beautiful, accented by two forts, one from the 17th century, the other from the 19th, that guard its entrance.

Trips across the bay to the city of **Niterói** on the far side, or to the islands within the bay, offer spectacular vistas looking back at Rio. The cheapest trip is by ferryboat, but more comfortable aerofoils also make bay trips (both the ferry and the aerofoils leave from Praça XV de Novembro).

Schooner trips take in various tourist points and leave every Sunday at 10am, also from Praça XV. Other options include a cruise on the historic *Laurindo Pitta*, which sails from the Espaço Cultural da Marinha.

Within the bay, the favorite stop is the **Ilha de Paquetá**, largest of its 84 islands. Visitors may rent bicycles or take a magical trip around the island by horse-drawn buggy.

Although *cariocas* can be dismissive about Niterói, the city does have attractions: the **Parque da Cidade**, at the end of a winding uphill road through a tropical forest, provides stunning views of the bay and the

mountains. At the foot of this hill is the Praia Itaipú, a beach that offers the same panoramic views of Rio. Niterói is also the site of the iconic **Museu de Arte Contemporânea, Niterói** (www.macniteroi.com.br; Tue–Fri and Sun 11am–7pm, Sat 1–9pm). Designed by Oscar Niemeyer, the spaceship-like building and its views are even more of an attraction than the modern art exhibits. The museum has an archive of over 1,500 works, mainly from the collector, José Sattamini, as well as visiting exhibitions. See it at night, when it is spectacularly lit. The museum also has its own restaurant and bistro, with live music on Friday and Saturday nights.

Sugar Loaf

Undoubtedly the most famous landmark on Guanabara Bay is **Pão de Açúcar ❶**, the granite prominence that rises 396 meters (1,300ft) high at the bay's entrance, and is known to the world as Sugar Loaf. The Amerindians called this singularly shaped monolith *Pau-na-Acuqua*, meaning high, pointed, isolated peak. To the Portuguese, this

Sacristy of Nossa Senhora da Glória do Outeiro.

On trips across the bay you will see the green-spired palace on the Ilha Fiscal.

TIP

Try to avoid visiting
Sugar Loaf between
10am and 11am, and
between 2pm and 3pm,
as this is when many of
the tourist buses arrive.
The best time to go is an
hour before sunset,
when you can see the
city as the light changes.

sounded like *pão de açúcar* (sugar loaf),
and its shape reminded them of the
clay molds used to refine sugar into a
conical lump.

In 1912, the first cable-car line was
installed from **Praia Vermelha ❷**, at
the base of Sugar Loaf, to its top in two
stages, the first stopping at the rounded
Morro da Urca (Urca Mountain),
which stands 218 meters (705ft) high.

Today, visitors are whisked up in
bubble-shaped cars manufactured in
Switzerland that were introduced in
June 2009, each of which holds up to
65 passengers and offers 360-degree
views. Each stage takes just three minutes, with cars starting out from the
top and the bottom simultaneously
and zipping past each other in the middle of the ride. Departures are from the
Praia Vermelho station, where tickets
are sold until 7.50pm, and are every
20 minutes from 8am to 8pm (www.
bondinho.com.br). The last car down is
at 9pm, or later if there are events.

From both the Morro da Urca
and Sugar Loaf, visitors have excellent views on all sides, with paths
leading to viewpoints. To the west

*Cable cars make the
trip up to Sugar Loaf
every 20 minutes.*

lie the beaches of **Leme ❸**, Copacabana, Ipanema, and Leblon, and the
mountains beyond. At your feet are
Botafogo and **Flamengo** leading to
downtown, with **Corcovado** peak
and the statue of Christ the Redeemer
behind. To the north, the bridge across
the bay connects Rio de Janeiro and
Niterói, with the latter's beaches
stretching away to the east. At any
hour of the day or night, the view is
quite extraordinarily beautiful.

It is estimated that since the first
cable-car journey in 1912, more than
40 million visitors had enjoyed the
trip to the top of Sugar Loaf by the
end of 2010.

The beaches

While not all of the bay's water is fit
for swimming, the beaches that encir-
cle it were once the principal attraction for *cariocas*. At the start of the
20th century, tunnels were constructed
linking bayside Botafogo with the
ocean beach of Copacabana, and Rio's
beach life found a new home. Since
then, the *cariocas'* endless search for
the best beach has carried them constantly south, first to Copacabana,
then to Ipanema and Leblon, then São
Conrado, Barra da Tijuca, and beyond.

With the passage of time, a day on
the beach has evolved from a tranquil
family outing into an all-encompass-
ing cradle-to-grave lifestyle of its own.
Today, the beach is not part of the life
of Rio – it *is* the life. The beach is a
nursery and a schoolyard, a reading
room, a soccer field, and a volleyball
court. It serves as a singles bar, restaurant, and rock concert hall; an exercise
center and office all at the same time.
It will even be the site of Olympic
activities in 2016. Occasionally, someone goes into the water, but only for
a refreshing pause before returning to
more important beach-based activities.

Cariocas read, gossip, flirt, jog, exercise, dream, think, and even close business deals on the beach. On a glorious
summer weekend, nearly the whole of
Rio spends some time on the beach.

And this isn't to say that they aren't on the beach during the week as well. One of the great mysteries of Rio is how anything ever gets done on a sunny day.

The great equalizer

Carioca sociologists claim that the beach is Rio's great equalizer, in addition to being its great escape valve. According to this theory, the poor who make up the majority of the city's residents, the inhabitants of its mountainside *favelas*, its housing projects and northern slums, have equal access to the beach and are therefore satisfied even though they are poor. Surprisingly enough, there is some truth to this simplistic and romantic notion, although the crime rate indicates that not all of the poor are satisfied with their lot. The beach, though, remains open to all and it is free.

But while they are democratic and integrated, Rio's beaches are not entirely classless. A quick passage along the sands of Copacabana and Ipanema will take you past small 'neighborhoods' of bathers, each

congregating in its own social type or group – gays, couples, families, teenagers, yuppies, celebrities, and so on. If you return the next day, you will find the same groups in exactly the same places. These 'beach-corner societies' have become a permanent characteristic of life in Rio de Janeiro.

Copacabana

Although aged, and in some places somewhat the worse for wear, **Praia de Copacabana** ❹ remains the centerpiece of Rio de Janeiro's beaches and the international tourist trade. Its classic crescent curve, anchored at one end by the imposing presence of Sugar Loaf, has made Copacabana a world-class picture-postcard scene for decades. Copacabana beach first gained fame in the 1920s after the opening of the high-class **Copacabana Palace Hotel** (see page 159). It was also in the early 1920s that gambling was legalized in Brazil, and Copacabana subsequently became home to many of Rio's liveliest casinos.

With gambling facilities and the continent's best hotel, Copacabana

Cargo ships at Guanabara Bay.

Playing volleyball on Ipanema Beach.

PONTE RIO-NITERÓI

An alternative way to visit Niterói is to take an exhilarating bus ride across the extraordinary Ponte Rio-Niterói – officially called the President Costa e Silva bridge, in honor of the man who ordered its construction. Buses run from the Rodoviária (bus station), and the fare is minimal. When winds are high, the bridge is closed to traffic, for obvious safety reasons. Automobile drivers should note that a small toll is payable at the Niterói end.

Inaugurated on March 4,1974, the six-lane bridge is a stunning sight. It is more than 13km (9 miles) long, of which almost 9km (5.5 miles) are over the water. Construction of the bridge, by a British company, began in 1969. It was financed by British banks, and the cost was estimated at around US$22 million (£14 million).

Rio's favelas

The *favela*, or shantytown, has become so much a feature of life in Rio that a visit to one of them is now included on many tourist itineraries.

Rocinha (Little Farm), Rio's largest *favela*, first sprouted in the 1940s, and is now a swarming anthill of narrow alleys, built on the side of a steep hill. Up to 250,000 people live in Rocinha.

In many ways, the *favela* is the heartbeat of Brazil's cities, a hotbed of musical talent, and the home of many of its most creative residents. The cultural input of the *favela* is rarely acknowledged. In fact, the Carnival would not exist if it were not for these communities as many of the main samba schools come from or are named after the *favelas*.

All Brazilian cities have *favelas*, but those in Rio are the most visible. They sprang up as a response to the chaotic expansion of the city. Property prices exploded, making it impossible for a poor family to buy or rent a house Downtown. At the same time, all the available work was

Residents of Favela das Canoas.

Downtown, and it was too expensive for poorly paid workers to take the two or three buses required to travel in from the cheaper suburbs. So, in the early 1900s, families began to build illegally on Rio's steep hillsides.

Around 70 percent of the people who live in Rocinha are from the impoverished northeast of Brazil. Often a family of six will live in one or two rooms with one bed for the adults and the children sleeping on the floor. Life expectancy is low compared to the national average. Some 80 percent of people in Rocinha are employed, and the vast majority have nothing to do with the drugs and violence for which their community was once famous.

In 2008, a new chapter was written in the history of Rio's *favelas* with the start of the pacification program introduced by Rio's mayor and governor. The first *favela* to be pacified was Dona Marta in Botafogo. By 2014 most of Rio's 800 *favelas* will have received the same treatment, and the lives of millions of people both inside and outside the *favelas* will have been changed, and hopefully for the better.

The results of the program have been far more positive for the *favelas* than the most optimistic projections. However, drug-traffickers, armed with sophisticated, modern weapons may have moved out of the *favelas*, but they are still around.

Visiting a favela

A visit to a *favela* can be an enlightening experience, but should only be done with a reputable operator, even after the recent improvements. The better agencies are allied with charitable organizations and plow at least some of their profits back into social projects. Marcelo Armstrong (tel: 21-3322 2727; www.favelatour. com.br) is a recommended operator who is trusted by the communities.

Over the years, many of the *favelados* have improved their property, so that a lot of them today have electricity and running water. Despite the harsh living conditions, almost all houses have a color television, often large-screen, and most have a stereo and the use of a mobile phone. There is even a thriving property business. The pacification has also seen the opening of bars and hostels looking to attract visitors, including foreigners. Before you book yourself in, just take a moment to question if you would be happy staying in a hostel in the poorest part of your own cities.

evolved into an international watering hole for the world's most glamorous celebrities. Black-tie evening at the Copa, as the hotel was baptized by the *cariocas*, became de rigueur for internationally famous figures, including such luminaries as Lana Turner, Eva Perón, Ali Khan, Marlene Dietrich, and Orson Welles. Even John F. Kennedy dropped in for a visit once in the 1940s.

Casino gambling was finally outlawed in Brazil in 1946, but the party rolled on into the 1950s. Copacabana suffered a slump in the 1960s, but with the construction of three major hotels and the refurbishing of others, including the landmark Copacabana Palace, the beach staged a comeback in the 1980s. Today, Copacabana beach has been widened by landfill, and still retains its magic, although Ipanema is an altogether more attractive and safer neighborhood to stay in.

Across its steaming sands on hot summer days pass literally hundreds of thousands of sun and water worshippers. Hawkers of beverages, food, suntan lotions, and hats sway across the beach, adding a musical accompaniment to the flow of colors with their singsong voices, whirling metal ratchets and the frantic rhythms that they beat on small drums. Bathers linger beneath multicolored beach umbrellas or canopies, then briefly refresh themselves in the ocean before crossing **Avenida Atlântica**, the beach drive, for a cool beer at one of the sidewalk cafés.

On any given summer weekend, up to half-a-million *cariocas* and tourists will descend on the locale to promenade on Copacabana; while on New Year's Eve, more than 3 million take to the streets and the sand to see in the new year. In February 2006 a crowd estimated at over 2 million turned up to watch a free concert given by the Rolling Stones. The crush of the beach is an extension of the crush beyond the beach. The quintessential Rio neighborhood, Copacabana consists of 109 streets on which more than 350,000 people live, squeezed close together into high-rises by the mountains at their back and the Atlantic in front. For this urban mass, the beach is their escape to an open space.

Copacabana Palace Hotel.

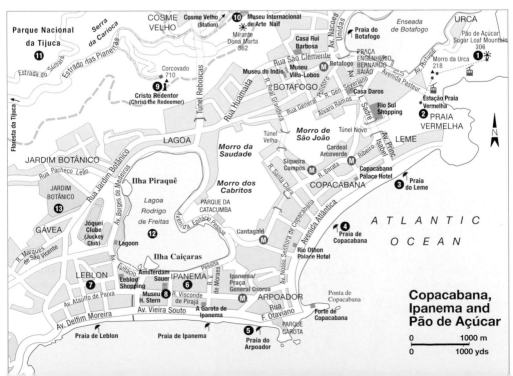

Find souvenirs in designer Gilson Martins' upmarket shop in Ipanema, which stocks a variety of bags and wallets.

Strolling on Ipanema's colorful sidewalk.

At the Ipanema end of Copacabana beach is a section called **Arpoador** , which is famed for its surfing. At the far end, standing sentinel at the end of Leblon, is the imposing **Dois Irmãos** (Two Brothers) mountain, a prominent feature in one of Rio's most spectacular natural settings.

Ipanema

Ipanema ❻ is an Amerindian name meaning 'dangerous waters.' It is home to a mixture of the traditionally wealthy and the nouveaux riches, although many of the latter have now moved on to Barra. The area began as an adventure in land development in 1894, marked by dirt roads running through the existing sand dunes, with a handful of bungalows along the sides of the roads. The neighborhood was mostly ignored until the crush of Copacabana became too much for its well-to-do residents, and they moved to the next beach south.

From the 1950s to the present day, Ipanema has undergone an extraordinary real-estate boom and population explosion, and since the 1960s, a surging army of high-rises have turned the Ipanema skyline into a smaller, lower version of Copacabana.

In the 1960s, the neighborhood was swept by a highly romanticized wave of liberalism. Rio's bohemians and intellectuals gathered at Ipanema's sidewalk cafés and bars to philosophize over the movements of the decade – the hippies, rock'n'roll, the Beatles, drugs, long hair, and free love. Humor was also present, expressed monthly through a satirical newspaper that proudly announced the founding of the Independent Republic of Ipanema. Two of the republic's prominent members were the poet Vinicius de Moraes and the songwriter Tom Jobim. One day, Jobim, in the spirit of the period, became enchanted with a beautiful *carioca* girl who walked by his habitual perch in an Ipanema bar. Each day for weeks, he followed her daily passage, and even invited his friend Moraes to join him. Inspired by her beauty, the two put their feelings into words and music, the result being the bossa nova classic, 'The Girl from Ipanema'.

This mystical blend of Camelot and Haight Ashbury received a severe blow with the 1964 military coup and the subsequent crackdown on liberals. Now, Moraes and Jobim are both dead, and the girl, Heloisa Pinheiro, is a late middle-aged businesswoman and mother of four. However, the story of the song's origin is commemorated in place names: the street down which Heloisa walked is now named after Moraes and the bar is called A Garota de Ipanema (The Girl from Ipanema), see page 99.

Despite its brevity, this period defined the modern *carioca* spirit – irreverent, independent, and decidedly liberal toward matters of the flesh and spirit. It also propelled Ipanema into the vanguard in determining *carioca* style, pushing Copacabana into second-class status.

Leblon

In the morning, joggers and cyclists rub shoulders – the former on the

sidewalk and the latter in the *ciclovia* (cycle lane) that runs the entire length of the beach and into town – while exercise-class participants go through their public gyrations. During the day, and for much of the evening, this is where the beautiful people of the city hang out.

Palm trees add to the intimate setting of Ipanema, as does (with a couple of notable exceptions) the lack of beach-front hotels and bars. At sunset, the paved sidewalk is crowded with lovers of all ages, strolling along hand in hand. Ipanema is less boisterous than Copacabana, and it preserves the romance of Rio more than any of the city's 22 other beaches.

The hotel that is the most notable exception on Ipanema beach is Fasano (www.fasano.com.br), on the corner of Avenida Vieira Souto and Rua Joaquim Nabuco. Since opening in 2007, it has been one of Rio's coolest addresses. Designed by Philippe Starck and Rogério Fasano, the hotel found itself hosting Madonna, Jay-Z, Beyoncé, and Alicia Keys on the eve of Carnival 2010. And the stars keep coming.

Ipanema and **Leblon** ❼ are essentially the same neighborhood; a canal linking the lagoon with the ocean divides the two, giving rise to separate names, but there is a shared identity. They remain Rio's center of chic and sophistication. If it's not 'in' in Ipanema and Leblon, then it's simply not 'in.' The city's poshest boutiques line the streets, and the trendiest are located on the main street, **Visconde de Pirajá**, and adjoining side streets running in both directions. Of these, **Rua Garcia d'Avila** is one of the best. Ipanema's shops cater to all tastes and all ages, offering leather goods and shoes in addition to clothing and gifts. Although this is not the cheapest area to shop in the city.

The end of 2006 saw the opening of the city's smartest and most fashionable shopping center, Shopping Leblon (www.shoppingleblon.com.br). With a main entrance on Avenida Afrânio de Melo Franco, Shopping Leblon has over 200 boutiques, which include one of the city's best book and music stores, a stylish food court with some restaurants offering views across the Lagoa to Corcovado, and four state-of-the-art movie theaters. The shopping center also offers free Wi-fi connection and plenty of comfortable areas in which to sit and work.

Since the 1980s Ipanema has been Rio de Janeiro's center for jewelry. Brazil is the largest producer of colored gemstones in the world, and samples of every variety and hue can be found on the block of Visconde de Pirajá between Garcia d'Avila and Rua Anibal Mendonça. This block is home to a number of jewelry stores, including the world headquarters of H. Stern, Brazil's leading jeweler and one of the largest in the world. The **Museu H. Stern** ❽ (www.hsterninrio.com; 113 Rua Garcia d'Avila; Mon–Fri 8.30am–5.30pm, Sat 8.30am–12.30pm; free and free taxi to museum from major hotels) houses a fascinating exhibition about everything to do with jewelry, and a free guided multilingual tour

FACT

The Copacabana Palace, which opened in 1923, was one of South America's first luxury hotels, and the first hotel in Rio built on the Atlantic shore rather than within the bay.

Doing acrobatics on Copacabana Beach.

is available. There is also the option – which many visitors take up – to buy exclusive jewelry at H. Stern prices.

Christ the Redeemer

Overlooking Rio's beach and city life is the world-famous statue of **Cristo Redentor** ❾ (Christ the Redeemer), standing with his arms outstretched atop **Corcovado** or Hunchback Mountain. To reach the 710-meter (2,330ft) summit, you could go by rented car or taxi, and transfer to vans for the last part of the journey, but the recommended method is the 3.7km (2.3-mile) Corcovado Railroad (www.corcovado.com.br), with the little trains leaving every 20 minutes (daily 8.30am–6.30pm) from the station in the **Cosme Velho** neighborhood, halfway between downtown and Copacabana.

The scenic ride climbs through tropical foliage, with views of the mountain and city below. From the upper station, an escalator takes visitors the short distance to the summit – although it's easy enough to walk as long as you are fit.

The palms lining the entrance to Jardim Botânico are more than 160 years old.

Located close to the train station in Cosme Velho is the **Museu Internacional de Arte Naïf do Brasil** ❿ (Rua Cosme Velho; www.museunaif.com.br; Tue–Fri 10am–6pm, Sat–Sun noon–6pm; halved if you have a Corcovado train ticket). The museum holds one of the world's largest and most complete collections of Naïve art, with more than 5,000 works dating back as far as the 15th century in its archives. Many paintings feature images of Rio and Brazil, including the huge canvas by Lia Mittarakis that you see as soon as you walk in.

On the top of Corcovado, the granite statue, which was given a general face-lift in 2010, is visible day and night from most parts of Rio, as long as there is no mist. Standing 38 meters (125ft) tall, it is the work of a team of artisans headed by French sculptor Paul Landowsky, and was completed in 1931. Since then it has competed with Sugar Loaf for the titles of symbol of Rio and best viewpoint. One decided advantage that Corcovado has over Sugar Loaf is that it provides the best view possible of Sugar Loaf itself. Towering over the city, Corcovado also looks down on Niterói, the southern beaches, and the beautiful Lagoa Rodrigo de Freitas see page 155.

For an even more spectacular panorama, take to the skies in a helicopter. Helisight (tel: 21-2511 2141; www. helisight.com.br) has three helipads and nine different flights available.

Enveloping Corcovado is the **Parque Nacional da Tijuca** ⓫, one of Rio's most enchanting natural attractions, a tropical reserve that includes 100km (60 miles) of narrow, two-lane roads, winding through the forest's thick vegetation, interrupted periodically by waterfalls.

Along the way are several excellent viewpoints not to be missed. The **Mesa do Imperador**, according to legend, is where Dom Pedro II brought his family for royal picnics so that they could look down directly at the lagoon and southern neighborhoods. The **Vista Chinesa** (Chinese View) looks toward the south with a sidewise glance at Corcovado, while the **Dona Marta Belvedere**, at 362 meters (1,190ft), just below the summit of Corcovado, gives views directly toward Sugar Loaf and back to Corcovado.

Back from the beaches

Inland from Ipanema lies the **Lagoa Rodrigo de Freitas** ⑫, often referred to simply as Lagoa. This natural lake, originally part of a 16th-century sugar plantation, provides a breathing space from the crowded southern beaches of the city. The lake will be the center for rowing activities during the 2016 Olympic and Paralympic Games. Around its winding shore, joggers, walkers, and cyclists beat a steady path, while at the same time enjoying the best of Rio's mountain scenery – Corcovado and the Tijuca Forest, Dois Irmãos mountain and the distant flat top of Pedra da Gávea.

The Lagoa has a number of kiosks where you can stop for a cold drink, snack, or even a full meal. The rowing stadium, **Lagoon** (www.lagoon.com.br), has also been totally redeveloped and now offers a selection of bars and good restaurants, plus a six-screen movie house, and the **Miranda Showhouse** (http://mirandabrasil.com.br/)

Toward the mountains, on the western edge of the lagoon, close to Lagoon, can be found Rio's **Jardim Botânico** ⑬ (Botanical Garden; www.jbrj.gov.br; daily 8am–5pm), an area of 140 hectares (340 acres) containing 235,000 plants and trees representing nearly 8,000 species. Created by Portuguese prince regent Dom João VI in 1808, the garden was used to introduce plants from other parts of the world, including tea, cloves, cinnamon, and pineapples. Many species of bird and other wildlife can also be seen. The tranquil garden is a refreshing respite from the heat and urban rush and tumble of Rio, and it deserves a long, studied walk through its many and varied examples of tropical greenery. The majestic avenue at the garden's entrance is lined with a double row of 134 royal palms, all more than 160 years old.

Located between the Jardim Botânico and the Lagoa is the city's magnificent Jockey Club, which offers race fans action on Saturday and Sunday afternoon and Monday and Friday evening. Foreign visitors are normally offered access to the palatial members' stand, which, like the course itself, dates from 1926.

São Conrado

More beaches extend south of Ipanema. The first, **São Conrado** ❶, rests in an idyllic natural amphitheater, surrounded on three sides by thickly forested mountains and hills – including the Pedra da Gávea (see page 156), a massive block of granite more impressive in shape and size than even Sugar Loaf, though it doesn't have the same iconic status.

São Conrado beach closes the circle on this small, enclosed valley. São Conrado can be reached from Ipanema

Cosme Velho station, from where you can access the rack railway to the summit of Corcovado.

The statue of Christ the Redeemer atop Corcovado mountain.

by a tunnel underneath Dois Irmãos mountain, but a far more interesting route is **Avenida Niemeyer**, an engineering marvel that was completed in 1917. The avenue hugs the mountain's cliffs from the end of Leblon to São Conrado. At times, it looks straight down into the sea with striking vistas of the ocean and Ipanema looking back. But the best view is saved for the end, where the avenue descends to São Conrado and suddenly, the ocean, the beach and the towering presence of Gávea emerge into sight. In Rio de Janeiro, the spectacular can become commonplace, but this is a view that startles with its suddenness and unmatched beauty.

On the cliff side of Avenida Niemeyer is the neighborhood of **Vidigal**, an eclectic mix of the super-rich and those who live in abject poverty. The smart mountainside homes of the former have been surrounded slowly by the ever-advancing shacks of the Vidigal *favela*.

Space, and the absence of the crush of Copacabana and Ipanema, are the main factors that separate the outlying beach areas from their better-known neighbors. Although it is compact in area, the relative lack of people means that São Conrado has an uncrowded openness that is further guaranteed by the 18-hole **Gávea Golf Course**, which runs right through the middle.

Conrado contrasts

São Conrado is a near-perfect microcosm of Rio society. On the valley floor live the middle- and upper-middle-class *cariocas* in the luxurious apartments, houses, and condominium complexes that line the beach front and flank the golf course. The privileged location of the links makes it one of the most beautiful in the world, and adds to the dominating presence of greenery in São Conrado.

But as lush as São Conrado is, the beauty of the whole area is marred by a development that contrasts starkly with its wealthier face. There is a swathe cut out of the hillside vegetation where **Rocinha**, South America's largest *favela* see page 150, spreads across the mountain from top to bottom. In this swarming anthill of narrow alleys and streets, at least 150,000 people live – and some estimates put it at double that number. Most of them inhabit tumbledown brick houses and shacks, pressed tightly together, side by side.

Flying over Rio

At the end of São Conrado, a highway surges past the massive Pedra da Gávea, where hang-gliders soar overhead. On the right, another road leads to the Tijuca National Park and Corcovado, passing through the thick tropical forest and providing memorable views of the beaches below. You may wish to experience the exhilarating sensation of jumping off a runway 510 meters (1,680ft) above sea level, soaring above the bay, and then gliding down to the beach. To fill this need, several of Rio's more experienced and trustworthy hang-glider

View down from the top of Rocinha favela.

pilots offer tandem rides. It is safer not to take rides with hang-gliders touting on the beach. Paulo Celani, of Just Fly, has nearly 20 years' experience in taking people on tandem flights (tel: 021-2268 0565; cell phone: 9985 7540; www.justfly.com.br). Hang-gliding over São Conrado even featured memorably in the 20th Century Fox animated comedy, *Rio*.

Barra da Tijuca

From São Conrado, an elevated roadway continues to the far western beaches, twisting along the sharply vertical cliffs where the mansions of the rich hang suspended at seemingly precarious angles. Emerging from a tunnel, you are suddenly face to face with the **Barra da Tijuca ❷**, firmly established as the city's most prestigious middle- and upper-middle-class suburb.

Since the mid-1980s, the height and density of the buildings in Barra, as it is commonly known, have increased dramatically. Prestigious high-rise blocks march toward the mountains on the western horizon. It is now a US-style city within the city, dubbed Brazil's Miami. Everything is more expensive here, and a car is pretty much a necessity for getting around. Barra is also where Latin America's largest shopping center, **Barra Shopping ❸** (www.barrashopping.com.br), is located. This is a thriving, opulent consumer paradise that acts as a magnet for Rio's discerning shoppers, and also includes a sizeable entertainment center and modern multiplex movie theater.

There are also a growing number of hotels that are already popular with visitors from other South American countries, who tend to be more relaxed about using a car in Rio, and therefore don't feel the need to be based in Copacabana. There are some new hotel properties being developed to be ready in time for the 2016 Olympic and Paralympic Games; the main Olympic Village and many of the sports will be located in Barra.

Barra's 18km (11-mile) beach fills up during the weekend. All along the beach drive, the **Avenida Sernambetiba**, the traffic is bumper-to-bumper as Rio's middle classes seek to escape the city streets.

At night, like the other Rio beaches, Barra comes alive. There are a number of popular nightclubs and bars in the neighborhood. There are also plenty of places to eat, from smart international restaurants, to fast-food outlets, to the multitude of shacks and trailers that line Avenida Sernambetiba (see page 163).

Barra's trailers

Barra's answer to Copacabana's sidewalk cafés are the beach-front trailers that sell cold drinks and hot food during the day to beach-goers. But on weekend nights, these same trailers become convivial meeting points. Large crowds gather around the more popular trailers, some of which are converted at night into samba centers called *pagodes*.

Originally confined to back yards in the lower-class northern neighborhoods, *pagodes* were simply samba

Watching the sun go down at Leblon.

sing-alongs where musicians, both professional and amateur, engaged in lively midnight jam sessions. In the move to the affluent southern zone of Rio, the *pagodes* have maintained their purist samba qualities, but have acquired commercial overtones, becoming in effect open-air samba bars.

For romantics, however, there can be no quibbling over the splendid image of Barra's beach-side trailers. With the surf crashing behind them, guitar and percussion instruments pounding out the samba in the night, and scores of fun-seekers singing along, it is just right for an evening out in Rio de Janeiro.

Dozens of motels have sprung up in the Barra region over the years. In Rio – as in the rest of the country – motels are designed for lovers, not for tourists, and rooms are rented by the hour and furnished with all the facilities a couple might desire, including saunas, whirlpools, and mirrored ceilings. Some of the motels in Barra outshine even the city's five-star hotels for unadulterated luxury and sheer indulgence.

Guaratiba

At the end of Barra beach is the **Praia dos Bandeirantes ❹**, a small beach with a natural breakwater creating the effect of a quiet bay. From Recreio, the road climbs sharply along the mountainside, descending to Prainha, a beach that is popular among surfers, and then to **Grumari**, a marvelously isolated beach where part of the movie *Blame It on Rio* was filmed.

From Grumari, a narrow, potholed road climbs straight up the hillside. At the top you will be treated to another unforgettable view – the expanse of the **Guaratiba** flatlands and a long sliver of beach stretching off into the distance, the Restinga de Marambaia, a military property that is off-limits to bathers.

Down the hill is **Pedra de Guaratiba** (60km/37 miles southwest of Rio), a quaint fishing village with a number of excellent seafood restaurants. From Barra to Guaratiba is an exhilarating day trip that can be topped by a leisurely two-hour lunch of shrimp or fish dishes at any of the Guaratiba restaurants, which are the favorites of the Rio in-crowd. There are two other attractions in the Barra and Guaratiba neighborhoods. The first is **Museu Casa do Pontal ❺** (3295 Estrada do Pontal; www.popular.art.br/museucasadopontal; Tue–Sun 9.30am–5.30pm), with more than 8,000 works of Brazilian folk art. The second is the **Sítio Roberto Burle Marx ❻** (tours, booked in advance Tue–Sun 9.30am and 1.30pm), the house and garden of the late, great

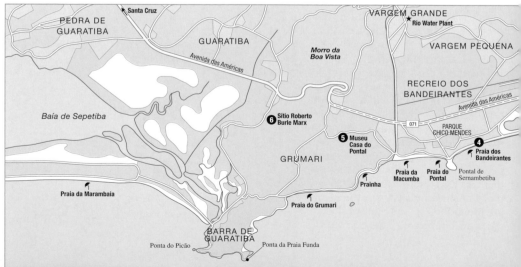

landscape architect. This was his home from 1949 till his death in 1994, when it was bequeathed to the nation (see page 161).

Nightlife

For all *cariocas*, an evening out is serious business. For many, in fact, it is more serious than the working day. To be in step with Rio time, a night out begins with dinner at 9pm or later. Most popular restaurants are still receiving dinner guests into the morning hours at weekends. Meals fall into two categories: small and intimate or sprawling and raucous. For an intimate dinner, French and Italian restaurants with excellent views are favored. For a sprawling, raucous evening, you will be best served by steak houses called *churrascarias*, where *cariocas* gather with small armies of friends around long tables practically overflowing with food and drink. At night, Copacabana is traditionally the king of Rio, although a far better and more sophisticated selection of bars, clubs, and restaurants can be found in Ipanema, Leblon, and around the Lagoa and in to Jardim Botanico.

Copacabana Beach is a good starting point. Sidewalk cafés run the length of Avenida Atlântica, and they act as gathering points for tourists and locals, where cold draft beer is the

favorite order. Copacabana at night is like an Eastern bazaar. Street vendors will be hawking souvenirs, paintings, wood sculptures, and T-shirts along the avenue. Prostitutes (female, male, and transvestite) prowl the broad sidewalk, with its serpentine designs.

The famous Copacabana Palace Hotel, known affectionately as 'the Copa,' was sympathetically refurbished in the 1990s and again in 2013, returning it to its glory days of the 1920s and 1930s, when it attracted the rich and famous from all over the world (see page 149). Indulge in a cocktail by the pool, or a meal in the Cipriani Restaurant, even if you can't afford to stay here. The Sofitel Rio Palace also has a cocktail bar, from where you can watch the sun set over Ipanema.

The suburb of Barra da Tijuca hugs the coast.

ATLANTIC OCEAN

São Conrado and Barra da Tijuca

Rio's 2016 Olympics

In August and September 2016, Rio de Janeiro will be the focus of world attention as it becomes the first South American city to host the Olympic and Paralympic Games.

On the morning of October 2, 2009 a crowd gathered on Copacabana Beach to hear the result of the bidding process to host the 2016 Olympic and Paralympic games. The decision was being made at a meeting of the International Olympic Committee (IOC) in Copenhagen. Four cities were on the shortlist. Along with Rio they included Chicago, Madrid, and Tokyo.

Since the shortlist had been announced in June 2008, Rio had been considered the outsider, but it had been slowly gaining momentum in the final months and weeks and, while still an outsider, might now come an honorable second to the hot favorite, Chicago. But news from Copenhagen suggested that Rio had made a stunning and passionate pitch to host the games, which would not just be for Rio and Brazil but for all of South America.

The Joao Havelange Stadium, which will host the athletics and opening ceremony for the 2016 Olympic Games.

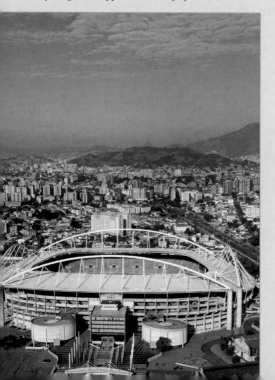

The first round of votes brought an unforeseen shock. Chicago was out, followed shortly after by Tokyo. There was now a nerve-racking wait of over an hour until the final announcement. The crowd on Copacabana, or following on TV and radio, started to believe something special was going to happen.

Jacques Rogge, president of the IOC, could be seen on Copacabana's giant screen holding the envelope. What he said would change the future for Rio. 'The games of the 31st Olympiad are awarded to the city of…' There was a slight pause as Rogge opened the envelope and turned the card to the camera, 'Rio de Janeiro.'

What might have seemed a wild dream a decade earlier was now a reality, Rio de Janeiro, the Marvelous City, would be hosting not only the FIFA World Cup in 2014 but also the Olympic and Paralympic Games in 2016.

Building for the future

Rio and its organizing committee quickly got to work. There would now be massive investment in the creaking infrastructure of the city. Everything from transportation and sanitation, to the games facilities would be built or upgraded, and that is what visitors to Rio will see in the run up to the games in 2016.

The majority of the Olympic and Paralympic activities will take place in four zones: Copacabana, Barra, Maracanã, and Deodoro.

Maracanã, which held the World Cup Final in 1950, and will again in 2014, is to host the opening and closing ceremonies. The Engenhão, which hosted the 2007 Pan-American Games, is having its capacity increased to host the athletics. Even the Sambódromo, home to the Carnival parade, will host the end of the marathon and the archery.

Rio will make full use of its natural beauty. Copacabana Beach will used for the beach volleyball, long-distance swimming, and the triathlon; the rowers will have the backdrop of the Lagoa Rodrigo de Freitas to compete against, and the yachtsmen and women will have Guanabara Bay.

The Olympic Village, the aquatic, hockey, tennis centers, and the velodrome are being built on the old site of the motor-racing circuit in Barra da Tijuca. The golf course is also being constructed in Barra. In total, the 2016 Olympic games will feature 28 sports in 36 disciplines.

The dates for the diary, if you are planning on coming to Rio for the Olympic Games, are August 5–16, while the Paralympic Games will take place from September 7–18. For more information visit www.rio2016.com. Book early.

Between Copacabana and Leme is the infamous red-light district. In the dark bars and clubs, even on the sidewalks, you will see Western men openly picking up prostitutes – seemingly oblivious to the risk of Aids, the desperation that causes people to become prostitutes, and the fact that many of the most attractive working women are, in fact, men.

Lapa

Lapa, in downtown Rio, was once the red-light district, but in recent years it has become an exciting area studded with live-music bars and restaurants. The crowd tends to be fairly young. Don't stray too far from the main streets if you want to be safe. Recommended venues include Carioca da Gema, Semente, and Rio Scenarium, all with a varied program of Brazilian music, from samba to bossa nova, in atmospheric settings.

Lapa is also home to the **Circo Voador** (Flying Circus; www.circovoador.com.br) music venue, originally a large tent where many leading Brazilian acts got their first break in the 1980s and 1990s. A purpose-built venue opened in 2000 and gave Circo Voador a whole new lease of life. Another major Lapa venue for music shows is the **Fundição Progresso** (www.fundicao progresso.com.br), set in a historical building that used to be a factory. The main theater can hold up to 5,000.

For full-scale extravaganzas, the other leading venues are Vivo Rio, next to the Modern Art Museum; the Imperator in Méier; and in Barra, the Citibank Hall, the HSBC Arena, and Barra Music, all showcasing the best in Brazilian and international attractions. The Plataforma I (www.plataforma.com), in Leblon, presents a nightly review of Brazilian song, dance, and Carnival that is pitched firmly at the foreign visitor.

For those of more erudite or classical tastes, venues of choice are more likely to be the Teatro Municipal and Sala Cecília Meireles in downtown Rio, and the Cidade das Artes (www.cidadedasartes.org), which opened in Barra in 2013.

Popular nightclubs include Miroir on Avenida Epitácio Pessoa, Lagoa;

Balcony Bar on the Copacabana Promenade.

ROBERTO BURLE MARX

Brazil's greatest landscape gardener, Roberto Burle Marx (1909–94), was a leader of opinion and style who did much more than design gardens; he also transformed the way people looked at spaces, through his use of varied textures and unusual plant groupings. Sítio Burle Marx, his farm and home in Rio's Barra de Guaratiba neighborhood, has more than 3,500 plant species, some of them extremely rare. Burle Marx, a flamboyant man with an adventurous approach to life, and a legendary quick temper, was a daring collector of non-plant material, too, and displayed old doors from demolition sites, bowsprit figures, clay pots, and chunky rocks to incredible effect around his house.

Other examples of his work can be seen in Flamengo Park, and on the colorful sidewalks of Copacabana.

The Sunday Hippie Fair sells crafts and souvenirs of all kinds.

Nuth Club on Avenida Epitacio Pessoa, Lagoa; 00 on Avenida Padre Leonel Franca, Gavea; Baronneti on Rua Barão da Torre, Ipanema; Melt, on Rua Rita Ludolf, Leblon; Black Bar, on Avenida General San Martin, Leblon; Nuth and Zero Vinte Um, on Avenida Armando Lombardi, Barra; Bukowski, on Rua Paulo Barreto, Botafogo; Rio Scenarium, on Rua do Lavradio in Lapa; Club Six, on Rua das Marrecas, Lapa; and Zozô, on Avenida Pasteur, Urca. Popular with the GLS community are Le Boy/La Girl on Rua Raul Pompeia, Copacabana and Dama de Ferro on Rua Vinicius de Moraes, Ipanema. It goes without saying that, as in any large city, what is hot and what is not will change on a monthly, even weekly, basis. If you are looking for jazz and bossa nova, the best call is Vinicius Bar on Rua Vinicius de Moraes, Ipanema; Miranda in Lagoon, Lagoa; and some of the venues in Lapa such as Lapa Café. To find out what is on, ask a local person or hotel concierge, or check the weekly Rio supplement of *Vejá* magazine.

Street scene in downtown Rio, an area also known as Centro.

Rio shopping

Rio de Janeiro's first major shopping center was constructed in the 1980s, and *cariocas* quickly adopted the idea of shopping in air-conditioned malls, happy to escape from the summer temperatures. Nowadays, many of the city's best shops and boutiques have gravitated away from Ipanema toward the top malls and shopping centers. The following are the principal centers.

Rio-Sul (www.riosul.com.br; Mon–Sat 10am–10pm, Sun 3–9pm) is in Botafogo, a short distance from Copacabana. With more than 400 stores, it has been completely refurbished and has high-level security. A good option for entertainment, too, with a food court, and several cinemas. This is the closest of the major malls to Copacabana.

Leblon Shopping (www.shopping-leblon.com.br; Mon–Sat 10am–10pm, Sun 3–9pm), Rio's smartest and most fashionable offers 200 boutiques, a stylish food court, and four state-of-the art movie theaters.

Barra Shopping (www.barrashopping. com.br; Mon–Sat 11am–10pm, Sun 3–9pm; free buses to and from major hotels), Latin America's largest shopping center in Barra da Tijuca closely resembles a US suburban mall.

São Conrado Fashion Mall (www. scfashionmall.com.br; Mon–Sat 11am–10pm, Sun 3–9pm), not far from the Sheraton Rio and Royal Tulip hotels. Smaller, with 130 stores, but more stylish than many of the others, with boutiques, restaurants, and art galleries.

Hippie Fair

The Ipanema Hippie Fair at Praça General Osorio (Sun 9am–6pm) is completely different – a lingering reminder of the flower-children days of the 1960s. On sale is a wide variety of woodcarvings, paintings, hand-tooled leather goods, and other gifts. Many vendors also set up stalls in the evening along Copacabana's Avenida Atlântica, an atmospheric place to browse when walking home after dinner.

RESTAURANTS AND BARS

Albamar
184 Praça Marechal Ancora, Centro
Tel: 21-2240 8378
Open: L daily until 5pm.
This is one of the city's oldest restaurants and a landmark in its own right. The historic building is the last remaining tower from the old Municipal Market. Seafood and typically Brazilian dishes are the speciality, but there is plenty of choice. Make a reservation to get a window seat with a view over the bay. **$$**

Bar Lagoa
1674 Avenida Epitácio Pessoa, Lagoa
Tel: 21 2523 1135
Open: L Sat Sun, D daily from 6pm.
A carioca institution since 1934. Good-value Art Deco bar for full meal or a drink, especially a beer or *caipirinha*, and a snack. Walters are famous for their surly manner, but it is all part of the charm. **$$**

Cais do Oriente
8 Rua Visconde de Itaboraí, Centro
Tel: 21-2233 2531
Open: L daily, D Tue–Sat.
Located in an interesting colonial house in the historic heart of downtown. Offers an eclectic mix of international, Asian, and Brazilian cuisine in the restaurant, as well as a bar, a garden area, and a lounge with nightly music shows. **$$$**

Casa da Feijoada
10 Rua Prudente de Morais, loja B, Ipanema
Tel: 21-2247 2776
Open: L&D daily.
Traditionally, *feijoada* is served on a Saturday in Rio, so here is the answer if you are not in town at the weekend. This restaurant specializes in Brazil's national dish made with black beans and various cuts of pork. Other Brazilian dishes on offer. **$$**

Celeiro
199 Rua Dias Ferreira, Leblon
Tel: 21-2274 7843
Open: L Mon–Sat.
Original and delightful salads made with organic vegetables, plus quiches, pies, and very good desserts. Opened in 1982, Celeiro was one of the first restaurants in Rio to cater for vegetarians, and remains one of the best. You pay by the weight of food that you eat. **$**

Cipriani
Copacabana Palace, Copacabana
Tel: 21-2545 8747
Open: L&D Mon–Sat, L Sun.
Elegant, classic but innovative Italian restaurant overlooking the glorious pool of the Copacabana Palace. One of Rio's, if not the world's, very best. Not the cheapest option, but a rare gourmet treat. If you want to make it extra special book 48 hours in advance for the Chef's Table. **$$$**

Confeitaria Colombo
32 Goncalves Dias, Centro
Tel: 21-2505 1500
Open: Mon–Fri 9am–8pm, Sat 9.30am–5pm.
Step back in time at this Art Nouveau Rio institution for light meals or a full buffet, but equally famous for its afternoon teas. First opened in 1894. A delightful branch, Café do Forte, is also operating in the Forte de Copacabana from 10am to 8pm with great views of Copacabana. **$$**

Fasano al Mare
80 Avenida Vieira Souto, Ipanema
Tel: 21-3202 4000
Open: L&D daily.
A highly rated Philippe Starck-designed restaurant located inside Rio's most hip and stylish hotel. Specializes in seafood and Mediterranean cuisine. One of Rio's best, but not cheap. **$$$**

Fogo de Chão
Avenida Reporter Nestor Moreira, Botafogo
Tel: 21-2279 7117
Open: L&D daily.
An excellent *rodizio* barbecue with a nice mix of other dishes thrown in, which is part of one of Brazil's top chains of barbecue houses. It's located in Botafogo with views across to Sugar Loaf. Make sure you are hungry when you go. **$$$**

Gero
157 Rua Anibal de Mendonça, Ipanema
Tel: 21-2239 8158
Open: L&D daily.
Gero is one of the hotspots on Rio's gastronomic map, and has been since opening in 2002. Part of the Fasano family that also owns and runs the hotel in Ipanema. Sophisticated classic and contemporary Italian cuisine. There is also a branch in Barra da Tijuca at 190 Avenida Erico Verissimo. **$$$**

Lagoon
1424 Avenida Borges de Madeiros, Lagoa
Tel: 21-2529 5300
Open: L&D daily
www.lagoon.com.br
Lagoon is an entertainment complex located in the old rowing stadium with views over the Lagoa. It sits exactly where the Olympic rowing will end in 2016. Here you have a selection of excellent restaurants such as Giuseppe Grill, Gula Gula, Pax Delícia, Quadrifoglio, and San Remo. **$$**

Olympe
62 Rua Custódio Serrão, Jardim Botânico
Tel: 21-2539 4542.
Open: L Fri-Sat, D Mon–Sat.
According to many, this is the best food in Rio, if not Brazil. Creative French cuisine with a Brazilian touch from friendly owner/chef Claude Troisgros and his son, Thomas. While Olympe is the flagship, Troisgros also offers the cheaper, but also excellent, CT Brasserie in São Conrado, CT Boucherie in Leblon, and CT Trattorie on the Lagoa. **$$$**

Porcão
Av. Infante Dom Henrique,
Attero do Flamengo
Tel: 21-3389 8989
Open: L&D daily.
If you choose just one barbecue house, this should be it. One of the most traditional *rodizio* barbecues in Rio, and still one of the very best. Wonderful food, but you need to be hungry. One of several branches, this one is located in the heart of Flamengo Park with views of Sugar Loaf. **$$$**

Quadrifoglio
19 Rua J.J. Seabra, Jardim Botânico
Tel: 21-2294 1433
Open: L Sun, D Mon–Sat.
Excellent, light, aromatic Italian cooking, served in comfortable and friendly surroundings. Quadrifoglio has been delivering high standards of cooking and service for over two decades. Also has a branch in the Lagoon entertainment complex. **$$$**

Siri Mole
50 Rua Francisco Otaviano, Copacabana
Tel: 21-2267 0894
Open: L&D Tue–Sun, D Mon.
This is one of the city's best spots to experiment with Brazilian cooking. Serves a number of Bahian specialties including a variety of *moquecas*, and seafood dishes. Bahian buffet offered for Saturday lunch. **$$**

RIO DE JANEIRO STATE

In the cool mountains above the city nestles Petrópolis, the former imperial summer retreat, while the coast is blessed with a string of gorgeous beaches and tropical islands.

The city of **Rio de Janeiro** ❶ has captured most of Brazil's glory through the decades, but the state of which it is the capital (also called Rio de Janeiro) is replete with attractions of its own. Like its capital, the state of Rio is an exciting contrast of forested mountains and sun-drenched beaches, all located within a few hours of the city.

Into the mountains

Dedicated as they are to beach life, Rio's residents also have the option of getting away from it all and making their escape to the cool, refreshing air of the mountains. This is especially appealing during the hottest months, and was the principal reason behind the founding of Rio's two leading mountain resorts, Petrópolis and Teresópolis. The pastel hues and green gardens of these two *carioca* getaways are a 19th-century imperial inheritance left by independent Brazil's first two rulers, emperors Pedro I and Pedro II.

Petrópolis ❷, a city of 315,000 only 65km (40 miles) from Rio, is a monument to Pedro II, emperor of Brazil from 1831 until his exile in 1889 (he died in France two years later). The city was first envisioned in the 1830s by Pedro I, who purchased land in the spectacular **Serra Fluminense** mountain range for a projected summer

palace. But it was his son, Pedro II, who actually built the palace and the quaint town surrounding it, starting in the 1840s. The idea, in pre-air-conditioning days, was to maintain a refreshing refuge from the wilting summer heat of Rio.

The road to Petrópolis is itself one of the state of Rio's prime scenic attractions. An engineering marvel, its concrete bridges soar over green valleys as the road curves around mountains and the flatlands below. From sea level in Rio, the highway climbs 810

Main Attractions

Petrópolis
Nova Friburgo
Búzios
Arraial do Cabo
Angra dos Reis
Ilha Grande
Paraty

The Imperial Palace at Petropolis.

meters (2,660ft) during the hour-and-a-quarter drive. Along the way, visitors can still glimpse traces of the old Petrópolis Highway, a perilous, cobblestoned roadway that used to keep workers constantly busy the whole year round making repairs.

Life in Petrópolis is centered on **Rua do Imperador**, a busy street, and the only part of town with buildings more than five stories tall. One of which is the recently refurbished **Grande Hotel Ⓐ** (www.grandehotel petropolis.com.br), built in 1930, that reopened in December 2011 after being closed for 36 years. Temperatures are lower here than in Rio, and the city's sweater-clad inhabitants give it an autumnal air during the cool months from June to September.

Perpendicular to Rua do Imperador is the Rua da Imperatriz, the city's lush boulevard that was used by Brazilian emperors of the past. The partially cobbled avenue is divided by a slow-moving canal, and horse-drawn carriages lined up for rent by the hour form an attractive old-fashioned taxi stand on its sun-dappled stones.

The area around the former royal Summer Palace, which is now the **Museu Imperia Ⓑ** (220 Rua da Imperatriz; www.museuimperial.gov.br; Tue–Sun 11am–6pm), is crowded with trees and shrubs and crisscrossed by carefully kept pathways. There is a spectacular sound-and-light show here on Thursday, Friday, and Saturday at 8pm. The rose-colored palace is one of Brazil's most interesting museums. Only a limited number of people are allowed into the museum at any one time, so you may have to wait a little while. Visitors are asked to wear specially provided felt slippers, in which they pad quietly over the gleaming jacaranda- and brazil-wood floors. The museum's humble furnishings, as well as its outward appearance, attest to the character of Pedro II, who for the most part avoided the traditional trappings of nobility. Its second-floor collection of personal artifacts, including a telescope and a telephone, is a reminder of Pedro's scientific dabblings.

Among other items of interest in the palace museum are the spectacular **crown jewels** – a glistening frame

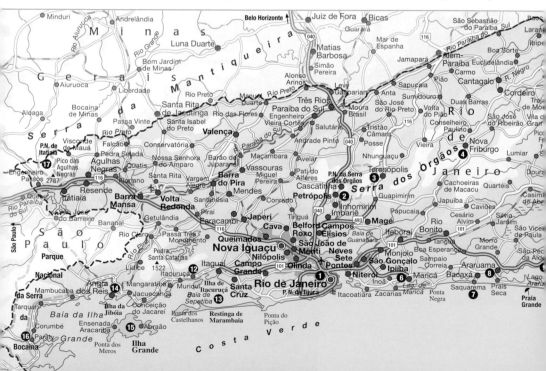

of 77 pearls and 639 diamonds – and the colorful skirts and cloaks of the emperor's ceremonial wardrobe, including a cape of bright Amazon toucan feathers. Royal photographs on the second floor, however, show that independent Brazil's last two emperors felt more at home in their conservative business suits than in flowing robes.

Cathedral and culture

A few blocks away, at Rua São Pedro de Alcântara, is the towering, French Gothic-style **Catedral de São Pedro de Alcântara** C (Tue–Sun 8am–8pm; free). This imposing structure was begun in 1884, but it took 37 years to finish the first stage, and another 48 years to complete the whole building.

The tombs of Dom Pedro II and his wife Dona Teresa Cristina are here, carved of exquisite Carrara marble. Both died in exile, and their bodies were returned here only in 1939, two decades after the decree banishing the royal family had been revoked.

The city is notable for its delightful rose-colored houses, including many that were once the dwellings of members of the royal family. Petrópolis is also known for its many overgrown private gardens and public parks, and the simple beauty of its streets. The **Casa da Ipiranga** D **– Instituto de Cultura** (http://casa daipiranga.blogspot.co.uk; tel: 24-9249 3319; Fri–Sun 1–6pm), at 716 Rua Ipiranga, is one of the few mansions open to the public. Visit it to marvel at the exquisite interior, to view its high-quality art exhibitions, and to have a coffee or lunch in its lovely restaurant, Bordeaux.

A few blocks beyond the cathedral, on Rua Alfredo Pachá, is the 1884 **Palácio de Cristal** (Crystal Palace) E, a glass-and-iron-framed edifice still used for gardening and art exhibitions. The palace was built almost entirely of panels shipped from France. Nearby is the unusual **Casa de Santos Dumont** F (22 Rua do Encanto; Tue–Sun 9.30am–5pm), which displays a collection of eccentricities reflecting the unusual personality of its former owner, the pilot and inventor *extraordinaire*, Alberto Santos-Dumont. The

The Tomb of Dom Pedro II.

Rio de Janeiro State

0   50 km
0   50 miles

ALBERTO SANTOS-DUMONT

The downtown Santos-Dumont Airport in Rio commemorates Brazil's most famous inventor. The son of a wealthy coffee-grower, Alberto Santos-Dumont moved to Paris at the age of 17, in 1891, to study engineering. There he led the life of a playboy until, seven years later, he took his first flight in a balloon. Santos-Dumont was enthralled, and went on to design a series of airships. He won the Deutsch Prize for flying from Saint-Cloud, round the Eiffel Tower and back – and gave half of his winnings to the poor.

Later, he built 14-bis, also known as Oiseau de proie (Bird of Prey), an ungainly aircraft resembling a series of linked box kites. In this craft, on October 23, 1906, he made the first fully documented heavier-than-air flight – in fact, the first self-powered flight, since the Wright Brothers had used a catapult system to get their craft airborne three years earlier. Santos-Dumont subsequently designed a monoplane, but lost interest in aviation soon afterwards. Sometimes he used his inventions to visit friends in the Paris suburbs, and he would tether a small airship to convenient lamp-posts near bars he wished to visit.

Santos-Dumont spent his last years back in Brazil. Tragically, he committed suicide in 1932, unable to come to terms with the use of aircraft in warfare.

TIP

Comfortable buses run between Rio and Búzios at regular intervals, from the Rodoviária Novo Rio. The bus company is Viação 1001 (tel: 21-4004 5001; www.auto viacao1001.com.br). There are also direct flights to Búzios at certain times of the year from Rio and São Paulo, as well as air taxi services.

house, which he designed himself, has just one room, no tables or kitchen (his meals were delivered by a hotel), and no interior staircases. There are all kinds of shelves, each designed for a specific purpose, and a special chest of drawers that he used as a bed.

Opened in 2012, the historical beer museum **Cervejaria Bohemia** Ⓖ (166 Rua Alfredo Pachá; Wed–Fri 11am–6pm, Sat–Sun 11am–8pm) is one of the city's newest attractions. It was Brazil's first brewery when it first opened in 1853. A full tour takes over two hours. Not surprisingly the attraction has its own bar that also serves food.

Other attractions include the sprawling Normandy-style **Palácio Quitandinha** Ⓗ (Tue–Sun 9am–5pm), a luxuriously appointed structure completed in 1944 as Brazil's leading hotel casino, and the largest in Latin America. But only a few months after its inauguration, gambling was outlawed, and has remained so ever since. Today, the striking complex, on the Rio–Petrópolis Highway 8km (5 miles) from Petrópolis, is a combination condominium and private club.

A bronze statue of Bardot gazes wistfully out to sea.

Mountain scenery

Just 57km (35 miles) from Petrópolis, at the end of a one-hour drive along steep and winding mountain roads, is Rio de Janeiro's other mountain gem, **Teresópolis** ❸ (pop. 150,000). Named after Pedro II's wife, the empress Teresa Cristina, it was planned in the 1880s but only incorporated in 1891, two years after the royal couple's exile.

The picturesque town, which is 92km (57 miles) from Rio on the broad **Rio–Teresópolis Highway**, clings to the edge of the **Serra Fluminense** at 870 meters (2,850ft). The main attractions, besides the cool air, are an encompassing, though distant, view of Rio's **Baía de Guanabara** and the city's proximity to the spectacular **Parque Nacional da Serra dos Orgãos**. The park is dominated by a ridge of sharp peaks, the tallest, **Pedra do Sino**, rising to 2,260 meters (7,410ft) above sea level. But the range's most striking summit is the rocky spike called **O Dedo de Deus** (The Finger of God). On clear days, the chiseled profile of the Serra dos Orgãos can be seen from many points

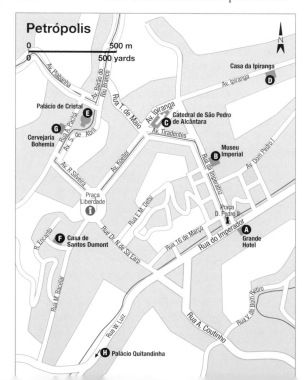

Petrópolis

0 — 500 m
0 — 500 yards

Casa da Ipiranga Ⓓ
Av. Ipiranga

Palácio de Cristal Ⓔ
Av. Piabanha
Av. Barão do Rio Branco
Rua T. de Maio
Av. Ipiranga

Ⓖ Cervejaria Bohemia
Rua A. Pachá
Av. S. de Abril

Ⓒ Catedral de São Pedro de Alcântara
Av. Tiradentes

Av. Koeller
Av. R. Silveira

Museu Ⓑ Imperial
Rua da Imperatriz
Av. Dom Pedro I

Praça Liberdade ⓘ
Rua E.M. Delsi
Praça D. Pedro II

Ⓕ Casa de Santos Dumont
Rua Dr. N. de Sá Earp
Rua 16 de Março
Rua do Imperador
Ⓐ Grande Hotel

R. Encanto
Rua M. Bacelar
Rua W. Luiz

Ⓗ Palácio Quitandinha
Rua A. Coutinho
Rua V. de Bom Retiro

in Rio itself. Walking trails, waterfalls, and swimming areas make the park a delightful place to spend a day.

Nova Friburgo ❹ (pop. 183,000) is a bustling city two-and-a-half-hours' drive from Rio. It was settled by a group of 400 Swiss (and later German) immigrant families in the 1820s, who came from the Swiss canton of Fribourg at the invitation of the exiled Portuguese king João VI. Today the Brazilian lingerie industry capital, it is notable for excellent cuisine (not all Germanic), dramatic views and trail hikes in nearby, near-virgin Atlantic forest areas, many reachable from the Lumiar–São Pedro da Serra-Sana region. The excellent 65km (40-mile) road that connects Nova Friburgo with Teresópolis is renowned for its many attractions, and fine restaurants and resort hotels, such as Rosa dos Ventos (tel: 21-2644 9900), Village Le Canton (tel: 21-2741 4200), and Fazenda Vista Soberba (tel: 22-2529 4053). In recent years, it has become faster and easier to drive between Nova Friburgo and the Sun Coast via a paved, spectacular mountain highway connecting Lumiar with Rio das Ostras near Búzios.

In 2011 Nova Friburgo and Teresópolis were at the heart of on one of Brazil's greatest natural disasters when flooding and mudslides killed more than 800 people.

Búzios

Located 190km (115 miles) east of Rio on the Costa do Sol (Sun Coast), **Armação dos Búzios** ❺ is a sophisticated international resort that for much of the year still tries to retain the air of a fishing village – although word has got around, and it's nothing like as quiet as it used to be, even off-season. The really busy time is the high summer, just before, during and after Carnival, when tranquil Búzios is overrun by tourists, including many cruise-ship passengers, and the population of 25,000 swells to 100,000. It is also one of the key weekend

destinations for Cariocas. It is best avoided at these times.

Its tranquility was partly due to the fact that it took so long to get there, but major road improvements, following the privatization of the highway linking Rio to Búzios, have reduced traveling time significantly, and the scenic drive can now be done easily in two-and-a-half hours, though holiday weekends still see massive traffic jams.

Búzios has undergone a major real-estate boom since the 1970s, but, fortunately, the city fathers have kept a firm hand on developers. Strict zoning laws limit building heights, with

Souvenirs are for sale, along with fresh produce, at the Brejal market, near Itaipava.

BRAZIL'S COLONIAL FAZENDAS

In the 19th century, when Brazil's major export was coffee, production was centered on large farms, or *fazendas*, in the hinterland behind Rio de Janeiro; land was often hacked out of the lush Atlantic rainforest of the Paraíba valley by slaves. The wealth generated turned the coffee barons into a new elite, who established luxurious and beautiful homes. When coffee production in the area began to decline in the 1880s, to be replaced by cattle, many *fazendas* changed hands, surviving as seats for new owners with independent incomes. Some of the handful of opulent *fazendas* remaining in the valley have been converted into country hotels and restaurants that offer an experience very different from the fast life of Rio city. Set in extensive grounds, they provide relaxation and comfort, with delicious home-produced food served in the silver-plate style of a bygone age. Several have facilities for pursuits such as horseback riding and canoeing.

Particularly recommended are two establishments in the former coffee-growing center of Valença: Pousada Fazenda São Polycarpo (tel: 24-2458 1190), beautifully decorated with 19th-century furniture and objets d'art; and Fazenda Pau d'Alho (tel: 24-2453 3033), which has no accommodations but serves an incomparable colonial-style afternoon tea (for which you should reserve in advance).

On Geriba beach, Búzios.

the result that Búzios has escaped the high-rise invasion that has scarred many Brazilian beach resorts. The fashionable homes that dot the beachscape blend, for the most part, with the picturesque houses of the fishermen. Much of the tourist accommodations in Búzios is foreign-owned *pousadas* or inns, small and quaint, although very sophisticated and often with pools, and fancy restaurants. In 2010, the area's largest hotel opened, the 329-room all-inclusive Blue Tree Park Búzios Beach Resort (see page 349).

The Bardot connection

According to the history books, **Búzios** was 'discovered' by the Portuguese at the beginning of the 16th century. Local people, however, know better. Búzios they say was actually discovered in 1964 by the French actress Brigitte Bardot, who had two well-documented stays in Búzios, parading her famous bikini-clad torso along the unspoiled beaches and, in

Surfers at Geriba beach in Búzios.

the process, spreading the fame of the little town across the globe. Búzios hasn't been the same since. After Bardot, it became a synonym for all that splendor in the tropics is supposed to be – white-sand beaches, crystalline water, palm trees and coconuts, beautiful people, and a relaxing, intoxicating lifestyle of careless ease.

What is amazing is that all this is true. Búzios is one of a handful of super-hyped destinations that doesn't delude or disappoint. It is not just as good as the posters. It is even better.

The beaches of Búzios

Altogether, there are 23 beaches in the Búzios area, some fronting quiet coves and inlets, others the open sea. The main distinction, though, is accessibility. Beaches close to the town, such as **Ossos**, **Do Canto**, and **Ferradura**, are easily reached on foot or by car.

As might be expected, the best beaches are those that require the most effort to reach, either via long hikes, sometimes over rocky ground, or by a drive along a potholed dirt road. At the end are treasures like **Tartaruga**, **Azeda**, and **Azedinha**, **Brava**, and **Forno**, known for their beautifully calm waters.

Visiting all the beaches by land is not only tiring but also unnecessary. The fishermen of Búzios have become part-time tour operators, and tourists can rent their boats by the hour or by the day. Sailboats can also be hired, as can cars and dune buggies, bicycles, motorcycles, and horses. Enthusiastic divers will find they can rent all the necessary equipment in town.

A typical Búzios day begins late (few people wake up before 11am) with a hearty breakfast at a *pousada*. Daytime activities center on the beach. Swimming, leisurely walks, or the exploration of distant beaches can be enjoyed, with the occasional break for fried shrimp or fresh oysters washed down with ice-cold beer or *caipirinha*, Brazil's national drink, composed of *cachaça* – a sugar-cane liqueur – slices of lime, and lots of ice. The more athletic might be tempted on to the links, as Búzios has an excellent and testing golf course.

As far as shopping is concerned, there is a variety of fashionable boutiques along cobblestoned **Rua José Bento Ribeiro Dantas**, better known as **Rua das Pedras**, or Stone Street, and also on **Rua Manuel Turibe de Farias**. And as many Brazilian and foreign-born artists have taken up residence in the town, it has also turned into a booming art mart.

Nightlife in Búzios

At night, the bohemian spirit of Búzios takes charge. Though small in size, the city is considered to be one of the best in Brazil for dining out, with more than 20 high-quality restaurants, some of which are rated among the country's finest. Gourmets have a wide array of cuisines from which to choose, including Brazilian, Italian, French, and Portuguese, as well as seafood and crêpes – a local favorite.

Sollar (Italian); Estáncia Dom Juan (barbecued meats); Cigalon (fine French cuisine); Sawasdee (Thai cooking); Satyricon (seafood); Salt (Mediterranean) and Patio Havana (seafood and a spectacular view) are among the top restaurants in Búzios. Other eateries – many superb – are constantly popping up see page 179. After dinner, the Búzios in-crowd gravitates to the city's bars, many of which have live entertainment. Both bars and restaurants are as well known for their owners as for their offerings. The city's numerous charms have waylaid dozens of foreign visitors since Bardot's first promenade. She left, but many of the others have stayed, opening inns, restaurants, and bars, and providing Búzios with an international air. Natives of Búzios have been joined by French, Swiss, Scandinavian, Argentine, and American expatriates, who vow they will never leave.

The lake region

Most people go straight to Búzios from Rio, but between the two places are several beautiful beach areas well worth exploring, starting with what

O Dedo de Deus in the Parque Nacional da Serra dos Orgãos.

is known as the lake region: a series of lagoons separated from the sea by lengthy sandbars. This is a favorite surfing area, as the sea along this unbroken coastline is marked by strong currents and large waves, so swimmers should be careful.

Close to **Maricá** ❻ is **Ponta Negra** beach, a spectacular, nearly deserted stretch of white sand and wild blue water. Major surfing competitions are held in nearby **Saquarema** ❼, one of the four beach resorts in the lake region. Here, horseback riding through scenic countryside is offered at the highly rated Nosso Paraíso *pousada* (tel: 22-9969 1969; www.nosso-paraiso. net). **Araruama** ❽ and **São Pedro da Aldeia** ❾ are popular among *cariocas* during vacation periods (especially Carnival), when the lake region's hotels and numerous campgrounds are filled to overflowing.

Salt flats are also visible off the side of the road along this stretch, culminating in a large area of flats at **Cabo Frio** ❿. This is officially the end of the lake region and the beginning of the Sun Coast.

People at a bar on Rua Das Pedras in Búzios.

Located 29km (18 miles) from Búzios, Cabo Frio is famed for the white, powdery sand of its beaches and dunes. In vacation season, Cabo Frio's population of 110,000 swells with visiting *cariocas*. Unlike Búzios, Cabo Frio is a historic city. Its 17th-century ruins include the **Forte São Mateus** and **Nossa Senhora da Assunção** church (both built around 1616), and the **Nossa Senhora dos Anjos** convent (built in 1686).

Arraial do Cabo

Only 18km (11 miles) from Cabo Frio is **Arraial do Cabo** ⓫, after Búzios the most beautiful attraction of the Sun Coast. Arraial has been discovered by the tourist trade. Once vacationers preferred to stay in Búzios and Cabo Frio, and just make day trips to Arraial, but now there is a range of *pousadas* and hotels to choose from.

Arraial has some of the clearest water in southern Brazil, making it the preferred site of scuba divers. The city is located at the tip of a cape with a variety of beaches, some with quiet waters and lush green mountain

backdrops, while others, the surfer beaches, are swept by strong winds that drive the waves high up the beach.

There are a number of licensed operators running diving tours from Arraial, which receives some 12,000 divers a year, attracted by the abundant underwater fauna, which benefits from the resurgence phenomenon that provides rich nutrients for the underwater food chain, and ensures visibility even at depths of 30 meters (100ft). Boat trips leave from the Marina dos Pescadores, at Praia dos Anjos.

Off the coast is the **Ilha do Farol**, site of a lighthouse but better known for the **Gruta Azul**, an underwater grotto with bright blue waters. The island, accessible by boat, also offers excellent views of the mainland.

Like Búzios, Arraial began as a fishing village, and is still known for the quality of the fresh catches brought in each day. The local fishermen climb to the top of sand dunes, from where they simply look into the water below in search of schools of fish, a testimony to the unspoiled clarity of the waters.

The Green Coast

On the southwestern side of the city of Rio, in the opposite direction from Búzios and the Sun Coast, lies a string of beaches and islands known collectively as the **Costa Verde** (Green Coast). This coast stretches for 260km (160 miles), as far as the border with São Paulo state. Named for the dense vegetation that dominates the coastline and descends right down to the sea, the Costa Verde is nature at its best: a splendid tropical mix of mountains, rainforest, beaches, and islands. Green, in every imaginable shade, surrounds you, invading even the sea with a soft turquoise hue.

Access to the Green Coast is along coastal highway BR 101, known as the **Rio–Santos Highway** after the two port cities that it connects. The scenic drive compares with the one down Spain's Costa Brava or California's State Road 1. At times, it seems almost as if you are going to take flight as the road rises high up a mountain side for a wide panoramic view, before winding steeply back down to the shoreline. This memorable route takes you past

TIP

There are a number of fast-track ferries that run passengers in small boats from Ilha Grande to Mangaratiba, where buses wait to deliver them to Rio hotels or direct to the airport. You can find current information on the harbor front in Abraão.

Angra dos Reis, once a busy port, is now a seaside resort.

THE GOLD TRAIL

From Paraty, you may like to follow the Gold Trail *(Caminho do Ouro)*, which is now open to visitors, retracing the routes taken by gold prospectors in the 18th century. This combines a bit of history, a bit of activity, and some splendid scenery. Specially adapted open trucks take you to the village of Penha, from where there is a 2.5km (1.5-mile) hike to a local farmhouse, accompanied by a *frigo-burro* (cooler-donkey), which carries cold drinks to keep you refreshed on the journey.

Departures are from the Teatro Espaço at 327 Rua Dona Geralda, Paraty (Wed–Sun 10am). Further information can be had on tel: 24-3371 1575. The cost is approximately US$10, with a further US$5 if you want the lunch provided at the farmhouse.

a national park, two nuclear power plants, tourist resorts, fishing villages, ocean-liner tanking stations, cattle ranches, a shipyard, and the town of Paraty – a stunning monument to Brazil's colonial past (see page 177).

The most enticing attractions along the Green Coast are the beaches. Some are small, encased by rocky cliffs, with clear, tranquil lagoons, while others stretch on for miles, pounded by rough surf. The entire area is a haven for sports enthusiasts, offering everything from tennis, golf, and boating to deep-sea fishing, diving, and surfing.

Although it is just about possible to see the Green Coast in a single day, to explore it thoroughly and truly enjoy its beauty, plan on two or three days, or more. Since the early 1980s, tourism has become the leading activity of the region, and there are a growing number of fine hotels and restaurants, even on some of the islands.

Tropical islands

The Green Coast begins 100km (60 miles) outside Rio de Janeiro city at the town of **Itacuruçá** ⓬ (pop. 3,700).

From the town harbor, schooners holding up to 40 people depart every morning for one-day excursions to the nearby tropical islands in the surrounding **Baía de Sepetiba** ⓭. The trips are reasonably priced, and you can buy a seafood lunch or buffet for an extra charge. The schooners stop at several islands, such as **Martins**, **Itacuruçá**, and **Jaguanum**, to allow passengers to swim or snorkel. Some of the smaller islands can be visited by hiring a boat and guide, usually a local fisherman (the islands of **Pombeba** and **Sororoca** are recommended). Also, for visitors who wish to stay on the islands, there are few acceptable hotels, including the Hotel Elias C, and Hotel do Pierre.

The highway continues past **Muriqui** to **Mangaratiba**, site of a large Club Mediterranée, the Portobello Resort Safari, and Porto Real. Further down the road is **Angra dos Reis** ⓮ (Kings' Cove), the Green Coast's largest city (pop. 130,000), which sprawls across a series of hills at the beginning of a 100km- (60-mile) -long gulf.

There are some 365 islands and 2,000 recognized beaches in the myriad of

Fishing boats at Manguinhos beach.

inlets, coves, and waterways around Angra dos Reis, including the large bays of Sepetiba and Ilha Grande. The water is delightfully warm and clear year-round, and is still a perfect sanctuary for marine life, despite evidence of gradually rising pollution from over-building, poor regulation of sanitation, and increased shipping traffic and commercial boatyards.

Spearfishing on the rocky shores and fishing in deeper waters are favorite pastimes. The tourist information center, opposite the bus station near the harbor, provides maps and information on hotels and boat tours. Hotel Frade & Golf Resort (see page 349) has the coast's only golf course (18 holes). Other top resorts in the region include the Vila Galé Eco Resort de Angra (see page 349) and the Pestana Angra Beach (see page 349).

Angra's tourist and accommodations infrastructure has improved significantly over the past decade, but it does not have the frenetic nightlife of Búzios. While there is a growing network of improved restaurants and bars in the city, most visitors tend to

remain in their hotels or *pousadas* in the evening, sometimes going by speedboat to islands such as Ilha do Arroz, Ilha de Itanhangá, and Chivas, where special night-time events and parties take place during peak season.

Fishing boats in Itacuruçá.

Ilha Grande

Some 90 minutes from Angra by boat is the paradisiacal **Ilha Grande** ⑮, a nature reserve with 192km (120 miles)

LITERARY FESTIVAL

In August 2003 Paraty became the latest city to host a literary festival comparable to those at Hay-on-Wye, Adelaide, Toronto, Berlin, and Edinburgh. The festival was begun by Liz Calder, co-founder of Bloomsbury Publishing, whose love for Brazil stems from the years she spent working as a model in São Paulo in the mid-1960s. Paraty's annual Flip festival (www.flip. org.br), in July or August, has become a prestigious event, consolidating a reputation as a truly international literary jamboree, attracting some of Brazil's, and the world's, finest authors, including Salman Rushdie, Ian McEwan, Hanif Kureishi, Martin Amis, Isabel Allende, Robert Crumb, Lou Reed, John Banville, Margaret Atwood, Nadine Gorimer, Paul Auster, Ariano Suassuna, Gilberto Gil, and Ruy Castro.

Sarongs and hammocks for sale in Vila do Abraão. The Parrot's Beak is in the background.

Spices at Paraty's market.

wooden-shuttered houses painted in bright primary colors.

Ilha Grande has become a very popular destination for well-heeled tourists and backpackers alike, with an increase in the number of chic *pousadas* and simple campgrounds, excellent restaurants, good, modest eateries, and atmospheric bars. From Abraão, small boats can be rented if you wish to visit more distant beaches such as lovely Lopes Mendes, Mangues, and Saco do Céu. Or take off on your own to explore one of the many well-marked nature trails that lead over the hills.

Lopes Mendes is considered one of the prettiest of all the Brazilian beaches. It is 3km of very fine, white sand that is lapped by very transparent blue water. Nobody lives on or near the beach, so it is nature at its best.

If you are fit and healthy, you could climb the 960-meter (3,150ft) peak called the **Bico do Papagaio** (Parrot's Beak), which resembles its name. If you do so, take water and mosquito repellent, and make sure somebody knows where you've gone. It's not

of coastline, spectacular flora and fauna, 106 beautiful beaches, idyllic coves, waterfalls, and mountain-trail walks. The island can be reached by ferryboats that operate from Mangaratiba and Angra and disembark at **Abraão**, the only town on the island – and a tiny one at that, with only about 500 permanent inhabitants. Abraão, despite a devastating mudslide in January 2010, is a delightful little place; its few narrow streets are lined with

a particularly difficult climb, but can take six hours; the weather can change rapidly, and the clouds and mist descend in no time.

Paraty

From Angra, the coastal highway flanks the gulf, running past two nuclear power plants, and the picturesque fishing village of **Mambucaba**. At the far end of the bay, about three and a half hours' drive from Rio (265km/165 miles), is **Paraty ⓰** (pop. 33,000; also spelt 'Parati'), a colonial jewel that, in 1966, was declared a national monument by Unesco and today delights visitors from other parts of Brazil and around the world.

Paraty was founded in 1660, and in the 18th century gained fame and wealth as a result of the discovery of gold and diamonds in the neighboring state of Minas Gerais. The precious stones were transported by land to Paraty and from there either on to Rio de Janeiro or by ship to Portugal. The city also served as the main stopping-off point for travelers and commerce moving between São Paulo to the south and Rio de Janeiro. For more than a century, Paraty flourished and its citizens prospered. Opulent mansions and large estates attest to the wealth of its residents.

After Brazil declared independence in 1822, the export of gold to Portugal ceased and a new road was eventually built, bypassing Paraty and connecting Rio to São Paulo directly. Paraty lost its strategic position and was forgotten. Although the town then became less prosperous, neglect meant that its colonial heritage was preserved. Today, that heritage awaits visitors in the form of colonial churches and houses in the relaxed, laid-back atmosphere of a town trapped contentedly in a time warp. But be careful how you go when exploring the town: the shiny, uneven paving stones in narrow roads that slope towards the center can easily throw you off balance.

Standing out among Paraty's churches is **Santa Rita** (built in 1722), a classic example of Brazilian Baroque architecture that was built for the freed mulatto population. Today the church also houses the small **Museu**

DRINK

Paraty and the surrounding area is a respected producer of cachaça, the sugar-cane liqueur that forms the basis of the caipirinha, and the town's shops are filled with bottles of the stuff, in all shapes, sizes, and colors.

A Beetle sits Outside one of the many brightly painted houses lining Paraty's streets.

de Arte Sacra (Museum of Sacred Art; Wed–Sun 9–11am, 2–5pm; free).

Paraty and its people have a great sense of identity, and this is well displayed in the stunning **Casa de Cultura** (Sun–Mon and Wed–Thu 10am–6.30pm, Fri–Sat 1–9.30pm). This is a monument to Paraty, and to its people, their simplicity, and their dignity.

All Paraty's streets contain hidden surprises: art galleries, handicraft shops, quaint *pousadas*, and colonial houses. From the outside, the *pousadas* look like typical whitewashed Mediterranean-style houses, with heavy wooden doors and shutters painted in bright colors. Inside, however, they open up on to delicately landscaped courtyards with pots of ferns, orchids, rose bushes, violets, and begonias.

Paraty is not known for its beaches, but schooners such as the 24-meter (80ft) *Soberno da Costa* make day trips to the nearby islands. There are about 65 islands and 300 beaches to choose from. Hotels and travel agents sell tickets for trips out, or you can just walk along the pier and make a deal with a local fisherman to take you.

Itatiaia

If heading toward São Paulo, there is an interesting detour on the state border to the **Parque Nacional de Itatiaia** ⓱ (off the Rio–São Paulo Highway). This beautiful nature reserve on the slopes of the Mantiqueira range was established in 1937. It was Brazil's first national park, and has a good infrastructure for tourists. Its forests are rich in wildlife, orchids, and bromeliads; it is a paradise for birdwatchers and has beautiful waterfalls and lakes.

Higher up in the mountains, the vegetation changes to grassland and brush, then to the lunar rocky landscape of the **Pico das Agulhas Negras** (2,787 meters/9,150ft). This is a great place for rock climbing and trekking. Near the park entrance, there is a natural history museum (Tue–Sun 10am–4pm). Recommended places to stay are the Hotel Donati (tel: 24-3352-1110), Hotel Simon (tel: 24-3352 1230/2214), Hotel Warabi (tel: 24-3387 1143), and Hotel do Ypê (tel: 24-3352 1453).

Vermelha beach near Paraty.

RESTAURANTS

Búzios

Brigitta's
131 Rua das Pedras, Centro
Tel: 24-2623 6157
Open: L&D daily.
The charming Brigitta's is a Búzios landmark. Shrimp and lobster figure prominently, but there are less expensive choices to be had, and all good. **$$**

Cigalon
265 Rua das Pedras, Centro
Tel: 22-2623 0932
Open: D Mon–Fri L&D Sat–Sun.
Enterprising French menu in a sophisticated and romantic setting overlooking the harbor. Something you might not guess from the discrete entrance off Rua das Pedras to the Pousada do Sol. Famous for its great desserts. **$$$**

Estância Dom Juan
178 Rua das Pedras, Centro
Tel: 22-2623 2169
Open: L&D daily.
One of the most popular spots on Rua das Pedras since opening in 1994. Melt-in-your-mouth beef, as you might expect from this Argentine owned establishment. Delightful setting occasionally livened up by a tango evening, which is normally on Wednesday evenings. **$$$**

Satyricon
500 Avenida José Bento Ribeiro Dantas, Orla Bardot
Tel: 22-2623 2691
Open: D daily, L&D Sun.
One of Búzios's, and Rio's, most traditional and reliable sophisticated seafood restaurants, which dates back to 1981. Italian and other international dishes also feature on the menu. Like many restaurants in Búzios, there are sea views from the best tables. **$$$**

Sollar
994 Avenida José Bento Ribeiro Dantas, Orla Bardot
Tel: 22-2623 5392
Open: L&D Wed–Sun.
Located within the Sollar Búzios *pousada* off Rua das Pedras, this is the brainchild of chef Danio Braga who is well known in Rio gastronomic circles for his creative Italian dishes, with a telling Brazilian touch. Last seen at the Locanda della Mimosa in Petrópolis, Braga's arrival in Búzios has not disappointed, so reserve in advance. **$$$**

Paraty

Banana da Terra
198 Rua Dr Samuel Costa
Tel: 24-3371 1725
Open: D Wed–Thu, L&D Fri–Sun.
Seafood served with local ingredients. Brave and at times exotic combinations that make for memorable meals. Lovely, traditional ambiance and good service. Considered amongst the town's best restaurants. Reservations recommended. **$$**

Bartholomeu
176 Rua Dr Samuel Costa
Tel: 24-3371 5032
Open: L&D daily.
A classy little restaurant with an 18th-century setting in the historic heart of the town. Argentine beef is a specialty, but the menu offers a nice selection of contemporary dishes based on local ingredients from the land and the sea. Bartholomeu is linked to the *pousada* of the same name, which has just five suites. **$$**

Merlin o Mago
376 Rua do Comércio
Tel: 24-3371 2157
Open: D Thu–Tue.
A touch of magic in a lovely 1780s building, the emphasis is on fresh ingredients. Menu reflects European, Asian and Brazilian influences. This really is very special, and one of the town's more formal restaurants. **$$$**

Porto Entreposto Cultural
14 Rua do Comércio
Tel: 24-3371 1058
Open: D daily.
Creative menu with obvious European and Brazilian influences. As you would expect being located in the historic heart of the town, the setting is very attractive and charming. One of the town's more sophisticated restaurants. **$$**

Petrópolis

Fazenda das Videiras
Estrada das Araras, Vale de Videiras
Tel: 24-2225 8090
Open: L Sun, L&D Fri–Sat.
Romantic, innovative quality French restaurant that is located in one of region's best and most romantic pousadas. A favourite with the Brazilian critics, and justifiably so. **$$**

Locanda della Mimosa
30 Alameda das Mimosas, Vale Florido
Tel: 24-2233 5405
Open: L Sun, L&D Fri–Sat.
Rated as one of Brazil's best Italian restaurants, and with good reason, although the fact that the owner and chef has moved on to Búzios, raises a few concerns. The fact that it's off the beaten track, in a pretty *pousada*, should not deter you if you are in the region. Friday evening the specialty is pizza. Brunch served on Sunday from 12.30–4pm. **$$$**

Majorica
754 Rua do Imperador
Tel: 24-2242 2498
Open: daily 11am–late.
A traditional steakhouse located in the center of Petrópolis, not far from the Imperial Palace. First opened for business in 1961. Rump steak remains the bestseller, but there are also dishes with sauces and good seafood options, too. Baclahau is a popular option. **$$**

Pousada da Alcobaça
298 Rua Dr Agostinho Goulão, Corrêas
Tel: 24-2221 1240
Open: daily 8am–late.
A delightful guesthouse on the outskirts of Petrópolis, about 15 minutes from the city center. Simply prepared, unpretentious, high-standard home cooking. Most vegetables are home-grown, and many of the ingredients are found in the mountain area, such as the trout, duck, and sausages. Feijoada is served on Saturdays, and there is also a monthly, traditional Portuguese cozido. **$$$**

Solar do Imperio
376 Avenida Koeler
Tel: 24-2103 3000
Open: L&D daily.
In downtown Petrópolis, this restaurant is beautifully appointed, and offers an attractive menu, including a very reasonably priced prix fixe lunch during the week. Menu includes both international and Brazilian favorites. Tea is served from 5pm on Friday and Saturday. The mansion that houses the 16-room hotel and restaurant dates from 1875. **$$**

Stained glass windows at Mercado
Municipal, São Paulo.

Banco do Estado de São Paulo, framed by the buildings of São João Avenue.

SÃO PAULO: CITY AND STATE

São Paulo state is Brazil's economic powerhouse.
Its capital is a vibrant place with an enormous
cultural mix, and some great restaurants, bars,
and clubs. And not far from the city you'll find
a mountain retreat and splendid beaches.

The state of São Paulo – Brazil's largest (pop. 42 million), most economically diverse, and wealthiest – includes a little bit of everything, from the smoky industries of São Paulo city, to beach resorts that rival Rio; from a string of pleasing mountain resorts, to a fertile farming area that is the most productive in Brazil.

The most striking element of São Paulo's modern development has been its speed. During the first three and a half centuries of recorded Brazilian history (1500–1850), São Paulo was a backwater, home to a few mixed-race traders and pioneers. Today, the state of São Paulo is Brazil's economic powerhouse and as such provides one-third of the country's GNP. Half of all Brazilian manufacturing concerns are members of the São Paulo industrial federation (FIESP), and around half of Brazil's 50 biggest privately held corporations and private banks are headquartered in the state. The state is also responsible for a disproportionately high consumption of such items as electrical power.

First settlements

São Paulo's story is as old as Brazil's. The coastal settlement of São Vicente was founded in 1532, the first permanent Portuguese colony in the New World. A generation later, in 1554, two

courageous Jesuits, José de Anchieta and Manuel da Nóbrega, established a mission on the high plateau 70km (42 miles) inland from São Vicente. They called the colony **São Paulo de Piratininga**. Much of São Paulo's traditional dynamism can be traced to the early isolation of settlements such as São Vicente and Piratininga, far away from the administrative and commercial center of the colony in the northeast region.

Since few European women were willing to accept the hardships of life

Main Attractions
Pátio do Colégio
Teatro Municipal
Liberdade
Pinacoteca do Estado
Museu de Arte de São Paulo
Museu do Futebol
Instituto Butantá
Ibirapuera

Busy São Paulo streets.

Socializing at Cristallo's café on the fashionable Rua Oscar Freire street in the Jardin Paulista area.

The Bovespa stock exchange.

on the windblown plateau, male colonists married Amerindian women and fathered hardy, mixed-race children who were accustomed to the privations of a frontier life and felt no attachment to faraway Portugal.

Within two generations, the remote colony of São Paulo de Piratininga had produced its own brand of frontiersman, known as the *bandeirante*. On his Amerindian side, the *bandeirante*'s heritage included pathfinding and survival skills. From his Portuguese father, he inherited a thirst for gain and a nomadic streak that sent him roaming across half a continent, in search of gold, diamonds, and indigenous people to sell as slaves to the colonists. Despite his less-than-noble motives, the *bandeirante* was instrumental in the conquest and establishment of the country's frontiers.

Bandeirante individualism was carried over to the political arena during the 19th century. Pedro I, the Portuguese emperor, was greatly influenced by his *paulista* advisers, led by José Bonifácio de Andrade e Silva. *Paulistas* are people born in São Paulo state; later in the century they led the fight against slavery and helped to establish the 1889 republic.

Economic growth

However, São Paulo's true vocation was business. Attracted by the growth of British textile manufacturing, *paulista* plantation owners first cultivated cotton in the early 19th century. Lacking a large slave population, however, the plantations soon faced a manpower shortage, and cotton production fell behind the American competition.

So, with money from the cotton boom, they diversified into coffee, a product enjoying increased world demand and little producer competition. São Paulo's climatic conditions and the fertile red soil called *terra roxa* proved ideal for the finicky coffee bush, and the stage was set for the state to become Brazil's richest.

Within a decade, coffee surpassed cotton as São Paulo's chief cash crop. Meanwhile, the labor-shortage problem was solved with large-scale European immigration, which began in the 1870s following a systematic campaign to attract settlers. Between 1870 and 1920, the campaign successfully attracted some 5 million immigrants. About half settled in São Paulo, most working for set contractual periods as coffee-plantation laborers.

Industry and migration

Coffee money rebuilt the once sleepy outpost of São Paulo de Piratininga. At the same time, the coffee barons began to look for investment hedges to protect themselves against a drop in world coffee prices. Their chief strategy, as in the past, was diversification, this time into manufacturing. Key elements were an innovative, dynamic business elite; ready capital from booming coffee exports; an enviable network of railroads; a first-class port; skilled, literate workers from the ranks of European immigrants; and, because of the web of rivers flowing down the coastal mountains, the Serra do Mar, ample sources of cheap hydroelectric power.

The stage was set for São Paulo's leap toward becoming both an industrial and a financial giant. World War I was the spark: lack of European manufactured imports left a vacuum filled by a rising class of entrepreneurs. The 1930s Depression began a process of internal migration that further fed the rapidly industrializing state's hunger for labor, and made São Paulo the world's fastest-growing major city during most of the 1960s and 1970s, with as many as 1,000 new residents arriving every day.

Independent streak

Meanwhile, São Paulo's tradition of political and intellectual independence continued into the 20th century. One of the first stirrings against the conservative old republic was a 1924 São Paulo barracks revolt led by some young army officers. In 1932, the entire state mobilized in a three-month civil war against federal intervention in state affairs.

Paulistas were also at the forefront of a nationalist intellectual movement that erupted in 1922, when the Brazilian government organized an exhibition in Rio de Janeiro marking the 100th anniversary of independence. A group of São Paulo artists and writers boycotted the official event, staging a parallel **Modern Art Week** at São Paulo's Municipal Theater.

This generation of intellectuals – the painter Anita Malfatti, novelist Mário de Andrade, critic Oswald de Andrade, sculptor Victor Brecheret, and composer Heitor Villa-Lobos – came to dominate 20th-century Brazilian arts and literature, and the continued mix of disparate elements, old and new, foreign and indigenous, is probably São Paulo's greatest charm.

São Paulo city

The state capital, also **São Paulo ❶**, is a city of contrasts. Its vast industrial park, one of the biggest and most modern in the world, attests to the force of the city's dynamo, its elegant apartments and mansions demonstrate the wealth of its powerful business elite, and its cultural and gastronomic scenes rival those of New York and London. But it also reflects Brazil's strong socioeconomic disparities. While the areas close to the city center are rich and developed, the periphery suffers from a lack of infrastructure and severe poverty. A sizeable part of the population survives on a total family income of US$250 or less a month. Yet, even for its poor, São Paulo is a 'carousel,' according to one of the city's most respected journalists, Lourenço Diaféria. 'São Paulo is a migrant city,' he notes. 'Many people manage to rise here, if only because their origins were so humble.'

Ethnic make-up

Despite the economic contrasts of São Paulo, its inhabitants share the

FACT

For the 2014 World Cup, São Paulo has gained a new stadium that is home to Corinthians. The Itaquera Arena, not far from the international airport, has a capacity of 68,000 for the cup, which will be cut to 48,000 after the tournament. It is also expected to get a new name.

A chariot with four bronze horses atop the Ipiranga Brazilian independence monument.

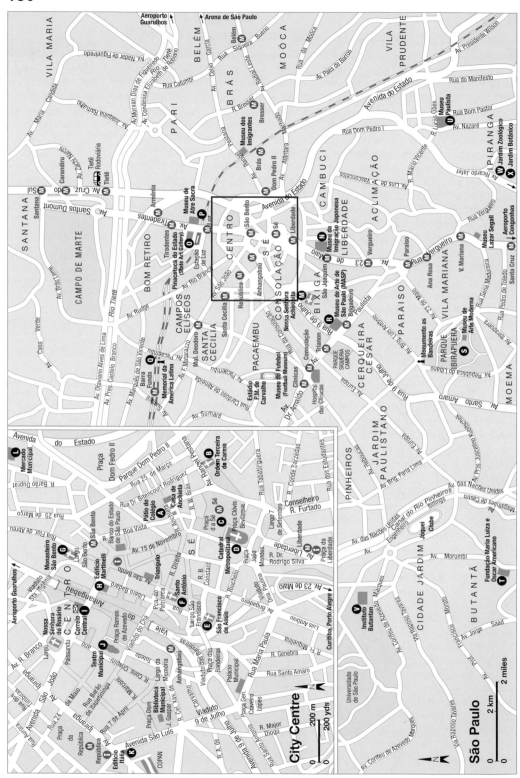

São Paulo

City Centre

usual Brazilian friendliness and *joie de vivre*. Much of this conviviality is attributed to Brazil's enormous ethnic diversity, which can be seen at its best in São Paulo. The city's 20 million inhabitants, almost 11 percent of Brazil's population, make it the fifth-largest city on Earth, smaller only than Tokyo, Mexico City, Seoul, and New York, and home to more ethnic communities than any other city in the region.

São Paulo is the third-largest Italian city in the world outside Italy, the largest Japanese city outside Japan, the biggest Portuguese city outside Portugal, the major Spanish city outside Spain, and the third-largest Lebanese city outside Lebanon – making the city a perfect host for games to be played during the 2014 World Cup. In contrast to other large Brazilian cities, black and mixed-race people make up less than 10 percent of São Paulo's population.

The business dynamo

São Paulo is the largest center of business-orientated tourism in the country, as well as its main entrance point. The city receives around 20 million visitors a year, 57 percent of whom come here on business. The city hosts 120 of the 160 largest trade shows in the country, and stands out for its sophisticated infrastructure, geared to the business traveler, with large hotel chains established in several of its neighborhoods.

Such a large influx of business travelers is mostly due to the fact that São Paulo is not only the headquarters of several of Brazil's main national and multinational banks and corporations (as has already been mentioned), but also has a modern, highly diversified industrial park that houses international blue-chip companies from important sectors such as automobile manufacturers, telecommunications, electronics, and food.

Agricultural activity is equally significant, and the Greater São Paulo region has a concentration of important agricultural distribution centers such as Mogi das Cruzes (40km/25 miles east of the city), and Biritiba Mirim, some 70km (45 miles) away.

The skyline of Sao Paulo.

In addition to this industrial and agricultural activity, São Paulo has been leaning more and more toward the provision of medical facilities and educational establishments, as well as specializing in the service sector, with large shopping malls, and leisure and cultural centers.

Historical center

The hard knot marking the center of São Paulo is a breezy esplanade and a handful of white-walled structures called the **Pátio do Colégio Ⓐ**. It was here that the hardy Jesuits Anchieta and Nóbrega founded the São Paulo de Piratininga mission in 1554. The houses and chapel were substantially reinforced during restoration work in the 1970s. The **Casa de Anchieta**, part of the complex, is now a cramped **museum** (www.pateocollegio.com.br; Tue–Sun 9am–noon, 1–5pm) displaying artifacts belonging to the village's earliest settlers.

It took nearly 100 years to add the first ring around São Paulo's humble settlement. In 1632, the **Igreja da Ordem Terceira do Carmo Ⓑ**

Statues of saints line the walls in Basilica de São Bento.

was built about 200 meters (660ft) from Anchieta's chapel, just behind the historic square, **Praça da Sé Ⓒ**. The Mannerist facade of the Carmo church is well-preserved, although largely hidden by office buildings and a fire station. On the south side of Praça da Sé, the **Catedral Metropolitana Ⓓ**, whose Gothic-Byzantine facade and 100-meter (330ft) spires were built in 1954, replaced a tottering 18th-century cathedral torn down by the city's Roman Catholic diocese in 1920.

In 1647 a building with another appealing Mannerist facade went up at one of the outlying points of the village – the pretty **Igreja de São Francisco de Assis Ⓔ**, located about 400 meters/yds from the Pátio do Colégio. A convent was attached in 1676. The complex is still bustling, and displays colonial-era woodcarvings and gold-leaf decoration.

In 1717 the **Igreja de Santo Antônio Ⓕ** was completed about half-way between the Pátio do Colégio and São Francisco. Restored in 2005, Santo Antônio's bright yellow-and-white

facade is a pleasing contrast to the gray office towers rising around it.

To the northeast of the center, in Largo São Bento, from where thousands of *bandeirante* expeditions were launched, is one of the city's oldest buildings, the **Monasteiro e Basílica de São Bento** , built in 1598. Its monks still sing angelic Gregorian chants, accompanied by one of the largest pipe organs in the country. These popular recitals can be enjoyed during some of the basilica's daily masses if you don't mind getting up early: Monday to Friday at 7am, Saturday at 6am and Sunday at 10am. Afterwards, make sure to try the fresh bread prepared by the monks at the monastery's bakery.

The 20th century brought a sweeping transformation to the old downtown. The peak coffee year of 1901 coincided with the inauguration of the brick-and-iron Luz train station, marked by an English-style clock tower and expansive gardens. The post-war years brought the **Banco do Estado de São Paulo**, modeled after New York's Empire State Building. Nearby, on **Avenida São João**, is the 30-story **Edifício Martinelli** ; the first great status symbol of São Paulo's Italian population, it was inaugurated in 1929. Just the other side of the tunnel stands the imposing **Correio Central**  (Central Post Office), built in 1920.

Municipal Theater

A few blocks south, on Rua Toledo, is the **Teatro Municipal** , an eclectic building whose Italian Renaissance and Art Nouveau styles evoke a miniature Paris Opera House. It was designed by the noted architect Francisco Ramos de Azevedo, and inaugurated in 1911 (a square close by is named after the architect). Isadora Duncan, Anna Pavlova, Maria Callas, Arturo Toscanini, Enrico Caruso, and Heitor Villa-Lobos, among other greats, performed under the 1.5-tonne Swiss crystal chandelier, and must

A fruit stall at Mercado Municipal.

have been impressed by the marble, bronze, and onyx decor. The spirit of an Italian opera singer is said to belt out forlorn solos from an upper window as his equally ghostly girlfriend clasps a lily and weeps.

West of here, on the southern corner of Praça de República, is one of the most potent symbols of the new São Paulo, the 42-story **Edifício Itália** , dating from 1965. The

FORMULA ONE MAGIC

Since Emerson Fittipaldi started the trend in 1972, armed with what was arguably the greatest Formula One design of all time, the Lotus 72D, Brazilians have won more championships than drivers of any other nationality except the British and Germans. Fittipaldi was followed by Nelson Piquet, winner of three world titles, and then by Brazil's most celebrated driver, Ayrton Senna. After winning three championships and dominating the sport, Senna died aged 34 during the San Marino Grand Prix in May 1994, and became one of Formula One's greatest legends.

Although he never won the world championship, Rubens Barrichello has driven in more Grands Prix than any other driver, while Felipe Massa, who was born in São Paulo, was just one corner away from winning the 2008 World Championship.

One motivating factor for Brazilian drivers is that Brazilians worship success, and world-conquering sportsmen become instant heroes. Yet it cannot be denied that, at its best, Brazilian driving is nothing short of magical. And that magic is more than capable of galvanizing crowds into a frenzy when a local driver wins at home. As one of the last races of the season, often the very last, the Grand Prix in São Paulo frequently decides the drivers' championship, as it did in 2008 for Lewis Hamilton, in 2009 for Jenson Button, and in 2012 for Sebastian Vettel.

rooftop restaurant, offers spectacular views over the city during the day, and a different, but equally spectacular view, at night.

To see another building designed by Ramos de Azevedo, this one in the Depression year of 1933, you must go to the northeast edge of the city center behind Praça Dom Pedro II. Here you will find the sprawling German-Gothic **Mercado Municipal** ❶ (www.mercado.municipal.com.br; Mon–Sat 6am–6pm, Sun 6am–4pm). This market is still in use, and worth a visit for its 55 pretty stained-glass windows, and wonderful displays of fresh produce. On the mezzanine level, the food court offers Spanish, Portuguese, Italian, Brazilian, Japanese, and Arab specialities.

City expansion

Until the mid-19th century, the quadrilateral of churches, embracing a dozen or so streets of one-story dwellings, was the full extent of the 'city'. The 1868 inauguration of the Jundiaí–Santos railroad to transport the cotton crop changed the face of São

Paulo for ever. Red brick and wrought iron crept into the city's previously rustic architecture. Workshops and warehouses grew up around the train station, near today's Luz commuter rail terminal.

The rise of coffee presaged even more growth. From 1892, when the first iron footbridge was flung across the downtown **Anhangabaú Valley**, through the 1920s, São Paulo added another ring of busy business districts and colorful neighborhoods. The coffee barons themselves were the first to build on the north side of the Anhangabaú, in a district called **Campos Elíseos**. Some of their Art Nouveau mansions, surrounded by high iron gates and gleaming with bronze and stained-glass finishings, can still be seen, although, overall, the neighborhood today is a shabby remnant of its glittering past. Later, more mansions were erected in nearby **Higienópolis** and then in an elegant row along **Avenida Paulista**.

Meanwhile, thousands of immigrants poured into neighborhoods that sprouted up around São Paulo's

Catedral Metropolitana.

old downtown. Vila Inglesa, Vila Economizadora, and others, their rows of red-brick houses and shops still neat and tidy, were civilized efforts to meet the city's urgent housing needs. But they didn't work.

By the time São Paulo's World War I industrial expansion began, Italian, Japanese, and Portuguese immigrants were crowded into cheek-by-jowl tenements in a ring of slums – **Brás**, **Bom Retiro**, **Bela Vista**, and **Liberdade** – circling the historic Downtown. Even today, these now cleaned-up neighborhoods contain tenements housing strong ethnic communities.

Distinctive communities

Bela Vista (popularly known as **Bixiga**), to the south of the center, is São Paulo's Little Italy. **Rua 13 de Maio**, Bixiga's heart, is a row of green-and-red *cantinas* and pretty little two-story houses. The parish church, **Nossa Senhora Achiropita** , is a squat mini-basilica graced by ornate columns and topped by an oversized dome. Achiropita is the setting of an annual festival (weekends in August)

celebrating wine, pasta, and music. Rua 13 de Maio is roped off as thousands gather for dancing, drinking (5,000 liters of wine are consumed), and eating (3 tonnes of spaghetti and 40,000 pizzas).

Bom Retiro, north of the historic center, near Luz station, retains vestiges of its past as São Paulo's Arab and Lebanese Christian neighborhood. Twisting Rua 25 de Março packs fabric and rug stores side by side in a noisy bazaar. Jewish, Muslim, and Christian merchants sip coffee together and chat as if Middle East tensions did not exist.

East of the city center, surrounding the cavernous Roosevelt commuter train terminal, is **Brás**. Predominantly Italian at the turn of the 20th century, Brás today houses thousands of migrants from the impoverished northeast. They are São Paulo's bus drivers, sun-seared road workers, and construction laborers. Their culture, rich with the sap of Brazilian folklore, can be seen on every street corner.

Nordestino (northeastern) accordion players perform nightly at the shabby north end of Praça da Sé. During the

Resident in Liberdade, the Japanese quarter.

LIBERDADE

A sprawling neighborhood centered around Rua Galvão Bueno, Liberdade, São Paulo's lively Japanese quarter, is home to 1.5 million Japanese, the largest population outside Japan. Liberdade's history began in June 1908, when the steamer Kasato Maru docked in Santos harbor with 830 Japanese immigrants on board. Their extraordinary journey from the coffee farms in the interior of the state to the founding of their own quarter in the city of São Paulo is recounted at the exceptional **Museu da Imigração Japonesa** (www.museubunkyo.org.br; Tue–Sun pm) on Rua São Joaquim. The building also houses a school that teaches the ritual of the tea ceremony.

Today, Liberdade is cherished by local people and tourists alike for its trendy shopping, top-quality oriental food and unbeatable atmosphere. To sample the cuisine, pay a visit to Kinoshita (405 Rua Jacques Felix), a traditional restaurant with innovations orchestrated by fashionable chef Tsuyoshi Murakami; or Sushi Yassu (98 Rua Tomás Gonzaga), which offers the best sushi in town, and a huge menu. Or try one delicacy at a time at the Oriental Street Fair on Sunday (9am–7pm) at Praça Liberdade (by Liberdade Metro). Day or night, Liberdade is full of life, color, and surprises. Visitors typically have only one complaint – they find it hard to believe they're in the heart of South America.

day, *repentistas* (guitar players who make up clever, rhyming lyrics on any subject suggested by onlookers) hold forth on the breezy **São Bento** esplanade. Bahian *capoeira* (Afro-Brazilian martial dance, see page 105) performers move to the eerie sound of the single-string *berimbau* outside the Anhangabaú subway station, and, at Praça do Patriarca, a *nordestino* herb salesman deals also in alligator skins, colorless elixirs, and Amazon spices sold from burlap sacks spread on the sidewalk.

From the 1940s onwards, São Paulo added more and more commercial and residential rings as it spiraled outward. **Higienópolis** and the **Jardins**, south of **Avenida Paulista**, became middle- and upper-class, high-rise apartment neighborhoods. Later, offices, apartments, and shopping centers formed another ring around elegant **Avenida Faria Lima**, just to the south of Paulista. In the 1970s, São Paulo jumped the **Pinheiros river** to start an even glitzier ring in hilly **Morumbi**, where landscaped mansions include the official residence of the state governor.

Brazilian sculpture in Pinacoteca do Estado.

Museums and galleries

Although São Paulo's citizens are known as workaholics, the city offers plenty of leisure pursuits. It has the best cultural attractions in the country, as well as excellent parks.

Behind the Luz train station and park (north of the center; Metro Luz or Tiradentes) is the **Pinacoteca do Estado** ⊙ (State Art Gallery; Praça da Luz 2; www.pinacoteca.org.br; Tue–Sun 10am–5.30pm; free on Sat), a beautiful neoclassical building designed by Ramos de Azevedo in 1905. What MASP (see page 193) does for Western art, the state gallery's 5,000-piece collection does for its Brazilian counterpart. Highlights include sculptures by Vitor Brecheret, creator of the *Bandeirantes Monument*, and Júnior's *A Leitura*, a portrait of a girl reading against a background of palm trees and striped awnings.

Across Avenida Tiradentes from the Pinacoteca do Estado is São Paulo's most important collection of colonial art and artifacts. The **Museu de Arte Sacra** ℗ (Avenida Tiradentes 676; Metro Armenia or Tiradentes; www.museuartesacra.org.br; Tue–Sun 11am–7pm) contains 1,000 pieces displayed in the former cloisters and chapel of the labyrinthine **Mosteiro da Luz**, and represents the evolution of sacred art in Brazil.

The main Baroque structure of the monastery was completed in 1774, although portions date from the late 17th century. The collection is completed by oil portraits of São Paulo's first bishops, gold and silver altar accoutrements, carved gold-leaf fragments of churches torn down by the juggernaut of 20th-century progress, and rare woodcarvings by Brazil's great 18th-century sculptor Antônio Francisco Lisboa, better known as Aleijadinho (see page 205).

To the west, the **Memorial da América Latina** ⊙, designed by Oscar Niemeyer on his traditional bold arcs of concrete, was built in 1989 (Metro: Barra Funda). The buildings house an

important **Latin American Cultural Center** (Tue–Sun 9am–6pm; free) with a museum, a library, an auditorium, and an exhibition center.

You need to go to the south of the city center (Metro Trianon-MASP) to visit MASP, the **Museu de Arte de São Paulo ®** (1578 Avenida Paulista; www.masp.art.br; Tue–Sun 11am–6pm). This is São Paulo's cultural pride, with nearly 1,000 pieces originating from Ancient Greece and contemporary Brazil. The unusual display arrangement – rows of paintings encased in smoked-glass slabs – was designed chiefly as a teaching aid. Detailed explanations on the back of each display put the artists and their work into historical perspective.

The museum is like an art history book – but offering the real thing instead of color plates. Raphael, Bosch, Holbein, Rembrandt, Monet, Van Gogh, Goya, Reynolds, and Picasso are just a few of the artists representing major European trends. The museum also includes a survey of Brazilian art from 19th-century court painters Almeida Júnior and Pedro Américo, to 20th-century Modernists Portinari,

Di Cavalcanti, and Tarsila do Amaral.

Further south is São Paulo's most important park and modern-art venue. **Ibirapuera ®** (Metro Vila Mariana or Paraiso and a short taxi ride) is a huge area of trees, lawns, and handsome pavilions, completed to celebrate São Paulo's 400th anniversary in 1954. Today, some 200,000 *paulistas* use its playgrounds, picnic areas, and sports complex on sunny weekends. At the front of the park are two of São Paulo's most noted monuments: the 72-meter (235ft) **Obelisk and Mausoleum** honoring heroes of the 1932 civil war, and Vitor Brecheret's **Bandeirantes Monument**, a tribute to the 17th-century pioneers (see page 36). Ibirapuera's low-slung curving pavilions, designed by Oscar Niemeyer, constitute São Paulo's most important cultural center (see page 193).

Off to the west, across from the imposing state governor's palace

The Museu de Arte de São Paulo mixes ancient Greek and contemporary Brazilian artworks.

Contemplating an exhibit in MASP.

ART IN THE PARK

The main showcase of the pavilions in Ibirapuera Park is a three-story rectangle of ramps and glass designed by Oscar Niemeyer, a building which hosts São Paulo's prestigious Bienal art show (www.bienal.org.br; Oct–Dec in even-numbered years). Held here since 1957, this is the world's largest regularly scheduled arts event, bringing together all that is new, experimental, and weird in the worlds of art and music.

The third floor of the pavilion displays a permanent collection of contemporary Brazilian art. Linked to the pavilion by an undulating breezeway, the **Museu de Arte Moderna** (www.mam.org.br; Tue–Sun 10am–5.30pm) plays host to changing exhibitions of work by Brazil's contemporary sculptors and painters.

El Cabriton y Amigos fashion store.

Museu do Ipiranga.

in Morumbi, the **Fundação Maria Luiza e Oscar Americano** ❶ (4077 Avenida Morumbi; www.fundacaooscar americano.org.br; Tue–Fri 11am–5pm, Sat–Sun 10am–5pm) is São Paulo's most bucolic setting for art appreciation. It's a lovely spot, but you will have to take a taxi to get there. Oscar Americano was a noted architect and collector who willed his estate to the public as an arts foundation when he died in 1974. The discrete glass-and-stone mansion displays works by Di Cavalcanti, Portinari, Guignard, 17th-century Dutch painter Franz Post, and many others, against a lush background of broad lawns and landscaped woods. A tearoom overlooks the ground-floor patio and is open until 6pm. String quartets and soloists perform in a small auditorium on Sunday afternoon.

Two more recent and highly rated museums are the **Museu da Lingua Portuguesa** (Praça da Luz; www.museu-dalingua-portuguesa.org.br; Tue–Sun 10am–5pm) and the **Museu do Futebol** (Praça Charles Miller; www.museu-dofutebol.org.br; Tue–Sun 10am–6pm).

The modern, interactive museum, located at the gates of the Pacaembu Stadium, is spread over three floors and tells the history of Brazilian football through an extensive archive of photographs, videos and historical objects. The museum covers not only the major Brazilian domestic teams, but also the national team that has on five World Cups.

Imperial reminders

In the tranquil suburb of Ipiranga, the sprawling **Museu Paulista** ❶ (Metro Vila Mariana and a short taxi ride; Avenida Nazaré s/n; www.mp.usp. br; Tue–Sun 9am–5pm) marks the spot where Pedro I declared Brazilian independence. An equestrian monument stands on the site where Pedro shouted, 'Independence or death!' before a small entourage. The emperor's remains are buried beneath the bronze-and-concrete landmark.

The massive, neoclassical museum building, also known as **Museu do Ipiranga**, is a hodgepodge of historical and scientific exhibits. One wing displays artifacts relating to Pedro and his family. Another includes furnishings, farm implements, and even horse carts from São Paulo's colonial past. Research by the University of São Paulo on Brazil's Amerindians has yielded material for several galleries, including an interesting display of pre-Columbian pottery from the Amazon island of Marajó.

Other exhibits honor the aviation pioneer Alberto Santos Dumont (who was born in Petrópolis), and the state militiamen who fought in the 1924 *tenentes* military revolt (see page 40). A separate gallery displays Pedro Américo's 1888 painting *Independencia ou Morte*, a romanticized portrayal of Pedro I's famous declaration quoted above.

To the southwest of the city, in the grounds of the São Paulo University, is the **Instituto Butantan** ❶ (Avenida Vital Brasil 1500; Metro Clínicas and a taxi ride; www.butantan.gov.

br; Tue–Sun 9am–4.30pm), founded in 1901, is one of the world's leading centers for the study of poisonous snakes. The slithery reptiles are everywhere – coiled behind glass in ornate kiosks, piled one on top of the other in grassy habitats, stuffed and mounted in display cases next to hairy spiders and scorpions. Part of the collection was destroyed by fire in 2010. Altogether, there are some 1,000 live snakes on the premises. Periodically, staff members will milk venom from their fangs.

Dining and shopping

For most *paulista* as well as foreign visitors, São Paulo is above all else a restaurant city. With its many ethnic communities, each with their own national dishes and restaurants, São Paulo has raised food appreciation to the level of worship. For the *paulista*, the substitute for Rio's beach life is an active nightlife centered on wine and dinner at one of the city's many restaurants. The largest concentration of good restaurants is in Jardim Paulistano, Cerqueira Cesar, and Itaim Bibi (see page 203). Although most restaurants open early, they do not fill up until 9 or 10pm on weekdays and even later at weekends. Wednesday and Saturday are *feijoada* days in São Paulo. *Feijoada* is one of the most traditional Brazilian dishes, and some say that it started with the African slaves who added bread and offal to the pieces of pork left over by their masters. Another theory is that it derives from European recipes such as Portuguese stews. This irresistible calorific bomb of black beans and several types of meat is best eaten at lunchtime, preferably when a digestive nap can be taken afterwards.

When *paulistas* are not working or dining out, they are usually shopping. **Rua Augusta**, around Rua Oscar Freire in Jardim Paulista, is the traditional headquarters for fashionable but pricey men's and women's wear. Forum, Zoomp, Osklen, and Ellus are famous boutiques. There are more boutiques in various galleries spread along Rua Augusta. **Rua Oscar Freire** and its surroundings

Café life on Rua Augusta.

FURTHER AFIELD

For those with time to go further afield (and who don't mind a relatively expensive taxi ride), there is a completely different side to São Paulo. The city has one of the world's largest zoos, with no fewer than 3,200 animals and 444 species, mostly occupying natural habitats. The Jardim Zoológico W (4241 Avenida Miguel Stéfano; www.zoologico.sp.gov.br; Tue–Sun 9am–5pm), noted for its tropical bird collection, attracts several million visitors annually.

On the same street as the zoo is the Jardim Botânico X (Botanic Garden; Tue–Sun 9am–5pm). There is public access to 360,000 sq meters (430,000 sq yds) of gardens, with two glasshouses containing hundreds of delicate plant species, including a prized orchid collection. The Botanic Institute here educates the public on the various ecosystems of Brazil.

North of the city, there is a delightful open space, the Horto Florestal, also known as Parque Albert Löefgren (931 Rua do Horto; daily 6am–6pm). Founded in 1896, the park has a playground, good walking trails, and the Pedra Grande viewpoint, which offers a beautiful view of the north of São Paulo city. Within the park, the Museu Florestal Octavio Vecchi (tel: 11-6231 8555; Tue–Fri 9–11.50am, 1.30–4.30pm; Sun 10am–3.30pm) displays a huge variety of native woods.

São Paulo has an ever-growing high-fashion scene.

The Osasco Orchestra performing.

(Rua Bela Cintra and Rua Haddock Lobo) are known as 'São Paulo's 5th Avenue,' where you can find designer names including Versace, Fendi, Montblanc, Armani, Kenzo, Thierry Mugler, Cartier, Bulgari, Christian Dior, and Tommy Hilfiger. A Saturday morning stroll through this area allows a fascinating glimpse into the lifestyle of the Brazilian rich and famous. Many excellent restaurants are also located in these streets, notably Fasano, Gero, Rodeio, and Antiquarius.

For antique-lovers the best bet is to visit one of the fairs that take place in museums and city squares at the weekend. The most famous are the MASP fair every Sunday at the Museu de Arte de São Paulo (1578 Avenida Paulista; 9am–5pm; free); and the fair in Shopping Center Iguatemi's parking lot (Avenida Faria Lima; Sun 9am–5pm; free).

But the *paulistano*'s first love is the shopping center. The largest is **Morumbi**. The oldest, the most elegant, and, for many, the best, is **Iguatemi**, on Avenida Faria Lima (there is also **JK Iguatemi** in Vila Olimpia); the most traditional is **Ibirapuera**, a boxy structure near the park; and the classy **Shopping Cidade Jardim** in Morumbi. There is also **Shopping Light**, an up-market mall with boutiques and eateries near the Anhangabau Metro station in the center of town, which is located in the old power company headquarters, built in 1929; also in the center, on Rua Vinte e Quatro de Maio, is **Galeria do Rock**, a shopping center just for rock fans. For outlet shopping, **Outlet Premium** is at 72 Km of Rodovia dos Bandeirantes, about an hour from the city center, between the Hopi Hari and Wet'n'Wild theme parks.

Nightlife

São Paulo has a seemingly infinite number of bars *(botecos)*, nightclubs, and discos. The choice of where to go depends on taste, money, season, age, and what is or is not currently trendy. São Paulo's nightlife comes alive around midnight. Be warned that instead of an entrance fee, many venues use a card with a pre-set minimum amount that you pay at the end of the night. Even soft drinks can be expensive, and some places also charge an 'artistic cover' to pay for the cost of the band.

The most varied nightlife, packed with the young and beautiful, can be found in **Itaim Bibi**, **Vila Olímpia**, and **Vila Madalena**, where artists, university students, and alternative minds meet for some of the best 'see and be seen' ambiance in town. One of the best draft beers is served in the south of the city at Original (137 Rua Grauna, Moema), but for an incredible night view of the city, Skye is champion. Attached to the restaurant of the same name, Skye is located on the roof of the Hotel Unique (4700 Avenida Brigadeiro Luis Antonio, Jardim Paulista; www.hotelunique.com.br). Varied live music can be heard at Grazie a Dio! (67 Rua Girassol, Vila

Madalena; www.grazieadio.com.br); and great dancing at the CB Bar (871 Rua Brigadeiro Galvao, Barra Funda; www.cbbar.com.br). For those looking for a truly romantic and classy venue, the Baretto at Hotel Fasano (88 Rua Vitorio Fasano, Jardim Paulista; www.fasano.com.br) is unbeatable, and was named best bar if the world by Wallpaper magazine. Bars on Rua da Consolação (between Alameda Jacé and Alameda Tietê) generally cater to a gay clientele.

Cigar aficionados should head for the Havana Club in Hotel Renaissance (2233 Alameda Santos, Cerqueira César) – a comfortable cigar lounge and bar with its own dance floor. For cowboys and cowgirls, there is Jardineira Beer (1051 Avenida dos Bandeirantes, Vila Olímpia).

Diverse entertainments

São Paulo's post-World War II growth (and money) has made it a magnet for world-class performers. A typical season might bring the Bolshoi Ballet, the New York Philharmonic, Beyoncé, Lady Gaga, Madonna, AC/DC, James Taylor, and many other stars to venues including the Anhembi Convention Center, the state-of-the-art Credicard Hall, Ibirapuera Gymnasium, HSBC Brasil, WTC Golden Hall, the Teatro Municipal, Direct TV Music Hall in Moema, Santana Hall in the north zone, and the most recent addition to São Paulo nightlife, Claro Live! House located in the Jockey Club. The Alfa Real Theater, next to the Transamérica Hotel, offers modern and comfortable facilities for the performing arts. Top Brazilian acts also perform in the more intimate setting at Tom Jazz in Higienópolis. (Check the local press for details, especially Veja São Paulo.)

São Paulo competes head-to-head with Rio when it comes to X-rated entertainment. Glitzy strip bars featuring explicit 'erotic' acts start on Rua Augusta near the Caesar Park Hotel, extending all the way to Rua Nestor Pestana downtown. Others are located on Rua Bento Freitas near the Hilton. In Itaim Bibi, near Ibirapuera, there is also the renowned Café Photo.

Hip cocktail bar Escape can be found in the popular nightlife area Itaim Bibi.

A restored steam locomotive at Paranapiacaba.

Mountain resorts

Like the inhabitants of Rio de Janeiro, São Paulo residents can vacation in the mountains or on the shore without leaving their state. At 1,628 meters (5,600ft), and 167km (103 miles) from São Paulo, in a lush valley of the Mantiqueira range, **Campos do Jordão** ② is São Paulo's chief mountain resort, with alpine chalets and winter weather. The month-long Festival de Inverno de Campos do Jordão (www.festivalcamposdojordao.org. br), held throughout July at the modern **Claudio Santoro Auditorium,** features programs of classical and popular music, and has become one of the most important musical events in the country.

Next door is the pleasantly landscaped **Felícia Leirner sculpture garden** (Tue–Sun 10am–6pm; free). On display are magnificent bronze and granite works by the Polish-born artist whose name it takes.

The hub of Campos do Jordão's busy downtown is a row of chalet-style restaurants and shops. Local products include metal, wood, and leather crafts. Nearby is a tranquil lake circled by horse-drawn carriages for hire. Yellow and brown trolleys carrying tourists occasionally rattle past.

Ringing the downtown area are around 50 hotels and dozens of summer homes belonging to the *paulistano* elite. The largest such abode, bearing the impressive name **Palácio Boa Vista**, is the state governor's winter retreat. A portion of this Tudor-style mansion has been converted into a **museum** (Wed–Sun 10am–noon, 2–5pm). Attractions of the museum include 19th-century furnishings, and oil paintings by *paulista* artists, including Tarsila do Amaral, Di Cavalcanti, and Cândido Portinari.

About 12km (7 miles) from downtown, Itapeva Peak offers an impressive view of the Paraíba river valley, where São Paulo coffee bushes first took root more than a century ago.

Somewhat closer to São Paulo, 60km (40 miles) north on the Fernão Dias Highway, and better organized for visitors, is **Atibaia** ❸, a mountain resort and São Paulo's peach and strawberry capital. A winter festival

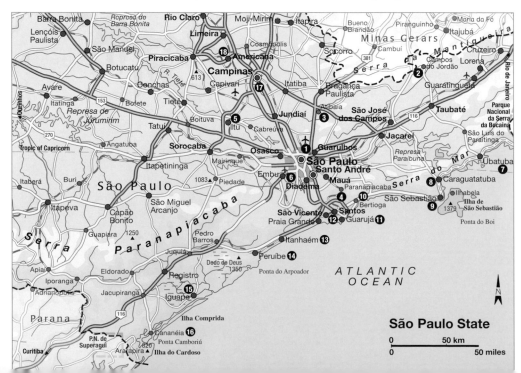

São Paulo State

0   50 km

0   50 miles

honors the lowly strawberry, selling everything from strawberry jam to pink strawberry liqueurs.

At 800 meters (2,600ft) above sea level, Atibaia's crisp, clean air attracts families in search of hotels with sports and leisure facilities, such as the Village Eldorado and the Estancia Atibainha. The younger crowd comes to Atibaia to practice hang-gliding or paragliding from the platforms of the stunning Pedra Grande.

The city's delightfully landscaped Parque Municipal features mineral-water springs, lakes, and a **railroad museum** (weekends and holidays 10am–6pm). Near the center is Atibaia's white-walled **Museu Historico Municipal João Batista Conti** (Praça Bento Paes; Tue–Sun 10am–5pm; free), dating from 1836.

Paranapiacaba

Some 60km (40 miles) from São Paulo, traveling toward the coast, is **Paranapiacaba** ❹, a quaint railroad outpost frozen in time. Built in 1867 by British railroaders, the brick-and-board station and row houses are a portrait of Victorian England. Even the tall clock tower is reminiscent of the one at Westminster. At a height of 800 meters (2,500ft), Paranapiacaba (which means sea view in the Tupi-Guarani language) was the last station on the Jundiaí–Santos line before the breathtaking plunge down the Great Escarpment. Paranapiacaba offers few amenities, however. There are no hotels or restaurants of note, only a few fruit and soft-drink stands. A **museum** (Tue; 9am–4pm) displays 19th-century train carriages and memorabilia.

Day trips

Quaint, prosperous **Itu** ❺, 100km (60 miles) from São Paulo on the Castelo Branco Highway, is another fresh-air paradise. The town's delights include 18th- and 19th-century row houses on pretty pedestrian streets, and a handful of cluttered antique

stores. The **Museu Republicano da Convenção de Itu** (Tue–Sat 10am–4.45pm, Sun 9am–3.45pm; free) off the main square exhibits colonial and imperial-era furnishings and artifacts. A small **Museu da Energia** (Tue–Sun 10am–5pm; free) tells the story of electricity.

Closer to São Paulo, 28km (17 miles) on the Regis Bittencourt Highway, is **Embu** ❻, the state handicrafts capital. Most stores open Tuesday to Sunday, 8am–6pm, and every Sunday the town's two main squares, and a network of pedestrian streets linking them, become a vast primitive-arts, handicrafts, and Brazilian food festival, when cars are not allowed in the town's center.

Ceramics, leather- and metal-worked handicrafts, woolen goods, lacework, knitted items, and colorful batiks are for sale at wooden stalls. On Largo dos Jesuitas, woodcarvers practice their craft in the open air, often surrounded by an audience. Rows of quaint 18th-century houses serve as stores for antique and rustic furniture.

In the Mountain resort of Campos do Jordão.

TIP

The coast road between São Paulo and Rio de Janeiro is truly spectacular. Easy enough to drive in one day, but if time is on your side try to spend two or three nights at different spots along the way.

Visitors can sample Bahian delicacies such as *vatapá* (a seafood or chicken stew) and coconut sweets at outdoor stalls, or choose from among a dozen interesting restaurants. Nearby, O Garimpo and Casa do Barao specialize in varied Brazilian cuisine.

Beach resorts

The beach resorts of São Paulo are not something for which the state is famous. Nevertheless, its stretch of the Rio–Santos Highway, one of the most beautiful in the country, offers the visitor more than 400km (240 miles) of beaches, which are regular retreats for affluent city workers during weekends and holidays.

Ubatuba 7, only 70km (40 miles) from Paraty in southern Rio de Janeiro (see page 177), is convenient for both São Paulo and Rio, although its charms are low-key rather than picturesque. A total of 85km (50 miles) of beaches curl around Ubatuba's inlets and islands. Boat trips take visitors to the Anchieta Prison ruins on one of the main islands, then continue up the coast to the eerie remains of Lagoinha

Sugar Plantation, partially destroyed by fire during the 19th century.

Caraguatatuba 8, 50km (30 miles) south of Ubatuba on State Highway 55, has almost as many beaches but fewer historical attractions than its northern neighbor. Its excellent Pousada Tabatinga offers several sports facilities just a step away from the sand.

São Sebastião 9, 25km (15 miles) south from Caraguatatuba on Highway 55, has an eclectic clutch of beaches distributed over some 100km (60 miles). Maresias and Camburi are good for surfing and eating out, with a lively nightlife. Boicucanga has more accommodation options and Barra do Una has good fishing, boat trips, and dining. Historical buildings and services are concentrated in the center of São Sebastião.

From São Sebastião, ferry boats take visitors to the village of **Ilhabela**, also called São Sebastião Island. The mountain scenery, waterfalls, beaches, and azure sea have made it popular with São Paulo's wealthy set. Ilhabela is also a byword for water sports, and every July it hosts one of the largest sailing events in South America.

Another 100km (60 miles) down Highway 55 is peaceful **Bertioga 10**, where there is some interesting flora and fauna. The **Forte São João**, with blazing white walls and miniature turrets, guards a narrow inlet. Its ancient cannons loom over passing pleasure craft. The fortress dates from 1547, and is considered the oldest in Brazil.

Thirty kilometers (18 miles) south of Bertioga is one of the most frequented towns on São Paulo's coast, the resort of **Guarujá 11**. **Enseada** is the most popular beach, a horseshoe of spray, sand, and gleaming hotels recalling Copacabana. Nearby is the more isolated **Pernambuco** beach. São Paulo's moneyed elite have made this their Malibu. Mansions of every architectural style – surrounded by broad lawns and closed in by fences, hedges, and guards – look out over surf and green and gray offshore islands.

An historical house façade.

Like São Paulo, Guarujá is a city for restaurant-goers. Highly recommended are Il Faro for Italian cuisine, Les Epices for French, Rufino's for seafood, and the bar and restaurant of the Casa Grande Hotel, a sprawling colonial inn on **Praia da Enseada**. Just a few blocks from the Casa Grande is the narrow area of **Praia de Pitangueiras**. Streets near the beach have been pedestrianized so that people can browse unhindered in the dozens of boutiques, and handicraft and jewelry stores.

Santos

Not far from downtown Guarujá, visitors can catch the car ferry across an oily inlet to **Santos 12**, São Paulo's chief port. *Santistas* don't try to hide the business end of their island – hulking tankers ply the narrow channels spewing oil; freight containers are piled in ugly pens or next to dilapidated warehouses. Unfortunately, this decay has spread from the port to the city's old downtown area. Historic **Igreja do Carmo**, with portions dating from 1589, is a gray

facade next to a broken-down train station. Nearby, a slum district has sprung up around the 17th-century **São Bento** church and its **Museu de Arte Sacra** (Rua Santa Joana D'Arc 795; Tue–Sun 2–5pm; free). The recently restored **Bolsa Oficial de Café**, in Rua 15 de Novembre houses a small but interesting coffee museum and café. There is also a football memorial dedicated to the city's greatest players.

The ocean side of Santos, however, shows the same whitewashed face as Guarujá. The **Museu de Pesca** (Fishing Museum; Tue–Sun 10am–6pm), near the Guarujá ferry landing, exhibits stuffed fish killed in nearby waters, an immense 91kg (200lb) octopus, and the bones of a 23-meter (76ft) whale, as well as fishing boats.

São Vicente, Brazil's oldest settlement, only 5km (3 miles) from Santos, was the first Portuguese permanent settlement (1532). The main Gonzaguinha beach is lined with white and pastel-colored houses, bars and outdoor restaurants. São Vicente is the gateway to Brazil's most crowded

Admiring the sunset at Ilhabela.

beach – **Praia Grande**, in season a seemingly endless stretch of spray, grayish-brown sand, and bobbing human bodies.

Another 60km (35 miles) south on Highway 55 is a very different scene: slow-moving **Itanhaém** , another of Brazil's oldest settlements. Parts of the gray, spooky Nossa Senhora da Conceição chapel date back to 1534.

Other beach towns south of São Vicente include pretty **Peruíbe** (80km/50 miles); **Iguape** (200km/120 miles), on a quiet inlet formed by Ilha Comprida; and remote **Cananéia** (280km/170 miles), which has a nature reserve and also offers boat excursions to nearby islands, which do have some isolated beaches.

Northern towns

Two urban centers in the northern interior are worth a brief visit (if you are passing that way). One is industrial **Campinas** (100km/60 miles from São Paulo), which grew wealthy from sugar and coffee. It is now the site of one of Brazil's best universities, Unicamp, a refuge for left-wing

teachers during the years of military repression. The city's fine neoclassical **Catedral Metropolitana** on Largo do Rosário dates from 1883. The main cultural venue, which has a noted symphony orchestra, is the **Centro de Convivência** (Praça Imprensa Fluminense).

Nearby **Americana** was the most successful of the Brazilian communities settled by Confederates fleeing the southern states of the United States after the Civil War (1861–5). They were drawn here by the prospect of cheap land, religious freedom, and the fact that slave labor – an institution that the war had brought to an end in the US – was still legal in Brazil.

For fans of aviation, some 250km/150 miles from São Paulo, outside São Carlos, is the **TAM Museum** (Rodovia SP 318, Agua Vermelha; www.museutam.com.br; Wed–Sun 10am–4pm), one of the largest aviation museums in the world to be owned and run by an airline. The museum reopened in 2010 after being closed for a long period for refurbishment and modernization.

The engraving of three Portuguese Galleons sailing ships on a wall of a historical building in downtown Santos.

RESTAURANTS

Baby Beef Rubaiyat
86 Alameda Santos, Paraíso
Tel: 11-3170 5100
Avenida Brigadeiro Faria Lima 2954, Itaim Bibi
Tel: 11-3165 8888
Open: L&D daily.
Elegant *churrascarias*, the first of which opened back in 1952, and among the city's best. Not a *rodizo*, but an à la carte grill, plus a large buffet selection. *Feijoada* served on Saturdays. The same group owns the Figueira Rubaiyat on Rua Haddock Lobo. **$$**

Cantaloup
474 Rua Manuel Guedes, Itaim Bibi
Tel: 11-3078 3445
Open: L&D Mon–Fri, D only Sat, L only Sun.
A real favorite: creative, contemporary food on an ever-changing menu served in a beautifully refurbished bread factory in Itaim Bibi. Elegant setting with high ceilings. Tables well spaced. **$$**

Capim Santo
471 Alameda Ministro Rocha Azevedo, Cerqueira Cesar
Tel: 11-3068 8486
Open: L&D Mon–Sat, L Sun.
Contemporary Brazilian cuisine from an à la carte dinner menu. Particularly good value is the lunchtime buffet with seafood, salad, and meat. Special children's menu. Also has a branch in the beach resort of Trancoso in Bahia. **$$**

Cheiro Verde
1413 Rua Peixoto Gomide, Jardim Paulista
Tel: 11-289 6853
Open: L daily.
In a city and country famous for its barbecue houses, vegetarians are well catered for here, in this a simple, friendly multi-award-winning natural restaurant. First opened in 1980 and moved to its current, more comfortable location in 2006. Seats 72. **$**

DOM
549 Rua Barão de Capanema, Cerqueira Cesar
Tel: 11-3088 0761
Open: L Mon–Fri, D Mon–Sat.
The best-known Brazilian restaurant among the serious global gourmets. It has won numerous awards and is often listed with the world's top ten restaurants. Creative, contemporary Brazilian cooking at its very best from, Alex Atala, one of Brazil's (and the world's) most talented and creative chefs. Outstanding. **$$$**

Fasano
88 Rua Vitorio Fasano, Cerqueira Cesar
Tel: 11-3062 4000
Open: Mon–Sat D only.
Since 1982, one of the most luxurious, elegant, and fashionably cool restaurants in São Paulo. Finest Italian cooking in the Fasano Hotel, which also has one of the city's great bars, Baretto. Also in the hotel is the less formal restaurant, Nonno Ruggero. **$$$**

Fogo de Chão
964 Avenida Moreiera Guimarães, Mocma
Tel: 11-5056 1795
Avenida Santo Amaro 6824, Santo Amaro
Tel: 11-5524 0500
Avenida dos Bandeirantes 538, Vila Olimpia
Tel: 11-5505 0791
Shopping Center Norte, Vila Guilherme
Tel: 11-2089 1736
Open: L&D daily.
Fogo de Chão is one of best-known and most respected chains of *rodizio* barbecue houses in Brazil. These are unquestionably four of the city's top rodizios – each one a carnivores' paradise. Go when you are really hungry. They can also be found in Rio, Brasilia, Salvador, and Belo Horizonte. **$$$**

Gero
1629 Rua Haddock Lobo
Tel: 11-3064 0005
Open: L&D daily.
A smart, fashionable bistro version of Fasano (see page 197), offering the same quality at a slightly lower price. In São Paulo the Fasano group is also responsible for the Gero Caffe and Armani Caffe in Shopping Iguatemi and the French bistro, Parigi, in Itaim. **$$**

Jardim de Napoli
463 Rua Dr Martinico Prado, Higienópolis
Tel: 11-3666 3022
Open: daily, all day.
This typical Italian cantina serves good pasta, and pizzas, which are considered the best in town. First opened for business back in 1949, this is one of São Paulo's best-known and loved restaurants. There is also a more modern branch in Higienópolis Shopping. **$**

Mani
210 Rua Joaquim Antunes, Jardim Paulistano
Tel: 11-3085 4148
Open: L&D Mon–Sat, L Sun.
Mani chef, Helena Rizzo, created an entire menu for the Brazilian airline TAM and is considered to be one of Brazil's most creative chefs. Her award-winning restaurant in Jardim Paulistano serves contemporary Brazilian food in truly charming surroundings. **$$$**

Massimo
1826 Alameda Santos, Cerqueira Cesar
Tel: 11-3284 0311
Open: L&D daily.
Timeless top-class Italian and international cuisine in spacious, elegant surroundings; excellent wines. One of the restaurants that, on opening in 1976, helped to build São Paulo's reputation as a gourmet centre. Popular *feijoada* buffet served on Saturday. **$$$**

Portucale
418 Rua Nova Cidade, Vila Olímpia
Tel: 11-3845 8929
Open: L&D Tue–Sat, L Sun.
Traditional, honest Portuguese specialities, always nicely presented. Any based on *bacalhau*, of which there were eight on the menu at the last count, is recommended.There are *Fado* shows at the weekend. **$$**

Rodeio
1498 Rua Haddock Lobo, Cerqueira Cesar
Tel: 11-3474 1333
Open: L&D daily.
Founded in 1958, Rodeio is one of São Paulo's most traditional and well-known barbecue houses and grills. It set the standards we now take for granted in Brazilian *churrascarias*. Mouth watering meats and other dishes are served from an à la carte menu. More relaxed and a lot less frenetic than other barbecue houses, Rodeio often becomes a firm favourite with people who have dined there. **$$**

BRAZILIAN BAROQUE

Brazil's exuberant tradition in Baroque art and architecture is one of the most memorable sights in the east of the country.

Unlike the monumental structures that sometimes overwhelm many Latin American capitals, Brazil's earliest public works of art are fresh, noble, and lively. The Baroque movement had three main centers in 18th-century Brazil: Salvador, Rio de Janeiro, and Minas Gerais.

The Jesuits, who sponsored the colonial explosion of Baroque in Bahia, were noted for their openness to new ideas and local trends, encouraging what many in Europe regarded as 'the secular opulence' of the Baroque aesthetic. Brazilian themes were brought to bear on the decorative arts, and great bunches of tropical fruits and wavy palm fronds formed an incongruous background to the traditional Bible stories depicted in paintings and woodcarvings. In Rio de Janeiro, the Baroque experience was less intense, as Rio was then secondary to the vice-regal capital of Salvador; and many colonial buildings were destroyed during an early 20th-century construction boom. The best surviving example is the Igreja de Nossa Senhora da Glória do Outeiro, dating from 1714 (see page 146).

It was in Minas Gerais that Brazilian Baroque reached its apex. Ouro Preto, the former state capital, is an architectural delight. The secret is the substitution of the curve for the line. The purest example, Ouro Preto's Nossa Senhora do Rosário dos Pretos chapel (see page 212), has a convex facade, ending in two bell-tower curves. Inside, the nave is an oval. Doors and windows are framed by elegant archways.

The Catholic Church invested heavily in elaborate interiors. Artists and architects were always trying to out do their rivals when commissioned to build a new church, as can be seen in this partial view of São Francisco Church in Salvador, Bahia.

The life of St Francis is depicted on this ceiling in the right hand chapel of São Francisco de Assis church in Ouro Preto.

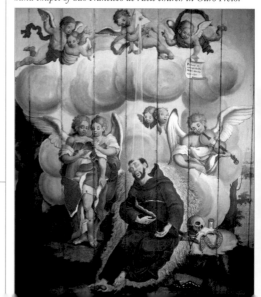

The statue of prophet Isaiah by Aleijadinho at the Bom Jesus de Matosinhos Sanctuary in Congonhas, Minas Gerais.

Glória's Church, Rio de Janeiro.

BRAZIL'S BAROQUE GENIUS

One reason for the artistic unity of *mineiro* churches is the dominance of one Baroque artisan – Antônio Francisco Lisboa (1730s–1814). The uneducated son of a Portuguese craftsman and a black slave woman, he became an individualistic sculptor and architect.

Struck by a crippling disease (which was probably leprosy) that left his hands injured, he was known as Aleijadinho – 'The Little Cripple.' Undaunted, he continued working by strapping a hammer and chisel to his wrists. Lisboa applied the principles of European Baroque that he learnt from books and missionaries. His greatest achievements are in Ouro Preto (see page 210) and in Congonhas do Campo in eastern Minas Gerais (see page 214), where he carved the 12 soapstone figures of the Old Testament Prophets and the 66 Stations of the Cross in wood.

Somewhat dramatically, recent scholars have suggested that the artist Lisboa never existed. No historical references to the man have been found outside of a single text, and that book is not contemporary with his works. There is no evidence of his designs as an architect, and even his parentage remains unproven.

The myth of the injured artist is an attractive figure, however, and many see his character as representative of a Brazilian culture.

Much of the blue tile work found in colonial buildings was inspired by azulejo tiles imported from Portugal.

The magnificent church of Saint Francis of Assisi, built in 1779 and considered one of Aleijadinho's masterpieces, is one of many Baroque churches to be found on the streets of Ouro Preto.

A interior detail of the Igreja de Nossa Senhora da Glória do Outeiro.

Aleijadinho's masterpiece, the chapel of São Francisco de Assis.

MINAS GERAIS AND ESPIRITO SANTO

Minas Gerais made its fortune from gold and diamonds, and spent much of it on splendid Baroque architecture. The less-visited state of Espírito Santo is home to three impressive nature reserves.

Brasília

Rio de Janeiro

T he state of Minas Gerais is a Brazilian giant. It covers 587,000 sq km (352,200 sq miles), and has nearly 20 million inhabitants. It is rugged and isolated, with a central plateau rising sharply from an escarpment that rims the entire eastern frontier.

Minas means mines, and everything from gold and diamonds to iron has flowed from its veins of mineral ore to the world. Even today, the streets of its quaint, ancient towns are pink with iron-ore dust and its rivers red with it.

Folklore contrasts the *mineiro* sharply with the extravagant *carioca* and the industrious *paulista*. The *mineiro* is said to be stubborn, cautious, hard working, and thrifty. He is also an assiduous preserver; he has kept not only the music-box churches of his Baroque past, but also saved family heirlooms and trinkets, which clutter his attic rooms.

São João del Rei residents have preserved the music, and even the instruments, of the 18th century, performing a liturgy of Baroque orchestral pieces every Holy Week. Yet *mineiros* are both conservative and progressive. The state contains Brazil's best-preserved colonial towns, but *mineiros* built the nation's first planned city, Belo Horizonte. And it was a group of *mineiros*, led by President Juscelino Kubitschek, who created the new capital, Brasília.

Ouro Preto's steep streets.

Colonial isolation

Much of the *mineiro* traditionalism can be traced back to the state's isolation in colonial times. Minas Gerais was established only when the gold rush began in 1695 (see page 35). The only line of communication with the rest of the world until the 19th century was by way of mule down the perilous Escarpment.

Isolation was so great that *mineiros* started their own farms and cottage industries. This versatility gave many of them a taste for democracy. The

Main Attractions

Belo Horizonte
Capela de São Francisco, Pampulha
Ouro Preto
Mariana
Congonhas do Campo
Tiradentes
Diamantina
Linhares

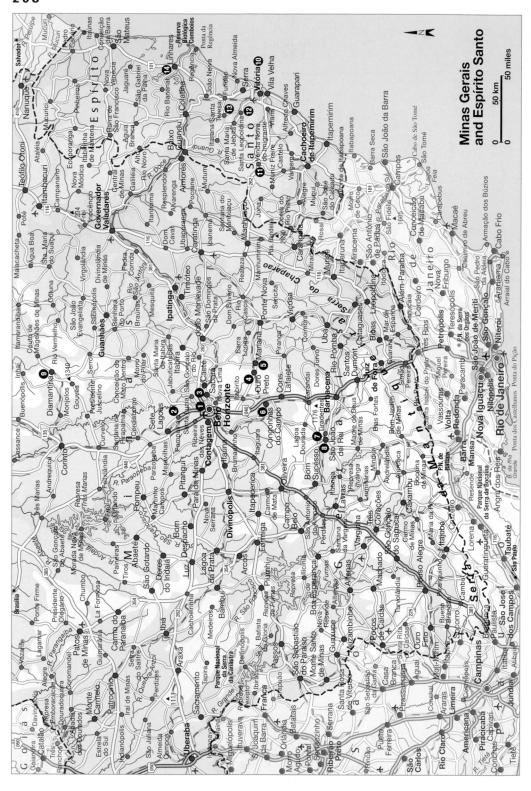

**Minas Gerais
and Espírito Santo**

French traveler Saint-Hilaire noted that 'there were scarcely any absentee landowners in Minas. The landowner worked side by side with his slaves, unlike the aristocratic owners in the rest of Brazil.' And *mineiro* poet Carlos Drummond de Andrade (see page 209) said: 'Minas has never produced a dictator and never will.'

Gold and diamond fever

In the 18th century, the gold of Minas Gerais was a colossus bestriding the world of commerce. About 1,200 tonnes of it were mined from 1700 to 1820. This fantastic amount made up 80 percent of all the gold produced in the world during that period.

Prospectors became spectacularly wealthy almost overnight. There were even some slaves who enriched themselves by clandestinely clawing the earth from underground mines. The legendary Chico Rei, who was a king in Africa before being brought to Brazil as a slave, vowed that he would recover his crown in the New World. That's exactly what he did, working feverishly in order to earn enough gold to purchase his own freedom and that of his large brotherhood.

The gold rush in Minas had ramifications abroad. Lisbon was flooded with gold coins minted at Ouro Preto's Casa dos Contos. But instead of investing their newfound wealth securely, the monarchy frittered away the fortune on opulent 'improvements.'

By the time Brazil's gold rush gave way to diamonds a few years later, Portugal had learnt its lesson. The Tijuco diamond mines were closed to prospectors. A governor was appointed, and a garrison sent to back up his decrees. But the plan didn't work. The prospect of riches makes men greedy. Governors like João Fernandes – who spent a vast sum building an artificial lake and a Portuguese sailing ship for his slave mistress, Xica da Silva – dealt in contraband. The diamonds themselves brought renewed wealth for only a short time.

Today, most visitors drive up from Rio de Janeiro, or fly to Belo Horizonte and travel from there to Ouro Preto and other places of interest, so Belo is where this suggested route will begin.

FACT

Mineiro Carlos Drummond de Andrade (1902–87) is regarded by many as the most influential of Brazil's 20th-century poets. You can see a life-sized statue of him beside Copacabana beach in Rio, the city he later made his home. The statue is famous for having the poet's glasses constantly stolen.

The interior of Nossa Senhora do Rosário dos Pretos.

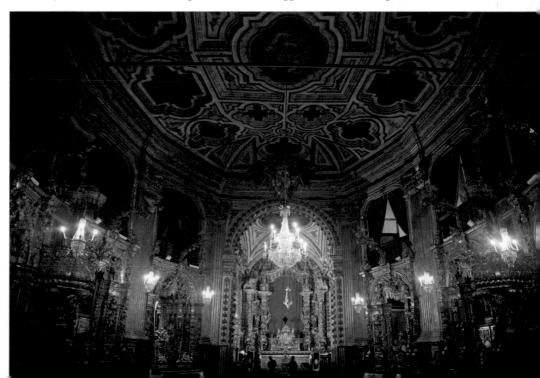

Baroque church door in Ouro Preto.

Niemeyer's Capela de São Francisco.

Belo Horizonte

Ouro Preto was Minas Gerais's capital until 1897, when *mineiro* statesmen inaugurated Brazil's first planned city, **Belo Horizonte ❶**. Compared with Ouro Preto, the bustling metropolis, with a population of 5.5 million, possesses little for sightseers, but it is a good base for visiting surrounding historic towns. It was one of the host cities for the 1950 World Cup, when the US famously beat England 1-0 at the Independência Stadium in Horto, and will again host games when the FIFA World Cup returns to Brazil in 2014. The city's Mineirão Stadium, in Pampulha, has been totally refurbished and modernized for the competition. One of the first events in the new stadium was a concert by Paul McCartney in May 2013. During the show, McCartney gave his first-ever live performance of a number of classic Beatles' tracks.

Also found in chic **Pampulha ❷** is the striking **Capela de São Francisco**, with its undulating roof and blue tiles, designed by Oscar Niemeyer in collaboration with Brazil's greatest modern artist, Candido Portinari (see page 115), who was responsible for the starkly painted images of St Francis and the 14 Stations of the Cross.

Lying in a wooded valley 23km (14 miles) north of Belo Horizonte is **Sabará ❸**, a Baroque treasure. A leafy suburb hides the town's bizarre, musty jewel, the oddly shaped chapel of **Nossa Senhora do O**. O's humble exterior belies its exuberant decor; every inch of wall and ceiling space is covered by woodcarvings, gold leaf, darkly mysterious paintings that depict various Bible stories, and delicate gold-hued oriental motifs. The Far Eastern figures reflect the experiences of Portuguese Jesuits in the Orient.

A few blocks from the chapel is Sabará's larger **Nossa Senhora da Conceição** parish church. Its squarish facade is redeemed by an explosion of rich interior decoration. The oriental theme is frequently used, especially on the design-crowded sacristy door.

Presiding incongruously over Sabará's main square is the ghostly stone shell of the **Igreja do Rosário dos Pretos**, which was abandoned when the gold mines ran down. A few blocks away is the precious **Igreja do Carmo**, a treasure trove of Aleijadinho works, including intricate soapstone pulpits and a bas-relief frontispiece. A pair of muscular male torsos, bulging with woodcarved veins, hold the ornate choir loft in place.

Ouro Preto

Although the riches produced by mining disappeared, the art remained. Today, the best place to see it is **Ouro Preto ❹**. Located 100km (60 miles) from Belo Horizonte, Ouro Preto was the center of the late 17th-century gold rush. First known as Vila Rica, it was just a mountain village when bands of adventurers from the Atlantic coast came in search of slaves and gold. Near Vila Rica they found a strange black stone and sent samples to Portugal. What they had unwittingly discovered was gold (the black coloration was

from iron oxide in the soil). Vila Rica was swiftly renamed Ouro Preto (Black Gold), and the gold rush was under way.

By 1750, Ouro Preto had a population of 80,000, which at that time was larger than that of New York City. Jesuit priests also arrived, bringing ideas and artistic concepts from Europe; they insisted that their churches, financed by the gold from the mines, be built in the Baroque style. Today, Ouro Preto has Brazil's purest collection of Baroque art and architecture. Six museums and no fewer than 13 churches set among low hills and picture-book cottages make Ouro Preto resemble a Grimm Brothers' fairy-tale town. In 1981 Unesco declared Ouro Preto a World Heritage Centre, a title it well deserves.

The fall of Tiradentes

In the town center is spacious **Praça Tiradentes A**, fronted by the imposing **Museu da Inconfidência B** (www.museudainconfidencia.gov.br; Tue–Sun noon–6pm). The cobbled plaza is rich in history. The severed head of patriot Joaquim José da Silva Xavier, nicknamed Tiradentes (Tooth-Puller) was displayed on a pole there in 1792. Xavier and six of his co-conspirators had plotted a coup to bring about Brazilian independence, but spies infiltrated the group and exposed the plan, and Tiradentes was executed.

The museum once served as the town hall and acted as the 'presidential palace' in the 1988 movie *Moon Over Parador*, which starred Richard Dreyfuss. Art and history are its current focuses. A macabre exhibit displays portions of the gallows used for Tiradentes's execution. Nearby is a copy of his death warrant. Some of his fellow conspirators are buried beneath masonry slabs on the first floor.

Another important building on Praça Tiradentes is the impressive church of **Nossa Senhora do Carmo C** (Tue–Sun noon–5pm; free), where the work of Aleijadinho can be seen.

This sturdy edifice was designed in 1766 by Aleijadinho's father, the engineer Manuel Francisco Lisboa. His son altered the plan while work was under way in 1770, incorporating the bell towers into the facade and adding an elegant archway over the main door. The changes were a compromise between conservative Mannerist traditions and the emerging Baroque style that Aleijadinho championed. The exuberant stone carvings of curlicues and soaring angels above the main entrance are particularly fine.

Sacred treasures

Next to the church is Carmo's richly endowed collection of sacred art, housed in the **Museu do Oratório** (www.oratorio.com.br; daily 9.30am–5.30pm). Aleijadinho's woodcarvings are prominent here, along with illuminated manuscripts and gleaming gold and silver altar accoutrements. A piece of bone labeled 'St Clement' floats eerily in a glass-and-gold reliquary.

Three blocks west of Carmo is the deceptively simple parish church of **Nossa Senhora do Pilar D**. The squarish facade hides Ouro Preto's most extravagant Baroque interior.

Statue of Tiradentes on Praça Tiradentes, the cobbled plaza in the town centre.

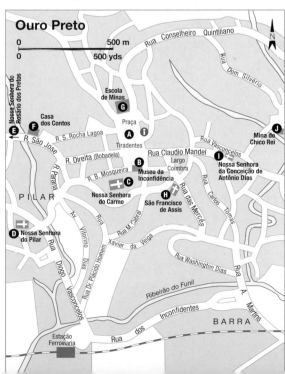

Ouro Preto

Praça Tiradentes at night.

Ouro Preto has been designated a Unesco World Heritage Centre.

Partly the work of the sculptor Francisco Xavier de Brito, Pilar's walls explode with rosy-cheeked saints and angels, their garments fluttering against the gold-leaf background.

Nossa Senhora do Rosário dos Pretos ⓔ, in the Rosário district farther west, produces the opposite effect. Its bold Baroque facade houses an almost bare interior. Rosário was built by slaves, who had accumulated enough gold to erect its stunning shell, but not to decorate the interior. But what a shell it is; the convex walls, curved facade, and shapely bell towers make Rosário Brazil's most brashly Baroque architectural monument.

Two other museums mark the route along cobbled streets back to Praça Tiradentes. The **Casa dos Contos ⓕ** (Mon 2–6pm, Tue–Sat 10am–6pm, Sun 9am–4pm), at the base of steep Rua Rocha Lagoa, was the tax authority during the gold-rush era. Gold coins, and the surprisingly sophisticated foundry for minting them, are displayed. At the top of the street is the sprawling **Escola de Minas** (College of Mine Engineering) **ⓖ**. The mineralogy museum inside (Tue–Sun noon–5pm; free) has an extremely interesting collection of precious stones, ores, and crystals – 23,000 pieces in total.

Aleijadinho's masterpiece

Just east of Praça Tiradentes is an Aleijadinho architectural masterpiece, the jewel-box chapel of **São Francisco de Assis ⓗ** (Tue–Sun 8.30–11.45am, 1.30–5pm), whose Baroque lines resemble those of Rosário dos Pretos. Extravagant relief work above the main entrance is a continuation of similar works at Carmo.

Inside are rare wood and soapstone carvings by Aleijadinho, characterized by the almond eyes, shapely anatomical features and ruffled garments of the high *mineiro* Baroque. The wall and ceiling paintings are by Manuel da Costa Athayde (1762–1837), whose works feature distorted human figures and realistic backgrounds. Painted surfaces and architectural features blend at the margins as if the painted-sky ceiling could open up for God's inspection.

Two blocks east is Ouro Preto's monument to Aleijadinho, the museum and church of **Nossa Senhora da Conceição de Antônio Dias** (www.museualeijadinho.com.br; Tue–Sun 8.30am–noon, 1.30–5pm). Aleijadinho is buried beneath a wooden marker near a side altar. The galleries behind the sacristy display his wood and soapstone carvings and the richly illustrated Bibles and missals he used to study European artistic models.

Still in Ouro Preto, you can visit the **Mina do Chico Rei** (Rua 108 Dom Silvério; daily 8am–5pm), a gold mine built by slaves in 1702, which fell into disuse following the abolition of

slavery in 1888. A small stretch of the 1,300-meter (4,265ft) gallery is accessible to visitors.

Between Ouro Preto and Mariana (8km/5 miles from Ouro Preto) is the more interesting **Minas da Passagem** (www.minasdapassagem.com.br; daily 9am–5pm), which was in use until the late 1980s. Demonstrations of the processing of gold ore are held here. This mine was dug out in the 18th century and has an 11km (7-mile) gallery, going down to a depth of 120 meters (394ft). Visitors can go down into the gallery by train as far as an underground lake. Minas da Passagem claims to be the largest gold mine in the world to allow visitors.

Mariana

The fascinating colonial town of **Mariana** , birthplace of Athayde, is 12km (7 miles) from Ouro Preto. The twin chapels of **Carmo** and **São Francisco**, and the magnificent **Catedral de Nossa Senhora da Assunção**, are smothered in the dark colors and mulatto figures of Athayde's opulent art. Especially noteworthy is

Aleijadinho's Prophet, in Congonhas do Campo.

Nossa Senhora do Rosário church.

The Passion and Death of Saint Francis. Athayde is buried under a wooden marker at the rear of Carmo. The cathedral has a German organ, built in 1701 and dragged by mule from Rio de Janeiro. Concerts are held on Friday at 11am and Sunday at 12.15pm. Behind the cathedral is Mariana's sacred-art museum, **Museu Arquidiocesano de Arte Sacra** (Rua Frei Durão; Tue–Sun 9am–noon, 1.30–5pm), which contains the largest collection of Baroque painting and sculpture in Minas Gerais.

Congonhas do Campo

Eastern Minas Gerais, more economically developed than the bleak *sertão,* also offers artistic treasures of the late *mineiro* Baroque. **Congonhas do Campo** ⑥, 80km (48 miles) from Belo Horizonte, is the site of Aleijadinho's two greatest masterworks of sculpture: the 12 life-sized outdoor carvings of *The Prophets,* located on the esplanade of the **Bom Jesus de Matosinhos Sanctuary**; and the 66 painted woodcarvings of *The Stations of the Cross,* housed in a series of garden chapels nearby. Carved entirely from soapstone, *The Prophets*

are stolid, gray, and severe. In their stylized postures and costumes, they possess a mythic quality, as if sculpted entirely from imagination.

While *The Prophets* seem suitably remote, the carved figures of *The Stations of the Cross* are vibrant and filled with emotion. The Christ statue, with its almond eyes and half-open mouth, skin pale and veined, and muscles strained, is as haunting as *The Holy Shroud.* The 12 Apostles, with their worried, working-class faces, probably sculpted after local residents, could well be an 18th-century jury.

Tiradentes

A further 80km (50 miles) to the south is the 1746 birthplace of Joaquim José da Silva Xavier. The town, appropriately named **Tiradentes** ⑦, preserves the colonial-era feeling better than almost any other in Minas Gerais. Pink-slate streets, an occasional horse-drawn cart, lace curtains, and brightly painted shutters contribute to a feeling of tranquility. The spacious **Museu Padre Toledo** (Rua Padre Toledo; Wed–Mon 9–11.30am, 1–4.40pm) contains period furnishings and sacred art. Nearby is the imposing **Igreja de Santo Antônio**, with gold-plated decoration and a stone frontispiece carved by Aleijadinho. Inside there is an 18th-century organ, a companion piece to the instrument in Mariana.

São João del Rei

Only 12km (7 miles) from Tiradentes is bustling **São João del Rei** ⑧. The São João train station, at Avenida Hemílio Alves 366, has been turned into a gleaming museum, the **Museu Ferroviário** (Tue–Sat 9–11.30am, 1–6pm), a fascinating reminder of old-fashioned rail travel. Hulking black and red Baldwin locomotives, dating as far back as 1880, are lined up in the roundhouse like oversized toys around a Christmas tree. Wood-paneled excursion cars feature porcelain fixtures and etched windows. The Victorian-style station is clean and authentic, right

Athayde's ceiling painting in São Francisco de Assis church.

down to the ear-splitting steam whistle and syncopated huff and puff of the old train that still makes tourist trips.

The town has seven churches. **Igreja do Carmo** recalls the Baroque masterpieces of Ouro Preto. The nearby cathedral, the **Basílica de Nossa Senhora do Pilar**, presents a blocky facade, and richly decorated walls and ceilings within. But the pleasing proportions and rounded towers of the **Igreja de São Francisco**, which has justifiably been hailed as Aleijadinho's most mature architectural triumph, is the town's proudest treasure. Double rows of swaying palm trees lead to a graceful esplanade of wide steps and curving balustrades.

São João del Rei is the nearest of the major historic towns to Rio de Janeiro, so if you are driving up from Rio, São João or Tiradentes will be a good option for a first-night stop in the region, or your last if heading back to Rio by road.

Diamantina

Heading north from Belo Horizonte (about 280km/175 miles), you come to a rugged hamlet many consider the equal of Ouro Preto in austere beauty and history – **Diamantina ⑨**. Bordering Brazil's semi-arid *sertão*, Diamantina is surrounded by iron-red hills rising to a rocky plain. This area is particularly rich in orchids; there are almost 300 species in the area, some of them very rare. The town's white-walled cottages and churches cascade down an irregular slope, producing a stark profile of wooden steeples.

The ornate wood and stone **Igreja do Carmo** across the square, was another gift from the diamond czar to his lover. Fernandes ordered the bell tower to be moved to the rear of the church when Silva complained its tolling kept her awake. Carmo's ceiling is covered by dark-hued paintings depicting Bible stories, which were favored by 18th-century *mineiro* painters, including José Soares de Araujo, whose work at Carmo and the nearby **Igreja do Amparo** recalls that of Athayde.

Colorful **Nossa Senhora do Rosário**, a block from Carmo, was built entirely by slaves, and the woodcarvings of the saints are black.

FACT

Diamantina was the headquarters of the diamond contractor João Fernandes and his slave mistress, Xica da Silva. Her stately home is located on Praça Lobo Mesquita. The story of Xica da Silva was told in Carlos Diegues' movie of the same name, released in 1976.

Bom Jesus de Matosinhos Sanctuary.

THE ROYAL ROADS

In the late 17th century it became clear that for Portugal to take full advantage of the mineral wealth being discovered in the state of Minas Gerais, it would need to get those riches quickly to the coast.

A road-building program got underway to build the Estrada Real, or Royal Road. The first route, the Caminho Velho (Old Road), was built in 1697 to link Ouro Preto, then called Vila Rica, down to the port at Paraty.

In 1701, the distance to the coast was cut by opening the Caminho Novo (New Road) from Ouro Preto down to Guanabara Bay in Rio. Then, with the discovery of diamonds in 1729, close to Diamantina, the Estrada Real was extended northwards from Ouro Preto.

Today the old royal roads are an attraction in their own right (www.institut oestradareal.com.br).

FACT

IBAMA, which was founded on the February 22, 1989, is the acronym for the very powerful and well-respected Brazilian Institute of Environment and Renewable Natural Resources (www.ibama.gov.br). It acts as the administrative arm of the Ministry of the Environment and is active throughout the entire Brazilian national territory.

Outside, the roots of a tree nearby have split Rosário's wooden crucifix, leaving only the bar and tip of the cross visible. Folklore says a slave accused of stealing was executed on the spot while protesting his innocence. He told onlookers: 'Something extraordinary will occur here to prove my truthfulness.' Soon after, buds appeared on the cross, eventually snaking into the ground and producing the sturdy tree.

Across from the cathedral is the informative **Museu do Diamante** (Tue–Sat noon–5.30pm, Sun 9am–noon). Period mining equipment, documents, and furnishings are displayed. Grisly implements of torture used against the slaves are kept in a back room. Also near the square is Diamantina's Public Library, noted for its delicate trellis and *muxarabiê* (a lattice-work casing covering a second-story balcony). A few blocks away, on **Rua Direita**, is the humble birthplace of President Juscelino Kubitschek (1902–76). Nearby is the **Casa da Glória**, a pair of blue and white stone structures linked by a wooden bridge. The site was the headquarters of Diamantina's royal governors.

Espírito Santo

The coastal city of **Vitória** , capital of the state of **Espírito Santo**, was founded in 1551, and has remained a relatively small town (pop. 313,000), its heart comprising an island connected to the suburbs by a series of bridges. There are a few buildings recalling its colonial past, and some beaches along the coast north and south of the city that are quite pretty. However, this state has not, as yet, been affected by the tourist boom that has brought so many changes to its neighbors Bahia and Minas Gerais, and, of course, to Rio de Janeiro.

The **Teatro Carlos Gomes** (Praça Costa Pereira) in Vitória was built as a faithful copy of La Scala in Milan. It frequently hosts music festivals as well as putting on plays. The **Catedral Metropolitana** (Praça Dom Luis Scortegagna), built in 1918, has beautiful stained-glass windows.

Outdoor pursuits

The lovely Alpine-like countryside around the village of **Venda Nova do Imigrante** (known simply as Venda Nova) , 113km (70 miles) west of Vitória, is popular for walking and mountaineering. About 70km (44 miles) northwest of Vitória is the Swiss-founded town of **Santa Leopoldina** , which offers a pleasant day trip from the capital.

A further 21km (13 miles) north lies the pretty hill town of **Santa Teresa** . Just outside it, the **Museu Biológico Professor Mello Leitão** (4 Avenida José Ruschi; Tue–Sun 8am–5pm) is a natural-history museum founded in 1949 by Augusto Ruschi, a world-famous expert on hummingbirds, who died in 1986. Set in an area of forests in which a vast variety of orchids proliferate, the museum has a small zoo attached, a hummingbird and butterfly garden, and grounds containing a wide variety of plants and trees.

In the colonial town of Diamantina.

Nature reserves

Close to **Linhares** ⑭, 135km (84 miles) from Vitória, is the **Reserva Biológica Comboios** (www.projetotamar.org.br; daily 8am–noon, 1–5pm; free), a fascinating nature reserve that was established to protect marine turtles, and which is part of the national Projeto Tamar. The project, which currently has 22 centers along the Brazilian coast, was set up in 1980 as a non-profit organization working to protect sea turtles from extinction. It has been very successful and has now widened its interests to cover sharks and all sea wildlife. There are a number of hotels and restaurants in Linhares itself.

There are two other nature reserves near Linhares. The **Reserva Florestal de Linhares** (e-mail: floresta@tropical. com.br), which is a private reserve; and the IBAMA-run **Reserva Biológica de Sooretama** (tel: 27-3371 9700/27-3763 2380). Both these reserves have been established to protect the rainforest and its incredible variety of plants (including numerous orchids), birds, and other wildlife. More than 370 species of bird have been recorded,

including the red-billed curassow. To visit either of these reserves, you will need special authorization, obtainable from the contacts above.

Further north, close to the border with Bahia state, is **Conceição da Barra**, a small town from which you can reach **Itaúnas**, with its lonely beaches and enormous sand dunes, some of them more than 30 meters (90ft) high. The dunes have buried the old town of Itaúnas, and only the church tower can still be seen above the sand.

Paragliders over the hills.

RESTAURANTS

PRICE CATEGORIES

Prices for a two-course meal for two. Wine costs around US$25 a bottle.
$ = under US$50
$$ = US$50–100
$$$ = US$100–150

Belo Horizonte

Alguidares
1037 Rua Pium-I, Anchieta
Tel: 31-3221 8877
Open: L&D Tue–Sun, D Mon.
Excellent Bahian and seafood in a simple but attractive restaurant, one of the best in Belo. **$$**

Fogo de Chão
1208 Rua Sergipe, Savassi
Tel: 31-3227 2730
Open: L&D daily.
Carnivores' paradise. Part of the leading chain of top rodizio barbecue houses. Make sure you are really hungry! **$$$**

Hermengarda
314 Rua Outono, Carmo Sion
Tel: 31-3225 3268
Open: D Tue–Sun, L Sun.
Interesting contemporary dishes using Brazilian ingredients in an extremely creative way. **$$**

Vecchio Sogno
75 Rua Martin de Carvalho, Santo Agostinho
Tel: 31-3292 5251
Open: L&D Mon–Sat, L Sun.
Award-winning Italian fare delivered in elegant surroundings. Generally considered to be the city's best restaurant. More modest is the group's highly rated *padaria* Casa Infinita on Rua Ceara. **$$$**

Ouro Preto

Bené da Flauta
32 Rua São Francisco de Assis, Centro
Tel: 31-35511036
Open: L&D daily.
Set in a lovely old colonial

house overlooking the church of São Francisco de Assis, one of Aleijadinho's masterpieces, this restaurant serves decent *mineira* and international dishes. **$$**

Tiradentes

Pau de Angu
Estrada Bichino Km4
Tel: 32-39948 1692
Open: L daily.
Traditional *mineira* cuisine is served in an old farmhouse just a 10-minute drive from Tiradentes in the direction of Bichinho. Leave space for the buffet of desserts. **$$**

Theatro da Villa
157 Rua Pe Toledo, Centro
Tel: 32-3355 1275
Open: D Tue–Sun
Creative dishes that more than live up to their wonderful and historic setting. Should be part of any visit to Tiradentes. Food is a mix of *mineira* and French. **$$$**

View from the Brazilian side at the Iguaçu Falls.

IGUAÇU FALLS

The Cataratas do Iguaçu is one of the natural wonders of the world, a place where you stand in awe of the power of nature. It is high on the list of places most visitors to Brazil want to see.

Main Attractions
Garganta do Diabo
Macuco Safari
Foz do Iguaçu
Itaipú Dam

The **Cataratas do Iguaçu ❶** (Iguaçu Falls) is one of the most powerful and extraordinary sights in the world. 'Poor Niagara!' exclaimed Eleanor Roosevelt on first setting eyes on it. Indeed, the statistics are confounding: 275 individual falls – some of which are more than 80 meters (260ft) high – plunge over a 3km (2-mile) precipice in an unending wall of spray, discharging, at the peak, a cascade of more than 6.5 million litres (1.7 million gallons) of water per second. At the heart of this unforgettable scene is the **Garganta do Diabo** (Devil's Throat), where 14 separate falls join forces, pounding down the 90-meter (295ft) cliffs in a deafening crescendo of sound and spray, crowned by a perpetual rainbow.

The falls are located on the Iguaçu river within a subtropical national park (a Unesco World Heritage Site) on the Brazilian/Argentine border, and can be reached from both countries. A half-day on the Brazilian side and a full day on the Argentine (Iguazú) side are recommended if you have the time.

Entrance to the Brazilian park is through a modern visitor center with a museum, shop, and ATM. From here, shuttle buses run to the falls (no cars are allowed in the park, but bikes can be rented at the gate), making an initial stop at the **Macuco Safari** – an unmissable experience. Aboard sturdy, 20-seater inflatable boats you can see up close the incredible power of the water from the base of these majestic falls. You will inevitably get thoroughly drenched, so it's advisable to wear a swimsuit, and take a plastic bag for your camera. There are lockers in which to store your other belongings. The final stop on the bus takes you to the start of a 1km (0.5-mile) wooden walkway, which gives a fantastic view of the Devil's Throat. When you reach the viewpoint, you find yourself surrounded by the roaring water, the mist, and white foam that boils up around the green of the jungle, and a

A toucan in the national park.

180-degree rainbow. It is an overwhelming (and at times wet) experience.

Just before you reach the visitor center there's a helipad offering 10-minute rides over the falls for around US$60. Opposite is the Parque das Aves, a bird park with huge aviaries housing, among others, the five species of toucan native to the region.

The Argentine side

In order to cross to the Argentine side – which you should certainly plan to do – you must pass border control at Ponte Tancredo Neves (check in advance if you might need a visa to enter Argentina). The procedure is fairly painless. Over 80 percent of the falls belong to Argentina, and the tourist infrastructure there is more advanced. Trains leave every 15 minutes for two trailheads, both of which offer extraordinary close-up views of the falls. From the Lower Circuit you can take a boat to Isla San Martín, where a steep trail winds among some lesser-visited falls and pools. A second train continues to the Devil's Throat walkway for a look down into the pounding waters.

To see the full force of the falls, go in January or February when the river is high. However, this is also when the humidity and heat are fierce, and the park is packed with tourists. From September to October, the water level is down but the temperature is pleasant and there are fewer people. Whenever you go, you are likely to get wet so take a raincoat or poncho – many people just wear a swimsuit in the wet season.

Most hotels in **Foz do Iguaçu ②** can organise excursions or transportation to and from the falls (see page 353 and page 374). Foz underwent a boom during the construction of the Itaipú dam and, because of its proximity to the falls, has a thriving tourist industry. If you want to spoil yourself, go to the Hotel das Cataratas (www.hoteldas-cataratas.com), part of the Orient-Express Group, located in the park in front of the falls. One major benefit of staying here is that you get to visit the falls before and after the public can enter the park. Also look out for their full moon tour. If you can't afford to stay at the hotel, you might want to try the restaurant or bar while visiting the falls.

TIP

If you are planning to visit the Argentine side of the falls, go early. Many large tourist groups initially work their way through the Lower Circuit, so take the train to the furthest station and visit the Devil's Throat first. You will find it less crowded. It's also best to visit during the week when there are usually fewer visitors.

The falls are at the border between Brazil and Argentina.

ITAIPÚ DAM

Built between 1970 and 1984, the **Itaipú dam** (www.itaipu.gov.br) was a joint construction project shared between Brazil and Paraguay, and is currently the world's largest hydroelectric plant. The dam itself is 8km (5 miles) in length and produces in the region of 27 billion kilowatts each year, providing a quarter of Brazil's electricity (and 80 percent of Paraguay's). There are a number of different tours of the dam, the most comprehensive of which takes 2.5 hours (daily 8am, 8.30am, 10am, 10.30am, 1.30pm, 2pm, 3.30pm, and 4pm). The shorter tour, about 1.5 hours, leaves on the hour from 8 am to 4 pm. There is also a special light show every Friday and Saturday evening at 8pm (9pm in the summer). More than 18 million people have visited since 1977. Book at reservas@turismoitaipu.com.br.

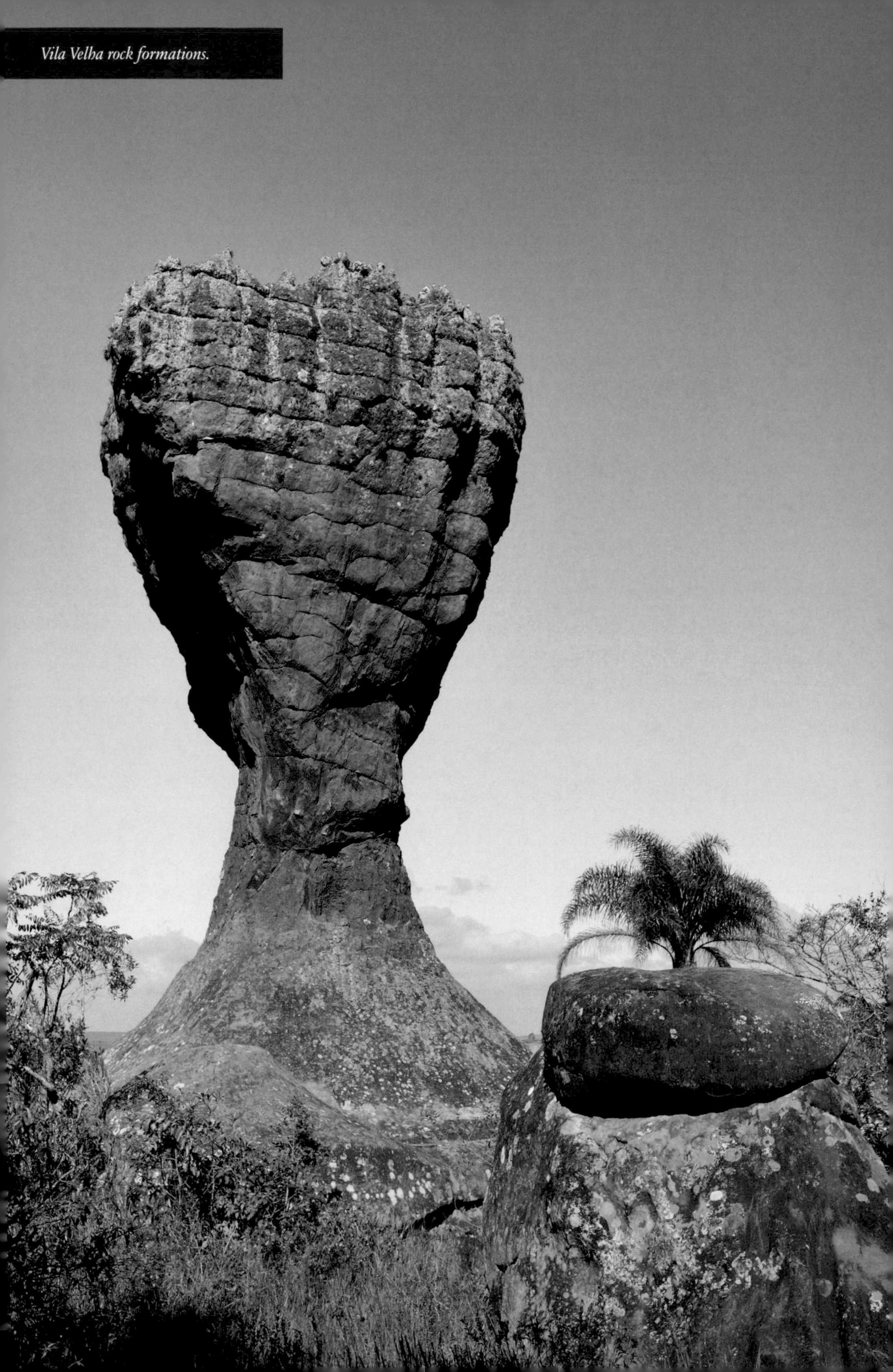

Vila Velha rock formations.

THE SOUTHERN STATES

This subtropical, prosperous region of Brazil has some spectacular natural attractions: most notably, the falls at Foz do Iguaçu and the Itaimbzinho Canyon, and a distinctive heritage, both European and gaucho.

The south of Brazil is different. Here, palm trees give way to pines, forested mountains are split by tranquil valleys, nature in general is more rugged, with roaring waterfalls and monumental canyons, and the temperate climate provides four distinct seasons, with cold weather, even snow, in the winter. The people, too, are different. Blue-eyed blonds replace the dark-featured types of the north and northeast, reflecting the deep European roots of the south.

The traditional breadbasket of Brazil, the south is a region of bounty. The farms and ranches of the states of **Paraná**, **Santa Catarina**, and **Rio Grande do Sul** are the country's leading grain producers. Paraná is home to Brazil's most extensive pine forests, and it is one of the country's largest producers of soya and wheat. Across the flat pampas of Rio Grande do Sul wander Brazil's largest cattle herds. In recent years, the south has drawn from its agricultural wealth to invest in industry, and today the region is the center of Brazil's booming textile and footwear industries. Together, the south's rich earth and surging industrial power have given the inhabitants of its three states a standard of living second only to the state of São Paulo.

It was no surprise to Brazilians that two cities from the south, Curitiba

and Porto Alegre, were chosen to host games during the 2014 FIFA World Cup. Both cities upgraded their existing stadiums. The 42,000-seat Arena da Baixada, in the case of Curitiba, and the 51,000-seat Estádio Beira Rio, located on the banks of the River Guaiba, in the case of Porto Alegre.

Paraná state and its capital

A combination of unleashed nature and pleasing urbanity are the trademarks of Paraná. It is here that you will find the wildly beautiful Iguaçu Falls.

Main Attractions
Vila Velha State Park
Paranaguá
Florianópolis
Porto Alegre
Missions

Boat docked near Florianópolis beach.

Curitiba ❸, the capital of Paraná state, is an urban planner's dream, with ample green space, wide avenues, flower-decked pedestrian malls, and a relaxed and comfortable pace of life.

Founded by gold-seekers in the 17th century, Curitiba today is a bustling metropolis with a population of 3.2 million, located atop an elevated plateau at 900 meters (2,800ft). In the latter half of the 19th century and the beginning of the 20th, Curitiba, together with the state as a whole, received an infusion of immigrants from Europe (Italians, Poles, Germans, and Russians), which transformed the city into a European outpost in the heart of South America. The profusion of fair-haired people on the city's streets, together with Curitiba's annual ethnic festivals, is proof of the mixed origins of its citizens. The city's best-known ethnic neighborhood is **Santa Felicidade**, founded in 1878 by Italian immigrants and today home to Curitiba's finest *cantinas*, traditional, informal Italian eateries, among which Madalosso is the most popular.

Aside from its deserved reputation as one of Brazil's cleanest cities, Curitiba

Ornate glasshouse in Curitiba's botanical garden.

is also a pedestrian's delight. A walking tour should begin at **Rua das Flores**, an extensive pedestrian mall in the city center, named after its beautiful flower baskets, and flanked by stores and boutiques, as well as inviting cafés, restaurants, and pastry shops.

Nearby is the historical center of Curitiba, concentrated in the blocks around Praça Garibaldi and the **Largo da Ordem**, the latter a cobblestoned square dominated by the **Igreja da Ordem Terceira de São Francisco das Chagas** (1737). This is the city's oldest church, known popularly as the Ordem Church. At night, the square comes alive with street musicians and outdoor cafés.

Every Sunday (9am–2pm) the historical center hosts a lively fair exhibiting good-quality local crafts, which is well worth a visit. There is more craftwork up the hill from the church in the **Garibaldi Mini Shopping**, which has handicrafts from all over Brazil, including woodcarvings, pottery, and leather and straw goods.

Back down the hill towards the Rua das Flores is the **Praça Tiradentes**, where Curitiba's neo-Gothic cathedral stands. Close to nearby **Praça Generoso Marques** is a walkway (with a glass roof), which is known as 'Rua 24-Horas,' where the shops, cafés, and bars stay open round the clock.

Vila Velha rocks

Some 80km (50 miles) west of Curitiba is the area's second great natural attraction, **Vila Velha State Park ❹** (Wed–Mon 8am–5.30pm). Sited majestically atop the plateau, with the wind whipping around them, is a series of fantastical rock formations, carved over 350 million years by the wind and rain. There are 23 separate formations, each identified by the object, animal, or human form that it appears to represent. Close by is another of nature's mysteries: the Furnas Craters, two enormous holes sliced into the rocky ground to a depth of almost 100 meters (330ft), half-filled with water.

Take your swimsuit, because in one of these natural wells an elevator has been installed so visitors can descend 54 meters (180ft) to water level.

A mini-train runs among the formations, but most visitors find it hard to resist a long, contemplative walk through the near-mystical site, with its haunting mixture of shadows and rocks, made even more atmospheric by the sound of the wind.

Train ride

Paraná is not known for its beaches but the train trip to the coast is one of the most breathtaking in Brazil. Completed in 1885, the railroad clings to the mountain sides, at times threatening to march off into space as it passes over viaducts and through tunnels during the long, slow, three-hour descent to the coastal plain (for the best views sit on the left side of the train when going down). The trip offers an unmatched tour through the best-preserved section of Brazil's Atlantic rainforest, a richly green tangle of trees and undergrowth broken occasionally by waterfalls.

Two trains make this unforgettable journey. The conventional one leaves Curitiba station daily at 8.15am (330 Avenida Presidente Afonso Camargo; tickets from the office behind the bus station) and arrives three hours later in **Morretes ⑤**, which is the best stop on the line (the final leg, Morretes to Paranaguá, does not have the same appeal as the rest of the journey and is only done by the weekend trains). The *litorina* (tourist train) leaves the same Curitiba station at 9.15am on Saturdays and holidays, and goes as far as Morretes, and at 7.30am on Sundays when it goes as far as Paranaguá. Reservations are highly recommended, especially in summer (Serra Verde Express, tel: 41-3888 3488; www.serra verdeexpress.com.br).

After such an adrenalin-packed journey, stomachs will be ready for a different sort of exploration, so it may be time to try the rich *barreado*, a local stew made of beef, pork, onions, and spices. The ingredients arc mixed in a clay pot, which is then sealed with manioc flour and water, and cooked for 12 hours until the meat becomes

EAT

In Morretes, one of the best barreados (a traditional slow cooked meat stew) can be found at Armazem Romanus (141 Rua Visconde do Rio Branco), and in Paranaguá at Casa do Barreado (38 Rua José Antônio da Cruz) and Danubio Azul (95 Rua XV de Novembro).

The train from Curitiba to Morretes.

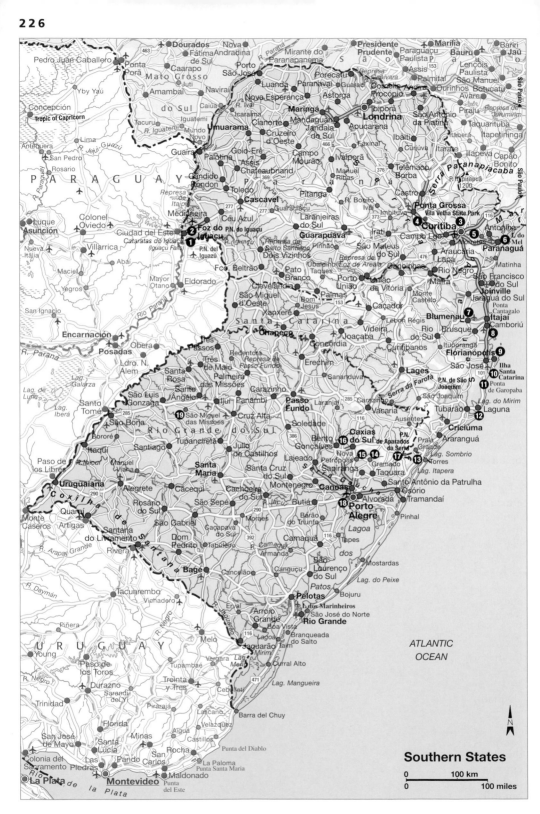

Southern States

0   100 km

0   100 miles

ATLANTIC
OCEAN

N

very soft, and has a luscious and quite unique flavor. The traditional *barreado* is served with manioc flour and slices of bananas and oranges.

Paranaguá

Founded in 1648, **Paranaguá** ❻ is one of Brazil's leading ports but, unfortunately, has preserved little of its historical past. What remains is located along **Rua XV de Novembro**, where an **archeological museum** (Tue–Fri 9am–noon, 1–6pm, Sat–Sun noon–6pm) is housed in the town's grandest building (completed in 1755), formerly a Jesuit college. The museum contains a selection of indigenous artifacts and items from colonial life.

The area's primary attraction is the **Ilha do Mel**, an island paradise that is reached by a 20-minute boat ride from the town of **Pontal do Sul**, an hour's drive from Paranaguá (boats from Paranaguá also make the trip, but it takes two hours). The island is a nature reserve with natural pools, grottoes, and deserted beaches. It is also home to the ruins of an 18th-century fort and a 19th-century lighthouse. There are no cars on the island, and transportation is either by foot along the many paths or by fishermen's boats. Its primitive, unspoiled nature has made the Ilha do Mel a popular spot for campers, for whom a flashlight and insect repellent are essentials. Visitors may also stay in one of the rustic *pousadas* on the island. Pousada das Meninas (www.pousadadasmeninas.com.br) and Grajagan Surf Resort (www.grajagan.com.br), in Nova Brasília, and Pousada Fim da Trilha (www.fimdatrilha.com.br) at Encantadas Beach are all recommended for their location and charm.

The best option for the return trip to Curitiba is the **Graciosa Highway**, a winding road that cuts through the verdant forest with explosions of wild flowers along the route. From the viewpoints, you can catch glimpses of the old mule trail used by the original Portuguese settlers to climb the mountainside to Curitiba. Real adventurers can still make this trip.

Santa Catarina

Or you can continue down the coast from Paranaguá into Santa Catarina. The smallest of the southern states, **Santa Catarina** is also the most boisterous. Its German heritage is apparent in the Bavarian architecture in inland **Blumenau** ❼, home to South America's liveliest Oktoberfest, a three-week blowout that attracts more than a million visitors, making it Brazil's second-largest festival after Rio's Carnival.

Blumenau is also one of Brazil's main textile centers, and offers an excellent 'direct from the factory' opportunity for buying clothes and household linen. Try Hering factory store (1421 Rua Bruno Hermann) or the CIC shopping mall (1395 Rua 2 de Setembro).

But the state's real treasure is its coastline, with miles of unspoiled white-sand beaches. The northern coastal resort of **Camboriú** ❽ has a long crescent beach that is a near-carbon copy of Rio's Copacabana, both for its landscape and its party atmosphere. During the summer holidays (December to February), Camboriú turns into a 'Mercosul meeting point,' where Argentines,

Fortress of Nossa Senhora dos Prazeres on Ilha do Mel.

Happy drinkers at the Blumenau Oktoberfest.

Paraguayans, and Uruguayans join Brazilians for weeks of sun, samba, and *caipirinhas*, the national drink.

Considered the capital that offers the best quality of life in the country, **Florianópolis** ❾ is the gateway to Santa Catarina Island. Before heading to the beaches, it is worth spending a day or two exploring the island's history and culinary delights in Florianópolis. The best place to start is the 1875 **Predio da Alfandega** (Customs Building; Mon–Fri 9am–6.30pm, Sat 8am–12.30pm; free) on Avenida Paulo Fontes, which is now a craft market. The neighboring **Mercado Municipal** (Mon–Fri 7am–7pm, Sat 7am–1.30pm; free) is where people meet to drink the excellent draft beer and eat *bolinhos de bacalhau* (salt-cod cakes) at Box 32.

Exploring Santa Catarina

Ilha Santa Catarina ❿ lies within an hour's drive from the city center, as it is linked to the mainland by the **Hercilio Luz Bridge**, one of the largest suspension bridges in the world. The island has 42 beaches, ranging from quiet coves to areas of roaring surf, and combines the aspects of a hectic capital with the delights of a laid-back fishing village. Here, life revolves around simple pleasures: swimming, sunbathing, eating, and drinking. The lifestyle, like the fish-based menu and the accent of local people, is inherited from the Azorean immigrants who first arrived on the island in 1750.

It is a quick 17km (10-mile) drive to **Santo Antônio de Lisboa**, the oldest and best-preserved Azorean village on the island. This is a great spot to watch the sunset, with the photogenic Hercilio Luz Bridge as a background.

Those in search of beach life during the day and a dance floor at night will find just what they want on the beaches to the north. They are well structured, with plenty of good hotels, restaurants, and shopping streets. Calm waters and a family atmosphere are found at Daniela beach or Lagoinha de Ponta das Canas. The most urbanized beaches are Jurere, Canasvieiras, and Ingleses, which are also favored by visiting Argentines.

The northern shore is home to one of the best-equipped beach resorts in the country, the Costão do Santinho

Graceful Hercilio Luz Bridge, one of the largest suspension bridges in the world.

Golf at **Praia do Santinho**. Good surf and beautiful people are to be found at Praia Mole and Joaquina, a world-famous surfing center that holds international competitions every year.

A few minutes away is the **Lagoa da Conceição**, a beautiful freshwater lake wedged between the island's mountain spine and the sea, with jet-ski and windsurfing facilities. Descendants of Azorean women still make lace in the traditional manner around the Rua das Rendeiras. There are lots of trendy stores, restaurants, and bars, some of them exceptional, such as the unpretentious **Um Lugar** (371 Rua Manoel Severino de Oliveira), which serves delicious, world-class gourmet seafood.

The island's southern beaches, such as Solidão, Naufragados and Lagoinha do Leste, are the most unspoiled and scenic. Many of them can be reached only by dirt roads or tracks that snake through some of the last stretches of preserved Atlantic forest left in the country. **Campeche** and **Armação** beaches are good choices for a day trip. Boats to Campeche Island leave from Armacão.

Nearby is the colorful village of **Ribeirão da Ilha**, site of one of the first Azorean settlements on the island, and home to some of the best seafood restaurants. Ribeirão da Ilha's fishermen specialize in the cultivation of oysters, the highlight of local menus such as that at Ostradamus (7640 Rodovia Baldicero Filomeno) or its neighbor, Rancho Acoriano. After indulging the taste buds, take a walk round the village to enjoy the beautifully preserved Azorean architecture.

Southern beaches

Back on the mainland, the principal southern beaches are on **Ponta de Garopaba** ⓫ – Garopaba, the neighboring Praia do Rosa (one of the most beautiful in the country), and Laguna. The largest concentration of cheerful, good-looking young Brazilians is found at Garopaba and Praia do Rosa. Surf shapes the local lifestyle, and the exceptional landscape of Praia do Rosa sets the scene for pretty little inns such as Quinta do Bucanero, and the Pousada Caminho do Rei.

TIP

The Ilha do Arvoredo, part of a biosphere reserve, has some of the best diving spots in the south of Brazil. Boats leave from Canasvieiras beach and take almost two hours to get to the island. Diving trips and courses can be arranged through the operators Acquanauta and Sea Divers in Canasvieiras.

Whale-watching trips can be very rewarding.

WHALE-WATCHING

Between July and November the Garopaba and Praia do Rosa region takes on a distinctive role. It turns into a breeding site for hundreds of southern right whales, which can be seen with their calves from the beach or up close on a boat trip. Praia do Rosa is home to the conservation project Baleia Franca (www.baleiafranca.org.br), created to study and to protect these special animals, and the old whaling station on Praia do Porto has been converted into a Whale Museum. The Vida Sol e Mar Resort (www.vidasolemar.com.br) in Praia do Rosa organizes whale-watching trips from Garopaba beach, as part of a package. Trips on 9-meter (30ft) boats last about two hours and are accompanied by a biologist from Baleia Franca with plenty of information to share.

Enjoying the scenery by horseback.

As Brazil's unofficial surfing capital, Garopaba became the headquarters of the top surf-gear manufacturers. One of the best is Mormaii, whose factory store can be found at the central Avenida João Orestes de Araujo.

The second-oldest town in the state, **Laguna** combines history, surf, and gorgeous beaches. Founded in 1676 as an outpost of the Portuguese crown, charged with protecting the region from the advance of Spanish forces, the little town continued to see bloodshed during the 1800s as a main center of the Revolucão Farroupilha, a Southern States revolutionary movement against Portuguese dominance. The main beach of Mar Grosso is built-up, but Farol de Santa Marta, 18km (11 miles) out of town, is a really beautiful spot.

Rio Grande do Sul

The southernmost state of Brazil, Rio Grande do Sul is also the most distinct. Bordering Uruguay and Argentina, it has developed a culture of its own, a mixture of Portuguese and Spanish together with Italian and German. The unique gaucho culture is the trademark of Rio Grande do Sul. Here, cowboys roam the southern pampas with their distinctive flat hats and chinstraps, their baggy pantaloon trousers, red neckerchiefs and leather boots, and the symbol of gaucho-land, the *chimarrão*, a gourd of hot maté tea.

Machismo runs strong, a heritage of the state's violent history. More than any other in Brazil, Rio Grande do Sul has seen the ravages of war. In the 18th and 19th centuries it served as a battleground for warring armies, revolutionaries, adventurers, and Amerindians, who marched back and forth across its grasslands, leaving a bloody stamp that has been transformed into legend.

Rio Grande is Brazil's leading manufacturer of leather footwear, and produces the country's finest wines. In addition, vast herds of cattle and sheep graze on its former battlefields, providing wool for the south's textile factories and beef for the succulent *churrasco*, the traditional Brazilian barbecue.

The landscape of Rio Grande do Sul is as rugged and uncompromising as its inhabitants. The state's 450km (280-mile) coastline is marked by pounding surf and rocky promontories, the best-known of which are located in the resort city of **Torres** ⓭.

The Serra Gaúcha

While Santa Catarina should not be missed for its beaches, Rio Grande's appeal is a few miles inland at its most famous mountain range, the **Serra Gaúcha**. Pine trees, lush green valleys, waterfalls, shimmering rivers, and awesome canyons distract the eyes of visitors as they wind their way through the *serra*. It was to this idyllic setting that thousands of German and Italian immigrants flocked in the late 19th century, establishing their homesteads along the valley floors. Today, many of the original stone and wood houses still stand as testimony to the hardy nature of the transplanted gauchos.

The crown jewels of the Serra Gaúcha are the cities of **Gramado** ⓮ and **Canela**. Both are slow-moving,

Gauchos preparing maté on a ranch.

Swiss-style mountain resorts where the residents of Brazil's non-stop southern cities escape the rush and indulge in upscale shopping, fondue-based restaurants, copious amounts of chocolate, and cozy inns and chalets tucked away beneath the pines. Good choices in Gramado are Saint Andrews; Varanda das Bromelias (www.varanadadas bromelias.com.br); Casa da Montanha (www.casadamontanha.com.br) and Serrano, or Pousada Cravo e Canela (www. pousadacravoecanela.com.br) in Canela.

Gramado hosts a prestigious Brazilian and Latin American film festival every August, but the area's main attraction is the **Caracol State Park** (daily 8.30am–5.30pm), 9km (5 miles) from Canela via Estrada do Caracol, where the dramatic **Caracol Falls** plunge 130 meters (400ft).

Some 30 minutes' drive away from Gramado and Canela is the small town of **Nova Petrópolis** ⑮, where the area's German heritage is prominent. In addition to the Bavarian architecture of the community's homes and public buildings, Nova Petrópolis's roots are visible in the **Immigration**

Park (Avenida 15 de Novembro; daily 8am–7pm; free), highlighted by a reproduction of a German colonial settlement of the 19th century.

The park also contains a bandstand and *biergarten* that are the center of festivities in January, February, and July, when the small hotels and inns of Nova Petrópolis, as well as Gramado and Canela, fill up with tourists.

Bento Gonçalves ⑯, 48km (30 miles) to the north, was founded in 1875 by Italian immigrants. The **Museu do Imigrante** (127 Rua Erny Dreher; Tue–Fri 8–11.15am, 1.30–5.15pm, Sat 1–5pm, Sun 9am–noon) documents its history. Today, Bento Gonçalves is the largest producer of fine wines in the country, as well as home to its only oenology university. Tours and tastings are available at a number of *adegas* (vineyards) in and around Bento Gonçalves. There is an annual wine festival in February and March in nearby **Caxias do Sul**.

Brazil's 'Grand Canyon'

The area's premiere attraction, three hours' journey from Bento Gonçalves,

Canela's cathedral.

An old country house in Bento Gonçalves.

Wine country

Although wine production came comparatively late to Brazil, when compared with its neighbors, it has started to make its mark – at least in the south.

Brazil's developing and improving wine industry is concentrated in the coastal mountains of Rio Grande do Sul, which is responsible for nearly 90 percent of national production.

The grapes and the wines produced from them were first brought to Rio Grande by Italian immigrants, who began to arrive in the 1880s. Since then, their descendants have carried on the tradition. Today, the cities and small farms of this area still retain an air of Italy about them. Cheeses and salamis hang from the ceilings of the prized wine cellars of the region's small farmers, many of whom make their own wine, cheese, and, of course, pasta. This culinary combination is also found in the area's restaurants, which are dominated by Italian cuisine.

The starting point for a visit to Brazil's wine country is Caxias do Sul, a booming industrial city tucked

Vineyards.

away in the mountains. Every even-numbered year, in February/March, Caxias hosts the region's Grape Festival, Festa da Uva (www.festanacionaldauva. com.br), during which the wine flows freely. It is worth a visit if you are in the area at this time. The leading vineyard in Caxias is the Château Lacave (on the BR-116 Km143; Tue–Sat 8am–7pm, Sun–Mon 10am–4pm), with its headquarters in a kitsch mock-European castle.

The areas around the principal cities are scattered with *cantinas* – local wineries that offer visits to their vineyards (January to March), and to their wine-production and storage areas, along with tastings and sales of wine. Some of the *cantinas* also have restaurants. Zanrosso and Tonet between Caxias do Sul and Flores da Cunha are highly recommended.

More tasting treats are to be found in and around Garibaldi and Bento Gonçalves, the recognized capitals of the wine-growing region. On the main road, just outside Garibaldi, is Maison Chandon (guided visits Mon–Fri 8.15–11.30am, 1.15–4.30pm, Sat 9.30am–3pm), Brazil's leading producer of espumante.

Other key producers

Other important producers of espumante are Cave Geisse, Georges Aubert, Peterlongo, and De Lantier. Continue on to Bento Gonçalves for a visit to the Cooperativa Vinicola Aurora (500 Rua Olavo Bilac; Mon–Sat 8.15am–5pm, Sun 8.30–11.30am). Bento is also home to several smaller, excellent producers, including Salton, Vinicola Miolo, and Casa Valduga. They all offer guided visits with generous tasting sessions at the end. Some, such as Casa Valduga (access via Km216 of RS-470 Highway; www.casavalduga.com.br) have built attractive little hotels in the grounds of the vineyards to accommodate enthusiastic guests.

The leading vineyards began to invest in quality in the mid-1970s because of growing local demand for good wines. Using imported varieties of grapes, increasingly high-quality products started to appear on the market. While the modernization process isn't yet complete, with most of the wine makers still adhering to the old tradition of oak barrels, some are stepping into the high-technology world of stainless-steel vats, which has substantially improved the quality of Brazilian wines, especially the whites. So marked is the improvement that several brands are now exported, and it is expected that, in time, Brazil's wines start challenging those of Chile and Argentina.

between the towns of Cambara do Sul and Praia Grande, is the **Aparados da Serra National Park** ⓱ (Wed–Sun 9am–5pm), about 120km (75 miles) from Canela. The view is well worth the effort of getting there, for suddenly, in the midst of pasture and forest, the earth seems to open up, revealing the enormous **Itaimbézinho Canyon**. Some 700 meters (2,200ft) deep, 7km (4 miles) long, and in places more than 2km (1 mile) wide, the canyon is the largest in Latin America. There are walking trails and horseback riding tracks running through the beautiful national park.

Itaimbézinho impresses not simply because of its amazing size but because of the varied shades of green that mark it out, from the light-green pasture to the deep-green forested cliffs. Waterfalls cascade down the canyon's sides.

Porto Alegre

The capital city of this southernmost state is **Porto Alegre** ⓲, a modern, commercial conurbation with a metropolitan population of 4.5 million – the largest metropolitan area in the south.

Located near the coast at the northern end of the Lagoa dos Patos, the city can be used as a jumping-off point for sojourns into the state's other areas. Gramado and Canela, the wine country and Rio Grande do Sul's beaches can all be visited in day trips from the capital city. Trips to the missions region and the pampas, however, require two days at least. Porto Alegre is also a stopover on the land route from Brazil to Argentina and Uruguay. It is a host city for the 2014 FIFA World Cup, with a strong soccer pedigree, two of its teams, Gremio and Internacional, being amongst the Brazilian elite. Both clubs have won the South American and World Club championships.

As befits its status as the capital of a beef-producing state, Porto Alegre offers excellent leather goods sold in downtown boutiques, plus steakhouses where you will be treated to the real mouth-watering Brazilian *churrasco*. Although far removed from the gaucho lifestyle, Porto Alegre provides visitors with a close-up look at their traditional music and dances at a number of popular nightspots.

The enormous Itaimbézinho Canyon.

The missions

The area known as 'the missions' lies due west of the Serra Gaúcha. Here, in the 17th century, with the authorization of the Portuguese and Spanish kings, Jesuit priests organized Guarani tribespeople into a series of settlements. The Jesuit fathers controlled the region for nearly a century, establishing centers of sophisticated culture as well as religion, and overseeing the construction of Amerindian cities, some of which had 5,000 inhabitants.

In 1750 the Treaty of Madrid solved the dispute between Portugal and Spain regarding the limit of their respective domains, and Portugal received the missions region. The Guarani did not recognize the treaty, and the relationship between the Jesuits and Portugal deteriorated fast. The Guaranitica War between the Guarani and Portuguese forces lasted until 1756, when the missions were attacked and overwhelmed. The Jesuits were expelled, and almost all the Amerindians were killed.

Roland Joffé's 1986 movie, *The Mission*, starring Robert De Niro

A visitor dances with Amerindian children in front of the ruins of the mission of São Miguel.

and Jeremy Irons, was based on this period, and the movie was filmed in the region as well as at the falls in Foz de Iguaçu.

Today, the ruins of the missions, notably **São Miguel das Missoes** ⓳, (designated a World Heritage Site), stand in dramatic solitude on the plain, all that is left of a once-thriving Amerindian community. Visitors to the mission region should stay in the city of **Santo Angelo**, 53km (32 miles) from São Miguel, from where day trips may be made to the ruins. Every evening, São Miguel mission offers a spectacular sound-and-light show, portraying the history of the area.

The Campanha

Across the windswept prairies of the **Campanha**, the legendary pampas, the gaucho cowboy still rides herd over the cattle and sheep that first brought wealth to Rio Grande do Sul. And *gaucho* tradition and culture are preserved in the southern cities that still seem to ring with the sound of cannon fire from the battles of the past.

RESTAURANTS

Curitiba

Capoani Café
906 Rua Comendador Araujo, Batel
Tel: 41-3018 6573
Open: L&D Mon–Sat.
Located in an old house that is the annex to one of Curitiba's most exclusive stores, Capoani serves both Brazilian and international cuisine. It is always well cooked and well presented in this charming bistro. Views to the garden. **$$**

Durski
254 Avenida Jaime Reis, São Francisco
Tel: 41-3225 7893
Open: L&D Tue–Sat, L only Sun.
Curitiba has a small, but vibrant Ukrainian community, and Durski serves a real Ukrainian feast – a cuisine with which most visitors may not be familiar, but which is well worth trying. One of Brazil's best wine lists. **$$**

Famiglia Caliceti Ristorante Bologna
1367 Alameda Dr Carlos de Carvalho, Batel
Tel: 41-3223 7102
Open: L&D Mon, Wed–Sat, L only Sun.
In a pretty house with a log fire and a winter garden, the Bologna has long been respected for its excellent pasta dishes. This is one of Curitiba's top Italian restaurants, and has been since first opening in 1972. **$$$**

L'épicerie
340 Rua Fernando Simas, Bigorrilho
Tel: 41-3079 1889
Open: D only Tue–Sat
A small French bistro, and one of the best in Curitiba, serving high-quality food at candlelit tables. Top spot for French classics since 2007. **$$**

Madalosso
5875 Avenida Manoel Ribas, Santa Felicidade
Tel: 41-3372 2121
Open: L&D Tue–Sat, L only Sun.
This claims to be the largest restaurant in Brazil, and is a popular stop with visitors. Not surprisingly, given that it can seat 4,800 customers and has 52 chefs. It offers a wide-ranging set menu with pasta, salads, chicken, liver, risotto, and fried polenta. But it's not the place for intimate dinners. **$$**

Scavollo
924 Rua Emiliano Perneta, Batel
Tel: 41-3225 2244
Open: D only daily, L Sat–Sun
Excellent pizza, and other Italian favorites, including steaks. Scavallo has been providing very good value for more than 25 years. Nice, comfortable ambiance. **$$**

Porto Alegre

Al Dente
210 Rua Mata Bacelar, Auxiliadora
Tel: 51-3343 1841
Open: D only Mon–Sat.
Some of the best Italian food in town; the highlight is the home-made pasta, which is always al dente. It comes with many sauces. Small, sophisticated, and cosy restaurant located in a period mansion. **$$**

Barranco
1578 Avenida Protásio Alves, Petrópolis
Tel: 51-3331 6172
Open: L&D daily.
An excellent, well-known and traditional barbecue house (not a *rodizio*) with an attractive outdoor area where tables are set under the trees. Very popular for Sunday lunch. Good wine list. **$$**

Le Bateau Ivre
805 Rua Tito Livio Zambecari, Mont Serrat
Tel: 51-3330 7351
Open: D Tue–Sat.
The Mediterranean influence is strong, leaning towards the classics of France, but with a Brazilian touch. A cozy restaurant often elected as one of the best in Porto Alegre. **$$**

Pampulhinha
1641 Avenida Benjamin Constant, Floresta
Tel: 51-3342 2503
Open: L&D Mon–Sat.
A top choice for fish and seafood for decades, with the *bacalhau* (salt cod) a particular favorite with local residents. Excellent selection of wines. **$$**

Steinhaus
415 Rua Coronel Paulino Teixeira, Rio Branco
Tel: 51-3330 8661
Open: D only Mon–Sat.
Many descendants of the German immigrant population consider this to be the city's best German restaurant (of which there are a good number). Regional and national Brazilian dishes are also on the menu. Good, attentive service. **$$**

Moqueca dish.

THE CENTER-WEST

This is a territory of vast open plains and pockets
of wetlands rich in wildlife, and it is also the
location of Brasília, the country's still futuristic
capital, which dates from 1960.

*The Niemeyer-designed
National Museum, Brasília.*

Apart from the federal district – Brasília – this region
can truly be described as Brazil's 'Wild West', whose
parallels with North America's eponymous land in
centuries past are manifold. *Bandeirantes* first traveled west
to push back the frontiers of discovered territory, seeking
gold but, for the most part, surviving by hacking down
swathes of jungle so they could run cattle on the land.

The vast *cerrado* (savannah plains, the terrain of most of
the region) is still sparsely populated, and many modern
day fortune hunters still claim their prize from the land and then move
on, while others stay to run huge isolated cattle
ranches. Dusty frontier towns, like the set of a
Western film, are spread thinly. There are even a
few Amerindians still living in the region.

Since 1960, the region has been home to Brazil's capital and has expanded rapidly. Intensive
soybean cultivation is the principal source of
income, with cattle-raising a close second. Today,
a staggering 85 percent of the population of 14
million live in urban areas. Most visitors, however, still come for adventure in an untamed land.

The chief attraction, especially for birdwatchers and fishing enthusiasts, is the Pantanal, an
enormous, seasonally flooded swamp with a
unique population of water birds. Tourists might
otherwise come to see spectacular canyons and
waterfalls, to ride on horseback through cowboy
country, to view the high plains from a hot-air balloon, to witness pioneering history, or to learn about Amerindian culture.

A family-friendly convertible.

You may wish to see Brasília. Modern, orderly, architecturally homo-
geneous Brasília – so incongruous in the middle of the empty *cerrado*
– was conceived as a symbol of national unity, located in the geographical center of the country, to replace Rio as the country's capital. It was
the vision of then-president Juscelino Kubitschek, and was intended to
provide the impetus to populate the west. But Brasília today, which celebrated its 50th anniversary in 2010, still has few links with the wild
country surrounding it.

The Warriors honors the laborers who built the city.

BRASÍLIA AND GOIÁS

Located in the very center of the country, at the edge of a formerly remote state cut by major river systems, the capital of Brazil is an impressive architectural monument that represents the realization of a dream.

For more than two centuries, the aim of Brazilian visionaries was to fill the vacuum in the center of their country with a new city. In 1891 Brazil's first republican government sent a scientific team to survey possible sites in Goiás, which is watered by three great rivers – the Amazon, the Paraná, and the São Francisco. For the same purpose, a later commission was sent, in 1946, to conduct an aerial survey. Yet until the election of president Juscelino Kubitschek in 1955, Brasília remained simply an idea.

Kubitschek made the development of Brasília the centerpiece of his campaign to modernize the country. The pace of the project was determined by politics; Kubitschek knew that if the city was ever to be completed, it had to be done by the end of his five-year term. He selected as his architect Oscar Niemeyer, a Communist and student of Le Corbusier. An international jury selected the city plan, which was the work of controversial architect Lúcio Costa, and Niemeyer designed all the major public buildings.

Building Brasília

The work began in September 1956 on the highest and flattest of the five sites identified by the aerial survey. The first task was to build a runway, which was used to bring in the initial building materials and heavy

equipment. **Brasília ❶** thus became the world's first major city conceived in terms of air access. Only after construction had begun was a road pushed through from Belo Horizonte, 740km (460 miles) to the southeast. A dam followed, and Lake Paranoá began to emerge. By April 1960, the city housed 100,000 people and was ready for its inauguration as capital. In 1987 it was declared a World Heritage Site by Unesco, and in 2002 an elegant triple-span steel bridge was built over Lake Paranoá – Juscelino

Main Attractions

Torre de Televisão
Memorial JK
Esplanada dos Ministérios
Congresso Nacional
Catedral Metropolitana
Palácio da Alvorada
Parque Cidade Sarah Kubitschek
Parque Nacional da Chapada dos Veadeiros

The iconic Congresso Nacional, Brasília

Guarding the official presidential residence.

Kubitschek Bridge. The city celebrated the 50th anniversary of its inauguration in 2010, and in 2014 it will host a number of the matches to be played in the FIFA World Cup. The matches take place in the city's new centrally located 71,000-seat **National Stadium** (Está**dio Nacional de Brasilia**) that hosted the opening game of the 2013 Confederations Cup (www.estadio nacionaldebrasilia.com.br).

Most visitors will come to Brasília the way Kubitschek first came – by plane. After flying over the semi-arid and sparsely inhabited Central Plateau, you see the city suddenly emerging as a row of white building blocks set along a gentle rise above the artificial lake. As it is a major domestic airline hub, it is relatively easy to include a quick visit to Brasília while travelling around the country.

Overland, the most spectacular approach is by road from the northeast. After driving through miles of red dust and gnarled scrub, known as *cerrado*, you reach a eucalyptus-lined ridge just beyond **Planaltina**, the oldest town in this region. Brasília is

Evening traffic in Brasília.

laid out in a gleaming arc in the valley below.

Like the United Nations Secretariat in New York, the present-day city is trapped in a 1950s vision of the future. Built around the automobile, its urban core is a complex of super-highways, which creates a hostile environment for pedestrians.

While under construction, Brasília captured the world's imagination, but soon afterwards, the world lost interest, and Brasília became synonymous with technocracy run wild. Yet to this day, the building of the city remains a matter of great pride among Brazilians. It was the only postwar project intended to serve the people, not industry; and it was entirely financed and built at the behest of an elected president, in a time of democracy. For all the flaws that are now evident, Lúcio Costa spoke for the majority of Brazilians when he asserted: 'The only important thing for me is that Brasília exists.'

City from above

The first recommended stop in Brasília is the 224-meter (735ft) **Torre de**

SOCIAL LIFE

Visitors staying in the hotel sector in the center of Brasília often get the mistaken impression that the city is completely dead at night. This is not the case: there is a lively scene in the bars, restaurants, and clubs concentrated along certain commercial streets in the residential wings – notably 109/110 South, 405/406 South, and 303/304 North.

Brasília's extremely fluid and casual social life is defined by the fact that it is a relatively affluent city and, as a modern, new creation, appeals to upwardly mobile young people. Although those who worked in the government sector in Rio de Janeiro – when that city was the capital – resented moving from the coast to Brasília, in recent decades many young professionals have moved here from other parts of Brazil.

Televisão Ⓐ (Television Tower; Tue–Sun 8am–8pm, Mon 2–8pm; free) at the highest point of the **Eixo Monumental** (Monumental Axis) that runs through the center of the city, close to the National Stadium. An informative map at the foot of the tower explains how the streets are laid out. An elevator to a viewing platform 75 meters (245ft) up the tower gives a bird's-eye view of Costa's plan: two gently curving arcs indicating the residential areas of the city, bisected by the Eixo Monumental containing the buildings of government. There is an arts and crafts market under the tower Friday through Sunday, and an impressive water show from the fountains in front.

Costa's plan has been variously described as a cross, a bow and arrow, and an airplane. Costa accepted all these interpretations, but said he really chose its shape to accommodate the curvature of the terrain above the lake, while emphasizing the civic buildings at the center of the city. Costa's design was selected because of its simplicity and suitability for a national capital.

Another good vantage point to view the city from is the distinctive Digital TV Tower, known as the **Flor de Cerrado** (Cerrado Flower), which opened to the public in 2012. The Niemeyer-designed tower, already located on high ground close to Sobradingo, on the road to Planaltina, has two observation platforms, including one restaurant. (Sat–Sun 9am–5pm; free). Due to the popularity of this attraction, it is expected that visiting hours will be extended in the future.

The government sector

Heading west from the center along the Eixo Monumental, you next come to the administrative seat of the Federal District in **Palácio do Buriti** Ⓑ, in pretty Praça Municipal. Continuing westward you reach the **Memorial JK** Ⓒ (Tue–Sun 9am–5.40pm), the memorial to Kubitschek. It was the first building in Brasília that the military allowed Niemeyer to design

after their takeover in 1964. The curious sickle-shaped structure on top of the monument, in which the statue of Kubitschek stands, seems more like a political gesture by Niemeyer than a symbol of Kubitschek's beliefs.

Inside the monument are Kubitschek's tomb and a collection of memorabilia about his life and the construction of Brasília. One showcase contains a summary of the unsuccessful entries in the competition to design the city, including a proposal to house most of its population in 18 enormous tower blocks over 300 meters (1,000ft) high, housing 16,000 people.

Heading in the other direction from the Television Tower, down the hill past the main bus terminal and central shopping mall, the Eixo Monumental opens on to the **Esplanada dos Ministérios** Ⓓ (Esplanade of the Ministries). A row of 17 identical pale-green box-shaped buildings runs down both sides of the vast open boulevard. Each building houses a different government department, whose name is emblazoned in gold letters on the front. Since every ministry has

Brasília's Juscelino Kubitschek (or JK) bridge.

Kubitschek stands aloft the Memorial JK, a striking Niemeyer design.

long since outgrown its original quarters, they have sprouted additions at the back, approved by Niemeyer and Unesco, connected in mid-air by concrete tubes to their mother ship. In the late 1960s, several buildings were subject to arson attacks, reportedly by disgruntled civil servants protesting against their forced move from Rio, although this rumor was never substantiated.

Niemeyer's best

Flanking the end of the Esplanade are Niemeyer's two finest buildings: the **Palácio do Itamaratí** Ⓔ (Mon–Fri 3–5pm, Sat–Sun 10am–3.30pm, guided tours only; free), now housing the Foreign Ministry, which floats in splendid isolation in the midst of a reflecting pool; and the **Palácio da Justiça** Ⓕ (Ministry of Justice; Mon–Fri 9–11am, 3–5pmfree), whose six curtains of falling water on the exterior echo the natural waterfalls around Brasília.

Beyond the Eixo Monumental is the **Praça dos Três Poderes** Ⓖ (Plaza of the Three Powers) – a dense forest of political symbols. Named after the three divisions of power under the Brazilian Constitution, the executive is represented by the **Palácio do Planalto** Ⓗ (Sun 9.30am–1.30pm; free), on the left, housing the president's offices, while the judiciary is represented by the **Supremo Tribunal Federal** Ⓘ (Supreme Court; Sat–Sun and holidays 10am–5.30pm; free) on the right.

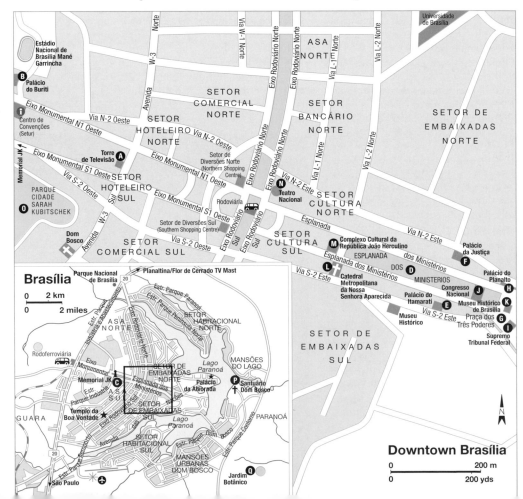

Downtown Brasília

Overshadowing both – architecturally if not politically – are the twin towers and offset domes of the **Congresso Nacional** ● (Chamber of Deputies: Mon–Fri 9–11.30am, 2.30–4.30pm, Sat–Sun and holidays 9am–1pm; Senate: Mon–Fri 9.30–11.30am, 3.30–4.30pm, Sat–Sun and holidays 10am–2pm). This is the building whose silhouette is the signature of Brasília. Even the former monarchy has a place in the plaza. The rows of tall imperial palms behind the congress building were transplanted from the Botanical Garden that Dom João VI created in Rio de Janeiro.

Around the plaza

There are a number of notable sculptures on the plaza. The basaltic head of Kubitschek protrudes from the marble walls of the small **Museu Histórico de Brasília** ● (Sun–Fri 9am–6pm), which is actually just a series of panels outlining the history of Brasília, and the most memorable sayings of Kubitschek, whose powers of hyperbole rivaled his talent for conceiving new cities.

In front of the Supreme Court is a blindfolded figure of Justice, sculpted by Alfredo Ceschiatti. Facing the Palácio do Planalto are the figures of *The Warriors* by Bruno Giorgi, a tribute to the thousands of workers and laborers who built Brasília. A note of whimsy is added to the plaza by Niemeyer's pigeon house, the **Pombal**.

The most recent addition to the plaza is the **Pantheon Tancredo Neves** (daily 9am–6pm), a tribute to the founding father of the New Republic, who died in April 1985 before he could be sworn in as president. Inside the darkened interior, designed by Niemeyer, is Brasília's most extraordinary and disturbing artwork. The mural, by João Camara, depicts the story of an uprising in the 18th century led by Brazil's best-known revolutionary, Tiradentes (Joaquim José da Silva Xavier), who, like Neves, was a *mineiro*. Painted in

seven black-and-white panels (rather like Picasso's *Guernica*), it is heavy with Masonic symbolism.

The iconic **Catedral Metropolitana da Nossa Senhora Aparecida** ● (Mon 8am–5pm, Tue–Sun 8am–6pm; free), at the western end of the Esplanada dos Ministérios, is an unusual concrete building with a spectacular, stained-glass domed roof. Nearby, the newest buildings on the Esplanada dos Ministérios are the Biblioteca Nacional Leonel de Moura Brizola (National Library) and the Museu Nacional Honestino Guimarães (National Museum), that together make up the **Complexo Cultural da República João Herculino** ●. These two buildings were completed in December 2006, following Niemeyer's original plans.

On the north side of the Eixo Monumental, near the Rodoviária, is the pyramid-shaped **Teatro Nacional** ● (daily 9am–8pm), where art shows and other exhibitions are held.

Further away, on the shores of Lake Paranoá, is the **Palácio da Alvorada** (Wed 3–5pm; free). The official

TIP

There are some specialized four-hour tours of Brasília's architectural landmarks. Contact the Bluepoint agency (tel: 61-3274 0033) for details. There is also the option of a two-hour bus tour of the city, which leaves from Brasília Shopping and covers most of the main sites. (Mon–Fri 10.30am, 2pm, 5pm, Sat–Sun 10.30am, 1pm, 3.30pm, 5pm).

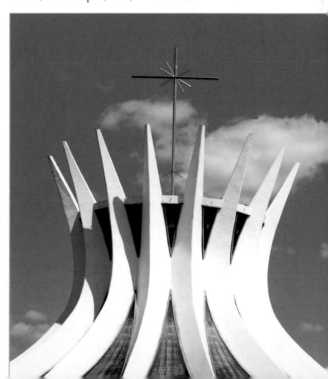

The design of Catedral Metropolitana is meant to represent two hands reaching up to heaven.

One of the four statues
of the Apostles outside
the Catedral
Metropolitana.

Inside the National
Museum, another of
Brasília's major
buildings designed by
Oscar Niemeyer.

presidential residence, the Alvorada is regarded as one of Niemeyer's masterpieces, and one of the first projects to be completed. It is a two-story, rectangular building whose main features are the marble columns that have become a symbol of Brasília.

Residential Brasília

To appreciate Brasília as a living city, you need to leave the center and visit the areas where people actually live – the purpose-built *quadras* that are arrayed along the city's north and south wings. Each *quadra* is made up of six to eight low-rise residential blocks, grouped around landscaped lawns and courtyards. Short commercial streets, which provide a range of basic services for the residents, are evenly interspersed between them. The *quadras* provide an essentially uniform standard of living across the city, which for many residents is a welcome respite from the urban jungles of Brazil's coastal cities.

Satellite cities

Lúcio Costa's original plan for Brasília gave the city a rigid shape. Once all the *quadras* planned for the north wing were built, the city proper could grow no further. The great surprise in the evolution of Brasília has been the explosive growth of the 'satellite cities' beyond its green belt. These were originally settled by construction workers from the northeast, who remained here after their contracted work in the city finished. Their numbers have since swelled with new migrants and lower-middle-class residents, who have sold the free apartments they were awarded in the pilot plan.

Today, Brasília proper accounts for only 22 percent of the population of the Federal District. Despite the egalitarian architecture and intentions of the pilot plan, the class barriers in the wider Federal District are even more rigid than in the rest of the country. The population is zoned by income into separate cities.

Leisure and pleasure

If you are looking for leisure and relaxation, go to the **Parque Cidade Sarah Kubitschek** Ⓞ (daily 9am–midnight), named after Juscelino Kubitschek's wife, and also known as Parque da Cidade (City Park). This is a vast, green area of 42 hectares (104 acres) in the centre of Brasília, close to the Torre de Televisão. Here local people and visitors alike come to exercise, sunbathe, meet friends, or just relax.

Further out, by Lake Paranoá, the **Pontão do Lago Sul** has shops, restaurants, bars, antique fairs, and piers. Younger visitors will probably favor Pier 21 (www.pier21.com.br; daily noon–1am), a shopping center full of bars, nightclubs, restaurants, cinemas, and bookstores.

Center of spiritualism

Brasília's spiritual life is as unusual as its social mores. Niemeyer's concrete cathedral along the Eixo Monumental represents Catholicism, the official faith. But closer to the city's true faith is the cult of Dom Bosco, an Italian

priest and educator who prophesied in 1883 that a new civilization would arise in a land of milk and honey on the site of present-day Brasília. His prophecy provided spiritual legitimacy for Kubitschek's secular dream of a new capital.

The first structure built on the city site, overlooking Lake Paranoá, was a small marble pyramid commemorating Dom Bosco's vision. Brasília's most striking church, the **Santuârio Dom Bosco** ⓟ (www.santuariodom bosco.org.br; daily 7am–7pm; free) in 702 South, is a cubic chapel with walls made entirely of blue-and-violet stained glass.

Brasília also enjoys a reputation as 'The Capital of the Third Millennium', by virtue of the 400-plus contemporary cults that flourish near here. Further south, at 915, is the extraordinary **Templo da Boa Vontade** (Temple of Goodwill; www.tbv.com.br/english/; daily 10am–6pm; free). Built in the form of a seven-sided pyramid in 1989 (seven is said to be the number of perfection), it is crowned with one of the world's largest crystals.

Vale do Amanhecer

Several New Age communities have been founded on the outskirts of Brasília. The largest and most accessible is the **Vale do Amanhecer** (Valley of the Dawn), south of Planaltina. Every Sunday, several hundred worshipers come here to be initiated into the commune established by 'Tia Neiva', a retired female truck-driver. The weekly parade of initiates, dressed in multicolored cloaks and veils, around a pond adorned with astrological symbols, is an eerie sight.

Parks and gardens

A short taxi ride away from the Dom Bosco church, to the southeast of the city, is the **Jardim Botânico** ⓠ (Setor de Mansões D. Bosco, Conjunto 12, Lago Sul; www.jardimbotanico.df.gov.br; Tue–Sun 9am–5pm), a pleasant place to discover the flora of the *cerrado* (savannah). To the north of the city is a 30,000-hectare (74,000-acre) nature reserve operated by the botanical gardens, the **Parque Nacional de Brasília** (daily 8am–4pm). This is an area of *cerrado* and low forest where

The magical interior of Santuârio Dom Bosco.

FACT

Many of the herbs and plants growing in the Pireneus range have medicinal properties, and have been used by the local population for generations. A number of these can be seen in Brasília during a visit to the Botanical Gardens.

The spider monkey's habitat stretches from Mexico down to Mato Grosso, which borders Goiás.

birds, wolves, monkeys, and armadillos find refuge. There are forest trails, natural swimming pools, and a visitor center.

Goiás state

The state of **Goiás** is an area of savannah and large rivers that attract growing numbers of keen fishermen and ecotourists. The riverbanks are densely forested and rich in wildlife. Much savannah land is being taken over by plantations of soybeans, and the state is now the center of a campaign to protect the *cerrado*.

The principal attractions of the state are the sister hydrothermal resorts of **Caldas Novas,** 172km (107 miles) from Goiânia, and **Rio Quente**, 43km (17 miles) away, along with its colonial towns and its beautiful national parks and nature reserves.

Pirenópolis ❷, a picturesque town 137km (85 miles) from Brasília, was founded in the 18th century to house gold miners. Its cobbled streets and fine Baroque houses make it well worth a visit. In the Pireneus mountain range, in which the town is set, blocks of quartz and sandstone have been sculpted by time and weather into spectacular shapes, on which grow lichens, moss, and cacti.

About 265km (165 miles) north of Brasília is the **Parque Nacional da Chapada dos Veadeiros ❸**, a nature reserve with numerous beautiful waterfalls, rock formations, and natural swimming pools.

Goiás ❹ (also known as Goiás Velho), 340km (212 miles) from Brasília, was the state's capital until 1937. Although it lost that status, it is interesting for its colonial architecture, with many well-preserved 18th-century churches and houses. In 2001 it was listed by Unesco, after a comprehensive restoration program.

Along the Araguaia river

Forming Goiás's western border is part of a river whose valley was described by Durval Rosa Borges, the author of *Araguaia, Heart and Soul,* as 'the Garden of Eden.' The Araguaia river is, in fact, 2,630km (1,634 miles) long, cutting Brazil in two, from the wetlands of the Pantanal across the *cerrado,* or central plains, to the Atlantic Ocean at Belém.

When the muddy floodwaters shrink in August to reveal immense white-sand beaches, 200,000 vacationing Brazilians descend on the river at **Aruanã ❺**, 530km (330 miles) west of Brasília, and **Barra do Garças ❻**, both in western Goiás state, to establish lavish campsites and sound systems for lively all-night parties. Even so, their presence is dwarfed by the Araguaia's vast scale.

The source of the river in southern Goiás is in the **Parque Nacional das Emas ❼**, from which it flows northward, forming a barrier between the states of Mato Grosso, Goiás, Tocantins, and Pará, dividing to form the fluvial **Ilha do Bananal ❽**. To the north of the island is the **Parque Nacional do Araguaia ❾**. During the low-water season, floating hotels operate on the river's tributaries.

RESTAURANTS

PRICE CATEGORIES

Prices for a two-course meal for two. Wine costs around US$25 a bottle.
$ = under US$50
$$ = US$50–100
$$$ = US$100–200

Addresses in Brasília look a bit odd if you are not used to them, but are really quite straightforward: Bloco means block, Casa means house, Conjunto means a group of buildings, and Loja means a unit. Most of the streets have numbers rather than names, eg 306 Norte (North), 402 Sul (South).

Alice Brasserie
Fashion Park, QI 17, Conjunto 9, Casa 17, Lago Sul
Tel: 61-3248 7743
Open: L&D Tue–Sat, L only Sun.
A delightful and popular, elegant French bistro that is considered by many people to be one of the best restaurants in Brasília. First opened back in 1996. Located, along with a number of other restaurants, in the Fashion Park. **$$**

Bargaço
Pontão do Lago Sul, QI 10
Tel: 61-3364 6090
Open: L&D daily.
A good and traditional Bahian and seafood restaurant, branches of which can also be found in Salvador, João Pessoa, Recife, and Belo Horizonte – and all of them are equally reliable. Nice view of the lake. **$$$**

Carpe Diem
104 Sul, Bloco D, Loja 1, Asa Sul
Tel: 61-3325 5301
Open: L&D (until 2am) daily.
There is a varied and well-priced menu, but Carpe Diem is best known for its *feijoada* on Saturday, which, since 1991, has become something of an institution in Brasília. Branches also at Brasília Shopping, Terraço Shopping, Casa Park and Pier 21. **$$**

Corrients 348
411 Sul, Loja 36, Bloco D
Tel: 61-3345 1348
Open: L&D daily, L only Sun.
Reliable, prime cuts of Argentine beef and other dishes inspired by Brazil's neighbor to the south. The group also has three restaurant of the same name in São Paulo and one in Curitiba. **$$$**

Dom Francisco
Setor de Clubes Esportivos Sul (SCES),Trecho 2, Conjunto 31
Tel: 61-3224 8429
Open: L&D Mon–Sat.
Dom Francisco serves both exotic and regional dishes. At the main address (above), which first opened in 1993, there is an excellent wine cellar, with more than 15,000 bottles from 14 countries, as well as great views across the lake. There are three other branches in town: at Patio Brasil, Park Shopping, and 402 Sul. **$$**

Feitiço Mineiro
306 Norte, Bloco B, Lojas 45/51
Tel: 61-3272 3032
Open: L&D (until last customer) Mon–Sat, L only Sun until 5pm).
Excellent regional cuisine from the state of Minas Gerais, hence the name. Feijoada a popular option on Saturday. Also, since 2005, offers a popular bar area, Bar do Fetiço, with snacks. **$$**

Piantella
202 Sul, Bloco A, Loja 34
Tel: 61-3224 9408
Open: L&D Mon–Sat, L only Sun.
Eat in pleasant, elegant and comfortable surroundings, in a venue that has been especially popular with

Feijoada – a stew of beans and pork.

politicians and diplomats for over 40 years. There's a good wine list to accompany dishes, and a good *feijoada* on Saturday. Not the cheapest option in town. **$$$**

Porção
Setor de Clubes Esportivos Sul (SCES), Trecho 2, Conjunto 35, next to Pier 21
Tel: 61-3223 2002
Open: L&D daily.
The largest and best-known barbecue restaurant in the city (it seats 900), set beside Lake Paranoá. There are more than 20 different cuts of meat, a generous buffet, and Japanese food as well. There are unlimited salads, to which you help yourself, and meat is sliced from skewers at your table, all at a set price. **$$$**

Trattoria da Rosario
Fashion Park, Bloco H, Loja 215 Lago Sul
Tel: 61-3248 1672
Open: L&D Mon–Sat. L only Sun (until 5pm).
Enjoy regional Italian food in one of the best restaurants in the capital. A veranda for eating outside opened in 2010. Popular with politicians and diplomats. **$$$**

Stalactites in a Geopark
Bodoquena-Pantanal cave.

THE PANTANAL

The Pantanal is an extraordinary place. Not only is the diversity of wildlife remarkable, but also the landscape and vegetation make it easy to see a great deal even on a brief visit.

The highlight of any visit to western Brazil is the **Pantanal** ⑩, a vast natural paradise that is one of the country's major ecological attractions. Pristine and biologically rich, the area comprises 230,000 sq km (89,000 sq miles), shared unequally between Brazil, Bolivia, and Paraguay, of seasonally flooded territory, offering a density of tropical wildlife unknown outside Africa. The word Pantanal comes from the Portuguese *pântano*, meaning swamp or marshland, but the region is in fact an immense alluvial plain, comprising rivers, lakes, grassland, forest, and savannah. The Pantanal crosses two states, Mato Grosso and Mato Grosso do Sul, and access to it is from the major towns of Corumbá and Campo Grande in the south, and Poconé and Cuiabá, a host city for the 2104 FIFA World Cup, and in the north.

Protecting the Pantanal

Scarcely populated, the majority of the Pantanal is privately owned (only 135,000 hectares/333,000 acres is national park), and the region's economy is sustained by extensive cattle farming, agriculture (soy, rice, and corn are grown) and, increasingly, tourism. Hunting is prohibited (although fishing is allowed with a permit, and some restrictions), but because of the nature of the terrain and, until fairly recently, lack of government enforcement or support, this area has been poorly policed.

A hyacinth-macaw egg can sell for more than US$10,000 and poachers, are still very active in the region.

Wildlife

It is the concentration, as well as the huge diversity, of wildlife that makes the Pantanal a naturalist's dream. Similar species are found here as in the Amazon, but owing to the lack of dense vegetation and, in the dry season, the birds and mammals around

Cattle drive in the southern Pantanal.

feeding areas such as watering holes, they are far easier to spot. Film crews trying to capture Amazon wildlife are frequently redirected to the Pantanal, where chances of sightings are better.

The area is home to an estimated 650 bird species, the majority of which are wading birds such as the graceful jabiru stork, which stands at 1.4 meters (over 4ft) tall, and the roseate spoonbill with its distinctive beak. Although the Pantanal offers sanctuary for migratory geese and ducks moving between Argentina and Central America, most of the water birds found here are residents that follow the changing water levels inside the huge swamp, in pursuit of the 250 species of fish that support them in the food chain.

Especially delightful are the 15 wonderfully colorful species of parrot, including the majestic hyacinth macaw (the world's largest parrot, at 1 meter/ 3ft long), as well as an incredible proliferation of toucans. These curious creatures, with their precise coloring and oversized beaks, often come to pick berries delicately from the fruit trees of your lodge as you sit at breakfast.

Glimpsing the mammals

You are more likely to catch a glimpse of the mammal inhabitants during the dry season. The capybara, dog sized with the blunt snout of a guinea pig, is the world's largest rodent – an adult can weigh around 80kg (175lbs). Capuchin and howler monkeys can often be seen and heard, and the extraordinary

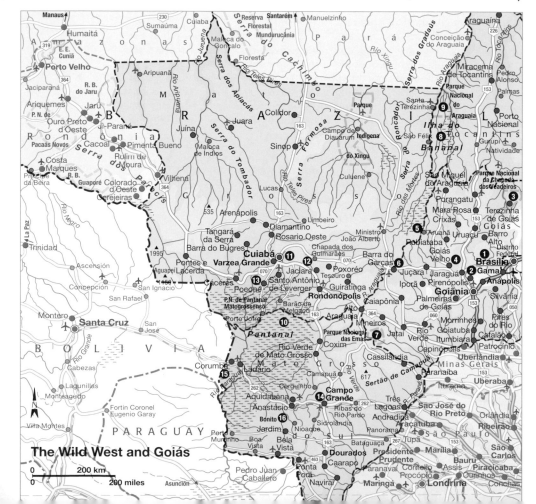

The Wild West and Goiás

giant anteater, with its long, delicate nose and majestic gait, emerges to feed at dusk. Armadillos, marsh deer, and coatis are other common sights, but you would be extremely lucky to see the elusive jaguar and puma, which leave paw prints in the dust.

The ubiquitous caiman lie open-mouthed, basking in the Pantanal sun, gorging themselves on fish, and waiting for the rains to come. And you may see the yellow anaconda, a greedy constrictor, which has been known to consume a whole capybara.

Rainfall cycles

Rainfall cycles are the key to the Pantanal: during the wet season (October to April) the River Paraguay and its tributaries burst their banks, spreading water into huge *baías*, or closed lakes where fish have been breeding. The waters activate ground vegetation and enable overhanging trees to produce fruit on which the fish gorge themselves, before swimming through open canals to spawn in the rivers, and attracting huge numbers of wading birds. Water levels can rise by 5 meters (16ft), leaving many

areas accessible only by boat or light aircraft. Mornings are usually dry and clear, with a steady build-up of clouds throughout the day, and a sustained, heavy burst of rain in the evening. Temperatures are around 24°C (75°F), and mosquitoes can be fierce.

In the long dry season, the waters recede the landscape changes completely, and the Pantanal becomes dusty and arid. Many fish are retained in small ponds, providing a crucial food source for the mammal and reptile inhabitants that congregate around the waterholes. In the heat, trees lose their leaves, and wildlife becomes easier to spot. Temperatures can drop to 10°C (50°F) at night, but during the day the sun is hot and persistent.

Cuiabá

Cuiabá ⑪, in the center of Mato Grosso, was the west's first settlement, founded in 1719 by a group of slave-hunters from São Paulo who struck shallow gold and diamond deposits. The resulting rush of prospectors made Cuiabá the third-most important city in Brazil. A century ago, the city found

The vicious teeth of a piranha.

An alligator comtemplates a butterfly.

THE HIGHWAY

From Poconé, the Trans-Pantaneira Highway, which is in a poor state of repair, runs 145km (90 miles) south-ward through the Pantanal to Porto Jofre. It crosses over 126 bridges. Begun in the 1970s, the Trans-Pantaneira highway was originally intended to link Cuiabá with Corumbá, but local political wrangling and pressure from environmentalists cut it short. Because the road runs parallel to the rivers, huge bodies of water collect beside it, ensuring sightings of alligators and birdlife even for those unwilling to get out of their cars.

Cargo boats also ply the 185km (115 miles) of the River São Lourenço to Corumbá. They run at irregular times, and usually transport cattle, not people, but they may take passengers if you are able to negotiate with the captain.

Tours and lodges

Accommodations in the Pantanal vary enormously, from hammocks slung beneath palapa roofs, to stylish, comfortable en suite cabins and eco resorts.

Access to the Pantanal is usually from Corumbá, Campo Grande, or Cuiabá. Lodges are reached by a combination of four-wheel-drive trips on paved and bumpy roads in the dry season, or occasionally by light aircraft or boat in the wet months.

Almost all lodges are full board, and transport to and from the lodge is included in the price. Two or three nights are recommended to make the most of the region, and lodges will include a tour early in the morning and another in the late afternoon, when it is cooler and there is more chance of spotting wildlife. There is usually a jeep safari, a boat trip, a night safari, a horseback ride, or a walk.

Budget travelers can book a guide locally on arrival at the airport or bus station in Corumbá, Campo Grande, or Cuiabá. Be very careful what you pay for: standards vary hugely, and while you may

Cabins on stilts are fairly typical as accommodation in the Pantanal.

not mind a few nights in a hammock, if your guide is not up to scratch, your trip will certainly not be all it could be. To guarantee quality of accommodations and guides, go for an all-inclusive trip at a reputable lodge. Some of the best are listed below.

From Campo Grande: **Pousada Aguape** is a delightful working cattle farm. Simple cabins, a nice pool, good food served buffet-style and friendly, English-speaking staff (tel: 67-3258 1146; www.aguape.com.br). **Refugio Ecologico Caiman** is a leading wildlife reserve, home to one of the most comfortable and tasteful lodges in the Pantanal, with immaculate cabins and great food. Tours are run by specialist bilingual guides with pick-ups from Campo Grande (tel: 67-3242 1450/11-3706 1800; www.caiman.com.br).

The popular **Pousada Refúgio** is one of the closest lodges to Bonito and halfway between Campo Grande and Corumbá. Accommodations are simple, but comfortable. The lodge offers a good series of tours (tel: 67-3306 3415; http://refugiodailha.com.br).

From Corumbá: **Passo do Lontra** is a large lodge on stilts on the banks of the Miranda river, 120km (75 miles) from Corumbá. Accommodations range from hammocks to beds in simple rooms, and comfortable cabins with en suite bathrooms and hot water. There is a large indoor restaurant. The lodge specializes in river and fishing trips (tel: 67-3245 2407; www.passodolontra.com.br).

Northern Pantanal

From Cuiabá: The **Araras Lodge** is 132km (82 miles) from Cuiabá (approximately two- and-a-half hours by road, of which 32km/20 miles is down a dirt track); it has 19 lovely, rustic, en suite rooms in a fantastic setting (tel: 65-3682 2800; www.araraslodge.com.br). Hotel **Porto Jofre** (245km/152 miles from Cuiabá) is a more formal affair, with 28 concrete cabins, a good-sized pool and enclosed dining room. Access is by small plane or boat in the wet season, or by car. There are motorboats for river trips and fishing (tel: 65-3637 1593; www.portojofre.com.br). **Pousada do Rio Mutum** comprises 22 neat, red-roofed chalets with en suite bathrooms and hot water, sheltered dining area and pool, set in relatively dense forest. The lodge is located at the point where the River Mutum merges with two lakes, so river otters are often seen (tel: 65-3052 7022; www.pousadamutum.com.br).

Pousada Piuval, 110km (68 miles) from Cuiabá, is another well-structured lodge close to the Rodovia Transpanteira. Well equipped for horseback riding and boat trips (tel: 65-3345 1338; www.pousadapiuval.com.br).

a new resource and acquired fame as a major supplier of exotic feathers to the milliners of Paris. Today, this prosperous city is a major starting point for trips into the Pantanal, and the capital of an immense logging, farming, and mining state. Little of colonial Cuiabá survives, but the cathedral church of Bom Jesus de Lapa has a small adjoining museum of religious artifacts.

For the 2014 FIFA World Cup, the city built a 43,000-seat stadium, Arena Pantanal, which also includes a shopping mall and convention center.

Chapada dos Guimarães

The **Museu do Indio Marechal Rondon** (Mon–Fri 7.30–11.30am, 1.30–5.30pm, Sat–Sun 7.30–11.30am) at the university entrance, 10 minutes' bus ride from the center, shows the artifacts and lifestyle of the Xingu tribes. Some of the items are on sale at a handicrafts shop run by FUNAI, the government Amerindian-affairs bureau. Other landmarks are the Governor's Residence and the **Fundação Cultural de Mato Grosso** (Praça da República 151; Mon–Fri 8am–5.30pm), in a historic mansion that houses three interesting museums: Antropológica, História Natural, and Cultura Popular.

Fish is Cuiabá's culinary forte. Piranha may be deadly in the water, but legend has it that in soup they possess aphrodisiac powers – try the *caldo de piranha* (piranha broth).

After the lowland heat, relief is close at hand 70km (45 miles) from Cuiabá. The **Chapada dos Guimarães National Park** is a rocky outcrop overlooking the flat plain, 800 meters (2,600ft) above sea level. In the misty cool of the Chapada's folded hills and monolithic rock formations are caves and stunning waterfalls. Local residents attest to the region's mystical qualities, and confirm frequent UFO sightings. These uplands provide one of the many water sources for the Pantanal marshlands.

Through the Gates of Hell

Later, the road curves through the **Portão de Inferno** (Gates of Hell) – a vertical drop that marks the edge of the escarpment. Overhead, tower pencil-like rock formations. Further

TIP

Cuiabá's main square, the Praça da República, is the location of Sedtur, the state tourism authority, which has a helpful visitor center. Two of the city's main tour operators offering tours to the Pantanal and Chapada are Lenda Turismo (www.lenda turismo.com.br) and Interativa Pantanal (www.interativapantanal. com.br/ingles/).

Jabiru stork in flight.

Entering the Pantanal.

on, admire the 86-meter (280ft) **Véu da Noiva** (Bride's Veil) waterfall from above, or walk for half an hour in the wooded canyon to reach its base. Further into the Chapada are the Casa de Pedra – a natural cave-house capped by an immense stone shelf – and the Caverna Aroe Jari, on whose walls are primitive paintings. You need a guide; they are easy to find, and will supply a flashlight. **Chapada dos Guimarães** ⑫, with the 200-year-old church of Santana, is a historical town that grew up to provide Cuiabá's miners with food. It is a good base for excursions into the surrounding countryside and the national park. Just outside town, a monument marks the geodesic center of South America.

Due south of Cuiabá, on state highway 060, is **Poconé** ⑬, a dry area given over to farming, that is another good jumping-off point for visiting parts of the Pantanal.

If you are short on time, it is possible to do a one-hour helicopter flight over the Chapada and parts of the Pantanal from Cuiabá. (Lenda Turismo; www.lendaturismo.com.br)

Cowboy towns and trains

Entry points for the southern Pantanal in Mato Grosso do Sul, are Corumbá and **Campo Grande** ⑭, the state capital. It began life in 1889, and is still an overgrown cowboy town. The **Museu Dom Bosco** (Rua Barão do Rio Branco 1843; daily 8.30am–5pm) has interesting Amerindian exhibits and a huge natural history collection.

In 2009, after a gap of nearly 20 years, the **Pantanal Express** (www.pantanalexpress.com) returned to action. The tourist train crosses 220km (140 miles) of the Pantanal west of Campo Grande to Miranda, 130km (80 miles) from Bonito. It's a ten-hour journey, with a two-hour stop for lunch at Aquidauana. Currently the train runs from Campo Grande to Miranda on Saturday, with a return journey on Sunday. More services are expected to be added, depending on demand.

Corumbá ⑮, on the Bolivian border opposite Puerto Suárez, was founded in 1778. From here there is access to the Pantanal by both road and river – even a brief boat trip gives a vivid impression.

A capybara.

Bonito

Crystal-clear rivers, waterfalls, and caves dot the landscape of the Serra do Bodoquena, and **Bonito** ⓰ has become the center of nature tourism in the area. The town is not particularly interesting, but with good bars, restaurants, and hostels, it is a good base from which to explore the natural attractions nearby. The extraordinary clarity of the water is due to the high concentration of carbonates, which bubble up from underwater springs from a limestone base, and calcify the impurities in the water, causing them to drop to the riverbed, leaving the rivers breathtakingly clear.

Most natural sights are on private land and charge a fee; since many are out of town, it's best to join an organized tour. Bonito is a protected area, and visitor numbers are limited. Places get booked up (and prices increase) in the Brazilian holiday season.

Rio da Prata is a stretch of almost transparent water 45 minutes' drive from Bonito. Most of it is only just over 1 meter (3ft) deep, and floating downstream, brushing against subaqua flora, face to face with curious fish, makes you feel as if you are in a giant aquarium. When you lift your head up out of the water, you are likely to see capuchin monkeys and toucans in the trees above. The Rio da Prata excursion includes river guides, and snorkeling equipment and wetsuits. The Rio Sucuri trip is similar but shorter, and accompanied by a small boat. This is the better option for those who feel less comfortable in the water.

Pools and lakes

Balneiro Municipal is a local, natural swimming pool (a five-minute moto-taxi ride from town) on Rio Formoso. There are changing rooms and a café, and the area is scrupulously clean.

At Estancia Mimosa (a 45-minute drive) you can hike through *ciliar* forest, which follows the banks of the river, stopping to bathe in waterfalls and natural pools.

Lagoa Azul is a lake inside a deep limestone cave that glows a brilliant blue when light from the cave's entrance is refracted in the limestone and magnesium. You can visit throughout daylight hours.

RESTAURANTS

PRICE CATEGORIES

Prices for a three-course dinner per person with a half-bottle of house wine:
$ = under $50
$$ = $50–100
$$$ = $100–200

In the Pantanal proper there are no restaurants as visitors eat at the lodge where they stay.

Bonito

Cantinho do Peixe
1918 Rua 31 de Marco
Tel: 67-3255 3381
Open: L&D Mon–Sat, L Sun.
As the name might suggest, freshwater fish from the Pantanal is the speciality here. Try the signature dish, a filet of pintado. **$**

Casa do João
664 Rua Nelson Felicio dos Santos
Tel: 67-3255 1212

Open: L&D Wed–Mon.
Considered one of the town's most reliable restaurants. Interesting menu of local produce, including the tail filet of a caiman, but you can also have a simple steak. Nice friendly atmosphere. **$**

Campo Grande

Fogo Caipira
145 Rua José Antonio
Tel: 67-3324 1641
Open: L&D Mon–Sat, L Sun.
Highly rated for its regional Brazilian cuisine that uses many ingredients from the Pantanal. The restaurant tries to reproduce the experience of eating at a typical *fazenda* (farm) of the region. **$$**

Vermelho Grill
6078 Avenida Afonso Pena, Bairro Chácara Cachoeira
Tel: 67-3326 7813
Open: L&D Mon–Sat, L Sun.
Charming grill house that is rustic and comfortable. The brainchild of a gaucho, this serves excellent meats from Rio Grande do Sul and a good selection of wines. **$$**

Cuiabá

Biba's Peixaria
508 Rua General João Severiano da Foseca, Araés
Tel: 65-3322 3174
Open: L&D Mon–Fri, L only Sat–Sun.
The place to try many of the fascinating freshwater fish found throughout the Pantanal region, as well as interesting side dishes. **$$**

Mahalo
359 Rua Presidente Castello Branco, Quilombo
Tel: 65-3028 7700
Open: L&D Mon–Sat.
Considered the city's best. Creative contemporary cuisine in a comfortable and modern setting mixing French and Brazilian influences. **$$**

The beach at Arraial d'Ajuda.

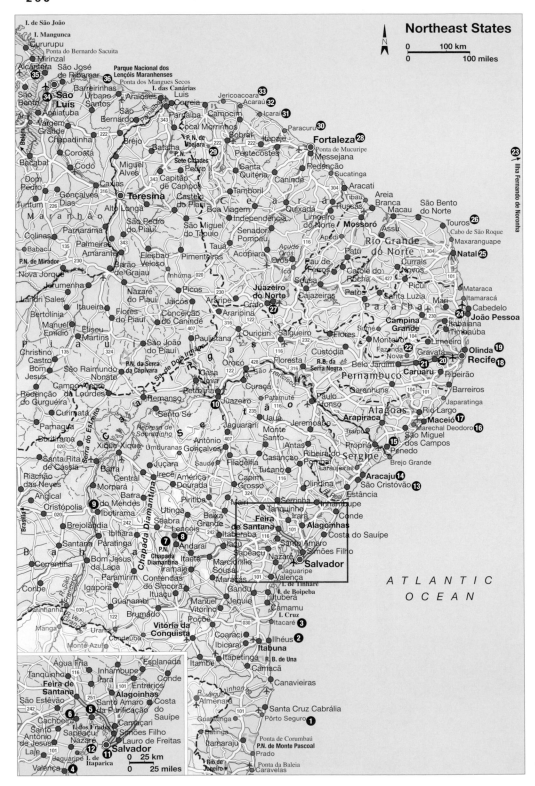

THE NORTHEAST

Northeastern Brazil comprises vast areas of scrubland,
idyllic beaches, and beautiful colonial towns, and its
vibrant culture is reflected in its festivals and music.

*The bust of a young child
in bronze.*

Travelers in the know have woken up to the potential of the northeast of Brazil as a tourist destination. Communications have been greatly improved with a network of modern airports and flight connections between the state capitals, and you can now fly direct to Salvador, Fortaleza, Natal, and Recife from a number of foreign cities. The attraction is obvious: quite simply, the northeastern coast is a paradise. It is warm and sunny year round, the glorious beaches are the best in Brazil, and certainly the least spoilt, and the wilderness areas are magical. The colonial towns are the oldest in the country, and *nordestinos* are a vibrant people whose distinctive Carnival and religious festivals rival Rio's.

Bahia, set apart from the rest of the northeast by its strong African roots, has a wonderfully rich heritage. Salvador, its capital, is one of the most favored destinations in Brazil, since word got around about the food, the music, and the festivals, as well as the colonial architecture.

*Taperapuã beach, a few
kilometres north of the settlement
of Porto Seguro, Bahia.*

The most populous and prosperous areas of the northeast are concentrated along the coast, where there is a strip of fertile land – as there is along the course of the São Francisco river, which runs through Bahia, Pernambuco, Sergipe, and Alagoas. The coastal economy benefits from agriculture, and from the income gained from tourists who visit the tropical beaches.

There is another aspect to the northeast, though: this is a predominantly parched territory of nine states, making up 18 percent of Brazil. It had its short-lived glory days at the beginning of the colonial period, when its economy was based on sugar-cane and cotton plantations. After competition killed off the sugar trade, the northeast went into decline, and was for many years neglected: the vast, arid *sertão* (scrubland) of the interior is a hard place to eke out a living. Today, state-funded development schemes are bringing benefits to those in greatest need, stemming the tide of migration to the cities, and the social problems this brings.

Reflecting the recent developments in the northeast, Fortaleza, Natal, Recife, and Salvador were all chosen to be host cities for the 2014 FIFA World Cup.

In the colonial city centre of Porto Seguro.

BAHIA

Bahia, where the Portuguese first landed, is said to be the most Brazilian of states. Today, its laid-back, colorful lifestyle attracts visitors, who come to explore the historic towns and arid interior landscape, and relax in idyllic beach resorts.

ahia is the soul of Brazil. In this northeastern state more than anywhere else, the country's cultures and races have mixed, producing, many believe, what is most authentically Brazilian.

It was at **Pôrto Seguro**, on the southern coast of Bahia, that Pedro Alvares Cabral first 'discovered' this land in 1500. A year later, on November 1 – All Saints' Day – the Italian navigator Amerigo Vespucci arrived in what is now **Salvador**, the capital of Bahia and, until 1763, also the capital of Brazil.

Bahia is the site of the country's first medical school, its oldest churches, its most important colonial architecture, and one of the largest collections of sacred art. Bahia is also the birthplace of many of Brazil's outstanding writers, politicians, and composers. Bahia-born novelist Jorge Amado's works have been translated into nearly 50 languages, and several of his books have become major films (including *Dona Flor and Her Two Husbands* and *Gabriela*). The music of Bahians João Gilberto, Caetano Veloso, Maria Bethania, Baden Powell, Dorival Caymmi, Gal Costa, Gilberto Gil, and more recently Carlinhos Brown, Margareth Menezes, Daniela Mercury, and Ivete Sangalo, is enjoyed by aficionados all over the world.

There is another side to Bahia, one that appeals to the spirit and the senses. The mysticism of Bahia is so strong, it pervades every aspect of life: it can be perceived in the way people dress, in their speech, their music, their way of relating to each other, even in their food. This mysticism is another reason Brazilians say that in Bahia lies the soul of their country.

The source of this mysticism was the original culture preserved by enslaved Africans. Today, the Pantheist religion of the African Yoruba tribe is still alive

Main Attractions

Porto Seguro
Trancoso
Ilhéus
Morro de São Paulo
Praia do Forte
Parque Nacional Chapada
  Diamantina

Street life in Porto Seguro.

and well in Bahia, and many white Bahians who are self-professed Catholics can be seen making offerings to the deities of the *candomblé* religion.

The phenomenon of syncretism, the blending of Catholicism with African religions, resulted when slaves, forbidden to express their religious beliefs, did so by worshiping their deities disguised as Catholic saints. Nowadays, you can still see the devout worshipping the African goddess Iemanjá as Our Lady, or the god Oxumaré as St Anthony.

Southern Bahia

The Portuguese first landed and established contact with the original inhabitants near today's **Pôrto Seguro ❶**, in the south of Bahia. Pataxo Amerindians still live near the town, fishing and fashioning handicrafts to sell to tourists. The area around **Monte Pascoal**, where the Portuguese had their first sighting of Brazil in 1500, is a densely forested nature reserve of original Atlantic rainforest. There are four national parks: Descobrimento, Monte Pascoal, Pau Brasil, and

Abrolhos (www.ilhasdeabrolhos.com.br) – the last a marine national park that is one of the best diving sites in Brazil, and a location for whale-watching.

The town of Porto Seguro (pop. 140,000) is 600km (373 miles) north of Vitória, in the state of Espírito Santo, and 722km (448 miles) from the state's capital, Salvador. It is one of the main middle-class tourist destinations for Brazilians; international travelers, too, have been coming here for many years. There are innumerable restaurants, bars, and dancehalls, and dozens of hotels and *pousadas* to suit every preference and budget. Some rather nice, sophisticated hotels, large and small, are now emerging all over other parts of southern Bahia, attracting large numbers of so-called 'discerning travelers' Nightlife is particularly lively during the summer and local holidays. Carnival here is a major celebration.

Across the bay by ferry is **Arraial d'Ajuda**, with *pousadas* and bars that swing with lively *forró* dancing. Twenty-five kilometers (15 miles) further south by *kombi* or bus is **Trancoso**, with colorful houses and a colonial church (1656) built around a grassy square, the Quadrado, with commanding views over the Atlantic. The magnificent beaches here attract droves of national and international tourists in the summer, and the whole area is an oasis of peace during the off-season, while remaining one of Bahia and Brazil's most sought-after upscale destinations for the international jet set.

Ilhéus

Some 264km (164 miles) north of Porto Seguro lies the most important city on Bahia's southern coast – the cocoa capital of Brazil, as well as one of the major export ports. **Ilhéus ❷** (pop. 220,000), some 468km (290 miles) from Salvador, was founded in 1534 and had its heyday in the early 20th century, due to the wealth produced by the cocoa plantations.

JORGE AMADO

Jorge Amado is one of Brazil's best-known 20th-century writers, and his work has been published in 55 countries in 49 languages. He was born in the town of Itabuna, 38km (24 miles) from Ilhéus, on August 10, 1912, one of four children. His father was a cocoa farmer, which gave Jorge his in-depth knowledge of rural life in Bahia. At the age of 10 he started a newsletter called A Luneta, which he distributed to family and neighbors, and only five years later, he was living in Pelourinho (see page 275), working as a crime reporter on a newspaper in the capital. In December 1933 he married Matilde Garcia Rosa, but it was Zélia Gattai, whom he met in 1945 after he and Matilde had separated, who was the great love of his life. Also a writer, she was his constant companion until his death.

Amado's prolific output was only matched by his political convictions. His strongly held views, his writings, and his connections with the Brazilian Communist Party, landed him in prison a number of times and also saw him live in exile. He was a keen traveler and a devotee of *candomblé*. Jorge Amado died on August 6, 2001 in Salvador, where, in accordance with his wishes, he was cremated and his ashes scattered around a mango tree in the gardens of his house in Rio Vermelho. There is a museum dedicated to him in Salvador (see page 275).

Beaches abound in the region, and the city's Carnival celebration is one of the liveliest in Bahia. Jorge Amado (see page 264), the foremost Bahian writer, was born nearby, and the city was the inspiration and setting for *Gabriela, Clove and Cinnamon*, one of his best-known works.

Olivença, 20km (12 miles) south of Ilhéus, is an excellent place to camp and 'take the waters.' Besides Carnival, major festivals in Ilhéus include St Sebastian's day (January 11–20), the city's birthday (June 28), and the cocoa festival (which lasts the entire month of October). Further south, Comandatuba Island has one of Brazil's best-structured beach resorts. The Transamérica Ilha de Comandatuba (www.transamerica.com.br) is set in tropical gardens and blessed with 21km (13 miles) of beaches; it also has its own airport, spa, and a very good golf course.

Itacaré

Itacaré ❸, 70km (43 miles) north of Ilhéus, has become one of the most popular destinations in Bahia. The little town (pop. 25,000) lies at the mouth of Rio das Contas, which starts at Chapada Diamantina (see page 270). Many restaurants and *pousadas* cater to the visitors who come here for the magnificent beaches and scenery. All forms of ecotourism are encouraged: diving, surfing, and walks through the Atlantic rainforest and the region's many deserted beaches. There are also excellent *pousadas* and some very exclusive resorts in the area, including the highly rated Txai and Itacaré Village.

Continuing north, the Maraú Peninsula is still a pristine and remote area, as access is not particularly easy. The magic of Maraú is its remoteness; it is ideal for those seeking peace and quiet. Some small *pousadas* and a couple of sophisticated resorts serve the area. At the extreme north of the peninsula is Barra Grande, which can get very busy during the season (by local standards), but nearby **Taipús de Fora**, considered by many to be the finest beach in Brazil, can be remarkably quiet and peaceful despite being one of the area's main attractions. It

Strings of beads made of seeds and shells in the colours of African gods.

High spirits in Arraial d'Ajuda.

Bahian cuisine

Bahian cooking is a unique Afro-Brazilian cuisine that is delicious and satisfying. Some dishes can be very peppery or rather heavy, so it is worth experimenting.

Though it contains contributions from the Portuguese colonists and the native Amerindians, by far the most important influence on Bahian cuisine came from the enslaved Africans, who not only brought their own style of cooking with them, but also modified Portuguese dishes with African herbs and spices.

Bahian cuisine is characterized by the generous use of *malagueta* chili peppers and *dendê* oil extracted from an African palm that grows well in the northeastern climate. Several Bahian dishes also contain seafood (usually shrimp), coconut milk, banana, and *okra* (ladies' fingers).

Moqueca is one of the region's most popular dishes. It is a mixture of shrimp – perhaps with other seafood as well – coconut, garlic, onion, parsley, pepper, tomato paste, and the ubiquitous *dendê* oil. These ingredients are all sautéed over a

A tasty Moqueca dish.

low flame and served with rice cooked in coconut milk – a creamy, delicious dish.

Other traditional dishes are *vatapá* – a spicy shrimp purée made with palm oil and nuts – and *carurú de camarão*, which contains both fresh and dried shrimp, as well as sliced okra.

In the better Bahian restaurants, these dishes are served with a hot *malagueta* sauce. Sometimes this is added directly to the dish in the kitchens, and the cook may ask you if you like your food *quente* (spicy hot). Until you get used to the strong flavors of the *dendê* and *malagueta*, it is best to say no. If the sauce is placed in a bowl on the table, as it often is, you can try a little at a time. Bahian hotels are a good place to kick off your culinary adventure, since they tend to go a little easier on the *malagueta*.

A sweet tooth

The women of Bahia are among the world's great confectioners. They concoct sweets from coconut, eggs, ginger, milk, cinnamon, and lemon. *Cocada*, a sugared coconut sweet flavored with ginger or lemon, is a favorite. *Ambrosia*, made with egg yolks and vanilla, and *quindim* (glistening little yellow desserts made from egg yolks, sugar, and ground coconut) are sweet delights. You can buy *cocada* from *baianas* throughout Salvador.

Baianas, usually dressed in white, set up shop daily in special shelters or at improvised tables where they sell *cocada*, *abará*, and *acarajé*, a traditional street food. You really should try this typical food, but do so at a place that has been recommended to you, or where you see plenty of local people eating, to be sure you are getting a fresh and well-prepared product.

Acarajé is made from shelled *fradinho* beans (similar to black-eyed peas), which are mashed together with ground shrimp and other ingredients and formed into a ball, then deep-fried in *dendê* (palm) oil. It is served split in half and then stuffed with *vatapá* or *caruru*, shrimps, and salad, and hot chili pepper if you wish. *Abará* is made from the same ingredients, but is not deep-fried. *Acarajé* is a wonderful treat to have between meals, especially if you have it with a beer at one of the beachfront bars.

For a Bahian culinary and cultural experience, you can't do better than go to one of Salvador's restaurants, many of which offer local cuisine, together with a folklore show (see page 283).

Good Bahian restaurants can also be found in many of the larger Brazilian cities, such as Rio and São Paulo.

offers large natural swimming pools of clear seawater, excellent for snorkeling, and 7km (4.3 miles) of deserted beach. The area can be visited on day trips from Itacaré.

Morro de São Paulo was once an isolated fishing village on the island of Tinharé, situated some 270km (168 miles) south of Salvador. A hippie hang-out, the village has become increasingly fashionable with Brazilian and international tourists, yet remains wonderfully relaxed, and there are no roads. Currently the *pousadas* are spread across five beaches. Primeiro Praia is the nearest to town and the action, while Quinta Praia is the quietest. Morro de São Paulo can be reached on regular two-hour fast catamaran transfers from Salvador or by small plane. Another island with great beaches is nearby **Boipeba** – reminiscent of Brazil 50 years ago, it is very quiet, with a laid-back lifestyle.

Further north, towards Salvador, 270km (168 miles) away is the town of **Valença ❹** (pop. 83,000), where the Una river meets the Atlantic Ocean. The town is the site of one of Brazil's first textile factories to use hydroelectric power. One of the best beaches in the region, 15km (9 miles) from Valença, is **Guaibim**, with a number of good seafood restaurants and bars.

North from Salvador

North from **Salvador** (see page 273) the Estrada de Coco (Coconut Road) takes you from the city's most distant beach, Itapoã. Along this road, lined with coconut palms, you will pass virtually unspoiled tropical beaches, including **Jaua**, **Arembepe**, **Jucuípe**, **Abaí**, **Guarajuba** (where the international resort, Vila Galé Mares, is located), and **Itacimirim**.

Some 85km (53 miles) from Salvador, at **Praia do Forte**, thousands of coconut palms stand on 12km (7 miles) of white sandy beach, protected against threats to the environment by a private foundation. Praia do Forte was once just a small fishing village.

The high street has now been paved, cafés, restaurants, shops, *pousadas* and hotels abound, including close by the Iberostar Bahia Resort (see page 356), Tivoli Ecoresort Praia do Forte, and the original Praia do Forte EcoResort. An increasing number of international tourists now visit the village. Even so, it remains a delightful place and, like most resorts, it can be blissfully quiet in the low season.

Praia do Forte is also the site of a major preservation center for sea turtles. The eggs are collected from nests on the beach at night and protected from predators (both humans and other animals) until the young are old enough to be set free in the sea and fend for themselves.

Continuing along from Praia do Forte, the road, now known as **Linha Verde** (Green Line), follows the coastline past spectacular, semi-deserted beaches all the way to the border with the state of **Sergipe**. It passes **Costa do Sauípe** (www.costadosauipe. com.br), a purpose-built resort with five luxury international hotels and a number of its own *pousadas*. The first

Hawksbill turtle at the Brazilian Sea Turtle Conservation Program (TAMAR) in Praia do Forte.

The sertão is a land that lionizes its folk heroes, and also has its own distinctive music. The two-part harmony of *música sertaneja* is simple, the chords rarely numbering more than three. Themes are of lost love, homesickness, bad weather, and death. No longer restricted to the sertão: popular variety shows on Brazilian television are now dedicated to this genre.

At the bridge that connects Cachoeira and São Félix.

phase was completed in 2000. In theory, fifty more hotels are planned in a series of five further building phases, but little seems to have progressed since the opening.

For golfers, the 18-hole golf course is worth noting (tel: 71-2104 7777; open to non-residents daily 7am–5.30pm). The region also has a number of other challenging and attractive courses.

The sertão

Situated inland, 200km (124 miles) from the coast, is the *sertão*, the northeast's drought-ridden scrubland region. This area has been the setting for a great deal of tragedy. Periodic droughts drive local farm laborers from the *sertão* to the coastal cities in search of food and work. When the rains return, so do the *sertanejos*. But often, the rains do as much damage as good: torrential downpours can easily cause massive flooding over this severely parched earth, which is too dry to absorb the rainwater. The *sertanejos* are a hardy people, loyal to their birthplace, and their land holds surprises for those willing to discover them.

A good place to start a trip to the *sertão* is in the Recôncavo da Bahia, the term used for the hot and humid region that surrounds Salvador's Baía de Todos os Santos. This region was once the source of much wealth, created by the sugar-cane and tobacco booms. Over several centuries slaves were brought from Africa to work the land. This heritage can be seen in the many historic towns in the region: Santo Amaro, São Félix, Jaguaripe, and, above all, Cachoeira. **Santo Amaro ❺** (pop. 60,000), a colonial town located some 80km (50 miles) from Salvador, was once a center of tobacco and sugar production. The town is revered by fans of Brazilian popular music as the home of singers and siblings Caetano Veloso and Maria Bethânia. While their international careers have taken them away from Santo Amaro, they return regularly. Their mother, Dona Cano, who turned 100 in 2007, and died in December 2012, continued to live in the village throughout her life and was a national figure in her own right.

Along Santo Amaro's cobblestone streets and tiny *praças* (squares), pink and white stucco colonial homes alternate with Art Deco facades painted in pastel colors, and decorated with raised geometric outlines in glittering white. These facades, testimony to the area's development and prosperity in the early part of the 20th century, can be seen in many of the small towns in the interior of the northeast.

Cachoeira

Colonial churches and monuments abound in **Cachoeira ❻** (pop. 34,000), 120km (74 miles) from Salvador, and a center of tobacco, cashewnut, and orange production. One of the main sites is the church of **Nossa Senhora da Conceição do Monte**, an 18th-century structure with a lovely view of the Paraguaçu river, and the village of São Félix on the opposite bank. The church is open to the public only in November. Don't miss the

Correios e Telégrafos, the post office, which has the best example of an Art Deco facade in town. Cachoeira also has souvenir shops, inns, and restaurants. The **Pousada do Convento** (www.pousadadoconvento.com.br), a 17th-century convent converted into a guesthouse, is especially interesting: the guest rooms were once nuns' cells, and the mausoleum is now a television lounge.

One of the most fascinating *festas* in Brazil is celebrated in Cachoeira and other parts of Bahia by the **Irmandade da Boa Morte** (Sisterhood of Our Lady of Good Death). It is not clear when this sorority was established, but it is certain that it goes back to the early 19th century and the days of slavery. Created to provide social assistance, particularly the provision of a dignified funeral, it lives on to this day. Membership is open only to black women over the age of 40, who must be devotees of both *candomblé* and the Virgin Mary. New sisters follow a strict three-year admission process. The sisterhood's main celebrations take place in the first fortnight in August, with an extensive program that includes processions to celebrate the death, burial, and resurrection of the Virgin. The celebrations combine African and Catholic rituals in a striking example of syncretism.

São Félix

Across the river, over the 300-meter (985ft) iron bridge that bears the grandiose name of Imperial Ponte D. Pedro I, is sleepy **São Félix**, with colonial architecture from the 17th–19th centuries. Some landmarks are the churches of Deus Menino and Senhor São Félix, the town hall, and the **Centro Cultural Dannemann** (Tue–Sun 8am–5pm; free) on the riverfront, with art exhibitions and displays of old machinery used for making *charutos* (cigars). You can see the skill involved in the making of hand-rolled cigars, and, of course, you can also buy the finished product.

Bahian cigars are highly regarded by connoisseurs.

In the **Casa da Cultura Américo Simas** (Mon–Fri 9am–noon, 2–5pm), in an old cigar factory, a number of courses are offered to local people.

Jaguaripe and Nazaré

Jaguaripe (River of the Jaguar, in the Tupi-Guarani language) lies on the eastern banks of the river of the same name, 240km (148 miles) from Salvador. It is fast becoming a center for ecotourism, and is also of historical interest, with religious and secular buildings, some dating from the early 17th century. From here you can go on a 45-minute cruise downstream to **Maragogipinho**, where a pottery was first introduced by the Jesuits more than 300 years ago. Today, though still a cottage industry, it is regarded as the largest in Latin America, and you can visit the workshops.

Once a year, during Holy Week, there is a large exhibition at nearby **Nazaré das Farinhas**, one of the busiest towns in the Recôncavo. The Recôncavo is one of the major

Portrait of a rural Bahian man.

Old colonial buildings in Cachoeira.

Cigars at Centro Cultural Dannemann, São Félix.

In Chapada Diamantina National Park.

centers of Bahia's strong agricultural economy. The state of Bahia produces grains, sugar cane and coconuts, and 95 percent of the country's cocoa output is harvested here. The town of **Camaçari** is home to one of Brazil's three petrochemical complexes, and industry in the region is booming.

Chapada Diamantina

The **Parque Nacional Chapada Diamantina ❼** was formed in 1985 and covers 152,000 hectares (600 sq miles). Altitude varies from 400 meters (1,300ft) to 1,700 meters (5,600ft) above sea level. The rainy season is from November to April, with heaviest rainfall between November and January. The driest time, and the best time to visit, is from August to October.

This region is one of the most beautiful in the Bahian countryside, and will appeal to all nature enthusiasts. Mountain springs help keep the drought away. Chapada is a mountain wilderness, best explored with a local guide. Orchids abound near the waterfalls, some of which can only be reached on foot. The **Cachoeira da Fumaça**, 66km (41 miles) from Lençóis, is 400 meters (1,300ft) high. It can be reached only by a very steep 7km (4-mile) walk. The **Gruta das Areias**, a grotto just over 1km (.6 mile) long, is lined with colored sands, which artisans use to fill glass bottles, creating delightful patterns. A stunning view of the region can be seen from on top of the **Pai Inácio Mountain**, where a host of exotic plants thrive. Small towns and villages, such as Mucugê and Igatú, give visitors an interesting insight into the history and lives of the people who inhabit this unusual region.

Lençóis

Situated in the heart of Bahia, 425km (265 miles) west of Salvador, just outside the national park, and serving as its main gateway, is one of the state's most distinctive attractions, the town of **Lençóis ❽** (pop. 10,000). Resting in the foothills of the **Sincorá Mountains**, Lençóis dates back to 1844, when diamonds were first discovered here. Hoards of fortune-seekers descended on the site, improvising shelters out of large cloth sheets, called *lençóis* in Portuguese, a name that has stuck. The diamond rush turned the little settlement into a boomtown. Lençóis society wore the latest Parisian fashions and sent their children to study in France. The French government even opened a consulate here. There are some interesting buildings in Lençóis, but its main attractions are the natural wonders nearby.

Though its folklore is unmistakably Bahian, Lençóis has its own peculiarities. Carnival is not a major event, but the Feast of São João in June is widely celebrated. Lençóis also has *jarê*, its own unique version of *candomblé*. *Jarê* celebrations occur in September, December, and January, in *candomblé* temples or the homes of its devotees.

Local handicrafts include lace, crochet, and earthenware. Lençóis has accommodations to suit all budgets and preferences, from campsites

and inns to attractive hotels such as Canto das Águas (www.lencois.com.br), with large tropical gardens by the river. Lençóis can be reached from Salvador by car and by a six-hour comfortable coach service (usually twice a day, depending on the season) with Real Expresso. It is also possible to take a one hour flight with Trip/Azul (www.voetrip.com.br) on Thursday and Sunday. There are also organized tours to the region.

Due west of Lençóis, 252km (157 miles) further along Highway 242, is the city of **Ibotirama** ❾, a fisherman's paradise on the legendary São Francisco river (see page 289). Its 26,000 inhabitants raise cattle and plant cassava, corn, beans, and rice, but when the drought comes, they depend on the river for food. Dozens of species of fish, including the piranha (seen as a delicacy), are here for the taking. Boats and canoes can be rented at the wharf.

Photographers can take a canoe out at the end of the day to photograph the spectacular sunset over the river's left bank. From March to October, the dry season, the water level drops, exposing sandy beaches on the islands of **Gado Bravo** (40 minutes upstream) and **Ilha Grande** (25 minutes downstream).

From Ibotirama, the São Francisco flows northeast to the **Sobradinho Dam**(see page 271). Close to the lake's northern edge is **Juazeiro** ❿ (pop. 240,000), 566km (352 miles) northwest of Salvador. During the colonial period, Juazeiro was a stopover for travelers and pioneers on their way to Salvador from the states north of Bahia. A township was officially founded in 1706, when Franciscan monks built a mission, complete with a chapel and a monastery, in a Cariri Amerindian village. By the end of the 18th century, Juazeiro had become the region's most important commercial and social center.

The folk art of the region is dominated by the *carranca*, the half-man, half-dragon wooden figurehead placed on boats to keep the devil at bay (see page 289). The *carrancas*, with their teeth bared in a silent roar, are carved from tree trunks and painted in bright colors. You will see miniature versions of them on sale as souvenirs.

FACT

At 320km (199 miles) long, with a surface of 4,220 sq km (1,630 sq miles), the Sobradinho Dam is one of the largest artificial lakes in the world. The wall is 41 meters (134ft) at its highest and 12.5km (7.7 miles) long. The lock measures 120 meters (394ft) by 17 meters (56ft), allowing navigation between towns in Minas Gerais and Pernambuco.

RESTAURANTS

PRICE CATEGORIES

Prices for a two-course meal for two. Wine costs around US$25 a bottle.
$ = under US$50
$$ = US$50–100
$$$ = US$100–150

Morro de São Paulo

Pimenta Rosa
Quatra Spiaggia, Ilha de Tinharé
Tel: 75-3652 1506
Open: L daily.
Popular location for lunch (served until 5pm), and located right at the start of the Fourth Beach of Morro de São Paulo. Creative Bahian cuisine. A good place to base yourself for a day at the beach. $$

Lençóis

Beco da Coruja
172 Rua da Rosário
Tel: 75-3334 1652

Open: L&D daily.
A restaurant that for once takes it for granted that vegetarians like interesting food as much as carnivores do. $
Burritos y Taquitos Santa Fé
58 Rua São Benedito
Tel: 75-3334 1105
Open: D only daily.
Simple restaurant that is the place to go for tasty and reliably good Mexican food. $
Neco's Bar Restaurante
15 Praça Maestro Clarindo Pacheco
Tel: 75-3334 1179
Open: L&D daily (until last customer). Delicious, home-made regional food in simple surroundings – but it should be ordered a few hours or even a day in advance. Popular on a Friday night with the locals. $$
Os Artistas da Massa
49 Rua da Baderna
Tel: 75-3334 1886
Open: L&D daily, (closed Oct–Nov).

Excellent and popular spot; authentic Italian pasta and other Italian dishes. Signature dish is the *nhoque de abóbora*.$$

Trancoso

Capim Santo
55 Rua do Beco, Quadrado
Tel: 73-3668 1122
Open: D Mon–Sat.
Laid-back and relaxed atmosphere. Located within the Capim Santo Pousada. Highly rated for its creative seafood and other options, although not the cheapest place in town. $$$
Mangia
6 Praça São João, Quadrado
Tel: 73-3668 1720
Open: D Wed-Sun.
Italian restaurant in the Quadrado with a chef from Italy via Buenos Aires. Small and concise menu that is based around what is interesting in the market that day. $$

SALVADOR

The capital of Bahia has a festive atmosphere and much to admire, from beautiful colonial churches to events like Carnival *afoxé* dance groups and numerous processions and rituals.

Salvador was first colonized some 30 years after Brazil was discovered. In 1530, King João III sent a group of colonists to stake claim to this new land and thereby strengthened the Portuguese presence against French and Dutch invaders. Salvador became the first capital of Brazil in 1549, when the Portuguese court sent Tomé de Sousa as the country's first governor general.

Perched atop cliffs, the tiny settlement was an ideal national capital because of its natural defenses. **Salvador** ⑪ has since lost economic and political importance but is renowned as the center of Afro-Brazilian culture, with a mixture of black and white races descended from Africans, Europeans, and Amerindians. With a population of nearly 3 million, Salvador, capital of the state of Bahia, is Brazil's third-largest city. Because life in Bahia revolves around Salvador, Brazilians frequently intermix the two, saying Bahia when they mean Salvador.

The religion and mysticism that are so much a part of Bahian life are reflected in the name Salvador, which means 'savior.' The peninsula on which the city was built, first discovered by Amerigo Vespucci in 1501, faces **Baía de Todos os Santos** (All Saints' Bay), named in honor of November 1, the day it was discovered.

Igreja da Ordem Terceira do Carmo church in Pelourinho, Salvador, Bahia.

What is most striking about Salvador is the way it assaults the senses: the sight of the gold-encrusted altars and panels of its churches; the inviting scent and exotic taste of the African-influenced food; the sounds of the street vendors' cries, the roar of traffic, the chant of fans at a soccer game (and Salvador is a host city for the 2014 World Cup), or enthusiasts at a political rally; and, most of all, the distinctive sounds and rhythm of Bahian music.

The best way to orient yourself in Salvador is to think of the town as

Main Attractions

Catedral Basílica
Largo do Pelourinho
Museu de Arte Sacra
Elevador Lacerda
Mercado Modelo
Nosso Senhor do Bonfim

divided into four: beaches, suburbs, and upper and lower cities. Downtown Salvador encompasses both the historical **Cidade Alta** (Upper City) and the newer **Cidade Baixa** (Lower City).

The Upper city

A walking tour of the Cidade Alta (Upper City) starts at **Praça da Sé** Ⓐ opening on to **Terreiro de Jesus**, home to three of Salvador's most famous churches. The largest, the **Catedral Basílica** Ⓑ, is a 17th-century Jesuit structure built largely of stone, with beautiful gold-leaf work on its main altar. Next to it are the 18th-century **São Pedro dos Clérigos** Ⓒ (St Peter's) and the 17th-century **Ordem Terceira de São Domingos** Ⓓ (Dominican). Shops in the area sell handmade lace and leather goods, and lovely primitive paintings.

Rising majestically from the adjoining square, **Praça Anchieta** is one of the world's most opulent Baroque churches. Paradoxically, it is dedicated to a saint who preached the simple, unencumbered life. The **Igreja e Convento de São Francisco** Ⓔ (St Francis) is an impressive 18th-century structure built of stone imported from Portugal. Its interior is covered from floor to ceiling with highly intricate carvings, thickly encrusted with gold leaf. In a side altar is the splendid statue of St Peter of Alcântara, which was carved from the single trunk of a jacaranda tree by Manoel Inácio da Costa, one of Brazil's most important Baroque artists. Blue and white hand-painted *azulejos* (tiles) depicting scenes from the life of St Francis, imported from Portugal in the late 18th century, adorn the porch. The Franciscan convent, which may be visited, is annexed to the church, and surrounds a delightful courtyard.

Next door, the **Ordem Terceira de São Francisco** Ⓕ (Church of the Third Order of St Francis) is noteworthy for its Spanish-style Baroque facade and the 18th-century tiles in the courtyard. Returning to the north side of Terreiro de Jesus, you will find the **Museu Afro-Brasileiro** Ⓖ (Afro-Brazilian Museum; www.mafro. ceao.ufba.br; Mon–Fri 9am–5pm, Sat

10am–5pm) in the old medical faculty. It has a fascinating collection of objects that highlight the strong African influence on Bahian culture, including musical instruments, masks, costumes, carvings, and other artifacts that are part of the *candomblé* religion. There are also some beautiful wooden panels carved by Carybé, an Argentine artist who fell in love with Brazil and adopted Salvador as his home.

Largo do Pelourinho

A short distance along **Rua Alfredo Brito**, on your right facing away from Terreiro de Jesus, you reach the **Largo do Pelourinho** ⓗ (Pillory Square), site of Salvador's best-preserved colonial buildings, whose colorful facades line the steep, meandering cobblestoned streets. The name recalls a time when pillories were set up here to punish slaves and criminals.

Today, Pelourinho is considered by Unesco to be the most important grouping of 17th- and 18th-century colonial architecture in the Americas. Once a fashionable district, the fortunes of its inhabitants gradually declined. However, Pelourinho is charming and distinctive. Many of the buildings have been renovated in recent years and converted into *pousadas* or restaurants, and the area is well policed.

The center of Praça José Alencar square is occupied by the **Casa de Jorge Amado** ⓘ (www.jorgeamado.org.br; Mon–Fri 10am–6pm; Sat 10am–4pm), a small museum-cum-library-cum-café, replete with books by one of Brazil's most famous novelists (his works have been translated into nearly 50 languages). The collection includes photographs, memorabilia and a video about the life of Amado (1912–2001), one of Bahia's most beloved sons (see page 264).

Next door is the tiny **Museu da Cidade** (City Museum; Mon, Wed–Sat 9am–6pm, Sun 9am–1pm), with a collection of Afro-Brazilian folkloric

items. On the top floor are mannequins dressed as the most important *orixás* (gods) of the *candomblé* faith, identified by their African names as well as their equivalent Catholic saint's name.

The **Senac Restaurant** ⓙ (see page 283; Mon–Sat 11.30am–3.30pm, 6.30–11pm, Sun 11.30am–3.30pm) on the square, which is run by a government hotel and restaurant school, is an excellent place to try the local food and see a Bahian folklore show (Thu–Sat at 7pm). The restaurant serves lunch and dinner and has a buffet section (Mon–Fri 11.30am–2.30pm) where your chosen food is charged by weight.

Just down the street from Pelourinho Square is the church of **Nossa Senhora do Rosário dos Pretos** ⓚ (Our Lady of the Rosary of Black People). Because slaves were not permitted to go into their masters' churches, they erected their own places of worship. At the bottom of Pelourinho Square is a flight of steps called the Ladeira do Carmo, which leads to the **Largo do Carmo** ⓛ (Carmelite

TIP

Inexpensive, air-conditioned buses run between Rio Vermelho and Pelourinho. There is also a good bus service from the airport all the way to Pelourinho, which is excellent value for money at about R$5 (US$2.50) for a 40-minute scenic journey, but be careful if you are carrying all your worldly goods.

The cobbled streets and colonial architecture of Largo de Pelourinho, Salvador.

The interior of Catedral Basílica on Terreiro de Jesus square, in Salvador.

Porto da Barra Beach.

Square). Scene of the resistance against the Dutch invaders, this block of buildings is the site of the Dutch surrender. The most interesting building is the **Igreja do Carmo** (Carmelite Church and Convent), dating from 1585. The convent has been partially transformed into a small **museum** (Mon–Sat 9am–1pm, 2–6pm). This area, called Santo Antônio, has enjoyed a renaissance in recent years. Several of the once-run-down buildings have been restored and now house small hotels and inns.

The Pelourinho has featured in a number of films and music videos, most notably Michael Jackson's *They Don't Really Care About Us* (1996) and Paul Simon's *Obvious Child* (1990).

Sacred arts

Still in the upper city, but in the opposite direction, are two museums, one of which is Salvador's best. The **Museu de Arte Sacra** (Museum of Sacred Art; Mon–Fri 11.30am–5.30pm) at 276 Rua do Sodré is housed in the 17th-century church and convent of **Santa Teresa**. *Baianos* claim this is the largest collection of sacred art in Latin America. Whether or not this is the case, it is easily the most impressive of the city's museums, and one of the most fascinating in Brazil.

The Baroque and rococo art is displayed in large, airy rooms, many of them lined with blue, white, and yellow tiles brought from Portugal in the 1600s. Proving that contraband was a part of secular life in the 17th and 18th centuries, many of the larger images of saints, carved from wood, have been hollowed out to hide smuggled jewels and gold. Paintings, ivory sculptures, and works in earthenware, silver, and gold are also displayed.

Going toward the Barra beach area, at 2490 Avenida Sete de Setembro, one of the city's main thoroughfares, you will find the **Museu Carlos Costa Pinto** (www.museucostapinto.com.br; Mon and Wed–Sun 2.30–7pm), in the **Vitória** district. Carlos Costa Pinto (1885–1946) was a wealthy businessman and art collector, and the museum is home to his family's collection of colonial furnishings, porcelain and jewelry, including crystal, hand-painted porcelain dishes, and opulent silver *balagandans* – clusters of charms that were pinned to the blouses of slave women to indicate their owners' personal wealth. Much of the flooring in the main rooms downstairs is of pink Carrara marble. At the entrance, museum staff place cloth slippers over your shoes to protect the floor.

Around Praça da Sé

Starting once more at Praça da Sé, but heading toward the Lower City, walk down Rua da Misericórdia to the church of **Santa Casa da Misericórdia**, which is decorated with lovely 18th-century Portuguese tiles. Inside is a **museum** (Mon–Sat 10am–4pm, Sun noon–4pm), containing church treasures and sacred art.

A short way down the street is the **Praça Municipal**, where the town council's and city hall's splendid

colonial buildings are. It leads you to Salvador's famous **Elevador Lacerda**, a massive elevator built in 1930 to link the Upper and Lower cities. From here there are excellent views of Baía de Todos os Santos (All Saints' Bay). The elevator whisks you down to the **Cidade Baixa**, the Lower City.

The Lower City

Straight ahead as you leave the elevator is the **Mercado Modelo ®**, which has occupied the former customs house, in its present form, since 1971, having twice been destroyed by fire. In this three-story building you will find stalls selling all kinds of local handicrafts and souvenirs.

The Mercado Modelo is one of Salvador's not-to-be-missed sites. Although it's undeniably touristy, it is the best place in town to purchase your souvenirs. As you stroll among the stalls, you will spot vendors of musical instruments playing their wares to entice you to buy. You may hear percussion instruments, or the single-stringed *berimbau*. There are also good displays of *capoeira*. You will be pressed to give them money, but the entertainment is well worth it. For refreshment, try one of the many types of fresh fruit juice.

Across the road from the market, keeping the bay to your right, walk down the street to the church of **Nossa Senhora da Conceição de Praia ❺**. Planned and built in Portugal in the early 18th century, this church was brought to Brazil piece by piece. It is the site of the annual religious procession held on December 8, one of the most important feast days in Salvador's Catholic calendar.

The Bonfim church

About 10km (6 miles) in the opposite direction stands the famous church of **Nosso Senhor do Bonfim** (Mon–Fri 8–6pm. Church services at other times; free). On the way to the church, you will pass the rustic **São Joaquim**

Market (Mon–Sat 6am–6pm, Sun 6am–noon; free). The market is fascinating, and has been improved following years of neglect, which had left it dirty and run-down.

The Bonfim church was built in 1745 and is one of the most popular sites for religious pilgrimage in the country. People come from throughout Brazil to pray for jobs or cures, or to give thanks for miracles attributed to Our Lord. As you enter the church, people will try to sell you a colorful ribbon printed with the words *Lembrança do Senhor do Bonfim da Bahia* (Souvenir of Our Lord of Good Ending of Bahia, see page 277).

Lacking the ornateness of Salvador's other churches, Bonfim is a favorite with both Catholics and *candomblé* practitioners. Don't miss the **Miracle Room**, which is filled with photographs of those who have reached a state of grace, and plaster casts of limbs or organs belonging to devotees cured through divine intervention.

Further down this same road is the church of **Monte Serrat**, a simple

The Igreja NS do Bonfim Church in Salvador was built by black slaves, hence the predominance of black saints on display.

A RIBBON FOR LUCK

One of the best-known souvenirs of Salvador and Bahia is a colored ribbon stamped with **Lembrança do Senhor do Bonfim da Bahia**. You should be given a ribbon by a person who will tie it around your wrist (or ankle) in three knots. Each knot represents a wish: when the ribbon falls off, it is said, your wishes will come true. Sold in various colors, the ribbon has a mystical side: each color symbolizes an *orixá* (or deity of the Yoruba religion). Dark green is for Oxossi, light blue for Iemanjá, yellow for Oxum, so the ribbon is a symbolic and spiritual link to a traditional part of Afro-Brazilian culture. Ribbons of different colors are also believed to have different powers, for example:

White: Peace, knowledge and calm. Wards off negative energy and increases positive energy. Can also represent innocence, and purity.
Red: Passion. Symbolizes love, desire, power, strength, and energy.
Green: Youth, vigor, and calmness; represents nature and new beginnings. Dark green equals masculinity, virility, and grandness.
Yellow: Wealth, riches, prosperity, knowledge, energy and optimism.
Orange: Personal and professional conquests, spontaneity.
Blue: Security, tranquility, harmony, good health, loyalty and subtlety.
Pink: Beauty, health, sensuality and romanticism, happiness in love.
Light Pink: Femininity. Love, friendship, fragility, delicacy, compassion.

16th-century chapel with Portuguese tiles. Nearby is the **Boa Viagem** church, the destination of Salvador's Our Lord of the Seafarers procession held every New Year's Day.

Salvador's beaches

A series of interconnecting streets and roads provides a non-stop promenade along Salvador's beaches, from the near-downtown Barra beach to the distant north-coast beaches, which are considered among Brazil's most beautiful. The city beach, **Barra** is famed less for its beauty than for the conviviality of its bars and sidewalk cafés. Barra is where many local people stop for a beer after work, and stay late into the evening. Barra is also good for shopping and has some 'apart-hotels,' which can be rented by the week or month and are usually much cheaper than hotels. The beach is protected by the gallant old fort **Santo Antônio da Barra**, with a lighthouse and an oceanography museum.

The next beach northward from Barra is **Ondina**, home to some big hotels. Inland from the beach, in the

same neighborhood, is the **Salvador Zoo** (www.zoo.ba.gov.br; Tue–Sun 8.30am–5pm). Next is **Rio Vermelho**, a picturesque, up-and-coming neighborhood where several good restaurants and new hotels have opened. The writer Jorge Amado lived here for six months of the year, until his death in 2001 (he spent the summer in Paris). There are coconut palms along the beaches as you travel northward, passing by **Mariquita** and **Amaralina**, where several restaurants are located.

At **Pituba**, you may see *jangadas*, primitive sail-driven fishing boats made of split logs roped together. Other beaches along this route include **Jardim de Alá**, **Armação de Iemanjá**, **Boca do Rio**, **Corsário**, **Pituaçu**, and **Patamares** (where there are also some good restaurants).

Piatã and **Itapoã**, the last beaches before the airport, are considered to be among Salvador's best. Itapoã may be slightly less crowded than Piatã, especially during the week, but in terms of natural beauty and opportunities for eating and drinking, they are equal. The statue of Iemanjá marks the border between the two beaches. One of the most beautiful sights in Salvador is the sunset viewed from Itapoã beach.

After dark

Nightlife in Salvador is concentrated partly around the cobblestoned streets of Pelourinho, where live music fills the air most nights of the week, but particularly on Tuesday, and there are concerts every night in summer – most of them free. There are nightclubs in the Barra area and along the beach drive. The Rio Vermelho district has good restaurants, bars, and nightlife.

The **Teatro Castro Alves** (www.tca.ba.gov.br), located at **Campo Grande** across from the **Hotel Tropical da Bahia** (www.tropicalbahia.com.br), is the place for ballet, theater, and musical performances, and has a

Party at Bombordo club, Porto Seguro.

seating capacity of 1,400. Large signs outside the theater list the current events. Occasionally, the Castro Alves is host to a Brazilian or foreign symphony orchestra, and you may find one of Brazil's top recording artists performing there. Look out for names such as Caetano Veloso, Maria Bethânia, and Gal Costa – *baianos* who, along with Gilberto Gil, are among Brazil's most popular singers and songwriters.

Soccer is a major form of entertainment in Salvador, as it is throughout Brazil. The city's main stadium is the Itaipava **Fonte Nova Arena** (www.itaipavafontenova.com.br), which was demolished in 2010 and totally rebuilt in time to host games for the 2013 Confederations Cup, the 2014 FIFA World Cup, and the 2016 Olympic Games. The stadium seats 55,000.

The local team, Esporte Clube Bahia, usually plays on Wednesday night and Sunday afternoon. Book a seat in the reserved area *(cadeiras especiais)*; it is more expensive but worth it. Tickets are available at the stadium on the day of the game.

You are advised to avoid the port area and the streets surrounding Pelourinho at night. For the very best in entertainment, day or night, do what the local people do: go to the beach. Pick one of the thatched-roof huts that function as bars on Pituba or Piatã beach, sit on a sawed-off trunk used as a stool, order your *batida* or *caipirinha* (cocktails made with fruit and *cachaça* – sugar-cane liqueur), and listen to the music played by your neighbors as you watch the waves roll in.

City of music

Throughout Salvador, and certainly on any beach, weekends are a time for music-making. Though much of the music you will hear today is commercial, and among the most popular in Brazil, some of it is influenced by *candomblé* (Afro-Brazilian ritual worship), in which the pulsating, hypnotic rhythm calls the gods into contact with their devotees. Groups of native Bahians, known as *baianos*, gather in bars to sing their favorite songs.

TIP

Some people prefer to spend a Carnival evening in a *camarote* (box) along the route. *Camarotes* range from the simple, affording a space from which to see the various bands pass by, to the sophisticated, with air conditioning, drinks, supper, and a disco/nightclub, guaranteeing a party until dawn. Prices vary according to the night of the week and facilities.

Elevador Lacerda and Mercado Modelo below.

Other clusters of amateur musicians play small drums and other percussion instruments, as well as the occasional guitar or *cavaquinho*, which has four strings and resembles a ukulele. Music and religion are as essential a part of the people's lives here as eating and sleeping. The year is organized around religious holidays. Street processions mark the celebrations. The religious calendar culminates in Carnival (see page 69), traditionally a last fling before the 40-day Lenten period of prayer and penance preceding Easter.

Carnival and *candomblé*

Officially, Carnival in Brazil lasts for four days, from the Saturday to the Tuesday before Ash Wednesday, but in Salvador the festivities start on the previous Wednesday and continue for a week. Preparation for the Carnival is practically a summer-long event. Clubs host pre-Carnival balls and hold *ensaios* (rehearsals).

If you visit during Carnival, don't expect to get much sleep: local people generate enough energy to keep going practically non-stop. Salvador's Carnival is a completely different experience from its counterparts in Rio de Janeiro and elsewhere in the country. For example, there are no samba schools competing for government money, and none of the extravagant costumes worn in Rio's samba parades. Here, the celebration is pure, wild fun: drinking, dancing, and music.

Though Carnival is an outgrowth of Christianity, mysticism also has its place. During Carnival, *afoxés*, groups of *candomblé* practitioners, take to the streets with banners and images of their patrons, usually African deities to whom they dedicate songs and offerings. One of the most famous and original *afoxés*, however, has chosen a different patron. Based in the center of the historical Pelourinho district, it is called *Filhos de Gandhi* (Sons of Gandhi), in honor of the Indian leader, and is dedicated to peace.

It is not only at Carnival time, though, that Salvador is home to joyful religious or popular celebrations. There is at least one important holiday each month, and if there is

A capoeira class.

no holiday during your stay, you can usually arrange to attend a *candomblé* ceremony (though they are not open to the public all year round), or a *capoeira* display. Travel agencies and some hotels can make reservations for folklore shows (including *capoeira*) and those *candomblé* ceremonies that are open to the public. You could also contact Bahiatursa, the state tourism board (tel: 71-3103 3103; www.bahia tursa.ba.gov.br), where operators, some of whom may speak English, can assist in making reservations.

Candomblé ceremonies are lively, spirited events with much music and dancing, but they are serious religious rituals and, as such, require respectful behavior and conservative dress – preferably in white or light colors – and no shorts or halter-neck tops. Also, cameras are strictly forbidden. Ceremonies usually take place at night and last at least three hours.

Capoeira, a martial art developed by the slaves, is a foot-fighting technique disguised as a dance (see page 105). Forbidden by their owners to fight, the slaves were forced to hide this pastime behind the trappings of a gymnastics display. Today, you can see this rhythmic exercise performed on street corners and in the Mercado Modelo in Salvador to the music of the *berimbau*, a one-stringed instrument resembling an archer's bow.

Saints' days

Among Salvador's festivals is that of **Procissão do Senhor Bom Jesus dos Navegantes**, a New Year's Day procession in honor of Our Lord of the Seafarers, when a flotilla of boats escorts the image of Christ to the **Boa Viagem beach**. Another takes place on the second Thursday in January, when *baianas* in brilliant white costumes ritually wash the steps of the church of **Nosso Senhor do Bonfim** (Our Lord of Good Ending), Salvador's most frequently visited church.

Iemanjá, the *candomblé* goddess of the sea, is honored on February 2, when *baianas* in white lace blouses and skirts send offerings, such as combs, mirrors, and soaps, out to sea on small handmade boats. This *orixá*

The interior of Igreja de Sao Francisco church is one of the most imposing in Portuguese-Brazilian Baroque gilt woodwork art (talha dourada).

A candomblé artefact for sale.

SALVADOR'S CARNIVAL

Carnival in Salvador is a highly organized affair. The Carnival *blocos* (blocks) are formed of a *trio elétrico* – national and local stars, soloists and bands, performing on stages perched atop enormous trucks, belting out music for dancing in the streets. They are followed by a support truck, which provides a bar, toilets, and a medical post. Each *bloco* permits around 3,000 participants to dance and have fun in a roped-off area with security protection as it makes its way through the streets at a slow pace, taking from five to seven hours to reach its destination. In order to join a Carnival *bloco*, an *abadá* kit is required: this comprises shorts and a T-shirt printed with the bloco's security symbol. The abadá is the access ticket, and is inspected carefully by the security team to prevent non-members joining in. They go on sale well in advance, and prices range from affordable to very high, depending on the popularity of the band.

Some revelers, known as *foliões pipoca* (popcorn dancers – an allusion to their jumping-up-and-down style of dance) follow behind the *bloco*, outside the roped area, enjoying the music without paying, but not enjoying the privileges or safety of bloco members. It is all great fun, and quite exhilarating, but do remember that care should be taken in such large crowds.

(goddess), who is perceived as vain, is placated to guarantee calm waters for the fishermen.

Festivities in June to celebrate the saints' days of St Antony, St John, and St Peter are collectively called *festas juninas* (June festivals), and were brought to Brazil by the Portuguese. St John's day is the most important, even rivaling Christmas. Finally, Nossa Senhora da Conceição da Praia (Our Lady of the Beach) is honored on December 8 with a Mass, a procession from the church dedicated to her, and popular festivities. (See page 75.)

Day trips from Salvador

Ilha de Itaparica 🄬 is a tropical island set in the Baía de Todos os Santos, where Club Med built its first hotel in Brazil. About 19,000 people live on the island, divided mainly between fishermen and wealthy weekenders, whose beach front mansions can often be reached only by boat. As it is a popular bolthole for middle-class Brazilians, hotels tend to be expensive, and the island gets very crowded during weekends and holidays.

There are several ways to reach Itaparica island: one is by ferry boat: they leave Salvador's port at regular intervals for the 45-minute crossing. You can also drive around to the other side of the bay and the bridge that links Itaparica to the mainland. This is a three-hour trip that may be extended to include stops at the fascinating historical towns of Santo Amaro and Cachoeira. Or you could take the passenger ferry from the Mercado Modelo in Salvador, which is great fun as long as you have good sea legs. Once on the island, you can rent a bicycle to do some exploring along its many beaches.

If your time is limited, take the day-long bay cruise that is sold by the top travel agencies in Salvador. The cruise includes transportation to and from your hotel and free *batidas* and soft drinks. Aboard the double-masted schooner *(saveiro)*, you will be in for a delightful surprise when you find that the guide and crew are also musicians. As the boat gently skims the calm waters of the bay between stops, the crew gathers at the prow to sing and play popular songs. Later in the day, after a fair number of *batidas*, nearly everyone is enthusiastically singing along and dancing.

After leaving Salvador, most of these boats make two stops. The first, in the late morning, is at **Ilha dos Frades**, a tiny and all-but deserted island inhabited by fishermen who have found a second, more lucrative source of revenue: the tourist trade. The boat anchors offshore, and visitors are brought ashore 10 at a time in rowing boats. Those who are not afraid of the jellyfish ('Their sting is just a little nip,' the local people say) can swim to the shore.

After an hour of exploring, drinking, or eating a snack at one of the improvised bars, or purchasing souvenirs, visitors are taken on to Itaparica Island for lunch and a walking tour. Then it is back to the boat for the return trip to Salvador, with a splendid view of the sunset over the city.

On Ponta de Areia beach.

RESTAURANTS

Salvador has a wide variety of restaurants, many with tables set in flower-decked courtyards. You can find some authentic Bahian cooking, often served in extremely large portions – some dishes are made for sharing – and prices are generally reasonable.

Alfredo di Roma
Atlantic Towers, Rua Morro do Escravo Miguel s/n, Ondina
Tel: 71-3331 7775
Open: L&D daily.
A good, well-dressed branch of the Rome original, in the Hotel Atlantic Towers. Consistently one of Salvador's best Italian restaurants, and a bonus in you want a change from the Bahian cuisine. The hotel also offers the less formal veranda area, Alfredo Cosí, which serves pizza. $$$

Conventual
Convento do Carmo Hotel, Rua do Carmo s/n, Pelourinho
Tel: 71-3327 8400
Open: L&D daily.
A stunning setting in the most luxurious hotel in town. There is a mix of traditional Portuguese and Bahian influences on the excellent and interesting menu. One of Salvador's more sophisticated restaurants. A chance to enjoy one of the city's most attractive hotels if you are not staying there. $$$

Fogo de Chão
4 Praça Colombo, Rio Vermelho
Tel: 71-3555 9292
Open: L&D daily.
Carnivores' paradise, but also offering an extensive salad bar and other dishes. Part of a leading chain of top Brazilian *rodizio* houses, and that means the meats keep coming. $$$

Manjericão
3-B Rua Fonte do Boi, Rio Vermelho
Tel: 71-3565 8305
Open: L only Mon–Sat.
Natural food served in a very relaxed and pleasant garden, or indoors close to the buffet. Normally around 20 dishes on offer daily, and you pay by the weight you eat. Excellent choice for vegetarian travellers. $

Maria Mata Mouro
8 Rua da Ordem Terceira de São Francisco, Pelourinho
Tel: 71-3321 3929
Open: L&D daily.
An eclectic menu of well-prepared contemporary and regional cuisine, served in the heart of the historical district in a house dating from the 18th century. Considered by some to serve Salvador's best *mouqueca* (seafood stew), which is praise indeed. Charming garden area at the back. $$

Paraíso Tropical
98 Rua Edgar Loureiro, Cabula
Tel: 71-3384 7464
Open: L&D daily.
One of the best Bahian restaurants in Salvador, especially for its signature *moquecas*. Slightly off the beaten track, this rustic restaurant is worth the effort if you are serious about having a Bahian culinary experience. $$$

Quattro Amici
35 Rua Dom Marcos Teixeira, Barra
Tel: 71-3264 5999
Open: D daily.
Considered one of Salvador's best and most consistent pizzerias, with 42 varieties offered. Located in a restored 19th-century building and equally popular with locals and visitors. Also has a branch in Salvador Shopping. $

Senac
13 Praça José de Alencar, Largo do Pelourinho
Tel: 71-3324 4564
Open: L only daily.
The city's catering school runs this self-service buffet restaurant, which offers a wide variety of interesting and well-prepared Bahian and Brazilian dishes. The buffet gives visitors an opportunity to try a lot of different Bahian dishes at one sitting. Well located in the Pelourinho, so it's popular. $$

Yemanjá
4655 Avenida Octávio Mangabeira, Jardim Armação
Tel: 71-3461 9010
Open: L&D daily.
Authentic Bahian dishes served in a pleasant and unpretentious atmosphere. This is one of Salvador's best-known restaurants, and popular with families and large groups. $$$

Moqueca, Bahia's famous fish stew

MISTURA FINA

The mix of races in Brazil is mainly European and African, but with Amerindian and many more exotic ethnicities, this is a wonderfully multicultural society.

Mistura Fina (exquisite mixture) is a proud term often used to describe Brazil's multiracial origins.

When the Portuguese founded Brazil, they had problems with trying to populate an area almost a hundred times larger than their mother country. To solve this, they adopted a policy of interbreeding with other races, and imported black Africans as slave labor to build the colony.

Slavery in Brazil was long lasting, but it was less rigorous than in the British colonies, and Afro-Brazilians were able to preserve much of their traditional culture. The result, many generations later, is that the majority of Brazilians are of mixed race, and in Brazilian culture, African roots are still very much alive.

Candomblé, *umbanda*, *macumba*, and spiritism all derive from African religions, and are often practiced in parallel with Christianity. A follower may go to church on Sunday and to the *terreiro*, where the African religions are practiced, on Friday.

Carnival was already a Portuguese tradition, but it was also intended to give slaves an annual respite, and an opportunity to express their heritage. Today, the whole population gets involved, but it still bears the hallmark of Africa. The rhythms of Brazilian music have strong African roots, transmuted into a distinctly Brazilian sound. The sensual bossa nova and samba, and their derivatives such as *lambada*, are reminiscent of African dances.

Brazil today without its African roots would be unthinkable; its culture would be poorer for the absence of the African essence, which is now part of every Brazilian soul.

Playing drums on the streets at Largo de Pelourinho.

Candomblé followers wear strings of beads made of seeds and shells in the colors of African gods.

The devoted may attend services at the local church, but it does not mean they are worshiping Catholic saints, as many people pay allegiance to multiple faiths.

Candomblé artefacts for sale in Bahia.

AFRO-BRAZILIAN ART AND CRAFTS

A great deal of Brazilian art and local crafts reflects an African heritage, and many pieces are derived from the skills and traditions that men and women brought with them from Africa over the centuries of their servitude. Wooden sculptures from the northeast region of Brazil, in particular, are strongly reminiscent of traditions and crafts from Africa.

The *carranca* figureheads that traditionally were believed to protect the boats on the São Francisco river, and which today can be found throughout the region as souvenirs, come from the figurative art traditions of Africa. Stylized statues in the same area are strongly reminiscent of the masks that proliferate in much of West Africa.

The faithful followers of *candomblé* are usually richly adorned with strings of beads in the colors of the African gods, as part of their religious costume. These are made of seeds or shells, and are similar to those that can be found in Africa. The beach-side stalls that sell them, largely in the northeast of Brazil, also carry a vivid range of T-shirts bearing traditional African designs.

The white robes can be traced back to the African slaves and have strong links to Candomblé, umbanda, macumba and other African influenced religions.

Colorful ribbons from the church of Senhor do Bonfim in Salvador represent a certain superstition and wish.

This pair of carved Orixa represents Oxum, the spirit of love, feminine beauty, fertility, and art, and Yansá, a warrior and spirit of the wind, sudden change, and the gates to the underworld.

SERGIPE AND ALAGOAS

Brasília
Rio de Janeiro

Great beaches, colonial towns, delicious seafood, and a host of festivals are luring increasing numbers of visitors to these two relatively unexplored states.

Main Attractions
São Cristóvão
Laranjeiras
Aracaju
Penedo
Marechal Deodoro
Maceió

Sergipe and Alagoas played a part in the rich sugar-cane period of Brazilian history, which began in the late 16th century. As in neighboring Bahia and Pernambuco, the population was divided between landlords and slaves – the latter brought here in growing numbers to work in the sugar mills and plantations. But there were numerous rebellions, and runaway slaves went into hiding in the forests where they formed independent communities, or *quilombos*, some of which flourished and lasted for decades.

The most famous, and largest, of these *quilombos* was the Republic of Palmares in the state of Alagoas, which lasted for 65 years, and had at one time almost 30,000 inhabitants. In 1694 the *quilombo* was destroyed and its inhabitants killed or taken back into slavery. The site of the republic has become a pilgrimage center, and a bust of its last leader, Zumbi, who was executed in 1695, now stands in Brasília.

Vestiges of the state's colonial past can also be seen in the sugar mills and once-grand farmhouses in the region, and in the ornate churches and other buildings in some historic towns.

Coastal attractions

Whereas neighboring northeastern states have largely substituted a tourist boom for the sugar-cane industry, Sergipe and Alagoas have been relatively late to the party, but tourism is beginning to take off. Between Recife and Salvador, the two most important cities in the northeast, lie 840km (525 miles) of beautiful coastline, which attract increasing numbers of visitors, and much of it is to be found in these two states.

The state capitals, Aracaju and Maceió, both have good urban beaches, and the stunning, unspoiled palm-ringed sands and deep-blue sea of Alagoas are among the best in the northeast. The dark green of Sergipe's waters are not as inviting, but the state more than

Palm trees ring the beach at Maceio.

compensates for this with two attractive historic towns.

São Cristóvão

Lying about 34km (20 miles) south of Aracaju is **São Cristóvão** ⓭, founded in 1590 by Cristóvão de Barros. It is the fourth-oldest city in Brazil, and has a number of well-preserved colonial structures, including the lovely Convento de São Francisco (1693), the Igreja e Convento do Carmo (1743–66), housing a striking **Museum of Votive Offerings** (Mon–Fri 10am-4pm; free), and Nossa Senhora da Vitória (late 17th century). The **Museu de Arte Sacra**, housed in the São Francisco convent, and, next door, the **Museu Histórico de Sergipe** (both Tue–Sun 1–5pm) are worth a look.

In 2010, São Cristóvão's town square, Praço São Francisco, was named a Unesco World Heritage site. This quadrilateral open space is surrounded by early colonial buildings such as the Convento e Igreja de São Francisco, Igreja de Santa Casa da Misercórdia, and the Palácio do Governo. These 18th- and 19th-century buildings create an urban landscape that reflects the history of the town since its origin. The square is an example of the typical architecture of the Franciscan order that developed in the northeast.

A visit to São Cristóvão is not complete without trying the biscuits, made by nuns, which are sold in the orphanage next to the church of Nossa Senhora da Visitação.

Most visitors come to São Cristóvão for the religious procession of Senhor dos Passos, which takes place two weeks after Carnival (February or March). Accommodations in the town are very simple, and there is just one restaurant of note.

Laranjeiras

Nearby **Laranjeiras** (23km/15 miles west of Aracaju) is another town that was founded on the sugar industry, and has preserved its heritage. It has the highest concentration of folkloric groups in the state, most notably the Grupo Folclórico São Gonçalo. It also has a rich Afro-Brazilian culture, and is home to the first Afro-Brazilian museum in Latin America, the **Museu Afro-Brasileiro de Sergipe** (Tue–Sun 10am–5pm), which opened in the 1970s. A number of groups in the town practice *candomblé*, and visits can be arranged through the museum.

Although only a small town, Laranjeiras has seven churches, notably Sant'Aninha (1875) and Comendaroba (1734). In the late afternoon you will see local people selling *acarajé* and other regional snacks in the town center. If you are thinking of staying in Laranjeiras, be aware that accommodations are hard to find.

Aracaju

A short way further north, the state capital, **Aracaju** ⓮, lies in the center of the Sergipe coastal strip. Founded in 1855, Aracaju (pop. 590,000) has a small but well-maintained historic center, with buildings that include the Cathedral of Nossa Senhora da Conceição. Opposite the cathedral, in a delightful colonial

Portrait of a man, Porto de Galinhas, Pernambuco. The town name translates as "Port of the Chickens."

A horse and cart in São Francisco.

Carranca figure head, Cachoeira, Bahia.

building, is the Tourist Center (Praça Olimpio Campos), which, apart from the local tourist information office, also houses a number of artisan stores with a varied selection of local crafts for sale at reasonable prices.

The city's interactive museum, **Museu da Gente Sergipana** (www. museudagentesergipana.com.br; Tue–Fri 10am–5pm, Sat–Sun 10am–4pm), located in a restored college building dating from 1926, tells the story of the local people of Sergipe and their lives. The museum was voted one of Brazil's best new museums in 2013.

There are better accommodations to be found at nearby Atalaia beach than in the center of town, with several modern beachfront hotels, including a popular Radisson, which opened in 2009. With an extensive promenade and a variety of restaurants, Atalaia makes a good base for exploring Aracaju, and for day trips to other beaches, such as Do Rabalo and Mosqueiro.

Northern festivals

Convento de São Francisco in Marechal Deodoro.

Aracaju is noted for the beauty of its beaches and the hospitality of its people, whose festival calendar is one of the fullest in the northeast. The numerous festivals are nearly always based on religious holidays, though they may often appear more secular than sacred. They include Bom Jesus dos Navegantes, a maritime procession of gaily decorated boats (January 1); São Benedicto, celebrated with folk dances and mock battles (the first weekend in January); the Festas Juninas, in honor of the three saints John, Anthony and Peter (vibrant celebrations throughout the month of June); Expoarte, a handicraft fair (the whole month of July); and Iemanjá, a religious procession in honor of the *candomblé* goddess, which is celebrated at different times in different cities, but here is held on December 8.

Delicious seafood and freshwater fish abound here, among which is Aracaju's main claim to fame, its freshwater shrimp (similar to crayfish in appearance), caught in the Sergipe river. Crab is another of this city's specialities, and for dessert, breadfruit compote or stewed coconut. The obligatory appetizer is a *batida*, made from sugar-cane

São Francisco river

Born from a spring in the Minas Gerais hills, the São Francisco, Brazil's third-largest river, has been vital in shaping the country's economic and cultural development.

In the 19th century, the 3,000km (1,800-mile) São Francisco river played a vital role in the development of the northeast, through which its reddish-brown waters flow, defining the border between Sergipe and Alagoas, where it empties into the Atlantic Ocean.

For many years the river was virtually the only major thoroughfare in the region, which lacked roads and railways. The river's role as primary mover of people and products has given it a place in Brazilian history and legend somewhat equivalent to that of the Mississippi in the US. From the 19th century until well into modern times, riverboats plied the São Francisco, carrying essential supplies to backwoods towns.

The villages and settlements that sprang up along the riverbanks during the colonial period had become important trading centers and commercial outposts by the mid-19th century. Today, the valley still serves as an agricultural oasis in an otherwise arid terrain. Along the banks you encounter farms producing fruits for export, including grapes, papaya, and mango. The Vale do Rio São Francisco is the only region in the world producing fine wines at a latitude of 88° from the.

Half-man, half-beast

Known as *Velho Chico* (Old Chico) to the local inhabitants, the São Francisco river is both admired and feared as the home of evil spirits. In order to protect themselves from these spirits, boatmen in the 19th century made wooden figureheads for their vessels, depicting fierce, ugly creatures that could warn a boat's crew of danger by emitting low moans. These figureheads, half-man, half-beast, are called *carrancas*. Only the older boatmen still believe in the powers of *carrancas*, but the legend lives on, and the figures are still attached to modern boats.

Two of the best places to purchase *carrancas*, carved from cedar wood, are Petrolina in Pernambuco (750km/465 miles from Recife) and neighboring Juazeiro in Bahia. The Oficina do Artesão (Final da Avenida Cardoso de Sa, Vila Eduardo, Petrolina) sells *carrancas* and other interesting wooden sculptures produced on-site by resident artists.

Boatmen offer daylong cruises to visitors. Trips begin in Penedo in Alagoas and Juazeiro in Bahia, and, directly across the river, Petrolina in Pernambuco, Ibotirama in Bahia, and Januária and Pirapora in Minas Gerais.

From Petrolina one can also visit a number of river islands, the most interesting of which is the Ilha de Massangano, where you can see Samba de Veio, one of the oldest folk groups in the region, established more than 100 years ago. The best time to see them is on the Dia dos Reis (January 6), when the group plays until dawn.

One gallant old paddle-wheel steamboat, the *Benjamim Guimarães*, which was built in the US in 1913 for use on the Mississippi, and fully restored in 2004, still makes jaunts down the São Francisco. Today it is used exclusively for tourists, and offers a three-hour trip on Sunday, sailing at 9am and covering 18km (11 miles) of the river (reservations at the port in Pirapora; tel: 38-3749 6155).

There are many villages along the São Francisco river.

Alagoas state is blessed with fine beaches.

liqueur *(cachaça)* and any one of a variety of local fruits and nuts – the best are mango, cashew, coconut, and *mangaba*.

Alagoas

Moving north along the BR-101 highway from Aracaju, you cross the state border between Sergipe and Alagoas, delineated by the immense São Francisco river (see page 289). Here, the town of **Penedo ⑮**, built in the 17th and 18th centuries, is a good place to stop on your way to the state capital, Maceió (see page 290).

Penedo's Baroque and rococo churches are its main attractions, in particular Nossa Senhora dos Anjos (1759) and Nossa Senhora da Corrente (1764). River trips downstream to the mouth of the São Francisco can be taken from Piacabucu (22km/14 miles from Penedo), or take the ferry across the river to Neópolis, where boat trips can be arranged at Brejo Grande (27km/17 miles from Neópolis).

A traditional jangada wooden fishing raft sails past a tropical beach.

Santana do São Francisco (3km/1.5 miles from Neópolis) is a good place to buy handmade earthenware and porcelain goods at the Centro de Artesanato,

a project run by members of the local community.

The road from Penedo to Maceió passes a variety of quiet, often deserted beaches, such as Japu, Miai de Cima, and Barreiras. Closer to Maceió, Praia do Gunga (45km/28 miles to the south) is a popular choice in the summer months. The beach is located at the point where the Roteiro lake meets the sea. It has a good infrastructure for visitors, with a number of stalls offering food and drinks. One of the busiest beaches close to the city limits is Praia do Francês, which is near the historic old town of Marechal Deodoro, the first capital of Alagoas.

Marechal Deodoro

Marechal Deodoro ⑯ itself is home to some lovely examples of Brazilian colonial architecture. Among the gems are the Convento de São Francisco (Monastery of St Francis), dating from 1684, and the church of Nossa Senhora da Conceição (1755).

Originally called Alagoas, the town was renamed after its most famous son, Field Marshal Manuel Deodoro da Fonseca (1827–92), who became, briefly, the first (non-elected) president of Brazil in 1891. He headed the military coup that deposed Emperor Dom Pedro II two years earlier, but his time in office was turbulent. Faced with strong opposition from the Congress, he handed over power to vice-president Floriano Peixoto after a few months, and died the following year.

Maceió

Between Sergipe and Pernambuco (to the north) lies the state of Alagoas, whose capital is **Maceió ⑰**, with a total population of 930,000. The city, founded in 1815, grew gradually out of a sugar plantation established there in the 18th century.

Maceió beaches are famous for the transparent, bright emerald-green of the water, especially at low tide on downtown **Praia Pajuçara**. Trapped between the beach and offshore

sand-bars, the water becomes an enormous wading pool. For a small sum, fishermen will take you out to the sand-bars in their *jangadas* (outrigger boats), with pools that are full of sea life.

Praia Pajuçara is considered one of the best urban beaches in Brazil, and is always busy. The city is struggling to keep up with the flow of tourists that descends upon it in summer; December is especially busy, when Maceió holds its Festival do Mar (Festival of the Sea) at Pajuçara. It is celebrated with a street and beach party that includes sporting events, folk dancing, and booths selling native handicrafts.

Maceió is a mostly modern town, but a few old buildings survive, including the **Pierre Chalita Sacred Art Museum** (Mon–Fri 8am–noon, 2–6pm), in the Palácio do Governo; the church of Bom Jesus dos Martirios (1870); and the Catedral de Nossa Senhora dos Prazeres (1840) on Praça Dom Pedro II.

North along the coast

Continuing north of Maceió toward the state border with Pernambuco is one of the most beautiful stretches of coastal road in the region. The palm tree-lined road hugs the coast for most of the distance, allowing easy access to a number of beaches. The section from Barra de Camaragibe to Porto de Pedras is reminiscent of bygone days, with little to disturb its serenity. The road passes through a series of small villages where local people sell craft goods, cakes, and tapioca from their porches. A series of discrete easy-to-miss dirt tracks will take you down to isolated beaches, which see few tourists even at the busiest of times.

The small town of **Porto de Pedras** makes a good base for visiting the beaches. The local restaurant here, Peixada de Marinete, specializes in excellent home cooking. The owner's signature dishes include lobster stew and a regional crab omelet (see page 291). Also popular is Pousadoa Patacho.

Beaches worth visiting include Praia do Toque and Tatuamunha. North of Porto de Pedras, almost on the border with Pernambuco, are the beaches of Japaratinga and Maragogi. The latter has been rated one of the top 10 beaches in Brazil by a respected national publication.

TIP

In the little resort of São Miguel dos Milagres, near Porto de Pedras, about one-and-a-half hours drive from Macio, you could pamper yourself at the lovely Pousada do Caju (tel: 82-3295 1103; www. pousadacaju.com), a luxurious retreat with just seven guest rooms, all with verandas, and a number of bungalows. There is also a pool, and Jacuzzi.

RESTAURANTS

PRICE CATEGORIES

Prices for a two-course meal for two. Wine costs around US$25 a bottle.
$ = under US$50
$$ = US$50–100
$$$ = US$100–200

Aracaju

Casquinha de Caranguejo
751 Avenida Santos Dumont, Atalaia
Tel: 79-3243 7011
Open: L&D daily.
A popular and relaxed beachfront spot specializing in crab. Other dishes include *badejo* fish with banana, seafood, and oysters. $$

O Miguel
340 Avenida Antionio Alves, Atalaia Velha
Tel: 79-3243 1444
Open: L&D Tue–Sun, L only Mon.
This down-to-earth but charming restaurant does an excellent *carne de sol* and *pirão de leite* and is considered the best and most consistent restaurant in Aracaju for regional cuisine. They will, however, be equally as happy to grill you a good steak. $$

Maceió

Carne de Sol do Picui
1140 Avenida da Paz, Jaraguá
Tel: 82-3223 8080
Open: L&D daily.
As the name suggests, *carne de sol* is the specialty and over a dozen variations are on offer. One dish can easily be enough for two. Located in the historic centre of Maceió, but stylish and modern. The restaurant has its own van for free transfers from the hotels. $$

Wanchako
93 Rua São Francisco de Assis, Jatiúca
Tel: 82-3377 6024
Open: L&D Mon–Fri, D only Sat.
A charming choice with an interesting menu laced with Peruvian influences (the chef makes regular trips to check on culinary developments). $$$

Porto de Pedras

Peixada da Marinete
100 Rua Avelino Cunha
Tel: 82-3298 1267
Open: L&D daily.
A simple but comfortable setting and great food (see page 291). Go for the chef's signature dishes that include *lagostada* – baby lobster stew – or *fritada de aratu* – crab omelet. No credit cards. $

São Cristóvão

O Sobrado
40 Praça da Matriz
Tel: 079-3261 1310
Open: L&D daily.
Luckily, the only restaurant of note in town is a relatively good one. Local food and dishes in an attractive colonial house. $

RECIFE AND PERNAMBUCO

Bustling Recife and beautiful, Baroque Olinda are
the main focuses of a state whose other attractions
include art and handicraft centers, and gorgeous
sandy stretches of beach.

When sugar was king, in the late 16th and early 17th centuries, Pernambuco was the richest state in Brazil. Sugar plantations and mills – *engenhos* – were centered in the region around Olinda, and Recife quickly developed as the ideal port for the export of the product. Slave labor was easy to come by, and political power came in the wake of economic dominance. When the economic importance of sugar dwindled, it was largely replaced by cotton, but by the mid-17th century, finds of gold and precious metal in the state of Minas Gerais were getting all the attention. The capital of the country was moved south, from Salvador, near the sugar plantations, to Rio de Janeiro, closer to the rich gold-mining areas, and Pernambuco and its capital, Recife, never regained their former glory.

Although political and economic power have moved south, Recife is once again becoming a booming center, this time for the fast-growing tourism industry. Good hotels and restaurants are attracting growing numbers of Brazilian and international visitors looking for beautiful beaches, colonial gems like Olinda, and a year-round warm climate.

Recife is one of the host cities for the FIFA World Cup and has built a 46,000-seater stadium, **Itaipava Arena**

Street life in Olinda.

Pernambuco (www.itaipavaarenapernam buco.com.br/en/), in the western suburb of São Lourenço de Mata. It is the centerpiece of what is known as Cidade da Copa. When the World Cup was last played in Brazil, back in 1950, Recife was the only city in the northeast to host games.

Coral-reef city

Recife ⑱, capital of the state of Pernambuco, is a metropolis of 3.7 million inhabitants. Its name comes from the Arabic word for 'fortified wall,'

Main Attractions
Boa Viagem
Olinda
Porto de Galinhas
Ilha Itamaracá
Nova Jerusalem

Hanging out in Olinda, one of the best-preserved historical cities in Brazil.

which in Portuguese has acquired the meaning of 'reef.' Recife's coastline, like much of the northeast, is characterized by barnacle and coral reefs running parallel to the mainland, between 90 meters (330ft) and 1km (0.5 mile) from the shore. The waves break on the far side of the reefs, making the water on the near side a shallow, saltwater swimming pool, tranquil and safe for bathers. On **Boa Viagem** beach in Recife you can wade out to the reefs at low tide, and barely get your knees wet.

In 1537, the Portuguese settled the coastal area of Pernambuco. A Dutch invasion a century later, under Prince Maurice of Nassau, brought with it a new era of art, culture, and urbanization to the town. Recife was once a maze of swamps and islets that Prince Maurice made habitable through the construction of canals. Now there are 39 bridges spanning the canals and rivers that separate the three main islands of Recife.

Recife on foot

A walking tour of Recife's historical district should begin, at the **Praça da República Ⓐ**, with the **Teatro Santa Isabel Ⓑ** (Mon–Fri 1–5pm), a neoclassical building dating from 1850, and one of the most beautiful in the city. Other 19th-century buildings on this square include the governor's mansion, the palace of justice, and the law courts, which double as the Catholic University's law school (the oldest one in Brazil).

Just across the street from the palace of justice is the Baroque **Capela Dourada Ⓒ** (Golden Chapel; chapel and adjoining sacred-art museum: Mon–Fri 8–11.30am, 2–5pm, Sat 8–11.30am). According to legend, it contains more gold than any church in Brazil, except Salvador's Igreja de São Francisco. Built in the late 17th century by laymen attached to the Franciscan Order, this is one of the most important examples of religious architecture in the country.

Eight blocks from the Santa Isabel Theater, down Rua do Sol, is the **Casa da Cultura Ⓓ** (www.casadaculturape.

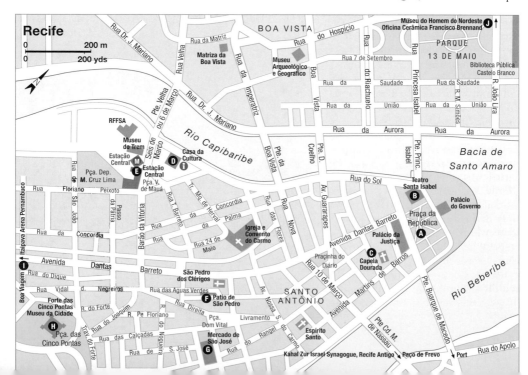

com.br; Mon–Sat 9am–7pm, Sun 9am–2pm), a three-story structure that served as a penitentiary for more than 100 years. In 1975 it was remodeled to become Recife's largest handicraft center. The prison cells have been turned into booths displaying articles ranging from leather and straw accessories to clay figurines, silk-screened T-shirts, and fruit liqueurs.

On Praça Visconde de Mauá, opposite the Casa da Cultura and next to the **Estação Central** ❺ (1888), is the **Museu do Trem** (Mon–Fri 9am–noon, 2–5pm), which traces the history of Brazil's railroads.

Four hundred meters/yds away, southeast along Rua Dantas Barreto, is the **Patio de São Pedro** ❻, the artists' corner of Recife, with music and folklore performances on weekends. It is a good place to buy local craftwork. The **Igreja de São Pedro** nearby is an interesting example of Baroque architecture. Continuing southeast, across Praça Dom Vital, you come to the **Mercado de São José** ❼ (Mon–Sat 5am–3.30pm, Sun 6am–noon), a busy market in a 19th-century building.

While downtown it is worth taking a short detour to the restored port area, Recife Antigo, where the cruise ships now dock. On Rua Bom Jesus can be found the Centro Cultural Judaico de Pernambuco and the **Kahal Zur Israel Synagogue** (tel: 81-3224 2128; Mon–Fri 9am–5pm, Sun 4–6pm). The reconstructed synagogue is built on the foundations of what was the oldest synagogue in the Americas, dating back to 1640, which served the first Jewish congregation in the New World. With the end of Dutch rule, in 1654, many of Recife's Jewish community fled from Brazil to New Amsterdam, which was to become New York.

Another major attraction in Recife Antigo is **Paço do Frevo** (Tue–Sun 9am–8pm), which is located in the old headquarters of the Western Telegraph Company in Praça do Arsenal da Marinha. Opened in 2013, the space is dedicated to the story of the

city's famous dance, *frevo*, a form that in December 2012 was recognized by Unesco as part of the Heritage of Humanity.

Frevo (from the Portuguese *ferver* to boil) is the centerpiece of Pernambuco's Carnival, combining a range of musical styles. In this festival there are no samba schools like those found in the south, and no electric instruments such as are found in Salvador. People dance in the streets, holding up parasols to help keep their balance. Groups portray *maracatu*, a typical northeastern legend that tells the history of the *candomblé* religion and its roots in the times of slavery.

The center of northeastern Carnival is Olinda, whose narrow streets are packed with delirious celebrants throughout the four-day festival.

At the southern end of Recife's downtown area, the massive, star-shaped **Forte das Cinco Pontas** ❽, built by the Dutch in 1630, houses the **Museu da Cidade** (Largo das Cinco Pontas; Mon–Fri 9am–6pm, Sat–Sun 1–5pm), with displays on the history of Recife.

The Igreja NS do Carmo church in Olinda was probably the first church built in Brazil by the Carmelite order.

In Recife's picturesque old town.

Tiles decorate an historic building in Olinda. The central part of town has been designated a World Heritage Site.

The view over the São Francisco monastery.

Taking a cab (or a lengthy walk) southwest from the Museu da Cidade along Avenida Dantas Barreto, you will eventually come to **Boa Viagem** . Most of the better restaurants and bars and nearly all the city's better hotels are located on or near the beach here. It is Recife's most beautiful beach, and also the center of its social life.

In the evening, the action is concentrated along the beach itself, and on Avenida Conselheiro Aguiar, one block inland. The street is home to a number of small bars and sidewalk cafés offering inexpensive drinks, nibbles, and plenty of live music.

There are a dozen museums in Recife, but one stands out: the **Museu do Homem do Nordeste** (Museum of Northeastern Man; Tue–Fri 8.30am–5pm, Sat–Sun and holidays 1–5pm) at 2187 Avenida 17 de Agosto . Founded by the late Gilberto Freyre (1900–87), Brazil's most reputable anthropologist, the museum is a tribute to the cultural history of this fascinating and unusual region. The museum has bilingual guides and is located in the **Casa Forte** district, 6km (4 miles) from downtown.

Another diverting stop in the same part of town, in the working-class district of **Várzea**, is the **Oficina Cerâmica Francisco Brennand** (www. brennand.com.br; Mon–Fri 8am–5pm), the workshop and studio of one of the northeast's best-known artisans. This immense atelier was a brick and tile factory until Francisco Brennand took it over. Brennand (b. 1927) is famed in Recife for his beautiful, hand-painted tiles, pottery, and vaguely erotic statuary, all eagerly bought both by local people and tourists. You can visit the workshop, and if you call ahead for a tour you may be lucky enough to be escorted by Mr Brennand himself (for details tel: 81-3271 2466).

Olinda

Time has stood still in neighboring **Olinda** , which stretches like an open-air museum across the hills overlooking Recife. The town is a treasure trove of Baroque art and architecture and, as such, was declared a World Heritage Site by Unesco in 1982. However,

many of the buildings are still await-ing or undergoing restoration.

Legend has it that the first Portu-guese emissary sent to govern the region was so enthralled by the beauty of these hills that he said 'O linda situ-ação para uma vila' (What a beautiful site for a settlement) – hence Olinda's name. By far the best way to explore Olinda is on foot. Narrow streets lined with brightly colored colonial homes, serenely beautiful churches, sidewalk cafés, and shops displaying ornate signs wind through the 17th-century setting of Olinda's hills.

Starting off at the **Praça do Carmo**, site of Brazil's oldest Carmelite church (built in 1580), continue up Rua São Francisco to the **São Roque** chapel, **Nossa Senhora das Neves** church, and the convent of **São Francisco** (Mon–Fri 8–noon, 2–5pm, Sat 8am–noon; free), dating from 1585, with Baroque frescoes depicting the life of the Virgin Mary. Turn left on Rua Bispo Coutinho to visit the **Seminário de Olinda** and the **Nossa Senhora da Graça** church – both well-preserved examples of 16th-century Brazil-ian Baroque architecture. This street opens out on to Alto da Sé, a hilltop square overlooking the ocean, and Recife, 6km (4 miles) away.

The **Igreja da Sé**, the first parish church in the northeast, was built at the time of Olinda's founding in 1537 and today is the cathedral of the archdiocese. Across from the cathe-dral, housed in the **Palácio Episco-pal** (1676) is the **sacred art museum** (Mon–Fri 9am–1pm), which contains a collection of panels portraying the history of Olinda. On weekend eve-nings, the Alto da Sé comes alive with outdoor cafés and bars.

As you turn down the Ladeira da Misericórdia, on your right is the church of the **Misericórdia** (daily 8am–noon, 2–6pm; free) dating from 1549. Its richly detailed wood-and-gold engravings are reminiscent of the French Boucher school. The building from which the **Mercado da Ribeira**

operates, on Rua Bernardo Vieira de Melo, was used in the 16th century as a slave market; it is now an excellent place to buy art. On the corner of Rua 13 de Maio is the **Museu de Arte Con-temporânea** (Wed–Mon 9am–5pm), an 18th-century structure that was originally designed to house prisoners of the Inquisition.

Most of Olinda's other historical buildings are open daily to visitors, with a two-hour lunch break, usually from noon–2pm. Accommodations can be found in luxury hotels and small inns, many of them historic mansions. Olinda can be used as a base for exploring the nearby beaches of Pernambuco and even Recife.

Porto de Galinhas

The name Pernambuco comes from the indigenous Tupi word paran-ampuka, which means 'the sea that beats on the rocks.' Indeed, the sea has played a major part in Pernambuco's history. Now, it's the beaches that attract large numbers of visitors, gen-erating an additional and much-val-ued source of income. Pernambuco's

Turquoise waters meet the blue sky along the beach in Brazil.

A figure from the Carnival celebrations in Olinda, where the streets become one large party scene.

coast stretches for 187km (116 miles) between the states of Paraíba to the north and Alagoas to the south. Visitors will find many glorious beaches, with sunshine and warm waters for most of the year.

As already mentioned, the best and most famous beach in Recife is Boa Viagem. Outside Recife, the most beautiful beaches lie to the south. **Porto de Galinhas**, next to the town of **Ipojuca**, 50km (30 miles) from downtown Recife, has gained an international reputation for its 18km (12-mile) expanse of soft, white sand, some world-class hotels and resorts, an attractive village, and excellent restaurants. A little further south, there are frequent surfing competitions during the summer months at Maracaípe. Continuing further, you will find Praia dos Carneiros; one of the most beautiful beaches along Pernambuco's coastline, it can be visited from Porto de Galinhas on a day tour.

To the north, the best beaches are found on **Ilha Itamaracá**, 53km (33 miles) from Recife, where local people spend their weekends. On the way,

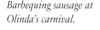

Barbequing sausage at Olinda's carnival.

along highway BR-101, is the historical town of **Igarassu**, much of which has been declared a National Monument. It is home to one of the oldest churches in Brazil, built in 1535, and dedicated to the twin saints of Cosme and Damião. The adjoining Franciscan monastery has one of the largest collections of Baroque religious paintings in the country, comprising more than 200 works. There are also a number of colonial houses, and Brazil's first Masonic hall.

Halfway across the bridge to Itamaracá sits a police checkpoint, a reminder that part of the island serves as an open prison for model inmates serving time at a nearby penitentiary. Married prisoners are allowed to live with their families, and all the inmates are engaged in some form of commerce. As you start down the island road, you will see lines of booths and small stores run by prisoners, selling postcards and crafts. Each man is identified by a number stenciled on to his T-shirt.

Before you reach Forte Orange, built by the Dutch in 1631, take the

MASTER CERAMICIST

The Caruaru ceramicist known as *Mestre* (Master) Vitalino – an acknowledgement of his status – was Vitalino Pereira dos Santos (1909–63), who lived in the Alto do Moura district, and became famous for his distinctive clay figures, mostly portraying poor rural workers of the northeast.

A group of other *bonequeiros* (dollmakers), who had also come to Caruaru from the surrounding countryside, gathered around him, making models in a similar style. Vitalino's five children worked with their father, and, after his death, continued the family tradition.

Two other interesting ceramicists whose work you can see in Caruaru are Luís Antônio and Manoel Galdino (the latter died in 1996), whose work has a more contemporary feel.

side road to **Vila Velha**, the island's first settlement, founded in 1534. This isolated village is tucked away in a coconut grove on the southern coast.

A number of colonial buildings, crowned by the 17th-century Nossa Senhora da Conceição church, line the square. If you're looking for a midday break, there are several regional and seafood restaurants. Splendid beaches line most of the island's shore.

Downtown Itamaracá and the historical Forte Orange district have some simple hotels and restaurants. Next to the old fort, there is a visitor center with displays on the work of the Manatee Project, which looks after injured manatees before returning them to the open sea.

Caruaru

The twice-weekly Caruaru handicrafts fair, and the backwoods town of Fazenda Nova (190km/118 miles from Recife), are the final destinations of an excellent day trip from Recife along the BR-232 highway that winds up the coastal mountain range to the resort town of Gravatá, and beyond.

Halfway to Gravatá, near **Vitória de Santo Antão**, looming on the left, is an enormous bottle with a crayfish on the label: the symbol of the Pitú *cachaça* distillery. The distillery hardly needs its bottle sign: its product, Brazil's distinctive sugar cane liqueur, can be smelled long before the bottle appears. Tours of the plant are available, and there are free tastings of the most famous brand of *cachaça* in the northeast.

From here to Gravatá it's 32km (20 miles) along a tortuous mountain road. The air becomes noticeably cooler, the vegetation more sparse. **Gravatá ⑳** is where Recife's wealthy have summer homes, and the fresh mountain air attracts visitors to its hotels and inns at the weekend. This is practically the last you will see of anything green, except for scrubland plants and lizards, until you return to the coast.

Ideally, a visit to Fazenda Nova should be made either on a Wednesday or a Saturday. On these two days, the next-door city of **Caruaru ㉑** turns into one great trading post, with rich and poor rubbing shoulders at the stalls. At one stand, a wealthy Recife matron may be choosing her hand-painted earthenware tea set, while at another, a toothless old man from the *sertão* will try to exchange a scraggly goat for a few sacks of rice, beans, and sugar.

People from outlying villages pay the equivalent of a few cents apiece for a place in a truck or a jeep to come to Caruaru just to do their weekly shopping. Others travel from distant states or foreign countries to purchase some of Brazil's most beautiful and artistic handicrafts.

The gaily-painted figurines, first created by the late Mestre Vitalino, are among the most popular items for sale, but beware of vendors who try to charge high prices, alleging that their figurines were made by the master himself. Vitalino wasn't *that* prolific (see pages and 298). What's on display here, and in Recife's Casa

Olinda's name fittingly means 'beautiful.'

da Cultura (where many of the same items are sold, but with less variety), was probably made by students of Vitalino. Caruaru's fair opens at about 9am and goes on until 5pm, and is considered the best of its kind in South America.

Nova Jerusalem

Fazenda Nova ㉒, a sleepy village that survived for years on what it could scratch out of the parched earth, took its place on the map in 1968 when the Pacheco family, with support from the state government, inaugurated **Nova Jerusalem** (www.novajerusalem.com.br). This open-air theater, which is designed to resemble the Jerusalem of AD 33, comes to life once a year, during Holy Week, when the Passion of Christ is re-enacted before tens of thousands of spectators (see page 300).

The setting is perfect: huge stages, each depicting a Station of the Cross, rise out of the sandy soil, looming over actors and spectators. The audience follows the players (500 in all, most of them village residents) from scene to scene, and becomes part of the Passion

Forte Orange on Ilha Itamaracá.

Play. Audience participation is at its height when Pontius Pilate asks the crowd, 'Who shall it be – the King of the Jews or Barabbas?' The actors do not speak. Instead, they mouth the recorded dialogue.

Giant statues

Just a short walk from the theater is the no-less-impressive **Parque das Esculturas** (daily 7am–5pm; free), a mammoth tribute to the northeast. In the park you will find immense stone statues, weighing up to 20 metric tonnes, representing both folk heroes and the ordinary people of the northeast. In one section, there is a washerwoman, a cotton picker, a sugar-cane cutter, and a lacemaker – each of them 3 to 4 meters (10 to 13ft) tall. In another section, Lampião, the legendary Robin Hood of the northeast, and his beloved, Maria Bonita, stand tall. There is also a collection of figures taken from Pernambuco's folk dances and celebrations, including an immense sea horse and his rider; a *jaraguá*, half-man, half-monster; and a *frevo* dancer.

THE NEW JERUSALEM

Nova Jerusalem (www.novajerusalem,com.br) in Pernambuco, the site of a Passion Play every Easter, is one of the largest open-air theater in the world. It occupies an area of 10 hectares (25 acres), and is surrounded by 3.5km (2.2 miles) of stone walls, with seven gates and 70 towers.

There had been a local Passion Play here for some time, but the huge theater was initiated by Plínio Pacheco in 1962. He was born in 1926 in the southernmost state of Rio Grande do Sul, and went to the town to visit a friend who was playing the part of Jesus in a production performed in the streets of the tiny village. There, he met Diva Mendonça, daughter of the organizer; they fell in love and married, and in the 1960s Plínio had the idea of building a miniature Jerusalem for the play.

RESTAURANTS

Olinda

Oficina do Sabor
355 Rua do Amparo, Amparo
Tel: 81-3429 3331
Open: L&D Tue–Sun.
For two decades Officina do Sabor
has been offering a creative mix of
international and regional cuisines
and produces excellent and mouth-
watering results. Considered the best
restaurant in Olinda and one of the
best in Recife; some would argue, it
is also the best in Brazil. Light and
informal setting. This is all about the
food. **$$$**

Porto de Galinhas

Beijupirá Restaurante
Rua Beijupirá s/n, Qd 9
Tel: 81-3552 2354
Open: L&D daily.
A culinary landmark in Porto de
Galinhas and Pernambuco. You can't
really say you have been to Porto da
Galinhas unless you treat yourself at
least once to the experience.
So book before you arrive. Inventive
seafood is a specialty, but there are
also good rice and chicken dishes.
There are branches now in Olinda
and Praia dos Carneiros.
$$$

La Crêperie
Rua Beijupirá (opposite Banco do Brasil)
Tel: 81-3552 1831
Open: L&D daily.
For 20 years La Crêperia has been
a good place to go for a crêpe (there
are more than 50 varieties on offer)
or for a fun and relaxed, informal
meal that can include pasta or
salads. **$$**

Domingos
Rua Beijupirá, Galeria Paraoby
Tel: 81-3552 1489
Open: L–late daily.
The chef and owner, Domingos,
arrived in Porto de Galinhas via
the Ouro Verde in Rio, and the
Hippopotamus nightclub in Recife. A
charming restaurant in the pleasant
setting of the Galeria Paráoby. It

offers an excellent and reasonably
priced menu of Brazilian and
international dishes. **$$**

Munganga Bistrô
32 Avenida Beira-Mar, Galeria Caminho
da Praia
Tel: 81-3552 2480
Open: L&D daily.
Sophisticated yet laid back,
Munganga Bistro is known for its
reputable wine list and a reliably good
menu based on seafood, which even
includes a shrimp curry. You can also
choose dishes from the menu of the
neighboring Paellero, which offers
meats as well as paella. **$$**

Recife

Boi Preto Grill
97 Avenida Boa Viagem, Pina
Tel: 81-3466 6334
Open: L&D daily.
This is the place for carnivores – a
great barbecue spot, rodizio style
(sliced at the table), with more that 25
cuts of meat on offer. Good salads as
well. **$$$**

Chez Georges
1483 Avenida 17 de Agosto,
Casa Forte
Tel: 81-3326 1879
Open: D Wed–Sat, L Sun.
Moved to a new house at the entry
to Poço da Panel in 2009, but has
kept its high standards. Both an
air-conditioned main restaurant,
and a garden for those who prefer
to sit outside. Excellent French/
Swiss cooking, with some heavy and
interesting local influences. **$$$**

Chica Pitanga
19 Rua Petrolina, Boa Viagem
Tel: 81-3465 2224
Open: L&D daily.
Considered the best self-service buffet
in Recife. Also offers good value for
what they serve. Close to Boa Viagem
beach it is popular with tourists and
local people, probably less crowded at
night. **$$**

Cozinhando Esondidinho
106 Rua Conselheiro Perett,
Casa Amarela
Tel: 81-8618 6781
Open: L&D Wed–Sun.
Simple, yet full of character, its chef,
Rivandro França, is considered
one of the stars of contemporary
northeastern cuisine and people
have been standing in line to get a

place to taste his dishes. Located
in the suburbs, the restaurant's
success may see it move to a more
central and larger location. **$$**

É
147 Rua do Atlantico, Boa Viagem
Tel: 81-3325 9323
Open: D Mon–Sat.
Intimate stylish restaurant for couples,
offering creative contemporary
Brazilian and international cuisine.
Considered one of Recife's best
since opening in 2004. International
standards. **$$$**

Famiglia Giuliano
3980 Avenida Engenheiro Domingos
Ferreira, Boa Viagem
Tel: 81-3465 9922
Open: L&D Fri–Sun, D only Mon–Thu.
Set in a replica medieval castle,
which is popular for events, this place
is rightly famous for its feijoada buffet
as well as its Italian inspired dishes.
$$$

Leite
147 Praça Joaquim Nabuco,
Santo Antonio
Tel: 81-3224 7977
Open: L&D Sun–Fri.
Located downtown by the banks of
the Capibaribe River, Leite must be
doing something right as it has been
in business since 1882, making it one
of Brazil's and South America's oldest
restaurants. Offers elegance and old
world charm, with Portuguese dishes
featured as well as Brazilian. Popular
for business lunches. **$$$**

Mingus
102 Rua Atlântico, Boa Viagem
Tel: 81-3465 4000
Open: L Sun, D Mon, L&D Tue–Sat.
Mingus offers excellent and
refined creative, contemporary
dining, leaning more towards the
classic French dishes. As the name
suggests, live music also plays its
part with a backdrop of live jazz and
MPB (Popular Brazilian Music).
$$$

Vittorina Pomodoro & Café
418 Rua Capitão Rebelinho, Pina
Tel: 081-3326 6023
Open: D daily, L Sun.
Under new management, Pomodoro
has managed to retain its position as
one of the best Italian restaurants in
the city. Quality Italian food with an
excellent wine list. Live piano music.
$$$

FERNANDO DE NORONHA

Fernando de Noronha is a little bit of paradise
on Earth, and those who visit never forget it.
Although the island now encourages tourism,
it is part of a protected reserve, and efforts are
made to ensure that it is not spoilt.

Main Attractions
Enseada dos Golfinhos
Praia do Sancho

Crystal-clear waters and an exuberance of corals, dolphins, lobsters, and colorful tropical fish, as well as wonderfully preserved beaches and virtually no pollution, make **Fernando de Noronha** ㉓ (www.noronha.pe.gov.br) a paradise for divers, surfers, and all nature-lovers, and a reminder that the world can still be a beautiful and peaceful place.

The island is formed from the tip of a mountain whose base is 4,000 meters (13,125ft) below sea level, and is part of a volcanic archipelago of 21 islands covering an area of 26 sq km (10 sq miles). It was discovered in 1503 by the Italian explorer Amerigo Vespucci, and given to Fernando de Loronha in 1504 by the Portuguese king, hence its name (with one letter changed). Because of its strategic position, the island was invaded in turn by the French, the Dutch, and the French again, before returning to Portuguese domination.

In 1938 it was turned into a prison, and during World War II Fernando de Noronha served as an American base. The army barracks from that period have been converted into a hotel.

In 1988 Fernando de Noronha became part of a Marine National Park covering an area of 112 sq km (43 sq miles), and protected by IBAMA, the Brazilian Institute for the Environment. This is the largest of the islands, and the only one that is inhabited. To visit any of the others, you need a special permit from IBAMA. Most visitors arrive on Fernando de Noronha by plane from Recife or Natal.

Wildlife highlights

Thousands of migratory birds stop off at the island on their way south. On a boat trip to the Enseada dos Golfinhos, hundreds of playful dolphins can be seen out at sea. Swimming is allowed only at the entrance to the bay so as not to disturb them, but lucky divers sometimes encounter the

A shoal of fish.

dolphins as they enter or leave the bay in the early morning or late afternoon.

Between January and June, tourists can observe marine turtles laying their eggs in the sand at night at Praia do Leão, and, with permission from the Tamar Project, they can help to monitor the baby turtles going out to sea.

But the greatest marvels are underwater, so it is unsurprising that scuba diving and snorkeling are the most popular activities for visitors. The sight of a myriad of multicolored fish and corals, sponges, and plants is unforgettable, and there are wrecks of sunken ships to visit. For the more adventurous, there is the possibility of meeting sharks on a night dive.

Horseback riding, mountain-biking, or trekking to more remote beaches are also popular. There are natural rock sculptures at the Baía dos Porcos beach, a waterfall at the glorious **Praia do Sancho** during the rainy season, and a natural swimming pool among the rocks at Praia do Atalaia.

The 18th-century Igreja Nossa Senhora dos Remédios, in the village of Vila dos Remédios, and the Forte de Nossa Senhora dos Remédios nearby, are all that remains of the island's checkered history. The Morro do Pico (323 meters/1,060ft), the island's highest point, offers a splendid view of the archipelago. Pleasant temperatures of around of 26°C (79°F) year-round, with a refreshing rainy season from February to July, complete the idyll.

Most of the island's 2,000 inhabitants are employed in local tourism, as guides, boatmen, drivers, or looking after one of the many *pousadas*. Accommodations have greatly improved in recent years and the local authority now rates the hotels and *pousadas* as one, two or three 'Dolphins.' A full list can be found at www.noronha.pe.gov.br.

Green tax

You can travel independently, or book through a travel agency or tour operator who may secure discounts on lodgings. The island has to import food and water from the mainland, so IBAMA discourages lingerers by charging an environmental-preservation tax based on length of stay. This can be paid in advance on the website.

TIP

There are a number of daily one-hour flights from Natal and one-and-a-half-hour flights from Recife with Trip Airlines (www.voetrip.com.br) and VARIG (www.varig.com.br). These connect with flights to all the major cities of Brazil, including Rio and São Paulo.

A gorgeous day in the archipelago of Fernando de Noronha.

Beach towels wave in the breeze in Natal.

THE FAR NORTHEAST

Fishing villages, modern cities, lunar dune-scapes, mestizo culture, fossil sites, and a place of pilgrimage – these are some of the images typical of the communities in Brazil's far Northeast.

The northern coastline of Brazil stretches along beautiful, semi-deserted beaches from dry Rio Grande do Norte all the way to the borders of the Amazon, and the *babaçu* palm groves of Maranhão state. Rio Grande do Norte and the small state of Paraíba just south of it were part of the sugar-cane boom of the early years of colonization, and declined with the demise of the *engenhos* (sugar mills).

Colonization in Ceará and Piauí came with the cattle ranchers in the late 17th century, but it is Ceará's beaches and fishermen that have made its fame. Maranhão was colonized by the French, then the Dutch, and only after their expulsion in the mid-17th century did the Portuguese show any interest, developing sugar and cotton plantations. Maranhão's economy now centers on *babaçu* plants, parts of which are made into food products (especially cooking oil), or added to fertilizers, cellulose, timber, and roofing materials, as well as being a biofuel.

These states are among the poorest in Brazil, but their natural beauties are unparalleled, and tourism – mostly in Ceará and Rio Grande do Norte, whose capitals, Fortaleza and Natal, host games during the 2014 World Cup – brings hopes of a brighter future.

A colonial house in Paraíba.

João Pessoa

Just over 100km (60 miles) north of Recife on the Atlantic coast lies **João Pessoa** ㉔ (pop. 740,000), the easternmost point of the Americas. The dozens of beaches in this region share two fortunate characteristics: they are protected from the pounding surf by rows of reefs, and from the tropical sun by lines of coconut palms.

Capital of the state of **Paraíba**, João Pessoa is the third-oldest city in Brazil, established in 1585. Tropical greenery is abundant in the city, especially palm

Main Attractions

Pipa
Natal
Canoa Quebrada
Fortaleza
Jericoacoara
São Luís

The Berimbau, an instrument which is used by Capoeira musicians.

João Pessoa's waterfront skyline.

trees, bougainvilleas, flamboyants, and other flowering trees. The lake in **Parque Solon de Lucena** downtown is ringed with majestic royal palms.

The lovely Baroque architecture exemplified by the church of **São Francisco** and the **Convent of Santo Antônio** contrasts with the futuristic design of the Tropical Tambaú Hotel, built in 1971, which looks like an immense flying-saucer set halfway into the Atlantic Ocean. All guest rooms look out on to the sea. At high tide, the waves nearly reach the windowsills. The city receives fewer tourists than other northeastern states, so its beaches are less crowded.

If you make a pre-dawn trek out to **Cabo Branco** (White Cape), 14km (8 miles) from the city, you can enjoy the knowledge that you are the first person in the Americas to see the sun rise. Nearby Praia da Penha is a fishing village with a 19th-century church.

One of the best beaches in the region is **Praia do Poço**, just 10km (6 miles) north of the Tropical Tambaú Hotel. Go there at low tide, when the ocean recedes to reveal the island of

Areia Vermelha (Red Sand). Rows of *jangadas*, the fishermen's primitive rafts that are an integral part of the scenery, take visitors to the island. Sea algae and schools of colorful fish glitter in the transparent water.

Further north, towards the border with Rio Grande do Norte, is **Baía da Traição**. The region has a number of deserted beaches and fishing villages, with simple restaurants and *pousadas*. Highlights include Coqueirinho and De Tamba beaches, where Potiguaras Amerindians sell crafts, and sweets made with local fruits.

Around Calcanhar Cape

Rio Grande do Norte, which borders Paraíba to the north, lies on the northeastern curve of the continent. En route to the state capital, Natal, you reach **Pipa** (80km/50 miles from Natal), the favorite of young, hip, northeastern Brazilians – a northeastern version of Búzios, if you like, Pipa started life as an ecological reserve, but during peak season and weekends visitors are equally attracted by the nightlife. It comprises several attractive

beaches, including Praia de Amor, where you can often see dolphins.

A more peaceful option is its generally overlooked neighbor, **Tibau de Sul**, a small village located at the point where the Tibau river reaches the sea. Across the river there is an impressive view of sand dunes, extending several kilometers along Guarairas beach. A small boat ferries tourists across.

Tibau also offers a fantastic gastronomic experience, courtesy of chef Tadeu Lubambo. Working as a photojournalist in the 1980s, Tadeu was the first outsider to live among the Xingu Amerindians. Today he welcomes eight guests each night to his house, Camamo, to enjoy a seven-course meal (see page 315).

Some 60km (38 miles) further north is **Eduardo Gomes**, home to Barreira do Inferno, the rocket launch center. A view of Barreira can be had from nearby **Cotovelo Beach**, one of the loveliest on the state's southern coast.

Natal ㉕ (pop. 950,000), 185km (110 miles) from João Pessoa, is not only the state capital but also another of the region's beach resorts. **Ponta Negra** is the most popular beach, with a wide variety of hotels, bars, and restaurants.

On Christmas Day 1599, Jerónimo de Albuquerque founded the city of Santiago here. It was later renamed Natal, which is Portuguese for Christmas. In 1633 the town was taken by the Dutch, who called it New Amsterdam. Its most famous monument, the star-shaped **Forte dos Reis Magos** (Three Kings Fort) was so named because construction began at Epiphany, January 6, 1600. Natal's **Museu Câmara Cascudo** (www.mcc. ufrn.br; Avenida Hermes da Fonseca 1398; Tue–Fri 9am–5pm, Sat 1–5 pm) has displays ranging from Amazonian Indian artifacts to objects used in *candomblé* rites.

Ribeira, on the riverfront, forms the oldest part of the city. Here, some of the buildings, including Teatro Alberto Maranhão, have been restored.

En route to Touros beach

The 100km (60-mile) drive from Natal north to Touros beach is an adventure, following a succession of semi-deserted beaches marked by sand dunes and coconut palms. You will pass by Maxaranguape, and Ponta Gorda, the site of Cabo de São Roque, where, on August 16, 1501, the first Portuguese expedition arrived, one year after the discovery of Brazil. The enormous sand dunes at **Praia do Genipabu** attract visitors from all over the country. Touring the dunes in beach buggies is a popular attraction, as are camel rides.

Touros ㉖, a town of 28,000, gets its name from the bulls that once wandered freely here. There is a handful of small inns, cafés, bars and restaurants where you can enjoy shrimp roasted in garlic butter, or fresh broiled lobster. In the evening, go to Calcanhar Cape, 8km (5 miles) away, to watch the sun go down and the Touros lighthouse come on. The island of Fernando de Noronha, a wildlife preserve, lies 290km (180 miles) northeast off the cape (see page 302).

A beach buggy on the sand dunes.

A lagoon near Natal.

Going inland

Most people continue along the coast from the cape to Fortaleza, but it is possible to make a trip inland by bus from Natal to **Juazeiro do Norte** ㉗. This is a religious center where pilgrims *(romeiros)* come to pay homage to Padre Cícero Romão Batista, who in 1889 wrought a miracle that earned him excommunication from the Catholic Church five years later. Padre Cícero consolidated his temporal powers, and in 1911 became a political leader whose army of *cangaceiros* defeated federal troops sent to arrest him. Pilgrims visit a 25-meter (75ft) statue of Cícero, with his characteristic hat and stick. The devotional tour begins in the **Capela de Socorro** where he is buried, and includes churches and the House of Miracles.

The Cariri valley's other townships are **Crato**, noted for its university, museums, and active cultural life; and **Barbalho**, whose hot springs offer more corporeal pleasures. The hilly **Chapada do Araripe**, due west of Juazeiro, 700 meters (2,200ft) above sea level, provides welcome relief, with waterfalls and natural pools, protected inside a national park.

East of Juazeiro, across the border in Paraíba, on the BR-230 5km (3 miles) from the town of **Sousa**, is the **Vale dos Dinossauros** (Dinosaur Valley; www.valedosdinossauros.com.br; daily 8am–5pm), which has the largest grouping of dinosaur footprints in the world. There is a visitor center here where you can hire a local guide.

Ceará's coast

If you are sticking to the coast, you will find that the state of **Ceará** has 560km (350 miles) of wonderful beaches backed by palms, sand dunes, and freshwater lagoons, where the favored residents of state capital Fortaleza spend strenuous weekends drinking beer, and cracking open crabs and lobsters while watching the *jangadas* bring the day's catch through the rollers. For the adventurous, the 800km (500-mile) drive between Natal and Fortaleza can be made almost exclusively along the shore in a beach buggy or Land Rover, stopping off in small villages on the way. The

The rocky shore of Praia das Fontes.

CEARÁ'S SALT

The economy of the Ceará region was based for many years on three things: subsistence agriculture and cattle rearing in the interior, and salt production on the eastern coast. The high winds that blow along this coast, and the high salinity of the sea water, make it an ideal area for the production of sea salt, which, in the days before refrigeration, was essential for preserving food, as well as being used in cooking.

The happy combination of beef and salt led to the invention of *carne de sol* (sun-dried or jerked beef), which is one of the most typical and most delicious regional dishes, and one you will find in many local restaurants. Salt is still produced around Fortaleza, although there is not such a high demand for it as there used to be.

drive will take you past innumerable beaches, each one more beautiful than the last. In the coastal villages, where offshore breezes blow constantly, lacemakers and embroiderers still ply their trade. But tourism and the weekend homes of city-dwellers are rapidly altering the coastal area.

Southeastern beaches

The southeastern coast of the state has a selection of attractive beaches, starting with **Canoa Quebrada**, some 60km (37 miles) from the border with Rio Grande do Norte and 10km (6 miles) from Aracati. During the 1970s, the lunar dune-scape of Canoa Quebrada attracted a generation of hippies from Brazil and abroad. They settled down in the fishermen's primitive houses, blending natural fruit juices, *forró* music, and free love with a village lifestyle that had changed little in 300 years. Development and its accompanying ills have followed a tourist influx, and the main avenue, Broadway, experiences an ever-growing trade in bars and restaurants. Fortunately, Canoa Quebrada's broad expanse of

beach, the dunes, and the crumbling red sandstone cliffs still retain something of their magic.

The eroded sandstone cliffs of **Morro Branco**, 70km (43 miles) north of Aracati and 85km (53 miles) south of Fortaleza, provide the raw material for craftsmen, while the less crowded beach here offers a welcome relief from Fortaleza's urban sprawl. Late in the afternoon, local fishermen visit the beach bars, proffering cooked lobsters. **Iguape**, 50km (30 miles) from Fortaleza, is famous for its lacemakers (ask to look at the Renaissance pattern) and the artificially colored sands from Morro Branco packed into bottles to depict landscapes.

Just a 34km (21-mile) drive south of Fortaleza is **Aquiraz**, Ceará's 17th-century capital, which contains the ruins of a Jesuit mission. It is home to an 18th-century church with the image of São José do Ribamar, the state's patron saint. The church ruins may be reached by way of a rum distillery.

Of the beaches still close to the city, **Prainha** is the most authentic. There are several seafood restaurants and

Traditional Brazilian sailboats on Canoa Quebrada.

TIP

If you are flying from Europe, and just looking to visit the Northeast, it is worth considering taking the direct TAP flights from Lisbon to Fortaleza, Natal, Recife, or Salvador. The flight time from Lisbon to Fortaleza is around seven hours, while just the flight from Rio de Janeiro, back up to Fortaleza, is around three-and-a-half hours.

bars stretching across the sand. The local fishermen here will take tourists for *jangada* rides. These traditional flat rafts with lateen sails are covered in advertising, as if they were racing cars, because in July, professionals compete in the Dragon of the Sea regatta.

The still urban, sophisticated resort of **Porto das Dunas** is worth checking out, as is **Beach Park** (www.beachpark. com.br; daily 11am–5pm, in winter it may close on Wed and Thu), the largest water park in Latin America. The resort also has its own four hotels, and own beach area.

Fortaleza's founder

The first attempt to colonize the arid *sertão* of Ceará, which separated Rio Grande do Norte from Maranhão, was in 1603. Amerindian fighter Pero Coelho de Souza led a mob of Portuguese soldiers and Amerindian warriors on a raid for slaves. He returned in 1606 but was driven off by a drought. Martim Soares Moreno was on the first expedition and was ordered by the governor general of Brazil to open up the region by befriending the Amerindians. By

Stalagmite formations in Parque Nacional de Ubajara.

1611 he was promoted to captain of Ceará and founded **Fortaleza** ㉘ by building the first fortress of São Paulo and a chapel by the Ceará river's mouth. The fortress stood Moreno in good stead when the French attacked that year – as did the Tapuia and Tupinambá tribes whom he had befriended. Fighting alongside the Amerindians, he drove off the French, then succumbed to the charms of Iracema, an Amerindian princess who is the city's muse and patron saint. Brazilian literati, led by José Alencar, rediscovered Amerindian history in a romantic movement that flowered just over a century ago with the novel *O Guarany*, and a short story retelling the tale of Iracema. In 1870 the story was adapted for Carlos Gomes's opera *Il Guarany*, the first internationally successful Brazilian opera.

Dutch invaders in 1649 built the foundations of a fort in what is now the center of Fortaleza. By 1654, the Dutch were driven out by the Portuguese, who rechristened the fort Nossa Senhora de Assunção. Fortaleza consolidated itself as a trading center for the cattle country of the interior.

Many of the Amerindian-fighting *bandeirantes* from São Paulo stayed behind, to establish immense cattle ranches that still exist today. In contrast to the sugar plantations of Pernambuco, Ceará's ranches used almost no African slave labor, and the region's culture is more influenced by its Amerindian-Portuguese *mestizo* past than African roots.

Fortaleza's seafront

Nothing remains of the original fortress that gave Fortaleza its name. With a population of 2.5 million, the city instead looks forward, as the aptly named **Praia do Futuro** indicates. Here, beach-front condominiums and bars have sprouted up, pushing visitors in search of unspoiled coastline away to beaches outside the sprawling city. Fortaleza's real strength is its selection of out-of-town beaches.

Praia do Futuro is a beach of two halves. The northern section, closer to Meireles, is not recommended for tourists, as it resembles a ghost town after dark. Petty crime is common in this section, and there is little or no policing. Nowadays, local people head to the southern part, where there is an appropriate infrastructure. Praia do Futuro is a lively spot on Thursday evening, when all the bars serve crab.

The main seafront hotels are on Avenida Beira Mar , which runs along **Praia do Meireles**, the main meeting place. At night, the noisy bars and broad sidewalks below the Gran Marquise and other hotels are packed with people drawn by the market, offering lace, ceramics, leather goods, and colored sand in bottles.

Fortaleza is a major exporter of lobster. Seafood restaurants along the oceanfront offer crab, shrimp, lobster, or *peixada* – the local seafood specialty. The best restaurants are located on the seafront or a few blocks back. One of the local favorites is Cantinho Faustino, also one of the city's best (see page 315). Northeasterners round off the night at hot, crowded dancehalls like Clube do Vaqueiro (Wednesday) and Parque do Vaqueiro (Friday), where couples dance the lively but seductive *forró*, accompanied by accordion music. The city's most famous, however, is Pirata, which is said to deliver 'the hottest Monday on the planet.' The restaurants and bars in restored historic buildings around the Centro Cultural Dragão do Mar (www.dragaodomar.org.br) often host live music.

The **MAC** (Museum of Contemporary Art; www.dragaodomar.org.br; Mon–Fri 1–6pm; free) and the **Ceará Memorial Museum** (Tue–Sun 10am–8pm; free) here have extensive displays of arts and crafts, and items on the history of Ceará; both deserve a visit.

The Praia do Meireles stretches from Mucuripe near the docks, where there's a lighthouse, to the breakwater at Volta de Jurema. The central section, **Praia de Iracema**, is marked by a modern sculpture of Moreno and his princess, but the beach is too polluted for swimming. However, its bars and restaurants are fun at night.

Handicrafts can be purchased at several locations, including the Centro de Turismo (350 Rua Senador Pompeu), in the tastefully converted old city jail; or sometimes more cheaply at the Mercado Central, which has more than 1,000 close-packed booths spread over several floors. The Ccart Center (1589 Avenida Santos-Dumont, Aldeota) has an excellent selection of arts and crafts from various regions of the state.

Another iconic attraction of Fortaleza is the Teatro José de Alencar, a cast-iron structure imported from Britain in 1910. Tours are available for a nominal fee.

West of Fortaleza, in the Ibiapaba hills, is the **Parque Nacional de Ubajara** ㉙, with caves that contain interesting stalagmite formations and a cable car that takes visitors up to waterfalls and lush green vegetation.

An Ubajara cable car.

Fortaleza's skyline at night.

EAT

Crab *(caranguejo)* is served in most of the *barracas* (kiosks) on the beach, usually boiled in water or coconut milk. It is given to you with a little wooden hammer, with which to break the shell and extract the meat.

Northwestern beaches

Northwest of Fortaleza, a series of beaches begins at **Barra do Ceará** – the river's mouth – but **Cumbuco** is the first port of call, 33km (20 miles) from the city. The attractions are the surfing beach and the dunes stretching inland as far as the black surface of the **Parnamirim** freshwater lagoon. At the beach bars, rides through the surf on sailing rafts are available.

There is no coastal road running north, but 85km (53 miles) from Fortaleza is **Paracuru** ❸⓪, reached from inland on the BR-222 federal highway. A lively community that enjoys a weeklong Carnival and regular surf and sailing regattas, the town is a favorite weekend spot. A few miles further is the less sophisticated **Lagoinha**, where rooms are available to rent in village houses. An intersection on the highway leading from BR-222 to Paracuru goes to Trairi, with access to the beaches of **Freixeiras, Guajiru**, and **Mundaú**.

Icaraí ❸❶ is 140km (87 miles) from Fortaleza, via the BR-222 intersection leading past Itapipoca, behind the Mundaú dunes and across the Trairi

A typical two story building with iron balconies and colorful façade in downtown São Luis.

river. Beaches include Pesqueiro, Inferno, and Baleia. **Acaraú** ❸❷, a further 90km (57 miles) from Fortaleza, is one of the most popular beach centers. The adjacent fishing village of **Almofala** also has a fine, unspoiled beach, and an 18th-century church, which for years was covered by sands.

The finest of Ceará's beaches is the remote **Jericoacoara** ❸❸, one of the picture-postcard images of Brazil's northeast. Declared a national park in 2002, it is a beautiful – even magical – spot. A short while ago, it was a paradisaical fishing village, cut off behind the dunes. Now, there is a plethora of good *pousadas* and restaurants catering to an influx of visitors that is bringing changes to a village that still remains small and friendly. The pure horizontals of sea, dunes, and sky are cut by coconut palms, and the village has no electricity or cars. A preservation order means that rare and endangered species are protected in the dunes and lagoons. Sea turtles come up the beach to lay their eggs, and the village has much of the mystique that Canoa Quebrada enjoyed a decade or so ago.

Reaching Jericoacoara (about 300km/190 miles from Fortaleza) is difficult because it is cut off by the dunes. The trip can be made by bus, then four-wheel-drive or beach buggy (tel: 88-669 2000/621 0211; www.jericoacoara.com.br) from Jijoca.

Repentistas

In gritty contrast to Fortaleza, the hinterland of Ceará is periodically racked by drought. When crops are ruined and landlords dismiss their *vaqueiros* (cowboys), they pack their belongings and head for the swollen cities in order to survive as best they can. Those who remain keep alive a strong oral culture derived from the troubadours. Village poets – *repentistas* – duel for hours to cap each other's rhymes with more extravagant verbal conceits. Traditions are also recorded in the *cordel* pamphlets, illustrated with woodcuts, whose humorous rhymes recount the

deeds of the anarchic cowboy-warriors – *cangaceiros* – and tell of local politics, and religious miracles.

Ancient sites in Piauí

The state of Piauí which sits between Ceara and Maranhão, has impressive geological monuments formed by erosion over millions of years. These can be visited at the **Parque Nacional Sete Cidades**, 180km (112 miles) from the inland capital, **Teresina**. The **Parque Nacional da Serra da Capivara**, in the southwest of the state, is the oldest archeological site in the Americas – more than 50,000 years old – and was declared a World Heritage Site by Unesco in 1991. Besides fossils of mastodons and giant ground sloths, it has the largest set of rock art in the world. The **Museu do Homem Americano** (tel: 89-3582 1612; www.fumdham.org.br; daily 6am–6pm) has interesting specimens of fossils and prehistoric tools.

São Luís

At the top of Brazil's northeast region, between the Amazon basin and the *sertão*, perched on the bayside of São Luís Island, is **São Luís 34**, capital of the state of Maranhão and another World Heritage Site. Legend has it that a serpent lives under the town, and that one day, once it has grown large enough, it will squeeze the island, causing it to sink. São Luís is enchanting, with a rich mix of history and culture. The city was founded in 1612 by French colonists, who first encountered the Tupinamba Amerindians on the island. The two groups lived in harmony until the French were driven out by the Portuguese three years later. In 1641 the Dutch invaded the island but were able to maintain their position for only three years. The mixed heritage manifests itself in the music of *tambor-de-criola* and *Bumba-Meu-Boi*. The *Bumba-Meu-Boi* celebrations on the feast days of São João (June 24) and São Pedro (June 29) form part of the June Festivals, and are on a par with Carnival in other cities. On

Friday evening (6–8.30pm) musicians and dancers gather in the Mercado da Praia Grande to perform the sensual *tambor-de-criola* in a tradition that has been handed down over generations.

The city is known for the brightly tiled, two-story homes that line its narrow, sloping streets. The blue, yellow, white, and green *azulejos* (tiles) were originally imported from Portugal, and have become the city's trademark. Cars have been banned from the most important streets, making it ideal for exploring on foot. Major points of interest include the **Cathedral** (1763), **Praça Remédios** (1860), **Capela de Santo Antônio** (1624), and the **Museu Historico e Artistico do Marânho** (Maranhão Art and History Museum; Tue–Sun 9am–3.30pm) in an early 19th-century villa. There are numerous stores in the historic center (known as Reviver) selling handicrafts as well as two peculiar local drinks: *Jesus* (a sweet, pink soft drink), and *Tiquira* (a *cachaça* made from manioc).

There is no shortage of good restaurants, but for an authentic gastronomic experience, visit a *base*. The term comes

Kitesurfing is a popular activity in the waters along the coast of Brazil.

An isolated bungalow in a peaceful lagoon.

from a time when there were no restaurants, and workers would visit the houses of local cooks for lunch. These houses were referred to as *bases*, and several still exist today, the most famous of which are A Diquinha and A Varanda (see pages 314 and 315). The town's best restaurant is Grand Cru on Avenida de la Touche.

Many of the best hotels and *pousadas* in the city are in the beach districts of Ponta d'Areia, Santo Antonio, Calhau, and Caolho. The last three form a continuous 5km (3-mile) stretch, with plenty of bars and restaurants. All these beaches have very strong undercurrents so inquire first before diving in.

Alcântara

A trip to São Luís is not complete without a visit to **Alcântara** ❸, originally a Tupinambá Amerindian village, which in the 17th century became the favored retreat for the landed gentry of Maranhão. Highlights include the **Museu Historica de Alcântara** (http://museucasaalcantara.blogspot.co.uk; Tue–Fri 9.30am–14.30pm, Sat–Sun 9.30am–14.30); Nossa Senhora do

Carmo church (1663); and the original Pelourinho (whipping post). The boat trip to Alcântara, 53km (33 miles) over choppy waters, takes 60 minutes. Boats leave the Terminal Hidroviario (Avenida Vitorino Freire) at around 9am, depending on tides. There are a number of *pousadas* in the town if you want to stay and enjoy the tranquility of Alcântara at night.

In the 1950s drought drove a group of *rendeiras* (lacemakers) from Ceará to set up shop in the small fishing town of **Raposa** (33km/20 miles north of São Luís). Their simple wooden houses, built on *palafiltas* (stilts) because of flooding from nearby mangrove swamps, serve as shops and homes. From Raposa you can arrange boat trips to the island of Curupu.

Lençóis Marahenses

With more than 155,000 hectares (382,000 acres) of sand dunes, **Parque Nacional de Lençóis Maranhenses** ❸ is an ecological paradise. During the rainy season (December to May) hundreds of crystalline lakes are formed. In September to October, wind speeds can reach up to 70km/h (45mph), so it is advisable to wear sunglasses to protect your eyes.

The journey from São Luís to **Barreirinhas** takes about three hours; follow the road just outside Lençóis Marahenses, Barreirinhas has become the main portal to the park, with numerous agencies offering a variety of excursions, including boat trips, four-by-four vehicle trips, and a 30-minute flight over the park (Operatur; tel: 98-3349 1898).

To get an idea of the simplicity of life here, take a boat to the tiny fishing village of Cabure along Rio Preguicas, stay at one of the *pousadas*, and eat in one of several good restaurants. But be warned: electricity comes from a generator, which is switched off at 10pm. On the way to Cabure you can stop off at Mandacaru to get amazing views of the national park from the top of the lighthouse.

Music-making at the bumba-meu-boi festival in São Luis.

RESTAURANTS

Fortaleza

Cemoara
166 Rua Joaquim Nabuco, Mercure
Apartments, Meireles
Tel: 85-3242 8500
Open: L&D Mon-Sat, L Sun.
Located in the Hotel Mercure, Cemora offers tasty seafood specialties. Probably some of the best *bolinho de bacalhau* (cod-fish cakes) in Brazil. Grilled lobster is a signature dish. $$$

Colher de Pau
1178 Rua Ana Bilhar, Varjota
Tel: 85-3267 3773
Open: L&D daily.
This Fortaleza institution, and award-winning restaurant, serves excellent regional food from both the interior of Ceará and the coast. *Carne de sol frita* (fried sun-dried beef) is recommended, as is the *peixe com molho da casquinha* (fish with crab sauce). $

O Cantinho do Faustino
1560 Frei Mansueto
Tel: 85-3267 5864
Open: L&D daily.
As real estate prices rocketed in Meirelles, Faustinho decided to move home and has relocated to the fish market. Still serving innovative Brazilian food with some delicious surprises. $$

João Pessoa

Bargaco
5160 Avenida Cabo Branco
Tel: 83-3247 1837
Open: L&D daily.
Specialises in Bahian cuisine (it has a branch in Salvador) and seafood. *Mini-acarajé* is an interesting innovation, while the lobster moqueca is considered a must. $$

Mangai
696 Avenida General Edson Ramalho
Tel: 83-3226 1615
Open: L&D daily.
Since opening in 1990, Mangai has developed over 200 recipes based on typical ingredients of the northeast. Excellent self-service spot with plenty of atmosphere. Popular Sunday breakfast from 7am. $

Natal

Âncora Caipira
474 Capos Salles, Petrópolis
Tel: 84-3202 9364
Open: L&D Tue–Sun.
Inspired by local specialties from the interior of the state, plus some more exotic dishes developed over the years by its talented chef. $$

Camarões
2610 Avenida Engenheiro Roberto Freire, Ponta Negra
Tel: 84-3209 2424
Open: L&D daily.
Given that Natal is one of the centers of the Brazilian shrimp industry, this is the place to head for. Hugely popular for seafood with shrimp, not surprisingly, a specialty. $$

Camamo
Tibau do Sul, Rio Grande do Norte
Tel: 84-3246 4195
Open: D daily.
Not located in Natal, but down the coast close to Tibau and Pipa, Camamo, offers one of the northeast's great gastronomic experiences. Chef Tadeu Lubambo welcomes limited number of guests each night to his house to enjoy a seven-course degustation menu that kicks off with a tropical *caipirinha*, and lasts about four hours. Hire a car and driver to take you and wait. $$$

São Luís

A Diquinha
62 Rua João Luís, Diamante
Tel: 98-3221 1568
Open: L&D daily.
Excellent home-cooking from Dona Diquiha in a very simple and modest restaurant, 10 minutes from center by taxi. $

Cabana do Sul
24 Rua João Pereira Damanasceno, Farol de Sao Marcos.
Tel: 98-3235 2586
Open: L&D daily.
Award-winning restaurant that serves the very best of Maranhense cuisine as well as other Brazilian and international dishes. A large but elegant restaurant that is popular with locals and visitors. Also has a branch at 10 Avenida Litoranea and one in the town of Imperatriz. $$

Prawns at Jamaica Beach Bar and Restaurant at Mundai Beach.

The Iguacu River.

Ka'apor girls.

THE AMAZON

In the north of Brazil, humanity is dwarfed by the continent's greatest river and its magnificent forested basin. Ecotours and river cruises from the once-splendid rubber towns of Belém and Manaus ply the Amazon and its tributaries.

Though it is not the longest river in the world, the **Amazon** is the world's *greatest* river. At the end of a 6,570km (4,080-mile) journey that begins in the Peruvian Andes, the river's massive mouth discharges a fifth of all the world's fresh water into the Atlantic, permeating the salt-water over 100km (60 miles) from the shore. And Amazonia is a vast, open-air greenhouse of global evolution, where a tenth of the world's 10 million living species make their homes. The River Amazon dominates Brazil, yet Brazilians are only beginning to discover it.

Early explorers

Amerigo Vespucci, an Italian adventurer much given to exaggeration, and after whom the Americas were named, claimed to have sailed up the Amazon in 1499. He was followed a year later by the Spaniard Vicente Pinzon, but the credit for the first voyage of discovery down the river goes to Francisco de Orellana. He set out by boat in 1542 on a short reconnaissance during an expedition in search of the legendary gold of El Dorado, for which he had joined forces with Gonzalo Pizarro, younger brother of Francisco, one of the conquistadors of Peru.

For six months, his boat was swept downriver through the excellent land and dominion of the Amazons, where his scribe Friar Carvajal was amazed by sightings of a matriarchal tribe, with bare-breasted women doing as much fighting as ten Indian men. It was these remarkable warriors who later inspired the name Amazons, after the women of Greek mythology who removed their right breasts to facilitate using a bow and arrow.

Amazonia began to excite scientific interest all over the world a century after its discovery, when, in 1641, a Spanish Jesuit called Cristóbal de

Main Attractions

Belém
Soure
Santarém
Manaus
Teatro Amazonas
Jungle Lodges
Roraima

A squirrel monkey enjoying some berries.

Amazonian plants and trees are rich resources.

A macaw.

Acuña published *A New Discovery of the Great River of the Amazons*, carefully recording Amerindian customs, farming methods, and herbal medicine, and concluding that – mosquitoes notwithstanding – it was one vast paradise.'

Botanical research

Bedrock scientific research in the Amazon was carried out by a trio of English collectors led by Alfred Russell Wallace, whose work on the diversity of Amazonian flora and fauna influenced Darwin's *On the Origin of Species*. Together with Henry Walter Bates and Richard Spruce, he set out in 1848 and discovered more than 15,000 species.

Another Englishman used his botanical skills in a way that was to cause the region's economic undoing when he broke Brazil's rubber monopoly. For a fee of £1,000 (about £80,000), adventurer Henry Wickham loaded 70,000 seeds of *Hevea brasiliensis* aboard a chartered steamer in 1876, and slipped them past customs in Belém, claiming

that they were rare plant samples, a gift for Queen Victoria. The seedlings sprouted under glass in London's Kew Gardens, and by 1912 had grown into the plants on which Malaya's ordered, disease-free rubber plantations were based.

Rubber riches

The properties of rubber, which had been discovered by the Omagua Amerindians, fascinated French travelers in the 18th century. Then Charles Goodyear's 1844 discovery of vulcanization, followed by Dunlop's 1888 invention of the pneumatic tire, caused a commercial explosion. As the price of rubber soared, production rose from 156 metric tonnes in 1830 to 21,000 metric tonnes in 1897. The cities were emptied of labor, and thousands migrated from the northeast to become rubber-tappers or *seringueiros*.

During the last decade of the 19th century, Brazil sold 88 percent of all exported rubber in the world, and for 25 years, around the turn of the 20th century, rubber made the Amazon

RIVER CRUISES

River cruises are a superb way to immerse yourself in the jungle. They all offer basic comforts such as en suite bathrooms and air conditioning to ease your passage into the rainforest. Most have a set itinerary: an early morning excursion into the forest (when it is most lively), followed by a few hours' cruise. In the mid-afternoon, smaller launches explore the river tributaries and the rainforest in more depth, and in the evening there is a talk on flora and fauna followed by flashlight caiman-spotting by canoe. The *Tucano*, operated by Ecotour Expeditions (www.naturetours.com), offers comfortable cabins on eight-night trips from Manaus along Rio Negro and Rio Branco. The smaller *Desavio*, operated by Amazon Cruises (www.amazoncruise.net), runs three- to four-day trips.

port of Manaus, 1,600km (1,000 miles) from the Atlantic, one of the richest cities in the world. A system of debt slavery was used to harvest Brazil's black gold over a vast area of Amazon jungle. The hundred or so rubber barons who controlled Manaus sent their laundry to Lisbon, and their wives and children to Paris.

However, British-controlled plantations in Asia undercut Amazon rubber prices just before World War I, and within a decade Manaus was a jungle backwater again. American industrialist Henry Ford attempted to compete with the British by organizing his own Amazon rubber plantation in 1927, but was unsuccessful (see page 328). You can still see one of Ford's two plantation sites, Belterra, near the Amazon river 825km (500 miles) from Belém.

Belém

With public parks, wrought-iron bandstands, *Beaux Arts* buildings, and mango-tree-lined avenues, **Belém ❶** retains more elegance of the bygone rubber era than its rival, Manaus.

During its *Belle Epoque*, French visitors to this city compared it favorably to Marseilles or Bordeaux. A city of 1.4 million set on the river's southern bank, one degree south of the Equator and 145km (90 miles) from the open sea, Belém is the gateway to the Amazon.

Between November and April it rains almost every day, but a breeze generally makes the humid climate tolerable. Belém is the capital of the state of Pará, which covers an area twice the size of France. It was properly linked to southern Brazil by the Belém–Brasília Highway only in 1960, and is still chiefly a port city for the export of tropical hardwoods, brazil nuts, jute, and other primary products.

A tour of the old city, whose narrow streets contain old houses fronted with Portuguese tiles, begins at the **Forte do Castelo ❹**, the nucleus of the original settlement of Santa Maria do Belém do Grão Pará, and now sadly run down. Adjacent is the 18th-century church of **Santo Alexandre ❺**, now a **museum of religious art**

A house perched on the Amazon river.

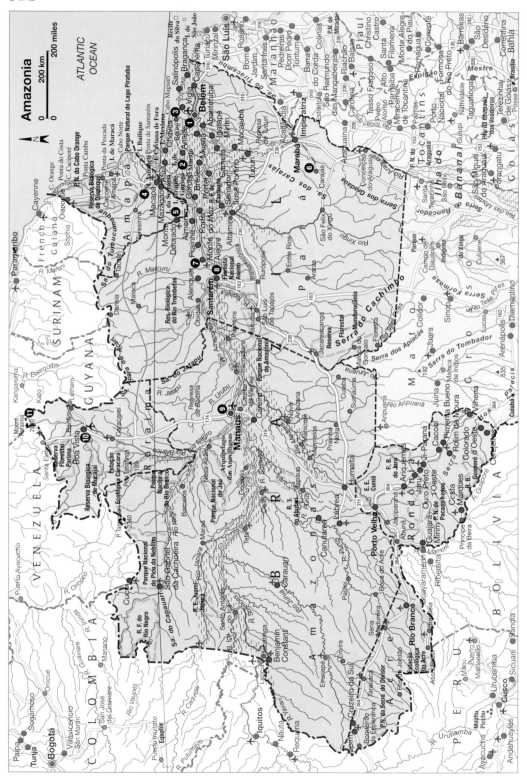

(Tue–Sun 10am–4pm). The cathedral church, **Catedral de Nossa Senhora da Graça ⓒ**, opposite the fort, contains sculptures in Carrara marble and paintings by Italian artist Pietro de Angelis.

One block away, on the south side of Praça Dom Pedro II, is the **Palácio Lauro Sodré ⓓ**, the former seat of government, which houses the **Museu do Estado do Pará** (State of Pará Museum; Tue–Fri 10am–6pm, Sat–Sun 10am–1pm). Built in the 18th century by the Italian architect Landi, it contains numerous examples of fine 19th-century furniture. Also on Praça Dom Pedro II is the current local government building, **Palácio Antônio Lemos ⓔ**. Dating from the late 19th century, the height of the rubber boom, it was built in Portuguese imperial style and houses an **art museum** (Tue–Fri 10am–noon, 2–5pm, Sat–Sun 9am–1pm), with many fine paintings and furnishings.

The **Ver-O-Peso ⓕ**, Belém's vast dockside market at the northern end of Avenida Portugal, is a showcase of Amazonia's prodigious variety of fish and tropical fruit. Fishing boats bring in their catch, which may include 90kg (200lb) monsters. The **Feira do Açaí** at the end of the market is the exclusive seller of the small and fashionable *açaí* berries that are the basis of much of Belém's cooking.

There are few souvenirs to buy inside the two food pavilions, but alongside them is a fascinating covered area of booths selling herbal medicines and charms used in African-Brazilian *umbanda* rituals. Sea horses, armadillo tails, and tortoise shells are piled up beside herbs that local people swear will cure rheumatism and heart problems. Also on sale are perfumes said to be guaranteed to attract men, women, money, and good fortune. Pickpockets can be a problem, and the area is best avoided after dark.

The east side

Continuing along the dockside, you will come to **Estação das Docas**. Here, the dilapidated warehouses have been transformed into an impressive cultural space with

Fishermen at the Ver-O-Peso market.

The lost city of El Dorado

The search for cities paved with gold is integral to the romance associated with the conquest and exploration of South America.

El Dorado, which means The Golden One, was the name given by Spanish explorers to a fabled Amazon king who ruled over the wealthy Kingdom of Manoa, deep in the jungle. The king himself was rumored to encrust his powerful naked body daily in gold dust, which he regularly washed off in a sacred lake.

Such tales of limitless riches spread abroad soon after Brazil's discovery by Europeans at the beginning of the 16th century. So it was that explorers such as Francisco de Orellana, the first European to traverse the entire Amazon basin, were less interested in national glory or the conversion of souls than in the gold of El Dorado. The Spanish Orellana, who had won his spurs fighting alongside Francisco Pizarro in Peru – where the conquistadors had helped themselves to copious amounts of Inca gold – became second-in-command on Gonzales

The Amazon, which is still home to many lesser-known Amerindian peoples, retains its mysterious lure.

Pizarro's 1540 expedition in search of Francisco's brother, new territories, gold, and cinnamon.

Pizarro was eventually forced, in the face of starvation and hostile Amerindians, to return to his base in Ecuador. But Orellana became separated from his patron, and with a smaller band of men, found favor with some Amazon tribes and glimpsed both tall, white-skinned Amazons and female warriors who, according to a man taken captive, lived in all-women villages and once a year invited men from surrounding tribes to a mating festival. Their leader, Orellana was told, ate with gold and silver utensils, and the villages were littered with golden female idols.

In search of civilization

The Portuguese explorer Francisco Raposo may have discovered the remains of El Dorado's kingdom, apparently devastated by an earthquake. His 1754 report describes relics of a great city, with stone-paved streets, elaborate plazas, and stately architecture, beautiful statues, hieroglyphics, and colorful frescoes – and a handful of gold coins.

In the early 20th century, Colonel Percy Fawcett (1867–1925), an eccentric English archeologist and explorer, whose lifelong obsession was to prove the existence of lost Amazonian civilizations, came across records indicating that a 16th-century shipwrecked adventurer, Diego Alvarez, had found numerous mines of gold, silver, and precious stones in the region.

This legendary city has never been rediscovered, yet Fawcett, described by colleagues as both a dreamer and a rascal, wrote in 1925: It is certain that amazing ruins of ancient cities, ruins incomparably older than those of Egypt, exist in the far interior of Mato Grosso.

Fawcett's fascination with the lost city of Z led him to venture several times into Brazil's deep interior. His final attempt began in May 1925, when he set out with his son Jack and a friend; all three were lost. Over the decades, a number of expeditions were mounted to try to discover what had happened to the men. The story of Fawcett's quest has been told by David Grann in *The Lost City of Z*, published in 2009, and subsequently turned into a film starring Brad Pitt.

Dreams of El Dorado continue. In 2009 detailed satellite imagery of the Amazon revealed more than 200 geometric earthworks carved in the upper Amazon basin close to Brazil's border with Bolivia. Spanning more than 250km (155 miles), some of these excavations have been dated to as early as AD 200, others to 1283.

restaurants, bars, and a theater. Near the customs house on **Praça Waldemar Henrique** ⓖ, the state tourism authority, **Paratur**, operates a visitor center and a **Feira do Artesanato** (Handicraft Fair) that is useful if you are looking for souvenirs. **Icoaraci** ⓗ, about half an hour from the city (the bus stop is two blocks from the Paratur office), is a center for modern ceramics that follows the pre-Columbian Amerindian *maroajara* pottery tradition, whose elaborate motifs are believed to have been borrowed from Inca culture.

Continuing along Avenida Presidente Vargas – the main shopping street – away from the port, you will come to the **Praça da República** ⓘ, then Belém's theater, the magnificent **Teatro da Paz** ⓙ (www.theatrodapaz. com.br; Tue–Fri 9am–5pm, Sat 9am–noon, Sun 9–11am; tours available). This restored theater, built in 1878 during the period of the rubber boom, is set in a green area complete with bandstand and the Bar do Parque – an agreeable place to sit and drink a Cerpa, the local beer.

About 15 minutes' walk inland from the Praça da República, along Avenida Nazaré, is Belém's most important church, the **Basílica de Nazaré** ⓚ, built in 1852, with impressive marble work and stained glass. It is the center of the Cirio de Nazaré religious procession which was instituted by the Jesuits as a means of catechizing Amerindians, and still draws over a million faithful on the second Sunday of every October. The venerated image of the Virgin was found in the forest near Belém in 1700. Continuing on, you will come to the **Museu Emílio Goeldi** ⓛ (376 Rua Magalhães Barata; www.museu-goeldi.br; Tue–Sun 9–5pm), which incorporates a highly regarded zoological and botanical garden, with many tropical species. The museum, founded in 1866, has a superb anthropological collection, and often has excellent temporary exhibitions about Amazon life. Further from the center but also worth a visit are the **Bosque Rodrigues Alves** (Tue–Sun 8am–5pm), botanical gardens that enclose an area of almost-natural forest, and a small zoo.

A colorful Amazonian plant.

AMAZON FACTS

A few interesting facts about the Amazon:

The official source of the Amazon, found in 1953, is on Mount Huagra in the Peruvian Andes.

The river is 6,570km (4,080 miles) long (only the Nile is longer) and its mouth is 330km (200 miles) wide.

The Amazon has 1,100 tributaries, including 17 that are more than 1,600km (1,000 miles) long.

In places, the Amazon is 110km (68 miles) wide; its lower course has depths of over 60 meters (297ft). Ocean-going freighters can travel 3,720km (2,310 miles) inland from the Atlantic to Iquitos, Peru.

The river system is the globe's largest body of fresh water. Total water flow is 160,000 to 200,000 cubic meters (42 to 53 million US gallons) a second, 12 times that of the Mississippi.

The Amazon basin is larger than that of any other river, and contains the world's largest rainforest. This spreads over nine countries, however, most of it lies within the boundaries of Brazil.

Amazonia supports 30 percent of all known plant and animal species, including 2,500 fish species, 50,000 higher plant species, and untold millions of insects.

The average annual rainfall is over 2,000mm (79ins), making the Amazon basin the wettest region in the world.

Ilha de Marajó

One of the world's largest river islands (48,000 sq km/18,535 sq miles), **Ilha de Marajó ❷**, at the river's mouth, is larger than Switzerland, yet has a population of just 250,000 people. They are far outnumbered by the herds of water buffalo (600,000 plus) that wallow in the flat, swampy northern area.

A government-owned ENASA ferry makes the four-hour trip to **Soure ❸** on the island's eastern tip (tel: 91-3211 6600). Air taxis from Belém Aeroclub do the trip in about 30 minutes. The best place to stay in Soure is the Hotel Ilha do Marajó (www.iaraturismo.com. br; tel: 91-4006 3852). The hotel can arrange trips to the Praia do Pesqueiro and Praia Araruna, beaches, whose water is part-river, part-ocean. A ferry crosses the river to Salvaterra, where a battered taxi continues to Joanes (where you can stay at the comfortable Pousada dos Guarás (www.pousada dosguaras.com.br).

First called the Ilha Grande do Joanes, Marajó was settled in 1617 by Franciscan monks who built a stone church here in 1665, the ruins of which survive beside the lighthouse. At nearby **Monserrat** there is another stone-built church containing Baroque images.

From Soure, day trips can be arranged to the **Providencia** and **Santa Caterina buffalo ranches**. However, buffalo farms in the island's interior, reachable only by boat, horse, or tractor, have far more wildlife than the populated coastal region. **Fazendas Laranjeira** and **Tapeira** both have private museums with archeological relics from ancient Amerindian sites.

Buffalo country

About 70 years ago, water buffalo were imported to the island as beasts of burden and to produce milk, meat, and for hides. They took to the place famously and bred extremely well. The buffalo had advantages over horses as their widely splayed hooves were much tougher and did not rot. They also had advantages over the delicate humped zebu cattle often to be found on Marajó because their

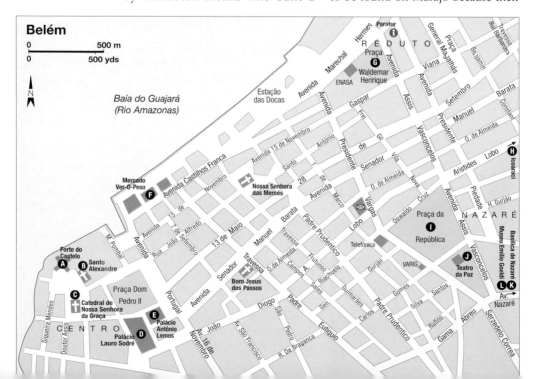

hide was much thicker, and that gave them the ability to shake off any hostile fauna.

Marajó is home to dolphins, capybaras, monkeys, birds, and alligators. But it is the great variety of snakes – from rattlesnakes to boas – that could be troublesome if the buffalos' hides were not so tough. The animals' qualities also include a gentle, placid outlook on life, which commended them to the local authorities who took some on for duty in the fire service and the police force. They can sometimes be seen on parade with the police, a pair yoked together pulling a cart, or individually, bearing a constable carrying his ceremonial lance, ready for action, perhaps to pull a farm implement or even a car out of the oozing mud. Their riders clearly have good relations with them, calling them each by its own name, guiding them gently with reins attached to a nose ring.

Now the Brazilian army is following up a good thing and using the water buffalo as pack animals in their numerous bases in Amazonia. They can easily carry supplies and munitions in remote areas, which may arrive by air but must eventually be moved by other means in the jungle, where there are no roads and little fuel, and rivers are often too shallow to navigate. They don't require petrol or special food. Buffalo eat anything, according to the army.

Straddling the equator

Macapá ❹, at the Amazon's northern mouth, stands on the equator, where you can straddle the marker line or *marco zero*. Nearby is a modest multipurpose stadium, known as the Zerão, in which one half of the pitch is in the northern hemisphere and the other in the southern hemisphere, the half-way line being the equator. Macapá has a large fort built of Lisbon brick by the Portuguese in 1782, and a thriving economy based on shrimp fishing and manganese mining. Planes leave Macapá for **Monte Dourado ❺** and the Jari Project, US billionaire Daniel K. Ludwig's ill-fated attempt to substitute the natural forest with plantations to mass-produce pulp to make paper.

Brazilian soldiers learn to ride water buffalos as part of a program to employ the animals in remote border posts where there are no roads for trucks.

An American dream

Amazonia is pockmarked with the ruins of the dreams of rich men. Two of them along the River Tapajós are memorials to the dreams of US automobile mogul Henry Ford.

In the 1920s Henry Ford bought 1 million hectares (about 2.5 million acres) of land on the Tapajós river, paying a lot more than he needed to. Ford called his tract of land Fordlandia and hoped it would be able to provide the rubber needed to make tires for the cars he manufactured in Detroit. Sadly, the land turned out to be no good for rubber trees, and after a few years it was abandoned to leaf blight, and sank back into the forest.

However, Ford's dream was not dead. He tried again further down the Tapajós, near its confluence with the Amazon. Belterra, as it was named, was supposed to be the success that would efface the failure of Fordlandia, and the car magnate was assiduous in the care of his employees, local and foreign.

Managers from the US were housed in a neighborhood called Vila Americana, in smart bungalows

The traditional method of rubber-tapping.

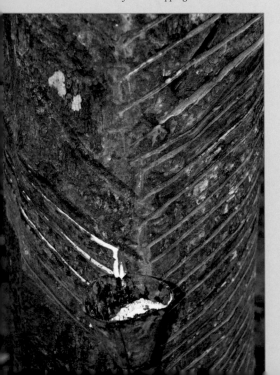

reminiscent of the houses of the workers of the British Raj in India.

Brazilian workers were not quite as well treated, but Ford did not exploit them as local bosses had done for decades, notably the rubber barons of the 19th century, who had operated a system of near-slavery. Ford paid good wages, three times what a laborer could earn in the nearby city of Belém, schools were built for workers' children, and water pipes were laid, but still there was very little rubber being produced.

One or two survivors of the Ford era linger on, one of whom bears out the account given by anthropologist Stephen Nugent in his excellent book, *Big Mouth: The Amazon Speaks*. The survivor remembers the days when he was a foreman and the planters from the United States were in charge.

There were very few of them and they didn't bring their families, he recalls. And they weren't much good at the very tricky task of planting trees. You can plant a rubber tree successfully in one spot, yet another one planted just a few meters away may wilt.

Three million trees

More than 3.5 million trees had been planted in the 1930s, but the operation was going too slowly, and it is estimated that it would have taken 1,000 years for the new area to be put under cultivation. After an expenditure of more than $10 million (about $150 million at today's rates), Ford walked away, and eventually the area was sold in 1945 to the Brazilian government at a loss of more than $20 million.

The authorities have kept the land as a resource for the neighborhood, and to this day, planning regulations decree that new houses have to be built in accordance with the plans that Ford brought with him from the United States. The remains are there to be seen: there are broad avenues, a sturdy church, and some remaining rubber trees, their trunks bearing the cuts from which the latex seeped out into the little cups that the workers emptied every day. There is also a signpost, almost covered by a forest creeper, indicating the way to Vila Americana, and the fire hydrants still showing that they were manufactured in Michigan.

A mile or two away is the little settlement of Pindobal, which served as a port for Belterra. Very few freight vessels tie up there these days, and the foreshore is left to families pottering about in their canoes, while local children play around the rusting wreckage of a bulldozer. Not much to show as the remains of a dream.

The Carajás project

The southeastern Amazon occupies a special place in the perennial dreams of economic greatness that have haunted Brasília's government planners: dreams that have become nightmares for conservationists. Development mega-projects that have consumed billions of dollars sprout across the region under the umbrella of the Carajás project, site of the world's largest and richest iron-ore deposit.

Conceived around an 18 billion-tonne iron-ore mine in the hills around **Carajás ❻**, 880km (547 miles) south of Belém, Brazil's moon shot in the Amazon includes the Tucuruí hydroelectric dam, an 890km (560-mile) railroad through the forest, and an immense complex supporting an aluminum smelting plant and a deep-water port. Carajás is owned and operated by the Brazilian company VALE (www.vale.com), the second-largest mining company in the world.

Those interested in Brazil's development and the bravura of the entrepreneurs can reach both Tucuruí and the Carajás mine at **Serra Norte** by plane from Belém. The treacherous terraces of the Serra Pelada gold mine, made infamous by Sebastião Salgado's photographs in the late 1980s, no longer exist. The mine is mechanized, and the *garimpeiros* (gold prospectors) are long gone.

Toward Manaus

Along the river from Belém, en route to Manaus, lies **Monte Alegre ❼**, a small village that became famous when the American archeologist Anna Roosevelt discovered pictographs and artifacts in caves in the area, which significantly altered existing ideas on human colonization in South America and the Amazon.

About 160km (100 miles) further upstream, **Santarém ❽** stands exactly halfway between Belém and Manaus, at the junction of the Tapajós and Amazon rivers. Founded in 1661 as a fort to keep foreign interests out of the mid-Amazon before the arrival of the Portuguese, Santarém was the center of a thriving Amerindian culture. Nearby lie the remains of the rubber plantations of **Belterra** and

Carajas Grande Iron Ore Mine as seen from the air.

Fordlandia, the latter now reclaimed by jungle (see page 328), expensive failures set up by the Ford Motor Company in the 1930s.

This mid-Amazon town has the comfortable Barão Center Hotel (www.baraocenterhotel.com.br) and Barrudada Tropical Hotel (see page 359) and riverboats that bring produce for the busy daily market along the waterfront. Most one-day boat tours travel up the Tapajós as far as **Alter do Chão**, site of the original settlement, and a superb beach some 38km (23 miles) from Santarém. The white-sand beach forms a curving spit that almost closes off the **Lago Verde** lagoon from the river. Also reachable by car, the village has a simple fish restaurant, a *pousada*, and

a number of weekend homes for Santarém's wealthy.

In Alter do Chão, the **Centro do Preservação de Arte Indígena** (Center for the Preservation of Indigenous Art; daily; free) exhibits art and crafts made by a number of Amazon tribes. Most hotels organize trips to the **Floresta Nacional do Tapajós** (National Forest Reserve), a well-preserved area of original forest.

Manaus

The city of **Manaus** ❾ is an oddity, an urban extravagance that turned its back on the rich surrounding forest and survived instead on federal subsidies, its exotic past, and today, increasingly, on tourism. Its moving spirit has always been quick riches. Once it

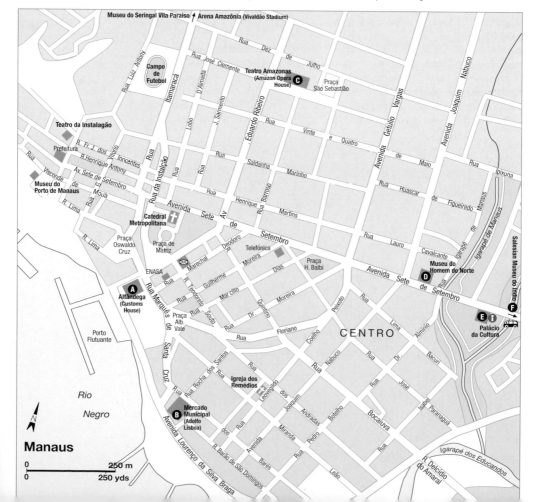

Manaus

had Art Nouveau grandeur; then, in the latter half of the 20th century, it acquired the image of a tawdry electronics bazaar, justified only by its status as a free port. Now, an ambitious restoration program is breathing new life into the city's architectural and cultural aspects, a program that helped it win the right to host games during the 2014 FIFA World Cup. The city's 44,000-seat Vivaldão stadium, or Arena Amazonia, has been rebuilt for the tournament. The port city's strategic position, close to the point where the three greatest tributaries form the Amazon river, means that it has long been the collecting point for forest produce from a vast area, and today is an important base for jungle tours.

Manaus still has reminders of its rubber wealth in the late 19th and early 20th centuries. British engineers in 1906 built the **Alfândega** Ⓐ (Customs House) out of Scottish bricks in an imperial style; and to accommodate the river's 14-meter (40ft) rise and fall, they assembled foreign-made sections of the floating dock.

The **Mercado Municipal (Adolfo Lisboa)** Ⓑ (daily 8am–6pm; free) on Rua dos Barés, southward along the dockside, is a busy market filled with regional produce, from exotic fruit to magic herbs to cure all ills. Handicrafts can also be bought there. The market is housed in an interesting cast-iron building, imported from Europe in 1882, which is a replica of the old Les Halles market in Paris.

Manaus is the capital of the state of Amazonia. The name means 'Mother of the Gods'.

Teatro Amazonas

The **Teatro Amazonas** Ⓒ (Amazon Opera House; www.cultura.am.gov.br; tours Mon–Sat 9am–4pm), located in the northern part of downtown Manaus, was begun in 1882, at the height of the rubber boom, after complaints from European touring companies that had been forced to play in smaller halls. Arriving there to sing during a cholera scare, the Italian tenor Enrico Caruso (1873–1921),

The Teatro Amazonas in Manaus.

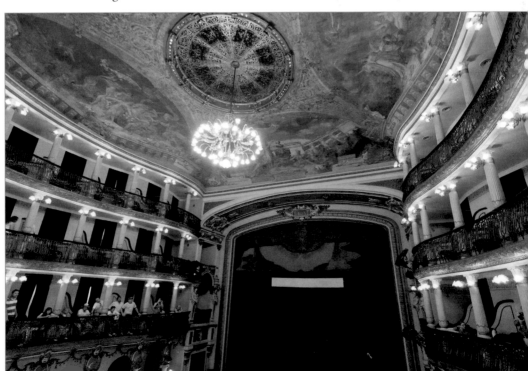

A walkway in a wooded area.

The meeting place of the waters from the Negro and Amazon rivers in the Amazon.

one of the greatest operatic stars of his time, returned to Europe without disembarking. After the grand inaugural performance of Ponchielli's *La Gioconda* in 1897, a month after the theater was completed, there were scant records of other operas being performed before the rubber boom collapsed.

The theater has been restored several times since it was constructed. The columns and banisters are of English cast iron, with stage curtains, chandeliers, and mirrors supplied by France. The marble came from Italy and the porcelain from Venice. Decorative motifs show the meeting of the Amazon waters and scenes from romantic literature about the Amerindians.

After many years of neglect, the theater was renovated in the 1990s, and functions as the venue for ballet, opera, and orchestral performances, including the Festival Amazonas de Opera (www.amazonasfestivalopera.com), which takes place in April and May, as well as being the location of the Amazonas Film Festival each November.

Another cultural center, the **Teatro da Instalação** hosts free music and dance performances (Rua Frei José dos Inocentes; tel: 92-3234 4096; www.culturamazonas.am.gov.br) in a restored historic building.

At 1385 Avenida Sete de Setembro, the **Museu do Homem do Norte** ⓓ (Museum of Northern Man; tel: 92-3232 5373; Mon 8am–noon, Tue–Fri 8am–noon, 1–5pm) gives a good idea of traditional Amazonian lifestyles. Also worth a look is the nearby **Palácio da Cultura** ⓔ (free), a wedding cake-like former palace, once seat of the state government, and now the venue for various cultural events.

Commercial hub

Though its rubber industry enjoyed a brief World War II recovery, Manaus was not rescued from lingering decay until 1967, when it was declared a free-trade zone. To take advantage of tax breaks, hundreds of factories were installed in the industrial zone. A *Zona Franca*, selling electronic consumer goods, also sprang up in the

city center, but prices will not excite foreigners.

The narrow streets of the port district are lined with stores selling goods to those who live on outlying tributaries. There is busy trade in some of the 1,500 different varieties of river fish and, in a separate section, Amerindian artifacts, *umbanda* items, and *guaraná* – a ginseng-like herbal energy preparation, which is also hugely popular as a soft drink. More Amerindian artifacts can be found at the **Salesian Museu do Indio** Ⓕ (296 Rua Duque de Caxias; Mon–Fri 9am–noon, 1–5pm, Sat 9am–noon).

Outside the center

A 20-minute ride out of the city along the Estrada Ponta Negra leads to CIGS, the army's training school for jungle warfare. There is a good zoo (Tue–Sun 9.30am–4.30pm) stocked with hundreds of Amazonian animals.

The **National Amazonian Research Institute** (INPA) carries out advanced studies with the help of many top foreign scientists. The aquatic mammals division (www.inpa.gov. br; Mon–Fri 9am–noon, 2–4pm, Sat–Sun 9am–6pm), located about 25 minutes by taxi along the Estrada do Aleixo, has an interesting collection of manatees, freshwater dolphins, and other species.

The **Tropical Hotel** (tel: 092-2123 5000; www.tropicalmanaus.com.br), situated on the Praia da Ponta Negra, 20km (12 miles) outside the city, became the social center of Manaus on opening in 1976. Its architecture is not exactly tropical, but the gardens, circular swimming pool, and, above all, the excellent swimming in the **Rio Negro** during the low-water season, make it a major attraction. The hotel operates daily boat tours 9km (5 miles) up the Rio Negro to **Lago Salvador** and the **Guedes Igarapé**. Visitors may fish, swim, walk the forest paths, and eat at a floating restaurant. An overnight stay at the lake allows time to travel up the *igarapé* (a forest backwater or creek) by motorized canoe, where you can go flashlighting

Toucans are primarily frugivorous, or fruit-eating, although they will occasionally snap up small bugs or insects for a snack.

Shipping bananas by boat.

At no point along its length is the Amazon river crossed by a bridge.

The Amazon parrot has a remarkable ability to mimic human speech.

boom. The base of the museum is actually the film set that was built for the film, *A Selva* (The Jungle), shot in 2001.

Day trips from Manaus

Several tour companies operate daylong river trips that follow a well-beaten track toward the **Lago Janauari** ecological park to see the *Victoria regia* giant water lilies (at their best from April to September). The boats then turn toward the meeting of the waters. The warm, clear waters of the Rio Negro collide with the silty Rio Solimões and run parallel without mixing for 20km (12 miles) in a great churning pattern through which tour boats pass. Some trips pause on **Terra Nova Island**, where river-dwellers demonstrate their rubber-tapping skills and sell souvenirs.

to see alligators. Next to the Tropical is the more modern Park Suites Manaus (see page 359), which offers fantastic views from the higher floors across the Amazon.

A popular attraction is Museu do Seringal Vila Paraiso (Tue–Sun 8am–4pm), a museum with a difference in that you will need to take a boat ride from Marina Davi, in Ponte Negra, to visit this recreation that looks at how people lived in the rubber plantations, the seringals, during the rubber

Two leading and reputable tour operators based in Manaus are Amazon Explorers (tel: 92-2123 4777; http://amazonexplorers.tur.br) and Swallows and Amazons (tel: 92-3622 1246; www.swallowsandamazonstours.com).

CRUISE SHIP PORT OF CALL

A trip along South America's mighty ocean-river should be high on every explorer's wish list, because its sheer scale boggles the imagination. Amazon cruise ships will show you the river in rather more comfort than the local boats, and there are plenty to choose from. Most run from Barbados and combine a few Caribbean calls with a stop at Santarém – where you can witness the marriage of the waters, as the coal-black Rio Negro merges with the café-crème Rio Solimões – before visiting Parintinss and Alter do Chão (home to an excellent museum charting Amazonian history and culture) en route to Manaus. If you can, choose a cruise that also calls at Devil's Island, off the coast of French Guiana. Home to the infamous prison described in the novel *Papillon*, it is a fascinating, and horrifying, place to visit, with its lightless isolation cells and haunting guillotine area.

Companies offering Amazon cruises include the de luxe small-ship operators Silversea Cruises and Seabourn Cruise Line (tel: 1-954-522 2299; www.silversea.com; or 1-80-929 9391; www.seabourn.com). If you prefer a larger ship (or a lower price), try Fred Olsen Cruises (tel: 44-1473 742424; www.fredolsencruises.co.uk), Saga Cruises (tel: 0800 096 0079; www.saga.co.uk), or Princess Cruises (tel: 0845 075 0031; www.princess.com).

Jungle lodges

To really appreciate the majesty of the Amazon, you will need to leave Manaus and go to stay at one of the many jungle lodges that sit in relatively close proximity to the city. A two-night minimum is recommended for a stay in a lodge. They will all include transportation to and from Manaus, excursions, guides, and meals (but not drinks), and most have a schedule of activities that includes short treks into the forest, canoe trips, piranha-fishing, torchlit caiman-spotting, and visits to local communities. The further into the jungle you go, the more pristine the forest, and the greater number of animal species you are likely to spot. Lodges range in comfort and cost. The following is a small selection that reflects the diversity on offer:

Considered one of the most comfortable and romantic of the lodges, **Anavilhanas Jungle Lodge** is located 184km (115 miles) from Manaus, close to Novo Airão. Transfer take about three and a half hours. The lodge has a mix of 16 stylish suites, plus eight cottages and four bungalows. It is in a privileged location as it borders two major protected ecological reserves, Jau and the Anavilhanas Archipelago (tel: 92-3622 8996; www.anavilhanas lodge.com).

The comfortable **Juma Lodge** (tel: 92-3232 2707; www.jumalodge.com) is located three hours from Manuas by van and boat, and offers 20 bungalows with views across the forest and a lake.

Four hours by road and boat from Manaus is the **Amazon Eco Lodge**, a remote, idyllic floating lodge. There are 18 simple but comfortable room, some with bathrooms, some with shared shower facilities, and a limited supply of electricity. A canopy platform allows a fantastic view over the rainforest as it comes alive at dawn and dusk (tel: 92-9964 6281; www.amazonlodgeamazonas.com.br).

The **Amazon Village** is three hours downstream from Manaus on the banks of the Purqucuara river. Rooms in thatched wooden bungalows are en suite with cold-water showers. There is a generator providing limited electricity, an alfresco restaurant, and a sun

Traveling by boat down the Amazon river is a unique experience to get up close to wildlife.

deck (tel: 92-3633 1444; www.amazon-village.com.br).

The **Uacari Lodge** is located in the Mamiraua Nature Reserve, the largest protected area of floodplain forest in Brazil, on the confluence of the Solimões and Japurá rivers. This floating lodge has 10 en suite rooms with solar-powered electricity. Because it is so remote, you are likely to see some rare Amazon species. Access is by a one-hour flight from Manaus to Tefé, then a four- to five-hour trip upstream by motorized canoe (tel: 97 3343 4160; www.pousadauacari.com.br).

Traveling by boat

Traveling by boat is a means of getting around, and is not the same as taking a river cruise. Though a growing number of roads are being built in the Amazon, rivers remain by far the most practical form of transportation for most people. Locals, and a few intrepid tourists, use the picturesque, cheap, and, in many ways, practical *gaiolas* that ply the waters of the Amazon river system. There is no better way to appreciate the character of the rural people of the Amazon than by travelling aboard a *gaiola*.

Though accommodations on board these riverboats are extremely basic, the open-sided decks festooned with hammocks are a logical solution to the slow, pitching gait of the boats and the sultry, humid climate. The movement of the boat keeps insects away, and many more passengers can be accommodated than by more conventional use of the space.

The trip from Manaus to Belém takes a little over a week – as long as there are no breakdowns. However, there are shorter trips that will give much the same flavor – one or two days are usually enough for most people – for example, **Santarém** to **Obidos**. On any *gaiola* it is advisable to take your own food, hammock, and bottled water. The food served on board is usually basic, often badly cooked, and occasionally inedible. Toilet facilities are extremely limited, and by the end of the journey they can be unpleasantly smelly. To offset these hardships, you will experience the closeness of the river and the forest at their most magical.

River choice

You will also be forced to come to terms with the pace of life in Amazonia, which is somewhere between very slow and stationary. It is better to travel upstream, because the boats keep closer to the edge of the river, where the current is slower. Traveling downstream, you may find yourself several hundred yards from either shore, with only a distant view of the vegetation. Bear in mind, however, that these trips are essentially a way of getting from A to B, and you will be lucky to see much wildlife.

For the less intrepid traveler there are better-equipped vessels with cabins and regular bunks. These are run by the government ENASA line, principally for tourists. These are luxurious by comparison with the *gaiolas*, with a bar, restaurant, and observation deck.

Jaguars are native to the Amazonian rainforest.

They even make stops to allow you to soak up the Amazon experience.

The most luxurious option, and an extremely comfortable way to experience a little of the Amazon, is on a three- or four-night cruise from Manaus on the Iberostar *Grand Amazon* (www.grandamazoncruises.com).

Whichever vessel you choose, a river voyage is an unforgettable experience. But unless you want your trip to include many frustrations and hours, or even days, spent waiting, you would be well advised to book a place on one of the tourist vessels, and pay for it in advance.

Those with time to spare can travel up the Solimões as far as **Benjamin Constant** and **Letícia** on the Peruvian–Colombian border, where it becomes the Marañón river. Launches from Manaus (subject to frequent delays) usually take about eight days.

Roraima

The Rio Branco drains Brazil's northernmost state, **Roraima**, whose dense forests and unmapped borders divide the Amazon and Orinoco river basins.

Until a highway was built from Manaus in 1977, with considerable loss of life owing to clashes with displaced Amerindian tribes, **Roraima's** capital, **Boa Vista** ⑩, was isolated from the rest of Brazil. Roraima is, according to legend, the location of the mythical El Dorado (see page 324). Mysterious **Mount Roraima** ⑪ is believed to have inspired Sir Arthur Conan Doyle's novel, *The Lost World*.

The 27,000-strong Yanomami Amerindian tribe – the continent's largest and least-acculturated indigenous group – occupies a region of jagged, forested peaks and chasms straddling the Brazil–Venezuela border in the **Parima** mountain range. The rare minerals on the Yanomami's land have attracted the interests of businessmen and illegal prospectors. It is estimated that 20 percent of the population was wiped out by attacks or disease during the 1970s and 1980s. In 1992, Yanomami land was finally demarcated, but at the time of writing, Brazil has not recognized tribal land-ownership, and the military is increasing its presence there

RESTAURANTS

PRICE CATEGORIES

Prices for a two-course meal for two. Wine costs around US$25 a bottle.

$ = under US$50
$$ = US$50–100
$$$ = US$100–200

Belém

Circulo Militar
Forte do Castelo, Praça Frei Caetano Brandão, Cidade Velha
Tel: 91-223 4374
Open: L&D daily.
Occupying a huge barrack room in the old fort, this restaurant offers a feast of regional dishes not to be missed. There's a good menu with plenty of choice, and good-humored waiters serve it at long tables. The dining room overlooks the Amazon river. **$$**
Dom Giuseppe
1420 Avenida Conselheiro Furtado,

Batista Campos
Tel: 91-400 8001
Open: L&D Mon–Sat, L Sun.
Top Italian dished with a distinctive Amazon accent. Located centrally and part of the Belém gastronomic scenery since 1992. One of the city's best wine lists. **$$**
Remanso de Peixe/Remanso do Bosque
2590 Travessa Barão do Triunfos/2350 Travessa Perebebuî
Tel: 91-3228 2447
Open: L&D Tue–Sat, L Sun.
Thiago Castanho is recognised as one of the best and most creative chefs when it comes to Amazonia cuisine. He started off with Remanso de Peixe, specialising in fish-based dishes. In 2001, he opened Remanso do Bosque, which sits in front of the city's Botanical Garden and offers dishes based on meat and pasta, as well as seafood. **$$**

Manaus

Banzeiro
102 Rua Libertador
Tel: 92-3234 1621
Open: L&D daily.
'Banzeiro' is an expression used in Amazonia for the waves formed in the rivers, especially when a boat passes. From this came the restaurant that many say offers the best Amazon cuisine in Manaus. Speciality is the rib of the tambaqui fish, and dishes that feature the pirarucu and matrinchã fish. **$$$**
Bistro Ananã
132 Travessa Padre Ghisland, Centro
Tel: 92-3234 0056
Open: D only Fri–Sat.
Hidden in the backstreets of the historic city center, Bistro Ananã only opens for dinner on Friday and Saturday, when it offers an extremely intriguing mix of contemporary and Amazon dishes and flavors. An attractive option. **$$$**

THE RICHES OF THE RIVER AMAZON

The world's greatest river and largest rainforest are estimated to contain one-tenth of the plant, animal, and insect species to be found on Earth.

The River Amazon is one of the greatest symbols of Brazil. It rises in the snows of the Peruvian Andes just a short distance from the Pacific Ocean. It then travels across the heart of South America – a distance of 6,570km (4,080 miles) – before it flows out into the Atlantic Ocean at the equator. It has about 1,100 tributaries, some of which, like the Araguaia and the Madeira, are mighty rivers in themselves. Just past Manaus, one of the most spectacular river sights is the meeting of the 'black waters' of the Rio Negro with the 'white waters' of the Rio Solimões, two other Amazon tributaries. The Amazon has a greater flow than any other river, depositing in the ocean each year about one-fifth of the world's fresh water.

At its mouth, the Amazon is 300km (185 miles) wide, a labyrinth of channels and islands, one of which has a greater landmass than Switzerland. The water flows with such force that it still tastes fresh 180km (110 miles) out into the ocean.

The Amazon's network of dark, dense jungles has often been referred to as the Great Green Hell. In the west of the Amazon basin, it is still possible to fly for several hours and see nothing below you but a carpet of tropical forest, broken only by rivers snaking their way through the trees. The Amazon has remained virtually unchanged for the past 100 million years, for it did not pass through the same ice ages that altered other parts of the world's landscapes. Some of the most remote areas are still inhabited by Amerindian groups who have never had contact with the world outside their own jungle, although such groups are increasingly rare as more and more forays are made into the rainforest.

The red uakari monkey is a very endangered species.

The Amazon basin covers seven million square kilometers (1.7 billion acres), of which an estimated five and a half million square kilometers (1.4 billion acres) are covered by the rainforest.

The Victoria Regis water lily is one of the most recognizable plants of the Amazon region. Its circular leaves can measure up to 2 meters (6ft) across and support a human or animal.

Devastating deforestation.

DEFORESTATION IN THE AMAZON

It has been estimated that about 20 percent of the Amazon forest – an area the size of France or twice the size of Colorado – has already been cut down, almost all of it over the past 40 years or so. Most of the destruction has taken place in the east of the basin, 'opened up' in the 1960s and 1970s when the military government built a vast network of roads. Cattle companies then moved in, slashing and burning the forest to sow pasture.

Avança Brasil was announced in 2001, a US$40-billion program that included the building of 10,000km (6,215 miles) of highways, electric dams, and power lines, but the program has been halted pending a review by the government. In recent years, the feeling is that the government has been taking more control over the illegal deforestation of the Amazon, and taking positive steps to protect this natural wonder.

So while the estimated loss of forest in 2004 was 27,423 sq km (10,600 sq miles), that fell to a loss of just 6,238 sq km (2,400 sq miles) in 2011, the slowest decline on record.

The Amazon River and its tributaries act as the region's main transport links; boats take over the roles of buses and trucks.

Clown tree frogs inhabit areas around bodies of water in the Amazon Basin, from Peru east through Brazil and the surrounding countries.

A boat at sunset on the Amazon.

INSIGHT GUIDES TRAVEL TIPS
BRAZIL

Transportation

Getting there 342
   By air 342
   By sea 342
   By bus 342
   Specialist tours 342
Getting around 343
   On arrival 343
   Domestic flights 343
   Brazilian airlines 343
   International airlines 343
   Trains 344
   Long-distance buses 344
   City buses 345
   The metro 345
   Taxis 345
   Hitchhiking 345
   Private transportation 346

Accommodations

Hotels 347
Budget accommodations 347
   Hostels 347
   Saving money 347
Charming hotels 347
Booking hotels 347
Hotel groups 347
Rio de Janeiro 348
Rio State 349
São Paulo City and State 350
Minas Gerais 352
Southern States 353
Brasília 354
Center West (Pantanal) 355
Bahia 355
Salvador 356
Sergipe and Alagoas 357
Recife and Pernambuco 357
The Far Northeast 358
Amazon 359

Activities

The arts 360
   Museums 360
   Art galleries 360
   Music and dance 360
   Theater 360
   Movies 361
Nightlife 361
Festivals 361
Sports 362
   Participant sports 362
   Spectator sports 363
Children's activities 363
Shopping 364
   What to buy 364
   Where to buy crafts 365

A – Z

Admission charges 366
Airport taxes 366
Budgeting for the trip 366
Business hours 366
Climate 366
Crime and safety 367
Customs and duty free 367
Disabled travelers 367
Electricity 368
Embassies and consulates 368
Entry regulations 368
Etiquette 369
Gay and lesbian travelers 369
Health 369
Internet 370
Lost property 370
Maps 370
Media 370
Money 371
Postal services 371
Public holidays 371
Public toilets 372
Religious services 372
Student travelers 372
Telecommunications 372
Time zones 373
Tipping 373
Tourist offices 374
Travel agents and
   tour operators 374
Websites 374
Weights and measures 375
What to bring 375

Language

Addressing people 376
Greetings 376
Pronouns 376
Getting around 377
Shopping 377
At the hotel 377
At the Restaurant 377
Money 378
Time 378
Numbers 378

Further Reading

History and travel 379
Fiction 379

TRANSPORTATION

ACCOMMODATIONS

ACTIVITIES

A – Z

LANGUAGE

TRANSPORTATION

GETTING THERE AND GETTING AROUND

Brazil is a very big country – larger than the continental United States or the European Union. The distance from top to bottom is similar to that from London to Central Africa. So even if places look close on the map – beware. Trying to fit in too much can mean spending your vacation on buses or in airport lounges.

Compounding your problem, moving around Brazil can be a slow business. Away from the main highways, bad road conditions can drag out journey times; and in big cities, traffic can be a nightmare. São Paulo to Rio is just 430km (270 miles), so it is five easy hours away on a good highway, but if you drive from the far side of one to the far side of the other at the wrong time of day, the urban crawl can almost double that time.

Most middle-class Brazilians insist on driving in town, even though some public transportation may be quicker – for example, city Metro systems and buses that use priority lanes. Of course, public transportation at rush hour is often impossibly crowded.

GETTING THERE

By air

Most major international airlines offer services to and from Brazil with a variety of routes (see page 343). Most direct in-coming flights head for São Paulo and then stop at Rio de Janeiro, although there is an ever increasing number of non-stop flights to Rio. Brasília, Belo Horizonte, Porto Alegre, Salvador, Fortaleza, Natal, and Recife also receive a limited number of international flights. Direct international flights link Brazil with both the east and west coasts of the United States, as well as with Florida and Canada, major cities in Europe, South America, Japan, the Gulf, and several African cities.

Brazil's main international carrier is TAM Airlines, which in 2011 merged with Chile's LAN to create LATAM, the largest airline in the southern hemisphere. Both airlines still fly under their respective brands and are members of the oneWorld alliance.

Flight time from the US is nine hours from New York, slightly less from Miami, and 12 hours from Los Angeles. Flights from Europe take 11 to 12 hours. Most international flights are overnight, so you arrive in Brazil in the early morning.

There is a variety of special package deals, some of them competitively priced. A travel agent will tell you what is available and make arrangements at no extra cost. See page 344 for details on Brazilian and South American air passes, which must be purchased outside Brazil.

Upon arrival, the airports have atms, currency-exchange facilities and information posts to help you find transportation or make a connecting flight.

By sea

There is no longer any regular ocean passenger service to Brazil, but it is possible to get there by boat. Costa (www.costacruise.com) is a major operator that runs many cruises up and down the Atlantic coast of South America during the European winter, and it – and a number of other cruise lines – will take on transatlantic passengers when the ships relocate between Europe or the Caribbean and Brazil. Other companies include Avalon Waterways, Celebrity, MSC, Oceania, P&O, Princess, Regent Seven Seas, Royal Caribbean, Saga, Seabourne, and Silversea. Several round-the-world cruise ships call at Brazilian ports, and reservations can be made for the trip to Brazil only. Special cruises travel up the Amazon river or visit Rio at Carnival time.

With the port development in Rio de Janeiro, it is expected that cruise ships will play an important roll in the accommodations for the 2016 Olympic games.

By bus

Long-distance bus services run between a few of the larger Brazilian cities and major cities in neighboring South American countries, including Asunción (Paraguay), Buenos Aires (Argentina), Montevideo (Uruguay), and Santiago (Chile). The highway from Manaus to Caracas has been paved, allowing a regular daily bus service. While undoubtedly a good way to take in the landscape, remember that the distances are great, and you may find yourself on a bus for several days and nights at a time. However, buses are usually of a high standard, in many cases providing toilets, food, and even almost-fully reclining seats.

Specialist tours

A wide variety of individual and group tours to Brazil are available. Some are all-inclusive packages with transportation, food and lodgings, excursions, and entertainment all arranged for you; some include only air transportation and hotel accommodations. There are also special-interest tours that include international travel to and from Brazil. These include boat trips on the Amazon river, fishing, and wildlife (including birdwatching) tours to the Pantanal, Mato Grosso in the center-west, and Carnival tours to Rio, Salvador, or Recife, as well as cultural tours focusing on dance, music, or art.

If you aren't on a tour where everything is planned, you might want to go on one of the readily available city sightseeing tours, boat outings to nearby islands, day trips to mountain and beach resort areas, and evening entertainment tour groups that take in a show.

Longer excursions can also be easily arranged once you are in Brazil – from Rio or São Paulo, for example, it is fairly easy to get on a tour to the Amazon or Pantanal, take a day trip by plane to Brasília or the Iguaçu Falls, or join a tour of the northeast or the colonial towns of Minas Gerais. However, in the peak season there may be a wait, as these excursions do get fully booked. Ocean cruising up and down the coast has grown rapidly in recent years, with a number of companies offering a variety of destinations. CVC (www.cvc.com.br), a major Brazilian travel agent and tour operator, normally has a large selection available, though it is best to book ahead for peak seasons. Language may be a problem, so if booking a local cruise you may wish to inquire in advance about English-speaking staff on board (see page 334).

GETTING AROUND

On arrival

At the airport, take a special taxi, for which you pay in advance at a fixed rate, and can use credit cards. There are fewer communication problems, no misunderstanding about the fare,

Getting from Sao Pãulo

São Paulo's international airport is 30km (18 miles) east of the city center in Guarulhos. There are efficient airport service buses (US$10) every 30 to 45 minutes from 5.30am to 11.40pm, stopping at Praça da Republica, the Terminal Tiete bus station, and the domestic Congonhas Airport. A taxi to the city center costs about US$80. Leave at least two hours before check-in time, longer at rush hour or if it is raining.

and if the driver takes you on the 'scenic route,' you won't be charged extra. If you take a regular taxi, check out the fares posted for the official taxis so that you will have an idea of what is a normal rate.

Most major Brazilian airports will also offer an efficient special airport bus service to take you into town. The routes normally includes stops at the larger hotels. Inquire at the airport information desk.

Some of the top-class hotels will send a driver to pick you up – it's best to arrange for this service when making your room reservation.

Domestic flights

Because Brazil is such an enormous country, it has a very good network of domestic flights. The airline industry in Brazil has gone through significant reorganization in recent years. Main domestic operators are TAM, Azul, and Gol/Varig, with, Trip, Brava, Pantanal, Passaredo, and Avianca offering budget or regional services. All of the larger lines fly extensive routes throughout the country and have ticket counters at the airports and ticket offices in most cities. At smaller airports in the more remote cities, these may only be staffed shortly before a flight.

Tickets can also be purchased at travel agencies and often at hotels, and reservations can be made by phone or on the airlines' websites. Information is usually provided in English as well as Portuguese. Airlines used to offer a toll-free service, but most now charge a premium rate.

Deregulation means that on some routes, flying is cheaper than traveling by bus. Discounts of up to 60 percent can be obtained for some internal flights. Travel agents in Brazil can give you details (see page 344). The large airlines also operate shuttle services between Rio and São Paulo (with flights every half-hour), Rio and Brasília (flights every hour), and Rio and Belo Horizonte (usually about 10 flights per day). The Rio to São Paulo shuttle between the airports of Santos Dumont (Rio) and Congonhas (São Paulo) is not available on the air pass. On domestic flights, checked baggage is limited to 20kg (44lb), and internationally accepted norms apply for hand luggage.

Brazilian airlines

A number of Brazilian airlines currently operate both domestic and

Flying in over Ipanema beach.

international flights: They include TAM, Gol, Azul, and Avianca . These, plus their subsidiaries and several budget airlines, are listed below.
Avianca
Tel: 11-4004 4040
www.avianca.com.br
Azul
Tel: 11-4003 1118
www.voeazul.com.br
Brava
Tel: 0800-=609 5800
www.voenht.com.br
Gol/Varig
Tel: 0300-115 2121
www.voegol.com.br
Pantanal Linhas Aéreas
Tel: 11-4002 5700
www.voepantanal.com.br
Passaredo
Tel: 0300-1001 777
www.voepassaredo.com.br
Rico
tel: 92-3652 1164
www.voerico.com.br
TAM
Tel: 11-4002 5700
www.tamairlines.com
Trip
Tel: 11-4003 1118
www.voetrip.com.br

International airlines

Most of the major international airlines have headquarters in São Paulo. Main contact numbers are as follows, but airlines now prefer you use their web sites rather than visit the offices:
Aerolíneas Argentinas
2441 Alameda Santos, 14th Floor
Tel: 11-2175 4200
www.aerolineas.com.ar
Aeroméxico
777 Avenida Paulista, 13th Floor,
Centro

Tel: 11-2344 3890
www.aeromexico.com.mx
Air Canada
949 Avenida Paulista, 13th Floor
Tel: 11-3254 6600
www.aircanada.com.br
Air Europa
332 Rua Rio Grande do Sul, Salvador
Tel: 71-3347 8899
www.aireuropa.com
Air France
222 Avenida Chedid Jafet, Block B,
2nd Floor
Tel: 11-4003 9955
www.airfrance.com.br
Alitalia
50 Avenida São Luix, 29th Floor
Tel: 11-2171 2171
www.alitalia.com.br
American Airlines
216 Rua Araújo, 9th–10th Floors
Tel: 11-3214 4000
www.aa.com.br
ANA
368 Rua da Consolação
Tel: 11-2141 2121
www.air-nippon.co.jp
Avianca
7059 Avenida Washington Luis
Tel: 11-4004 4040
www.avianca.com.br
British Airways
745 Alameda Santos, 7th Floor
Tel: 11-3145 9700/0300 7896140
www.britishairways.com
Delta Airlines
222 Avenida Chedid Jafat, Block B
Tel: 0800 221121
www.delta.com
Emirates
92 Rua James Joule, 7th Floor
Tel: 11-5503 5000
www.emirates.com
Ibéria
216 Rua Araújo, 3rd Floor
Tel: 11-3258 5333/11 3237 1100
www.iberia.com.br
JAL
542 Avenida Paulista, 3rd Floor,
Paraíso
Tel: 11-251 5222
www.br.jal.com/pt
KLM
222 Avenida Chedid Jafat, Block B
Tel: 11-4003 1888
www.klm.com
Lan Chile
247 Rua da Consolação, 12th Floor
Tel: 11-3259 2900/0300-788 0045
www.lan.com
Lufthansa
1356 Rua Gomes de Carvalho, 2nd
Floor, Itaim Bibi
Tel: 11-3048 5800
www.lufthansa.com
South African Airlines
852 Alameda Itú, 1st Floor
Tel: 0800-118 383

www.flysaa.com
TAP
453 Avenida Paulista, 14th Floor
Tel: 0800-727 2347/0300-210 6060
www.tap-airportugal.com.br
United Airlines
777 Avenida Paulista, 89th Floor
Tel: 0800-162 323
www.united.com.br

Trains

Except for crowded urban commuter railways, trains are not a major form of transportation in Brazil, and rail links are minimal. There are a few train trips, however, which are tourist attractions in themselves, either because they are so scenic or because they feature antique steam-powered trains. Their schedules can be rather erratic, however, so check carefully before going to catch one of these trains.

In the southern state of Paraná, the 110km (66-mile) Curitiba–Paranaguá railroad (www.serraverdeexpress.com.br) is famous for spectacular mountain scenery (see page 225). The first part of the trip, to Morretes, is the most beautiful.

A return trip can be done in a day. Bear in mind that you may not see much on a cloudy day.

The same company also runs the Pantanal Express (www.pantanalexpress.com) that operates on a route between Campo Grande and Miranda (see page 256).

In the state of Minas Gerais, antique steam locomotives haul passengers the 12km (7 miles) between São João del Rei and Tiradentes on a narrow-gauge railway from Friday to Sunday, and holidays (see page 214).

Air passes

Air passes are a good idea if you are going to be traveling a great deal around a country the size of Brazil. Ask your travel agent about them, as they must be purchased outside Brazil, and before you arrive. The cost depends on the number of flights, the season, and the region the cover. Each pass is only available for the flights of the issuing airline. The Brazilian carrier with the widest domestic network is TAM Airlines, which offers both a Brazil and South America Airpass. Details of the TAM Airpass can be found on its international website: www.tamairlines.com

Long-distance buses

Comfortable, on-schedule bus services are available between all major cities, and even to several other South American countries. Remember that distances are great and bus rides can be long – in other words, several days. But you could break up a long journey with a stop along the way.

On most routes there are three classes available. You can take a regular bus, with upholstered, reclining seats; an executive bus, with more comfortable seats; or the top-rate sleeper (leito) bus, which has wider and fully reclining seats with foot rests, as well as coffee and soft drinks on board.

On some routes, there may be just one bus a day (such as the Rio–Belém route, a 52-hour trip) or just one or two a week. Iry to buy your ticket in advance through a travel agent or at the bus station.

In São Paulo's Estacao da Luz train station.

There is a local bus service to the smaller, more isolated towns. This is quite a different experience and will leave you with no doubts that you are in a still-developing country. Almost always overcrowded, buses bump along dirt roads, picking up passengers who wait along the roadside, often with large bundles they are taking to market. Those who travel standing up – often for three to four hours or more – are charged the same as those who paid for a numbered seat. For the visitor, it may be a new experience, but you certainly have to admire the endurance and patience of the people for whom this precarious system is the only form of getting around.

City buses

Since just a small percentage of Brazilians can afford cars, public transportation is used a great deal. Some larger cities have special air-conditioned buses connecting residential areas to the central business district, including routes from airports and bus stations that swing by many of the larger hotels. You will be handed a ticket as you board. Take a seat and an attendant will come around to collect your fare, which will be extremely modest by North American and most European standards.

Your hotel may be helpful in providing information about bus routes, but most hotels discourage tourists from riding anything but the special buses.

The regular city buses are very cheap. Get on (often quite a high step up) and after paying the cobrador, who will give you change, move through the turnstile. Try to have your fare handy – several people may board at your stop and all have to get through the turnstile before they can sit down. This is also a favorite bottleneck for pickpockets who can jump out the back door as the bus takes off, so be alert to what's going on around you.

If you travel standing up, be sure to hold on tight. Some bus drivers (especially in Rio and São Paulo) can be very inconsiderate, jamming on the brakes suddenly, careening around

Travel translated

Entrada = Entrance
Saída = Exit
Unitário = Single
Ida e volta = Return/Round trip

corners at full tilt, etc. Signal when you want to get off by pulling the cord (some buses have buttons).

The metro

Rio de Janeiro and São Paulo have excellent, though not extensive, subway services, with bright, clean, air-conditioned cars. Maps in the stations and in each car help you to find your way without needing to communicate in Portuguese.

Lines radiate from the city center, and the service is further extended by bus links, often with train and bus combination tickets. Subway extension bus lines are marked 'integração.'

São Paulo (www.metro.sp.gov.br) has five main metro lines, all color coded, that link with a further seven train lines, three of them crossing at Estação da Luz and two underneath the Praça da Sé at the city's heart.

The north–south Line 1 (blue) connects Tucuruvi and Jabaquara; Line 2 (green) extends from Vila Madalena to Imigrantes; the east–west Line 3 (red) runs from Palmeiras/Barra Funda to Itaquera; Line 4 (yellow) goes from Estação da Luz to Vila Sônia; Line 5 (lilac) runs from Largo Treze to Capão Redondo. They run from 4.40am to just after midnight, and until 1am on Saturday night, and there are stops at the inter-city bus stations and bus link-ups to the Guarulhos International Airport.

Rio's two lines (www.metrorio.com.br) reach out from downtown as far south as Praça General Osório station in Ipanema, and to the north as far as Pavuna, with stops near the Sambódromo, Maracanã and Olympic Stadium. The metro is a quick and safe way to get between Ipanema, Copacabana and the historic and business center of the city.

The Rio subway, which is being expanded out to the start of Barra da Tijuca in time for the 2016 Olympic and Paralympic games, operates Monday–Saturday 5am–midnight and Sunday 7am–11pm. There are extended hours over Carnival and at New Year.

Both the Rio and São Paulo metros have helpful websites (see page 345). Other Brazilian cities to operate a metro service include Belo Horizonte, Brasília, Porto Alegre, and Recife.

Taxis

Taxis are probably the best way for visitors to get around in the cities. Of course, it's easy to get 'taken for

Daylight robbery

Be on guard against robberies on crowded buses, which occur frequently, even in broad daylight. If you are determined ride the regular city buses, try at least to avoid the rush hour, when passengers on certain lines are packed tighter than the proverbial sardines in a can.

Don't carry valuables; keep your shoulder bag in front of you, and your camera inside a bag. Avoid calling attention to yourself by speaking loudly in a foreign language. In other words, be discreet.

a ride' in a strange city. Whenever possible, take a taxi from your hotel, where a member of staff can inform the driver where you want to go.

Radio taxis are slightly more expensive, but safer and more comfortable. Although the drivers of the cabs you flag down in the street won't rob you, some occasionally try to overcharge or take you the long way around. Try to find out the normal fare for a given destination – most trips will be just a few dollars. Airport taxis charge high rates by Brazilian terms, but you will probably still find fares relatively low compared with North America or Europe.

In the street, if possible get a cab at a ponto, an organized rank where the drivers are all known to each other. There is no standard color for taxis in Brazil – in Rio they are yellow, in São Paulo they are white, but in other places they may look like regular cars with meters.

Radio taxis calculate a certain percentage above the meter rate (about 50 percent). If you hail a taxi at the curbside, be sure that the No. 1 tariff shows on the computerized display when the driver resets the meter. The No. 2 tariff indicates that the meter is set at a 20 percent higher rate – chargeable after 8pm and on Sundays and holidays and going beyond certain specified city bounds or up steep areas. Cab drivers can also use the No. 2 rate during the month of December to earn the '13th-month salary' that Brazilian workers receive each year as a sort of a Christmas bonus.

Hitchhiking

The basic rule about hitchhiking is – don't. There is no real hitchhiking tradition in Brazil, with the exception

Diving in off a chartered pleasure boat around Paraty.

River trips

Local boat tours and excursions can be taken in coastal and riverside cities. There are also longer trips available. Amazon river boat trips may last a day or two, or a week or more (see page 320). These range from luxury floating hotels to more rustic accommodations. Boat trips can also be taken on the São Francisco River in the northeast and in the Pantanal marshlands of Mato Grosso, popular for the incomparable bird and other wildlife. A lot of towns have local ferry services across bays and rivers and to islands.

of a few very specific circumstances – police and army cadets in uniform, truck-stop girls, and perhaps students on one or two specific routes between campus and city center, etc. While it might sound like fun to try to 'introduce a foreign custom,' and it is a shame to mistrust the whole of humanity because of a warped minority, the bottom line is: not in Brazil. Be you single or a couple, male or female, you're asking for trouble. It is not worth the risk.

Private transportation

Rental car services

Car rental facilities are available in the larger cities. Both **Avis** and **Hertz** operate in Brazil; www.avis. com.br, tel: 11-2155 2847 with a large number of outlets across Brazil; or www.hertz.com.br, tel: 11-2246 4300, São Paulo office open Mon–Fri 6am–11.45pm. Another option is Yes; www.yesrentacar.com.br; tel: 0800-709 2535.

The largest Brazilian national chains are: **Localiza** (www.localiza. com; 24-hour reservations, tel: 31-324 7761/0800-979 2000); and **Unidas** (www.unidas.com.br; 0800-121 121). Note the Unidas website is in Portuguese only. There are also good regional companies, especially in the northeast resorts for renting beach buggies.

Rates vary depending on the type of car. Some companies bill a flat daily rate, while others bill by mileage. Major international credit cards are accepted by these companies. Some will charge extra if you rent a car in one city and hand it back in another. Check exactly what you are getting on your insurance – it's worth paying more to be covered for all

eventualities.

Arrangements can be made at the airport as you arrive, through your hotel, or at the agencies. An international driver's license is helpful, but you can also rent a car with your own country's driver's license. For a relatively modest additional fee, you can hire a driver with the car.

Driving

Motoring in Brazil may seem chaotic compared with the rest of the world. Rio drivers are especially notorious for their erratic lane changing, in-town speeding and disregard for pedestrians and other drivers on the road. Be on the defensive and expect the unexpected. Although it doesn't seem to deter local drivers, speeding fines can be huge (several hundred dollars) even for going slightly over the limit, which can change erratically. There are speed cameras on many roads.

In the big cities, parking can be a difficult business downtown. A good solution in Rio is to park your car near an out-of-town subway station and take the metro into the city center. Wherever you park in Brazil, always lock your car. Never leave anything visible inside; even if you don't think of it as valuable, someone else might, and they might suspect that there are other items to be had as well.

It seems that wherever you park in the cities, within seconds a freelance car 'guard' will appear, either offering to keep an eye on your car in the hope of receiving a tip or even demanding that you pay him in advance for his (dubious) vigilance. The fee is quite modest; a few coins will usually be enough. It's best to pay up, or you risk finding some slight damage to the car upon

your return.

Licensed guards have been introduced in Rio and São Paulo; they will supply a receipt that covers a certain period of parking time.

The highways, especially the interstates, are generally quite good, but are crowded with more trucks than you will have ever seen. These huge vehicles bog down traffic on winding, climbing stretches of road in the mountains. Be aware that there are different rules of the road. It is polite to beep your horn when overtaking, and flashing your lights is a warning, for example.

If you plan to drive a lot in Brazil, buy the excellent Quatro Rodas (Four Wheels) Guia Brasil road guide, complete with road maps, city and regional itineraries, and hotel and restaurant listings (in Portuguese), which is available at most newsstands. The same company produces a more detailed Guia Estradas, with larger-scale road maps of the whole country, plus a range of individual state maps.

It is against the law to drink and drive in Brazil. There is zero tolerance. If in any doubt take a taxi. Don't risk it.

Road safety

While they are at all other times a polite, decent people, something happens when Brazilians get behind the steering wheel, especially in Rio. Be very cautious when driving, and when crossing streets be prepared to make a dash. Despite the tightening of traffic regulations, most drivers expect pedestrians to watch out for themselves and move out of the way.

ACCOMMODATIONS

HOTELS, YOUTH HOSTELS, BED & BREAKFAST

HOTELS

There is no shortage of excellent hotels in Brazil. The larger cities and resort areas, especially, have hotels run to international standards, with multilingual staff. At all grades, rooms are usually clean and the staff are polite. A Continental-style breakfast is normally included in the price. Rates fluctuate according to demand and location, so our price guide is only approximate. Expect higher prices in Rio during the 2016 Olympics.

In Rio there is a bed-and-breakfast association called Cama e Café, which focuses mainly on the Santa Teresa district, but this has not yet caught on elsewhere. However there are a growing number of good hostels throughout Brazil.

It is always best to book well in advance, especially during Carnival or a major holiday. In peak months (Jan–Feb and July), hotels may be booked up by Brazilian vacationers. There may also be a minimum required length of stay during the high season.

As Brazil is hosting the FIFA World Cup in 2014 and the Olympic and Paralympic Games in Rio in 2016, there are a number of new hotels opening, but also a number of existing properties, especially in Rio, which are closed or restricting room numbers for refurbishment or expansion programs.

In places where no hotels are listed here, or for a wider selection, you will find the Quatro Rodas *Guia Brasil* guide, available at newsstands, useful. Be aware that motels are often rented out by the hour for trysts.

BUDGET ACCOMMODATIONS

Hostels

Hostels are getting better in Brazil, especially in Rio, as they become a more acceptable choice. Oztel, listed below, is an example.

The Casa do Estudante do Brasil, at 9 Praça Ana Amelia, Castelo, Rio de Janeiro; tel: 21-2220 7423, has a list of hostels in 10 Brazilian states that are registered with the International Youth Hostel Federation (www. hihostels.com) and charge just a few dollars. There is no age restriction. Also check Hostel Brasil, with more than 100 hostels throughout Brazil on its books (www.hostel.org.br).

Saving money

Big savings can be made on room rates by visiting places when the main target audience is not. For example visit Brasília, São Paulo, and other business centers at the weekend as most hotels are aimed at business travelers. The opposite is true for the beach or tourist destinations, so if you don't need to go to Búzios at the weekend, then don't. Go in the week, and you may get a much better deal.

Probably the only city this does not work for is Rio, which has both leisure and business demand, but a rate at a hotel in downtown Rio may still be better at the weekend.

CHARMING HOTELS

The Roteiros de Charme is a small group of hotels and pousadas. They are generally of a high standard and usually in historical buildings. Attractive, intimate, and with good food, these establishments are likely to offer the most memorable accommodations of your trip. For more information, tel: 21-2287 1592; www.roteirosdecharme.com.br.

BOOKING HOTELS

Because Brazil is so hooked up to the internet, even the most basic hotels normally have a web site with a booking engine. A good selection of mainstream hotels in Brazil can be found on all the major international hotel booking sites, making the booking of hotels and pousadas in Brazil fairly straight forward and reliable.

HOTEL GROUPS

Most of the major international hotel groups operate in Brazil, with the French group Accor, for example, offering hundreds of hotels throughout Brazil. International brands operating in Brazil include Best Western, Golden Tulip, Grand Hyatt, Hilton, Holiday Inn, Iberostar, Ibis, Inter-Continental, Marriott, Mercure, Novotel, Orient Express, Radisson, Ramada, Royal Tulip, Sofitel, Starwood, and Tryp.

There are also a number of Brazilian chains such as Atlântica (www.atlanticahotels.com.br), Blue Tree (www.bluetree.com.br), Estanplaza (www.estanplaza.com.br), Fasano (www.fasano.com.br), InterCity (www.intercityhoteis.com.br), Othon (www.othon.com.br), Transamérica (www.transamerica.com.br), Tropical (www.tropicalhotel.com.br), and Windsor (www.windsorhoteis.com.br), to name a few.

RIO DE JANEIRO

Arpoador Inn
177 Rua Francisco Otaviano, Ipanema
Tel: 21-2523 0060
www.arpoadorinn.com.br
Small (50 rooms), simple, a bit dated,
but good value because it is in one
of the most beautiful spots in Rio,
right by the sea and Ipanema Beach.
First opened for business back in
1974. Beach-front rooms are much
quieter. **$$**

Caesar Park
460 Avenida Vieira Souto, Ipanema
Tel: 21-2525 2525
www.sofitel.com
Now under the management of
Sofitel. Of a high international
standard, the 23-floor, 221 room
Caesar Park was for many years, the
top hotel in Ipanema and is still one
of the city's best. Well situated in the
heart of Ipanema and on the beach
front. Roof top pool. One of Rio's
leading business hotels. **$$$$**

Cama e Café
5 Rua Pascoal Carlos Mango, Glória
Tel: 21-2225 4366
www.camaecafe.com.br
Cama e Café is not in itself a hotel
but a company that offers bed and
breakfast in a number of charming,
historic buildings, mainly in and
around the Santa Teresa area.
The properties vary in level of
sophistication and facilities, but the
hotel's website gives a very clear
indication of what is on offer. **$–$$$**

Copacabana Palace
1702 Avenida Atlântica, Copacabana
Tel: 21-2548 7070
www.copacabanapalace.com.br
An iconic oasis of calm with a superb
Italian restaurant, excellent pool
area and spa, and some of Rio's best
and most comfortable rooms. Good
business facilities. Great service. Best
afternoon tea in Brazil. Classic luxury
in the heart of Copacabana beach.
One of the world's great hotels. Part
of the Orient-Express group. **$$$$**

Excelsior Windsor Copacabana
1800 Avenida Atlântica, Copacabana
Tel: 21-2195 5800
www.windsorhoteis.com.br
This once-traditional hotel has been
refurbished by the ever-expanding
Windsor Hotel Group, and offers
excellent value as a beach-front
executive hotel. Located on the same
block as the Copacabana Palace.
Rooftop pool. **$$$**

Fassano
80 Avenida Vieira Souto, Ipanema
Tel: 21-3202 4000

www.fasano.com.br
Rio's most fashionable (and
expensive) boutique hotel since
opening in 2007. Good enough for
Madonna, Jay-Z, Beyoncé, and Alicia
Keys to visit, and all at the same
time. Highly rated restaurant, Fasano
al Mare, and bar, Barretto Londra.
Exclusive infinity pool on rooftop
and spa. Located in Ipanema, so
surrounded by interesting bars and
restaurants. **$$$$**

Royal Tulip São Conrado
222 Rua Prefeito Mendes de Morais, São
Conrado
Tel: 21-3323 2200
www.royaltulipriodejaneiro.com
Once a good, reliable Inter-
Continental hotel with full resort
facilities. The facilities are still the
same, but it now operates under the
Royal Tulip banner. Next to the São
Conrado Fashion Mall. **$$$$**

Ipanema Inn
27 Rua Maria Quitéria, Ipanema
Tel: 21-2523 6092
www.ipanemainn.com.br
A reliable mid-priced hotel, well
located for sightseeing. The rooms
are small but comfortable, and it's
just round the corner from the beach.
Lots of nice restaurants and bars
close by. **$$**

Ipanema Plaza
34 Rua Farme de Amoedo, Ipanema
Tel: 21-3687 2000
www.ipanemaplaza.com.br
Popular with regular visitors to Rio,
who appreciate its location and
facilities in the heart of Ipanema, just
one block from the beach and close
to many bars, restaurants and shops;
140 rooms. Rooftop pool. **$$$**

JW Marriott
2600 Avenida Atlântica, Copacabana
Tel: 21-2545 6500
www.marriott.com.br/riomc
Classic and stylish JW Marriott
that is very popular with American
visitors, those who are in town both
for business and for leisure. Try to
get a beach view as an atrium view is
nothing special when you are staying
on Copacabana Beach. **$$$$**

Marina All Suites
696 Avenida Delfim Moreira, Leblon
Tel: 21-2172 1100
www.marinaallsuites.com
Famous for its eight signature design
suites, the result of a promotion for
leading Brazilian interior designers.
Modern and stylish, Marina All
Suites is located on the beach front
at Leblon, and considered one of
the area's best, although there are

concerns that standards are slipping,
and not what they were. **$$$$**

Oztel
91 Rua Pinheiro Guimaraes, Botafogo
Tel: 21-3042 1853
www.oztel.com.br
One of a new breed of fashionable,
cool and comfortable hostels. Good
dorms, as well as suites. Nice bar
with snacks. TV room. Free Wi-fi.
Breakfast included. **$**

Porto Bay Rio Internacional
1500 Avenida Atlântica, Copacabana
Tel: 21-2546 8000
www.portobay.com
Modern Copacabana beach-front
hotel, popular with both business
and leisure travelers. Even standard
rooms have balconies and sea views,
and there's a nice rooftop pool with
great views over Copacabana and the
beach. Top spot for New Year. Part of
Porto Bay group. **$$$$**

Praia Ipanema
706 Avenida Vieira Souto, Ipanema
Tel: 21-2141 4949
www.praiaipanema.com/
A beach-front hotel on the border
of Ipanema and Leblon with a nice
rooftop pool deck. Well-located and
well-priced for such a desirable
location. Close to good, fun bars and
restaurants, as well as the beach. **$$$**

Rio Hostel Ipanema
18 Rua Caning, Casa 1
Tel: 21-2287 2928
www.riohostelipanema.com
Friendly hostel with dormitory
beds, two blocks from the beach at
Ipanema. Lovely staff; tours offered. **$**

Santa Teresa
660 Avenida Alm Alexandrino, Santa Teresa
Tel: 21-3380 0200
www.santateresahotel.com
Stylish, award-winning boutique hotel
in the bohemian district of Santa
Teresa. Located in an old coffee-
plantation mansion. It's no good if
you want to be on the beach front,
but it offers stylish accommodations
and a very special atmosphere. Good
restaurant and bar. Very different from
other Rio properties, and very special
if you don't need to be on the beach
front. A member of Relais e Chateau.
$$$$

Sheraton Barra
3150 Avenida Lucio Costa, Barra da Tijuca
Tel: 21-3139 8000
www.sheraton-barra.com.br
Reflecting the growing importance
of Barra da Tijuca, the Sheraton was
the first of a number of hotels to open
here back in 2003. It's a beach-front
resort, and all the rooms have both

sea views and balconies. Hotels in Barra will be the closest to events at the Olympic Village and Rio Centro Convention Center, but a little out of the way for general sightseeing. Sheraton also offers the Sheraton Rio Hotel & Towers (www.sheraton-rio.com) on the coast road between Ipanema and São Conrado. A top resort hotel that offers excellent accommodations and facilities. $$$$

Sofitel Rio Palace
4240 Avenida Atlântica, Copacabana
Tel: 21-2525 1232
www.accorhotels.com.br
This is a very good conference and business hotel with beautiful views over Copacabana and the usual high Sofitel standards of style and service. There are 388 rooms and 52 suites. Nice pool area, with stunning views down Copacabana Beach. Le Pre Catelan is one of Rio's best restaurants. $$$$

La Suite
501 Rua Jackson Figueiredo, Joá
Tel: 21-2484 1962
www.lasuiterio.com
Very classy little French-run guesthouse with just seven rooms. There's an infinity pool, from which there are views back over Leblon and Ipanema. The only disadvantage is that the location means you need to have a car or take taxis. $$$$

Windsor Asturias
14 Senador Dantas, Centro
Tel: 21-3873 8888
www.windsorhoteis.com.br
Nicely maintained, well-priced executive hotel in downtown Rio. Cute sundeck with small pool. Just around the corner from Cinelandia and the metro that takes you straight to Copacabana and Ipanema. Also around the corner is the evening hotspot of Lapa. A good option if you want to save money and catch the sights. Good choice if you are working downtown. $$

Windsor Atlântica
1020 Avenida Atlântica, Leme
Tel: 21-3873 8888
www.windsorhoteis.com.br
The landmark beach-front building, known to many as having once been the Meridien, closed for a number of years for a total upgrade. The all-new hotel was reopened by the Windsor group at the end of 2010 and with 545 rooms; it is one of Rio's largest and has re-established itself as one of the city's best. There are two pools, one on the 39th floor. Good for business or leisure. $$$$

Windsor Leme Palace
656 Avenida Atlântica, Leme
Tel: 21-2122 5900
www.windsorhoteis.com.br
Traditional beach-front hotel that was refurbished in 2009 when it was the Leme Othon. Now under the Windsor banner, standards will improve further. The location at the quieter, Leme end of Copacabana, makes it convenient for the city. Only negative is lack of pool or sundeck. Windsor now offers a total of 12 hotels in Rio, with more on the way. $$$

RIO STATE

Angra dos Reis

Hotel Frade & Golf Resort
BR-101 Sul, Km 123
Tel: 24-3369 9500
www.fradevilas.com.br
Good resort facilities and on its own beach. One of Brazil's first resort properties that has expanded its offerings over the years. Features an 18-hole golf course, a marina, and water sports. $$$

Pestana Angra Beach
3700 Estrada Vereador Benedito Adelino, Retiro
Tel: 24-3364 2005
www.pestana.com
Attractive waterfront boutique hotel; 27 exclusive bungalows all with breathtaking ocean and island views. Pool, spa and Jacuzzi. Water sports. $$$

Vila Galé Eco Resort de Angra
8413 Estrada do Contorno, Praia de Tangua
Tel: 24-3379 2800
www.vilagale.pt
World-class all-inclusive hotel; stunning location in the grounds of the old Tangua Estate, and on its own beach; 307 rooms and 11 suites. Four restaurants and four bars. Meeting facilities for up to 1,900. $$$$

Búzios

Blue Tree Park Búzios Beach Resort
Praia de Tucuns, Búzios
Tel: 22-2623 1763
www.bluetree.com.br/hotel/blue-tree-park-buzios/
With over 335 rooms, this is the largest hotel in the region. An excellent all-inclusive resort on a stunning beach, the management of which has been taken over by Blue Tree from Breezes. Kids Club, mini golf, and water sports. Free transfers into Búzios. $$$$

Casas Brancas Boutique Hotel & Spa
10 Morro do Humitá
Tel: 22-2623 1458
www.casasbrancas.com.br
A hip and charming all-white boutique hotel nestled in hills overlooking the bay of Búzios, with a highly rated spa. Classy, well equipped rooms. Nice restaurant, Café Atlantico and just a short walk into town. The resort has its own beach club and lounge, Rocka, at Praia Brava. $$$$

Insolito Boutique Hotel
Rua E1, Lotes 3 and 4, Praia da Ferradura
Tel: 22-2623 2172
www.insolitos.com.br
Not the cheapest option, but one of the best and most sought-after *pousadas* in Búzios, if not Brazil. Wellness Center. Water sports. Isolito has its own beach club on the sands below; 12 very stylish and comfortable rooms. $$$$

Pousada Hibiscus Beach
Rua 1, 22 Quadra C Praia de João Fernandes
Tel: 24-2623 6221
www.hibiscusbeach.com.br
Individual Polynesian-style bungalows set among tropical plants, all with balcony and sea views. Very relaxing. British-run. $$$

Cabo Frio

La Plage
40 Rua dos Badejos, Peró
Tel: 22-2647 1746
www.laplage.com.br
Cabo Frio's main beach-front property at Praia do Peró. La Plage has 85 rooms with sea views. $$$

Pousada Portal do Sol
76 Rua Francisco Paranhos, Algodoal
Tel: 22-2643 0069
www.portaldosolpousada.com.br
A well-located moderately priced inn close to the Teatro Muncipal and only 200 meters/yds from Praia do Forte. $$

Ilha Grande

Pousada O Pescador
Vila do Abraão

PRICE CATEGORIES

Price categories are for a double room. Breakfast is usually, but not always, included:
$ = under US$120
$$ = US$120–250
$$$ = US$250–400
$$$$ = over US$400

TRANSPORTATION

ACCOMMODATIONS

ACTIVITIES

A – Z

LANGUAGE

Tel: 24-3361 5114
www.opescador.org/en
A simple, charming little place, right
on the beach. Breakfast included, and
it has one of the best restaurants on
the island serving Italian and Brazilian
dishes. **$**

Itacuruçá
Hotel do Pierre
Ilha de Itacuruçá
Tel: 21-2253 4102
www.hotelpierre.com.br
Twenty minutes by boat from the
mainland. Fifty-one rooms, slightly
dated, but all with verandas
overlooking the sea and bay.
Restaurant, bars, and sporting
facilities. **$$$**

Itatiaia National Park
Hotel Simon
Parque Nacional, Km 13
Tel: 24-3352 1122
In a beautiful setting within the park,
with an orchid garden attached.
Helpful advice given on getting around
the park and birdwatching. **$$$**
Hotel do Ypê
Parque Nacional, Km 16
Tel: 24-3352 1453
www.hoteldoype.com.br
On the park road, with good meals,
including a poolside barbecue on
Saturday, included in room rate.
Indoor and outdoor pools and 16
cabins. Birdwatching. **$$$**

Nova Friburgo
Bucsky
Estrada Niterói–Nova Friburgo, Km 76.5,
Mury
Tel: 24-2522 5052
www.hotelbucsky.com.br
Comfortable, cozy, 4-star hotel with
70 rooms. A short distance from
town. Pool. Tennis. Gardens. Meals
included. **$$$**
Fazenda Gamelo Eco Resort
RJ 160 – Estrada Cantagalo, Cantagalo
Tel: 21-2220 3731
www.gamela.com.br
Well-equipped and friendly eco-
resort for families, great for an active
weekend. **$$$**
Pousada Vale das Flores
224 Rua Jacy Linhares Ramos, Braunes
Tel: 22-2526 3503

www.valedasflores.com
Pleasant, medium-priced inn with
beautiful views over the valley.
The pousada has 19 suites with
mountain views, a sauna and a pool.
Owner runs off-road tours. **$$**

Paraty
Casa do Rio Hostel
120 Rua Antônio Vidal
Tel: 24-3371 2223
www.paratyhostel.com
A hostel located in a gorgeous house
by the river. Linked to Hostelling
International. Two blocks from historic
heart of Paraty. Room for 70 people. A
number of private rooms. **$**
Picinguaba
130 Rua G, Vila Picinguaba
Tel: 12-3836 9105
www.picinguaba.com
Stunning *pousada*, on its own beach
in an eco-reserve 30 minutes south
from Paraty. Just nine simple, but
comfortable rooms with private
balcony. A very special place; no TV or
internet. **$$$**
Pousada Corsário
26 Rua João do Prado
Tel: 24-3371 1866
www.pousadacorsario.com.br
Peaceful spot with riverside tropical
garden and pool. Thirty-nine rooms.
Owners also have properties in Búzios
and Santo André. **$$**
Pousada do Ouro
145 Rua Dr. Pereira
Tel: 24-3371 4300
www.pousadaouro.com.br
Central, discreetly luxurious
accommodations in the historic center
of Paraty. Some of the 39 rooms are
located in the villa of the pousada.
Pool. Sauna. Bar terrace. **$$$**
Pousada do Sandi
1 Largo do Rosario
Tel: 24-3371 2100
Reservations, tel: 11-2503 0195
www.pousadadosandi.com.br
For over 20 years, considered one of
Paraty's top *pousadas*. Colorful and
comfortable; 25 rooms including a
master suite and junior suite; highly
rated restaurant, Pippo, inspired by
the 1960s and the movies of that
time. Located in the heart of the
historic center. Asian day spa. **$$$**

Petrópolis
Grande Hotel
545 Rua do Imperador, Centro Historico
Tel: 24-2244 6500
www.grandehotelpetropolis.com.br
Excellent choice for people looking to
stay in the heart of Petrópolis itself,
just around the corner from the main
attractions like the Museu Imperial.
Sixty-seven modern rooms in a
beautifully restored hotel dating from
the 1930s, which had been closed for
45 years prior to reopening in 2011.
Lobby reflects the building's elegant
and historic past. **$$$**
Locanda Della Mimosa
30 Alameda das Mimosas, Vale Florido
Tel: 24-2233 5405
www.locanda.com.br
Luxurious *pousada* on the outskirts
of Petrópolis, on the road to Itaipava,
with one of the region's best
restaurants and wine cellars. Good
base to explore the area. Nice pool.
$$$
Pousada da Alcobaça
298 Rua Agostinho Goulão, Correas
Tel: 24-2221 1240
www.pousadadaalcobaca.com.br
One of the top *pousadas* in town,
although 15 minutes from the center
of town, with lovely gardens, a great
restaurant, pool, sauna, and tennis
court. Eleven rooms. **$$**
Tankamana
Estrada Julio Capua, Vale do Cuiaba
Te: 24-2232 2900
www.pousadatankamana.com.br
One of the region's best-equipped
pousadas; 16 delightful individual
chalets. Highly rated restaurant
offering contemporary Brazilian and
international cuisine. Private cinema.
A top choice for a weekend break. **$$$**

Teresópolis
Hotel Village Le Canton
12 Estrada Teresópolis–Friburgo, Km 12,
Vargem Grande
Tel: 21-2741 4200
www.lecanton.com.br
Nestled in a green valley, this is
one of the most traditional and
well-equipped resorts in the Rio
mountains. Excellent cuisine, smooth
service, and beautiful rooms. Top-
notch spa. **$$$**

SÃO PAULO CITY AND STATE

São Paulo
Emiliano
384 Rua Oscar Freire, Cerqueira César
Tel: 11-3069 4369
www.emiliano.com.br

Consistently one of the city's leading
boutique hotels, in the heart of São
Paulo's top shopping area. There are
38 stylish rooms and 19 suites, a
fitness center, and a spa. Emiliano

has a top Italian restaurant plus
champagne and caviar bar. Good for
business and pleasure. **$$$$**
Grand Hyatt
13301 Avenida das Nações Unidas,

Morumbi
Tel: 11-2838 1234
www.saopaulo.grand.hyatt.com.br
Superbly equipped, classy Grand Hyatt offering great service for business or leisure stays. Close to Morumbi Shopping. Interesting restaurant and bar annex, which is equally popular with tourists and locals. Leading choice for Formula 1 Grand Prix weekend. **$$$$**

Hilton Morumbi
12901 Avenida das Nacoes Unidas, Morumbi
Tel: 11-2845 0000
www1.hilton.com
One of the world's top Hiltons. Located next to the Grand Hyatt in Morumbi with 487 rooms and suites. Indoor rooftop pool on 28th floor. Choice of restaurants and bars. Great infrastructure. **$$$$**

Holiday Inn Anhembi
100 Rua Prof Milton Rodrigues, Anhembi
Tel: 11-2107 8844
ww.holidayanhembi.com.br
Large hotel, with 780 rooms, that is really aimed at those attending an event at the Anhembi exhibition center with little time to enjoy the city. Saves being stuck in traffic. Not a lot in the area, so not the choice if you are not going to Anhembi. **$$$**

Hospedaria Mantovani
269 Rua Eliseu Guilherme, Paraiso
Tel: 11-3889 8624
www.residenzamantovani.com.br
Recommended budget option in good central neighborhood near Avenida Paulista. Looking after people on a limited budget for over four decades. Rooms are modest, but all have a bathroom. No air conditioning. **$**

Inter-Continental São Paulo
1123 Avenida Santos, Cerqueira Cesar
Tel: 11-3179 2600
Reservations tel: 0800-118 003
www.intercontinental.com/saopaulo
Considered one of the most luxurious in town and recently renovated. Located one block from Avenida Paulista. The hotel has 195 rooms and 38 suites, fine dining at Tarsila restaurant, and a pool. Excellent service. It was a favorite with President Lula. **$$$$**

Normandie Design
1187 Avenida Ipiranga, Ipiranga
Tel: 11-3311 9855
www.normandiedesignhotel.com.br
Budget hotel with style. Good value, in the heart of old São Paulo, although not to everyone's taste in terms of style and location. 162 rooms **$$**

Pergamon
80 Rua Frei Caneca, Consolação
Tel: 11-3123 2021
Reservations tel: 0800-551 056
www.pergamon.com.br
Combines comfort with art and design; Pergamon is good value for the standard offered. There are 120 rooms and a Brazilian restaurant.. Located near Rua Augusta. **$$$**

Porto Bay L'Hotel
266 Alameda Campinas, Jardim Paulista
Tel: 11-2183 0500
www.portobay.com
Classic European style and excellent service. Located in a residential area close to Avenida Paulista, this hotel has 75 executive rooms and eight suites, a spa, and small pool. Classy and charming. **$$$$**

Pousada Dona Zilah
1621-1633 Alameda Franca, Jardim Paulista
Tel: 11-3062 1444
www.zilah.com
Yes, you can find a rustic *pousada* in the center of São Paulo. Friendly and affordable in an upmarket part of town, the Jardins. An interesting option. **$$**

Radisson Faria Lima
625 Avenida Cidade Jardim, Itaim Bibi
Tel: 11-2133 5960
www.radisson.com/saopaulobr
Good standard and popular Radisson. Located on the corner of Cidade Jardim and Faria Lima, a few blocks from Iguatemi Shopping Mall. Best known for its exclusive women's floor. 202 rooms. **$$$**

Tivoli Morfarrej
1437 Alameda Santos, Cerqueira César
Tel: 11-3146 5900
www.tivolihotels.com
A total renovation and the introduction of the Tivoli brand have restored it to one of the city's best. The hotel's 220 rooms include a presidential suite that is one of the largest in Latin America. The Arola Vintetres restaurant and bar on the 23rd floor has views of Avenida Paulista, and the Spa by Banyan Tree is considered one of the best in Brazil. **$$$$**

TRYP Higienópolis
371 Rua Maranhão, Higienópolis
Tel: 11-3665 8200/3665 8201
www.tryphotels.com/en/tryp-hotels-brazil.html
Upmarket neighborhood. A good-value option for both business and tourism. Close to Shopping Patio Higienopolis. Pool and 252 rooms. Reflecting the business power of São Paulo, TRYP offers another seven properties in the city. **$$$**

Unique
4700 Avenida Brigadeiro Luis Antonio, Jardim Paulista
Tel: 11-3055 4710
www.hotelunique.com.br
São Paulo's most stylish and sought-after boutique hotel designed by Ruy Ohtake. It has a fitness center and a great pool area with city views.. The equally stylish Skye bar and restaurant is one of São Paulo's best. DJ from 9 pm. 85 rooms and 10 suites. **$$$$**

Atibaia

Estancia Atibainha
I Via Dom Pedro, Km 55
Tel: 11-3331 3114
www.hotelestanciaatibainha.com.br
A popular spot for weekend breaks, although it does have a business center and a health club. There are 95 chalets with one or two bedrooms, seven pools, tennis, horseback riding; trails. **$$$**

Campos do Jordão

Grande Hotel Campos do Jordão
3549 Avenida Frei Orestes Girardi, Capivari
Tel: 12-3668 6000
Reservations tel: 0800-770 0790
www.grandehotelsenac.com.br
A traditional casino turned into a luxurious hotel in breathtaking natural surroundings. Art Nouveau-style decor. Good infrastructures for adults and children, who even have their own restaurant. The adult restaurant, Araucária, is highly rated and one of the best in the region. **$$$$**

Vila Casato
297 Rua André Kotchkoff, Villa Capivari
Tel: 12-3663 7341
www.villacasato.com.br
A mansion transformed into a luxurious pousada. One of the best in Brazil and top choice for many in Campos do Jordão. Italian styling. Six suites. Spa. **$$$$**

Caraguatatuba

Pousada da Tabatinga
Estrada Caraguatatuba–Ubatuba, Praia Tabatinga
Tel: 12-3884 6010
www.hotelpousadatabatinga.com.br
Stylish eco resort on a great beach, with all facilities. Fifty-four comfortable and well-equipped suites. Relaxed restaurant. **$$$$**

Guarujá

Casa Grande Hotel Resort & Spa
1001 Avenida Miguel Stefano, Praia da

PRICE CATEGORIES

Price categories are for a double room. Breakfast is usually, but not always, included:

$ = under US$120
$$ = US$120–250
$$$ = US$250–400
$$$$ = over US$400

TRANSPORTATION

ACCOMMODATIONS

ACTIVITIES

A – Z

LANGUAGE

Enseada
Tel: 13-3389 4000
www.casagrandehotel.com.br
A well-equipped, colonial-style hotel with resort and spa facilities, located 70km from São Paulo, or just 15 minutes by helicopter. This is a landmark hotel for Paulistas heading for the coast, and a good choice for families. Four bars and five restaurants. Good pool and beach services.. 268 rooms. **$$$$**

Delphin Hotel
1295 Avenida Miguel Stefano, Praia da Enseada
Tel: 13-3797 6000
www.delphinhotel.com.br
More modest than the Casa Grande, and dated but also on the beach front, for a quick break from São Paulo. **$$$**

Sofitel Jequitimar Guaruja
1100 Avenida Marjori da Silva Prado, Praia de Pernambuco
Tel: 13-2104 2000
www.accorhotels.com
Opened in 2007, this modern hotel is giving Casa Grande a run for its money. Luxury resort property with

highly rated Le Spa. Five restaurants and three bars, including the highly rated dinner-only Les Epices, and one for the children. Pool, water sports, tennis, and golf. 301 rooms. **$$$**

DPNY Beach Hotel
7668 Avenida José Pacheco do Nascimento, Praia do Curral
Tel: 12-3894 3000
www.dpnybeach.com.br
Luxury, award-winning stylish beach-front hotel and spa with plenty of charm; aimed at a crowd that wants to party and be seen. There is a large pool and deck, a beach club, water sports, and nice gardens. The Troia restaurant is highly regarded in its own right, and there is also a sushi bar and Sunday brunch. 83 luxury suites. **$$$$**

Pousada Canto da Praia
793 Avenida Forca Expedicionaria Brasileira, Praia de Santa Teresa
Tel: 12-3896 1194
www.cantodapraiailhabela.com.br
Relaxed, rustic elegance in a converted fisherman's house located right beside the ocean. Five suites. **$$$**

Avenida Palace
10 Avenida Presidente Wilson, Gonzaga
Tel: 13-3289 3555
www.avenidapalace.com.br
Modest, dated, yet pleasant and comfortable, right on the beach front. Restaurant overlooks the beach. 94 rooms. **$$**

Mendes Plaza
42 Avenida Floriano Peixoto, Gonzaga
Tel: 13-3208 6400
www.mendeshoteis.com.br
A central, modern, upmarket option, with good facilities. Split between two towers are 240 well-equipped rooms split between two towers. Pool and pool bar. **$$$**

Ubatuba

Solar das Aguas Cantantes
Estrada do Saco da Ribeira s/n, Praia do Lázaro
Tel: 12-3842 0178
www.solardasaguascantantes.com.br
This is an attractive hotel, with gardens, pool, and a good seafood restaurant. 20 basic rooms. **$$$**

MINAS GERAIS

Belo Horizonte

Belo Horizonte Othon Palace
1050 Avenida Afonso Pena, Centro
Tel: 31-2126 0000
www.othon.com.br
One of Belo's most traditional hotels; large and impersonal, but with 295 spacious, comfortable rooms and suites, all facilities, and central location. The Varandão Bar and Restaurant on the 25th floor offers panoramic views of the city. **$$$$**

Comodoro Tourist
508 Rua dos Carijós, Centro
Tel: 31-3201 5522
www.comodorotouristhotel.com.br
Very basic, dated but central accommodations that offer good value for money. 60 rooms. **$$**

Ouro Minas Palace
4001 Avenida Cristiano Machado
Tel: 31-3429 4001
www.ourominas.com.br
Considered one of the best in town, with a modern business complex and health center, and 301 elegant rooms spread over 25 floors. Ouro Minas is known for its good service. Part of the Summit Hotel and Resorts group. Quinto do Ouro restaurant, fitness center and pool. **$$$$**

Royal Savassi Boutique Hotel
699 Rua Alagoas, Savassa
Tel: 31-2138 0000
www.royalhoteis.com.br

Well-located modern business hotel with 84 rooms. One of four very acceptable options in Belo Horizonte offered by the Royal Towers group. **$$$**

Diamantina

Diamante Palace
1050 Avenida Sílvio Félicio dos Santos
Tel: 038-3531 1561
www.diamantepalace.com.br/
Comfortable hotel with 48 rooms, located at the entrance to the town. Restaurant with panoramic views and a bar. **$**

Pousada do Garimpo
265 Avenida da Saudade, Consolação
Tel: 038-3532 1040
www.pousadadogarimpo.com.br
Probably the area's best-equipped hotel; basic but pleasant with 58 rooms and a small pool. Good service. Ten-minute walk to town center. **$$**

Ouro Preto

Estalagem das Minas Gerais
Rodovia dos Inconfidentes, Km 87
Tel: 31-3551 2122
www.sescmg.com.br/
In its own grounds, 6km (4 miles) outside Ouro Preto, with panoramic views, restaurant and pool. Good for families who need space. 160 rooms and 48 chalets. **$$$**

Grande Hotel de Ouro Preto

164 Rua das Flores
Tel: 31-3551 1488
www.grandehotelouropreto.com.br
The great Oscar Niemeyer designed this attractive, Modernist hotel in the 1940s, which contrasts with its colonial setting. Restaurant with panoramic view over city. Centrally located, with a pool, also designed by Niemeyer, and deck. 35 rooms. **$$**

Luxor Ouro Preto
16 Rua Dr. Alfredo Baeta
Tel: 31-3551 2244
www.luxorhoteis.com.br
Converted colonial mansion in the historic center, a five-minute walk from Praça Tiradentes. 18 rooms. **$$$**

Pousada do Mondego
38 Largo de Coimbra
Tel: 31-3551 2040/3551 3094
www.mondego.com.br
An attractive old building dating from 1747 in the colonial heart of town, with well-furnished and comfortable rooms. The place to stay to really soak up the historic atmosphere of Ouro Preto. 24 rooms, some with views over the city. **$$$**

Solar do Rosario
270 Rua Getulio Vagas, Rosario
Tel: 32-3551 5200
www.hotelsolardorosario.com.br
Charming and very comfortable converted colonial house. Slightly away from the center of town. If street

noises worry you, ask for a room overlooking the courtyard. **$$$**

Solar da Ponte
Praça das Merces
Tel: 32-3355 1255
www.solardaponte.com.br
Tiradentes is one of the best places to be based for exploring the historic towns of Minas Gerais, and without question the best place to . stay in Tiradentes is this delightful colonial mansion, which opened as a pousada in 1974. Just 18 really attractive rooms. Garden with pool. **$$$**

SOUTHERN STATES

Plaza Blumenau
818 Rua 7 de Setembro
Tel: 47-3231 7000
Reservations, tel: 0800-471 213
www.plazahoteis.com.br
A luxury, old-fashioned hotel, considered by many to be the best in town, with business facilities. Good service. Terrace Restaurant. Pool. Located on main street. **$$$**

Pousada Quinta dos Marques
200 Rua Gravataí
Santa Teresinha
Tel: 54-3282 9812
www.quintadosmarques.com.br
Designed for pure and sensual indulgence, the charming *pousada* offers many delights, including massages in the middle of the forest. Pool and 12 rooms. **$$$**

Deville Rayon
1424 Rua Visconde de Nacar, Centro
Tel: 41-2108 1100
www.deville.com.br
Located close to 'Rua 24-Horas,' and the business heart of the city, this is considered one of the best hotels in town for both business and leisure travel. Spa, fitness center, and heated pool. 136 rooms. **$$$**
Four Points by Sheraton
4211 Avenida Sete de Setembro, Agua Verde
Tel: 41-3340 4000
www.starwoodhotels.com
Aimed at the business traveler, with 165 well-equipped, modern rooms. Indoor pool. Spa. Cantanzaro Italian restaurant. Good brunch. Good central location. **$$$**
Mercure Curitiba Golden
2044 Rua Desembargador Motta, Batel
Tel: 41-3322 7666
www.mercure.com
Well located and well priced to take advantage of the city's better restaurants and bars in the Batel area. The city also offers four other Mercure hotels. All well-priced online. **$$$**

Blue Tree Towers Florianópolis
2304 Rua Bocaiuva, Centro
Tel: 48-3251 5555
www.bluetree.com.br
Great sea views at a hotel conveniently located among bars, restaurants, and shopping centers, including Beria Mar, in the town center. Rooftop pool. Part of the Brazilian Blue Tree group. 95 rooms. **$$$**
Costão do Santinho Resort & Spa
Rodovia Vereador Onildo Lemos 2505, Praia do Santinho
Tel: 48-3261 1000
www.costao.com.br
Award-winning resort that is considered one of the most comprehensive and luxurious in the south. Sports facilities include golf, tennis, canoeing, swimming, and soccer. **$$$$**
Il Campanario
1760 Avenida dos Buzios, Jureré Internacional
Tel: 48-3261 6000
www.ilcampanario.com.br
Sophisticated upmarket resort hotel with excellent facilities within a luxury condominium. Minimum three-day stay in high season. Best rooms in the city. Opened its doors in 2009. **$$$$**
Intercity Premium
1210 Avenida Paulo Fontes, Centro
Tel: 48-3027 2200
www.intercityhotel.com.br
Modern executive hotel located close to Florianópolis' historical market; 121 rooms with bay views. Pool. Wi-fi. **$$**
Pousada da Vigia
291 Rua Conego Walmor Castro, Praia da Lagoinha
Tel: 48-3284 1789
www.pousadavigia.com.br
Built on a rise above the beach, this charming pousada, known locally as the Governor's house, has beautiful sea views. Two suites have their own sun decks; seafront rooms have balconies. Heated swimming pool. Jacuzzi. Delicious breakfasts. **$$$**
Pousada Penareia
207 Rua Hermes Guedes da Fonseca, Praia da Armação
Tel: 48-338 1616
www.pousadapenareia.com.br
Ideal for couples having an indulgent holiday. Some rooms have air conditioning, hydro, and large verandas. Overlooking beach with beach deck. Peaceful. **$$$**
Quinta das Videiras
113 Rua Afonso Luis Borba, Lagoa da Conceição
Tel: 48-3232 3005
www.quintadasvideiras.com.br
Romantic and charming boutique hotel based on a 19th-century Portuguese residence. Close to bars and restaurants. Impeccable service. No children under 12. 11 rooms. **$$$**

Bourbon Resort
Avenida das Cataratas, Km 2
Tel: 45-3521 3900
www.bourbon.com.br
Traditional, large, well-equipped family-focused resort with a pool and spa. Convention center, Located close to the entry to the park. 310 rooms and suites. **$$$**
Hotel das Cataratas
Iguaçu National Park
Tel: 45-2102 7000
www.hoteldascataratas.com
The only hotel actually in the park and overlooking the falls. Gives access to the falls when the park is closed, including at night when falls can be viewed in the moonlight. Colonial-style building totally refurbished since being taken over by Orient-Express group. Delightful pool area. Restaurants and bars are open to non-guests. Worth the price if this may be your only visit to the falls. **$$$$**
Nadai Confort
1332 Avenida República Argentina
Tel: 45-3521 5050
www.nadaiconforthotel.com.br
Centrally located, well priced, comfortable executive hotel; pool and sauna. Kids club. 139 rooms and suites. **$$**

Gramado

La Hacienda Estalagem
4200 Estrada da Serra Grande (access on RS-115, Km 37 to Taquara)
Tel: 54-3295 3025
www.lahacienda.com.br
Sophisticated, attractive replica of the farms established by European immigrants in the 1800s. Six cottages for up to four people. Delightful restaurant. Own trails and tracks. **$$$$**

Saint Andrews
171 Rua das Flores,
Tel: 54-3295 7700
www.saintandrews.com.br
A member of Relais e Chateau, this is one of the most luxurious and sophisticated small hotels in Brazil. Amenities include lovely gardens, a library, indoor pool, spa and sauna. In a beautiful setting, overlooking Quilombo Valley. 11 suites. **$$$$**

Serrano Resort
1480 Avenida das Hortênsias
Tel: 54-3295 8000
www.gjphoteis.com.br
Award-winning, comfortable, and traditional resort and convention hotel. Good base from which to explore the charms of Gramado and surrounding area. 272 rooms. **$$$$**

Laguna

Laguna Tourist
Praia do Gi Km 4
Tel: 48-3647 0022
www.lagunatourist.com.br
A large, modern hotel on, and over looking, the beach. It has good views and great facilities. Best in area. **$$$**

Nova Petrópolis

Recanto Suiço
2195 Avenida 15 de Novembro
Tel: 54-3281 1229
www.recantosuico.com.br
Small, cozy, traditional, Swiss-style hotel. Fifteen air-conditioned rooms in chalets, a bar, restaurant, and swimming pool. **$$**

Porto Alegre

Embaixador
354 Rua Jerônimo Coelho, Centro
Tel: 51-3215 6600
www.embaixador.com.br
Comfortable, traditional and classical, if dated, business hotel; efficient service. Fitness center. 182 rooms. **$$$**

InterCity Premium
2105 Av. Borges de Medeiros, Bairro Praia de Belas
Tel: 51-3022 9100
www.intercityhoteis.com.br
Well-located modern, well-priced executive hotel from the InterCity group, which also offers InterCity Express Porto Alegre. Bistro restaurant. Rooftop pool with panoramic views of the city. 120 rooms. **$$$**

Plaza São Rafael Hotel
Avenida Alberto Bins 514, Centro
Tel: 51-3220 7000
Reservations, tel: 0800-512 244
www.plazahoteis.com.br
A luxury hotel, one of the best in Porto Alegre, with the best convention facilities. Located in the old downtown area. Some rooms have lovely the river views. **$$$$**

Sheraton
18 Rua Olavo Barreto Viana, Moinhos de

Vento
Tel: 51-2121 6000
www.starwoodhotels.com
Modern hotel with 170 tastefully decorated guest rooms. Located in an exclusive neighborhood of Porto Alegre, close to good restaurants, bars, and Moinhos Shopping Center. Nice city views, a bistro restaurant, health club, and pool. **$$$$**

Praia Rosa/Garopaba

Pousada Caminho do Rei
Caminho do Alto do Morro s/n
Tel: 48-3355 6062
www.caminhodorei.com.br
Lovely place, built in the 1980s. Glorious views; nine comfortable rooms in bright, clean colors. Nice pool deck with views over the sea. Home theater and sauna. **$$**

Quinta do Bucanero
Estrada Geral do Rosa s/n (off BR-1-1)
Tel: 48-3355 6056
www.bucanero.com.br
Attractive, romantic, relaxing *pousada* in a glorious setting close to the Praia do Rosa beach (about 70km/45 miles from Florianópolis). Just ten rooms, each with a balcony and panoramic views. There is a small pool as well as beach service. Part of Roteiros de Charme. No children under 14. **$$**

Vida Sol e Mar
Estrada Geral da Praia do Rosa, Imbituba
Tel: 48-3355 6111
www.vidasolemar.com.br
An attractive and homely beach village and eco-resort that pioneered special trips for whale-watching in the region; there is also birdwatching and horseback riding. The Mediterranean restaurant has views over Praia do Rosa. **$$$**

BRASÍLIA

Carlton
Setor Hoteleiro Sul, Quadra 5, Bloco G
Tel: 61-3224 8819
www.carltonhotelbrasilia.com.br
Standard and slightly dated business hotel in a convenient location with all the usual facilities. Pool. 195 rooms. **$$$**

Golden Tulip Brasília
Setor Hoteleiro Norte, Trecho 01, Lote 1B, Bloco A–B
Tel: 61-3429 8000
www.goldentulipbrasiliaalvorada.com
Part of the same complex as the grander Royal Tulip (see page 355), but not right on the lake as it sits behind its more luxurious sister hotel. Leisure facilities shared between the two hotels, including marina and spa. About a 15-minute drive to Downtown

(and the sights) or the airport. 448 rooms. **$$$**

Kubitschek Plaza
Setor Hoteleiro Norte, Quadra 2, Bloco E, Asa Norte
Tel: 61-3329 3333/3329 3655
www.kubitschek.com.br
Very comfortable, if a little dated, well situated for exploring the heart of Brasília. Like many hotels in Brasília, look for special deals at the weekend. Part of the Plaza Brasília group that operates the Manhattan Plaza, Brasília Plaza, and St Paul Plaza in the city. **$$$$**

Meliá Brasíl 21
Setor Hoteleiro Sul, Quadra 6, Bloco D
Tel: 61-3218 4700
www.solmelia.com
Modern, international business hotel,

centrally and conveniently located for seeing the city's sights. Pool and fitness center. Norton Grill and Churchill Lounge Bar. One of Brasília's top choices. **$$$**

Nacional
Setor Hoteleiro Sul, Quadra 1, Bloco A
Tel: 61-3321 7575
www.hotelnacional.com.br
The Nacional is old-fashioned, and dated, but a landmark in its own way.. Opened in 1961 as the city's first luxury hotel, over the years it has hosted kings, queens and other heads of state, including Jimmy Carter when he was the US president. **$$**

Nobile Lakeside Convention & Resort
Setor Hoteleiro Norte, Trecho 01, Lote II

Tel: 61-4062 5323
www.nobilehoteis.com.br
Pleasantly situated by the lakeside, this is a modern resort that has a marina where you can rent jet-skis and boats. Good value, and there are excellent resort facilities. Nice pool area. **$$$**

Royal Tulip Brasília
Setor Hoteleiro Norte,
Trecho 01, Conjunto 1B,
Bloco C
Tel: 61-3424 7000
www.royaltulipbrasiliaalvorada.com
A large (395-room) modern hotel, by the lake, with excellent facilities

and a convention center. Many rooms with lake views, and all have balconies. One of the best hotels in the city, although not the most central. Large pool area overlooking the lake. Previously the Blue Tree Park. **$$$$**

CENTER WEST (PANTANAL)

Bonito

Muito Bonito
1448 Rua Cel. Pilad Rebua
Tel: 67-3255 1645
www.muitobonito.com.br
Attractive and simple hostel on main street. Comfortable rooms; helpful English-speaking owner can arrange excursions to the Pantanal and to the attractions around Bonito. **$**

Zagaia Eco-Resort
Rodovia Bonito–Três Morros, Km 0
Tel: 67-3255 5500
www.zagaia.com.br
Upmarket, a little way out of town, popular with Brazilian visitors. Modern, comfortable apartments; large pool, good leisure facilities, and restaurant. **$$**

Campo Grande

Bristol Exceler Plaza
444 Avenida Afonso Pena, Amambaí
Tel: 67-3312 2800
www.bristolhoteis.com.br
Smart, modern, comfortable high-rise with pool, tennis, good breakfast, friendly service. Just out of town; convenient for airport if you are going to have to overnight in Campo Grande before or after traveling to a lodge in the Pantanal. 102 rooms. **$$**

International
223 Allan Kardec
Tel: 67-3784 4900
www.hotelintermetro.com.br

Good, modern budget hotel near the bus station. Small pool, 100 impersonal but comfortable rooms, all conveniences. Incredible buffet breakfast. Five minutes from the airport if needed for a stopover. The group also owns and operates the Hotel Metropolitan. **$$**

Corumbá

Pousada do Cachimbo
4 Rua Alen Kardec, Bairro Dom Bosco
Tel: 67-3231 4833
www.pousadadocachimbo.com.br
A five-minute drive from town, this traditional farmhouse, which became a pousada in 1980, has 14 air-conditioned apartments, a pool, and views over the river. Friendly, helpful staff. **$$**

Cuiaba

Deville Cuiabá
1000 Avenida Isaac Povoas
Tel: 63-3319 3000
www.deville.com.br
Centrally located executive hotel of a good standard. Look for deals at the weekend. One of the city's best and most comfortable, modern option if having to overnight in Cuiaba before or after visiting a lodge in the Pantanal. Fifteen minutes from the airport. Pool and spa. 174 rooms. **$$$**

Intercity Premium Cuiabá
64 Rua Presidente Arthur Bernardes,

Bairro Goiabeiras
Tel: 65-3025 9900
www.intercityhoteis.com.br
Modern executive hotel close to the city's best bars and restaurants. Spacious rooms. Solid choice for stopovers. **$$$**

Gran Odara Hotel
8344 Avenida Miguel Sutil, Ribeirão da Ponte
Tel: 65-3616 2014
http://en.hotelgranodara.com.br/hotel
New luxury hotel for the World Cup in 2014. A good option for overnighting on the way to or from lodges in the Pantanal, or if in town on business. Fitness center and spa. **$$$$**

Mato Grosso Palace Hotel
170 Rua Joaquim Murtinho
Tel: 65-3614 7000
www.hotelmt.com.br
Comfortable but simple rooms, and a very central location. Good breakfast spread. Price may be the main attraction. 136 units. **$$**

Paiaguas Palace hotel
1718 Rubens de Mendonça
Tel: 65-3642 5353
www.hotelmt.com.br
A large (262-room), centrally located, executive hotel with good facilities. Comfortable and clean rooms. Wi-fi. Same owner as Mato Grosso Palace. Look for online deals, especially at weekends. **$$$**

BAHIA

Arraial d'Ajuda

Arraial d'Ajuda Ecoresort
Ponta do Apaga Fogo
Tel: 73-3575 8500
www.arraialresort.com.br
Excellent upmarket eco-resort offering elegant rooms and facilities. Rooms have ocean, river, or garden views. Guests have free entry to the neighboring water park. Special green fees at Terravista Golf Club. **$$$$**

Maitei
475 Estrada do Mucuge

Tel: 73-3575 3877
www.maitei.com.br
Sophisticated yet unpretentious property with 17 rooms and magnificent sea views. Located above the beach. **$$$**

Ilhéus

Transamérica Ilha de Comandatuba
Estrada P/Canavieiras, Km 77, Una
Tel: 73-3686 1122
www.transamerica.com.br
Constantly listed amongst Brazil's

best resort properties. A top-class resort hotel, 75km (45 miles) from Ilhéus with 363 rooms, including

PRICE CATEGORIES

Price categories are for a double room. Breakfast is usually, but not always, included:
$ = under US$120
$$ = US$120–250
$$$ = US$250–400
$$$$ = over US$400

suites and bungalows. Amenities include a highly rated golf course, tennis center, and a spa by Clarins. **$$$$**

Itacaré

Txai
Itacaré
Tel: 73-2101 5000/11-2627 6363
www.txai.com.br
One of the country's best, most fashionable, and most exclusive boutique resorts. As popular with the international jet set as wealthy Paulistas. Shamash Spa. 14 apartments, 26 bungalows. **$$$$**

Lençóis/Chapada Diamantina

Hotel Canto das Aguas
01 Avenida Senhor dos Passos
Tel: 75-3334 1154
www.lencois.com.br
Delightful, comfortable hotel in superb gardens with pool. Close to historic center and a great base from which to explore the Chapada Diamantina. Considered the best in the region. **$$$**
Hotel de Lençóis

747 Rua Altina Alves
Tel: 71-3334 1102
www.hoteldelencois.com.br
Pleasant garden and pool; extra large rooms make it good for families. Set above the town and another solid choice for visiting the Chapada. 50 rooms. **$$**

Pôrto Seguro

Poty Praia Hotel
140 Rua dos Ibiscos,
Praia de Taperapuan
Tel: 73-3679 1203
www.poty.com.br
One of the best budget alternatives in town offering 60 comfortable and functional rooms close to the beach. An option to the many, large resort properties in the region. **$$**

Praia do Forte

Iberostar Bahia Resort
Rodovia BA 099, Km 56,
Praia do Forte
Tel: 71-3676 4300
www.iberostar.com.br
Large, well-equipped resort and spa, one of the largest in Brazil (536

rooms), 56km (36 miles) north of Salvador and close to pretty town of Praia do Forte. All-inclusive property. Golf course. **$$$**

Trancoso

Etnia Pousada
Trancoso
Tel: 73-3668 1137
www.etniabrasil.com.br
A small, very exclusive pousada in the delightful wooded surroundings of the 'global village' of Trancoso. Offers eight themed bungalows with terraces and private gardens. Also has its own fashionable boutique. **$$$**
Villas de Trancoso
Trancoso
Tel: 73-3668 1151
www.villasdetrancoso.com
A private villa retreat, pousada and boutique hotel on a stunning beach 1.5km (1 miles) from Trancoso. Just five private villas, plus one larger house that can accommodate up to eight guests. One of the region's best. Bordering the Terravista golf course. **$$$$**

SALVADOR

Bahia Othon Palace
2456 Avenida Oceânica, Ondina
Tel: 71-2103 7100
www.othon.com.br.
Traditional Salvador hotel from the 1970s, so slightly dated compared with more modern properties, but rooms larger than newer builds. Good location for beach and sightseeing. Comfortable rooms; good ocean and city views. **$$$$**
Catherina Paraguaçu
128 Rua João Gomes Rio Vermelho
Tel: 71-3334 0089
www.hotelcatharinaparaguacu.com.br
Charming, well-located family-run budget hotel set in an old mansion from the 19th century. Lively neighborhood with bars and restaurants. **$$**
Club Med Itaparica
Rodovia Bom Despacho, Nazaré, Km 13,
Ilha de Itaparica, Vera Cruz
Tel: 71-3881 7141
www.clubmed.com.br
Located on the magical island of Itaparica, across the bay from Salvador, with all expected Club Med facilities. This was one of the first resorts of an international standard to open in Brazil. A destination in its own right, however, not the place to base yourself for

sightseeing in Salvador. **$$$$**
Pestana Bahia
216 Rua Fonte do Boi, Rio Vermelho
Tel: 71-2103 8000
www.pestana.com
Same owner as the Convento do Carmo. Comfortable, modern seafront hotel with panoramic views from all rooms. Something of a modern landmark since first opening as the Meridien in the 1970s. 410 rooms and 20 suites. **$$$**
Pestana Convento do Carmo
1 Rua do Carmo, Pelourinho
Tel: 71-3327 8400
www.pestana.com
Luxurious and stylish hotel in a restored 16th-century convent that has been setting new standards for accommodations and service in Salvador. One of the city's best and most attractive places to stay and soak up the history in comfort and style. **$$$$**
Pousada Redfish
1 Ladeira do Boqueirão,
Santo Antônio
Tel: 71-3241 0639
www.hotelredfish.com
Attractive and functional pousada in restored historical house, a short walk from the Pelourinho. Rebuilt

and run by an English artist. Good breakfasts. **$$$**
Solar dos Deuses – Suítes de Charme
12 Largo do Cruzeiro do São Francisco
Tel: 71-3322 1911
www.solardosdeuses.com.br
Another pleasant and comfortable pousada in the heart of the historic center, located in a building dating back to the 17th century. The seven suites are named after the candomblé gods. **$$**
Tropical da Bahia
1537 Avenida 7 de Setembro, Campo Grande
Tel: 71-3352 4856
www.tropicalbahia.com.br
Traditional if slightly dated hotel close to the city center with 275 rooms spread over 12 floors. An excellent location for Carnival. **$$$$**
Villa Bahia
Largo do Cruzeiro do São Francisco 16
Tel: 71-3322 4271
www.lavillabahia.com
Lovely boutique hotel in the old town set in two mansions. Seventeen rooms carefully renovated to preserve their historical spirit. Two garden courtyards with plunge pool. Charming restaurant. A gem. **$$$**

SERGIPE AND ALAGOAS

Aracaju

San Manuel Praia
75 Rua Niceu DantasAtalaia
Tel: 79-218 5200
www.sanmanuelpraiahotel.com.br
A pleasant and modest budget hotel just one block from beach. Wi-fi and courtyard pool. The hotel has 67 rooms and suites, some with beach views. **$**

Pousada Praia e Mar
433 Avenida Santos Dumont, Atalaia
Tel: 79-3243 4520
www.hotelpraiaemar.com.br
A nice, simple budget hotel near the beach with 37 functional rooms. Well located for beach and sightseeing. **$**

Radisson Aracaju
40 Rua Dr. Bezerra De Menezes, Atalia
Tel: 79-3711 3300
www.atlanticahotels.com.br

An efficient, modern hotel on Atalia beach. Well located, well maintained, and popular for both business and leisure travelers; one of the city's best-equipped to cater for both markets. **$$$**

Maceió

Hotel Praia Bonita
943 Avenida Dr. Antônio Gouveia Pajucara
Tel: 82-2121 3700
www.praiabonita.com.br
Well located, modest but comfortable hotel overlooking Pajucara beach, which is across the road. Ask for a room at the front with a sea view. Close to restaurants and artisan market. Small pool. **$$**

Radisson Maceió
40 Rua Dr. Bezerra De Menezes, Atalia
Tel: 82-3202 4900

www.atlanticahotels.com.br
A modern business and leisure hotel from the expanding Atlantica group. Like many cities in the Northeast, Radisson is offering both business and leisure travelers the facilities and service they require. This property is on the city's best beach but also offers a rooftop pool with views over the ocean and beach. **$$$**

Ritz Praia Hotel
1300 Rua Eng. Mario de Gusmao Ponta Verde
Tel: 82-2121 4600
www.ritzpraia.com.br
Budget accommodation, pleasant rooms with air conditioning, TV and Wi-fi; 50 meters/yds from beach. English spoken. Bar and dip pool on roof with views to beach and ocean. 53 rooms. **$**

RECIFE AND PERNAMBUCO

Olinda

Pousada do Amparo
199 Rua do Amparo
Tel: 81-3439 1749
www.pousadadoamparo.com.br
An attractive, stylish *pousada* in an historic building. Luxury rooms are available on request, and most are shown on the website. A branch of the wonderful Beijupirá restaurant operates in the *pousada*, with views over Olinda and Recife. **$$$$**

Pousada dos Quatro Cantos
441 Rua Prudente de Moraes Carmo
Tel: 81-3429 0220
www.pousada4cantos.com.br
Small, simple, and pleasant, in a 19th-century mansion in the historic center. Just two suites and sixteen rooms. Sits on the corner of what is the heart of Olinda's carnival activities. **$$**

Sete Colinas
307 Rua São Francisco
Tel: 81-3439 6055
www.hotel7colinas.com.br
In the historic heart of Olinda, with delightful gardens and a pool area. Four suites and 44 basic, but comfortable rooms. Has its own museum of 19th century furniture. **$$$**

Porto de Galinhas

Hotel Armação
Lot. Merepe II, Quadra G1, Lote 1 A
Tel: 81-3311 6000
www.hotelarmacao.com.br
Family-run hotel in a great location on

one of the best parts of one of Brazil's best beaches; three pools (one on the beach), tennis, live entertainment. Just 2km (1.2 miles) from the center of Porto Galinhas. Excellent value. **$$$**

Nannai Beach Resort
Access via Km 2 on PE-009 Praia de Muro Alto
Tel: 81-3552 0100
www.nannai.com.br
Upmarket beach-front Polynesian-style resort, including some bungalows with private pools. Has set the levels for the other top resorts in the area to aspire to. Top spa destination. Pitch and putt golf. Tennis. **$$$$**

Pousada Tabapitanga
Access via Km 3 on PE-009 Praia do Cupe
Tel: 81-3552 1037
www.tabapitanga.com.br
Forty-five comfortable and colorful chalet-style bungalows with air conditioning, directly on the beach, just 5km (3 miles) from Porto de Galinhas. Ocean view restaurant. **$$**

Summerville Beach Resort
Gleba 6a, Praia de Muo Alto
Tel: 81-3302 5555
www.summervilleresort.com.br
First five-star resort in the region on opening in 2000. Apartments, suites, and bungalows. Extensive grounds and pool area. An excellent child-friendly resort for families, with a children's club, playground, and even a children's restaurant. 202 rooms. **$$$$**

Recife

Hotel Atlante Plaza
5426 Avenida Boa Viagem, Boa Viagem
Tel: 81-3302 3333
www.atlanteplaza.com.br
One of the best and most reliable hotels in Recife, right on the Boa Viagem seafront. Panoramic elevator. 241 rooms and 18 suites. **$$$$**

Beach Class Suites
1906 Avenida Boa Viagem, Boa Viagem
Tel: 81-2121 2626
www.beachclasssuites.com
Modern executive hotel located on Boa Viagem beach close to the best restaurants. Spectacular beach views. Large rooms. Lively area of the beach. **$$$**

Best Western Manibu Recife
919 Avenida Conselheiro Aguiar, Boa Viagem
Tel: 81-3084 2811
www.hotelmanibu.com.br
A well-run hotel that offers excellent value for money for those on a limited budget but who want to stay in and around Boa Viagem. Small rooftop pool. Good restaurants close by. **$$**

Cult Hotel
755 Avenida Conselheiro Aguiar,

PRICE CATEGORIES

Price categories are for a double room. Breakfast is usually, but not always, included:
$ = under US$120
$$ = US$120–250
$$$ = US$250–400
$$$$ = over US$400

Boa Viagem
Tel: 81-2123 2777
http://culthotel.com.br
Simple hotel-cum-art gallery, with the emphasis on local culture. Located close to Boa Viagem beach, Cult Hotel offers something a little different and more imaginative than the standard city and beach hotels. Owner also runs the very budget Hotel das Art. 60 rooms. **$$$**

Dorisol Recife Grand Hotel
1624 Avenida Bernardo Vieira de Melo, Piedade
Tel: 81-2122 2700
www.dorisol.com/dorisol-recife-grand-hotel/hotel.html
The Dorisol is a modernish hotel located right on Praia de Piedade, to the south of the city. Take note if you want to be in Boa Viagem. All 198 rooms, all with have sea views. Two

pools. **$$$**
Mar Hotel Recife
451 Rua Barão de Souza Leão, Boa Viagem
Tel: 81-3302 4444
www.marhotel.com.br
A modern, standard business hotel, 10 minutes' walk from the beach at Boa Viagem. There are rooms with balconies, and a good pool area. Good restaurant choice close by. 214 rooms. **$$$**

THE FAR NORTHEAST

Fortaleza

Gran Marquise
3980 Avenida Beira Mar, Meirelles
Tel: 85-4006 5000
www.granmarquise.com.br
One of Fortaleza's most elegant and well-equipped hotels. Also well located. Popular for both business and leisure travelers. New executive floors added in 2012. Its Nostradamus restaurant is one of the best in the city. **$$$$**
Praiano Palace
2800 Avenida Beira Mar, Meirelles
Tel: 85-4008 2200
www.praiano.com.br
Refurbished, four-star, although possibly three by European and US standards. The Thames restaurant serves regional and international dishes. **$$$**
Seara Praia Hotel
Avenida Beira Mar, Meirelles
Tel: 85-4011 2200
www.hotelseara.com.br
Good five-star hotel, although parts could be refreshed. All rooms have a sea view. The Azul de Prata restaurant specializes in dishes with a French influence. Access to large swimming pool. Well located. **$$$**
Vila Galé Fortaleza
4189 Avenida Dioguinho, Praia do Futuro
Tel: 85-3486 4400
www.vilagale.pt
A well-equipped modern resort hotel, close to the beach at Praia do Futuro. It's a little way from the town center and the main nightlife, but there is hotel shuttle bus. 300 rooms. **$$$**

João Pessoa

Caiçara
235 Avenida Olinda, Tambaú
Tel: 83-2106 1000
www.hotcaicara.com
An efficient budget hotel, part of Best Western chain; 10 minutes from center, one block from the beach. Roof top pool. 104 rooms. **$$**
Littoral Hotel & Flats
2172 Avenida Cabo Branco,

Praia de Cabo Branco
Tel: 83-2106 1100
www.hotellittoral.com.br
Rooms with sea views; smallish pool. The Malagueta restaurant offers Brazilian and international dishes. **$**
Tropical Tambaú
229 Avenida Almirante Tamandaré, Praia de Tambaú
Tel: 83-2107 1900
www.tropicalhotel.com.br
A landmark hotel since 1971 and one of the few survivors of what was the Tropical hotel group. Hotel offers comfortable, old school accommodations at a reasonable price, given its location and infrastructure. Design made it a city landmark. **$$**
Verdegreen
255 Avenida João Maurício, Manaíra
Tel: 83-3044 0000
www.verdegreen.com.br
Modern, functional eco-hotel for both business and leisure travelers. Generally high standard of service and a good base for exploring the area. **$$$**

Natal

Manary Praia Hotel
9067 Rua Francisco Gurgel, Ponta Negra Beach
Tel: 84-3204 2900
www.manary.com.br
Luxury boutique beach-front hotel on Ponta Negra, one of the city's and the northeast's nicest. Sets the standards for others in the region to follow and match. Air conditioning and internet connection in rooms. Good tours of the region. Pool. **$$$**
Ocean Palace
Via Costeira Km 11, Ponta Negra Beach
Tel: 84-3220 4144
www.oceanpalace.com.br
Comfortable, if in places dated, five-star beach-front hotel at Ponta Negra. Popular with Brazilian holidaymakers. Wi-fi internet in rooms. Good pool area. **$$**
Pestana Natal Beach Resort
5525 Avenida Senador Dinarte de Mariz, Via Costeira

Tel: 84-3220 8900
www.pestana.com
Modern, well-equipped and well-maintained all inclusive beach resort from the Pestana group. Minimum stay required in high season. **$$$**
Praia Azul Mar
92 Rua Francisco Gurgel, Ponta Negra Beach
Tel: 84-4005 3555
www.praia-azul.com
A more modest beach-front apart-hotel, close to local restaurants. Rooms have safe, cable TV, internet access. Good value option. **$$**
Serhs Natal Grand
6045 Avenida Senador Dinarte Medeiros Mariz, Via Costeira
Tel: 84-4005 2000
www.serhsnatalgrandhotel.com
Large beach-front property. Excellent facilities for families. One of the city's most modern and well-looked-after resorts. All rooms have sea views. **$$$**

Pipa

Marinas Tibau Sul
301 Avenida Gov. Alusio Alves
Tel: 84-3246 4111
www.hotelmarinas.com.br
Luxury individual chalets with views of the river and sand dunes. Large pool. Fishing and horseback riding facilities. Good tours. **$$**
Toca da Coruja
Avenida Baia dos Golfunhos, Pipa
Tel: 84-3246 2226
www.tocadacoruja.com.br
One of the northeast's first outstanding boutique hotels, which is set in its own lovely gardens, close to the beach. Not the cheapest option, but one of the best. Highly rated restaurant, Oca Toca. **$$$**

São Luís

Pestana São Luis
1 Avenida Avicênia, Praia do Calhau
Tel: 98-2106 0505
www.pestana.com
Modern, attractive and elegant hotel that appeals equally to business and leisure travelers. Located on a beach

10 minutes from the historic center. Best-equipped in São Luis. 124 rooms. **$$$**

Pousada Portas da Amazonia
129 Rua do Giz, Praia Grande
Tel: 98-3222 9937
www.portasdaamazonia.com.br
The name says it: 'Doors to the Amazon.' A pleasant *pousada*, well located in an attractive 19th-century colonial building. Twenty-nine rooms including eight master rooms with views over the historic center. A special experience. **$$**

Rio Poty Hotel
Avenida dos Holandeses s/n, Ponta D'Areia
Tel: 98-3311 1500
www.riopotysaoluis.com.br
Large, modern hotel on Ponta D'Areia beach. All 142 rooms have panoramic sea views. Beauty salon, hydromassage and saunas on offer; two restaurants and three bars. Wi-fi. Convention center. **$$**

AMAZON

Belém

Beira-Rio
4804 Avenida Bernardo Sayão, Guamá
Tel: 91-4008 9000
www.heirariohotel.com.br
Located 15 minutes from the town center on the Guamá river, which won't suit everyone coming to Belem on business. Pool and air conditioning. **$$$**

Hilton Belém
882 Avenida Presidente Vargas, Praça da República
Tel: 91-4006 7000
www.hilton.com
Dated when compared with some of the new kids on the Belém block, but still considered one of the city's best. Located in Belém commercial center next to the Teatro da Paz. **$$$**

Radisson Maiorana Belem
321 Avenda Comandante Bras do Aguir, Nazare
Tel: 91-3205 1399
www.radisson.com/www.atlanticahotels.com.br
Radisson Belem hotel is located in the charming Nazare neighborhood, and close to Belem's popular tourist and business districts. This modern hotel, which opened in 2012, offers the amenities travelers expect, including wireless internet access, onsite restaurant, fitness center, and indoor pool. Spacious guest rooms. **$$$**

Regente
485 Avenida Governador José Malcher, Nazaré
Tel: 91-3181 5000
www.hregente.com.br
Not the newest or the best, but offers modest but comfortable, three star hotel accommodations. Convenient location. **$$**

Zoghbi All Suites Hotel
100 Rua Ferreira Cantão
Tel: 91-3230 3555
www.zoghbi.com.br
Clean, friendly and modest, all-suite hotel, with small pool and restaurant. Good value and well located for both business and leisure travelers. **$$**

Manaus

Ana Cássia Palace
14 Rua dos Andradas Centro
Tel: 92-3303 3637
www.hotelanacassia.com.br
A simple budget hotel. Dated, but pleasant and centrally located. Small pool and sauna. **$$**

Caesar Business
654 Avenida Darcy Vargas, Bairro do Chapada
Tel: 92-3306 4700
www.accorhotels.com/
Solid three- to four-star business class hotel, centrally located in Manaus. Good, reliable choice if you need to overnight before going on to one of the lodges. Part of the Accor group. Pool and sauna. 229 rooms. **$$$**

Iberostar Grand Amazon
Porto de Manaus, Centro
Tel: 92-2126 9927
www.grandamazoncruises.com
A floating hotel of sorts. With 74 modern air-conditioned cabins and suites, all with private balconies from which to enjoy views of the Amazon, the ship does three- and four-night cruises from Manaus of the Rio Negro and Rio Solimões. **$$$**

Manaós
881 Avenida Eduardo Ribeiro, Centro
Tel: 92-3633 5744
www.hotelmanaos.com.br
Budget hotel next to the Teatro Amazonas; 39 basic air-conditioned rooms. **$$**

Park Suites Manaus
1320 Avenida Coronel Teixeira A, Praia da Ponta Negra
Tel: 92-3306 4500
www.atlanticahotels.com.br
A good option for business and leisure travelers. On the banks of the Rio Negro, close to the Tropical, of which it used to be almost a form of annex, the higher rooms have stunning views across the river and forest. Nice pool overlooking the river. **$$$**

Taj Mahal Continental
741 Avenida Getúlio Vargas, Centro
Tel: 92-3627 3737
www.grupotajmahal.com.br
Modern executive hotel in the center of town with 170 spacious rooms and suites. Hotel boasts a revolving rooftop restaurant that is open to non-residents of the hotel. **$$$**

Tropical
1320 Avenida Coronel Teixeira, Praia da Ponta Negra
Tel: 92-2123 5000
www.tropicalhotel.com.br
Landmark hotel and resort in its own park 12km (7 miles) from the center of Manaus, on the banks of the Amazon and River Negro. Still the number one choice for most leisure visitors to Manaus. Swimming pool and tennis courts. 556 rooms. **$$$**

Macapá

Ibis Macapá Hotel
303 Rua Tiradentes Centro
Tel: 96-3217 1350
www.accorhotels.com
Standard, modern Ibis chain hotel, that delivers everything you expect. Is probably now the most reliable and comfortable option in Macapá. **$$$**

Pousada Ekinox
1693 Rua Jovino Dinoá
Tel: 96-3223 0086
www.ekinox.com.br
Very popular little *pousada* in the center. Good base for visitors. Friendly, with a good restaurant. Wi-fi. **$$**

Santarém

Barrudada Tropical Hotel
74120 Mendonça Furtado, Liberdade
Tel: 91-222 2200
www.barrudadatropicalhotel.com.br
Choice is limited in Santarém, so while dated and nothing that special, Barrudada will tick most of the boxes if you need to spend a few nights in the city. Used to be VARIG's Hotel Tropical. **$$**

PRICE CATEGORIES

Price categories are for a double room. Breakfast is usually, but not always, included:
$ = under US$120
$$ = US$120–250
$$$ = US$250–400
$$$$ = over US$400

ACTIVITIES

THE ARTS, NIGHTLIFE, FESTIVALS, SPORTS, CHILDREN'S ACTIVITIES, AND SHOPPING

THE ARTS

Museums

Brazil's historical museums are unlikely to be at the top of most visitors' list of attractions. There are not enough resources available for proper upkeep and acquisitions – although there are some notable exceptions. Those worth visiting are described in the Places section of this book, with opening times. Temporary exhibitions are announced in the major Brazilian newspapers under Exposições.

Art galleries

Those showing the work of contemporary artists abound in the larger cities, especially Rio de Janeiro and São Paulo. The art museums also organize periodic exhibitions. Shows are listed in the papers under Exposições.

The Bienal (Biennial Art Exposition) held in São Paulo every two years (2014, 2016, etc.) from September to December, is Latin America's largest contemporary art show.

Music and dance

Music is Brazil's forte. A variety of musical forms have developed in different parts of the country, many with accompanying forms of dance. While the Brazilian influence (especially in jazz) is heard around the world, what is known of Brazilian music outside the country is just the tip of an iceberg (see page 98).

Take in a concert by a popular singer or ask your hotel to recommend a nightclub with live

Brazilian music: bossa nova, samba, choro and serenata are popular in Rio and São Paulo – each region has something different to offer. If you are visiting at Carnival, you'll hear and see plenty of music and dancing in the streets, mostly samba in Rio and frevo in the northeast. There are also shows all year long that are designed to give tourists a taste of Brazilian folk music and dance.

A rock concert in Brazil is something not to be missed if that is your taste in music. The atmosphere is unimaginable, as the audience almost becomes part of the show, a seething, vibrant, ever-moving mass of enjoyment. The music is a magical blend; undeniably rock, yet at the same time Brazilian, with Latin rhythms pumped out by swollen percussion sections seamlessly and effortlessly merging with the power of electronic amplification.

There are an increasing number of rock festivals in Brazil, of which the most famous is Rock in Rio, which currently takes place every couple of years (www.rockinrio.com/rio/).

The classical music and dance season runs from Carnival through to mid-December. Besides presentations by local talents, major Brazilian cities (mainly Rio, São Paulo, and Brasília) are included in world concert tours by international performers. One of the most important classical music festivals in South America takes place in July each year in Campos do Jordão in the state of São Paulo.

If you want to attend a live music performance, check in the weekend section of the local paper, under the heading Lazer (Leisure), which will give listings of clubs, theaters, bars and dancehalls holding concerts.

Capoeira

A uniquely Brazilian activity, *capoeira* is a relic from slavery days, when fighting, and especially training for fighting, by the slaves had to be hidden. *Capoeira* is a stylized fight-dance, with its own accompanying rhythms and music, using the feet a great deal to strike out, and requiring a graceful agility. This tradition has been kept alive chiefly in Salvador and Rio, where there are academies teaching *capoeira* (you can watch the classes free of charge). You can arrange to see a presentation or you may catch a street group performing on a beach or in a busy square (see page 105).

Theater

In order to enjoy theater, you really do have to understand the language. Rio de Janeiro and São Paulo, in particular, have busy seasons starting after Carnival and running to November.

Getting tickets

Online ticket services:
Ingresso.com: Good for advance purchase of movie tickets nationwide, also shows, and some theme parks. www.ingresso.com.br.
Ingresso Fácil: Specializes in sporting events including football matches in Rio, São Paulo, and Belo Horizonte. www.ingressofacil.com.br.
Ingresso Rapido: Tickets for shows, concerts and events across Brazil. www.ingressorapido.com.br.

Movies

Most major international films are released on the principal Brazilian circuit more or less simultaneously with their release in Europe and the US. Recent years have seen a revolution in the cinema business with the advent of modern, multiscreen venues often located in shopping centers, which means easy parking, more comfort and a wider choice. Prices in major cities are around US$15 for recent releases. People over 60 and students with the appropriate ID pay half.

Most foreign films are shown with original soundtrack and Portuguese captions (legendado), but beware – more and more films, particularly those appealing to children, may also have dubbed versions (dublado) in some theaters. Good listings will indicate 'L' and 'D' or 'Leg' and 'Dub.'

Some Brazilian films are very good (see page 108). The country is slowly gaining prominence in the industry with films such as Fernando Meirelles' City of God, which received four Oscar nominations in 2004, and José Padilha's Tropa de Elite (Elite Squad). However, unless you understand Portuguese, it's better to see Brazilian movies abroad or during film festivals, where they may have subtitles.

There are various annual film festivals: the Rio festival (Festival do Rio) takes place in September and October; São Paulo's in October; and Gramado – a small town in southern Brazil – hosts a major six-day event in August.

NIGHTLIFE

For information on nightlife in the main cities, see the relevant chapters in the Places section of this book. But beware, what is hot and happening one week can be deserted the following week. The legal drinking age in Brazil is 18, and some bars and

Celebrating Carnival in Rio.

clubs may ask young people for ID. Carry a photocopy of your passport rather than the real thing. Many nightclubs will not allow you to enter if wearing shorts. Prostitutes frequent some establishments – particularly those popular with tourists.

Major centers such as Rio and São Paulo offer all kinds of after-hours activity, including restaurants, bars, and clubs that stay open into the early hours. Brazilians love partying so even in smaller towns there is often a club open late at weekends, but beware – away from the tourist routes, people tend to go to sleep earlier, particularly during the week.

Some bars with live music charge for entry, typically US$5–15 for a decent attraction, while others may set a similar minimum spending limit per person (consumação mínima). This is technically illegal and the object of a constant battle by consumer protection agencies.

Live music in bars is usually some strain of Brazilian – samba, choro, frevo, pagode, sertanejo (country music), and the ubiquitous MPB, the latter standing for Popular Brazilian Music, and covering a host of styles including 'tropicalized' rock'n'roll.

As befits a global melting pot, São Paulo offers a wide variety, from jazz and electronic music to venues specializing in 'cover bands' from the 1960s and 1970s, such as The Doors, Led Zeppelin, and Pink Floyd. There are numerous bars and restaurants with food and music from other Latin American countries, and many offering Arabic food and shows.

FESTIVALS

Besides national holidays, many religious or historical events are commemorated locally. Each city celebrates the date on which it was founded and the day of its patron saint. Many villages and neighborhoods stage their own regional folk celebrations – usually with music, dancing, and stalls selling food and drinks associated with the event. Some of the most important festivals are listed below (see page 371).

January

1 New Year's Day
National holiday. Bom Jesus dos Navegantes a four-day celebration in Salvador starts with a spectacular boat parade.
6 Epiphany
Regional celebrations, mostly in the northeast.
3rd Sunday – Festa do Bonfim. One of the largest in Salvador.

February

2 Iemanjá Festival in Salvador. The Afro-Brazilian goddess of the sea corresponds with the Virgin Mary (also see New Year's Eve).

February/March

Carnival
National holiday celebrated on the four days leading up to and including Ash Wednesday. Dates vary depending on the date of Easter (see page 69). Most spectacular in Rio, Salvador, and Recife/Olinda.

March/April

Good Friday
National holiday. Colonial Ouro Preto puts on a procession; a Passion Play is staged at Nova Jerusalem.

April

21 Tiradentes Day
National holiday in honor of the

Splashing in the sea at Copacabana beach in Rio.

TRANSPORTATION

ACCOMMODATIONS

ACTIVITIES

A – Z

LANGUAGE

martyred hero of independence. Celebrations in his native Minas Gerais, especially Ouro Preto.

June

15–30 Amazon Folk Festival
Held in Manaus.

June/July

Bumba-Meu-Boi
Processions and street dancing in Maranhão, late June/early July.
Festas Juninas
Street festivals in June and early July in honor of saints John, Peter, and Anthony, featuring bonfires, dancing, and mock marriages.

August

Festa do Peão Boiadeiro
In Barretos, São Paulo state. The world's largest annual rodeo.

What's on

Major city newspapers have daily listings: Folha de São Paulo and Estado de São Paulo in São Paulo, O Globo in Rio. The Veja national newsweekly has regional supplements with good listings of restaurants and shows. Also, the Friday edition of the Folha de São Paulo has a handy comprehensive booklet covering the week ahead, listing cinemas, theater performances, shows, concerts, etc., with selected restaurants. It's all in Portuguese, but not too difficult to get the gist of. Most of the information is also on their websites.

Other websites
Guia da Semana (weekly guide) offers listings and reviews for cinema, shows, theater, and more in São Paulo, Rio de Janeiro, Belo Horizonte, Salvador, Porto Alegre, Brasília, Curitiba, Florianópolis, and many other cities. (Portuguese only); www.guiadasemana.com.br
Samba & Choro lists dozens of bars and dancehalls throughout Brazil that have live shows of samba and choro, two essential musical styles. There are separate pages for Rio and São Paulo. Listings include some traditional old establishments (in Portuguese only); www.samba-choro.com.br.
Veja is the most comprehensive and best guide. http://vejabrasil. abril.com.br/rio-de-janeiro/, http:// vejasp.abril.com.br, or http://veja. abril.com.br.

Festival Literaria Internacional Parati (flip)
International literature festival in idyllic Paraty, south of Rio. Attracts international authors for a laid-back, long weekend of discussion.

October

Oktoberfest
In Blumenau, staged by descendants of German immigrants.
Cirió
Religious procession in Belém.
12 Nossa Senhora de Aparecida
National holiday honoring Brazil's patron saint.

December

31 New Year's Eve
Millions gather on Rio de Janeiro beaches to watch spectacular firework displays, and to offer gifts to the goddess Iemanjá.

SPORTS

Participant sports

Aquatic sports
A large variety of aquatic sports can be enjoyed in Brazil. Almost any coastal town has boat rental facilities and many resort hotels rent sailboats, fishing tackle, jet-skis, diving gear and surf and windsurfing boards. Sailboats, speedboats or schooner-like Brazilian saveiros, can all be rented complete with equipment and crew. In Rio, go to the Marina da Gloria.
Excursion clubs arrange whitewater canoeing, kayaking and sailing outings. Rapids-shooting rafting excursions can be arranged through hotels in Rio.

Diving
Diving equipment and tuition are available. Some of the more spectacular places to dive include Fernando de Noronha island, off Brazil's most northeastern point, and the coral Abrolhos archipelago off the coast of southern Bahia. More accessible are the Sun Coast, east of Rio de Janeiro (Cabo Frio, Búzios), and the Green Coast between Rio and São Paulo (Angra dos Reis, Paraty).

Surfing
Brazil's seemingly endless coastline offers good opportunities for surfing. Saquarema, in the state of Rio de Janeiro, is the site of international championships.

Swimming
Ocean swimming is a delight, especially in the north and northeast, where the water is warm all year round. Many hotels have swimming pools, as do the private clubs. Be aware that many city beaches can be polluted.

Fishing
There is a large variety of fish, both ocean and freshwater varieties, all along the coast as well as in the rivers and the flooded Pantanal marshlands. Fishing equipment can be rented along with a boat and guide, and special fishing excursions are organized. The website www.brasilfishing.com. br is a useful resource. Professional fishermen in the northeast will sometimes take an extra passenger or two on their *jangada* rafts.

Climbing and caving
There are plenty of peaks to climb in Brazil. In Rio you can even climb the city's landmarks, Sugar Loaf mountain and Corcovado. There are excursion clubs that arrange outings to nearby mountainous regions and areas where you can go spelunking (caving). Contact one of the following:
Centro Excursionista Brasileiro, 2–8 Avenida Almirante Barroso, Centro, Rio de Janeiro CEP230031, tel: 21-2252 9844; www.ceb. org.br; **Sociedade Brasileira de Espeleologia** Caixa Postal 7031, Campinas SP, Cep 13076, tel: 19-3296 5421; www.sbe.com.br.

Cycling
Since the 1992 environment conference in Rio, good cycling facilities have been developed, including a cycle lane running the length of the Copacabana, Ipanema, Leblon, São Conrado and Barra beaches, and on to the center of Rio.

Ecotourism
This term is frequently used to describe any kind of nature or adventure tourism, and does not necessarily mean any consideration has been given to the environment. There are genuinely ecologically concerned tours on offer, but others may involve anything from catching caiman in the Amazon to fishing for piranha in the Pantanal, neither of which are sustainable activities.

Golf
Golf is not big in Brazil and there are a limited, but growing, number of public courses, and it is gaining in popularity. It is played mostly in the states of São

Paulo and Rio de Janeiro, , and there are an increasing number of courses linked to the resorts in the northeast. Country clubs are quite exclusive but you can normally arrange through a top hotel to play as a visitor. Golf has been reinstated as an Olympic sport for the 2016 games in Rio, for the first time since 1904, and a new course is being built in Barra da Tijuca.

Hang-gliding

Hang-gliding is popular, especially in Rio, where modern-day Daedaluses leap off the mountains and soar on air currents before landing on the beach below. Inexperienced flyers can go tandem with an instructor. In some places paragliding is available. Contact the AVLRJ (Associação de Vôo Livre do Rio de Janeiro; www.abvl.com. br) or Just Fly (www.justfly.com.br; tel: 21-2268 0565/21-9985 7540).

Hiking and camping

If you want to go hiking and camping, contact the Camping Clube do Brasil, 75 Rua Senador Dantas, 29° Andar, Rio de Janeiro, tel: 21-3479 4200 or 0800-227 050; www.campingclube. com.br. They have campsites throughout the country and they organize treks in out-of-the-way parts of Brazil. If you prefer to backpack on your own, check the maps available from the IGBE – Brazilian Institute of Geography and Statistics – tel: 0800-218 181; http://loja.ibge.gov.br or Quatro Rodas.

Horseback riding

The Pantanal, home of Brazilian cowboys, is a popular place for horseback riding, and a good way to see local wildlife. The old gold trails in the mountains in the southern states offer scenic rides. The country's long, open beaches are ideal for galloping along the surf.

Hunting

Hunting is illegal in Brazil. The only shooting of wildlife permitted is the kind done with a camera.

Running

Runners have a beautiful place to keep in shape while in Rio: the town beaches have wide sidewalks, with the distance marked in kilometers along the way. In São Paulo, Ibirapuera Park is a favorite spot.

The biggest races are the Rio Marathon in July (www.maratonadorio. com.br) and the São Paulo Marathon in April or May (www. maratonadesaopaulo.com.br). São Paulo and Brazil's most famous race,

Volleyball-playing locals on Ipanema beach.

however, is the São Silvestre held on January 1 (www.saosilvestre.com.br).

Tennis

Some of the larger hotels have tennis courts. There are a few public courts, but the game is played mostly at clubs. Since the charismatic 'Guga,' Gustavo Kuerten won the French Open on a number of occasions and became a top player, interest in tennis in Brazil has been on the increase.

Trekking

There are lots of places to trek in the country, whether hiking through lush forest trails, exploring scenic national parks, or climbing through mountainous regions. A local guide is usually advisable.

Volleyball

On the beaches, especially in Rio, you can spend many hours being entertained by the skill of volleyball players (Brazil has won both world and Olympic titles). The atmosphere is relaxed, though the games are often skilful, and you may be able to join in.

Spectator sports

Soccer (futebol)

This is Brazil's national sport and a passion that unites all ages and classes. During the World Cup, the country grinds to a halt as everyone tunes in to watch the matches on television.

If you're a soccer fan, arrange through your hotel to see a professional game – there are organized tours. The boisterous fans are often as interesting to watch as the actual game itself.

Especially exciting are the games

between top rival teams in Rio's Maracanã Stadium, which was totally rebuilt for the 2014 World Cup; or in São Paulo's Pacaembu Stadium, Morumbi or the new World Cup Stadium. There is rarely any violence, but it is better to get a reserved seat rather than sit in the packed bleachers (uncovered stadium seating). Many hotels can book tickets and transport – worthwhile to avoid the crush.

Most weekend afternoons you can see a fast and furious 'sand lot' match between neighborhood teams on Brazil's beaches or in the parks.

Horse racing

Horse racing is popular, and several cities have tracks. The top prize event, called the Grande Premio do Brasil, is held in the first half of August at the Rio de Janeiro track (tel: 21-3534 9000; www.jcb.com.br). In São Paulo, contact the Jockey Club (tel: 11-2161 8300; www.jockeysp.com.br).

Motor racing

Brazil is a rarity in that it is on both the Formula One and Indy Car racing circuits. The Formula One Grand Prix, which often decides the Championship, normally takes place in October or November at São Paulo's Interlagos circuit, while a street circuit is built in São Paulo to host the São Paulo Indy 300 race in May. Brazilian drivers are prominent in all categories.

CHILDREN'S ACTIVITIES

Brazilians love children, and they tolerate them to an extent that can occasionally exceed limits expected by some other cultures. If you go to a restaurant that caters to families at a weekend lunchtime, don't be surprised to have children wander up and say hello, or run around shrieking.

Major cities have children's theater and cinema – see listings in What's On – but these will be in Portuguese, and expect foreign films to be dubbed.

Theme parks are popular. Two in or around São Paulo are:

Hopi Hari, Bandeirantes Highway SP-348, exit Km 70.5. Large, fun park 70km (44 miles) north of São Paulo. There are activities for all ages: magic castles stuffed with Brazilian folklore and legends, carousels, Wild West shows, and a Rio Bravo raft ride. Current cost is US$30 per day for entry and most rides. Closed Mon and some weekdays; times vary. Tickets from tel: 4007 1134 or online at www.hopihari.com.br.

Wet'n'Wild, Estrada de Bandeirantes SP-348, Km 72, 72km (45 miles) north of the city. Water fun park. Entry US$30, additional charge for some attractions. Open in summer Tue–Sun 10am–6pm. Tickets available on tel: 11-4496 8000 or online, at www.wet nwild.com.br.

In Rio de Janeiro:

Rio Water Planet, 24000 Estrada de Bandeirantes. Large water park for all ages. Current cost is US$50 per day for entry and most rides. Open daily 10am–5pm. Tickets at the door, or tel: 21-2428 9000, or online at www.riowaterplanet.com.br.

Bookshops

Rio de Janeiro

FNAC
Barra Shopping, 4666 Avenida das Americas, Loja B, 101–16.
www.fnac.com.br
Superstore with great selection of books and music.

Leonardo da Vinci
185 Avenida Rio Branco, Loja 2.
www.leonardodavinci.com.br
Traditional store with a wide selection of books about Brazil, also art and photography.

Livraria Argumento
417 Rua Dias Ferreira, Leblon.
7777 Avenida das Américas, Barra.
www.livrariaargumento.com.br
Art and travel; also literature and children's books.

Livraria da Travessa
Shopping Leblon, 290 Avenida Afrânio de Melo Franco, Leblon.
572 Rua Visconde de Pirajá, Ipanema.
44 Avenida Rio Branco, Centro.

Barra Shopping, 4666 Avenida das Américas, Barra.
www.travessa.com.br
Leading chain of Rio bookstores. CDs and DVDs as well.

São Paulo

Cultura
2073 Avenida Paulista, Conjunto Nacional.
www.livrariacultura.com.br
Wide selection of books on all topics, including many about Brazil. Major Brazilian chain with six other stores in São Paulo as well as Brasília, Fortaleza, Porto Alegre, and Recife.

FNAC
901 Avenida Paulista, Bela Vista.
34 Praça dos Omaguás, Pinheiros.
1089 Avenida Roque Petroni Junior, Morumbi.
www.fnac.com.br
Superstores with a great selection of books and music.

SHOPPING

What to buy

Gemstones and jewelry

One of the major attractions of shopping for gemstones in Brazil, besides the price, is the tremendous variety. Brazil produces amethysts, aquamarines, opals, topazes, and many colors of tourmalines, as well as the more precious diamonds, emeralds, rubies, and sapphires.

Some 65 percent of the world's colored gemstones are produced in Brazil, which is also one of the world's major gold producers. Brazil today is one of the top jewelry centers in the world, and costs are attractive because the operation is 100 percent domestic, from the mining of the gems to the cutting, crafting, and designing of jewelry.

The value of a gemstone is determined largely by its color and quality, not necessarily by its size. When choosing a gem look for color, cut, clarity and cost. The stronger the color, the more valuable the stone. Buy from a reliable jeweler, where you will get what you pay for, and can trust their advice.

The two leading jewelers operating nationwide are H. Stern (www.h stern.net) and Amsterdam Sauer (www.amsterdamsauer.com), but there are reliable smaller chains. Top

Shopping for clothes in a fashion boutique on Rua Oscar Freire street, in the Jardins area of São Paulo.

jewelers have shops in the airports and shopping centers, and many hotels.

Leather goods

Shoes, sandals, bags, wallets, and belts are all good buys. Although found throughout the country, some of the finest leather comes from the south. Shoes are plentiful, and handmade leather items can be found at street fairs or covered markets.

Wooden objects

Brazil has beautiful wood. Gift shops sell items such as salad bowls and trays, and woodcarvings can be found at craft fairs. The grotesque *carranca* figureheads, unique to São Francisco riverboats, are difficult to fit into your suitcase but very unusual. Be aware, though, that items may be made from endangered tropical hardwoods. It is not illegal to export them, but the industry is contributing to the mass deforestation of the Amazon.

Musical instruments and CDs

A fun thing to take home is one of the peculiar percussion instruments that you hear samba bands playing, usually on sale at street fairs. From Bahia comes the berimbau, a simple instrument consisting of a wire-strung bow and a gourd sound box. It has a characteristic sound, but is surprisingly difficult to master. If you enjoy Brazilian music, buy CDs, too, or buy them online.

Fashion

Boutiques in most cities are clustered in certain districts, and shopping malls enable you to visit many shops in less time. If you want something uniquely Brazilian, buy lace or embroidery from the northeast, or a tiny bikini or a beach cover-up.

T-shirts are everywhere, from beautifully designed and expensive ones to humble but colorful screen-printed ones. They are excellent value and usually of good quality.

Paintings

These can be bought at galleries as well as crafts fairs and markets. Brazilian Primitive, or Naïve, paintings are popular (see page 119).

Religious articles

Popular amulets include the figa (a carved clenched fist with the thumb between the index and middle fingers) and the Senhor do Bonfim ribbons (to be wrapped around a wrist or ankle and fastened with three knots) from Salvador (see page 277).
Also from Salvador come bunches of silver fruits, which Brazilians hang in their homes to ensure there is always plenty of food on the table.

Coffee

Ground and roasted Brazilian coffee can be found at any supermarket or bakery. You can get coffee packaged in a handy carton at the airport.

Where to buy crafts

Handicrafts shops and markets are plentiful. In most larger towns in the northeast and the Amazon there is a central craft market or a craft center. A few of these are listed below.

Rio de Janeiro

Pé de Boi
55 Rua Ipiranga, Laranjeiras
Tel: 21-2285 4395.
www.pedeboi.com.br
Velho Chico
303 Rua Visconde de Pirajá, Ipanema
Tel: 21-2523 6305.
The Hippie Fair
Praça General Osório, Ipanema. Sunday. Lively, touristy, handicrafts market that attracts artisans from across Brazil.
www.feirahippieipanema.com

São Paulo

Amoa Konoya Arte Indígena
1002 Rua João Moura
Tel: 11-3061 0639.
www.amoakonoya.com.br
Fabulous collection of Indian handicrafts from the Amazon and other parts of Brazil. Baskets, bows and arrows, feather, wood, and clay

Regional crafts

Ceramics are a particularly good purchase in the northeast, where clay bowls, water jugs, and other items are commonly used in the home. Also from the northeast come primitive clay figurines depicting folk heroes, customs and celebrations. Marajoara ceramic pieces, decorated with geometric patterns, come from the island of Marajó at the mouth of the Amazon river.

Beautiful handmade lace and embroidered clothing are produced mostly in the northeast, especially in the state of Ceará, while Minas Gerais is a traditional producer of handmade weavings and tapestries.

Also in Minas Gerais, soapstone items are on sale everywhere. Both decorative and utilitarian objects – cooking pots, toiletry sets, quartz and agate bookends and ashtrays

– can be found in many of the souvenir stores.

Straw and natural fibers (banana leaves, palm bark) are fashioned into baskets, hats, bags, mats, etc., especially in the northeast.

Indian handicrafts are mainly made in the northern Amazon region and include adornments (necklaces, earrings), utensils (sieves, baskets), weapons (bows, arrows, spears), and percussion instruments (like the 'rain sticks' that imitate the sound of falling rain) made out of wood, fibers, thorns, teeth, claws, colorful feathers, shells, and seeds.

Cotton hammocks are popular all over Brazil, but the best place to buy them is in the north and northeast, where they are used extensively instead of beds. They are sometimes finished with lacy crocheted edgings.

objects, and CDs of Indian music.
Arte Nativa Aplicada
184 Rua Dr Melo Alves
Tel: 11-3088 1811.
Textiles, table mats, and lamps in interesting tribal patterns.
Casa do Amazonas
460 Alameda dos Jurupis, Moema
Tel: 11-5051 3098.
Large variety of Indian art and crafts.
Jacques Ardies
579 Rua Morgado de Mateus
Tel: 11-5539 7500.
www.ardies.com
Primitive and Naïve art.
Kariri
877 Rua Arthur de Azevedo, Jardim Américas
Tel: 11-3064 6586.

Traditional doll souvenirs in Paraty.

www.depositokariri.com.br
A wide range of Brazilian crafts – basketware, painted clay folkloric figures, and wooden sculptures.
São Paulo Craft Fairs
MASP: Sunday. Under the masp art museum. Antiques.
Liberdade: Sunday. Plants, crafts, food, and clothes, in the Japanese district of the city.
Praça Benedito Calixto: Saturday. Hippie Fair, with crafts, Indian clothes, pottery, and jewelry.
Praça de Republica: Saturday. Paintings, clothes, jewelry, gemstones.
Embu: Sunday. In a small town southwest of the city. Arts, crafts, food, and plants, plus live music.

TRANSPORTATION • ACCOMMODATIONS • ACTIVITIES • A – Z • LANGUAGE

A – Z

A HANDY SUMMARY
OF PRACTICAL INFORMATION

A

Admission charges

Museums and galleries normally charge a small entrance fee, typically US$1.50–10. There may be reductions for students, but this cannot be relied upon, and there are some free days. Churches are free but usually appreciate a donation.

Airport taxes

Domestic flights carry an embarkation tax of roughly US$7–10, depending on the size of the airport. On international flights out of Brazil you pay roughly US$35. In addition, some companies may have fuel and security surcharges. Check with your travel agent when buying your ticket to find out if all these are included.

B

Budgeting for the trip

Allow US$120 upwards a day for two people for accommodations, starting at the hostel or 'cheap and cheerful' level; US$25 per person a day upwards for basic meals in snack bars and inexpensive restaurants, without alcohol; obviously meals in better restaurants cost a lot more (see Restaurant sections at the end of relevant chapters). Allow around US$15 a day for getting around Rio or São Paulo, based on one taxi ride and the rest by bus or Metro.

Business hours

Offices in most cities open Monday–Friday 9am–6pm, sometimes with a very long lunch hour. Banks open Monday–Friday 10am–4pm. *Casas de câmbio* (currency exchanges) usually operate 9am–5pm.

Most stores are open Monday–Friday 9am–6.30pm or 9am–7pm, and Saturday until 12.30 or 1pm. They may stay open much later depending on their location. The shopping centers are open Monday–Saturday 10am–10pm as a rule (and many also open on Sunday), although not all the shops inside keep the same hours. Large department stores are usually open Monday–Friday 9am–10pm and 9am–6.30pm on Saturday. Most supermarkets are open 8am–8pm. Some stay open 24 hours a day, seven days a week.

Post offices are open Monday–Friday 9am–5pm and 9am–1pm on Saturday. Some larger cities have one branch that stays open 24 hours a day. Many pharmacies stay open until 10pm, and larger cities will have 24-hour drugstores.

The 24-hour and 12-hour clocks are both in common usage.

C

Climate

Almost all of Brazil's 8.5 million sq km (3.3 million sq miles) of territory lies between the equator and the Tropic of Capricorn. Within this tropical zone, temperatures and rainfall vary from north to south, from coastal to inland areas, and from low areas (the Amazon river basin and the Pantanal, as well as along the coast) to higher altitudes. If you are coming from the northern hemisphere, you should remember that seasons are inverted (ie Brazil's summer is your winter), although at this latitude, seasons are less distinct than they are in temperate zones, unless you are heading to the far south of the country.

If you are heading south during the Brazilian winter, make sure you have the right clothing, as at night temperatures can drop below freezing. Even in northern parts of Brazil you may want to carry a jumper or wrap if you are going to be sitting for a long period in an air-conditioned office, restaurant, or concert hall. (See page 375).

Rain, when it comes, can be short and dramatic. Take your lead from the Brazilians. They seem to know if the rain is here to stay, or if you only need to shelter for a few minutes.

The north

In the Amazon river basin jungle region, the climate is humid equatorial, characterized by high temperatures and high humidity, with heavy rainfall all year round. Although some areas have no dry season, most places have a short respite between July and November, so that the rivers are highest from December through to June. Average temperature is 24–27°C (75–80°F).

The east coast

The Atlantic coast from Rio Grande do Norte to the state of São Paulo has a humid tropical climate, also hot, but with slightly less rainfall than in the north, and with summer and winter seasons. The northeastern coast, nearer to the equator, experiences little difference in summer/winter temperatures, but more rainfall in the Brazilian winter, especially April–June. The coastal southeast receives more rain in summer (December–March). Average temperature is 21–24°C

(70–75°F), being consistently warm in the northeast, but fluctuating in Rio de Janeiro from summer highs of more than 40°C (104°F) down to 18°C (65°F), with winter temperatures usually around the 21°C (70°F) mark.

The interior

Most of Brazil's interior has a semi-humid tropical climate, with a hot, rainy Brazilian summer (December–March) and a drier, cooler winter (June–August). Year-round average temperature is 20–28°C (68–82°F). São Paulo, at an altitude of 800 meters (2,600ft) above sea level, and Brasília, over 1,000 meters (3,300ft) above sea level on the Central Plateau, as well as mountainous Minas Gerais, can get quite cool: although the thermometer may read a mild 10°C (50°F), it will not feel so balmy indoors if there is no heating.

The mountainous areas in the southeast have a high-altitude tropical climate, similar to the semi-humid tropical climate, but rainy and dry seasons are more pronounced and temperatures are cooler, averaging from 18–23°C (64–73°F).

Part of the interior of the northeast has a tropical, semi-arid climate – hot with sparse rainfall. Most of the rain falls during three months, usually March–May, but sometimes the season is shorter, and in some years there is no rainfall at all. The average temperature is 24–27°C (75–80°F).

The South

Brazil's south, below the Tropic of Capricorn, has a humid, subtropical climate. Rainfall is distributed regularly throughout the year, and temperatures vary from 0–10°C (32–50°F) in winter, with occasional frosts and a rare snowfall, to 21–32°C (70–90°F) in summer.

Crime and safety

Sadly, personal crime, in the form of pickpocketing and theft from hotel rooms, is common in parts of Brazil, particularly in bigger cities. But with a little caution and common sense, most visitors manage to avoid trouble.

When traveling, always carry valuables and money in a money belt, worn out of sight underneath clothing, and don't wear a flashy watch or expensive jewelry. Be especially alert in crowded places, such as rush-hour subway stations, city buses, beaches, and markets. Seek advice from your hotel about local areas to avoid at night. A good general rule is to avoid the beach after dark.

Thieves often operate in teams, and are masters at diversionary tricks. If carrying expensive camera equipment, never let it out of sight, and be wary of strangers telling you, for instance, that you have stepped in something smelly, and offering to assist you.

Leave valuables in your hotel safe if one is available, but check to see that they are actually put away, and ask for a list of items deposited. Make sure that you can get access to them at all hours, if checking out very early or late.

Take photocopies of your passport and important documents and, if traveling with a friend, keep copies of each other's documents.

Always report any losses or injuries to the police and ask for a written report of the incident for insurance purposes. But make sure that your claim is completely honest as a number of tourists are now serving time in Brazilian jails for making false robbery and insurance claims.

Tourist police (delegacia de proteção ao turista) can be contacted in the following cities:
São Paulo: tel: 11-3257 4475
Aeroporto de São Paulo, Congonhas: tel: 11-5090 9032.
Aeroporto Internacional de São Paulo, Guarulhos: tel: 11-2611 2686
Rio de Janeiro: tel: 21-2332 2924
Salvador: tel: 71-3116 6817
Fortaleza: tel: 85-3101 2488

Customs and duty free

You will be given a declaration form to fill out on the plane before arrival. Customs officials spot-check some incoming 'nothing to declare' travelers. If you are coming as a tourist and bringing articles obviously for your personal use, you will have no problem. As with most countries, food products of animal origin, plants, fruit, and seeds may be confiscated.

You can bring in US$500-worth of anything brought from abroad, except liquor, which is limited to one bottle (each) of wine and spirits.

If you are coming on business, it's best to check with the consulate as to what limitations or obligations you are subject to. Professional samples may be brought in as long as the quantity does not lead customs inspectors to suspect that they are, in fact, for sale.

Electronic devices worth no more than US$500 can be brought in on a tourist visa and need not leave the country with you – they can be left in the country as gifts.

There is a Duty Free shop at all major airports receiving international flights. Arriving passengers have a US$500 limit, but the shops are virtually a one-chain monopoly and most prices are not wonderful.

D

Disabled travelers

Airlines provide free wheelchair reception for passengers with disabilities who request it in advance. Laws in Brazil require public places to be wheelchair-friendly, but not all are. Many major city centers are gradually equipping all crossings with curb ramps, and some more modern city buses can accommodate wheelchair entry and exit. Some elevators in more modern buildings have Braille numbering for buttons. Travelers with disabilities should expect difficulties, but can also expect friendly help. Many facilities in Rio will be totally upgraded in preparation for hosting the Paralympics in 2016.

CLIMATE CHART

Brasilia

°C	J F M A M J J A S O N D	mm
40		175
30		150
25		125
20		100
15		75
10		50
5		25
0		0

Manaus

°C	J F M A M J J A S O N D	mm
35		280
30		240
25		200
20		160
15		120
10		80
5		40
0		0

Rio de Janeiro

°C	J F M A M J J A S O N D	mm
40		175
30		150
25		125
20		100
15		75
10		50
5		25
0		0

◼ Maximum temperature
☐ Minimum temperature
— Rainfall

E

Electricity

Voltage is not standard throughout Brazil, but most cities use 127V; Brasília, Florianópolis, Fortaleza, Recife, and São Luís use 220V; Manaus uses 110V.

If you can't do without your shaver, hairdryer or personal computer, inquire about the voltage when making hotel reservations. If you plug an appliance into a lower voltage than it was made for, it will function poorly, but if you plug it into a much stronger current it can overheat and short-circuit. Many appliances have a switch so they can be used with either 110-v or 220-v (110-v appliances work normally on a 127-v current). Many hotels have adapters, and some have more than one voltage available.

Embassies and consulates

A full list of embassies and consulates can be found on the Brazilian Foreign Office website.

Australia
19 Forster Crescent, Yarralumla, Canberra, ACT 2600
Tel: 6126-273 2372
http://camberra.itamaraty.gov.br/en-us/
Canada
450 Wilbrod Street, Ontario, K1N 6M8
Tel: 1-613-237 1090
http://ottawa.itamaraty.gov.br/en-us/
Ireland
Harcourt Centre, Europa House, Block 9, Harcourt Street, Dublin 2
Tel: 353-1-475 6000
http://dublin.itamaraty.gov.br/en-us/
New Zealand
10 Brandon Street – Level 9, PO Box 5432, Wellington
Tel: 644-473 3516
www.brazil.org.nz
South Africa
Hillcrest Office Park, Pretoria
Tel: 12-366 5200
http://pretoria.itamaraty.gov.br/en-us/
UK
14 Cockspur Street, London SW1Y 5BL
Tel: 0207-747 4500
www.brazil.org.uk
Consulate: 3 Vere Street, London W1G 0DG
Tel: 020-7659 1550
http://cglondres.itamaraty.gov.br/en-us/
US
Washington, DC: 3006 Massachusetts Avenue, NW, DC 20008

Tel: 202-238 2805
Fax: 202-238 2827
http://washington.itamaraty.gov.br/en-us/
Atlanta: 3500 Lenox Road, Suite 800, GA 30326
Tel: 404-949-2400
http://atlanta.itamaraty.gov.br/en-us/
Boston: 20 Park Plaza, MA 02116
Tel: 617-542 4000
http://boston.itamaraty.gov.br/en-us/
Chicago: 401 North Michigan Avenue, Il 60611
Tel: 312-464 0244
http://chicago.itamaraty.gov.br/en-us/
Houston: 1233 West Loop South 1150A, TX 77027
Tel: 713-961 3063
http://houston.itamaraty.gov.br/en-us/
Los Angeles: 8484 Wilshire Boulevard, Suites 730–711, Beverly Hills, CA 90211
Tel: 213-651 2664
http://losangeles.itamaraty.gov.br/en-us/
Miami: 80 SW Eighth Street, Suite 2600, FL 33130
Tel: 305-285 6200
http://miami.itamaraty.gov.br/en-us/
New York: 1185 Avenue of the Americas, 21st Floor, New York, NY 10036
Tel: 917-777 7777
http://novayork.itamaraty.gov.br/en-us/
San Francisco: 300 Montgomery Street, CA 94104
Tel: 415-981 8170
http://saofrancisco.itamaraty.gov.br/en-us/

Foreign Embassies and Consulates In Brazil

Embassies are found in Brasília, where consulates are located, and also in Rio and São Paulo and some other cities. Many countries also have diplomatic missions in several cities. Call before visiting because they frequently keep unusual hours. If you're coming to Brazil on business, remember that your consulate's commercial sector can be of great assistance.

Australia
Brasília:
SES, Avenida das Nações, Qd 801, Conj. K, Lote 7
Tel: 61-3226 3111
www.brazil.embassy.gov.au
São Paulo:
456 Alameda Ministro Rocha Azevedo, 2nd Floor
Tel: 11-3085 6247
Canada
Brasília:
SES, Avenida das Nações, Qd 803, Lote 16, s1. 130

Tel: 61-3424 5400
www.canada.org.br
São Paulo:
12901 Avenida Nações Unidas, 16th Floor, Torre Norte
Tel: 11-5509 4321
Ireland
Brasília:
SHIS, Qd 12, Conj. 5, Casa 09
Tel: 61-3248 8800
São Paulo:
2006 Avenida Paulista, Conj. 514 (Cerqueira Cesar)
Tel: 11-3287 6362
New Zealand
Brasília:
SHIS Qd 9, Casa 1
Tel: 61-3248 9900
579 Alameda Campinas, 15th Floor
Tel: 11-3148 0616
South Africa
Brasília:
SES, Avenida das Nações, Qd 801, Lote 6
Tel: 61-3312 9500
www.africadosul.org.br
1754 Avenida Paulista
São Paulo
Tel: 11-3265 0449
UK
Brasília:
SES, Avenida das Nações, Qd 801, Conj. K, Lote 8
Tel: 61-3329 2300
www.ukinbrazil.fco.gov.uk
Rio de Janeiro:
284 Praia do Flamengo, 2nd Floor, Flamengo
Tel: 21-2555 9600
São Paulo:
741 Rua Ferreira de Araújo, 2nd Floor
Tel: 11-3094 2700
US
Brasília:
SES, Avenida das Nações Unidas, Qd 801, Lote 3
Tel: 61-3312 7000
www.embaixada-americana.org.br
Rio de Janeiro:
147 Avenida Pres. Wilson, Centro
Tel: 21-3823 2000
São Paulo:
500 Rua Henri Dunant, Chácara Santo Antônio
Tel: 11-5186 7000
Recife
163 Rua Gonçalves Maia, Boa Vista
Tel: 81-3416 3050

Entry regulations

Visas

Tourist visas used to be issued routinely to all visitors upon arrival, but Brazil now has a reciprocity policy: if Brazilians need a visa in advance to visit your country, you will need a visa in advance to visit Brazil. US citizens need to apply for a visa in advance; European Union citizens do not. Your airline or travel agent should be able to tell you if you need a visa; or contact a Brazilian consulate or embassy. Do not take it for granted that you do not need a visa.

If you do not need a visa in advance, your passport will be stamped with a tourist visa upon entry. This permits you to remain in the country for 90 consecutive days. If you apply for a visa in advance, you have up to 90 days after the issue date to enter Brazil. Upon entry, you will get a tourist visa allowing you to stay in Brazil for up to 90 days.

If you are traveling to several countries and not going straight to Brazil, the entry visa needn't be issued in your home country, but it's still a good idea to allow for enough time in order to avoid surprises and hassles. The 90-day tourist visa can be renewed once only for another 90 days. To get an extension, go to the immigration section of the federal police.

Temporary visas for foreigners who will be working or doing business in Brazil allow a longer stay than a regular tourist visa. If you are a student, journalist or researcher, or employed by a multinational company, contact the Brazilian consulate or embassy in your country well before you plan to travel. It is usually difficult – or even impossible – to change the status of your visa once you are in the country. If you come with a tourist visa, you will probably have to leave the country to return on another type of visa.

Permanent work visas and residency visas normally require the applicant to have a job offer in a senior position from a Brazilian company, or in a small group of professions that are determined by the government. Application must be made from outside Brazil and the process is lengthy and bureaucratic.

Etiquette

Generally speaking, social customs in Brazil are not vastly different from those you will find in 'Western' countries, but Brazilians can be both awkwardly formal and disarmingly informal.

Surnames are little used. People start out on a first-name basis, but titles of respect – senhor for men and most frequently dona for women – are used not only to be polite to strangers but also to show respect

A hat-seller on the beach in Búzios.

to someone of a different age group or social class. In some families, children even address their parents as o senhor and a senhora instead of the Portuguese equivalent of 'you.'

While handshaking is a common practice at introductions, it is also customary to greet friends, relatives, and even complete strangers to whom you are being introduced with hugs and kisses. The 'social' form of kissing consists usually of a kiss on each cheek. However, in most circles men do not kiss each other, rather shaking hands while giving a pat on the shoulder with the other hand. If they are more intimate, men will embrace, thumping each other on the back. Although this is the general custom in Brazil, there are subtleties about who kisses whom that are governed by social position.

Brazilians are incredibly kind people in general. You will encounter offers of help wherever you go. Ask for directions and you are likely to be taken there in person.

Brazilians are also generous hosts, ensuring that guests' glasses, plates, or coffee cups are never empty. Besides the genuine pleasure of being a gracious host, there is the question of honor. Even poor people like to put on a good party.

Although Brazil is definitely a male-dominated society, machismo takes a milder and subtler form than is generally found in neighboring Hispanic America.

Expect schedules to be much more flexible than you may be used to. It is not considered rude to show up half an hour late for a social engagement. Except in the larger cities, even business appointments are often leisurely when compared with the US or Europe. If you are there on business, don't try to include too

many in one day, as you may well find your schedule badly disrupted by unexpected delays.

G

Gay and lesbian travelers

Brazil is a generally tolerant country, and both Rio and São Paulo have Gay Parades that have become major annual events with a Carnival atmosphere, attracting people of all kinds of minorities. Gay and lesbian travelers will not feel discriminated against in major city centers, and Rio is often voted the 'Best Global Destination' in gay publication and website polls. However, as in most countries, the more remote rural areas tend to be conservative.

H

Health

A yellow-fever certificate may be required if you are arriving from certain South American and African countries. This is subject to change, so check with the Brazilian Consulate. If you plan to travel in areas outside of cities in the Amazon region or in the Pantanal in Mato Grosso, however, it is recommended that you have a yellow-fever shot. This protects you for 10 years, but is effective only after 10 days, so plan ahead. Be sure to get a certificate for any vaccination. It is also a good idea to protect yourself against malaria in these same jungle areas: there are drugs that will provide immunity, and most need to be taken for several days before visiting the area. Consult your doctor or local public-health service.

TRANSPORTATION

ACCOMMODATIONS

ACTIVITIES

A – Z

LANGUAGE

Don't drink tap water in Brazil. The water in the cities is treated and is sometimes quite heavily chlorinated, but people filter water in their homes. Any hotel or restaurant will have inexpensive bottled mineral water, both carbonated (com gas) and uncarbonated (sem gas). If you are out in the hot sun, make an effort to drink extra fluids. Coconut and other fruit juices or mineral water are good for replacing lost fluids.

Don't underestimate the tropical sun. There is often a pleasant sea breeze, and you may not be aware of how the sun is baking you until it's too late. Use an appropriate sunscreen (filtro solar) – there are many international brands on sale in Brazil.

Prescription drugs are available in abundance – frequently without a prescription – and you may even find old favorites that have been banned for years in your country. Bring a supply of any prescription drugs that you take regularly, but simple things like aspirin, antacids, plasters, sunscreen, and suchlike, are easy to obtain. However, there have been cases of falsification of medicines, so it's best to buy drugs in larger chain stores or in the big cities. Drug stores also sell cosmetics; sanitary protection can be purchased in any drug store or supermarket.

Some US health insurance plans cover any medical service you may require while abroad, but you should check with the company, and if not, ensure you have private medical insurance before traveling, which is something visitors from the UK and elsewhere should always do.

Medical emergencies

If you need a doctor while in Brazil, your hotel should be able to recommend reliable professionals who often speak several languages. Many of the better hotels have a doctor on duty. Your consulate will also be able to supply you with a list of physicians who speak your language.

I

Internet

Brazil is one of the most web-savvy and connected countries on the planet and has helped to make Portuguese the most used language on the internet after English. Ninety-five million people in Brazil use the internet. Internet cafés are found throughout the country, although service can be slow in smaller beach resorts. Many larger hotels offer internet and Wi-fi facilities free to their guests. This means it is easy to stay in touch via email.

The importance and size of the Brazilian internet market is reflected by Yahoo! and Google setting up Portuguese-language search engines for Brazil.

While a lot of the web content on Brazil is in Portuguese, major websites tend to offer pages in English. A Brazilian web address will often end '.com.br'.

L

Lost property

Lost and found in Portuguese is *achados e perdidos*. There is an *achados e perdidos* point at most major airports and bus stations. However, remember that Brazil is a country with widespread poverty, and most valuables lost in the street or on public transport are gone for good. Your documents may be returned, depending on your luck, but it is sensible to leave your passport in your hotel safe and carry a simple photocopy.

The Brazilian mail service – *Correios* – runs a nationwide document-return service, and people who find lost items can simply drop them in a public mailbox. There is an online service to check whether documents have been handed in: www.correios.com.br. Tel: 3003-0100.

M

Maps

The Quatro Rodas publisher (part of the Abril group) has a nice range of state maps, and various national guidebooks. The ibge (Brazilian

A Rio newsstand.

Left luggage

This is *guarda volumes* in Portuguese. It is available at most major airports and bus stations, normally of the rent-a-locker variety, sometimes with a store-room option for larger items. Most hotels will also look after you baggage if you have to check out early prior to a late night flight.

National Geographical Institute) sells more detailed maps in its own shops.

Media

Newspapers and magazines

With the majority of people content to catch up on the news via the internet or TV, the demand to import newspapers and magazines has fallen away. The *Miami Herald*, the Latin America edition of the *International Herald Tribune*, and the *Wall Street Journal*, are available on some newsstands in the big cities, as are news magazines such as *Time* and *Newsweek*. At larger newsstands and airport bookshops you will find a larger selection of international publications, including German, French, and English magazines.

You may want to buy a local paper to find out what's on in town. Besides the musical shows, there are always numerous foreign movies showing in the original language with Portuguese subtitles. Entertainment listings appear under the headings of *cinema*, *show*, *dança*, *música*, *teatro*, *televisão*, *exposicões*, etc. *Crianças* means 'children.' It is not difficult to understand the listings, even if you speak no Portuguese.

If you do know some Portuguese and want to read the Brazilian newspapers, the most authoritative and respected include: São Paulo's

Folha de São Paulo, Estado de São Paulo, Gazeta Mercantil, and Rio's *O Globo.* There is no nationwide paper, but these wide-circulation dailies reach a good part of the country. The colorful weekly magazine *Epoca,* along with *Veja* and *Isto E,* are also good sources of information.

Television and radio

Brazilian television mostly features light entertainment programs like quiz shows, comedies, and soaps. It is big business, with Brazil exporting programs around the world. There are a staggering 185 million viewers in the country.

There are twelve national and several hundred local networks, which bring television to nearly all parts of Brazil. There are also seven networks, which are government-controlled. These are for educational purposes or to show what is happening in parliament. Brazil's giant TV Globo is the fourth-largest commercial network in the world. With more than 40 stations in a country with a high illiteracy rate, it has great influence over the information to which many people have access (see page 111).

Only about a third of all television programs on open network channels in Brazil are imports, and these are mostly from the US. Foreign series, specials, sports coverage, and movies are dubbed in Portuguese, except for

Photography tips

Digital photography has taken over Brazil, just like the rest of the world, and there are places to print photos or record them on to a CD in most shopping centers and downtown areas of larger cities. Additional memory cards are available in larger cities for most common international standards. Thirty-five-mm film is still available in larger centers, although it is increasingly difficult to find. The same goes for developing.

Light can be very strong, and during the middle of the day the near-vertical sun can result in strong contrasts. Better results are often obtained earlier in the morning, or toward the end of the afternoon.

Don't walk around with your camera hanging around your neck or over your shoulder; it is an easy target for a snatcher. Carry it discreetly and never leave it unattended on the beach. If you have expensive equipment, it's a very good idea to have it insured.

some of the late-night movies and musical shows.

Most hotels and many middle- and upper-class homes in the cities receive cable television offering hundreds of channels, including most of the global favorites such as CNN, BBC World and ESPN. It is even possible to watch American breakfast television while in Brazil. At present, cable television is one of the fastest-growing media industries in the country.

There are several thousand radio stations around Brazil, which play international and Brazilian pop hits, as well as a variety of Brazilian music reflecting regional tastes. A good deal of American and British music is played; classical music programs are also popular, including Sunday afternoon operas in some areas.

The Culture Ministry station often has some interesting musical programs. All Brazilian broadcasts are in Portuguese.

Money

The currency is the *real* (plural, *reais*), which is made up of 100 *centavos.* Exchange rates are subject to a great deal of fluctuation as the *real* was the currency that most increased its value from 2009 to 2012.

The use of commas and decimal points in Portuguese is the opposite of what you may be used to. In Portuguese, one thousand *reais* is written R$ 1.000,00.

ATM machines can be found throughout Brazil, including in airports, and major shopping areas usually accept Visa and MasterCard/Cirrus cards. The major banks that provide ATM services include HSBC, Itaú, Santander, and Banco do Brasil. There will usually only be one international machine at a branch, and it may not be clear which one, so keep trying. Using ATMs is the easiest way to obtain foreign currency. You can exchange dollars, yen, pounds, and other currencies at accredited banks, hotels, and tourist agencies. If you can't find one of these, some travel agencies will exchange your currency, although this is, strictly speaking, an illegal transaction. The few hotels that exchange traveler's checks give a poor rate.

Banks will not exchange *reais* or traveler's checks into foreign currency. The only exception to this is the Banco do Brasil, which has branches at international airports. As you leave the country, they will exchange back, at the official rate, 30 percent of the currency

you exchanged at a similar airport branch bank on your way into Brazil, if you show the receipt for the initial exchange. You cannot get traveler's checks cashed into dollars.

Most hotels will accept payment in traveler's checks or by most major credit cards. Many restaurants and shops take credit cards; the most frequently accepted are American Express, Diners Club, MasterCard, and Visa, which all have offices in Brazil. You may also be able to pay with dollars. Hotels, restaurants, stores, taxis, and so on, will usually quote an exchange rate.

P

Postal services

Post offices are generally open Monday–Friday 9am–5pm and 9am–1pm on Saturday, and are closed on Sunday and holidays. In large cities, some branch offices stay open until later in the evening. The post office in the Rio de Janeiro International Airport is open every day from 7am–8pm. Post offices are usually designated with a sign reading *Correios* or sometimes ECT (for *Empresa de Correios e Telégrafos* – Postal and Telegraph Company).

An airmail letter to or from the US takes about a week to arrive. To the UK, it may take at least two weeks. In the more densely populated areas, domestic post is usually delivered a day or two after it is mailed. National and international rapid mail service is available, as well as registered post and parcel services (the post office has special boxes for these). Stamps for collectors can also be purchased at the post office.

You can have mail sent to you at your hotel. Although some consulates will hold mail for citizens of their country, they tend to discourage this practice.

Public holidays

January New Year's Day.
February/March Carnival. Dates vary, depending on date of Easter (see page 69).
March/April Good Friday.
April 21 Tiradentes Day.
May 1 Labor Day.
May/June Corpus Christi. Date varies: ninth Thursday after Easter.
September 7 Independence Day.
October 12 Nossa Senhora de Aparecida – Brazil's patron saint.
November 2 All Souls' Day.

November 15 Proclamation of the Republic.
November 20 Black Consciousness Day.
December 25 Christmas Day.

Public toilets

Toilets are always found in shopping centers, hotels, restaurants, airports, bus stations, the better snack bars, better gas stations, and the like. You won't find any in the street or in other public places, except for a few along Copacabana beach.

R

Religious services

Catholicism is the official and dominant religion in Brazil, but many people follow religions of African origin. Of these, *candomblé* is the purest form, with deities (the *orixás*), rituals, music, dance, and even language very similar to those practiced in the parts of Africa from which it was brought. *Umbanda* involves a syncretism with Catholicism in which each *orixá* has a corresponding Catholic saint. Spiritualism, also widely practiced in Brazil, contains both African and European influences. Many Brazilians who are nominally Catholic attend both Afro-Brazilian and/or spiritual and Christian rites.

Candomblé is practiced most in Bahia, while *umbanda* and spiritualism seem to have more mass appeal. In Salvador you can arrange through your hotel or a local travel agency/tour operator to see a ceremony – visitors are welcome as long as they show respect for the belief of others. Ask permission before taking any photographs.

If you wish to attend a service at a church of your faith while in Brazil, many religious groups can be found

in the larger cities, and, besides the ever-present Catholic churches, there are many Protestant churches throughout Brazil. Evangelical churches have expanded their presence dramatically, and have their own radio stations as well as large churches. Because of the diplomatic personnel in Brasília, there is a large variety of churches and temples. Rio de Janeiro and São Paulo both have several synagogues, as well as churches with services in foreign languages, including English.

Your hotel or your country's consulate should be able to help you to find a suitable place of worship.

S

Student travelers

There are Student Travel Bureaus in Rio (550 Rua Visconde de Pirajá, Loja 201; tel: 11-2512 8577) and São Paulo (2923 Avenida Brigadeiro Faria Lima; tel: 21-3071 1244), and in a number of other cities (www.stb.com.br/atendimento/lojas-stb.aspx). The law says that students can buy cinema and theater tickets at half-price, but most places insist on seeing ID issued by a local student union. By all means try a foreign student ID, but don't bank on it being successful.

T

Telecommunications

Telephone

Brazil's once creaky telephone service has improved dramatically since privatization in the 1990s. Virtually all parts of the country are covered, and virtually all numbers have been standardized on an eight-digit format, plus an area code.

Dialing intercity requires the use of a two-digit 'operator code' to select the carrier. Embratel, a national carrier uses code 21 and can connect between most cities, but depending on where you're calling from and to, there may be cheaper options.

When dialing intercity the order is: '0' to indicate intercity, then operator code (21 or other IDD/direct dialing code; see page 373), then city code, then number. So to call, say, São Paulo from Rio (where 11 is the São Paulo city code) using Embratel, you dial 0 21 11 xxxx xxxx. Confusingly, if you were dialing Rio from São Paulo, it would be 0 21 21 xxxx xxxx. Each of the cell phone (mobile phone) services also has their own code.

This is not the case with every phone, however, as some companies and hotels have already built the long-distance code into their system so you would dial as before, 011 + phone number.

So, accepting that the obvious is not always obvious, if you have to call long-distance within Brazil, ask hotel staff or the owner of the phone which is the best – and cheapest – long-distance server.

Payphones in Brazil use phone cards, which are sold at newsstands, bars or shops, usually located near the phones. The phone card, *cartão de telefone*, comes in several values. The most common is a 30-unit card, but 90-unit cards can also be bought.

The sidewalk *telefone público* is also called an *orelhão* (big ear) because of the protective shell that takes the place of a booth – yellow for local or collect calls, blue for direct-dial, long-distance calls within Brazil. You can also call

Emergency numbers

National (free) numbers:
Ambulance: 192
Police: 190
Fire: 193
Civil Defense: 199
São Paulo
Women's police station (specializing in crimes against women, staffed by female officers – *Delegacia da Mulher*): tel: 11-3976 2908; State highway police: tel: 11-3327 2727.
Rio de Janeiro
Women's police station: 21-2332 9994
Tourist police: tel: 21-3399 7171
Coastguard (Salvamar) tel: 21-2253 6572
State highway police: tel: 21-3399 4857

Pushing a fruit cart in Olinda.

Useful telephone numbers

International calling and enquiries

Direct dialing – 00 + operator code + country code + area code + phone number.
000333 or 0800-703 2100 – information regarding long-distance calls (area codes, directory assistance, and complaints).
0800-703 2111 – international operator (Embratel), to place person-to-person, collect, and credit-card calls. Operators and interpreters who speak several languages are available.
000334 or 0800-703 2100 – information regarding rates. International rates go down 20 percent

8pm–5am (Brasília time) Monday–Saturday and all day Sunday.
To access your US phone company:
Connect: **000-8012**; Sprint: **000-8016**; AT&T: **1-800 437 0966 ext. 60330** (English); 1-800 541 5281 ext. 59859 (Spanish).

Domestic calling and inquiries

Direct dialing (IDD) – 0 + operator code + area code + phone number. Embratel's code is 21; Tim 41; Intelig-Tim 23, Oi 31; Covergia 32; Vivo 15; CTBC 12; Brasil Telecom 14; GVT 25.
Direct-dial collect call, long distance – **90** + operator code + area code + phone number. A recorded message

will tell you to identify yourself and the city from which you are calling after the beep. If the party you are calling does not accept your call, you will be cut off.
107 – operator-assisted collect calls from payphones (no token needed).

Other service numbers

102 – local directory assistance.
Area code + 102 – directory assistance in that area.
108 – information regarding rates.
0800-55135 – telegrams (local, national, and international).
138 – wake-up service.
130 – correct time.

from a *posto telefônico*, a telephone company station (at most bus stations and airports), where you can either use a phone card, or make a credit card or collect call.

For international calls, country codes are listed at the front of telephone directories. For long-distance domestic calls, area codes within Brazil are listed on the first few pages of directories.

Domestic long-distance rates are reduced from 8pm–6am and from Monday–Friday 6–8am and 8–11pm, Saturday 2–11pm and Sunday and holidays 6am–11pm.

Brazil has national coverage for cell phones (mobile phones), in major urban centers, and the centers of more affluent smaller towns. However, not all operators or systems cover all regions. The main national operators are Vivo, Caro, Tim, Oi, and Nextel, and there are now around 180 million subscribers in Brazil.

Phones from other countries may be used temporarily in Brazil provided they can operate on 1800-MHz using GSM or TDMA. Before leaving home, check with your service provider to find out if your phone and payment plan will allow you to use international roaming in Brazil. It is also advisable to check out what charges will apply – for example, if a local call in Brazil will be billed at an international rate.

Another option, if you plan phoning much within Brazil, is to buy a prepaid phone and keep charging it up. Phones can be purchased in shopping centers and larger supermarkets. Or bring an unblocked phone with you, and simply buy a local SIM card. There is a national register of prepaid cell phones, to try to prevent use by criminals, so be prepared to show your passport. Credits can be bought

in many places – the ubiquitous lottery shops are a favorite, also gas stations and news-stands.

Fax

Email dominates communications, but a fax can be sent from some post offices, and most hotels have telex and fax services for their guests. Fax services are also available at travel agents, office-services bureaux, and many other outlets. The prices charged for sending and receiving faxes vary widely.

Time zones

There are four different time zones in Brazil.
Two hours behind GMT: The archipelago of Fernando de Noronha, 350km (220 miles) off the Atlantic coast.
Three hours behind GMT: The western extension of Brazil's main time zone – in which 50 percent of the country lies – is a north–south line from the mouth of the Amazon river, going west to include the northern state of Amapá and the entire southern region. Rio de Janeiro, São Paulo, Belém, and Brasília are all located in this zone.
Four hours behind GMT: Another large zone encompassing the Pantanal states and most of the north.
Five hours behind GMT: The far western state of Acre, and the westernmost part of Amazonas.
Daylight Saving Time is in use, with clocks being set ahead in October and back to standard time in February or March. This, confusingly, means that time differences do not remain the same. Daylight Saving Time is only used in certain parts of Brazil, and takes place in the other half of the year in the northern

hemisphere. Therefore, the time in Rio de Janeiro, for example, is often only two hours behind GMT, and the time difference between São Paulo and Rio and most of continental Europe can swing from three to five hours.

States located in the following regions currently use Daylight Saving Time: Center West (Mato Grosso, Mato Grosso do Sul, and Goiás), Southeast (Espírito Santo, Minas Gerais, Rio de Janeiro, and São Paulo), South (Paraná, Rio Grande do Sul, and Santa Catarina) and North (Tocantins),

Tipping

Hotels and the more expensive restaurants will automatically add a 10 percent service charge to your bill, but this doesn't necessarily go to the individuals who served you and were helpful to you. Don't be afraid of overtipping – most employees earn a pittance and rely on the generosity of tourists.

Tipping taxi drivers is optional; most Brazilians don't. Again, a driver who has been especially helpful or waited for you should be awarded appropriately. At the airport, tip the last porter to help you – what you pay goes into a pool.

A 10 to 20 percent tip is typically expected in barbershops and beauty salons. Gas-station attendants, the people who shine your shoes, etc. should be tipped a small amount, again, depending on the level of service.

If you are a house guest, leave a tip for any household help (who cooked or laundered for you while you were there). Ask your hosts how much would be appropriate to give them. A tip in dollars will be especially appreciated. A small gift brought from home will certainly be welcome, and may even be better.

Tourist offices

Each state has its own tourism bureau, as do the major cities such as Rio and São Paulo. Addresses for some of these offices in the main cities are listed below.

Embratur
SCN Quadro 02, Bloco G Ed, Brasília, DF 70712
Tel: 21-3429 7777
www.visitbrazil.com

Belém/Para
Paratur, Praça Waldemar Henrique
Tel: 91-3212 0669
www.paratur.pa.gov.br

Belo Horizonte/Minas Gerais
Belotur, Rua Aimorés, Belo Horizonte, 30140
Tel: 31-3277 9777
www.minasgerais.com.br

Brasília/DF
Setur, Setor de Divulgação Cultural, Centro de Convenções, Setur, 3rd Floor
Tel: 61-3214 2742
www.setur.df.gov.br
Information Center: Airport

Florianópolis/Santa Catarina
249 Rua Felipe Schmidt, Florianópolis, SC 88010
Tel: 48-3212 6300
Fax: 48-3212 6315
www.sol.sc.gov.br

Fortaleza/Ceará
Setur, Avenida Gal Afonso Alburquerque Lima, Ed. Seplag, 60830-120 CE
Tel: 85-3101 4688
www.ceara.gov.br

Manaus/Amazonas
321 Rua Saldanha Maringo, Manaus, 69010
Tel: 92-3182 6250
Fax: 92-3182 6251
www.visitamazonas.am.gov.br
Information Center: Airport

Porto Alegre/Rio Grande do Sul
156 Rua General Camara, 90010-230, RS
Tel: 51-3288 5400
www.turismo.rs.gov.br
Information Center: Airport

Recife/Pernambuco
Empetur, Avenida Professor Andrade Bezerra, Olinda, PE, 53111 1970
Tel: 81-3182 8300/3427 8000
www.empetur.pe.gov.br
Information Centers: Airport, Bus Station, Casa da Cultura

Rio de Janeiro
272 Rio Convention and Visitors' Bureau, Rua Guilhermina Guinle, RJ 22270
Tel: 21-2266 9750
www.rcvb.com.br

Riotur, Praça Pio X 119, RJ, 20040 (Rio city only)
Tel: 21-2271 7000/0800 285 0555
www.rioguiaoficial.com.br
Information Centers: International Airport, Copacabana.
TurisRio, 30 Rua Acrer Centro, RJ 20081
(State of Rio de Janeiro)
Tel: 21-2333 1037
www.turisrio.rj.gov.br

Salvador/Bahia
Bahiatursa, 650 Avendia Simon Bolivar, BA 41750
Tel: 71-3117 3000
www.bahiatursa.ba.gov.br; www.saltur.salvador.ba.gov.br
Information Centers: Airport, Bus Station, Convention Center, Mercado Modelo, Porto da Barra, Pelourinho, Shopping Barra, Shopping Iguatemi

São Paulo
SPTuris, 1209 Avenida Olavo Fontoura, SP 02012
Tel: 11-2226 0400
Fax: 11-2226 0404
www.spturis.com
www.turismo.sp.gov.br
Information Centers: Praça da República, Praça da Liberdade, Praça da Sé, Praça Ramos de Azevedo, Avenida Paulista in front of Top Center and at corner of Rua Augusta, Shopping Morumbi, Shopping Ibirapuera

Travel agents and tour operators

Brazil

Brazilian Incoming Travel Organization
www.bito.com.br
Body representing the major Brazilian ground operators.
Brazil Tour Operators Association
www.braziltouroperators.org
Body representing Brazilian specialist tour operators in the US.
Latin American Travel Association
www.lata.org
Body representing Brazilian and Latin American specialist tour operators in the UK and Europe.

Rio de Janeiro

Brazilian Incentive & Tourism
56 Barão de Ipanema, 5th Floor, Copacabana
Tel: 21-3208 9000
www.bitourism.com
Offers a comprehensive program of tours that covers the whole of Brazil.

São Paulo

Freeway
322 Rua Cap. Cavalcanti
Tel: 11-5088 0999
www.freeway.tur.br

Trips to Fernando de Noronha, Bahia, and the Amazon. Ecotourism, trekking, climbing, and diving expeditions.
TAM Viagens
Tel: 11-3274 1313
www.tamviagens.com.br
One of the largest Brazilian travel companies, linked to the national airline. Stores throughout Brazil.

Iguaçu

Iguassu Falls Tour
Rua Ignacio Sottomaior, Foz do Iguaçu
Tel: 45-9104 7001
www.iguassufallstour.com
Offers a comprehensive set of packages to the falls, as well as excursions to Paraguay and the Itaipú dam.

Cuiabá (Pantanal)

Anaconda
606 Avenida Isaac Póvoas, Cuiabá
Tel: 65-3028 5990
www.anacondapantanal.com.br
Trips in the northern Pantanal.

Salvador

Tatar Turismo
274 Avenida Tancredo Neves, Centro Empresarial Iguatemi, Bloco B, Salas 222–4
Tel: 71-3450 7216
www.tatur.com.br
Specialized tours in the state of Bahia. Cultural and ecological trips in the northeast and to Fernando de Noronha.

Recife and the Northeast

Luck
4030 Rua Pinto Lula Cardoso Ayres, Recife
Tel: 81-3366 6262
www.luckreceptivo.com.br
Specialized tours in the northeast.

Natal

Manary Ecotours
9067 Rua Francisco Gurgel, Praia de Ponta Negra
Tel: 84-3204 2900
www.manary.com.br

Manaus (Amazon)

Swallows and Amazons
992 Rua Ramos Ferreira, Manaus
Tel/fax: 92-3622 1246
www.swallowsandamazonstours.com
Company offering good Amazon tours.

W

Websites

Below is a list of some Brazilian websites likely to be useful for travelers, and if you are looking for the obvious in Brazil, try '.com.br' rather than '.com':

Brazilian government
www.brazil.gov.br

Brazilian Embassy
(Washington)
http://washington.itamaraty.gov.br/en-us/

Brazilian Embassy
(London)
www.brazil.org.uk

Embratur
(Brazilian Tourist Board)
www.visitbrasil.com

Estado de São Paulo (newspaper/links)
www.estado.com.br

Folha de São Paulo (newspaper/links)
www.folha.com

Google Brasil
www.google.com.br

O Globo
(newspaper/links)
www.oglobo.com.br

IBGE (Brazilian Official Statistics)
www1.ibge.gov.br

INFRAERO (Airport authorities)
www.infraero.gov.br

Itamaraty (Foreign Office)
www.itamaraty.gov.br

Latin American Travel Association
www.lata.org

League of Samba Schools
http://liesa.globo.com

Rio Convention and Visitors' Bureau
www.rcvb.com.br

Rio Tourist Board Guide
www.rioguiaoficial.com.br

Salvador Tourist Board
www.emtursa.com.br

São Paulo Tourist Board
www.spturis.com

Veja (news magazine)
veja.abril.com.br

2014 FIFA World Cup
www.fifa.com/worldcup/index.html

2016 Olympic Games
www.rio2016.org.br

Weights and measures

The metric system is used throughout Brazil, and temperature is measured on the centigrade or Celsius scale (°C). Other measuring units are used in rural areas, but people are familiar with the metric system.

What to bring

Brazilians are very fashion-conscious, but are casual dressers. What you bring will depend on where you will be visiting and your holiday schedule. São Paulo tends to be dressier, while in small inland towns people are more conservative. If you are going

to a jungle lodge, you will want sturdy clothing and perhaps boots. If you are in Brazil on business, a suit and tie for men, and suits, skirts or dresses for women are the office standard. Bring a summer-weight suit for office calls: linen is smart and cool, but liable to crease. Generally speaking, suits and ties are used less the further north you go in Brazil, even by businessmen. Although some restaurants in the downtown business districts of the larger cities require a tie at lunch, other restaurants have no such regulations.

If you like to dress up, there are plenty of places to go to in the evening in the big cities. But avoid ostentation and expensive or flashy jewelry. There are many desperately poor people in Brazil, and unwitting foreign tourists make attractive targets for both pickpockets and purse-snatchers.

Shorts are acceptable for men and women in most areas, especially near the beach or in resorts, but they are not usually worn in downtown areas of cities. Most churches, and some museums, do not admit visitors dressed in shorts, and the traditional gafieira dancehalls will not admit those dressed in shorts, especially men. Jeans are acceptable and are often worn, but can be too hot.

If you come during Carnival, remember that it will be very hot, and you will probably be in a crowd and dancing non-stop. Anything colorful is appropriate. If you plan to go to any of the balls, you will find plenty of costumes in the shops – you might want to buy just a feathered hair ornament, flowered lei (garland) or sequined accessory to complete your outfit. Many women wear no more than a bikini and make-up. Most men wear shorts – with or without a shirt – or sometimes a sarong.

If you are traveling in the south

Classic Brazilian footwear: Havianas thongs.

Bikini rules

Don't forget to pack your swimsuit. Or buy a tiny local version of the string bikini, called a *tanga*, for yourself or someone back home – there are stores that sell nothing but beachwear. New styles emerge each year, in different fabrics and colors, exposing this part or that. The tiniest are called *fio dental*, or dental floss.

Topless sunbathing on Brazil's beaches has never really caught on. Women should avoid exposing their breasts on the beach; for most Brazilians, this is regarded as offensive behavior. Despite their open attitude towards sex, it is worth remembering that Brazilians are a deeply Catholic and often conservative people.

Decently dressed women get ogled, too. Brazilian men don't go in for catcalls, but draw their breath in sharply between clenched teeth, and murmur comments as the women pass by. Brazilian women don't let this cramp their style.

or in the mountains, or to São Paulo in winter, it can be quite chilly. Even in the areas where it is hot all year round, you may need a light sweater, jacket, or sweatshirt, if not for the cooler evenings, then for the chilly air conditioning in hotels, restaurants, and offices. Rain gear is always worth taking with you – Brazilians tend to use umbrellas more than raincoats. Seaside hotels will usually provide you with sun umbrellas and beach towels.

As on any trip, it is sensible to bring a pair of comfortable walking shoes. Sandals and beach thongs (flip-flops) are comfortable in the heat, and they're very convenient for getting across the hot sand from your hotel to the water's edge. If there's one thing that gives Brazilians the giggles, it's the sight of a *gringo* going to the beach in shoes and socks. But as Brazil produces the popular Havaianas flip-flops, and sells them very cheaply, you may as well wait until you get there to buy them.

There is nothing better for the summer heat than cotton, and since Brazil produces linen and exports cotton you might want to pack the bare essentials, and acquire a new wardrobe.

When buying clothes, remember that some natural fabrics will shrink. *Pequeno* = Small; *Médio* = Medium; and *Grande* = Large (often marked 'P', 'M', and 'G'). *Maior* means larger; *menor* means smaller.

LANGUAGE

UNDERSTANDING THE LANGUAGE

Although Portuguese, not Spanish, is the language of Brazil, a knowledge of Spanish will go a long way. You will recognize many similar words, and some Brazilians will understand you if you speak in Spanish. You will, however, find it difficult to understand them. Although many upper-class Brazilians know at least some English or French and are eager to practice on foreign visitors, don't expect people on the street to speak your language. An effort by a foreigner to learn the local language is always appreciated. Pronunciation can be confusing. For example, 'r' is pronounced 'h,' so that 'Rio' sounds like 'Hee-o.'

At most large hotels and top restaurants you can get by in English with very few problems. But if you like to wander around on your own, you might want to invest in a good dictionary; the Berlitz Pocket Dictionary is a useful one, light and easy to carry around.

ADDRESSING PEOPLE

First names are used a great deal in Brazil. In many situations in which English-speakers would use a title and surname, Brazilians often use a first name with the title of respect: *Senhor* for men (written *Sr* and usually shortened to *Seu* in spoken Portuguese) and *Senhora* (written *Sra*) or *Dona* (used only with first name) for women.

There are three second-person pronoun forms in Portuguese. Stick to *você*, equivalent to 'you,' and you will be all right. *O senhor* (for men) or *a senhora* (for women) is used to show respect for someone of a different age group or social class, or to be polite to a stranger. As a foreigner, you won't

offend anyone if you use the wrong form of address. But if you want to learn when to use the more formal or informal style, observe how others address you, and be guided by that. In some parts of Brazil, mainly the northeast and the south, *tu* is used a great deal. Originally, in Portugal, *tu* was used among intimate friends and close relatives, but in Brazil, it is equivalent to *você*.

If you are staying for some time and are serious about learning the language, there are plenty of Portuguese courses for non-native speakers. Meanwhile, here are some of the most essential words and phrases.

GREETINGS

Tudo Bem, literally meaning 'all's well,' is one of the most common forms of greeting: one person asks, '*Tudo bem?*' (or '*Tudo bom?*') and the other replies, '*Tudo bem*' (or '*Tudo bom*'). This is also used to mean 'OK,' 'all right,' 'will do,' or as a response when someone apologizes, as if to say, 'That's all right, it doesn't matter.' '*Ta legal*' is a formal slang expression commonly heard. It means 'OK' or 'That's cool.' Other forms of greeting are:
Good morning (good afternoon) *Bom dia (boa tarde)*
Good evening (good night) *Boa noite*
How are you? *Como vai você?*
Well, thank you *Bem, obrigado*
Hello (to answer the telephone) *Alô*
Hello (common forms of greeting) *Bom dia, boa tarde, etc.*
Hi, hey! (informal greeting also to get someone's attention) *Oi*
Goodbye (very informal and most used) *Tchau*

Goodbye (literally 'until soon') *Até logo*
Goodbye (similar to 'farewell') *Adeus*
My name is (I am) *Meu nome é (Eu sou)*
What is your name? *Como é seu nome?*
It's a pleasure *É um prazer*
Pleasure (used in introductions as 'Pleased to meet you') *Prazer*
Good! Great! *Que bom!*
Health! (the most common toast) *Saúde*
Do you speak English? *Você fala inglês?*
I don't understand (I didn't understand) *Não entendo (Não entendi)*
Do you understand? *Você entende?*
Please repeat more slowly *Por favor repete, mais devagar*
What do you call this (that)? *Como se chama isto (aquilo)?*
How do you say...? *Como se diz...?*
Please *Por favor*
Thank you (very much) *(Muito) Obrigado (or obrigada, if a woman is speaking)*
You're welcome (literally 'it's nothing') *De nada*
Excuse me (to apologize) *Desculpe*
Excuse me (taking leave or to get past someone) *Com licença*

PRONOUNS

Who? *Quem?*
I (we) *Eu (nós)*
You (singular) *Você*
You (plural) *Vocês*
He (she) *Ele (ela)*
They *Eles (Elas)*
My (mine) *Meu (minha)* **depending on gender of object**
Our (ours) *Nosso (nossa)*

Your (yours) *Seu (sua)*
His (her/hers) *Dele (dela/deles)*
Their, theirs *Delas*

GETTING AROUND

Where is the...? *Onde é...?*
beach *a praia*
bathroom *o banheiro*
bus station *a rodoviária*
airport *o aeroporto*
train station *a estação de trem*
post office *o correio*
police station *a delegacia de polícia*
ticket office *a bilheteria*
marketplace *o mercado*
street market *feira*
embassy (consulate) *a embaixada (o consulado)*
Where is there a...? *Onde é que tem...?*
currency exchange *uma casa de câmbio*
bank *um banco*
pharmacy *uma farmácia*
(good) hotel *um (bom) hotel*
(good) restaurant *um (bom) restaurante*
snack bar *uma lanchonete*
bus stop *um ponto de ônibus*
taxi stand *um ponto de taxi*
subway station *uma estação de metrô*
service station *um posto de gasolina*
newsstand *um jornaleiro*
public telephone *um telefone público*
supermarket *um supermercado*
department store *uma loja de departamentos*
boutique *uma boutique*
jeweler *um joalheiro*
hairdresser (barber) *um cabeleireiro (um barbeiro)*
laundry *uma lavanderia*
hospital *um hospital*
doctor *um médico*
A ticket to... *Uma passagem para...*
I want to go to... *Quero ir para...*
How can I get to...? *Como posso ir para...?*
Please take me to... *Por favor, me leve para...*
Please call a taxi for me *Por favor, chame um taxi para mim*
I want to rent a car *Quero alugar um carro*
What is this place called? *Como se*

Forms of transport

taxi *taxi*
bus *ônibus*
car *carro*
plane *avião*
train *trem*
boat *barco*

Emergencies

I need... *Eu preciso de...*
a doctor *um médico*
a mechanic *um mecânico*
transportation *condução*
help *ajuda*

chama este lugar?
Where are we? *Onde estamos?*
How long will it take to get there? *Leva quanto tempo para chegar lá?*
Please stop here (Stop!) *Por favor, pare aqui (Pare!)*
Please wait *Por favor, espere*
What time does the bus (plane, boat) leave? *A que horas sai o ônibus (avião, barco)?*
Where does this bus go? *Este ônibus vai para onde?*
Does it go via...? *Passa em...?*
Please let me off at the next stop *Por favor, deixe-me na próxima paragem*
Airport (bus station) tax *Taxa de embarque*
I want to check my luggage (on a bus, etc.) *Quero despachar minha bagagem*
I want to store my luggage (at a station) *Quero guardar minha bagagem*

SHOPPING

Do you have...? *Você tem...?*
I want... please *Eu quero... por favor*
I don't want... *Eu não quero...*
I want to buy... *Eu quero comprar...*
Can you help me please? *Pode ajudar-me, por favor?*
It's not quite what I want *Nao è bem o que quero*
Where can I buy...? *Onde posso comprar...?*
cigarettes *cigarros*
film *filme*
a ticket for... *uma entrada para...*
a reserved seat *um lugar marcado*
another the same *um outro igual*
another different *um outro diferente*
this (that) *isto (aqui)*
**something less
expensive** *algo mais barato*
postcards *cartões postais*
paper (envelopes) *papel (envelopes)*
a pen (a pencil) *uma caneta (um lápis)*
soap (shampoo) *sabonete (xampu or shampoo)*
toothpaste *pasta de dente*
sunscreen *filtro solar*
aspirin *aspirina*
How much? *Quanto?*
How many? *Quantos?*
How much does it cost? *Quanto*

custa? Quanto é?
That's very expensive *É muito caro*
a lot, very (many) *muito (muitos)*
a little (few) *um pouco (poucos)*
handbag (purse) *bolsa/saco*
money purse *porta-moedas*
wallet *carteira*

AT THE HOTEL

I have a reservation *Tenho uma reserva*
I want to make a reservation *Quero fazer uma reserva*
A single room (A double room) *Um quarto de solteiro (Um quarto de casal)*
With air conditioning *com ar condicionado*
I want to see the room *Quero ver o quarto*
suitcase *mala/bolsa*
room service *serviço de quarto*
key *chave*
the manager *o gerente*

AT THE RESTAURANT

waiter *garçon*
maître d' *daitre*
I didn't order this *Eu não pedi isto*
The menu (the wine list) *O cardápio (a carta de vinhos)*
breakfast *café da manhã*
lunch *almoço*
supper *jantar*
the house specialty *a especialidade da casa*
carbonated mineral water *água mineral com gás*
uncarbonated mineral water *água mineral sem gas*
coffee *café*
tea *chá*
beer (bottled) *cerveja*
beer (draft) *chope*
white wine (red wine) *vinho branco (vinho tinto)*
a soft drink (juice) *um refrigerante (suco)*
an alcoholic drink *um drink*
ice *gelo*
salt *sal*
pepper *pimenta*
sugar *açúcar*
a plate *um prato*
a glass *um copo*
a glass of wine *uma taça de vinho*
a cup *uma xícara*
a napkin *um guardanapo*
bread *pão*
egg *ovo*
fish *peixe*
crab *caranguejo/aratu*
herring *arenque*
lobster *lavagante*

seafood *marisco*
meat *carne*
beef *carne de boi*
chicken *frango*
ham *presunto*
lamb *borrego*
liver *fígado*
mutton *carneiro*
pork *porco*
stew *guisado*
vegetables *legumes*
potatoes *batatas*
aubergine (eggplant) *beringela*
avocado *abacate*
beans *feijãos*
broad beans *favas*
carrots *cenouras*
garlic *alho*
ginger *gengibre*
lettuce *alface*
well done *bem passado*
medium rare *ao ponto*
rare *mal passado*
baked *cocido no forno*
home-made *caseiro*
fumado *smoked*
I'm a vegetarian *Eu sou vegetariano/a*
I don't eat meat/fish *Eu não como carne/peixe*
The bill, please *A conta, por favor*
Is service included? *Está incluído o serviço?*
I want my change, please *Eu quero meu troco, por favor*
I want a receipt *Eu quero um recibo*

MONEY

bank *banco*
cash *dinheiro*
Do you accept credit cards? *Aceita cartão de crédito?*
Can you cash a traveler's check? *Pode trocar um traveler's check? (cheque de viagem)*
I want to exchange money *Quero trocar dinheiro*
What is the exchange rate? *Qual é o câmbio?*

TIME

When? *Quando?*
What time is it? *Que horas são?*
Just a moment please *Um momento, por favor*
What is the schedule? *(bus, tour, show, etc.) Qual é o horário?*
How long does it take? *Leva quanto tempo?*
hour *hora*
day *dia*
week *semana*
month *mês*
At what time...? *A que horas...?*

At one o' clock (two, three) *A uma hora (duas, três)*
An hour from now *Daqui a uma hora*
Which day? *Que dia?*
yesterday *ontem*
today *hoje*
tomorrow *amanhã*
this week *esta semana*
last week *a semana passada/*
next week *a semana que vem*
the weekend *o fim de semana*
Monday *segunda-feira (often 2a)*
Tuesday *terca-feira (often 3a)*
Wednesday *quarta-feira (often 4a)*
Thursday *quinta-feira (often 5a)*
Friday *sexta-feira (often 6a)*
Saturday *sábado*
Sunday *domingo*

NUMBERS

Ordinal numbers are written with ° ie a degree sign after the numeral, so that 3° *andar* means 3rd Floor.
BR followed by a number refers to one of the federal interstate highways, for example BR-101, which follows the Atlantic coast.

1 *um*
2 *dois*
3 *três*
4 *quatro*
5 *cinco*
6 *seis*
7 *sete*
8 *oito*
9 *nove*
10 *dez*
11 *onze*
12 *doze*
13 *treze*
14 *quatorze*
15 *quinze*
16 *dezesseis*
17 *dezessete*
18 *dezoito*
19 *dezenove*
20 *vinte*

Addresses

The following will help you understand Brazilian addresses and place names:
Al. or *Alameda* = lane
Andar = floor, story
Av. or *Avenida* = avenue
Casa = house
Centro = the central downtown business district, also frequently referred to as a cidade (the city)
Cj or *Conjunto* = a suite of rooms, or sometimes a group of buildings
Estr or *Estrada* = road or highway
Fazenda = ranch, also a lodge
Lgo or *Largo* = square or plaza
Lote = lot
Pça or *Praça* = square or plaza
Praia = beach
Rio = river
Rod or *Rodovia* = highway
R or *Rua* = street
Sala = room

21 *vinte um*
30 *trinta*
40 *quarenta*
50 *cinquenta*
60 *sessenta*
70 *setenta*
80 *oitenta*
90 *noventa*
100 *cem*
101 *cento e um*
200 *duzentos*
300 *trezentos*
400 *quatrocentos*
500 *quinhentos*
600 *seiscentos*
700 *setecentos*
800 *oitocentos*
900 *novecentos*
1,000 *mil*
2,000 *dois mil*
10,000 *dez mil*
100,000 *cem mil*
1,000,000 *um milhão*

Read the menu with our language guide.

FURTHER READING

HISTORY AND TRAVEL

Birds of Brazil, by Ber van Perlo. Brazil's bird diversity is one of the richest in the world. Here is the guide.
Brazil, by Michael Palin. A good primer, written in the same chatty tone as the 2012 TV series.
Brazilian Adventure, by Peter Fleming. In 1925, Colonel Fawcett – soldier, spy, and legendary explorer – embarked on a journey into the dark and uncharted heart of Brazil in search of the lost 'City of Z.'
The Brazil Reader, by Robert M. Levine and John J. Crocitti (eds). The Brazil Reader offers a fascinating guide to Brazilian life, culture, and history.
A Concise History of Brazil, by Boris Fausto. Covers almost 500 years of Brazilian history.
A Death in Brazil, A Book of Omissions, by Peter Robb. Delving into Brazil's baroque past, Peter Robb writes about its history of slavery and the richly multicultural society.
The Lost City of Z, by David Grann. Journalist David Grann interweaves the stories of Fawcett's quest for 'Z' with his own journey into the jungle.
Lula of Brazil, by Richard Bourne. Full-length portrait of the South American political phenomenon.
The New Brazil, by Riordan Roett. The story of South America's largest country as it evolved from a remote Portuguese colony into a regional leader.
Walking the Amazon: 860 Days. One Step at a Time, by Ed Stafford. Ed Stafford set off to become the first man ever to walk the entire length of the Amazon.

FICTION

Brazil, by John Updike. In the dream-Brazil of John Updike's imagining, almost anything is possible if you are young and in love.
The Brothers, by Milton Hatoum. Set in Manaus during the rubber boom.
City of the Beasts, by Isabel Allende. A coming-of-age tale set in the Amazon jungle.
City of God, by Paulo Lins. The novel on which the award-winning film was based: life and violence in a Rio slum.
Dom Casmurro, by Machado de Assis. A sad and darkly comic novel about love and the corrosive power of jealousy.
Dona Flor and Her Two Husbands, by Jorge Amado. One of the classics from Brazil's best-known novelist.
Elite Squad, by Luiz Eduardo Soares. The book behind the award-winning film of police corruption in Rio.
Soulstorm, by Clarice Lispector. Short stories by writer noted for her blend of suspense and romance.

CIVILIZATION AND SOCIETY

Amazon Frontier: The Defeat of the Brazilian Indians, by J. Hemming. Chronicles the first 150 years of Europeans exploring the Amazon.

Send Us Your Thoughts

We do our best to ensure the information in our books is as accurate and up-to-date as possible. The books are updated on a regular basis using local contacts, who painstakingly add, amend and correct as required. However, some details (such as telephone numbers and opening times) are liable to change, and we are ultimately reliant on our readers to put us in the picture.

We welcome your feedback, especially your experience of using the book 'on the road.' Maybe we recommended a hotel that you liked (or another that you didn't), or you came across a great bar or new attraction we missed.

We will acknowledge all contributions, and we'll offer an Insight Guide to the best letters received.

Please write to us at:
Insight Guides
PO Box 7910
London SE1 1WE
Or email us at:
insight@apaguide.co.uk

At the End of the Rainbow? Gold, Land and People in the Brazilian Amazon, by G. Macmillan. This book explains how gold fever came to grip the Amazon and considers the changes it has brought to the region.
Brazil on the Rise: The Story of a Country Transformed, by Larry Rother. A view of Brazil from the New York Times' Rio bureau chief.
Disinherited Indians in Brazil, by Fiona Watson, Stephen Corry, and Caroline Pearce (eds). The story of Brazil's Indian population.
Fazendas: The Futebol: The Brazilian Way of Life, by Alex Bellos. Entertaining combination of history and anecdote that will fascinate those who have an interest in football.
Great Houses and Plantations of Brazil, by Fernando Tasso Fragosa Pires and Nicholas Sapieha. A picture book that traces the development of Brazil's sugar and coffee plantations and cattle ranches.
Murder in the Rainforest, by Jan Rocha. Using eyewitness accounts, this work tells the story behind the Haximu massacre, a fateful meeting between a group of young Yanomami Indians and Brazilian gold miners.
Oscar Niemeyer: Curves of Irreverence, by Styliane Philippou. A look at the work of Brazil's greatest architect.
Rio de Janeiro, by Ruy Castro. Brazilian essayist reveals his personal Rio, with fascinating anecdotes.
Travelers' Tales Brazil, by Annette Haddad and Scott Doggett. Fifty essays on the country's commingling of cultures.

OTHER INSIGHT GUIDES

Insight Guides cover nearly 200 destinations, providing information on culture and all the top sights, as well as superb photography. *Insight Guide: South America* covers the whole subcontinent, from Colombia to Tierra del Fuego. Other Insight Guides on South America include: *Argentina, Chile and Easter Island, Ecuador and the Galápagos*, and *Peru*.

beaches 228, 229
Lagoa da Conceição 229
Praia do Santinho 229
Ribeirão da Ilha 229
Santo Antônio de Lisboa 228
Ilhéus 264, 355
immigrants 22, 40, 66, 184, 224, 230
German community 22
Italian community 23
Japanese community 23, 191
Middle Eastern community 23
immigrrants
Japanese community 187
industry 42, **49**, 55, 184, 185, 223, 270
internet 370
Ipojuca 298
Irmandade da Boa Morte 269
iron ore 55, **56**, 57, 62, 66, 207, 329
Isabel de Orléans e Bragança 20
Itacaré 265, 356
Itacimirim 267
Itacuruçá 174, 350
Itacuruçá island 174
Itaimbézinho Canyon 233
Itaipú Dam 66
Itaipú dam 221
Itanhaém 202
Itatiaia national park 178
Itaúnas 217
Itu 199
Museu da Energia 199
Museu Republicano da Convenção de Itu 199

J

Jackson, Michael 104
Jaguanum island 174
Jaguaripe 269
Jaua 267
Jericoacoara National Park 312
Jesuits 24, 36, **36**, 211
missions 234
Jesus, Isabel de 119
jet-skiing 229
João III 36, 273
João Pessoa 305
accommodations 358
Convent of Santo Antônio 306
Parque Solon de Lucena 306
restaurants 315
São Francisco 306
João VI 37
Jobim, Tom 99, 102, 152
John Paul II, Pope 139, 142
Jorge, Seu 102, 106
Juazeiro 271
Juazeiro do Norte 86, 308
Capela de Socorro 308
Jucuípe 267
jungle 320, 321, 324, 335

K

Kaneko, Taro 114
Kubitschek, Juscelino 42, 49, 120, 138, 207, 216, 239, 241

L

Lagoa Azul 257
Lagoinha 312
Lago Salvador 333
Lago Verde 330
Laguna 229, 230, 354
Landowsky, Paul 154
language 17, 35
Laranjeiras 287
Museu Afro-Brasileiro de Sergipe 287
Le Corbusier 120
Lee, Rita 103
left luggage 370
legends and mythology 289, 313
Lençóis 270
Lençóisa 356
Lençóis Maranhenses National Park 314
Letícia 337
Lima, Walter, Jr 109
Linhares 217
Linha Verde 267
Lisboa, Antônio Francisco. See Aleijadinho
Lisboa, Manuel Francisco 211
Lobato, Monteiro 115
Lopes Mendes 176
Loronha, Fernando de 302
lost property 370
Lubambo, Tadeu 307
Ludwig, Daniel K. 327
Lula da Silva, Luiz Inácio 27, 38, **45**, 46, 55, 57

M

Mabe, Hugo 114
Mabe, Manabu 114
Macapá 327, 359
Maceió 286, 290
accommodations 357
Pierre Chalita Sacred Art Museum 291
Praia Pajuçara 290
restaurants 291
Malan, Pedro 55
Malfatti, Anita 114, 185
Mambucaba 177
Manaus 321, 330, 334
accommodations 359
Alfândega 331
Mercado Municipal (Adolfo Lisboa) 331
Museu do Homem do Norte 332
National Amazonian Research Institute 333
Palácio da Cultura 332
restaurants 337
Salesian Museu do Indio 333
Teatro Amazonas 331
Teatro da Instalação 332
zoo 333
Manet, Edouard 115
Mangaratiba 174
Maragogipinho 269
Maranhão 63, 305, 313
Maraú Peninsula 265
Marechal Deodoro 290

Mariana 87, 213
Carmo 213
Catedral de Nossa Senhora da Assunção 213
Museu Arquidiocesano de Arte Sacra 214
São Francisco 213
Maria, Tania 102
Maricá 172
Marinho, Roberto 111
Marius, Ferreira Louis 119
markets
arts and crafts market (Brasília) 243
Caruaru 299
Central (Fortaleza) 311
Ipanema Hippie Fair (Rio) 162
Mercado Modelo (Salvador) 277
Mercado Municipal (Florianópolis) 228
Mercado Municipal (São Paulo) 190
Municipal (Adolfo Lisboa) (Manaus) 331
Predioda Alfandega (Florianópolis) 228
Ribeira (Olinda) 297
São Joaquim (Salvador) 277
São José (Recife) 295
Ver-O-Peso (Belém) 323
Martins, Aldemir 118
Martins island 174
Massa, Felipe 189
mata atlântica 65
Mato Grosso 251, 253
Mato Grosso do Sul 251
Maurice, Prince of Nassau 294
media 370
medical emergencies 370
Medici, Emílio Garrastazu 44
Meirelles, Fernando 109
Mendes, Chico 62
Menezes, Margareth 104, 105
Menininha do Gantois, Mãe 83
Mercury, Daniela 104
Miller, Charles 89
Minas Gerais 35, 66, 87, 117, 133
mining 329
missions, the 234
Mistura Fina 284
monasteries and convents
Convento de Santo Antônio (Rio) 139
Convento de São Francisco (Salvador) 274
Convent of Santo Antônio (João Pessoa) 306
Monasterio e Basilica de São Bento (São Paulo) 189
Mosteiro de São Bento (Rio) 140
Nossa Senhora dos Anjos (Cabo Frio) 172
São Francisco convent (Olinda) 297
money matters 371
budgeting for your trip 366
tipping 373
Monserrat 326
Monte Alegre 329
Monte Dourado 327

Monte, Marisa 105
Montenegro, Fernanda 109
Monte Pascoal 264
Moog, Vianna 21
Moraes, Vinicius de 99, 102, 152
Morais, Prudente de 39
Morretes 225
Morro Branco 309
Morro de São Paulo 267
motor racing 189, 363
mountain-biking 303
movies 361
movie theaters
   in Rio 143, 153, 157, 162
Mundaú 312
Muriqui 174
museums and galleries 7, 360
   archeological museum
      (Paranaguá) 227
   Bolsa Oficial de Café (Santos) 201
   Casa da Ipiranga – Instituto de
      Cultura (Petrópolis) 167
   Casa Daros Rio (Rio) 143
   Casa de Anchieta (São Paulo) 188
   Casa de Cultura (Paraty) 178
   Casa de Jorge Amado (Salvador)
      275
   Casa de Santos Dumont
      (Petrópolis) 167
   Casa dos Contos (Ouro Preto) 212
   Ceará Memorial Museum
      (Fortaleza) 311
   Centro Cultural Dannemann (São
      Félix) 269
   Centro do Preservação de Arte
      Indígena (Alter do Chão) 330
   Cervejaria Bohemia (Petrópolis)
      168
   Complexo Cultural da República
      João Herculino (Brasília) 245
   Espaço Cultural da Marinha (Rio)
      140
   Fundação Cultural de Mato
      Grosso (Cuiabá) 255
   Fundação Maria Luiza e Oscar
      Americano (São Paulo) 194
   Latin American Cultural Center
      (São Paulo) 193
   MAC (Fortaleza) 311
   Museu Afro-Brasileiro de Sergipe
      (Laranjeiras) 287
   Museu Afro-Brasileiro (Salvador)
      274
   Museu Arquidiocesano de Arte
      Sacra (Mariana) 214
   Museu Biológico Professor Mello
      Leitão (Santa Teresa) 216
   Museu Câmara Cascudo (Natal)
      307
   Museu Carlos Costa Pinto
      (Salvador) 276
   Museu Casa do Pontal (Rio) 158
   Museu Chácara do Céu (Rio) 146
   Museu da Cidade (Recife) 295
   Museu da Cidade (Salvador) 275
   Museu da Energia (Itu) 199
   Museu da Gente Sergipana
      (Aracaju) 288
   Museu da Imigração Japonesa
      (São Paulo) 191
   Museu da Inconfidência (Ouro
      Preto) 211
   Museu da Lingua Portuguesa (São
      Paulo) 194
   Museu da República (Rio) 147
   Museu de Arte Contemporânea
      (Niterói) 147
   Museu de Arte Contemporânea
      (Olinda) 297
   Museu de Arte de São Paulo (São
      Paulo) 193
   Museu de Arte do Rio (MAR) (Rio)
      140
   Museu de Arte Moderna (MAM)
      (Rio) 141
   Museu de Arte Moderna (São
      Paulo) 193
   Museu de Arte Sacra (Paraty) 178
   Museu de Arte Sacra (Salvador)
      276
   Museu de Arte Sacra (Santos)
      201
   Museu de Arte Sacra (São Paulo)
      192
   Museu de Arte Sacre (São
      Cristóvão) 287
   Museu de Pesca (Santos) 201
   Museu do Diamante (Diamantina)
      216
   Museu do Estado do Pará (Belém)
      323
   Museu do Folclore Edison
      Carneiro (Rio) 147
   Museu do Futebol (São Paulo) 89,
      194
   Museu do Homem Americano
      (Serra da Capivara National
      Park) 313
   Museu do Homem do Nordeste
      (Recife) 296
   Museu do Homem do Norte
      (Manaus) 332
   Museu do Imigrante (Bento
      Gonçalves) 231
   Museu do Indio Marechal Rondon
      (Cuiabá) 255
   Museu do Indio (Rio) 143
   Museu do Ipiranga (São Paulo)
      194
   Museu Dom Bosco (Campo
      Grande) 256
   Museu do Oratório (Ouro Preto)
      211
   Museu do Seringal Vila Paraiso
      334
   Museu do Trem (Recife) 295
   Museu Emílio Goeldi (Belém) 325
   Museu Ferroviário (São João del
      Rei) 214
   Museu Florestal (São Paulo) 195
   Museu Histórico de Brasília
      (Brasília) 245
   Museu Histórico de Sergipe (São
      Cristóvão) 287
   Museu Historico Municipal João
      Batista Conti (Atibaia) 199
   Museu Histórico Nacional (Rio)
      141
   Museu H. Stern (Rio) 153
   Museu Imperia (Petrópolis) 166
   Museu Internacional Arte Naïf do
      Brasil (MIAN) (Rio) 119
   Museu Internacional de Arte Naïf
      do Brasil (Rio) 154
   Museum of Votive Offerings (São
      Cristóvão) 287
   Museu Nacional de Belas Artes
      (Rio) 142
   Museu Nacional (Rio) 143
   Museu Padre Toledo (Tiradentes)
      214
   Museu Paulista (São Paulo) 194
   Museu Republicano da
      Convenção (Itu) 199
   Museu Villa-Lobos (Rio) 143
   Palácio Antônio Lemos (Belém)
      323
   Palácio Boa Vista museum
      (Campos do Jordão) 198
   Palácio de Cristal (Petrópolis) 167
   Palácio Episcopal (Olinda) 297
   Pierre Chalita Sacred Art Museum
      (Maceió) 291
   Pinacoteca do Estado (São Paulo)
      192
   railroad museum (Atibaia) 199
   railroad museum (Paranapiacaba)
      199
   Salesian Museu do Indio
      (Manaus) 333
   Santo Alexandre museum (Belém)
      321
   TAM Museum (Americana) 202
music and dance 7, 98, 284, 360.
   See also nightlife, theaters and
   concert venues
   bossa nova 102
   classical music 360
   contemporary 103
   folk music 98
   frevo 73, 295
   fusion of genres 99
   musical instruments 100, 277,
      281, 364
   música sertaneja 268
   opera 310
   Salvador music scene 279
   samba 71, 100, 144
   samba schools 72, 101
   tambor-de-criola 313
   traditional gaucho 233
   Tropicalia 103

N

Nação Zumbi 107
Nascimento, Milton 103
Natal 261, 305, 307
   accommodations 358
   beaches 307
   Forte dos Reis Magos 307
   Museu Câmara Cascudo 307
   Ponta Negra 307
   restaurants 315
National Federation of Afro-
   Brazilian Tradition and Culture
   (FENATRAB) 83
national parks. See also nature
   reserves
   Abrolhos Marine 264

Aparados da Serra 233
Araguaia 248
Chapada Diamantina 270
Chapada dos Gimarães 255
Chapada dos Veadeiros 248
de Brasília 247
Emas 248
Fernando de Noronha 302
Itatiaia 178
Jericoacoara 312
Lençóis Maranhenses 314
Serra da Capivara 313
Serra dos Orgãos 168
Sete Cidades 313
Tijuca (Rio) 154
Tumucumaque 64
Ubajara 311
National Reconstruction Party 46
nature reserves. See also national
 parks
 Comboios 217
 Florestal de Linhares 217
 Ilha Grande 175
 Sooretama 217
naturereserves
 Ilha do Mel 227
Nazaré das Farinhas 269
Negro, Rio 320, 333, 334
Neiva, Tia 85
Neves, Tancredo 44
Nicola, Norberto 118
Niemeyer, Oscar 120, 147, 192,
 193, 210, 241
nightlife 98, 361. See also under
 major towns
Niterói 147
 Museu de Arte Contemporânea
 147
 Parque da Cidade 147
Nóbrega, Manuel da 183
Northeast 63. See also Far
 Northeast
Nova Friburgo 169, 350
Nova Petrópolis 231, 354
 Immigration Park 231
Novo Hamburgo 23
Nugent, Stephen 328

O

Obidos 336
O Dedo de Deus 168
Ohtake, Tomie 114
oil 63
Oiticica, Helio 116
Olinda 73, 293, 296, 301
 accommodations 357
 Carnival 295
 Igreja da Sé 297
 Mercado da Ribeira 297
 Misericórdia 297
 Museu de Arte Contemporânea
 297
 Nossa Senhora da Graça 297
 Nossa Senhora das Neves 297
 Palácio Episcopal 297
 Praça do Carmo 297
 São Francisco convent 297
 São Roque 297
 Seminário de Olinda 297

Olivença 265
Olodum 104
Olympic Games. See sports
opening hours. See business
 hours
Orellana, Francisco de 319, 324
Os Ipanemas 102
Os Mutantes 103
Ouro Preto 20, 35, 87, 204, **210**
 accommodations 352
 Casa dos Contos 212
 Escola de Minas 212
 Igreja de Nossa Senhora do Pilar
 211
 Igreja de Nossa Senhora do
 Rosário dos Pretos 20, 204
 Mina do Chico Rei 213
 Minas da Passagem 213
 Museu da Inconfidência 211
 Museu do Oratório 211
 Nossa Senhora da Conceição de
 Antônio Dias 213
 Nossa Senhora do Rosário dos
 Pretos 212
 Praça Tiradentes 211
 restaurants 217
 São Francisco de Assis 212

P

Pacheco, Ana Maria 113
Pacheco, Plínio 300
Padilha, José 110
Pagodinha, Zeca 101
Pai Inácio Mountain 270
Palmares 20
pampas 66, 230, 234
Pancetti, José 115
Pantanal 129, 239
 accommodations 254
 restaurants 257
 sightseeing flights 256
 tours 254
Pantanal Express 256
Paracuru 312
paragliding 199
Paraguay, River 253
Paraíba 305
Paraná 66, 129, 223
Paranaguá 227
 archeological museum 227
Paranapiacaba 199
 railroad museum 199
Paraná River 241
Paranoá, Lake 241
Paraty 75, 173, 175, 177, 350
 Casa de Cultura 178
 Museu de Arte Sacra 178
 restaurants 179
 Santa Rita 177
Paredes, José Nogueira 70
Parima 337
Parintins 79, 334
parks and gardens. See
 also national parks, state parks,
 theme parks, water parks
 Bosque Rodrigues Alves (Belém)
 325
 Felícia Leirner sculpture garden
 (Campos do Jordão) 198

Horto Florestal (São Paulo) 195
Ibirapuera Park (São Paulo) 193
Immigration Park (Nova
 Petropólis) 231
Jardim Botânico (Brasília) 247
Jardim Botânico (Rio) 155
Jardim Botânico (São Paulo) 195
Pampulha (Belo Horizonte) 120
Parque Cidade Sarah Kubitschek
 (Brasílias) 246
Parque da Cidade (Niterói) 147
Parque das Esculturas (Fazenda
 Nova) 300
Parque Solon de Lucena (João
 Pessoa) 306
Parnamirim 312
Partido dos Trabalhadores (PT) 46
Paula Rodrigues, Francisco de 39
Pavanelli, Ernani 119
Pedra do Sino 168
Pedro I 39, 165, 184, 194
Pedro II 38, 39, 165
Pelé 90, 144
Penedo 290
Penha 173
Pennacchi, Fulvio 116
people 17, 284. See
 also Amerindians, immigrants;
 See also immigrants
 bandeirante 184
 of African descent 18
 of Minas Gerais 207
 of Rio 137
 of São Paulo 185
 Paulistas 184
Pereira dos Santos, Nelson 108
Pereira dos Santos, Vitalino 298
Pernambuco 200
Pernambuco state 35, 36, **293**,
 297
Peruíbe 202
Petróleo Brasileiro (Petrobras) 55
Petrópolis 38, 165
 accommodations 350
 Casa da Ipiranga – Instituto de
 Cultura 167
 Casa de Santos Dumont 167
 Catedral de São Pedro de
 Alcântara 167
 Cervejaria Bohemia 168
 Grande Hotel 166
 Museu Imperia 166
 Palácio de Cristal 167
 Palácio Quitandinha 168
 restaurants 179
 Rua do Imperador 166
photography 271
Piauí 305, 313
Pico das Agulhas Negras 178
Pindobal 328
Pinheiro, Heloisa 99, 152
Pinheiros river 192
Pinzon, Vicente 319
Pipa 306, 358
Piquet, Nelson 189
Pirenópolis 248
Pizarro, Gonzales 324
Planaltina 242
Planalto Central 63
plantlife. See also rainforests

biodiversity 64
giant water lilies 334
orchids 215, 216, 270
Poconé 251, 256
politics. See government and
politics
Pombeba island 174
Ponta de Garopaba 229
Pontal do Sul 227
Ponta Negra 172
population 49
Portão de Inferno 255
Portinari, Candido 115, 210
Porto Alegre 223, 233, 235, 354
Porto das Dunas 310
Porto de Galinhas 298, 301, 357
Porto de Pedras 291
Pôrto Seguro 263, 264, 356
postal services 371
Prado, Vasco 118
Praia do Forte 267, 356
Praia do Genipabu 307
Praia do Poço 306
Praia do Rosa 229
Praia Grande 202
Prainha 309
Prestes, Júlio 40
Providencia buffalo ranch 326
public holidays 361, 371
public toilets 372

Q

Quadros, Jânio 42
quilombos 286

R

rail travel 344
Pantanal Express 256, 344
scenic routes 225, 344
rainforests 64, 173, 217, 225, 264,
320, 338. See also Amazon,
jungle
Raposa 314
Raposo, Francisco 324
Recife 118, 129, 261, 293
accommodations 357
Boa Viagem beach 294, 296
Capela Dourada 294
Carnival 73
Casa da Cultura 294
Casa Forte 296
Estação Central 295
Forte das Cinco Pontas 295
Igreja de São Pedro 295
Itaipava Arena Pernambuco 293
Kahal Zur Israel Synagogue 295
Mercado de São José 295
Museu da Cidade 295
Museu do Homem do Nordeste
296
Museu do Trem 295
nightlife 296
Oficina Cerâmica Francisco
Brennand 296
Paço do Frevo 295
Patio de São Pedro 295
Praça da República 294
restaurants 301

Teatro Santa Isabel 294
Várzea 296
Recôncavo da Bahia 268
Regina, Elis 98
Rego Monteiro, Vicente do 115
Rei, Chico 209
religion 81, 190, 280, 372
Amerindian beliefs 82
candomblé 83, 83, 263, 280
Evangelicals 85
Islam 85
jarê 270
Judaism 86
Roman Catholicism 81
umbanda 83
Vale do Amanhecer movement 84
religious services 372
repentistas 312
Resende, José 113
Reserva Biológica Comboios 217
Reserva Biológica de Sooretama
217
restaurants. See also food and
drink
Amazon 337
Bahia 271
botequims 97
Brasília 249
Far Northeast 315
Minas Gerais 217
Pantanal area 257
Pernambuco state 301
Rio 163
Rio de Janeiro State 179
Salvador 275, 283
São Paulo 195
Sergipe and Alagoas 291
Southern States 235
restrooms 372
Revolucão Farroupilha 230
ribbons, symbolic 78, 277
Rio da Prata 257
Rio de Janeiro 36, 65, 129, 133
accommodations 146, 348
Arco do Teles 141
Arcos da Lapa (Carioca Aqueduct)
145
Arpoador 152
Avenida Atlântica 151, 162
Avenida Niemeyer 156
Avenida Sernambetiba 157
Baía de Guanabara 147
Barra da Tijuca 148, 157, 160
Barra Shopping 157, 162
beaches 148, 155, 158
Biblioteca Nacional 142
Botafogo 148
botequims 97
buses 149
cable-cars 148
Carnival 70, 144
Casa Daros Rio 143
Casa Rui Barbosa 143
Catedral Metropolitana 139
Cidade das Artes 161
Cidade do Samba 72, 144
Cinelândia 142
Circo Voador 161
Convento de Santo Antônio 139
Copacabana 148, 149, 160

Copacabana Palace Hotel 149,
159
Corcovado 148, 154
Corcovado Railroad 154
Cosme Velho 154
Cristo Redentor 154
Dois Irmãos 152
Dona Marta Belvedere 155
Downtown 139
Engenhão 144, 160
Espaço Cultural da Marinha 140
favelas 149, 150, 156
ferries 147
Flamengo 146, 148
Fundição Progresso 161
Gávea Golf Course 156
Glória 146
Grumari 158
Guanabara Bay 160
Guaratiba 158
history 137
Igreja da Nossa Senhora da
Candelária 140
Igreja da Ordem Terceira de São
Francisco de Paula 140
Igreja de Nossa Senhora da Glória
do Outeiro 204
Igreja de Nossa Senhora da
Penha 76
Igreja de São Francisco da
Penitência 139
Ilha de Paquetá 147
Ipanema 148, 152
Ipanema Hippie Fair 162
Jardim Botânico 155
Jardim Zoológico 143
Lagoa Rodrigo de Freitas 155,
160
Lapa 145, 161
Largo da Carioca 139
Leblon 148, 152
Leblon Shopping 162
Leme 148
Maracanã 144, 160
Maracanã Stadium 89
Mesa do Imperador 154
Morro da Urca 148
Mosteiro de São Bento 140
movie theaters 143, 153, 157,
162
Museu Casa do Pontal 158
Museu Chácara do Céu 146
Museu da República 147
Museu de Arte do Rio (MAR) 140
Museu de Arte Moderna (MAM)
141
Museu do Folclore Edison
Carneiro 147
Museu do Indio 143
Museu Histórico Nacional 141
Museu H. Stern 153
Museu Internacional Arte Naïf do
Brasil (MIAN) 119
Museu Internacional de Arte Naïf
do Brasil 154
Museu Nacional 143
Museu Nacional de Belas Artes
142
Museu Villa-Lobos 143
nightlife 145, 157, 159

Nossa Senhora da Glória do Outeiro 146
Nossa Senhora do Carmo 141
Odeon 143
Ordem Terceira do Monte do Carmo 141
Paço Imperial 141
Palácio do Catete 146
Pão de Açúcar 147
Parque Nacional da Tijuca 154
Pedra de Guaratiba 158
Petrobrás 145
Praça Tiradentes 139
Praça XV de Novembro 141
Praia dos Bandeirantes 158
Praia Vermelha 148
Real Gabinente Português de Leitura 140
restaurants 157, 163
Rio-Sul 143, 162
Rocinha 150, 156
Rua do Ouvidor 23
Rua Garcia d'Avila 153
Sala Cecília Meireles 161
samba schools 72
Sambódromo 71, 144, 160
Santa Teresa 145
São Conrado 148, 155
São Conrado Fashion Mall 162
shopping 153, 157, **162**, 365
sightseeing flights 154
Sítio Roberto Burle Marx 158
Teatro Municipal 142, 143, 161
Tiradentes Palace 141
transportation 345
trolleys 145
Vidigal 156
Visconde de Pirajá 153
Vista Chinesa 155
Rio de Janeiro State 165
Rio Grande do Norte 305, 306
Rio Grande do Sul 23, 66, 118, 129, **230**, 232
Rio Quente 248
Rio–Santos Highway 173
Rio–Teresópolis Highway 168
Rocha, Glauber 108
Rodrigues, Virginia 104
Romão Batista, Padre Cícero 308
Rondon, Cândido Mariano da Silva 25
Roosevelt, Anna 329
Roosevelt, Eleanor 220
Roraima 337
Rosa Borges, Durval 248
Rousseff, Dilma 22, 47
royal roads 215
rubber 49, 320, 328
running 363

S

Sabará 210
Igreja do Rosário dos Pretos 210
Nossa Senhora da Conceição 210
Nossa Senhora do Ó 210
sailing 200
Saldanha, Carlos 110
Salgado, Sebastião 117, 327, 329
Salles, Walter, Jr 109

salt 308
Salvador 36, 129, 261, 263, **273**
accommodations 356
Amaralina 278
Armação de Iemanjá 278
Barra 278
beaches 278, 279
Boa Viagem beach 281
Boa Viagem church 278
Boca do Rio 278
Campo Grande 278
Carnival 70, **73**, 279, 280, 281
Casa de Jorge Amado 275
Catedral Basílica 274
Cidade Alta 274
Cidade Baixa 274, 277
Corsário 278
Elevador Lacerda 277
ferry to Ilha de Itaparica 282
Festa do Bonfim 78
festivals 281
Igreja do Carmo 276
Igreja e Convento de São Francisco 87, 274
Itaipava Fonte Nova Arena 279
Itapoã 278
Jardim de Alá 278
Largo do Carmo 275
Largo do Pelourinho 275
Mariquita 278
Mercado Modelo 277
Monte Serrat church 277
Museu Afro-Brasileiro 274
Museu Carlos Costa Pinto 276
Museu da Cidade 275
Museu de Arte Sacra 276
nightlife 278
Nossa Senhora da Conceição de Praia 277
Nossa Senhora do Rosário dos Pretos 84, 275
Nosso Senhor do Bonfim 277, 281
Ondina 278
Ordem Terceira de São Francisco 274
Patamares 278
Pelourinho 278
Piatã 278
Pituaçu 278
Pituba 278
Praça Anchieta 274
Praça da Sé 274
Praça Municipal 276
Procissão do Senhor Bom Jesus dos Navegantes 78, 281
restaurants 275, 283
Rio Vermelho 278
Rua Alfredo Brito 275
Salvador Zoo 278
Santa Casa da Misericórdia 276
Santa Teresa 276
Santo Antônio da Barra fort 278
São Joaquim Market 277
São Pedro dos Clérigos 274
Senac Restaurant 275
Teatro Castro Alves 278
Terreiro de Jesus 274
transportation 275
Vitória 276

Samico, Gilvan 118
Sangalo, Ivete 104
Santa Catarina 129, 227
Santa Caterina buffalo ranch 326
Santa Leopoldina 216
Santarém 329, 334, 336, 359
Santa Rosa, Thomaz 116
Santa Teresa 216
Museu Biológico Professor Mello Leitão 216
Santo Amaro 268
Santo Angelo 234
Santos 66, 201, 352
Bolsa Oficial de Café 201
Igreja do Carmo 201
Museu de Arte Sacra 201
Museu de Pesca 201
São Bento 201
Santos-Dumont, Alberto 167
São Cristóvão 287, 291
Museu de Arte Sacra 287
Museu Histórico de Sergipe 287
Museum of Votive Offerings 287
Praço São Francisco 287
Senhor dos Passos procession 287
São Félix 269
Casa da Cultura Américo Simas 269
Centro Cultural Dannemann 269
São Francisco river 65, 261, **289**
São Francisco River 241
São João del Rei 214
Basílica de Nossa Senhora do Pilar 215
Igreja de São Francisco 215
Igreja do Carmo 215
Museu Ferroviário 214
São Luís 313, 315, 358
São Miguel das Missoes 234
São Miguel dos Milagres 291
São Paulo 23, 65, 113, 129, 133, 185
accommodations 350
airport shuttles and taxis 343
Anhangabaú Valley 190
Avenida Faria Lima 192
Avenida Paulista 190
Avenida São João 189
Banco do Estado de São Paulo 189
Bandeirantes Monument 193
Bela Vista 191
Bixiga 191
Bom Retiro 191
Brás 191
Campos Elíseos 190
Casa de Anchieta 188
Catedral Metropolitana 188
Correio Central 189
Edifício Itália 189
Edifício Martinelli 189
Fundação Maria Luiza e Oscar Americano 194
Galeria do Rock 196
Higienópolis 190
Horto Florestal 195
Ibirapuera Park 193
Ibirapuera shopping center 196
Igreja de Santo Antônio 188